THE CORRESPONDENCE OF EMERSON AND CARLYLE

THE CORRESPONDENCE OF

Emerson AND *Carlyle*

EDITED BY

Joseph Slater

COLUMBIA UNIVERSITY PRESS

NEW YORK AND LONDON 1964

Joseph Slater is Professor of English and Chairman of the Department of English at Colgate University.

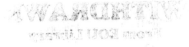

PREFACE

This is a new edition of what was probably the best-known correspondence of the nineteenth century. The early editions, though available in most libraries, have long been out of print and like many other late-Victorian books are now loose-leaved and dog-eared. Also, naturally, a considerable number of letters that were then unknown or cautiously withheld can now be published. But what seems to me the chief justification for a new edition rather than a reprinting of the old is that the editorial methods of Charles Eliot Norton, who first made a book of the correspondence, were very different from those of contemporary scholars.

Norton's edition, well suited to its time and purpose, was a selection from the letters then available; it omitted freely any passages that might have bored or offended; it regularized spelling and corrected grammar, diction, and arithmetic; and it was only slightly disfigured by footnotes. My edition treats the letters as if they were sacred scripture. It alters nothing and excludes nothing; it even includes, as a sort of apocrypha, letters to Lidian Emerson, Jane Carlyle, and Dr. John Carlyle. Whatever was offensive in 1883 has ceased to be so. Whatever was boring is now an illumination of the past and of the lives of two great artists. If that trite example of triviality, a laundry list, had appeared in a postscript I should have been happy to publish it, with footnotes. I feel as Carlyle did about the lives of the great: "We want to know what time [they] got up in the morning and what sort of shoes and stockings [they] wore."

In the matter of footnotes I have been almost as piously profuse as the seventeenth-century scholar Matthew Poole, into whose *Annotations upon the Holy Bible* "the sacred text is inserted, and various readings annexed; . . . the more difficult terms . . . are explained; seeming contradictions reconciled; questions and doubts resolved; and the whole text accommodated to the use of vulgar capacities." In case my annexations and explanations strike some readers as discourteous, I confess that the capacity which I used as a measure was my own.

I have copied the letters as exactly as the practicalities of printing justify. Only photography can transmit the visual pleasures, the immediacy, and the dramatic and graphological values of manuscript. But much of the taste of a letter can be preserved in print if misspellings, repetitions, omissions, abbreviations, and eccentricities of punctuation are doggedly reproduced. Such reproduction I have accomplished, I think, except that I have put canceled passages into the footnotes and followed twentieth-century American practice in combining quotation marks with other marks of punctuation. Where the manuscript is torn, as it often is from the breaking of the seal, I have used brackets and suspension points [. . .] to represent the missing syllable or words; where I am confident that I know what is missing, I have supplied it, in brackets, as in "[for]tnight."

My introduction has very limited aims. It makes no comment on the major works of Carlyle and Emerson except as they are mentioned or echoed in the correspondence. It does not attempt to analyze the deep and reciprocal influences that moved between the writers or to argue, as it well might, that their two sets of collected works constitute a kind of correspondence. It is merely an introduction to this volume of letters. Three chapters are biographical; they recount as fully as possible the three meetings which frame and bisect the correspondence. One chapter tries to simplify and clarify the business—or, as Carlyle called it, "bibliopolical"—relationship which seems on first encounter confusing and tedious. Another fills in the political background of the latter half of the correspondence, which many readers have thought to be darkened by Carlyle's contempt for democracy and America and by Emerson's resentful silence. Yet another gives the history of Norton's edition. The last chapter is concerned with the literary values of the correspondence and with a way of reading which I think enhances those values.

Whenever possible I have based my texts on the manuscripts. With one exception I have used all those I know of. Since most of the manuscripts of both sides of the correspondence are owned by the Ralph Waldo Emerson Memorial Association, I acknowledge my indebtedness here. Unless a footnote says otherwise, all of the letters in this edition are owned by the Association and are published by its generous permission. Other owners to whom I wish to state my gratitude are Mr. John Cooley, Mr. Daniel Maggin, the National Library of Scotland, the University of Edinburgh, the Victoria and Albert Museum, the Berg Collection of the New York Public Library, the Yale University Library, the Columbia University Library, the Princeton University Library, the Historical Society of Pennsylvania, the Library of Congress, the Folger Shakespeare Library, the Harvard College Library, and, especially, for a hundred courtesies, the Houghton Library of Harvard University. Professor Eleanor Tilton kindly sent me one of the missing letters, an Emerson note of introduction. It did not, alas, get into print.

I am grateful for financial assistance from the Research Council of Colgate University. For direction, advice, guidance, and kindness, I am indebted to the late Professor Ralph L. Rusk, to Professor Edward Waldo Forbes, to Professor Lewis Leary, and to Miss Carolyn Jakeman. In the endless—or unended—task of identifying quotations and allusions I have incurred more debts than I can pay or even list, but I set down here a few names of representative men whose learning I have pilfered: Professor Herbert Huscher of the Julius-Maximilians-Universität, Würzburg; the late Professor J. Milton French; and Professors Kenneth W. Cameron, W. T. H. Jackson, Paul Fussell, C. F. Main, and Charles Sanders. I have had the learned editorial assistance of Miss Elisabeth Shoemaker of Columbia University Press.

In the footnotes I have used many abbreviations, either self-explanatory or explained at their first appearance. The most important I list here for convenience of reference:

RWEMA	The Ralph Waldo Emerson Memorial Association
NLS	The National Library of Scotland
MS 521	Manuscript Volume 521
Works TC	Centenary Edition of the Works of Carlyle
Works RWE	Centenary Edition of the Works of Emerson
Let RWE	The Letters of Emerson, edited by Rusk

The appearance of the letter *n* after a reference to Rusk's edition of the letters means that I have taken information from one of his notes;

there are many such *n*'s. I regularly abbreviate the dates of letters as, for example, C.11.13.47, which means Carlyle's letter of November 13, 1847.

There would perhaps be something unseemly in my saying that the correspondence of Carlyle and Emerson is "for" my wife; but at least my part of this book is.

JOSEPH SLATER

Poolville, New York
June, 1964

CONTENTS

Illustrations follow page 52.

INTRODUCTION

I

PRELUDE

1827-1833

The Reverend Ralph Waldo Emerson of Boston sailed for Malta on Christmas day 1832. He had recently resigned from the ministry of the Second Church (Unitarian) and was traveling for his health. But it was not physical health alone that the young clergyman sought. His spirit still ached from the death of his wife two years before. His mind was still agitated by the religious doubts which had led to his resignation, a resignation not merely from the Second Church but ultimately from all organized religion and all orthodoxy. He needed diversion, leisure, and perspective if he was to design, in his thirtieth year, a new pattern of life and thought. And so he carried ruins to ruins; he marched through museums, inspected cathedrals, crossed the Alps, and filled his journal with travel notes.[1]

Marble and gilded monuments, however, were not enough: he needed the powerful rhyme of scholarly discourse. When he looked back later on this pilgrimage to the European past, he realized that, more than anything else, he had wanted to talk with the men whose books had freed him from the New England past. But the first months of his journey were, in this regard, far from satisfactory. In Italy he spoke mainly with his own countrymen and with Walter Savage Landor. Goethe, who had counseled his brother William in a similar spiritual crisis nine years before,[2] was dead, and so he did not go to Germany. In Paris on July 11 he complained to his journal:

A man who was no courtier, but loved men, went to Rome,—and there lived with boys. He came to France, and in Paris lives alone, and in Paris seldom speaks. If he do not see Carlyle in Edinburgh, he may go to America without saying anything in earnest, except to Cranch and to Landor.

[1] The basic sources of this narrative, to which I shall not ordinarily refer, are *The Life of Ralph Waldo Emerson* by Ralph L. Rusk and Emerson's own accounts in his *Journals*, ed. Edward Waldo Emerson and Waldo Emerson Forbes, and in *English Traits*, vol. V of *The Complete Works of Ralph Waldo Emerson*, ed. Edward Waldo Emerson.

[2] Rusk, *Life*, p. 107.

The name Carlyle, which occupied such a startlingly prominent place on this intellectual itinerary, had been unknown to Emerson until two months before his departure from Boston, but the anonymous essays which Carlyle had published in the British quarterlies had for years been highly regarded by him and by other American scholars. In 1827 George Ripley had discovered "the untold treasures of German thought" through Carlyle's article "State of German Literature" and had read it again "times without number."[3] James Freeman Clarke and Margaret Fuller had begun to study German in 1832, "attracted towards this literature, at the same time, by the wild bugle call" which they later learned had been sounded by Thomas Carlyle.[4] And Emerson, as early as 1827, had urged his brother to read the *Edinburgh Review* article on Richter because it presented the German writer as a stylist very much like Mary Moody Emerson, their brilliant and eccentric aunt.[5]

Unfortunately, the record of Emerson's reading of Carlyle is, after this early and familiar beginning, a meager one. In 1830 he had copied into his journal a passage from Carlyle's translation of *Wilhelm Meister*. In 1831 he had read the articles on German literature which appeared in the *Edinburgh Review* and the *Foreign Quarterly Review,* and he had been especially interested in "Characteristics."[6] By October 1, 1832, Carlyle's voice, though still anonymous, had become distinctive and recognizable. "I am cheered and instructed," Emerson wrote in his journal,

by this paper on Corn Law Rhymes in the Edinburgh by my Germanick new-light writer, whoever he be. He gives us confidence in our principles. He assures the truth-lover everywhere of sympathy. Blessed art that makes books, and so joins me to that stranger by this perfect railroad.

By October 19, when Emerson read the *Fraser* review of the Goethe-Schiller correspondence, he had learned the stranger's name and had come to think of him as almost a friend:

[3] Joseph Slater, "George Ripley and Thomas Carlyle," *PMLA*, LXVII (June, 1952), 342.

[4] *Memoirs of Margaret Fuller Ossoli*, I, 114.

[5] *The Letters of Ralph Waldo Emerson*, ed. Ralph L. Rusk, I, 218. This work will hereafter be referred to as *Let RWE*.

[6] MS, Alexander Ireland to Emerson, January 8, 1878, owned by the Houghton Library, Harvard University.

If Carlyle knew what an interest I have in his persistent goodness, would it not be worth one effort more, one prayer, one meditation? But will he resist the Deluge of bad example in England? One manifestation of goodness in a noble soul brings him in debt to all the beholders that he shall not betray their love and trust which he has awakened.

During the critical days of his own resistance to orthodoxy, Emerson's thoughts had turned frequently to Carlyle. On October 22, 1832, the day after his final sermon, he had had dinner with an English clergyman who brought recent news about "Carlisle . . . a German bred scholar." Within a week he had copied passages from the *Fraser* article "Luther's Psalm" which seemed relevant to his own heterodox position. On October 28, when the proprietors of the Second Church had voted to accept his resignation, Emerson had been reading Carlyle's *Life of Schiller*. On November 13 he had been at the Boston Athenaeum reading the *Foreign Quarterly Review* article "Goethe's Works" and memorizing an early, pre-*Sartor* quotation which it contained from *Die Kleider: ihr Werden und Wirken*.

It was appropriate that Emerson should turn thus to Carlyle's current periodical essays for help in a time of trouble, because that trouble was to a considerable degree the work of their predecessors. In his first letter to Carlyle, Emerson wrote of those early articles as "by far the most original and profound essays of the day." In the preface to the Boston edition of *Critical and Miscellaneous Essays* he reminded American readers of "pages which, in the scattered anonymous sheets of the British magazines, spoke to their youthful mind with an emphasis that hindered them from sleep." Since Emerson was not given to flattery or careless use of the superlative, these sentences say much about the influence of Carlyle in America. An examination of the early works themselves argues, even in the absense of biographical evidence, that they had much to do with the making of Emerson's mind and with his departure from his Unitarian pulpit.

Whether he saw the first of these, the *Life of Schiller*, before 1832 is uncertain, although the book was easily available and well known. George Ripley owned a copy of the London edition of 1825 which he had found "in a neglected corner of a Book-seller's shop" and which he "soon diffused through a wide circle of friends." [7] When Emerson did read *Schiller* in 1832, in the midst of his ecclesiastical difficulties, he

[7] Slater, "Ripley," p. 342.

seems to have been chiefly concerned with biography, with "Schiller himself"; if he read Ripley's copy earlier, in 1826 or 1827, he must have prized it rather as an introduction to German literature and thought. It was a comfortable and undemanding introduction, to be sure, for the anonymous author himself had not, as he said, penetrated far into "the arcana of transcendentalism," but it was full of exciting names and recondite allusions and it quietly assumed that "many things are true which cannot be demonstrated by the rules of *Watt's Logic*." It was enriched, too, with provocative digressions, of which the most notable, perhaps, were attacks on the doctrines of compensation and universal philanthropy.

About the availability of the British periodicals there can be little question. Emerson himself was a subscriber, after 1829, to the *Edinburgh Review,* and he was able to find most of the others, as he wrote, "every month" in "our reading rooms." [8] The articles on German literature which appeared there in 1827 and 1828 must have spoken with startling directness to the imagination of the young Emerson. In them Richter appeared not merely as an exotic and an eccentric but as a man who "independently of all dogmas, nay perhaps in spite of many . . . is, in the highest sense of the word, religious." [9] Fichte was presented as a prophet of the Divine Idea of which Literary Men are the true interpreters, a "perpetual priesthood." [10] Werner, a convert to Catholicism, was defended at least from charges of inconsistency: "consistency perhaps is no such brilliant virtue." [11] A fragment quoted from Novalis's Notebook read

There is, properly speaking, no Misfortune in the world. Happiness and Misfortune stand in continual balance. Every Misfortune is, as it were, the obstruction of a stream, which, after overcoming this obstruction, but bursts through with the greater force.[12]

And a passage from his *Pupils at Sais* contained this commandment: "let man honor Nature as the Emblem of his own Spirit." [13]

The frequent brilliance and provocativeness of these essays were not so important, however, as the reflection—or refraction—in them of the new light that was shining in Germany. "State of German Litera-

---

[8] See below, E.5.14.34, n. 1.

[9] *The Works of Thomas Carlyle,* Centenary Edition, XXVI, 22. This will be referred to hereafter as *Works TC.*

[10] *Ibid.,* p. 58.   [11] *Ibid.,* p. 138.   [12] *Ibid.,* XXVII, 40.   [13] *Ibid.,* p. 35.

ture" concluded with an exposition of Kant, judiciously called "loose and popular," which yet claimed a first-hand knowledge of the *Kritik der reinen Vernunft* and which made the distinction between *Vernunft* and *Verstand* seem not only clear but exciting. The essay "Novalis" included a section on philosophical idealism, a glance at Fichte's *Ich* and *Nicht-Ich,* an introduction to the Kantian conception of space and time as mere categories of the understanding, and a loose and popular definition of *transcendental*—"ascending beyond the senses"—which was to be adequate for most of the needs of New England transcendentalism.

With "Signs of the Times" in 1829 Carlyle spoke to readers of the *Edinburgh Review* not as cultural ambassador from Germany but as a native prophet and on matters of the greatest seriousness. These must have been the anonymous pages which, brighter even than Germanic new light, kept New England awake, for the signs which Carlyle reported were ominous indeed. This was, he said, an Age of Machinery not only in the world of things but in the world of the spirit. No major task could now be undertaken without meetings, committees, prospectuses, and public dinners. Education, once "an indefinable tentative process, requiring a study of individual aptitudes and a perpetual variation of means and methods," had become predictable, standardized mass production. Worship, where it existed, was "mechanically explained into Fear of pain or Hope of pleasure"; morality was a "calculation of the profitable"; thought had become "not Meditation but Argument"; and poetry had been explained by a contemporary scientist as "a product of the smaller intestines."

In New England as well as Old, this must have seemed an accurate diagnosis of the spiritual malady of the nation. And, perhaps because New England was still close in time and space to a very different world, the therapy which Carlyle proposed must have seemed a workable one. For, he reminded his readers, things had not been always thus. All great achievement in the past, in art, in science, in religion, had been the work of individuals—Shakespeare, Newton, Luther; had been spontaneous and instinctive; had resulted from ideal and not from material causes. The chief source of modern ills was that men had "lost faith in individual endeavour" and had embraced instead the fatuous belief that "happiness depends entirely on external circumstances." Let them, Carlyle prescribed, subordinate, though not abandon, their machinery; let them have hope and sure faith. To reform the world, to reform a nation, no wise man will undertake; and all but foolish men know, that the only solid though a far slower reformation, is what each begins and perfects on *himself*.

Documentary evidence that Emerson knew this most Emersonian of Carlyle's essays is slight but persuasive. On September 10, 1831, he concluded a sermon by quoting a quatrain,

> Knowst thou yesterday, its aim & reason
> Work'st thou well Today, for worthy things
> Then calmly wait Tomorrow's hidden season
> And fear not thou. what hap so e'er it brings

which he could hardly have known except from the first paragraph of "Signs of the Times." [14] It is a translation—although not identified as such by either Carlyle or Emerson—from Goethe's *Zahme Xenien,* IV, 1179–83. It does not appear in any other article by Carlyle, nor is there reason to believe that it is a translation by another hand. But surely internal evidence alone would be sufficient to establish "Signs of the Times" as a potent factor in the development of Emerson's ideas.

That he was familiar with the almost equally important essay "Characteristics" of 1831 there can be no doubt. His brother Charles, and consequently Emerson himself, knew in October, 1832, that Carlyle was "the author of the Characteristics article." [15] Emerson in Edinburgh in August, 1833, showed so strong an interest in the essay that Alexander Ireland, his companion in that city, remembered it forty-five years later.[16] Such response is less likely to have been evoked by Carlyle's artistry than by his bold statement of two ideas which were, or were to become, fundamental in Emerson's thinking. The first, that the "healthy Understanding . . . is not the Logical, Argumentative, but the Intuitive," had been suggested in "Signs of the Times" and was implicit in much romantic thought but had not before, in English, been so clearly related to the processes of intellectual creation:

Of our Thinking, we might say, it is but the mere upper surface that we shape into articulate Thoughts;—underneath the region of argument and conscious discourse, lies the region of meditation; here, in its quiet mysterious depths, dwells what vital force is in us; here, if aught is to be created, and not merely manufactured and communicated, must the work go on.

[14] I am indebted for this information and for the text of Emerson's quotation to Professor Kenneth W. Cameron. The sermon is numbered 126 and is owned by the Ralph Waldo Emerson Memorial Association, hereafter referred to as RWEMA.

[15] Rusk, *Life,* p. 165.   [16] See above, p. 4, n. 6.

The second, as old as Heraclitus, was here given new value for an age of revolution:

All human things are, have been and forever will be, in Movement and Change. . . . In some provinces, it is true, as in Experimental Science, this discovery is an old one; but in most others it belongs wholly to these latter days. How often, in former ages, by eternal Creeds, eternal Forms of Government and the like, has it been attempted, fiercely enough, and with destructive violence, to chain the Future under the Past; and say to the Providence, whose ways with man are mysterious, and through the great deep: Hitherto shalt thou come, but no farther! A wholly insane attempt; and for man himself, could it prosper, the frightfullest of all enchantments, a very Life-in-Death.

There were parts of "Characteristics," surely, which did not call forth immediate assent from Emerson. There was a gibe at Socinian preachers which must in 1831 have stung him a little. More important, there was a new statism or societism, based on the subordination of the weak to the strong and sharply contemptuous of constitutions, republics, and democracies, which even a New England conservative must have resisted. But resistance and dissent are phlogistic elements, and they must have heated the transatlantic influences which brought the simmering Emerson to a boil.

Whatever the extent of his intellectual indebtedness, Emerson, from the beginning of his European journey, had Carlyle very much on his mind. In quarantine at Malta, condemned to a fortnight of shipboard waiting, he consoled himself with a quotation, "Time brings roses," which he attributed to "friend Carlyle." In Rome one evening in April, at a party given by his college friend Horace Gray, he met a young Frenchman named Gustave d'Eichthal, a Saint-Simonian socialist, who had been for some years in correspondence with Carlyle and had visited him in London. That very evening, it would seem, d'Eichthal wrote Emerson a letter of introduction to Carlyle. The next day he came to Emerson's hotel with an introduction to another friend, John Stuart Mill, which asked that Mill also introduce Emerson to Carlyle.[17] Thus doubly sure of achieving his major objective, Emerson went north to Florence to see Walter Savage Landor. He was delighted by Landor's brilliance and friendliness but disappointed by his unwillingness to give credit where it was due: "Sir James Mackintosh he

---

[17] *Let RWE*, I, 374n.

would not praise, nor my Carlyle." [18] With rather a sharp pen Emerson reported to his brother Charles that Landor's conversation was not the equal of his writing: "It is a mean thing that literary men, philosophers, cannot work themselves clear of this ambition to appear men of the world. . . . I hope better things of Carlyle." [19]

Soon after his arrival in London on July 21, Emerson went to India House with d'Eichthal's note to Mill. He may have had to make two visits, for Mill in a letter to Carlyle on August 2 mentioned "one or two conversations" with "an American named Emerson," but he got his introduction and learned that Carlyle was not in Edinburgh but in a place called Craigenputtock.[20] On August 5 he went to Highgate to pay his respects to an older prophet. That visit, however, was "rather a spectacle than a conversation": Coleridge, he found, "was old and preoccupied, and could not bend to a new companion and think with him." More sight-seeing followed—Oxford, Kenilworth, Warwick—before Emerson reached Edinburgh on Friday the 16th. There he presented another letter of introduction, to the physician John Gairdner, an important Unitarian layman.[21] Gairdner, too busy to look after an obscure American, handed him over to a literary young man named Alexander Ireland. On Sunday Emerson preached a sermon at the Unitarian chapel, which Ireland thought remarkable for "originality" of thought and "consummate beauty" of expression. The rest of the weekend the two young men spent in sight-seeing, in literary talk— Coleridge, Goethe, Montaigne, and "especially Carlyle, of whom Emerson expressed the warmest admiration"—and in discovering the precise location of Craigenputtock, which, they finally learned from the secretary of the university, was a farmhouse in the county of Dumfries, southwest of Glasgow.[22] During the next week Emerson traveled slowly through the country of Scott and Burns. He spent the night of the 24th in Dumfries. The next day, Sunday, he hired a gig at the inn and rode

[18] Typescript copy of Emerson's manuscript journals: Pocket Note Book. Journals of Travel 1833, p. 24.

[19] Let RWE, I, 383.

[20] H. S. R. Elliot, Letters of John Stuart Mill, I, 60. This is an inference: Mill knew Carlyle's address, but Emerson might easily have learned it himself from an article in the June issue of Fraser's Magazine (VII, 706) which disclosed that it was "a place rejoicing in the melodious title of Craigenputtock."

[21] DNB, article on Alexander Ireland.

[22] Ireland, In Memoriam: Ralph Waldo Emerson, pp. 140–47.

sixteen miles through "wild and desolate heathery hills" to Craigenputtock.

Most literary men of Carlyle's stature would have found little cause
for rejoicing in the letter from Mill which announced the intended
visit: "Emerson . . . appears to be a reader and admirer of your writings, . . . but . . . I do not think him a very hopeful subject." [23]
Carlyle, despite the anonymity of his writings, was at the age of thirty-
eight by no means unknown and was not without honor in his own
country. *Fraser's Magazine* had just published a portrait of him by
Maclise and had identified him as "the thunderwordoversetter" of

Wilhelm Meister, and other works, so Teutonical in raiment, in the structure
of sentence, the modulation of phrase, and the roundabout, hubble-bubble,
rumfustianish (*hubble-bubblen, rümfustianischen*), roly-poly growlery of style,
so Germanically set forth, that it is with difficulty we can recognize them to be
translations at all.[24]

He had access to the literary society of Scotland; he had met, and dis-
dained, the literary society of London; he had been a correspondent
of Goethe and, recently, of Mill. But Craigenputtock, where he and
his wife Jane had lived for almost five years, was a lonely place, and
the political and literary salients which he occupied were even lonelier. Readers and admirers he doubtless possessed, but they had not
beaten a path to his door. And so the arrival of an admirer, even a not
very hopeful one, would be a memorable event. It was, said Jane, "the
first journey since Noah's Deluge undertaken to Craigenputtock for
such a purpose." [25] Whatever the man turned out to be, the Carlyles
decided, he should be asked to stay overnight. And when the rusty
hired gig pulled up at the gate, interrupting their Sunday dinner, they
persuaded their visitor to send the driver back to Dumfries.

Emerson, when he had delivered his letters and given a brief account
of himself, was pleased to find that Craigenputtock was not as wild
and desolate as the hills which surrounded it. There was a piano, tuned
only two days before; there were books and a servant; there was a wife,
"a most accomplished and agreeable woman"; and Carlyle himself was

[23] Elliot, *Letters of John Stuart Mill,* I, 60.
[24] *Fraser's Magazine,* VII (June, 1833), 706. This was one of a series called "Gallery
of Literary Characters." The article, unsigned, was the work of William Maginn:
see William Bates, *The Maclise Portrait Gallery* (New York, 1883), p. 174.
[25] James Anthony Froude, *Thomas Carlyle: First Forty Years,* II, 210.

no Teufelsdröckhish eccentric but an easy and intellectual man of the world.

He was tall and gaunt, with a cliff-like brow, self-possessed and holding his extraordinary powers of conversation in easy command; clinging to his northern accent with evident relish; full of lively anecdote and with a streaming humor which floated every thing he looked upon.[26]

The two men walked together for miles through the hills, looked south into Wordsworth's country, and talked. It was for talk that Emerson had come, it was talk that the eremitical Carlyle chiefly needed, and in twenty-four hours they went, as Carlyle said, "thro' the whole Encyclopedia." [27]

Their talk began, probably, with people. They had common acquaintances: Mill—whose mind, Carlyle said, was the best he knew—and d'Eichthal. And Emerson might easily have met, but had not, Carlyle's brother John, who was a friend of d'Eichthal's and who had been living in Rome at the time of Emerson's visit there.[28] The Carlyles told the story of their epistolary friendship with Goethe: the very chain that Mrs. Carlyle wore about her neck had been a gift from him, and she had been sorely disappointed when the miscarriage of Carlyle's book on German literature had prevented their visit to Weimar. In this warm household Emerson's New England reticence thawed, and he spoke of his dead wife.[29]

They talked about books and about the sad state of contemporary letters. Emerson was delighted with the playfulness and irreverence of Carlyle's literary gossip and with the broad Scots in which it was spoken; he was puzzled by his perversities of tastes ("Scott, Mackintosh, —Jeffrey;—Gibbon; even Bacon are no heroes of his . . . but Burns & Samuel Johnson"); he was offended by his ignorance of Plato and his disparagement of Socrates; but chiefly he was impressed by the multifariousness of his literary experience. For modern literature Carlyle had little hope. Not only was most of it intrinsically worthless, but news-

---

[26] Emerson, *Works*, V, 15.

[27] In addition to the obvious sources, this paragraph is based on Lawrence and Elisabeth Hanson, *Necessary Evil, the Life of Jane Welsh Carlyle*, p. 178; Charles Eliot Norton, ed., *Letters of Thomas Carlyle 1826–1836*, p. 371; Alexander Carlyle, ed., *Letters of Thomas Carlyle to John Stuart Mill*, p. 66; and *Let RWE*, I, 394.

[28] Norton, ed., *Letters of Thomas Carlyle 1826–1836*, p. 371.

[29] Hanson, *Necessary Evil*, p. 178.

papers and publishers had so debased criticism that now no book would sell. He knew for a fact, he said, that Colburn and Bentley of London had spent £10,000 in one year on puffs.[30]

Repeatedly their talk turned to the questions of government and society with which Carlyle was increasingly concerned and for which his answers were increasingly authoritarian. The American principle, he feared, was mere negative rebelliousness, tolerable perhaps in a country where even the bootblack ate roast turkey, but not in England. To Craigenputtock itself there now came beggars, wanderers from the swarming cities, for whom alms were not enough, who needed a government which would set them to tilling the idle moors. If the governing classes persisted in the selfish abdication of their duties—and only a few days ago an army officer had paid five pounds for the right to kill grouse on the Craigenputtock moors [31]—then perhaps the burning of haystacks was a wise and necessary activity.

In religious discussion it was Emerson who took the lead. He spoke of the strange new forces—Swedenborgianism, for example—which were changing the New England mind. And he had questions to ask. What were the theological implications of "Characteristics," he wanted to know; and what did the last paragraph of "State of German Literature," which asserted that the "dwelling and birthplace" of religion "is in the soul of man," indicate with regard to Carlyle's own "religious development"? To such interrogation Carlyle gave most unsatisfactory replies: he was not competent to say, he was waiting to see. Always loath to engage in theological argument, he must have been especially uncomfortable with this restless Unitarian, for Unitarians, he had long felt, were "hollow men" with "a certain mechanical metallic *deadness* at the heart of all of them." [32] As the two men sat on a hill and looked southward into Cumberland, Emerson began embarrassingly to talk of the immortality of the soul. Carlyle, though reluctant, did not finally evade the issue. He believed, he said, and he based his belief on the subtle interrelationship of past and present and the merely relative existence of time: "Christ died on the tree; that built Dunscore kirk yonder; that brought you and me together." An honest answer, Emer-

---

[30] Emerson, Typescript journals (Journal F. 1836–1837, p. 9).

[31] Froude, *Thomas Carlyle: First Forty Years*, II, 373.

[32] Carlyle, *Letters to Mill*, pp. 67, 20.

son thought; but his final judgment was that he "had met with men of far less power who had yet greater insight into religious truth." [33]

And so the talk flowed on—Wordsworth and the earl of Lonsdale, Whitehaven and London, Coleridge and Hazlitt, the coronation of William IV and the death of Nero—until nearly twenty-four hours had passed and the gig returned from Dumfries in time to make connection with the evening coach for the south. Carlyle wrote down Emerson's address in his notebook. He did not ride with his guest to the top of the hill, but "preferred to watch him mount and vanish like an angel." [34] Emerson wrote that night at his inn: "A white day in my years. I found the youth I sought in Scotland, and good and wise and pleasant he seems to me." Carlyle two days later wrote to his mother: "one of the most lovable creatures in himself we had ever looked on. He . . . talked and heard talk to his heart's content, and left us all really sad to part with him." [35] On September 10 he reported to Mill on "Emerson, your Presentee":

A most gentle, recommendable, amiable, wholehearted man. . . . A good 'Socinian' understanding, the clearest heart; above all, what I loved in the man was his health, his unity with himself; all people and all things seemed to find their quite peaceable adjustment with him, not a proud domineering one, as after doubtful *contest,* but a spontaneous-looking, peaceable, even humble one.[36]

And Emerson, waiting at the Star and Garter in Liverpool for his ship to sail, wrote in his journal: "Ah me! Mr. Thomas Carlyle, I would give a gold pound for your wise company this gloomy eve."

But something had happened on that August weekend which is not to be accounted for by records of conversation or by the immediate judgments which each man made of the other, something which neither man was conscious of, perhaps, for many years to come. It was rather Jane Carlyle who felt and expressed the emotional significance of that meeting: "It was like the visit of an angel; . . . and though he staid with us hardly twenty four hours, yet when he left us I cried—I could not help it." [37] Loneliness, obscurity, personal affinity, sensibility, frankness: these had somehow combined to transmute the base metals

---

[33] *Let RWE*, I, 394.   [34] Cabot, *A Memoir of Ralph Waldo Emerson*, I, 197.
[35] Froude, *Thomas Carlyle: First Forty Years*, II, 374.
[36] *Letters to Mill*, pp. 66–67.
[37] Richards, "Longfellow in England," *PMLA* (1936), 1129, LI.

of respect-paying, conversation, and acquaintanceship into silver and gold. Almost half a century later, Carlyle was to say to an American friend: "Give my love to Emerson. I still think of his visit to us at Craigenputtock as the most beautiful thing in our experience there." [38]

Back in Boston, Emerson, though still unsettled and uncertain, began to rebuild his life. He lived in various temporary lodgings and preached irregularly in other men's pulpits; more important, he made his first appearances as a secular lecturer. He wrote "The Rhodora" and worked at *Nature*. On May 14, 1834, he carefully composed an epistle to Carlyle.

[38] Conway, *Emerson at Home and Abroad*, p. 63.

II

BIBLIOPOLY

1835-1847

The occasion for that first epistle was the publication in *Fraser's Magazine* of the fourth installment of *Sartor Resartus*. Emerson had learned at Craigenputtock that *Sartor* was finally to appear in print. From Liverpool he had sent in a subscription to the magazine; from Boston during the winter he had written Fraser some much-needed words of encouragement: "Send me *Fraser* so long as 'Sartor' continues in it." [1] Now in the spring he was writing the author "thanks evermore" for a book which showed that "one living scholar is self-centered & will be true to himself though none ever were before." It was with *Sartor Resartus,* then, that the correspondence of Carlyle and Emerson began, and it was around *Sartor* that there developed the quasi-commercial relationship between the two men which was to be the strongest buttress of their friendship.

In this first venture into what Carlyle called bibliopoly, Emerson was merely advocate and distributor. He recommended *Sartor* to his friends as "a noble philosophical poem." [2] When Carlyle sent him extra copies of the "stitched pamphlet" made up of offprints from *Fraser's,* Emerson gave them to "three greedy receivers": his aunt, Sarah Ripley, Lydia Jackson, who was soon to become his second wife, and the clergyman Frederic Henry Hedge. [3] Hedge, long an admirer of Carlyle, had already considered bringing out an American edition of *Sartor,* [4] but he now found himself anticipated by a younger enthusiast, a recent graduate of Harvard, Le Baron Russell, who had read Miss Jackson's stitched

[1] Conway, *Thomas Carlyle,* p. 72. Since this sentence is Conway's version of Carlyle's recollection, thirty years later, of Fraser's oral quotation from Emerson's letter, it may not be verbatim.

[2] In a letter to James Freeman Clarke printed in Holmes, *Ralph Waldo Emerson,* p. 79.

[3] See below, 11.20.34; see also Caroline H. Dall, *Transcendentalism in New England.*

[4] *Let RWE,* I, 433n.

pamphlet. Russell was so "carried away by it, and so anxious to own a copy" that he consulted the Boston publisher James Munroe about the practicalities of making the *Sartor* papers into a book. Subscribers, said Munroe, were the first necessity, and so Russell, with the help of a college friend, set about soliciting subscriptions.[5]

Meanwhile, on March 12, 1835, Emerson, at the request perhaps of Russell and his friend, perhaps of other zealots, had written Carlyle for fifty or a hundred copies of the Fraser offprint pamphlet to test the appetite of the American public. Fraser, who knew a failure when he saw one, shrieked at such commercial folly and would yield only four copies. The Boston publisher was less cautious: when, with little difficulty, Russell had accumulated one hundred and fifty subscriptions, he found that Munroe was willing to bring the book out as a commercial venture. He wrote to Emerson for a preface and received three paragraphs of discriminate praise which were printed anonymously.[6] And so the book was published, in a printing of five hundred copies, priced at one dollar. On April 8, 1836, Emerson mailed Carlyle a copy of the first edition of *Sartor Resartus*.

Carlyle's immediate reaction to this American beneficence was expressed in a letter now missing. But fortunately the book itself was entangled in postal complications and Emerson was obliged to send a second copy, and so there exists in Carlyle's letters of November 5, 1836, and February 13, 1837, almost the freshness of first thanks. When the first copy finally arrived, ransomed from the post office at more than twice its price, Carlyle was writing his article "Mirabeau," and he contrived to include in it a graceful and ironic bow to his American friends: he introduced a long passage from *Sartor* with the parenthesis, "we quote from a New-England Book."

The New England book did well. By September 17, 1836, Emerson could report that the first edition was entirely sold and widely read. On March 31, 1837, he wrote that a second edition was in the book stores and that twenty-five copies had been ordered by benighted Old England. On September 13, he reported a total sale of 1,166 copies. But the book's success brought financial profit to James Munroe and Com-

[5] Holmes, *Ralph Waldo Emerson*, p. 82.

[6] *Ibid.* Emerson indicated that he had found the eccentricity and exoticism of the book distasteful at first but that these faults were unimportant when weighed against the "wit," "mastery," and "splendor" of the prose and the critical insight and "purity of moral sentiment which inspire the work."

pany only, not to Carlyle, who complained that in the past four years he had earned only £50 by his writing, and Emerson was somewhat embarrassed at being involved in an act of benevolent piracy. He instructed Munroe not to reprint *The French Revolution* until the English edition had had a chance at the American market.

On October 22, 1837, while he was as yet the only American owner of the new book, Emerson spoke of his plans to Elizabeth Peabody, who had once been a pupil of his and who was soon to be the proprietress of the most distinguished bookstore in America. She chided him for his lack of enterprise: "You might have made $500 for the man out of his Sartor." [7] Two days later Emerson went to Boston and made the rounds of the publishers with the announcement that he wished to bring out an American edition of *The French Revolution* at his own risk and for the benefit of the author. The best terms were offered by the firm of C. C. Little and James Brown: two volumes of about five hundred pages each could be manufactured at an estimated cost of $1.18; the publishers, who were also booksellers, would receive twenty percent of the retail price of $2.50; Emerson could have as many volumes at cost as he could find subscribers for. By October 31, Emerson had accepted the offer of Little and Brown and written a prospectus for them to print:

Sir,—I have engaged Messrs. C. C. Little and James Brown to publish an American edition of THE HISTORY OF THE FRENCH REVOLUTION, by THOMAS CARLYLE. In addition to the wish of presenting to the public a work of great intrinsic value, I have the hope of securing a private benefit to the author, to whom all the profits arising from it will be transmitted. With this view, the publishers have made with me a liberal contract, by which they relinquish to the author all profit on the sale of such copies as shall be subscribed for. May I ask your aid in procuring, and transmitting to them, at 112 Washington street, the names of any subscribers.

R. W. Emerson.

TERMS

The Work will be published in two volumes, large 12 mo. of from 450 to 500 pages each. It will be printed on a new type and good paper, and strongly done up in cloth, and delivered to subscribers at $2.50 a copy.[8]

[7] *Let RWE*, II, 99; and R. W. Emerson and W. H. Furness, *Records of a Lifelong Friendship*, p. 2.
[8] *Let RWE*, II, 99.

On November 1, he sent Little and Brown, perhaps along with the prospectus, a list of thirty-nine prospective subscribers—clergymen, writers, and intellectuals, in New York, Philadelphia, and Louisville, and throughout New England from Bangor to Springfield.[9] The next day he made a report to Carlyle which concluded: "I shall sustain with great glee the new relation of being your banker and attorney."

The book was published on Christmas Day, and Emerson soon found himself involved in other than financial and legal relations. He wrote a review for the *Christian Examiner*.[10] He sent review copies to editors, among them William Cullen Bryant of the New York *Evening Post*. He sent ten copies to his brother for private sale in New York so that Carlyle might have the five dollars which would otherwise have gone as booksellers' commissions.[11] He impressed his boyhood friend, the Reverend W. H. Furness, as distributor for the Philadelphia subscribers.[12] By February 9, 1838, he could write to Carlyle that half of the edition of one thousand had been sold, two hundred copies to subscribers, and that he hoped to send seven hundred dollars at the end of June.

The dissemination of the Boston edition of *The French Revolution* was, considering its high price and its formidable reputation, remarkably successful—copies were sold in such outposts of the intellectual life as Vicksburg and New Orleans—but the financial harvest was not so early or so great as Emerson had expected. It was the end of July before he gathered any money from the publishers and then the sum was not $700.00 but $242.22, with which he bought a £50 bill of exchange. Carlyle was absent from Chelsea on his annual retreat into Scotland when Emerson's letter enclosing the bill arrived, and so it was Jane who received the first money that *The French Revolution* had earned its author. A "very wonderful thing indeed," she thought it, "which brought a sort of tears into my eyes." [13]

Although Carlyle's own acknowledgment came tardily from Ecclefechan late in September, it was written in warm gratitude and it gaily proposed the purchase of "something permanent" with the American pounds, something to be called "either *Ebenezer or Yankee-*

---

[9] MS owned by RWEMA.   [10] See below, E.2.9.38, n. 4.   [11] *Let RWE*, II, 104.

[12] R. W. Emerson, *Records of a Lifelong Friendship*, p. 4.

[13] Froude, ed., *Letters and Memorials of Jane Welsh Carlyle*, I, 75.

doodle-doo." In a letter written from London in November, *Yankee-doodle-doo* took more definite form as *Yankee,* "a sharp little nag," on which Carlyle intended to flee the demons of dyspepsia. But literary history was not, unfortunately, to be adorned by an English horse named *Yankee:* it was Citoyenne, the gift of a wealthy *Yorkshire* admirer, that carried Carlyle through the London suburbs in the summer of 1839.[14] These first transatlantic pounds did not, however, disappear unrecorded among the domestic expenditures of 5 Cheyne Row. With his New Year's Day letter to his mother Carlyle sent a tithe of the sum which had finally emerged from the Barings' bank:

I send my dear Mother five off the fore-end of it; the "kitlin ought to bring the auld cat a mouse" in such a case as that,—an American mouse! It is very curious that cash should come in that way to good Annandale industry from across three thousand miles of salt water, from kind hands that we never saw.[15]

Eventually, of course, *The French Revolution* was to bring Carlyle a great deal more cash from kind hands across the salt water. On February 4, 1839, a letter from Concord arrived in Chelsea with a bill of exchange for £100 and the news that Little and Brown's edition had been sold out before the first of the year. This letter not only moved Carlyle to deeply serious expressions of gratitude—"there never came money into my hands I was so proud of. . . . Thanks to the mysterious, all-bounteous Guide of men, and to you my true Brother, far over the sea!"—but also produced a deep blush on the face of James Fraser, his laggard London publisher. Fraser, although seventy-five copies of his first edition remained unsold, was beginning to talk of a second. It occurred to Carlyle that this might well be an Anglo-American edition, stereotyped from that of Little and Brown so that the task of proof-reading should be forever done. When stereotyping proved to be too expensive, Carlyle proposed to print at his own expense five hundred copies of Fraser's second edition for the American market and ship them in sheets to whatever publisher Emerson should strike a bargain with. Little and Brown accepted each of these proposals in turn, amending the second one to include binding by Fraser in London, and the books were finally shipped ("bound in red cloth, gilt," Carlyle wrote) in September, 1839. They cost Carlyle £95, plus freight. They cost Emerson, at the customs office, $243, and they were sadly altered,

---

[14] *New Letters of Thomas Carlyle,* ed. by Alexander Carlyle (London, 1904), I, 169.
[15] *Ibid.,* p. 145.

somehow, from the bright colors Carlyle had seen to "a sober green," but Little and Brown pronounced them satisfactory and hoped to sell them all, at a net profit to Carlyle of $1.10 a copy, within six months.

Concurrently with these operations, during all of 1838 and 1839, Emerson was engaged in even more complicated bibliopoly on behalf of Carlyle. The sale of the Boston *French Revolution* was so profitable that publishers began to talk of reprinting the early periodical articles and reviews. Alarmed lest Carlyle gain fame without dollars, Emerson undertook, early in February, 1838, to make a selection from this miscellany and have it published under terms such as he had arranged for *The French Revolution*. A similar plan had occurred, somewhat earlier, to another Bostonian, Ellis Gray Loring, who had long been an admirer of Carlyle's work.[16] Applying through Harriet Martineau, who introduced him as "a wealthy young lawyer, of great worth," he asked Carlyle to send him a catalog of the periodical writings and promised that the venture would be "profitable," a word which Miss Martineau, who was an authority on New England, took to mean about five hundred dollars.[17] Carlyle, unaware that Emerson had any plans for the essays, sent catalog and consent. It was not until around March 10, just as Emerson was about to make final arrangements with a publisher, that he learned of Loring's parallel enterprise. Unfortunately, the two plans were not identical: Emerson had intended a selection, Loring a complete collection in chronological order. Carlyle wrote to say that he would prefer a selection, but his letter, dated March 10, did not reach Concord until May 9, by which time Emerson had acceded to the insistence of Loring and other Carlyleans and a firm of Cambridge printers was at work on the first two volumes of the complete *Critical and Miscellaneous Essays*.

This first edition of the volumes which came to be known as *Miscellanies* was even more a cooperative and amateur effort than the first edition of *Sartor* had been. The task of reading proof was done by two young Harvard graduates who were living in Cambridge, Henry S. McKean, an engineer, and Charles Stearns Wheeler, a student in the Divinity School. "With regard to what I have done in this business," Wheeler wrote to Emerson on June 21, 1838, "I will simply say that it has been a labor of love; and that Mr. Carlyle is welcome to the commercial profit he gets from it, in pay for the intellectual profit that

---

[16] See below, E.4.30.35.   [17] *New Letters*, I, 106–7.

falls to my share." [18] Copies of *The Foreign Review,* in which many of the early articles on German literature had appeared, were lent by the Rev. Convers Francis. Again Emerson wrote a prospectus and had it sent to likely purchasers.[19] And as the date of publication drew near he wrote a brief introduction which he called "Advertisement" and signed "R. W. E. Concord, June 24, 1838."

Financial and legal arrangements seem to have been left largely in Emerson's now experienced hands. This time, he found, there was competition among publishers. The best offer was made by James Munroe and Company, who proposed an edition of one thousand priced at $2.50 a volume with a net profit to Carlyle of $1.00 a volume. For such liberality, however, there were compensations. Emerson himself was obliged to pay or guarantee the costs of paper and printing, and these obligations eventually put rather a severe strain upon his *rentier* economy. On October 20, 1838, he received this letter from Munroe:

Your note for $311.25 given to Wilkins & Carter for Paper for Carlyle's Miscellanies is payable on Tuesday next the 23d. The amount received of subscribers & Copies sold for Cash is $147.20 leaving a balance of $164.05. We shall depend upon you to put us in funds in season to meet the note as we have no money on hand unappropriated at this time.[20]

On July 8, 1839, he wrote to his brother William: "I am in terror growing every moment for a certain paper maker's bill of $500, to be paid for Carlyle's book July 15." [21] At least once he had to borrow money to meet these extraordinary expenses. But Munroe was honest, the *Miscellanies* prospered, and the laws of compensation continued to operate: during the lean summer of 1841, Emerson was kept out of debt by the payments which finally came from the publishers.[22]

The first two volumes were published on July 14, 1838.[23] They contained in approximately chronological order the essays written before 1831 and, although Emerson had thought them neither the best nor the most likely to succeed, they were very successful: within two weeks two hundred and fifty sets had been sold. By October 17 Emerson could report that half of the edition was gone and that it was both influential and well received. The third and fourth volumes were published on July 1, 1839; they contained material as recent as the

---

[18] MS owned by RWEMA.   [19] *Let RWE,* II, 123.   [20] MS owned by RWEMA.
[21] *Let RWE,* II, 206.   [22] *Ibid.,* p. 454.   [23] *Ibid.,* p. 143n.

review of Varnhagen von Ense's *Memoirs* which had appeared in the *London and Westminster* the preceding December. They were bought even more eagerly than their predecessors, Emerson wrote, and there was, as he had expected, special enthusiasm for the essays on Johnson and Scott.

A month before the first Boston *Miscellanies* went on sale, Carlyle proposed the importation of two or three hundred copies to make an English edition. His old publisher Fraser had been talking half-heartedly for some time about a collection of the early essays, but Carlyle had now taken his business to the more enterprising firm of Saunders and Ottley, who were willing to undertake the binding and sale of American sheets. To this proposal Emerson quickly agreed: five hundred copies of Volumes I and II were still in sheets and Carlyle could have as many as he wished. But Jane Carlyle disagreed. She thought that Americans knew best how to make money out of her husband's books. And then Saunders and Ottley grew hesitant and prudent. As a result it was not until November, when the first copies of Volumes I and II arrived in London, that Carlyle was able to make up his mind. He would buy two hundred and sixty copies of all four volumes at cost, bound (but with the pages uncut or rough-cut, after the English fashion), and have them sold for him by Fraser. This imported edition did not arrive in England until the summer of 1839; by December 8 it was entirely sold and Fraser, understandably, because by the "Rules of the Trade" he was to receive somewhat more than half of the £500 the books had brought into his till, lamented that Carlyle had not ordered a thousand. "This thousand," Carlyle wrote, "he now sets about providing, by his own industry, poor man."

The American edition was not so quickly exhausted. Bills of exchange from Munroe continued to arrive in Emerson's letters as late as March, 1844. "America," wrote Carlyle in acknowledgment of that final payment, "is like an amiable family teapot; you think it is all out long since, and lo, the valuable implement yields you another cup, and another!" And when the Boston teapot was empty there was a cup to be had from Philadelphia. In January, 1845, Carey and Hart, publishers of that city, offered to buy what remained of the Boston *Miscellanies,* or, astonishingly in an age of piracy, to pay Carlyle £50 for his permission to publish an edition of their own. Because only thirteen sets of the Munroe edition remained, Emerson accepted the latter alternative, and Carlyle wrote in approval: "You have made another brave bargain for me . . . '*Euge! Papae!*' "

Brave bargains of this sort had become, even before 1846, a stable element in the Carlyle-Emerson relationship. On December 8, 1839, for example, when Fraser was about to publish the essay "Chartism" as a booklet, Carlyle blandly wrote to Emerson, "I mean to send you the Proofsheets of this thing, to do with as you see cause." And Emerson, quickly and expertly, struck a bargain with Little and Brown which was to bring Carlyle in time one hundred and fifty American dollars. But there was more to transatlantic bibliopoly than the making of bargains. Two publishers, four books, various editions, various and complex financial arrangements, debts, interest: these were the elements in a commercial tangle which Emerson by 1840 needed professional help to cope with. From that time on his letters regularly enclosed statements in the neat hand of Nichols, Munroe's clerk, "of the mutual claims between the great houses of T. C. & R. W. E." Too few of these enclosures have survived to permit a final auditing of the account, but even one—that of April 25, 1839, for example—is sufficient to show the depth of Emerson's financial involvement, the breadth of his activity as promoter-advertiser-circulation manager, and the intensity with which he scrutinized the pettiest details. And one sentence of thanks is sufficient to show that Carlyle did not misread those columns of figures: "will you forgive me if I never do verify this same account, or look at it more in this world except as a memento of affection, its arithmetical ciphers so many hierograms, really sacred to me!" [24]

When Emerson's first volume of *Essays* reached England in 1841, Carlyle did not, surprisingly, recognize at once the opportunity to make a payment on his large transatlantic debt. It was the timorous Fraser who first suggested an English reprint of 750 copies with a preface by Carlyle and half of the profits for Emerson. But Carlyle wrote the preface, read the proof, clipped reviews, kept track of sales, and took pleasure in being able to write, "There man! Tit for tat." The half-profits, when they came, were modest enough, only one hundred and twenty-one dollars. The *Essays* were bought, however, by five hundred Englishmen; they received the honor of a piratical reprint; and they aroused another publisher, John Chapman, to write to Concord for new manuscripts. Chapman's letter arrived opportunely in August, 1844, as Emerson was reading the proof sheets of his second volume of *Essays*,[25] and so, Fraser having in the meantime died, Chapman became Emerson's English publisher. For *Essays, Second Series* Carlyle again read proof and wrote an *imprimatur*. "The reciprocity," as he had said, was *"not all on one side."*

Piracy had become by this time a major hazard to transatlantic bibliopoly, which necessitated for Carlyle and Emerson the development of evasive and defensive maneuvers. The sheets of *Heroes and Hero-Worship*, sent early from London as usual, somehow went astray and did not arrive in America before the first copies of the book itself had reached the New York publisher Appleton. Despite Emerson's protest, Appleton reprinted the book and announced his intention of doing the same with all future publications of Carlyle. To meet the threat, Emerson proposed that Carlyle have his manuscripts copied by a scrivener and sent to America in time for simultaneous publication. So in 1843 *Past and Present* arrived in Concord, partly in sheets, partly in the scrawly hand of "a poor young governess, confined to a horizontal posture, and many sad thoughts, by a disease of the spine," and Emerson set about publishing an American edition. But piracy had entered a new phase. Cheap reprint houses in New York and Philadelphia fell instantly on all English books of importance, published them in pamphlet or newspaper form, and within a few hours had them, as Emerson said, "hawked by a hundred boys in the streets of all our cities for 25, 18, or 12 cents." Since under these conditions no publisher would buy an English book, Emerson once again employed Little and Brown to print an edition "on our own account." He ordered 1,500 copies, set a competitive retail price of seventy-five cents, wrote a prefatory notice that this was the authorized edition, requested the major pirates to respect private property,[26] and hoped for a profit of three hundred dollars. These measures were successful for only a few weeks. After that a minor pirate named Colyer launched an edition at twelve and a half cents which captured most of the American trade. Emerson's *Past and Present* paid for itself but produced little profit: after four

[25] *Let RWE*, III, 265*n*.

[26] Harper and Brothers replied on May 9, 1843: "Upon the receipt of your favour of April 26th, we intended to say, by return of mail, what we *now* beg leave to say, that we shall not interfere with the arrangements referred to, as having been made by you, for Mr. Carlyle's benefit" (MS owned by RWEMA).

years and a publisher's auction there were still sixty-three copies un-sold. In this failure and in the pirating of *Essays,* Carlyle read the end of his bibliopolic relations with Emerson: "Such chivalrous interna-tional doings must cease between us."

Emerson, however, had one more maneuver to propose: perhaps the pirates could be beaten by their own methods. Let Carlyle, he wrote on February 29, 1844, send over a manuscript copy of *Cromwell* as soon as it is finished, so that James Munroe may "print a cheap edition such as no one will undersell, & secure such a share of profit to the author as the cheap press allows." But the last words of *Cromwell* were not written for a year and a half, and Carlyle, more than ordinarily exhausted, fled a few days later to Scotland without sending either manuscript copy or sheets. "I forbid you," he wrote, "to plague your-self any farther with these . . . Booksellers." He was followed to Scot-land, however, by reproving letters from Emerson, and so on his return he had his publishers despatch a copy to Concord, one month before publication, by way of the New York publishing house of Wiley and Putnam. These circumstances of time and place made it impossible, or dangerous, for Emerson to employ the slow Boston presses of Munroe. Instead he accepted the offer which Horace Greeley of the New York *Tribune* had made two months before:

A note from Miss Fuller informs me that you have just received the sheets of Carlyle's "Life of Cromwell." If you have not arranged for their publication, and can assure us a month's start of other American publishers, I would like to issue the work in 25 cent numbers—probably 4—and then in a compact volume. We will give half the clear profits, if any can be made on it.[27]

But this promising plan was frustrated by a muddle which led finally to the end of bibliopolic chivalry. Wiley and Putnam announced to Greeley that they intended to keep Emerson's copy of *Cromwell* until they had brought out a reprint of their own for which they had the approval of Chapman and Hall, Carlyle's London publishers. Greeley "said what he thought proper on the occasion, but of course without effect." [28] Emerson, angered at piracy so flagrant and at interference with the mails, asked his brother, a New York lawyer, "to commence usual proceedings against these men." [29] Carlyle, infuriated, wrote to his publishers for an "explicit contradiction" of the claims of Wiley

[27] E.10.14.45, MS owned by RWEMA.   [28] E.12.10.45, MS owned by RWEMA.
[29] *Let RWE,* III, 316.

and Putnam which could be "published in the New York papers; to point out the said Wiley and Putnam there, and stamp them publicly for the hungry thievish hyaenas that they are." [30] But Chapman and Hall explicitly and apologetically confirmed what Wiley and Putnam had said: misunderstanding a remark of Carlyle's and ignorant of Emerson's plans, Chapman had sold Wiley and Putnam an advance copy for £50 and suggested that Emerson's copy be tardily delivered.[31] By the time the epithets had settled, it was clear that the publishers were all honorable men. Perhaps a general feeling of embarrassment moved Wiley and Putnam to make a generous offer for the second edition of *Cromwell* and Emerson and Carlyle to accept. By the summer of 1846, at any rate, relations were so good that Carlyle granted Wiley and Putnam a near monopoly in American publication of his works. This establishment of a regular commercial connection meant for Emerson a considerable step towards retirement from the irregular literary agency which he had undertaken eleven years before.

A further and even more important step was the enlistment of E. P. Clark, a Boston banker, as Carlyle's American auditor and financial plenipotentiary. Clark, "a Carlylese of that intensity that . . . he has collected a sort of album of several volumes, containing illustrations of every kind, historical, critical, &c, to the *Sartor*," [32] had become involved in Carlylean bibliopoly as early as the summer of 1843 and had been promising for years to make a complete audit of the Carlyle-Emerson accounts. This old business was never actually accomplished, but Emerson had enough faith in Clark's good will to suggest, when the contract with Wiley and Putnam was being drawn up, that all new business be submitted to his "audit and umpirage." This suggestion both Clark and Carlyle accepted, and eventually the two men entered into a formal commercial relationship. "My dear Sir," Carlyle wrote to Clark on March 18, 1847,

Tho' I have long known you, in a very kind manner, thro' Mr Emerson and otherwise, and have even made use of you as a practical Friend, our relation, very genuine in itself, has been hitherto a silent one. But now, it would appear, the time for speech too has come. I have a piece of real business to entrust you with. . . .

Last year, as you are aware, in a Contract made with the Messrs Wiley & Putnam Booksellers of New-York, . . . I took the liberty to nominate you as

---

[30] C.12.29.45, MS owned by the Pierpont Morgan Library.   [31] *Let RWE*, III, 325.

[32] See below, E.10.30.43. This album is now owned by the Harvard College Library.

my representative with them in all pecuniary matters that were to arise in consequence. . . .

Of Messrs W. & P.'s intention to keep these terms, as regular merchants and honourable men, I have no reason to entertain the smallest doubt. But it becomes important for me, as you will perceive,—apart even from the probably very considerable *pecuniary* interests involved in the business,—to ascertain for myself, with the completest possible assurance, that the terms *are* accurately kept; that no portion of the concern which is really mine in this matter be in any way huddled into twilight and confusion, but that it be all really seen into, managed, and made the best of. . . .

Now if you, as a real man of business, will undertake this charge for me, I shall, at all times, with the completest satisfaction I could have in it, be able to assure myself that it is actually getting itself done; that I personally need give myself no more trouble about it. The function to be performed is this simple one; . . . but it is a thing, too, which cannot be done without trouble, without exertion, scrutiny and locomotion; in fact the whole charge I am struggling to put upon you is founded on work, on trouble.

For which reason, and according to an old principle of mine, I find it altogether indispensable that the man who undertakes this service for me must expect and receive *his due professional wages.* . . . Tell me you undertake the business professionally, for due wages, then the matter is already settled, and you are fully installed and authorized, and I shall be free of care thenceforth;—and over above all wages you will have done me a favour which I shall deeply acknowledge. . . .[33]

Clark did undertake the business professionally, as even a less intense Carlylese might have done, with Wiley and Putnam and with other publishers, and Emerson found himself free from most of the "exertion, scrutiny, and locomotion" of selling another man's books.

Bibliopolic relations between Carlyle and Emerson did not, of course, abruptly cease in 1847. There was unfinished business like the loss of Carey and Hart's £50 draft. There was new business like finding an American publisher for John Carlyle's translation of Dante. In the search for missing papers by and about Margaret Fuller, Carlyle acted as Emerson's agent. Emerson got himself involved in an ugly quarrel between Carlyle and the Harpers. But there was no real need for commercial chivalry. Carlyle's poverty, never very severe, was no longer even a subject for rhetoric. His obscurity had lifted after *The French Revolution* and his name now appeared as frequently as that of Dickens in the literary gossip columns of American newspapers. Even piracy, although in the absence of international copyright laws it was still a

[33] MS owned by the Houghton Library of Harvard University.

menace, had subsided under moral and economic pressures, and American publishers were accustomed to pay generously for "authorized editions" of important English books. Whatever the causes (and other, deeper ones may perhaps be found in the events of the next few years), bibliopoly was not after 1847 a major subject of the Carlyle-Emerson correspondence or a central element in the Carlyle-Emerson relationship.

But central and fundamental to that relationship it had indeed been. Emerson's labors had brought Carlyle money (payments of £655 are recorded in the letters) at a time when it was genuinely useful; more important, they had brought him fame and followers abroad at a time when he lacked both at home; most important, they represented a sustained benevolence which left Carlyle—for the reciprocity *was* mainly on one side—a permanent debtor. It was less the memory of one bright day at Craigenputtock than gratitude for many dull years of bibliopoly which kept this friendship alive when, after 1847, personal friction and political difference brought it close to death.

INTERLUDE
1847-1848

In the winter of 1847 Emerson began seriously to consider invitations he had received from admirers in Lancashire who wished him to make an extended English lecture tour. The enterprise was laden with much domestic difficulty for a man so committed and involved as Emerson, but it was professionally and personally very attractive. Among the strongest of its personal values was surely the prospect of a reunion with Carlyle. The letter of January 31, 1847, which told Carlyle about the possibility of the journey suggested in its very gaiety that Emerson had already made his decision.

Somebody or somebodies in Liverpool & Manchester have proposed once or twice, with more or less specification, that I should come to those cities to lecture. And who knows but I may come one day? Steam is strong & Liverpool is near. . . . Then I have a very ignorant love of pictures, and a curiosity about the Greek statues & stumps in the British Museum. So beware of me, for on that distant day when I get ready, I shall come.

Carlyle's reply glowed with encouragement and invitation:

If you will travel like a private quiet person, who knows but I, the most unlocomotive of mortals, might be able to escort you up and down a little. . . . There is a spare-room always in this House for you,—in this heart, in these two hearts, the like. . . .

And his later letters were equally warm:

A prophet's chamber is ready for you in Chelsea, and a brotherly and sisterly welcome, on whatever day at whatever hour you arrive.

On July 31 Emerson sent a letter of acceptance to Lancashire and wrote Carlyle, "In my old age I am coming to see you." On October 5, leaving his household in the hands of Henry Thoreau, he sailed for Liverpool aboard the packet *Washington Irving*.

The reunion had a farcical prologue. When Emerson's July letter arrived, the Carlyles were traveling in the north. It followed them to

Derbyshire, failed somehow to be delivered there, and was sent back to Chelsea, where Jane Carlyle found it on or shortly after her return in the middle of September.[1] She sent it to Carlyle, who was by then in Scotland with his mother. He, reading it on September 27, nearly two months after it had been written, was distressed by what must seem a breach of hospitality and friendship: "I fear I must have got into a mess with Emerson . . . the truest friend or among the truest I now have." But he was tired; he had passed "one of the wearisomest days ever spent by mortal"; and he instructed his wife to answer the letter for him.[2] Jane, too, had been spending wearisome days. After her return she had "suffered horribly from irritation, nausea, and languor."[3] Then she had spent the last week of September at Addiscombe, one of the country houses of the Ashburtons, where her sufferings had been ignored, as if she were a hypochondriac. By October 9 she could report that some preparations had been made: "I have been in a pretty mess with Emerson's bed, having some apprehensions he would arrive before it was up again. The quantity of sewing that lies in a lined chintz bed is something awfully grand!"[4] But neither she nor Carlyle had written the letter.

By the time Carlyle reached Chelsea the social situation was desperate: Emerson, if he had sailed, as he first planned, "about the 1 October," would already be nearing Liverpool or London. But to which port and by what ship he was coming Carlyle did not know and could

[1] *Letters and Memorials,* I, 291. In the National Library of Scotland there is a letter from Jane Carlyle to her husband which gives more details about the mishap. It is dated in the hand of Alexander Carlyle, who was usually accurate in this regard, September 25, 1847. "Here is a letter for you—from Emerson—I think—which you ought to have received that Sunday morning at Buxton, and which Postie has recovered with infinite pains. The fact of its existence was revealed to me in this accidental manner—Mrs Piper said one day she would have done so&so only that when she wrote to ask me about it I had sent no answer—I replied that no letter from her had ever reached me—that was strange, she said, for her husband sealed her letter into *the shilling one* that was forwarded to the post office at Buxton— I said to the best of my recollection you got *no* letter at Buxton—and certainly could not have got *that* one or *I* would have got the enclosure— When she told her Husband he affirmed that a shilling-letter—American he thought—had been forwarded to Buxton in time to reach you there on the Sunday morning—and after much writing or signing of papers the enclosed has been looked up—" (Manuscript Volume 603).

[2] Thomas Carlyle, *Letters to His Wife,* ed. Trudy Bliss, p. 238.

[3] *Letters and Memorials,* I, 297.

[4] *Ibid.,* p. 305.

not at the last minute ascertain. The man who was arranging Emerson's tour, however, Alexander Ireland, now editor of the Manchester *Examiner,* might reasonably be assumed to have such information. On October 15 Carlyle wrote Emerson a letter of welcome which was full of indignation at the delinquent Derbyshire postmaster, silent about other delinquencies, equivocal about dates, and, perhaps in part as a result of these embarrassments, extraordinarily warm. He addressed it "to R W E: on the instant when he lands in England" [5] and enclosed it in a letter to Ireland with "solemn charges" to have it "delivered duly." [6]

On Friday, October 22, Ireland learned by telegraph that the *Washington Irving* was off Holyhead in Wales, about sixty miles from Liverpool. Since the *Examiner* was published on Fridays, he was unable to go to Liverpool himself. Instead he sent a young assistant, Francis Espinasse, with an explanatory note which enclosed the letter from Carlyle. In Liverpool, Espinasse was informed that the ship would not arrive for two days, and so he returned to Manchester and sent the letter by mail. But he had been misinformed. Late Friday evening the *Washington Irving* anchored in Liverpool harbor, and Emerson went ashore with the captain by boat, to find not only no greeting from Carlyle but no instructions from Ireland. He took a room at the Waterloo Hotel and waited. On Saturday he sought out the Unitarian minister James Martineau, brother of his friend Harriet, and had tea with him. On Sunday he heard him preach. Finally on Monday morning the vagrant letters arrived: Ireland's a friendly invitation to spend the weekend in Manchester and "talk over your campaign," Carlyle's "so hearty a welcome & so urgent an invitation to house & hearth, that [Emerson] could no more resist" it than he could "gravitation." He went immediately to Manchester, where he talked with Ireland for an hour or two and found that the campaign would not begin for a week. Then he took the train for London, probably the fast train, which traveled the 212 miles in an astonishing six hours. By ten o'clock that evening the door at 5 Cheyne Row was opened for him "by Jane Carlyle, and the man himself was behind her with a lamp in the entry." [7]

Emerson's first impression was that the Carlyles had changed little

[5] *Let RWE,* III, 422.   [6] *New Letters,* II, 51.

[7] *Let RWE,* III, 442*n*, 422–23, 426, 428; and Francis Espinasse, *Literary Recollections and Sketches,* p. 156.

since he had seem them at Craigenputtock fourteen years before. Talk began immediately and did not cease until one in the morning. It started again at breakfast and continued during an afternoon walk through the center of the city, "Carlyle melting all Westminster & London down into his talk & laughter as he walked." That evening Dr. John Carlyle, who had just finished his translation of the *Inferno,* came for dinner, and there was more talk, until late. Thus, at any rate, ran the pleasant report which Emerson sent to his wife. He had not, he wrote, fully understood Carlyle in the single day of the Craigenputtock visit. Carlyle's writings did not give an adequate account of his personality, nor was it to be understood by analogy with New England intellectuals. Carlyle was more like "a very practical Scotchman, such as you would find in any sadler's or iron dealer's shop" or like Hugh Whelan, the Emerson's gardener:

Suppose that Hugh Whelan had had leisure enough in addition to all his daily work, to read Plato, & Shakespeare, & Calvin, and, remaining Hugh Whelan all the time, should talk scornfully of all this nonsense of books that he had been bothered with,—and you shall have just the tone & talk & laughter of Carlyle.[8]

Emerson stayed with the Carlyles until Friday, and his letters to his wife, then and later, showed only faint shadows of dissatisfaction with these old friends. His letter of thanks, written from Manchester on November 5, mentioned "astonishment" and "consternation," but its tone was intimate and affectionate. The reunion had evidently been, for Emerson, more successful than reunions generally are.

For Carlyle the experience was somewhat different. This act of hospitality was an obligation but also an annoyance: it broke in upon his privacy and disrupted his rigid schedule of work. By good luck he finished an article for *Fraser's,* an edition of some newly discovered letters of Cromwell, just an hour before Emerson arrived, but he knew, as he said in a letter to his mother next day, that the visit "would put an end to work for some time!" He was dismayed to find that Emerson planned to stay "till next week" and exhausted by the torrent of talk that flowed through his house. He had urgent letters to write—to his mother, whom he had put off with a short note the day before; to his sister, who must be told about the fate of the box of honeycomb which

[8] *Let RWE,* III, 424.

he had brought back with him from her house: "She *leaked,* my lassie, leaked about a matter of two pounds, we guessed,—but only into some shirts and such like, mostly *dirty* ones too!"; and there all the while was Emerson in the same room, rummaging through his books, waiting impatiently for talk to begin again. But Emerson still seemed, on that first day, "a very fine fellow, whom it is pleasant to talk with," "a fine brave gentle ingenious creature." [9]

Two days later, Jane Carlyle wrote to her friend Lady Ashburton:

He is come then, is here, this Yankee seraph. We have seen him "face to face and (over) soul to (over) soul." For two days I have lived in the *manna* of his speech, and now I have escaped to my bedroom, to *bathe my head* in *cold water,* and report progress to you.

So far all has gone better than you "predicted"; they do not *hate* one another *yet:* C. still calls Emerson "a most polite and gentle creature, a man of really seraphic nature, tho' on certain sides of him overlaid with mad rubbish" and Emerson still (in confidence to me) calls C. "a good child (!) in spite of all his deification of the *Positive,* the *Practical,* most astonishing for those who had first made acquaintance with him in his books!" [10]

And Carlyle wrote to the same "high lady" on November 3, a few days after Emerson's departure:

His sad Yankee rule seemed to be, that talk should go on incessantly except when sleep interrupted it: a frightening rule. The man, as you have heard, is not above bargain, nor if one will be candid, is he fairly much below it. A pure-minded elevated man; *elevated* but without breadth, as a willow is, as a reed is; no fruit at all to be gathered from him. A delicate, but thin pinched triangular face, no jaws nor lips, lean hook-nose; face of a *cock* . . . No getting into any intimacy with him, talk as you will. You have my leave to fall in love with him, if you can! And so he plays his part: gone to lecture in Lancashire; to return hither he knows not when: it is privately hoped he may go to Rome! I wish him honestly well, do as I am bound respect him honestly; but *Friends,* it is clear, we can never in this world, to any real purpose be.[11]

The Carlyles were not notably temperate letter-writers. Cattiness and backbiting are part of the peculiar flavor of their correspondence, as are caricature, whim, and rhetorical exuberance, and they always wrote to Lady Ashburton at higher than normal pitch. But these two letters

[9] NLS, MS 521 and MS 512.
[10] Iris Origo, "The Carlyles and the Ashburtons," *The Cornhill Magazine,* CLXIV (1950), 461–62.
[11] *Ibid.,* p. 461.

about Emerson seem somehow genuine in their denial of friendship. They are supported, too, by a letter which Carlyle wrote on November 8 to his mother, with whom he was always at his most sober and charitable:

Emerson is lecturing both at Manchester and Liverpool, as you have heard. I rather think his popularity is not very great hitherto; his doctrines are too *airy* and thin for the solid practical heads of the Lancashire region. We had immense talking with him here; but found he did not give us much to chew the cud upon,—found in fact that he came with the *rake* rather than the *shovel*. He is a pure high-minded man, but I think his talent is not quite so high as I had anticipated.[12]

For the time being, at any rate, the Craigenputtock warmth with which the Carlyles welcomed Emerson in October had cooled into something between disenchantment and mocking repudiation. It is hardly likely that such a change was the result of differences in temperament or the ordinary tensions of hospitality.

There seems, in fact, to have been a quarrel—if we may consider Emerson capable of quarreling—over fundamental matters of politics and morality. The time was one of acute political crisis, at home and abroad, about which Carlyle had a deep, personal sense of urgency and involvement. Emerson, he must soon have discovered, held beliefs of a bland and innocent sort which directly contradicted his own; worse, Emerson not only rejected his solution to the problems of the time but scoffed at it. Francis Espinasse, who saw Emerson in Manchester immediately after the London visit, perceived a little "irritation" in him which he thought a consequence of his "refusal to fall down and worship" Carlyle's hero Cromwell.[13] And Emerson, in a letter to Elizabeth Hoar late in December, wrote: "Carlyle takes Cromwell sadly to heart. When I told him that he must not expect that people as old as I could look at Cromwell as he did, he turned quite fiercely upon me." [14] This, presumably, was the clash which Emerson recounted, more fully and dramatically, to George Searle Phillips:

Emerson said that he had just visited Carlyle—who had grown so fierce & savage that he should be afraid of trusting some of his more gentle & spiritually minded friends in his presence. His denunciations of high & sacred things are so terrible, he said, that they could not fail to do harm to any young,

[12] NLS, MS 521. [13] Espinasse, *Literary Recollections and Sketches*, p. 161.
[14] *Let RWE*, III, 460.

unbalanced persons who did not know from what deep sincere depths all that denunciation sprung. Carlyle, he said, had grown impatient of opposition, especially when talking of Cromwell. I differed from him, he added, in his estimate of Cromwell's character, & he rose like a great Norse giant from his chair—and, drawing a line with his finger across the table, said, with terrible fierceness: Then, sir, there is a line of separation between you and me as wide as that, & as deep as the pit.[15]

Such ferocity was surely not engendered by a disagreement over historical fact or interpretation of personality. To Carlyle discipline and dictatorship were as necessary for salvation in the nineteenth century as they had been in the seventeenth, and one's attitude toward Cromwell was a measure of one's spiritual health and worldly wisdom. Emerson's moral optimism, his anarchism, his pacifism might seem merely evidence of idiocy; his dismissal of Cromwellism as childish must have been intolerable heresy which bordered on personal affront.

Not seriously disturbed by the clash, determined merely to meet Carlyle again with "the most serene skeptical calmness," Emerson traveled about, preaching his airy doctrines to the solid practical heads of the north, until March, 1848. He was busier with lectures than he had ever been in New England, he was lionized by both transcendentalists and capitalists, and he was studying the anatomy of an extremely complex society: he found little time to write to Carlyle. The letters he did write, and those which came from Carlyle, were as easy and cordial as any in the correspondence, as if nothing had gone wrong in London, as if they had 3,000 miles of sea to travel and not 212 miles of rail. But when the northern lecturing was over and the time came for Emerson to return to London, the prophet's chamber in Chelsea did not have quite the gravitational pull it had had in October. To Carlyle's warm invitation of February 28, "your room is standing vacant ever since you quitted it,—ready to be lighted up with all manner of physical and moral fires that the place will yield; and is in fact *your* room, and expects to be accounted such," Emerson replied with perhaps skeptical calmness that he had taken rooms in the house of his publisher, John Chapman.

The second London visit began almost as favorably as the first. On his first day in the city Emerson went, a self-invited guest, to dinner at the Carlyles'. Three days later Carlyle and his brother called at Emer-

[15] Phillips ("January Searle"), *Emerson, His Life & Writings*, p. 47.

son's rooms, and there was talk about the new French Revolution and the revolutionary rumblings of Chartism.[16] On March 9 Emerson wrote to Ireland that he found Carlyle "in the best humour at the events in France. . . . I think him a most valuable companion, and speaking the best opinions one is likely to hear in this nation. It is by no means easy to talk with him but there is little need of that." [17] On the 18th Emerson was delighted to receive a call from Jane Carlyle at his rooms in Chapman's house. "A noble child," he called her, for having come so far and climbed three flights of stairs to see him. He did not know that her kindness was unintentional, that she "had *not* come to see him—far from it," as she reported to John Forster, but had been looking for another bookseller named Chapman to inquire about the success of Geraldine Jewsbury's new novel.[18]

Later that month Carlyle introduced Emerson into the aristocratic houses which he frequented. "On Thursday," he wrote to his sister Jean, March 26,

I had again an eight-o'clock dinner to execute at the Barings', on occasion of Emerson,—or rather Emerson was but the *excuse* of it, for he kept very quiet; mild modest eyes, lips sealed together like a pair of pincers, and nobody minded him much; we had quantities of Lords, Town-wits (Thackeray &c), beautiful ladies;—and I, as usual, got a most sick head and heart by it.[19]

Emerson took some satisfaction in finding that his friend's fierce jeremiads were not taken very seriously in those exalted circles. "All his methods," Emerson wrote to his wife, "include a good deal of killing, & he does not see his way very clearly or far." [20]

By April, 1848, the friendship was again in serious danger. This time it was Emerson who took offense. "I seldom see Carlyle," he wrote to his wife, "& I do not see him with much pleasure: he is always strong, but always pounding on the same strings, one endless vituperation of all people & things in the modern world." [21] Once again the offense was in matters of politics and morality: Emerson seems to have heard more than enough of killing and vituperation. In his journal he began to apply to Carlyle such phrases as "arrogance and contempt," "brag and conceit." [22] He wrote this account of his friend's conversation:

[16] *Let RWE*, IV, 34.
[17] Alexander Ireland, *In Memoriam: Ralph Waldo Emerson*, p. 202.
[18] *Letters and Memorials*, I, 244–45.   [19] NLS, MS 512.
[20] *Let RWE*, IV, 43.   [21] *Ibid.*, p. 49.   [22] *Journals*, VII, 348, 367.

His sneers and scoffs are thrown in every direction. He breaks every sentence with a scoffing laugh,—"windbag," "monkey," "donkey," "bladder," and let him describe whom he will, it is always "poor fellow." I said, "What a fine fellow you are to bespatter the world with this oil of vitriol!" [23]

He entered this sketch of Carlyle's character: "I find C always cunning: he denies the books he reads; denies the friends he has just visited; denies his own acts & purposes;—By God, I do not know them—and immediately the cock crows." [24] On April 25, after dinner at Lincoln's Inn Fields with Forster, Dickens, and Carlyle, he wrote a brief statement of the Carlylean social philosophy: "Carlyle is no idealist in opinions, but a protectionist in political economy, aristocrat in politics, epicure in diet, goes for murder, money, punishment by death, slavery, and all the pretty abominations, tempering them with epigrams." [25] Beyond this point, for Emerson, bitterness could hardly go, and friendship hardly survive.

Fortunately, Emerson was a very busy man. He was meeting most of the writers in London, not as a pilgrim but as a distinguished visitor. He was enjoying a considerable degree of lionhood, or at least utilizing it for the study of English traits. Fortunately, too, he had chosen the month of May for a trip to revolutionary Paris. And when he returned, on June 3, he found himself involved in a course of lectures which his friends, among them Carlyle, had arranged in order to introduce him to the fashionable audience of London.[26] On June 8 he sent his wife, without ironic or hostile comments, a copy of the *Spectator* which contained two protectionist articles by Carlyle.[27] Business and absence had perhaps been effective medicine for a sick friendship.

The friendship was strong enough, at any rate, to survive the critical period of Emerson's London lectures. After the first lecture the Carlyles and young Espinasse went to Emerson's lodging with words of congratulation. "Very Emersonian," Carlyle managed to say, instead of the "moonshiny discourses" and "intellectual sonatas" which represented his private opinion. When Carlyle ridiculed him for merely reading from the platform instead of suffering the torments of improvisation, Emerson kept a pacific silence.[28] In spite of genuine distaste, which became shock and moral indignation when they heard

[23] *Ibid.*, pp. 347-48. E. W. Emerson prints this passage as if written in 1847, but the reference to Milnes, etc., indicate 1848 as the correct year.
[24] Typescript journals, XVII (Journal LM, p. 103).   [25] *Journals*, VII, 441.
[26] Rusk, *Life*, p. 351.   [27] *Let RWE*, IV, 81.
[28] Espinasse, *Literary Recollections and Sketches*, p. 161.

Emerson assert that even in a brothel man "is on his way to all that is great & good," [29] the Carlyles continued to attend his lectures. And Emerson was sufficiently pleased by seeing them there to interpret as "loud Scottish Covenanter gruntings of laudation, or, at least of consideration" [30] what James Froude heard as "a loud, kindly contemptuous laugh." [31] Carlyle even attended a second series of lectures priced for the middle class, and although he complained to Lady Ashburton of the unselect and unaristocratic audience and of his boredom with "the High Child," [32] he accepted a seat on the platform directly behind the speaker. Emerson found this intrusion "odious," but he seems to have complained only to his wife. On the evening of July 1, the day after Emerson's final lecture, the Carlyles went to Chapman's house for "a sort of farewell party." And perhaps, Emerson told his wife, Carlyle would go with him to Stonehenge before he sailed. They had talked about it.[33]

Carlyle did go. And the weekend that the two men spent sight-seeing in Hampshire and Wiltshire was one of the most important periods in the history of their friendship. They took with them all their polarities of character, all their conflicts, but these were somehow muted by tolerance, by good humor, perhaps by the thought that this too was a sort of a farewell party. The Stonehenge trip was a recapitulation and a coda; it was also a resolution of discord.

They left London on Friday, July 7, and traveled by train to Salisbury. They talked of travel, of art, of science. Carlyle spoke of the superiority of English culture to American. Emerson, although he agreed, argued that by the necessities of geography the future was American "and that England, an old and exhausted island, must one day be contented, like other parents to be strong only in her children." [34] This was dangerous material, but they handled it without explosions. They went by carriage from Salisbury to Amesbury, where they stopped at the George Inn, which had been recommended by Hazlitt, Dickens, and Forster.[35] There they had a dinner which perhaps served as a lightning rod for Carlyle's wrath: "whale-blubber mutton

---

[29] *Ibid.*, p. 164. This version of the brothel sentence is from Phillips, *Emerson,* p. 7.

[30] *Let RWE*, IV, 85.   [31] Froude, *Thomas Carlyle: Life in London,* I, 269.

[32] Origo, "The Carlyles and the Ashburtons," p. 463.   [33] *Let RWE*, IV, 94.

[34] Emerson, *Works,* V, 275. Unless otherwise indicated, facts about the Stonehenge trip are taken from chapter xvi of Emerson's *English Traits.*

[35] MS letter, TC to John Forster, owned by the Victoria and Albert Museum.

and old peas," he called it when he wrote his wife.[36] Then they walked two miles across the barren downs to Stonehenge. They "found a nook sheltered from the wind . . . where Carlyle lighted his cigar," they paced and counted the stones, they speculated about ancient Britain, and their "petty differences of nationality" seemed to Emerson to melt away. Carlyle was subdued and gentle and introspective. "I plant cypresses wherever I go," he said, "and if I am in search of pain, I cannot go wrong." (He had worn a thin coat on a chilly night.) [37] Back at the inn, he borrowed some note paper from Emerson and catalogued for his wife the sufferings of the day. He had been "obliged to *talk* all the way to Salisbury" . . . whale blubber . . . dreadful cold . . . no cream for the tea . . . not sleepy . . . doomed to travel to Wilton tomorrow in a *dogcart* . . . "Good night, my own poor Jeannie,— ah me!" But there was no rancor in the letter, and Emerson was painted accurately and amiably in its *chiaroscuro* postscript:

I wonder how your Chopin prospered; how your concert-tickets, etc.! Emerson is healthy; full of cheerfulness, at least, of unsubduable placidity: if I could get a little sleep, I should do weel enough yet. "Why art thou cast down, my soul; what should discourage *thee?*"
Good night, Dearest.[38]

Next morning the dogcart came and they went again, for half an hour, to Stonehenge. There "the local antiquary, Mr. Brown" pointed out the "astronomical" and "sacrificial" stones, and Emerson remembered seeing American masons move blocks quite as large for "the substructure of a house in Bowdoin Square, in Boston." As the dogcart carried them across the downs to Wilton, Carlyle fumed at the unfaithful stewardship of the landowners who kept the country for sheep when English workers were hungry and idle. (Emerson later learned that the land was untillable.) At Wilton the travelers visited the great manor house of the earls of Pembroke, from the present incumbent of which, Sidney Herbert, Carlyle had obtained a letter of admission in London. They inspected the portraits and the statuary, walked through the grounds, and returned to "a table laid . . . with bread, meats, peaches, grapes, and wine." Then they took the coach to Salisbury, for the cathedral, and the train to Bishopstoke, where their friend Arthur Helps met them and drove them to his house at Bishops Waltham.

[36] Trudy Bliss, ed., Carlyle, *Letters to His Wife*, p. 246.
[37] *Ibid.*   [38] *Ibid.*, p. 247.

It rained on Sunday. Emerson, Carlyle, and Helps sat in armchairs in the study, "disagreeing to the utmost, amicably," while wind and rain beat against the window.[39] Was there, the Englishmen provocatively asked, such a thing as an American idea? Emerson, provoked, replied that there was, but an idea in comparison with which French communism would seem solid and practicable. And he "sketched the Boston fanaticism of right and might without bayonets or bishops, every man his own king, and all coöperation necessary and extemporaneous." [40] With the bit in his teeth he raced beyond "the dogma of no-government and non-resistance" to a rejection of propaganda even for the good.[41] When luncheon was announced he was bravely defending the possibility of universal and permanent peace.[42] Carlyle received this Emersonian moonshine with astonishing mildness. He seemed, Emerson thought, impressed by some of the supporting anecdotes, and he gaily refused, on the ground that he was "altogether too wicked," to be the first to leave the study for luncheon. Emerson, in reply, planted his back against the wall, and Helps was obliged to terminate the boyish scuffle by announcing that he was the wickedest and would lead the way.

Late Sunday afternoon, after a visit to Winchester, Carlyle and Emerson took the train for London. That evening Carlyle, answering a letter from James Marshall of Leeds, included a brief, calm, and balanced judgment of the

Transatlantic Friend . . . who, after some months sojourn in these parts, is on the point of turning homeward again. A man of genius and worth in his American way; somewhat *moonshiny* here and there in the results he arrives at, but beautiful in speculation if you leave practise *out*,—in fact a kind of modern-antique "American Gymnosophist," for whom we are bound to be thankful.[43]

Sometime the next day, before Emerson took the train for Coventry, Carlyle gave him a copy of Anthony Wood's *Athenae Oxonienses* and, as he wrote in his journal on July 12, "parted with him in peace."

A spiritual *son* of mine? Yes, in a good degree, but gone into philanthropy and other moonshine; for the rest, a dignified, serene, and amiable man of a

[39] MS, Helps to Emerson, May 9, 1853, owned by RWEMA.
[40] Emerson, *Works*, V, 398.
[41] Charles Gavan Duffy, *Conversations with Carlyle*, p. 201.
[42] Espinasse, *Literary Recollections and Sketches*, p. 165.
[43] MS owned by the British Museum.

certain indisputable natural faculty, whose friendliness to me in this world has been great.[44]

A week later, in the same mood but with greater elaboration, he wrote his sister Jean a summary of Emerson's second visit:

Emerson, as perhaps you know, is gone to America again; left Liverpool by the steamer of Saturday last. He was very kindly treated by the people he got among; and is a man who praises everything, and in a languid kind of way is *content* with everything. I think he goes home very happy with his journey here. I found him very amiable, gentle-minded, sincere of heart; but withal rather *moonshiny, un*practical in his speculations, and it must be confessed a little wearisome from time to time! The things and persons he took interest in, were things generally quite of the *past tense* with me; and the best I could do generally was to listen to such psalmodyings as those of his *without* audibly wishing them at the Devil! He got among a poor washy set of people chiefly, "friends of humanity" &c—to keep wide *away* from whom is my most necessary struggle here,—so in fact I have not had very much relation to him at all; and as he sedulously keeps the peace with all mortals, and really loves me very well, I managed without difficulty to keep the peace to him; and our parting was altogether friendly. Poor Emerson,—I shall not see him again; and, alas, what good could the sight of him do me, or of me do him? That is the sad lot of mortals in this world. He zealously assured me of many deep (silent) friends in America; but I answered that for that very reason I ought to continue silent to them, and never behold them in the body: if they once found what a "fiery ettercap" I was, and how many of their delightful philanthropies I trampled under my feet, it would be a great vexation to both of us!—I attended all Emerson's Lectures here,—pleasant *moonshiny* discourses, delivered to a rather vapid miscellany of persons (friends of humanity, chiefly), and was not much grieved at the ending of them: after which, near ten days ago, I accompanied him into Wiltshire (100 miles) to visit a strange old Druid Monument called *Stonehenge* (concerning which visit I wrote Jamie an account the other day), and so, after gifts given and kind wishes expressed or understood, we parted in peace.[45]

On July 15, after a few days with George Eliot, Arthur Hugh Clough, and other friends of humanity, Emerson sailed from Liverpool. During his last few minutes in England, he walked the deck with young Clough and talked about Carlyle. "You leave all of us young Englishmen," said Clough,

[44] Froude, *Thomas Carlyle: Life in London,* I, 270.

[45] NLS, MS 512. "Ettercap" is a Scottish word meaning "spider"; Carlyle's allusion here is to chapter LXIV of *Waverley.* If the letter to Jamie is still in existence, I do not know its whereabouts.

without a leader. Carlyle has led us into the desert, and he has left us there."
Emerson said to him, "That is what all the young men in England have said
to me"; and he placed his hand on Clough's head and said, "I ordain you
Bishop of all England, to go up and down among the young men, and lead
them into the promised land." [46]

In his stateroom, however, as tokens of a relation in which lost leader-
ship and spiritual filiation were unimportant, Emerson had not only
Athenae Oxonienses but also the proofs of John Carlyle's *Inferno*,
for which he had undertaken to find an American publisher.

The friendship of Emerson and Carlyle had altered greatly in the
eight months since the *Washington Irving* anchored at Liverpool.
Whatever elements it had contained of sentimentality and hero worship had been burned out of it and replaced by irony and tolerance. It
had been tempered in disillusionment. The two men now knew the
worst about each other and were not to be shocked or shaken by the
deepest disagreement. Perhaps, too, they knew their debt to the Atlantic Ocean, for Carlyle's friendship, like his love, flourished best on
paper. They did not meet again till 1872, and that meeting was an
epilogue.

[46] Reported by Edward Everett Hale in an address in Brooklyn, May 24, 1893;
printed in his *Works*, VIII, 262. Emerson may have told this story on January 25,
1849, during a "whole afternoon" which he spent with Hale while waiting for a
train in Worcester, Mass. See E. E. Hale, Jr., *Life and Letters of Edward Everett
Hale*, I, 189. Clough, although he wrote to Thomas Arnold on July 16 that he
had seen Emerson "pass rapidly down the Mersey on his way home," did not
mention the ordination (*The Correspondence of Arthur Hugh Clough*, ed. Frederick
L. Mulhauser, I, 215). Another apocryphal but plausible story of the 1847–48 visit
might be thought of as a theological counterpart to this ecclesiastical tale of
Clough's. It was most fully told by George Eliot in a letter of October 19, 1851: "I
must tell you a story Miss Bremer got from Emerson. Carlyle was angry with him
for not believing in a devil, and to convert him took him amongst all the horrors
of London—the gin-shops, etc.—and finally to the House of Commons, plying him
at every turn with the question, 'Do you believe in a devil noo?'" (Gordon S.
Haight, ed., *The George Eliot Letters*, I, 372. The same story appears in Richard
Garnett's *Life of Thomas Carlyle*, p. 124, where it is attributed to Caroline Fox, but
I do not find it in her *Memories of Old Friends*.

SILENCES

1848-1872

In 1903 a newspaper reviewer of Mead's *The Influence of Emerson* wrote that there had been far more friction between Emerson and Carlyle than was generally realized. "At one time," the reviewer remembered, "when Carlyle's temper was particularly bad," Emerson said, " 'I have let silence answer him so far, and shall until he has a better mind.' " [1] This speech has an Emersonian ring and it seems at first to solve one of the puzzles of the Carlyle-Emerson relationship. From 1848 to 1872 the correspondence was marked by long and ominous silences, often of a year, once of three years, and almost always on the part of Emerson. But the letters which Emerson let silence answer were in no sense bad tempered: after 1848 Carlyle was consistently warm, kind, and conciliatory. If Emerson was offended, the cause must be sought outside the correspondence and outside the area of personal relations.

In the summer of 1848 Carlyle had told Emerson of his plans for "writing a newspaper or at least short off-hand tracts to follow each other rapidly on the political questions of the day." [2] The result of these plans was the publication, early in 1850, of the *Latter-Day Pamphlets*, angriest and extremest of Carlyle's attacks on democracy and on America, which might well have provoked a sensitive American democrat to punitive silence. "What great human soul," asked Carlyle about America,

what great thought, what great noble thing that one could worship, or loyally admire, has yet been produced there? None: The American cousins have yet done none of these things. "What have they done?" growls Smelfungus, tired of the subject: "They have doubled their population every twenty years. They have begotten, with a rapidity beyond recorded example, Eighteen Millions of the greatest *bores* ever seen in this world before,—that hitherto is their feat in History!"—And so we leave them, for the present; and cannot predict the success of Democracy, on this side of the Atlantic, from their example.[3]

[1] See p. 25 of a Columbia University scrapbook containing clippings on Emerson from the period 1903–19.

[2] *Let RWE*, IV, 86.   [3] *Works TC*, XX, 21.

To this the abolitionist Elizur Wright replied with a pamphlet entitled *Perforations in the "Latter-Day Pamphlets" by one of the "Eighteen Millions of Bores,"* which attacked Carlyle as ignorant and reactionary and concluded: ". . . we will take in good part the broad hint to make our calls shorter and less frequent at Cheyne Row." Emerson sent Carlyle a copy, without comment.[4] Emerson's friend Sam Ward took the hint and pointedly avoided Cheyne Row even when he had a letter from Emerson to deliver. This snub Emerson thought "fine vengeance"; he showed Ward the letter in which Carlyle protested against such unfair treatment.[5] The pamphlets themselves, however, Emerson declared "sturdy" and "wonderful," although he "often dissented" and regretted Carlyle's ignoring of "the benevolent necessity that rounds us all in." Four years later he chided another traveling friend, George P. Bradford, for not calling at Cheyne Row: "What possesses you to avoid Carlyle? We cannot afford to pass by such men, & he is kind of heart." [6]

More offensive, perhaps, than the *Latter-Day Pamphlets* was Carlyle's *Occasional Discourse on the Nigger Question,* which was published in *Fraser's Magazine* in December, 1849, but which Emerson may not have seen till it appeared as a pamphlet in 1853. This was a fierce neofeudalist attack upon the doctrines of racial equality and economic freedom; it advocated a new serfdom, rather than chattel slavery, for all inferior races and classes, a new order of work and obedience; and it was studded with invocations to the State which must have had an ugly sound in Concord. It appeared, too, during the time when Emerson's humanitarianism was hardening into abolitionism, when that "filthy enactment," the Fugitive Slave Law, had made isolation impossible, when *liberty* in the mouth of the compromising Daniel Webster sounded like *love* in the mouth of a courtesan. But somehow Emerson seems not to have resented the uncompromising words of Carlyle. Perhaps they seemed to him mere literary fantasy, too remote from the real world of American politics to require an answer.

For Emerson, as for most Americans, the realities of politics and war came, in the late fifties, to dominate and distort all other realities. In 1859 he told a Boston audience that the hanging of John Brown would "make the gallows as glorious as the cross." [7] On December 8, 1862, he wrote to Carlyle: "Here we read no books. The war is our sole & doleful

---

[4] *New Letters and Memorials of Jane Welsh Carlyle,* ed. Alexander Carlyle, II, 20.
    [5] *Let RWE,* IV, 236–37.   [6] *Ibid.,* p. 459.   [7] Rusk, *Life,* p. 402.

instructor." By September 26, 1864, the war had taught him that there
were no Northerners of intelligence and virtue who were sympathetic
to the Confederacy but only "the wild Irish element, imported in the
last twenty-five years into this country, & led by Romish priests, who
sympathize, of course, with despotism"; that the Confederates themselves were "the enemies of mankind"; and that "the battle for Humanity is, at this hour, in America." The war, he wrote, was a poem.

For Carlyle, the war was a tragic farce, a stupid and bloody answer
to the question which he had treated in his Occasional Discourse of
twelve years before. Early in 1862 he wrote to his brother: "No war
ever raging in my time was to me more profoundly foolish-looking:
neutral am I to a degree, I for one." [8] But his neutrality was, as he
might have said, all on one side. The South was ruled by a brave,
ruthless, responsible aristocracy, almost exactly what he desired for
England. The whole structure of Southern society rested upon a denial
of liberty and human equality. When such values were involved, Carlyle
could not fail to wish for a Southern victory, and his partisanship is
clearly evident in a private letter which he wrote to the Confederate
agent John Thompson [9] or in a single sentence from a letter to Joseph
Neuberg: "I am considerably relieved to hear that Vicksburg (for whh
the Yankee Editors were hallelujahing afflictively loud on Saturday) is
still *un*taken!" [10] In action, however, and in public utterance, Carlyle
preserved a decent neutrality. He listened sympathetically not only to
Thompson but to Moncure Conway, another Virginian, who was an
unofficial propagandist for the North. His only published writing on
the war, *Ilias (Americana) in Nuce,* printed in *Macmillan's Magazine*
in August, 1863, must have seemed to most readers merely a contemptuous damning of both houses:

Peter of the North (to Paul of the South): Paul, you unaccountable scoun-
drel, I find you hire your servants for life, not by the month or year as I do.
You are going straight to Hell you,—
Paul: Good words, Peter. The risk is my own, I am willing to take the risk.
Hire you your servants by the month or the day, and get straight to Heaven;
leave me to my own method.
Peter: No, I won't. I will beat your brains first: And is trying dreadfully
ever since, but cannot yet manage it.

[8] NLS, MS 525, letter dated January 30, 1862.
[9] MS owned by the Princeton University Library, dated March 27, 1865.
[10] NLS, MS 553.

Only a careful student of Carlyle's opinions would have known that servantship for life was offered seriously as a solution for both the Negro problem and the labor problem.

But there were many careful students of Carlyle in the North, disciples even, who had been awakened and freed by his transcendentalism and who now felt themselves betrayed by his sympathy with despotism. A measure of their hurt and anger is the eloquent "Letter to Thomas Carlyle" which appeared in *The Atlantic Monthly* of October, 1863, in answer to Carlyle's August nutshell of political wisdom. The writer, D. A. Wasson, identified himself as such an early disciple, one who twenty years before, "alone there in the remote solitudes of Maine," had read *Sartor Resartus* "afoot and on horseback, sleeping with it under my pillow and wearing it in my pocket till pocket and it were worn out" and who was still a believer in Carlyle's greatness.

You are great, but not towards us Americans. Towards us you are little and insignificant and superfluous. Your eyes, though of wondrous efficacy in their way, blink in our atmosphere like those of an owl in broad sunlight; and if you come flying here, it is the privilege of the smallest birds—of which you are quite at liberty to esteem me one—to pester you back into your mediaeval twilight.

He told in highly emotional terms the story of a young slave who had been whipped for disobedience because she had refused the sexual demands of her aged master, and he charged Carlyle with complicity.

Yes, Thomas Carlyle, I hold you a party to these crimes. *You,* YOU are the brutal old man who would flog virgins into prostitution. You approve the system; you volunteer your best varnish in its commendation; and this is an inseparable and *legal* part of it.[11]

In this context, Emerson's reactions seem remarkably tolerant. Carlyle's attitude was "unfortunate," he said, "but no more than could be expected" in a writer who "purposely made exaggerated statements merely to astonish his listeners." [12] In his journal he wrote, "Each of the masters has some puerility, as Carlyle his pro-slavery whim." [13] To Carlyle he wrote no direct comment but merely a mild and oblique reproof for having been "cited for one moment on the side of the

[11] *The Atlantic Monthly*, XII, 497–504. Wasson clipped the article and sent it to Carlyle, who thought it "curious" and him a "clever man, but nearly gone insane on the Nigger Question" (NLS, MS 517).

[12] Ireland, *Emerson*, p. 203.   [13] *Journals*, X, 52.

enemies of mankind." Two years after the war Carlyle, in his political valedictory, *Shooting Niagara: and After,* demonstrated that his opinion of American affairs was quite unreconstructed:

A continent of earth has been submerged, for certain years, by deluges as from the Pit of Hell; half a million (some say a whole million, but surely they exaggerate) of excellent White Men, full of gifts and faculty, have torn and slashed one another into horrid death, in a temporary humour, which will leave centuries of remembrance fierce enough: and three million absurd Blacks, men and brothers (of a sort), are completely "emancipated;" launched into the career of improvement—likely to be "improved off the face of the earth" in a generation or two!

Emerson's reply, if he made one at all, came three months later in a letter inviting Carlyle to make the long-postponed American visit: "I have long ceased to apologize for or explain your savage sayings about American or other republics or publics, and am willing that anointed men bearing with them authentic charters shall be laws to themselves, as Plato willed." Those are not the words of a man who would punish heresy by excommunication.

What is more, there is evidence of a positive sort that Emerson did not, deliberately, let silence answer the letters of Carlyle. Even during the worst periods of tension and of gaps in the correspondence other channels of communication remained open. These correspondents were writers of books, and their new volumes continued to cross the Atlantic, maintaining a kind of dialogue—or even argument—in buckram: *Latter-Day Pamphlets* and *Representative Men* in 1850, *The Life of John Sterling* in 1851, *Memoirs of Margaret Fuller Ossoli* in 1852, *English Traits* in 1856, the early volumes of *Frederick the Great* in 1858, and *The Conduct of Life* in 1860.

When Emerson's second volume of poems arrived in Chelsea Carlyle did his best to read them. "The charm of them is certainly not poetic," he wrote to his brother on July 1, 1867; "prosaic *intellectual puzzles* rather, whh now & then are worth trying to guess; sometimes *not.*" [14] Three years later he acknowledged Emerson's "Two pretty *volumes* of *Collected Works*" as "a pleast salutatn from you—whh set me upon reading again what I thot I knew well before." Salutations these books were in a double sense, for each flyleaf carried a message: in a volume of *Frederick,* "To R. Waldo Emerson esq/ (Concord, Massachusetts):/

[14] NLS, MS 526.

From an old Friend/ T. Carlyle/ Chelsea, 6 Decr, 1858—"; in another volume of the same work, "To R. Waldo Emerson Esq (Concord, Mass.)/ with kindest regards from an Old Friend/ T. Carlyle (Chelsea, 15 Feby 1865)"; in the first volume of the "Library Edition" of Carlyle's *Collected Works*, "To Ralph Waldo Emerson Esq (Concord, Mass-achtts), in loving memory of a long friendship:/ T. Carlyle Chelsea, 26 Jany 1869"; [15] and in *Society and Solitude*, "To the General in Chief from his Lieutenant, March 1870." [16] Thus inscribed, each book became a kind of printed letter, an assurance that the silence was not so deep or ominous as it seemed.

Despite the *Latter-Day Pamphlets*, visitors continued to arrive in Chelsea bearing introductions from Emerson and news of Concord. Even during the war there was an "Emerson man" who, Carlyle wrote to his brother, "came back, insisting on 'a walk' with me; and got his poor heart shocked by my views upon the Nigger Question, upon Philanthropy &c &c: a good creature but extremely mad." [17] And often the visitors brought messages, as Edward Everett did, for example, from Carlyle: "Emerson never writes to me, or not once in many months, the sinful man; please give him my regards if he ever come athwart you"; [18] or Arthur Hugh Clough from Emerson: "If you see Carlyle, give my love to him. I shall write to him soon, perhaps today." [19] The year after the war Emerson gave the foreign correspondent George W. Smalley a letter of introduction to Carlyle with the warning, "You must not be surprised if you find him inhospitable to American ideas, and perhaps to Americans." But Smalley found that "Carlyle's manner when he spoke of Emerson was gentle and affectionate," that he insisted on his love for America, "the true America, the country which has given birth to Emerson and Emerson's friends," [20] and that he was even willing to believe that the victory of the Northern armies had proved the righteousness of the Northern cause—all of which Smalley reported to Emerson when he returned.[21] That same year Horatio

[15] These volumes are now in Emerson's study in the museum of the Concord Antiquarian Society.

[16] This volume is in Carlyle's house in London.

[17] NLS, MS 517. The visitor may have been Moncure Conway.

[18] *Let RWE*, IV, 486n.

[19] *The Correspondence of Arthur Hugh Clough*, II, 487, letter dated July 24, 1854.

[20] See clipping of a London *Times* article by Smalley in Columbia University Library scrapbook on Emerson, 1903–19.

[21] George W. Smalley, *London Letters*, I, 291.

Nelson Powers told Emerson of Carlyle's surly reply to the compliments of an American railroad capitalist—"I do not believe a word of it. I don't believe that you care for me or for what I've written"—and noted that Emerson was "exceedingly . . . amused." [22] In February, 1871, Moncure Conway wrote from London: "Carlyle is not so well lately: sleeps badly. He is never so happy as when he has received a letter from you." [23]

Ever since 1846 Emerson and Carlyle had maintained a sort of visual communication by means of photographs; in the lean years after the war photographs sometimes crossed the ocean when letters did not. Often they were carried by travelers, by the Unitarian minister William Rounseville Alger, for example, who on November 27, 1865, wrote Emerson that he had brought him "one of the latest" pictures of Carlyle.[24] George Smalley, on his way home in the autumn of 1866, called again in Chelsea and received a photograph inscribed for Emerson. When Emerson learned that Smalley had not suggested the gift his "beautiful, strong face lighted up. He held the picture in a grasp that was almost a caress, and he said, 'Thank you, you could have brought me nothing I should so much value.' " [25] On October 31, 1868, after almost two years of silence, Carlyle signed and sent, probably by one of "the eighteen million," a photograph which Emerson framed and hung on the wall of his study.

In the early seventies, in his own childless and bereft seventies, Carlyle became a friend of the Emerson family. Emerson's children, who had learned to recognize Carlyle's bold handwriting almost as soon as they learned to read, were now making their own transatlantic pilgrimages and carrying their father's greetings to Cheyne Row. In September, 1871, Emerson announced that his son Edward was soon to pass through London on his way to study medicine in Germany. "Give him your blessings," he wrote, "& tell him what he should look for in his few days in London, & what in your Prussia. He is a good youth. . . ." Next August Edward paid another visit to Carlyle at a

[22] Horatio Nelson Powers, "A Day with Emerson," *Lippincott's Monthly Magazine*, XXX (November, 1882), 479.

[23] MS letter owned by RWEMA, dated February 4, 1871.

[24] MS letter owned by RWEMA.

[25] Smalley, London *Times* article in Columbia University scrapbook on Emerson, 1903–19.

country house where he was staying, and Carlyle reported to John Forster: "We had a son of Emerson's here, for two days; a fine intelligt good yg fellow; who speaks of London for his winter school." [26] On January 19, 1872, Emerson wrote that his daughter Edith was coming, with her children and her husband, Col. William H. Forbes, who had been "an officer in the Masstts Cavalry, & [done] good service in Virginia, in the War of the Rebellion." He had given her, he wrote, a "secret counsel," which he hoped Carlyle would "permit her to carry out."

The secret counsel seems to have been that she ask Carlyle to have his picture taken with her five-year-old son Ralph. This Carlyle did, at any rate. He took the family sight-seeing, too, to Westminster Abbey; he introduced Edith to Lady Ashburton and to Dean Stanley; and he wrote letters of introduction to friends in Scotland.[27] The following August, shortly before she sailed for home, Edith called again in Chelsea with Edward and her husband but found that Carlyle was out of the city. She wrote him then, from the steamer *Hecla*, an affectionate letter of farewell. "I have not sent your picture," she said,

for I preferred to have the pleasure of carrying it to Father. Perhaps you remember that I asked if you were willing that copies of it should be given to one or two gentlemen who had asked for it, but I waited for Father's permission also, and learned that, as I had thought, he preferred that his treasure should be his alone, so the duplicates I spoke of will be saved for my original purpose which was to make sure that there should be a reserve, that the children may have them when they grow up.

What Emerson thought of his treasure is not recorded, but one can easily imagine—it was later published as the frontispiece of Volume X of the *Journals*—that the bearded, brooding old man and the bright boy seemed to him a symbol of the longevity and the complexity of a friendship.

Photographs, messages, and flyleaf inscriptions do not, however, entirely bridge the clefts in the latter part of the correspondence. They do not counterbalance the heavy antagonisms that might well have made Emerson feel this a time to keep silence. An entry in his journal of 1865 indicates that he found Carlyle's opinions a real obstacle to the maintenance of the correspondence: "I have neglected badly Carlyle, who is so steadily good to me. Like a Catholic in Boston, he has put

[26] MS owned by the Victoria and Albert Museum.   [27] NLS, MS 1773.

himself by his violent anti-Americanism in false position, and it is not quite easy to deal with him." [28] And a fragment of a letter to Carlyle exists, probably a rough draft of that of January 23, 1870, which puts the matter even more strongly:

How can I write to you? Your mood is not mine & you choose to sit like Destiny at the door of nations, & predict calamity, & contradict with irresistible wit your own morale, & ridicule shatter the attempts of little men at humanity & charity & uphold the offender.[29]

But these emotions, however deeply they were felt, could not have been the main source of Emerson's inaction. Vindictiveness and retaliation were not elements of his character. Even less was he capable of repeatedly attributing a punitive silence to inertia or incapacity. He was, however, as slothful and dilatory as most letter writers, and during the fifties and sixties he permitted himself to become a very busy man. All his life he had suffered from a lack of vitality; perhaps long before 1866 he felt the approach of the god Terminus and knew the necessity to economize his failing powers. His correspondence diminished; it became more and more limited to business and domestic matters; and difficult, demanding, delicate letters to Carlyle, for which rough drafts and revisions were often necessary, simply did not get written.

The correspondence, however, remained precious to him. He had kept all, or almost all, of Carlyle's letters. In June, 1870, he sent seventy-seven of them to Edith Forbes to be copied for binding. "I have been reading over a great many of these letters," he wrote, "& am delighted with the hope of having them in a book." He planned to make an index.[30]

[28] *Journals,* X, 122.   [29] See below, E.1.23.70, n. 1.   [30] *Let RWE,* VI, 121.

EMERSON AS A YOUNG CLERGYMAN
A miniature painted by Sarah Goodridge in 1829,
four years before the Craigenputtock meeting

CARLYLE IN 1832
A drawing by Daniel Maclise,
published in *Fraser's Magazine*
in June, 1833, two months before
the Craigenputtock meeting

I

AN ACCOUNT, IN EMERSON'S HANDWRITING, OF HIS BIBLIOPOLIC ACTIVITIES
ON CARLYLE'S BEHALF

(See E.4:25:39)

II

A DAGUERREOTYPE OF EMERSON
TAKEN IN ENGLAND IN 1848

THE DAGUERREOTYPE WHICH CARLYLE
SENT TO EMERSON IN 1846
(See C.4.18.46, C.4.30.46, and E.5.31.46)

III

CARLYLE AT 70
(See C.6.14.65 and E.1.7.66)

JANE CARLYLE AT 64
(See C.6.14.65 and E.1.7.66)

CARLYLE AT 70
(See C.6.14.65 and E.1.7.66)

EMERSON AT 70
A photograph taken in London in the spring of 1873

CARLYLE AT 76, WITH EMERSON'S GRANDSON
RALPH FORBES
(See E.1.19.72, n.2)

VII

EMERSON AT HIS WRITING TABLE
A photograph taken in October, 1879

VIII

POSTLUDE
1872-1882

On July 24, 1872, Emerson made an entry in his journal: "House burned." The very brevity of his statement indicated, perhaps, the severity of the shock which he had suffered. All members of his household had escaped injury, nearly all his books and manuscripts had been rescued, and the damage to the house itself was not irreparable, but within a short time Emerson began to show serious symptoms of mental and physical decline. So alarming to his family was the intensification of the mild aphasia with which he had been for some years afflicted that in September they persuaded him to consult a physician. In 1872, as in 1833, doctors and laymen agreed upon the curative powers of foreign travel. The friends who gathered together the astonishing sum of seventeen thousand dollars for the rebuilding of Emerson's house urged that part of the money be used for a holiday abroad. At first Emerson was unwilling that his English friends should see him as he then was—bald, weak, and vague—but he wanted to see his son Edward in London, and he let himself be persuaded that his English visit might be a brief and clandestine prelude to a winter in Egypt. On October 23, accompanied by his eldest daughter, Ellen, he sailed for the third time for Liverpool.[1]

Carlyle did not learn the news until Emerson was halfway across the Atlantic. On the evening of November 1, Edward Emerson, dining at John Forster's house with Carlyle and the Irish poet William Allingham, announced, perhaps on impulse, that his father would arrive in Liverpool early the next week. Carlyle immediately offered as London lodging the room which Emerson had occupied twenty-five years before, but Edward thought it unlikely that his father's health would permit him to accept. [2] Edward was right. When Emer-

[1] Rusk, *Life*, pp. 452–59.
[2] Carlyle, *New Letters*, II, 291. Reporting this news to his brother, Carlyle added: "I do not think he will accept nor indeed can regret if he don't; so feckless fidgetty and dreary is my own way of life here" (NLS, MS 527).

son arrived in London at noon on Wednesday, November 6, he went directly to the house in Down Street where Elizabeth Hoar had recently stayed and engaged rooms for Ellen and himself.[3]

The next morning, carrying Edward's directions, which loss of memory had made necessary, Emerson found his way from Piccadilly to Chelsea.[4] Carlyle gazed seriously at him for a moment and then embraced him. "I am glad to see you once more in the flesh," he said. They sat down in the study and talked steadily for more than two hours. Carlyle seemed to Emerson very aged in appearance but strong in spirit and person. His speech was still witty and depreciatory and his memory still flawless. Emerson regretted, when he wrote to his wife, that Ellen's sprained ankle had prevented her being there to report accurately the "outpouring . . . on persons, events, & opinions," [5] but Ellen heard enough at second hand to write that her father had "had a truly delightful day with Mr. Carlyle." [6]

During the remainder of Emerson's week in London there were at least two more meetings. On Saturday Carlyle came to call at the Down Street rooms. Ellen found him "young and sound looking after the photographs." She had difficulty understanding his Dumfriesshire dialect, but she wrote to her mother, "he kept Father . . . laughing." [7] That evening Emerson said to William Allingham: "Carlyle called today—his humour runs into everything, hearty laugh, excellent company—has always something memorable to say in choice language." [8] On Tuesday Charles Eliot Norton, who had attempted the day before to arrange a dinner for Emerson and Carlyle, took Emerson to luncheon at the home of Burne-Jones and drove him afterward to Carlyle's.[9] That afternoon Emerson took one of the "walks with Carlyle in London" which he mentioned to his wife in a letter from Cairo;[10] "a long talk, and do muddy walk," Carlyle called it in a letter to his brother: "very gentle, clear and pure on his part; but less of real heart interest coming out of it than one ex-

[3] *Let RWE,* VI, 226; MS, Ellen to Lidian Emerson, November 8, 1872, owned by RWEMA.

[4] MS, Ellen to Lidian Emerson, November 8, 1872.   [5] *Let RWE,* VI, 226–27.
[6] MS, Ellen to Lidian, November 8, 1872.   [7] *Ibid.*
[8] William Allingham, *Diary,* p. 216.
[9] Norton, *Letters,* ed. Sara Norton and M. A. De Wolfe Howe, I, 503; and MS, Ellen to Lidian, November 8, 1872.
[10] *Let RWE,* VI, 231.

pected." [11] Perhaps there was only one walk: the records of that November visit are neither clear nor complete. But there seem to have been no quarrels. Emerson's obvious ill-health may have softened Carlyle's temper. The visits may have been too short for the reviving of old antagonisms. At any rate, to Lidian Emerson in Concord Carlyle's reception of her husband seemed "most lovely and touching—he is as tender as he is savage." [12]

Winter in France, Italy, and Egypt had much the effect that Emerson's friends had hoped for. By March he and his daughter were back in Paris, and Carlyle learned at third hand of his "safe arrival . . . with 'his age renewed' by his Egyptian winter, and in particular, instead of the utterly bare, or slightly woolly scalp, a visible coat of hair again." [13] The Egyptian winter seems also to have renewed Emerson's optimism or at least to have made him more eloquent and less cautious in his expression of it. Charles Eliot Norton, who crossed the Atlantic with him in May, found him "the greatest talker in the ship's company," and noted that

his optimistic philosophy has hardened into a creed, with the usual effects of a creed in closing the avenues of truth. He can accept nothing as fact that tells against his dogma. His optimism becomes a bigotry, and, though of nobler type than the common American conceit of the preeminent excellence of American things as they are, has hardly less of the quality of fatalism. To him this is the best of all possible worlds, and the best of all possible times. He refuses to believe in disorder or evil. . . . "I have never known," he said to me, "what it was to be ill for a whole day." [14]

Good health, or the illusion of it, loquacity, and dogmatic optimism might be considered amiable weaknesses in most quarters, but they were not likely to produce peaceful discussion in Cheyne Row.

A year after Emerson's death Frederic Henry Hedge wrote: "Emerson confessed to me, after his return from Europe in 1873, that, during his sojourn in London, he found talking with Carlyle so uncomfortable and exasperating that he ceased to visit him." [15] Hedge's statement is undoubtedly accurate, but Emerson's is rendered somewhat suspect by the inaccuracy of his memory and it is not fully sus-

[11] NLS, MS 527, letter dated November 13, 1872.
[12] MS, Lidian to RWE, November 25, 1872, owned by RWEMA.
[13] Carlyle, *New Letters*, II, 296.   [14] *Letters*, I, 503.
[15] "The Correspondence of Carlyle and Emerson," *The Christian Register*, LXII (March 15, 1883), 164.

tained by the records of this last London sojourn. Emerson and Ellen returned to their Down Street rooms on Saturday, April 5.[16] Next day they called at Carlyle's house. Emerson was "looking a great deal better for his Winter voyage," Carlyle thought; "very gentle, very amiable, clear and wonderfully happy." "I do not get much solid talk with him," he wrote, "nor indeed does [it] much avail me when I do. His daughter . . . is a pleasant looking, rational person, probably over thirty. . . ." [17] Sometime early in that week Emerson went for a walk with Carlyle but found him neither gentle nor happy nor amiable. On Wednesday both men were dinner guests at the home of James Anthony Froude. The next day, when Carlyle called, Emerson was out; [18] he was paying—or did at some time on that Thursday pay— the visit to Norton which led to a paragraph in Norton's journal on "the difference between Emerson and Carlyle":

Life and its experience and its teachings have led them along widely diverging paths; the outcome of their creeds and philosophies is so unlike as to limit their mutual sympathies. They have fewer opinions and sentiments in common than they had forty years ago. They will be friends to the end; but neither is dependent for sympathy on the other. But how few are the deep unbroken friendships founded on intimate sympathy! Happy the man who has one friendship of this sort! [19]

After church on Easter Sunday, April 13, Emerson and Ellen went again to Cheyne Row. This time Carlyle was far more agreeable than he had been the week before. He showed Ellen an early daguerreotype of her father which she longed to steal for its resemblance to Edward and which she thought she might ask for as a bequest. Carlyle's house seemed to her the most "interesting and pleasant" she had seen on her travels. "Father has been very happy," she wrote to her mother, "in the remembrance of this call." [20] The following Saturday Emerson and Ellen called again, but Carlyle was out. On Thursday, April 24, as the London visit was drawing to a close, Emerson went to breakfast with Gladstone, and then bade goodbye to Carlyle. "Father . . . spent the forenoon with Mr. Carlyle," Ellen wrote, "with real comfort." [21] Discomfort and exasperation were certainly important elements in the Carlyle-Emerson relationship that April, as they had been

[16] Rusk, *Life*, p. 473.   [17] NLS, MS 527, letter to John, April 12, 1873.
[18] MS, Ellen to Lidian, May 1, 1873, owned by RWEMA.
[19] *Letters*, I, 477.   [20] MS, Ellen to Lidian, May 1, 1873.   [21] *Ibid.*

since 1847, but they seem not to have dominated it even at the end nor to have forced Emerson to cease his visits.

Carlyle during the April meeting was consistently tolerant and friendly. He recognized, of course, that the intellectual and temperamental gulf between Emerson and himself had widened to oceanic breadth, but he was able to contemplate it calmly. On April 19, when he had been seeing Emerson off and on for about two weeks, he said to Norton:

There's a great contrast between Emerson and myself. He seems verra content with life, and takes much satisfaction in the world, especially in your country. One would suppose to hear him that ye had no troubles there, and no share in the darkness that hangs over these old lands. It's a verra strikin' and curious spectacle to behold a man so confidently cheerful as Emerson in these days.[22]

He paid his share of visits to Down Street and reported in friendly fashion what he heard there: Emerson was, as always, "excellent, pure, & placid," faulty only in that he was at ease in Zion; Ellen was "a much more determined kind of person . . ."

at least so I judge from this trait of her, that she openly expresses her utter weariness & disgust at the Nigger, & has one hope concerning him, that he will utterly perish out of the way of the United States, where he is nothing but a superfluity & a nuisance.[23]

Once when five days had passed without a visit from Emerson he wrote anxiously to Norton "about the question of his health you mentioned when we last met." [24] After Emerson's farewell visit Carlyle wrote to his brother in Dumfries:

Emerson . . . came down hither day before yesterday, sat about a couple of hours, talking cheerfully in his mild, modest, ingenious but rather theoretic way; and then rose inexorably to go for Forster's who had asked him to dinner for this (Saturday) night, but was to find him inexorably engaged elsewhere. So he went his way, and it is probable I shall see him no more. . . . I think sometimes the Edinburgh University people should give him a Public Dinner. . . . Should you be writing to Masson, you might fling out a hint? [25]

[22] *Letters*, I, 484.   [23] NLS, MS 527, letter to John Carlyle, May 7, 1873.
[24] MS, April 18, 1873, owned by the Houghton Library of Harvard University.
[25] Carlyle, *New Letters*, II, 297. John Carlyle replied that there was little chance of a public dinner: "All the professors, with few exceptions, are out on holiday till the middle of May when the summer classes begin" (NLS, MS 1775E).

On April 28, at about three o'clock in the afternoon, Allingham called at Carlyle's house to accompany the old man, as he frequently did, on his daily walk. This day it was to be a visit to Emerson. But they were late in starting. Carlyle spent fifteen minutes poking a brass wire through the stem of a new clay pipe in an effort to get a satisfactory draft. Finally he gave up, called for another pipe, and smoked it before he would go out into the streets. They walked through Hyde Park, talking of Masson and Milton and then of Emerson. "A mild, pure, gentle spirit," Carlyle said, who, though he might with some justice be accused of having spent his life making sentences, had "made golden sentences, diamond sentences, sentences to be always grateful for." At Hyde Park Corner, three blocks from Down Street, Carlyle looked at the clock and saw that the time was half-past five. It was too late now, he said, for the visit to Emerson, and he turned toward Knightsbridge where the Chelsea omnibus stopped. Allingham, cursing the half-penny clay pipe,[26] did not know that Emerson and Ellen had left London the day before. Carlyle was in his seventy-eighth year.

After 1873 Carlyle and Emerson did not meet again, and their correspondence quickly came to an end. On June 20, 1873, Emerson sent a note of introduction for his boyhood friend George P. Bradford, "who knows your mind," he wrote, "better than most Americans, though he has never seen your face." He had forgotten that twice before he had introduced Bradford to Carlyle and only two years ago had identified him as "an early and late friend of mine, who once stopped at your door and values himself on having seen you." On April 2, 1875, Carlyle wrote in a letter to Edith Emerson Forbes,

I wish you had told me something about your Father's health & procedures in these his years of rest; but I always vaguely hear from time to time that he still keeps his health tolerably and of his constant friendship to me and the kind of silent but sacred covenant that exists between us two to the end & has at all times been so precious to me, I never have any questioning.[27]

[26] Allingham, *Diary,* pp. 223–24. It is clear from Rusk, *Life,* p. 476, that the Emersons had left London on the 27th. The accuracy of Carlyle's memory even in old age suggests that Allingham's date may be incorrect. But this entry in his *Diary* fits closely with other entries, and a memory slip on Carlyle's part seems no more implausible than the senile infirmity of purpose which the anecdote otherwise indicates.

[27] Norton, *Letters,* II, 137.

But although no more letters passed between Carlyle and Emerson, the remaining years of the friendship were not entirely silent or uneventful. Emerson had entered what he called his "threescore-and-tenship" on the voyage from Liverpool to Boston, and he was very much aware of the need to put his affairs in order. On November 11, 1873, he wrote to Charles Eliot Norton, who had been his companion on that voyage,

I shall like to know that I may confide to you the entire file of Carlyle's letters to me from 1835 to 1872—nearly a hundred, I believe—that you may hereafter make what disposition or destruction of them you shall find fit.[28]

And Carlyle replied, when Norton wrote to him for his concurrence,

I entirely agree with Emerson in his disposal of these letters, and have or can have no feeling on the subject, but that if he was going to do anything at all with the stuff he could not in the world have found anybody better to take charge of it than yourself. . . . I charge you with my friendliest, fraternal salutations, and thanks to Emerson.[29]

Such salutations passed frequently across the ocean during the final years of the friendship. On April 23, 1874, Carlyle wrote Norton of his pleasure in the news that Emerson had been named a candidate for the rectorship of Glasgow University and his hope "that we may once more behold the face of Emerson in this world." [30] With the letter he sent a print of a supposed portrait of John Knox in which he had recently become much interested; it was inscribed, "The one Portrait I ever cd believe to be a Likeness of Knox—T. Carlyle, Feby 1874." Emerson received the gift from Norton in Cambridge the night he delivered his second Divinity School Address; [31] he had it framed and hung it in his Concord study. On December 5, 1875, Emerson

---

[28] *Ibid.*   [29] *Ibid.*, pp. 138–39.

[30] MS, Carlyle to Norton, April 23, 1874, owned by the Houghton Library of Harvard University. Carlyle's first reaction to this affair, less polite and more characteristic, was expressed in a letter to his brother John on April 4: "Emerson has actually consented to stand candidate for the Glasgow Rectorship, and is contented to cross and re-cross the Atlantic for the sole purpose of delivering an address to the poor *gorbs* of student creatures there; a fact I had vaguely heard of, but could only ascribe to Emerson's great ignorance of the kind of phenomenon he wd actually encounter here. . . . The . . . request that I or any grown-up man should 'speak the decisive word' or at all appear in such a water-gruel transaction appeared to me completely foolish, and so I spoke no word at all in the matter, nor shall . . ." (NLS, MS 528).

[31] Norton, *Letters*, II, 43.

wrote in his journal, "Thomas Carlyle's 80th birthday";[32] three months later he received a medal which had been struck in England to commemorate that event.[33]

At about the same time, Carlyle received a copy of *Letters and Social Aims*. His opinion of it was reported to Norton by his niece Mary Aitken, who was not only his amanuensis but, increasingly, his letter-writer:

He has read Emerson's new Book & thinks of it pretty much what you do; he told me a minute ago to tell you more precisely what he thought of it; & then added characteristically "Oh no, you need not say that after all, for I have a real affection for Emerson." [34]

In 1878 Emerson sent the pamphlet edition of his address *The Fortunes of the Republic;* Carlyle's opinion of that work was recorded—phonetically—by an American visitor, Thomas Wentworth Higginson: "I've just noo been reading it; the dear Emerson, he thinks the whole warrld's like himself,; and if he can just get a million people together and let them all vote, they'll be sure to vote right and all will go vara weel." [35] Early in 1878 Emerson received a direct report on Carlyle from Alexander Ireland:

It will interest you to know that in May last I spent part of an evening with Mr Carlyle at Chelsea, I was truly glad to find him looking so hale for a man of 83. Anyone, not knowing him, might easily have taken him for a hill-side sheep-farmer, with healthy weatherbeaten face, & homely air & speech; he stoops in walking more than he did when you saw him in 1873, but his memory & talk are as ready & notable as ever—only his laughter is not so Titanic as it used to be. . . . I have recently got an enlarged photographic likeness of him—very good & real, taken about a year ago—If you would care to have one, it would give me much pleasure to send it to you.[36]

It was perhaps this photograph which George Parsons Lathrop saw Emerson receive: "He gazed long at it, and then with a smile of

[32] *Journals*, X, 445.　　　[33] *Ibid.*, p. 450.

[34] MS, Mary Carlyle Aitken to Norton, February 2, 1876, owned by the Houghton Library of Harvard University. A more precise statement of Carlyle's opinion was, presumably, that which he sent to his brother on March 25: "I . . . read it over with a kind of agreeable stimulus that Emerson's fragmentary glitterings generally yield; but I *learnt* nothing from it strictly speaking; nor I doubt will you beyond what we already know of him" (NLS, MS 528).

[35] T. W. Higginson, *Carlyle's Laugh and Other Surprises*, p. 10.

[36] MS, Ireland to RWE, owned by Houghton Library.

beautiful tenderness said slowly: 'Poor boy! He grows older and older!' " [37]

On September 19, 1878, Moncure Conway wrote to Emerson that recently, in company with Bayard Taylor, he had paid a visit to Carlyle: "He always asks after you and your family when I see him, and I wish Ellen or Edward would write to me that I may carry him better information next time than I did last." [38] In almost immediate response there came a letter from Edith, not to Conway but to Carlyle himself, a long, detailed, and affectionate report on Emerson, his wife, his children, and his grandchildren.

Father is very well and very happy. Mother often says that he is the happiest person she ever knew—he is so uniformly in good spirits, and waking each morning in a joyful mood. His only difficulty is that he is very apt to be unable to think of the word he wishes to say, and this failure of his memory is so annoying to him that he is unwilling to go into society at all.

Ellen, she said, was now her father's right hand, indispensable in whatever work he was still able to do. William Forbes took care of all his business affairs. Edward, the physician, lived close by and watched over his parents. And there were many grandchildren: she herself had five boys and a girl.

I often wish I could spend a month or two in England—but not without my children and their school days must not be interrupted yet. I wish I could call upon you. I often long to do so and wish that Father still had direct communication with you.[39]

Communication of an indirect sort continued until the last. In 1879 Norton offered to send Carlyle an engraving of a portrait of Emerson, and Mary Aitken replied for her uncle, who was sitting beside her reading *Henry VI:* "He says I am to tell you that he will like very much to have the Engraving of his dear old friend Mr Emerson." [40] In 1880 Moncure Conway, returning to America for a visit, stopped at 5 Cheyne Row to bid farewell to Carlyle and receive a farewell message for Emerson. "Give my love to Emerson," Carlyle said, "I still think of his visit to us at Craigenputtock as the most beautiful thing in

[37] New-York *Daily Tribune,* April 30, 1882, p. 4.
[38] MS, Moncure Conway to RWE, owned by Houghton Library.
[39] NLS, MS 1773, letter dated October 6, 1879.
[40] MS, Mary Carlyle Aitken to Norton, May 11, 1879, owned by Houghton Library.

our experience there." [41] And Norton, in that same year, in his last letter to Carlyle, wrote what may well have been the last words that Carlyle read about Emerson:

I have not seen Emerson since the winter, but I heard lately that he was physically well. His memory is quite shattered, and at times his mind moves as in dreams. I was told of his speaking the other day of the pleasure he had once had in a visit from you at Concord.[42]

Carlyle died first. His niece, sitting at his bedside, "often thought of what Emerson says about 'Circles.' Each stage of his illness seemed a circle and at the last his life seemed to be like a circle, which death would complete. . . ." [43] The news traveled fast. The Massachusetts Historical Society, of which Carlyle had been an honorary member, learned of his death in time to prepare a memorial ceremony for its meeting of February 10, 1881, the very day, as it happened, of the burial at Ecclefechan. Emerson, although the nature of his illness was well known, was asked to read a paper. He accepted. With the help, presumably, of Ellen and of his friend James Elliot Cabot, he put together some unpublished pages from his letters and journals of thirty years before and called them "Impressions of Thomas Carlyle in 1848." On the afternoon of February 10 he sat, with Ellen beside him, at a small table in the Dowse Library in Boston and read the passages which she indicated.

Thomas Carlyle is an immense talker, as extraordinary in his conversation as in his writing,—I think even more so.
He is not mainly a scholar, like the most of my acquaintances, but a practical Scotchman. . . .

He stumbled over long words. When he seemed entirely defeated, Ellen would make the sounds silently and he would imitate her lips.

Young men, especially those holding liberal opinions, press to see him . . . they will eat vegetables and drink water, and he is a Scotchman who thinks English national character has a pure enthusiasm for beef and mutton . . . they praise moral suasion, he goes for murder, money, capital punishment, and other petty abominations of English law . . .

[41] Moncure Conway, *Emerson at Home and Abroad*, p. 63.
[42] Norton, *Letters*, II, 112.
[43] MS, Aitken to Norton, March 26, 1881, owned by Houghton Library.

He read loudly enough for all to hear, but even so his audience drew into a circle about him.

Carlyle has, best of all men, in England, kept the manly attitude in his time. He has stood for scholars, asking no scholar what he should say . . . he has carried himself erect, made himself a power confessed by all men, and taught scholars their lofty duty. He never feared the face of man.[44]

Two days afterward, Ellen wrote to her sister that it had been "a very pleasant occasion," [45] but when, later in the month, Norton proposed and Cabot approved a repetition of the reading at Cambridge, she had to refuse. "There are more mistakes each time," she wrote to Norton, "and he forgets to speak loud." Besides, he had already forgotten the proposal.[46]

During the sleepy final year of his life Emerson must have dreamed and said much about his years of friendship with Carlyle. He must have read or known of the poignant volume of *Reminiscences* which Froude gave to the publishers a few months after Carlyle's death. But the recorded facts of that year are very few. Sometime in 1881 he sent £10 to the committee which was erecting the Carlyle monument in London.[47] And in April, 1882, the month of his death, when his mind was so clouded that he could hardly remember Longfellow, whose funeral he had attended the week before, he pointed to a photograph of Carlyle which hung on the wall and said, "That is my man, my good man!" [48]

[44] Ralph Waldo Emerson, "Impressions of Thomas Carlyle in 1848," with a note by George E. Ellis, *Scribner's Monthly*, XXII (1881), 89–92.
[45] Rusk, *Life*, p. 503.
[46] MS, Ellen Emerson to Norton, February 26, 1881, owned by Houghton Library.
[47] Moncure Conway, *Autobiography*, II, 282.
[48] E. W. Emerson, *Emerson in Concord* (Boston, 1889), p. 194.

VI

THE FIRST EDITION

The history of the book called *The Correspondence of Thomas Carlyle and Ralph Waldo Emerson* may be said to begin in 1870 when Emerson decided to have his ninety or so letters from Carlyle copied and bound.[1] Three years later he asked Charles Eliot Norton to accept the bequest of the Carlyle letters for whatever "disposition or destruction" of them seemed suitable. This Norton did, with Carlyle's approval: "Accept it . . . I pray you; lock it by in some drawer till I have vanished; and then do with it what to your own just mind shall seem best." [2] In 1875 Emerson's daughter Edith Forbes asked Carlyle to bequeath to her the Emerson half of the correspondence, and Carlyle gave the necessary instructions to his executors.[3] Long before the death of either correspondent, then, there was a kind of tacit agreement that when the time came this correspondence should be made into a book.

The time came sooner than might have been expected. On April 29, 1882, the day before Emerson's funeral, there appeared in *Harper's Weekly* an advertisement for a pirated edition—two volumes for thirty cents—of James Anthony Froude's new book, *Thomas Carlyle: a History of the First Forty Years of His Life*. This biography, so Carlylean in its ruthlessness, so un-Victorian in its publication of private matters, was a source of shock and offense to many readers. Norton, for one, thought it cynical, treacherous, and "artfully malignant." [4] He proposed to edit and publish the Carlyle-Emerson correspondence as soon as possible in the hope that he could thus help to "redress the wrong that Froude had done." [5] Emerson's family approved, and Mrs. Forbes turned over to Norton the letters which she had inherited from Carlyle.

[1] *Let RWE*, VI, 121. Emerson was of course conscious from the beginning that the correspondence was a valuable one: in 1848 he spoke to George Searle Phillips about "some letters from [Carlyle] which would prove of the very highest importance hereafter" (Phillips, *Emerson*, p. 47).

[2] Norton, *Letters*, II, 138.   [3] *Let RWE*, VI, 121*n*.

[4] *Letters*, II, 135.   [5] *Ibid*., 137.

At first Norton seems to have been attracted by the offer of Thomas Bailey Aldrich, editor of *The Atlantic Monthly,* to publish the correspondence serially in that magazine, but the Emerson family preferred it to "make its first appearance as an independent book." [6] Norton then asked several publishers for terms. "I think it will form two volumes," he wrote to H. O. Houghton on July 24, ". . . 12mo of 350 pp. each or thereabouts. The letters will require very little editing, and I hope to be able to get the book ready for publication in December,—to begin to print by the first of October." Any profits, he said, would go to Emerson's family.[7] The best offer was made by J. R. Osgood and Company, and Norton accepted it.[8]

But the book was not ready for the printers by the first of October. Norton and Mrs. Forbes discovered when they came to examine the packet of Emerson letters that at least thirty-four were missing.[9] About this time, British magazines—*The Herald, The Athenaeum,* and *The Academy*—began to publish copies of the missing letters, and it was obvious that the originals had been stolen. Carlyle's niece suspected a German named Frederick Martin [10] who had once been employed by Carlyle as an amanuensis and who five years before had attempted to publish an unauthorized and in large part plagiarized biography of his former employer.[11] Moncure Conway, to whom Norton wrote for assistance in this crisis, was acting at the time as a kind of London agent for Harper and Brothers. In this capacity he was approached by Martin and offered for publication the manuscript of Carlyle's journal of his tour in Ireland in 1849. So furtive was Martin's behavior that Conway too became suspicious. He learned from the editor of *The Athenaeum* that the four Emerson letters which that magazine had printed had been bought under similar circumstances and selected from a large number offered for sale. It began to appear that thirty-four letters from Emerson, written, most of them, in Concord before 1840 had found their way into the underworld of London.[12]

Conway became a detective. He learned that Martin had been

[6] Norton to H. O. Houghton, June 24, 1882. MS owned by the Houghton, Mifflin Company.

[7] *Ibid.*   [8] *Ibid.,* August 3, 1882.   [9] Conway, *Autobiography,* II, 370, 374.

[10] MS, Mary Aitken Carlyle to Norton, September 26, 1882, owned by Houghton Library.

[11] D. A. Wilson and D. W. MacArthur, *Carlyle in Old Age,* pp. 410–12.

[12] Conway, *Autobiography,* II, 371.

using the name of "Beckerwaise" and that he was a member of a ring which operated through "William Anderson, dealer in Autographs and Manuscripts, Toronto Villa, Torriano Avenue, London, N.W." On a Sunday late in August Conway, accompanied by a friend from Concord, paid a cautious visit to Torriano Avenue. He was told that the manuscripts were not there but that the woman who had them would come to his house if he wished. She came the next day, "middle-aged, crafty, and very timorous," bringing only four letters. But Conway and his wife gave her tea, "treated her like a lady," and agreed to buy four letters for ten pounds if they might have their choice of the letters she possessed. Tea, courtesy, and perhaps Conway's ecclesiastical manner won her confidence. She left the four letters, and the Conways copied them. When she came back next she brought so many letters that the Conways had to sit up all night. She came again, she ate cake and drank sherry, until Conway had copies of twenty-seven letters, which he sent by registered mail to Norton. On November 20 he consulted Sir James Stephen, one of Carlyle's executors, about the possibility of legal action, but the situation did not seem clear enough for that.[13] The four, or more, letters he had bought he sent to Mrs. Forbes in February. By that time the ring had begun to sell the letters in other cities—three were published in the New-York *Daily Tribune* on October 22—and Mrs. Forbes wrote Conway that she hoped to "pick up the others by degrees." [14] When the book was published, she inscribed a copy to "Mr and Mrs Moncure D. Conway/ With grateful acknowledgment of their kind help in the recovery of these letters." [15] Norton wanted to include in his introduction a full account of the adventure of the stolen letters, but Conway persuaded him to omit all details which might frighten the ring,[16] and so there appeared only this discreet statement: "My best thanks and those of the readers of this Correspondence are due to Mr. Moncure D. Conway, for his energetic and successful effort to recover some of Emerson's early letters which had fallen into strange hands."

Norton's work as editor was done with remarkable speed. He could not take time to advertise for lost letters or wait until Mrs. Forbes

[13] *Ibid.*, pp. 371–73. The date of the trip to Toronto Villa may be established by a MS letter from E. W. Emerson to Conway, September 12, 1882, owned by the Columbia University Libraries.

[14] MS, February 7, 1883, owned by CUL.   [15] Owned by CUL.

[16] Conway, *Autobiography*, II, 375.

had bought back those that had been stolen. A lengthy introduction seemed to him unnecessary—or worse:

The letters seemed to me to form a complete and unique whole, needing no addition from any other hand. Who was I that I should patch on a piece of my work to a canvas like this? . . . The sentiment of the book was too intimate for a third person to intervene in it.[17]

And he saw little need to append explanatory footnotes to names, allusions, and quotations. It was necessary, however, to find time for excision and polishing. Norton deleted long passages which he thought would be tiresome: detailed accounts of business with publishers or lists of errors in the American editions of Carlyle's books. He deleted passages which would have given offense to Cambridge neighbors or to English writers: Carlylean exclamations of "ass," "ape," "blockhead," or "bore"; a disparaging comment by Emerson on Moncure Conway, which was indeed an embarrassment; a Carlylean burlesque of Bronson Alcott. And he scrupulously marked almost every deletion. He corrected or regularized punctuation, spelling, capitalization, and arithmetic. Occasionally he felt obliged to touch up Emerson's diction and idiom: he changed "wifey" to "wife," and he omitted the "not" in a sentence which seemed excessively Yankee, "I think they will not have but about one hundred copies more to sell."

There were 173 letters altogether, eighty-nine by Carlyle, eighty-four by Emerson. They were printed in two volumes of 363 and 383 pages respectively. Norton's modest "Editorial Note" was dated January 29, 1883. The book was published by James R. Osgood and Company of Boston. It was advertised for sale in the New-York *Daily Tribune* on February 24 as "doubtless the most interesting correspondence ever published."

The publication of the Carlyle-Emerson correspondence was, certainly, one of the most interesting literary events of 1883. The book was widely, fully, and favorably reviewed. Critics seemed to feel that they were present at the unveiling of an important literary monument, and they wrote with suitable sweep and finality. Richard Herne Shepherd in *The Gentleman's Magazine* called it "a history of one of the most beautiful and remarkable friendships hitherto recorded in literary annals." Alexander Ireland in *The Academy* thought it "certain to take a permanent place among the records of literary

[17] Norton, *Letters*, II, 146.

friendship." E. P. Whipple, writing in *The North American Review*, saluted it as "a book which is destined to last for a century or two, at least."

Norton's work as editor called forth some disapproval. Ruskin wrote in a private letter to Norton that he was "much disappointed at having no word of epitaph" on Carlyle and Emerson.[18] Frederic Henry Hedge, in his *Christian Register* review, complained that the Rowse portrait, which Norton had used as a frontispiece, failed "utterly with its milky mildness and placid vacuity to give us the Emerson we knew and revered." Edward Fitzgerald, in a letter to Fanny Kemble, regretted that Norton had not inked out more of Carlyle's caricatures.[19] Shepherd, in *The Gentleman's Magazine*, thought that there was too little "substitution of stars or dashes for names." *The Saturday Review*, too, complained of inadequate expurgation; many sharp "passages about living people," it said, "might better have been consigned to the waste-paper basket of oblivion." But on the whole Norton was praised for tasteful and unobtrusive performance of his duties.

Unfavorable comment on the correspondence itself grew largely out of emotional reactions to the correspondents. Ruskin found Emerson's letters "infinitely sweet and wise," but he was "vexed . . . and partly angered" by Carlyle's with their "perpetual 'me miserum'." [20] *The Saturday Review*, also, was offended by Carlyle's lamentation and whining, and E. P. Whipple in *The North American Review* had much to say about his reactionary politics. G. E. Woodberry in *The Atlantic Monthly* blamed Emerson for the decline of the correspondence. "It is pitiful," he wrote, "to read Carlyle's appeals against his friend's silence," and he charged Emerson with never having known "the love that clings and yearns." But some critics made more objective complaints. The reviewer in *The Nation* found little of "literary and speculative interest" and recommended the book only as "a memorial of literary friendship" and "very pleasant reading." *The Spectator* thought Carlyle and Emerson had refused to face basic moral and philosophical problems. James Freeman Clarke was

---

[18] *Letters . . . to Charles Eliot Norton*, II, 190.
[19] *Letters and Literary Remains*, IV, 272.
[20] Ruskin, *Letters . . . to . . . Norton*, II, 189.

"rather startled at the stately, elaborate style on both sides. . . . Even the impetuous T. C.," he wrote, "appears daunted by R. W. E."[21] And Hedge was disappointed to find so much book business and so little "purely intellectual commerce."

The most eminent and the most surprising criticism of the *Correspondence* was made not in a magazine but in a lecture which was given at Chickering Hall in Boston on December 1, 1883.[22] Matthew Arnold had read "the two thick volumes" in October as he crossed the Atlantic for an American lecture tour, and his lecture on Emerson, composed at sea and in American railroad trains and clubs,[23] became to a considerable degree a review of those volumes. He chose as much, almost, of his illustrative material from the *Correspondence* as from the *Essays*. He concerned himself almost as much with Carlyle as with Emerson. He made the inevitable evaluations and comparisons:

As Wordsworth's poetry is, in my judgment, the most important work done in verse, in our language, during the present century, so Emerson's *Essays* are, I think, the most important work done in prose. His work is more important than Carlyle's.[24]

And he made the suggestion, startling for 1883 but widely accepted thereafter, that the best of Carlyle was to be found in his letters: "I should not wonder if really Carlyle lived, in the long run, by such an invaluable record as that correspondence between him and Emerson."[25]

But only one review, that written by Henry James, Jr., for *The Century Magazine* of June, 1883, had any real distinction as literary criticism. Like all the reviewers, James told in some detail the story of the friendship of Carlyle and Emerson and quoted copiously from their letters. Like the others, he was impressed by the sharpness of the contrasts between the two friends. But he brought into his criticism no partisan or defensive attitudes: he was not interested in rescuing Carlyle from Froude, whose work he regarded as "deeply interesting" and illuminating, nor in demonstrating Emerson's moral superiority to Carlyle. He brought, rather, a novelist's interest in the

[21] *Autobiography, Diary, and Correspondence,* p. 377.
[22] New-York *Tribune,* December 2, 1883, p. 2.
[23] Arnold, *Letters,* ed. G. W. E. Russell, III, 134, 136, 141.
[24] *Discourses in America,* p. 196.
[25] *Ibid.,* p. 167.

subtlety and complexity of the personalities behind the letters and a novelist's sense of the importance of period and place. With nice balance and sensitivity he weighed difference in style:

The violent color, the large, avalanche-movement of Carlyle's style—as if a mass of earth and rock and vegetation had detached itself and came bouncing and bumping forward—make the efforts of his correspondent appear a little pale and stiff. There is always something high and pure in Emerson's speech, however, and it has often a perfect propriety—seeming, in answer to Carlyle's extravagances, the note of reason and justice.[26]

And he suggested the broader literary qualities of the book:

We seem to see them from a distance; the united pair presents itself in something of the uplifted relief of a group on canvas or in marble. . . . There was something almost dramatic in the beginning of their friendship. Emerson, a young Bostonian, then unknown, went to Europe for the first time in 1833. . . . The reader at this point of the correspondence feels a certain suspense: he knows that Carlyle never did come to America, but like a good novel the letters produce an illusion.[27]

The first sentence of James's review announced that this correspondence was a literary work of enduring value; the review itself was distinguished enough in seriousness, insight, discrimination, and grace to be a proper vehicle for such an announcement.

The *Correspondence* seems to have been a popular as well as a critical success. There was sufficient profit from the sale of the first edition so that Norton thought it worth while to make over to Emerson's widow the share due to himself as editor.[28] By the end of 1884 seventeen new letters, thirteen by Emerson and four by Carlyle, had turned up, and Norton had them published by Ticknor and Fields in a supplementary volume for the owners of the first edition. In 1886 a second edition was published by Houghton, Mifflin Company, and in 1899 a third, each with additional letters which brought the final number to one hundred and ninety-one.[29] The success of the book was not limited to America. The first edition was published simul-

[26] "The Correspondence of Carlyle and Emerson," *Century Magazine*, XXVI, 271.
[27] *Ibid.,* pp. 265–67.
[28] Penciled note by Miss Sara Norton in a copy of *The Letters of Charles Eliot Norton* owned by the Houghton Library.
[29] Advertising pages in the back of the Supplement announce a "New revised edition of 1885, with 100 additional pages of newly-found letters." I have not seen this edition. Although Norton's "Note" to the Supplement is dated December 31, 1884, the volume was copyrighted in 1885 and dated 1886.

taneously in Boston and London; it was reviewed in Chicago and in Berlin. As early as April 27, 1883, the publisher Huschke of Weimar wrote Leslie Stephen that he planned to bring out a German edition, without royalties,[30] but this project seems never to have been carried out: no German translation is mentioned by Karl Federn in his chapter "Carlyle und Emerson in ihrem Briefwechsel" in *Essays zur Amerikanischen Literatur* (Halle, 1899). In 1912 a French translation by E. L. Lepointe, abridged but more fully annotated than Norton's edition, was published in Paris by Librairie Armand Colin.

The *Correspondence* was not quickly forgotten, and it did not lose its power as it grew old. Thirty-eight years after its publication it could still evoke emotional and even extravagant praise from its readers. A few months before his death in 1921 John Burroughs, who had been one of the earliest critics of the book, wrote in his journal: "Have been reading again the correspondence of Emerson and Carlyle. What an experience it has been! I feel lonesome." [31] In April of that year J. M. Sloan wrote in *The Landmark,* the organ of the English-Speaking Union, that "there is not in all literature a more worthy or more inspiring record of friendship" than the Carlyle-Emerson correspondence and that it was worth more than many political treaties to the cause of Anglo-American amity.[32] In the same year, the St. Louis Hegelian Denton J. Snider wrote, with perhaps unphilosophical enthusiasm, that the *Correspondence* seemed to him "much more vital, more original and far-reaching than any of old Plutarch's rather external parallels." [33] But even the most restrained of readers would, by 1921, have agreed that the letters of Carlyle and

---

[30] MS, Stephen to Norton, July 5, 1883, owned by the Houghton Library.

[31] Clara Barrus, *The Life and Letters of John Burroughs,* II, 406.

[32] Reprinted in *Littell's Living Age,* CCCIX (1921), 486–89.

[33] In *A Biography of Ralph Waldo Emerson,* p. 287. The paralleling or coupling of the names of Carlyle and Emerson began very early in the notion of British readers that Emerson was a sort of American Carlyle. The distinction between the two was made clear by Lowell in *A Fable for Critics* in 1848 and by Emile Montègut in the *Revue des Deux Mondes* in 1850, but their names continued to be closely associated in the literary mind. In 1869 a "Carlyle and Emerson Association" was formed in Auckland, New Zealand, which had as its object "the diffusion of useful knowledge among the members by means of a lending library consisting of Books of an elevating tendency" (MS, James Leask Sinclair to RWE, October 28, 1869, owned by the Houghton Library). The deaths of the two friends within fifteen months brought forth a good deal of elegiac comparison in the newspapers; John Burroughs wrote an article entitled "Carlyle and Emerson" for *The Critic* in 1882

Emerson had become one of the classic documents of nineteenth-century literature.

(II, 140), and John Tyndall, in 1882, ended his speech "On Unveiling the Statue of Thomas Carlyle" (*New Fragments*, p. 397) with a plea "that somewhere upon the Thames Embankment could be raised a companion memorial to a man who loved our hero, and was by him beloved to the end. I refer to the loftiest, purest, and most penetrating spirit that has ever shone in American literature—to Ralph Waldo Emerson, the life-long friend of Thomas Carlyle." The publication of the *Correspondence* gave, for a time at least, a marmoreal, Demosthenes-and-Cicero aspect to the Carlyle-Emerson relationship. Three months after the book appeared *The Atlantic Monthly* published a poem by the journalist Montgomery Schuyler entitled "Carlyle and Emerson":

> A bale-fire kindled in the night,
> By night a blaze, by day a cloud,
> With flame and smoke all England woke,—
> It climbed so high, it roared so loud.
>
> While over Massachusetts' pines
> Uprose a white and steadfast star;
> And many a night it hung unwatched,—
> It shone so still, it seemed so far.
>
> But Light is Fire, and Fire is Light;
> And mariners are glad for these,—
> The torch that flares along the coast,
> The star that beams above the seas.

In 1900 James Joyce, in his *Fortnightly Review* essay "Ibsen's New Drama," listed as "those giants" who before Ibsen had held "empire over the thinking world in modern times" only Rousseau, Carlyle, and Emerson.

VII

THE ART OF
THE LETTERS

The correspondence of Emerson and Carlyle is in some ways a unique correspondence—unique in that it was carried on equally by two writers of equal rank and of the first rank, or at least the second; that it is almost a lifelong correspondence and yet a continuous one; and that it is both personal and philosophical, concerned with both private and public affairs, with life and with principle. But uniqueness is not really important. It does not justify comparisons with Plutarch, or predictions of "a century or two" of life, or even a new edition eighty-one years after the first one. Such justification can be found only in the light which the letters throw on the mind and the face of the past and in the value which they may themselves possess as literature.

Perhaps the most evident, though not the most important, virtues of the correspondence are its breadth and variety of content. It is concerned with autobiography, biography, gossip, business, politics, philosophy, religion, criticism, aesthetics. There are few subjects under the nineteenth-century sun that are not reflected in it, and there are few works of fiction or fact which tell a fuller story of the life of the mind in the nineteenth century.

Because the correspondents were separated, except for nine months, by the Atlantic Ocean, their letters cover the years from 1834 to 1872 with the continuity and completeness of autobiography. But because each writer knew from the first—or almost the first—that his letters would be read with affection, the book has a warmth and an immediacy seldom attained by autobiography. Carlyle announces his removal to London:

Let me explain, what you long to know, how it is that I date from London. Yes, my friend, it is even so: Craigenputtock now stands solitary in the wilderness, with none but an old woman and foolish grouse-destroyers in it; and we for the last ten weeks, after a fierce universal disruption, are here with our household-gods.

And Emerson, in a very different idiom, announces some forensic activity:

I have written & read a kind of Sermon to the senior class of our Cambridge Theological School a fortnight ago; and an address to the Literary Societies of Dartmouth College; for though I hate American pleniloquence, I cannot easily say *No* to young men who bid me speak also. And both these are now in press. The first, I hear is very offensive. I will now try to hold my tongue until next winter.

There is hardly an important event in the mature life of either man which is not thus vividly and characteristically recorded.

The correspondence crackles with news and gossip of the literary world. Dr. Channing has been reading *Sartor:* Gladstone has quoted from *The American Scholar:* there is going to be a new magazine called *The Dial;* Harriet Martineau has written a novel; New England is going in for reform; George Ripley is talking up an ideal agricultural-cultural community; London seethes with Chartism; a young man named Thoreau is writing very good poetry; Alcott is coming to England, and Horace Mann—with his bride, Mary Peabody—, and Henry James, and Margaret Fuller; and Emerson plans to build a cabin on his woodlot at Walden Pond.

The correspondence is a portrait gallery. In it hang English men of letters—Wordsworth, Southey, Rogers, Sterling, Milnes, Dickens, Thackeray, Tennyson, Browning, Landor—richly, boldly, fantastically painted or caricatured:

Southey's complexion is still healthy mahogany-brown with a fleece of white hair, and eyes that seem running at full gallop. . . . Old Rogers with his pale head, white, bare, and cold as snow, will look on you with those large blue eyes, cruel, sorrowful, and that sardonic shelf-chin.

And on the opposite wall, painted rather in water colors than in oils, hangs transcendental New England:

Henry Hodge is a recluse but catholic scholar in our remote Bangor, who reads German & smokes in his solitary study through nearly eight months of snow in the year, and deals out, every Sunday, his witty apothegms to the lumber-merchants & township owners of Penobscot River, who have actually grown intelligent interpreters of his riddles by long harkening after them.

Occasionally the same subject, Daniel Webster or Alcott or Margaret Fuller, is painted by both artists, and there is an instructive contrast in style and vision.

These are literary letters, full of the practical business of literature, full also of speculation, prejudice, theory, general principles, technical analysis, and unvarnished opinion. Carlyle writes of Emerson's second volume of *Essays:*

By the bye I ought to say, the sentences are very brief; and did not . . . always entirely cohere for me . . . did not, sometimes, rightly stick to their foregoers and their followers; the paragraph not as a beaten *ingot,* but as a beautiful square *bag of duck-shot* held together by canvas!

And Emerson says of *Sartor:*

Believe . . . that men are waiting to hear your Epical Song; and so be pleased to skip those excursive involved glees, and give us the simple air, without the volley of variations.

Carlyle lays down the law on poetry in words which may have had some effect on Emerson's essay "The Poet":

At bottom "Poetry" is a most suspicious affair for me at present! You cannot fancy the oceans of Twaddle that human creatures emit upon me in these times; as if when the lines had a jingle in them, a Nothing could be Something. . . . what is the use of putting your accusative *before* the verb, and otherwise entangling the syntax; if there *is* really an image of any object, thought, or thing within you, for God's sake let me have it the *shortest* way, and I will so cheerfully excuse the *omission* of the jingle at the ends.

And Emerson announces the best book of 1855, a volume on which that same essay "The Poet" had not been without influence:

One book, last summer, came out in New York, a nondescript monster which yet had terrible eyes and buffalo strength, & was indisputably American,— which I thought to send you; but the book throve so badly with the few to whom I showed it, & wanted good morals so much, that I never did. Yet I believe now again, I shall. It is called "Leaves of Grass,"—was written and printed by a journeyman printer in Brooklyn, N.Y. named Walter Whitman; and after you have looked into it, if you think, as you may, that it is only an auctioneer's inventory of a warehouse, you can light your pipe with it.

Emerson's first letter was accompanied by a dual selection of books from the new world; Carlyle's last letter, almost forty years later, contains a strong injunction to read Ruskin's *Fors Clavigera.*

But the letters are not exclusively or even primarily literary. They are concerned also with metaphysics and morality and social justice. Emerson here makes early statements of his familiar themes: Optimism, Compensation, Independence of Society, Self-trust. Carlyle clamors for Silence, and preaches his doctrines of Fact and Work and the Identity of Might and Right, Real and Ideal. Repeatedly and centrally, the letters deal with the problems of politics. Carlyle writes:

I was much struck with Plato, last year, and his notions about Democracy. . . . I, for my own part, perceive the use of all this too, the inevitability of all this; but perceive it (at the present height it has attained) to be disastrous withal, to be horrible and even damnable. That Judas Iscariot should come and slap Jeasus Christ on the shoulder in a familiar manner; that all the heavenliest nobleness should be flung out into the muddy streets there to jostle elbows with all. . . .

And Emerson reports on democracy in wartime:

The leaders were prompted & corrected by the intuitions of the people,—they still demanding the more generous & decisive measure, & giving their sons & their estates, as we had no example before. In this heat, they had sharper perceptions of policy, of the ways and means, & the life of nations. . . . We were proud of the people. . . .

In almost every letter two major minds are engaged, not only with each other but with the major problems of their time.

This, at a glance, is what the correspondence is about. A closer examination, through the microscope of the index for example, demonstrates that it is a document of the greatest importance both for the study of Carlyle and Emerson and for the history of thought and taste in the nineteenth century. But merely documentary values do not give a book, beyond the library stacks, the classic status which has been claimed for this one. The correspondence of Marx and Engels lives in one world, the correspondence of Horace Walpole in another, the letters of John Keats in still another. Where the correspondence of Carlyle and Emerson lives, or will live, is essentially a literary question which must be answered in terms of the texture and tone of the letters and the shape and structure of the book as a whole.

The virtues of Emerson as a letter writer are not immediately apparent. He was, in 1834, a very mature and self-reliant young man. His comments on Wordsworth and Coleridge, in the privacy of his journal, show him remarkably unawed by his elders and betters; and he talked with the Carlyles at Craigenputtock as an equal. He was an experienced and accomplished writer: already his journal contained blocks of prose which he would use later for the *Essays* and

English Traits. But he was quite untested. He had published little but a boyish essay on the middle ages, long forgotten.[1] He had written sermons, but his career in the ministry had been a brief and parochial one. He had written letters, but only to his family, his college friends, his ministerial colleagues. When on May 14, 1834, he took pen in hand, it was a formal ministerial pen and a hand stiffened by embarrassment.

He did not trust himself to intuition; he listened rather to the courtly muses of Europe, and made a careful first draft of his letter:

My dear Sir,—There are some purposes we delay long to execute simply because we have them more at heart than others, and such an one has been for many weeks, I may say months, my design of writing you an epistle. Some chance wind blew your name to me two or three years ago as the author of the papers which I had long before distinguished, as indeed it was very easy to do, from the mass of English Periodical Criticism that comes every month to our reading rooms. . . .[2]

This he polished and improved. After "some chance wind" he inserted "of Fame" to give a touch of elegance and abstraction. He crossed out the clause "that comes every month to our reading rooms": it was perhaps too specific, too temporal and local. He had compared the content and form of *Sartor Resartus* to "the world in a birchbark canoe," but that was both bold and concrete and he struck it out. He was well enough pleased with this sentence, however: "I comprehend not why you should lavish in that spendthrift style of yours Celestial truths"; and he copied it into the epistle which went to Craigenputtock.

But if the rhetoric of this American scholar was timid, imitative, and tame, his message was quite the opposite. He teased Carlyle for his use of the neologism "environment." He vigorously, or, as he said, saucily, attacked the extravagances of Carlyle's style and attributed them, accurately, to the isolation and alienation of the artist. He displayed an impressive and unfashionable erudition in allusions not only to Matthew and *Hamlet* but to Coleridge, Montaigne, and *Wilhelm Meister*. And along with this first letter he sent as odd a pair of books as ever crossed the ocean: Webster's *Reply to Hayne* and Sampson Reed's *Growth of the Mind*, a psychological-philosophical essay by a Swedenborgian druggist of Boston.

[1] Rusk, *Life*, p. 96. [2] Rough draft, owned by RWEMA.

Such freshness and originality of mind must inevitably, or so it would seem to a clothes-philosopher, demand new styles in rhetoric. But Emerson was, as Carlyle once put it, close-buttoned. He changed slowly. For years his letters were disfigured by sentences like this: "Now as to the welcome hint that you might come to America, it shall be to me a joyful hope." He was capable of quoting, as a message from his wife to Jane Carlyle, a sentence which all by itself would have been enough to keep the Carlyles on their own side of the Atlantic: "Come, & I will be to you a sister." He clung to the abstract. An obituary paragraph on his brother Charles concluded thus: "He postponed always a particular to a final and absolute success, so that his life was a silent appeal to the great and generous." He clung to his method of rough draft and revision, in spite of his recognition that he had "a formidable tendency to the lapidary style." In the first draft of a letter written in 1839 he told of "the existence here of one or two great men. Bronson Alcott is a majestic soul and the only man with whom conversation is possible." This he rendered even more affected and pretentious in his final draft: "A man named Bronson Alcott is a majestic soul with whom conversation is possible." And in both drafts he continued: "He is capable of truth, & gives me the same glad astonishment that he should exist which the World does." In the essays and poems Emerson's lapidary style turned out some very precious stones; in the letters it produced—far too often—rhinestones and millstones.

But a number of influences were at work early in the correspondence to change Emerson from a writer of epistles to a writer of letters. The first of these was business. As Carlyle's American agent, Emerson had to concern himself with the facts of paper, print, dollars, and piracy. He wrote letter after letter in which lapidarianism and abstraction might have been more than rhetorically disastrous. He wrote impromptu in the corner of a publisher's shop; he wrote in haste to enclose a draft from his banker Abel Adams or to get a question into the mail bag before the *Great Western* sailed. As early as 1835 he wrote a long letter on the lecture business in America:

So let us suppose we have 900 persons paying $3 each, or $2,700. If it should happen, as it did in Prof. Silliman's case, that many more than 900 tickets were sold it would be easy to give the course in the day *and* in the evening. . . . If the lectures succeed in Boston, their success is insured at Salem, a town thirteen miles off, with a population of 15,000.

This is businesslike; and it is so colloquial that it needs an under-lined *and* if it is to be understood at first reading. In the press and intimacy of business, the pernicious first drafts became less and less frequent, and Emerson wrote to Carlyle as freely as he wrote to his brothers.

Another influence was the correspondence itself. For every letter of Emerson's there was one from Carlyle proclaiming by example and precept the importance of Facts. When *The American Scholar* first arrived in England, Carlyle could write only the most enthusiastic praise, but after a second or third reading he suggested that Emer-son's "next work ought to be a *concrete* thing; not *theory* any longer, but *deed.*" After the Divinity School address he wrote: "I long to see some concrete thing, some Event, Man's Life, American Forest, or piece of Creation, which this Emerson loves and wonders at, well Emersonized; depictured by Emerson." After the appearance of the first number of *The Dial* he complained, "For me it is *too* ethereal, speculative, theoretic. . . . I will have all things condense themselves, take shape and body, if they are to have my sympathy." And even-tually the world of Emerson did take shape. A frank and warm letter invited the Carlyles for a year's visit to the big house in Concord with its garden, its orchard, its forty young pine trees, its three servants, and reminded them that they would be no burden to a man who had $22,000 at six percent. The boy Waldo had appeared in the letters at five months as merely "a lovely wonder"; the girl Ellen, at a year, was "the softest & gracefullest little maiden alive, creeping like a turtle with head erect all about the house."

And finally there is the influence, hard to calculate but surely im-portant, of Emerson's artistic and public success. In 1834 he was an unemployed Unitarian minister. In 1836 he was the author of a "little book" entitled *Nature;* in 1837 he delivered that latest form of in-fidelity *The Divinity School Address;* in 1841 he polished and pub-lished his lectures as *Essays:* he had become the equal of Carlyle or of any man, not merely in potentiality but in achievement.

Carlyle's letter of praise for *The American Scholar* had made him nearly jump for joy. "Fine things about our poor speech at Cam-bridge," he wrote boyishly, "fine things from *Carlyle*—scarcely could we maintain a decorous gravity on the occasion." But soon he was less concerned about gravity, although he was hardly ever indecorous. He made a jest from time to time: his hope for Carlyle in the American book business was the vulgar one of dollars—"that innate idea of the American mind." His lectures he wrote of as "a good spur to the sides of that dull horse I have charge of." When the Carlyles complained of ill-health, he threatened to report them to the vegetarian Alcott—"who will have his revenge." Year by year his letters took on a lighter tone. He described the daguerreotype which had been made on his forty-third birthday as giving him "the air of a decayed gentleman touched with his first paralysis." His letter of congratulation on the completion of *Cromwell* was easy, deft, and graceful. His letters announcing the second trip to England had a boyish gaiety which he could not have commanded when he was a boy: "And who knows but I may come one day? Steam is strong and Liverpool is near. . . . So beware of me, for on that distant day when I get ready I shall come. . . . In my old age I am coming to see you."

During the fifties and sixties Emerson's letters attained something of the excellence which Carlyle's had had from the beginning of the correspondence. Mastery of the art of the letter Emerson was never to achieve. Essentially poet and preacher, he was never at his best in informality. Even forty years of correspondence with Carlyle never quite freed him from the forced smile, the dry, nervous cough of the man who is at home only in the study and the pulpit. But as he grew older, his letters came more and more to express the full range of his feeling and his experience. They recorded in detail a lecture trip to Kentucky, Ohio, and the Upper Mississippi, or a sixty-mile sleigh ride to give a lecture in frontier Milwaukee; and Carlyle applauded them as *letters*, which he had not done before: "your . . . wild dashing portraiture of things as they are . . . under your light caricature, the outlines of a right true picture." They expressed his indignation over slavery, his deep involvement in the war, his sympathy when the news came of Jane Carlyle's death. His sentences and images were now easy and unforced:

But I was going to say, my neglect of your request will show you how little saliency is in my weeks & months. They are hardly distinguished in memory other than as a running web out of a loom, a bright stripe for day, a dark stripe for night, &, when it goes faster, even these run together into endless grey.

From the beginning Emerson's letters bore the special marks of his genius: they were—whatever their shortcomings—brilliant, bold, and sweet. At the last, or at their best, they spoke for him with a human voice which was, as Carlyle said, "charmingly vivid and free."

Carlyle did not, during the years of his correspondence with Emerson, greatly change or improve his epistolary style. By 1834 he was already a mature writer. In the ten years of contribution to *The Edinburgh Review* and *Fraser's Magazine* which lay directly behind him, he had written his most influential and important work and had tailored and retailored the clothes he was to wear, with only a few alterations, for the rest of his career. His style was perhaps even better suited to informal letters than to the exposition of *Allerlei-Wissenschaft,* and the first letter which he sent to Emerson might well have traveled not in a postbag from Chelsea but in one of the six considerable paper bags from Weissnichtwo. It might, too, have been dictated forty years later to Mary Aitken and signed shakily in pencil.

"A noble letter," Emerson exclaimed, and sent it to New York for his brother to read. It was an active volcano of a letter: personal, egotistical ("let me explain, what you long to know, how it is that I date from London"); but warm and friendly ("your old Bed stands in a new room here, and the old welcome at the door"); parenthetical, exclamatory, underlined for emphasis with schoolgirl prodigality; learned, allusive—adorned, or rather splashed, with quotations from or references to *Wilhelm Meister,* Juvenal, Matthew, Diogenes, Teufelsdröckh, Frederick the Great; newsy ("Gustave d'Eichthal [did you hear?] has gone over to Greece"); factual; concrete and specific ("solitary in the wilderness, with none but an old woman and foolish grouse-destroyers in it; and we for the last ten weeks. . ."). No wonder indeed that this letter was passed about, copied, and read by half of transcendental New England.

The faults of Carlyle's letters are as obvious as their virtues or as the faults of *Sartor Resartus:* "On the whole, Professor Teufelsdröckh is not a cultivated writer." He is extravagant and overbearing; at his worst he can be blatant and affected. These are perhaps the natural faults of Carlyle's personality and his method of letter writing. He never blotted out a line. His sentences are full of parenthetical afterthoughts, qualifications, and corrections. He approaches the end of his paper with surprise and dismay: "What a pity this poor sheet is done! I had innumerable things to tell you about people whom I have seen, about books. . . ." To save paper and thus to save postage for Emerson, he fills his margins with microscopic postscripts and he cross-hatches headings and salutations. Such improvisation gives entrance to the mannerism of the moment, to archaisms or exoticisms, and in a writer of Carlyle's temperament it encourages rhapsody and rant. But even in these faults there are, as Emerson must have found, compensations. Some of Carlyle's happiest dramatic effects are achieved by throwing the cold water of deprecation on a passage which suddenly seems too purple:

Forty years of age; and extremely dyspeptical: a hopeless-looking man. Yet full of what I call desperate-hope! One does verily stand on the Earth, a Star-dome encompassing one; seemingly accoutred and enlisted and sent to battle, with rations good, indifferent or bad,—what can one do but in the name of Odin, Tuiskone, Hertha, Horsa and all Saxon and Hebrew Gods, fight it out?—This surely is very idle talk.

But the method which produced such idle talk produced also much true talk, that approximation of speech which is the essence of a good letter and which is often so difficult for men of letters. "By the bye," Carlyle writes, in mild remorse at having told Emerson that he liked Unitarians a good deal less than atheists,

how very good you are, in regard to this of Unitarianism! I declare I am ashamed of my intolerance:—and yet you have ceased to be a Teacher of theirs, have you not? I mean to address you this time by the secular title of Esquire; as if I liked you better so. But truly, in black clothes or in white, by this style or by that, the man himself can never be other than welcome to me. You will further allow me to fancy that you are now wedded. . . .

With the ease and inclusiveness of table talk his letters weave together transcendentalism and domesticity. In the warmth of composition he can see himself, implausibly, as a Scotch uncle to the household in Concord:

I do believe, if I live long, I shall get to Concord one day. Your wife must love me. If the little boy be a well-behaved fellow, he shall ride on my back yet; if not, tell him I will have nothing to do with him, the riotous little imp that he is. And so God bless you always, my dear friend!—Your affectionate
T. Carlyle

These warm, extemporaneous, colloquial, spoken letters are not, however, as they might well be, formless. The sentences, despite their alarums and excursions, their Teutonic length and complexity, are drawn tight by careful, elaborate punctuation; they are beaten into paragraph-ingots, and they stick rightly to their foregoers and followers. Even crosshatched postscript paragraphs are likely to be fitted out with topic sentences.

Nor did improvisation and colloquialism produce in Carlyle's prose the insipidity of ordinary speech. His diction is, like Teufelsdröckh's, both idomatic and rich, and his prose echoes with a contrapuntal allusiveness. Sensitive to the ancestry and consanguinity of his words, he plays with them etymologically: "My other Manuscripts are scratchings and scrawlings;—children's INfant souls weeping because they never could be born." He writes scarcely a sentence which has not above it the overtone of quotation or reference, "encyclopediacal allusion," as Emerson wrote, "to all knowables." Sometimes he merely quotes, or misquotes, a famous line of verse: "Tomorrow to fresh fields and pastures new." Sometimes he weaves phrases and images into a more complex pattern: "Were I to give you my actual *view* of the case it were a view such as Satan had from the pavilion of the Anarch old. Alas, it is all too like chaos: confusion of dense and rare; I also know what it is to drop *plumb:* fluttering my pennons vain,— for a series of weeks!" Sometimes his references must have been as meaningless to Emerson as they are to a twentieth-century reader: "I am for some practical subject too; none of your pictures in the air, or *aesthetisches Zeug* (as Müllner's wife called it, Müllner of the 'Midnight *Blade*')." But for the most part he is canonical, deft, and pertinent. Of a slovenly reprinting of *The French Revolution* he writes: "Fraser 'finds the people like it'; credat Judaeus"—which any educated man would quickly complete with *Apella non ego*. Of a bank draft for one hundred pounds, the result of American bibliopoly, he writes: "The miraculous draught of Paper I have just sent to a sure hand in Liverpool"; and the former clergyman in Concord must have smiled at a pretty turn in the game of allusion.

Such elegancies and ornaments are set against a sturdy fabric of concreteness. The doctrine of Fact which he preaches perennially to Emerson he practices in his own letters. He cannot write about a packet of Margaret Fuller's manuscripts without adding the physical details, as if he were a Dutch painter or a postal clerk: "[Loose Package in brown paper, tied with string and sealed (by M. F.): dimensions 10 inches by 3 and by 7½; weight 3 lbs minus 1½ oz.]." He writes in time and space at an hour, at a place: "Adieu my friend:

it is silent Sunday; the populace not yet admitted to their beer-shops, till the respectabilites conclude their rubric-mummeries. . . . we have wet wind at North-east, and a sky somewhat of the dreariest"; or "My wife, who is just gone out to spend the day with a certain 'celebrated Mrs Austin' . . . charged me very specially to send you her love"; or " 'Post passing!' I must end in mid-course"; or "Here at the moment a miserable Italian organ-grinder has struck up the *Marsellaise* under my window."

More important than the concreteness of Carlyle's letters—or their spontaneity, their idiosyncrasy, their vocality—is the freshness of their diction and metaphor. Never, or hardly ever, is the word that comes to Carlyle's pen the familiar or expected one. On every page, almost in every postscript, there are words that seem specially created for the occasion, even though the occasion itself may be trivial and routine. A short and ordinary sequence from the letter of November 11, 1845, to take a random example, mentions an engraver who is now in the house working on the *Cromwell* frontispiece and "requiring new indoctrination,—poor fellow!" In ten days it will be over, the *Cromwell* affair, a worthless experience "except for the little fractions or intermittent fits of pious industry there really were in it"; but, before then, Carlyle and his wife will be off to visit the Ashburtons, "the Lord-Ashburtons, in fact; more properly the younger stratum of that house . . . the bustle of moving is already begun." And what good news is the promise of a new book by Emerson: "to one man here it is ever as an *articulate voice* amid the infinite cackling and cawing."

Carlyle's more explicit and elaborate figures are similarly startling in their newness and aptness. Of Harriet Martineau he writes, in two separate letters:

A genuine little Poetess, buckramed, swathed like a mummy, into Socinean and Political-Economy formulas, and yet verily alive in the inside of that! . . . Behold now Unitarian mechanical Formalism was to have its Poetess too; and stragglings of genius were to spring up even thro' that like grass thro' a Macadam highway!

Charles Sumner seems to him "inoffensive, like a worn sixpence that has no physiognomy left," and in Daniel Webster he sees an "amorphous crag-like face; the dull black eyes under their precipice of brows, like dull anthracite furnaces, needing only to be *blown;* the mastiff-mouth, accurately closed." Frederic Henry Hedge has

a face like a rock; a voice like a howitzer; . . . [he] came to me with tall
lank Chapman at his side,—an innocent flail of a creature, with considerable
impetus in him: the two when they stood up together looked like a circle and
tangent, in more senses than one.

And in very different figures, but no less vividly, he can write a letter
of condolence: "Such a Brother, with such a Life opening round him,
like a blooming garden where he was to labour and gather, all vanished suddenly like frostwork, and hidden from your eye!"

The action which crowds Carlyle's letters is intense and dramatic,
intensified and dramatized. Holiday trips to Scotland are desperate
flights, with life or sanity at stake. The fugitive arrives at his mother's
cottage on no ordinary day but "on the longest day of June" and falls
exhausted into a hypnotic sleep: "all was unearthly. . . . The gushing of my native brooks, the *sough* of the old solitary woods, the great
roar of old native Solway (billowing fresh out of your Atlantic, drawn
by the Moon): all this was a kind of unearthly music to me." The
arrival of a poor photograph of Emerson brings not merely a request
for a portrait but a dark fantasy of the sort which shadowed all of
Carlyle's days, if not all of his letters:

Here is a genial, smiling energetic face, full of sunny strength, intelligence,
integrity, good humour; but it lies imprisoned in baleful shades, as of the
valley of Death; seems smiling on me as if in mockery, "Dost know me friend?
I am dead, thou seest, and distant, and forever hidden from thee; I belong
already to the Eternities, and thou recognizest me not! On the whole it is the
strangest feeling I have. . . .

A visit from Count D'Orsay makes not merely a piece of social intelligence but a *scene* in which "the emperor of European Dandies" en-
counters "the Prophet of spiritual Sanscullotism":

He came rolling down hither one day, many months ago, in his sun-chariot, to
the bedazzlement of all bystanders; found me in dusty grey-plaid dressing
gown, grim as the spirit of Presbyterianism (my Wife said), and contrived to
get along well enough with me.

Even when a letter is written many months after the action which it
reports, it has—as do Carlyle's astonishing reminiscences of his childhood—the sharpness and immediacy of a diary. But sometimes the
immediacy is real, the action occurs between salutation and signature,
and the letter becomes something like a dramatic monologue. On
April 30, 1860, Carlyle writes about a matter of business in which

he feels he has been ill-used by the publisher Harper. It is a hasty letter, angry, furious, possessed:

To Mr Cabot be so good as say that Harper of New-York is to me Harpy, odious, rapacious. . . . The wretched mortal wrote to me again and again, while the question with me was not of lucre but of life or death; and in every letter you saw the mingled physiognomy of owl, raven and unclean birds . . . my wish then strongly was, and still is, that I could in some way signify to him, "Avaunt, unclean bird, come not between the wind and me again! Be so extremely obliging as to steal any property of mine you can find not guarded by the gallows, and to hold your tongue about it, and not trouble me with any dialogue at all!"—

Then, after half a paragraph of subsidence, there is a double dash.

——You will need to translate all that into rational deliberate speech; and deliver it mildly, with my gratitude, and other good human feelings (whʰ are not wanting, had I time to state them) to Mr Cabot. Nay the poor devil Harper, he too ought to have justice; and I am not the least angry at him, while he keeps wide of me! Besides I remember, it was not he at all that wrote; but some hungry feathered being (probably in moult at the time) whom he keeps here in London. God give us patience with all creatures feathered and unfeathered,—at least till we can get a chance to suppress (and extinguish by good methods) the intolerable kinds of them!—

"No time to re-read," says a postscript. "I suppose you can decipher." It was surely not Carlyle's purpose, consciously, in this letter or elsewhere, to portray his own complex, mercurial, tormented personality; but he used the only kind of pen with which such a portrayal can be made, a swift, possessed, unconscious pen. Of all the portraits in the gallery of his letters, the best one is his own.

There *are* portraits in those letters, and the sights and sounds of Victorian England, the feel and smell of life. A bank draft from Emerson is dropped into the brass slit at Barings', a letter for Emerson into the leather bag at the North and South American Coffee House. The last word of *The French Revolution* is written "one night in early January, when the clock was striking ten, and our frugal Scotch supper coming in!" Emerson's *American Scholar* arrives at Cheyne Row "one snowy night in January"; his Dartmouth College Oration is read "over dinner in a chophouse in Bucklersbury, amid the clatter of some fifty stand of knives and forks." Carlyle sits reading books, his wife sewing beside him, "with the light of a sinumbra, in a little apartment made snug against the winter"; he rides over Surrey with a leather valise behind him and a mackintosh before, "very singular to see." Yeomanry captains in Yorkshire cultivate milk-white mustachios. Daniel Webster has "a mastiff-mouth, accurately closed." Milnes is "a pretty little robin-redbreast of a man," Heraud "a loquacious scribacious little man of parboiled greasy aspect." Sounds and smells and words, a thesaurus of words, palpable, accurate, newly cut, recut, never combined in quite this way before: they reproduce the smoke, the grit, the salt, the blood of Carlyle's life; they make him seem in these letters less a historian, or a critic, or a prophet, than a novelist.

But Carlyle's letters to Emerson are not, considered singly, better than those he wrote to Sterling, and they lack, of course, the intensity and the subtlety of those he wrote to his wife. Emerson's letters to Carlyle are not *his* best letters: he wrote as well to Margaret Fuller; he wrote better to his brothers. And it would be rash to say that either man at his best wrote better letters than Gray or Byron. The special values of *The Correspondence of Emerson and Carlyle* lie in the whole rather than in the parts. By circumstances of geography and biography, by accident, or—to use the language of Carlyle and Emerson—by the Poetry of History, by the Artistry of Life, by the Design of Nature, these letters have a structure which makes it possible to read them as a single work of art. Henry James felt in them the quality of fiction, and perhaps they *should* be read as though they were fictional. Indeed, unconsciously, now intensifying and now simplifying, the fanciful reader does tend to transform the correspondence into an epistolary novel.

The story they tell is one which, long before Henry James, is concerned with international episodes, transatlantic sketches, and ambassadors. It is a story in which the Atlantic itself is constantly present, as barrier and as channel of communication. The letters are full of the names of the ships, swift packets and swifter steamships, which carry them and at least one of their writers. It is a story of places: a chophouse in Bucklersbury, a summer beach at Nantasket, the Solway Firth and the Musketaquid River, Ecclefechan and Staten Island. London is almost a character in the story, a roaring chaos where "brownstout, in quantities that would float a seventy-four, goes down the throats of men"; and three thousand miles away stands the antithetical village of Concord where the moon shines on pines and alderbushes and little girls may safely walk across the fields to Walden Pond.

There are human characters, too, many of them. Half of literary London appears in the letters, caught by the "portrait-eating, portrait-painting eyes" of Carlyle. Half of literary Boston comes to Cheyne Row bearing letters of introduction from Emerson. And there are families: Carlyle's mother, smoking her pipe at Scotsbrig; Emerson's mother, "whitest, mildest, most conservative of ladies"; Lidian Emerson, who "hardly stores a barrel of flour or lays her new carpet without some hopeful reference to Mrs Carlyle"; Emerson's children, creeping like turtles, walking to Walden, studying medicine at Harvard; Emerson's brothers who die of tuberculosis; Carlyle's brother John, traveling physician to Scottish and Irish nobility, translator of Dante; and Jane Carlyle, who was there at Craigenputtock in 1833, who is rarely absent from the correspondence, and who herself writes the book's warmest words of affection.

The two protagonists—and the story *is* a Plutarchian one—are as opposite in character as London and Concord. Poor and rich, high and low, hot and cold, dark and light: such antitheses pervade the book at every level of thought and action. In London, as at Craigenputtock, the Scottish peasant complains of poverty (he can afford only one servant); the Concord Brahmin is sympathetic, and embarrassed. In 1834 Carlyle is a writer of international, if uncertain, reputation, the friend and correspondent of Goethe; Emerson is an unknown provincial, unsuccessful at the only profession he has attempted. Carlyle is a fiery, intolerant, pagan Covenanter, Emerson a cool ex-Unitarian drifting toward theosophy and strange gods; Carlyle an empiricist, Emerson an extreme idealist and quasi-mystic; Carlyle extravagant in manner, speech, and dress, Emerson close-buttoned; Carlyle dyspeptic and discontented, full of the stupidity and suffering of the world, his letters heavy with keening and denunciation, Emerson tight-lipped in his own sorrows, hopeful in the worst of times, able to see good even in war. In principles as in temperament they stand poles apart, in politics especially in this most political of centuries. Carlyle, even in the thirties, is moving toward a position which can be described as neo-feudalism or proto-fascism. As the years pass, he attacks democracy and capitalism and defends autocracy, slavery, and the Confederacy.

Emerson, the most radical of individualists and libertarians, is driven, despite his dislike of parties and mass action, into abolitionism, equalitarianism, and the defense of what he would have been pleased to call free enterprise.

Contrasts in character and belief are intensified by cunning parallels in action. "Curious," writes Carlyle: "your Course of Lectures 'on Human Culture' seems to be the very subject I am to discourse upon here." When Emerson writes about the vast power of the Mississippi, Carlyle is curiously able to reply with a report on his own ascent of the Rhine. Emerson's letter announcing the death of his son is answered by one edged in black and mailed from Scotland where Carlyle has gone after the death of his wife's mother to dispose of her house and possessions. Emerson's mother dies in November, 1853, Carlyle's on the following Christmas Day. Carlyle writes that he is doing a biography of John Sterling; Emerson replies, "I am trying to make a sort of memoir of Margaret Fuller." These parallels are not merely curiosities of coincidence: they give shape to the action; they also serve to illuminate character. Emerson's reaction to the death of his mother is that of a man of fifty; Carlyle's reaction to *his* mother's death is that of a boy.

The plot of the story is the course of this unlikely friendship. It begins, not with Emerson's first letter of May, 1834, but with a scene on the Scottish moors the preceding summer which the reader comes to know well through flashback and repeated reference. Five years afterward it was an incandescent memory for Jane Carlyle:

"Forgotten you"? O no indeed! if there were nothing else to remember you by, I should never forget the Visitor, who years ago in the Desart descend on us out of the clouds, as it were, and made one day there look like enchantment for us, and left me weeping that it was only *one* day.

Thirty-three years later Emerson could "recall vividly the youthful wife, and her blithe account of her letters & homages from Goethe, & the details she gave of her intended visit to Weimar, & its disappointment." The Craigenputtock meeting is both prelude and statement of major theme.

The first two letters are propitiously timed. Emerson's, saucily critical of the style of *Sartor Resartus,* carries also praise for the contents of the book and homage to its author, and it arrives at a moment when Carlyle feels his work has earned only neglect and abuse. "Blessed," he exclaims, "is the voice that amid dispiritment stupidity and contradiction proclaims to us: *Euge!*" And his reply arrives in Concord shortly after Emerson has learned of the death of his brother Edward in Puerto Rico. A token of "fraternal friendliness," Emerson thought it, "a bright light in a solitary & saddened place."

With the relationship thus firmly founded in emotion, the book moves into a long section of development and elaboration through good works, through bibliopoly. Here, to be sure, there is some tediousness. Letter after letter is filled with business details: negotiations with publishers, sales, profits, reprinting, stereotyping, proofreading, lists of errata. Letters cross and duplicate one another so that the line of the story is often, throughout the first or bibliopolic half of the book, obscured. But at frequent intervals, especially in this section, come exciting announcements of work in progress, of publication, and then of the book itself, already crossing the ocean in the hold of the *Great Western*. There are dramatic events. A friend borrows the manuscript of *The French Revolution* and returns a few nights later with "distraction (literally) in his aspect." And the heterodox Divinity School Address produces such a storm in the Massachusetts washbowl that Emerson warns Carlyle to postpone his promised visit lest he too become embroiled.

The story is quickened and varied by the traditional methods of the novelist. There are subplots, continued stories that run through an exchange of three or four letters: the comic episode of Alcott's visit to Carlyle; the tragic, and much longer, story of John Sterling, who reads *Nature,* falls "overhead in love with a certain Waldo Emerson," and takes the book with him to Madeira where the doctors have ordered him for his lungs. There is suspense. Will Carlyle really kill himself, as he fears, with the torments of lecturing and the agony of composition? Will he ever, really, come to America? This latter uncertainty, as Henry James pointed out, is sustained with remarkable effectiveness throughout the book. In his first letter Carlyle says: "Who knows but Mahomet may go to the Mountain? It occasionally rises like a mad prophetic dream in me that I might end in the Western Woods!" And Emerson, with boyish enthusiasm, plans living quarters in his house, lecture tours, a college at Concord, the editorship of a new magazine to be called *The Transcendentalist* or *The Dial*. But no, not this year, perhaps next, year after year; until at almost the very last Carlyle writes his thanks for yet another "potential welcome, and flinging wide open of your doors and your hearts to me at Concord. The gleam of it is like sunshine in a subterranean place. Ah, me, ah, me!"

The bibliopolic sections of the book are not, however, mere tedium and statistics which must be relieved by suspense, subplot, and vivid incident. A footnote is perhaps necessary to make it clear that Emerson went into debt in order to finance the American edition of *The French Revolution*. But even the least imaginative reader must soon realize that these columns of figures represent a noble work of generosity and affection. When the first fifty pounds arrive from America Jane Carlyle weeps, and her husband writes, in his native dialect, "May ne'er waur be amang us!" By the close of 1841 Carlyle's financial situation is so much improved that he can write to Emerson for advice on investments. Emerson's reply, perhaps the most dramatic of all the letters, demonstrates the contiguity here of business and the deepest places of life. Buy no Southern stocks, Emerson says, possibly Illinois, but best of all Massachusetts. "If you wish to invest money here, my friend Abel Adams, who is the principal partner in one of our best houses, Barnard, Adams, & Co. will know how to give you the best assistance & action the case admits." Here there is a space, as if the writer had wished to separate his paragraphs by more than indentation, and then: "My dear friend, you should have had this letter & these messages by the last steamer, but when it sailed my son a perfect little boy of five years and three months had ended his earthly life." Carlyle's answer begins: "This is heavy news that you send me," and concludes: "Adieu, my good kind Friend, ever dear to me, dearer now in sorrow."

In the second half of the book, after prosperity and piracy have put an end to what Carlyle calls "chivalrous international doings" in the book business, the letters come in pairs, expostulation and reply, and the tempo of the story becomes more rapid. *The Dial* crosses the ocean and draws lively and accurate fire. Sterling dies. Tennyson appears. The second volume of *Essays* gets written, criticized, and defended. Emerson dares to send across a volume of poems. *Cromwell* is finished at last. And now there is talk of gray hair and spectacles. Half solemnly, half gaily, they exchange daguerreotypes. "Do you," writes Carlyle, as he looks at his own photograph, "do you bethink you of Craigenputtock, and the still evening there? I could burst with tears, if I had

that habit: but it is of no use." And Emerson writes, "In my old age
I am coming to see you."

But when the packet *Washington Irving* arrives in Liverpool in
October, 1847, Carlyle is not there to meet it. Emerson's letter has
ominously miscarried and Carlyle must send his welcome by another
hand. During the ten months of Emerson's lecture tour in Britain, the
correspondence is of course fragmentary: invitations, notes, a letter or
two on forensic matters. But when it resumes, late in 1848, there can
be no doubt that something has gone wrong. "Of one impression we
fail not here," Carlyle writes: "admiration of your pacific virtues, of
gentle and noble tolerance, often sorely tried in this place! Forgive me
my ferocities. . . ." And in another letter: "O forgive me, forgive me
all trespasses,—and love me what you can!" What ferocities? What
trespasses? asks the reader whose pleasure has not been spoiled by
footnotes and introductions. He suspects politics to be the root of the
evil, but he considers the possibility of quarrels over theosophy and
poetry or of animosity resulting from Carlyle's inability to share his
pulpit. The discussions of corn meal and cookery which dominate the
correspondence just after Emerson's return seem at first reassuringly
trivial; at second thought they seem a significant evasion of dangerous
topics. But complex and ambiguous as the situation may be, one thing
is clear: the crisis of the friendship and of the book occurs off stage
and unrecorded.

The darkness of this crisis hangs over the correspondence for the
next eighteen years. The letters come at longer intervals now, a year
or more apart. It is Carlyle who writes and Emerson who answers, late.
Lethargy, indifference, hostility, all seem possible reasons for Emerson's silence and sources of the suspense which is a central element
of this part of the book. From Carlyle there are fierce attacks on democracy, and apologies to Emerson for opinions which are so clearly
offensive:

Tho' I see well enough what a great deep cleft divides us, in our ways of
practically looking at this world,—I see also (as probably you do yourself)
where the rock-strata, miles deep, unite again; and the two poor souls are at
one . . . has not the man Emerson, from old years, been a Human Friend to
me? Can I ever forget, or think otherwise than lovingly of the man Emerson?

From Emerson there is no comment on the deep cleft, only a cool,
close-buttoned silence. Not until the end of the war does he write of
Carlyle's Confederatism, and even then he writes obliquely:

I have in these last years lamented that you had not made the visit to America, which in earlier years you projected and favored. It would have made it impossible that your name should be cited for one moment on the side of the enemies of mankind.

But silence, whatever the cause, is sharper than invective. A sentimental and deeply involved reader might well feel in this part of the book, as George Woodberry did, that "judged in the High Court of Friendship Emerson's sins were scarlet"; [3] any reader sensitive to fictional, or human, values must feel the tensions of the relationship and speculate about what constitutes sin in the classical conflict between friendship and principle.

But the war passes and letters continue to come, although Carlyle's hand is now shaking badly. Photographs come too, among them one of Jane Carlyle, who has been in bad health. Emerson is encouraged by it: "I recognized still erect the wise friendly presence first seen at Craigenputtock." But his next letter, in the spring of 1866, begins: "I have just been shown a private letter from Moncure Conway to one of his friends here, giving some tidings of your sad return to an empty home. We had the first news last week. And so it is." Carlyle's reply is written from France in January of 1867:

It is a long time since I last wrote to you; and a long distance in space and in fortune,—from the shores of the Solway in summer 1865, to this niche of the Alps and Mediterranean today, after what has befallen me in the interim! A longer interval, I think, and surely by far a sadder, than ever occurred between us before, since we first met in the Scotch moors, some five and thirty years ago.

Death, old age, memory: these combine, it seems, to brush away the barricades of politics, to build a bridge across the cleft.

The last letters are full of words and acts of reparation. When Carlyle writes again, three years later, fearful that his correspondence with Emerson has gone out along with the other lights of a "now dusky and lonely world," it is to offer his library of Cromwell and Friedrich books to some New England library as testimony of his good will. And now the correspondence revives. There is business again, and letters pass once and twice a month: "My old Emerson again, not a feature of him changed, whom I have known all the best part of my life." Once more there is talk of philosophy and criticism and politics and voyages:

[3] MS, Woodberry to Norton, February 26, 1883, owned by the Houghton Library.

I thought I read in what you say of not making the long promised visit hither, a little willingness to come. . . . Every reading person in America holds you in exceptional regard, & will rejoice in your arrival. They have forgotten your scarlet sins before or during the war.

And Carlyle replies:

I may confess to you . . . that in my occasional explosions against "Anarchy," and in inextinguishable hatred of *it,* I privately whisper to myself, "Could any Friedrich Wilhelm, now or Friedrich, or most perfect Governor you could hope to realize, guide forward what is America's essential task at present faster or more completely than 'anarchic America' herself is now doing?" *Such* "Anarchy" has a great deal to say for itself.

Carlyle's last letter seems, in its advocacy of Ruskin's "fierce lightning-bolts" and "divine rage," almost a conscious abdication and valediction; it concludes, like so many of his earlier letters but somehow differently, with a lament that the end of the paper has come: "Alas, alas . . . and I had still a whole wilderness of things to say." Emerson's last letter has, in its evidence of mental decline, a sad but unsentimental finality; it seems also to say, in its announcement of one last visitor from Concord to Chelsea, that discords have been resolved and that a pattern has been completed.

The Correspondence of Emerson and Carlyle is a story of ideas, of conflict and compromise; it is a story of friendship, of quarrel and reconciliation; essentially it is a story of the victory of life over principle. But most important, it is, or tells, a story. Like some pieces of driftwood and some lives, like the simultaneous deaths of Adams and Jefferson, it is a work of nature which is very much like a work of art.

THE CORRESPONDENCE

1834

Boston, Massachusetts 14 May, 1834

My dear Sir,

There are some purposes we delay long to execute simply because we have them more at heart than others, & such an one has been for many weeks I may say months my design of writing you an Epistle.

Some chance wind of Fame blew your name to me perhaps two years ago as the author of papers which I had already distinguished, (as indeed it was very easy to do,) from the mass of English periodical Criticism as by far the most original & profound essays of the day [1] the works of a man of Faith as well as Intellect sportive as well as learned & who belonging to the despairing & deriding class of philosophers was not ashamed to hope & to speak sincerely. Like somebody in Wilhelm Meister,[2] I said, this person has come under obligations to me & to all whom he has enlightened. He knows not how deeply I should grieve at his fall if in that exposed England where genius always hears the devil's whisper "All these kingdoms will I give thee,—" [3] his virtue also should be an initial growth put off with age. When therefore I found myself in Europe I went to your house only to say "Faint not— the word you utter is heard though in the ends of the earth & by humblest men; it works, prevails." Drawn by strong regard to one of my teachers I went to see his person & as he might say his environment [4] at Craigenputtock. Yet it was to fulfil my duty, to finish my mission, not with much hope of gratifying him; in the Spirit of "If

---

[1] See above, Introduction, pp. 5, 77.

[2] In the first draft, "enlightened" was "exhorted." The passage Emerson had in mind was a speech made by Madame Melina to Wilhelm (*Lehrjahre*, VII, viii): "O, mein Freund, ein guter Mensch verspricht durch seine Gegenwart nur immer zu viel! Das Vertrauen, das er hervorlockt, die Neigung, die er einflösst, die Hoffnungen, die er erregt, sind unendlich, er wird und bleibt ein Schuldner, ohne es zu wissen" (*Goethes Sämtliche Werke*, XVIII, 253).

[3] Cf. Matt. 4: 9.

[4] The *NED* gives Carlyle as the first to use "environment" in its present concrete sense. Emerson enclosed the word in quotation marks in the first draft of this letter.

I love you what is that to you?" [5] Well, it happened to me that I was delighted with my visit, justified to myself in my respect, & many a time upon the Sea in my homeward voyage I remembered with joy the favored condition of my lonely philosopher,—his happiest wedlock, his fortunate temper, his steadfast simplicity, his all means of happiness not that I had the remotest hope he should so far depart from his theories as to expect happiness. On my arrival at home I rehearsed to several attentive ears what I had seen & heard, & they with joy received it.[6]

In Liverpool I wrote to Mr Fraser to send me his Magazine & I have now received four numbers of the Sartor Resartus [7] for whose light, thanks evermore. I am glad that one living scholar is self-centred & will be true to himself though none ever were before; who, as Montaigne says, "puts his ear close by himself, & holds his breath, & listens" [8] And none can be offended with the self subsistency of one so catholic & jocund. And 'tis good to have a new eye inspect our mouldy social forms, our politics, & schools, & religion. I say *our,* for it cannot have escaped you that a lecture upon these topics written for England may be read to America. Evermore thanks for the brave stand you have made for Spiritualism in these writings. But has literature any parallel to the oddity of the vehicle chosen to convey this treasure. I delight in the contents, the form which my defective apprehension for a joke makes me not appreciate I leave to your merry discretion. And yet did ever wise & philanthropic author use so defying a diction? As if society were not sufficiently shy of truth without providing it beforehand with an objection to the form. Can it be that this humour proceeds from a despair of finding a contemporary audience & so the Prophet feels at liberty to utter his message in droll sounds.[9] Did you not tell me, Mr Thomas Carlyle, sitting upon one of your broad hills, that it was

[5] Emerson called this a "saying" when he used it in his essay "Love" (*Works,* II, 180), but he probably found it in *Wilhelm Meisters Lehrjahre* in a speech of Philine to Wilhelm: "Und wenn ich dich lieb habe, was geht's dich an?" (*Goethes Sämtliche Werke,* XVII, 273).

[6] Cf. Matt. 13: 20.

[7] The fourth installment of *Sartor Resartus* appeared in *Fraser's Magazine* for March, 1834. It concluded with ch. 7 of bk. II.

[8] Cf. ch. 20 of bk. II of the *Essays.*

[9] In September, 1833, in a letter to Mill, Carlyle had written a remarkably similar explanation of the eccentricities of *Sartor Resartus:* "I never know or can even guess what or who my audience is, or whether I have any audience: thus too naturally I adjust myself on the Devil-may-care principle" (D. A. Wilson, *Carlyle to "The French Revolution,"* p. 338).

Jesus Christ built Dunscore kirk yonder.[10] If you love such sequences, then admit, as you will, that no poet is sent into the world before his time; that all the departed thinkers & actors have paved your way; that (at least, when you surrender yourself) nations & ages do guide your pen, yes & common goose-quills as well as your diamond graver. Believe then that harp & ear are formed by one revolution of the wheel; that men are waiting to hear your Epical Song; and so be pleased to skip those excursive involved glees, and give us the simple air, without the volley of variations. At least in some of your prefaces you should give us the theory of your rhetoric. I comprehend not why you should lavish in that spendthrift style of yours Celestial truths. Bacon & Plato have something too solid to say than that they can afford to be humorists. You are dispensing that which is rarest, namely, the simplest truths—truths which lie next to Consciousness & which only the Platos & Goethes perceive. I look for the hour with impatience when the vehicle will be worthy of the spirit when the word will be as simple & so as resistless as the thought, & in short when your words will be one with things. I have no hope that you will find suddenly a large audience. Says not the sarcasm "Truth hath the plague in his house." [11] Yet all men are *potentially* (as Mr Coleridge would say) [12] your audience & if you will not in very Mephistophelism repel & defy them, shall be actually & whatever the great or the small may say about the charm of diabolism a true & majestic genius can afford to despise it.

I venture to amuse you with this homiletic criticism because it is the sense of uncritical truth seekers to whom you are no more than Hecuba,[13] whose instincts assure them that there is Wisdom in this grotesque teutonic apocalyptic strain of yours, but that tis hence hin-

---

[10] This speech is recorded more fully in *English Traits*: "Christ died on the tree; that built Dunscore kirk yonder; that brought you and me together. Time has only a relative existence" (*Works RWE*, V, 18). See also *Sartor Resartus* (*Works TC*, I, 196).

[11] An Italian proverb: "Il vero ha il morbo in casa." Emerson probably found the English version in Vicesimus Knox's *Elegant Extracts . . . Prose* (London, 1797), where it is followed by an explanatory parenthesis, "*i.e.* is carefully avoided" (Kenneth W. Cameron, "Emerson, Thoreau, *Elegant Extracts*, and Proverb Lore," *The Emerson Society Quarterly*, I Quarter [No. 6, 1957], 28, 35).

[12] Coleridge made frequent but, according to the *NED*, not unusual, use of "potential" and its derivatives. Perhaps this is an allusion to the Carlyle-Emerson conversations of August 25 and 26, 1833, which came shortly after Emerson's visit to Coleridge.

[13] *Hamlet*, act II, scene 2, line 585.

dered in its effect. And though with all my heart I would stand well with my Poet, yet if I offend, I shall quietly retreat into my Universal relations wherefrom I affectionately espy you as a man, myself as another.

And yet before I come to the end of my letter I may repent of my temerity & unsay my charge. For are not all our circlets of will as so many little eddies rounded in by the great circle of Necessity & *could* the Truth-Speaker perhaps now the best Thinker of the Saxon race, have written otherwise? And must not we say that Drunkenness is a virtue rather than that Cato has erred.[14]

I wish I could gratify you with any pleasing news of the regeneration, education, prospects of man in this Continent. But your philanthropy is so patient so farsighted that present evils give you less solicitude. In the last six years Government in the United States has been fast becoming a job, like great Charities.[15] A most unfit person in the Presidency has been doing the worst things & the worse he grew the more popular. Now things seem to mend. Webster, a good man & as strong as if he were a sinner, begins to find himself the Centre of a great & enlarging party & his eloquence incarnated & enacted by them. Yet men have not hope that the Majority shall be suddenly unseated. I send herewith a volume of Websters that you may see his Speech on Foots Resolutions, a speech which the Americans have never done praising.[16] I have great doubts whether the book reaches you, as I know not my agents. I shall put with it the little book of my Swedenborgian druggist, of whom I told you.[17] And if, which is hardly to be hoped, any good book should be thrown out of our vortex of trade & politics, I shall not fail to give it the same direction.

[14] Cf. Seneca, *Moral Essays* (Loeb Classical Library), II, 282: "Catoni ebrietas obiecta est; facilius efficiet, quisquis obiecit ei, crimen honestum quam turpem Catonem."

[15] Emerson had remarked in his Journal (III, 276) a month before that charitable enterprises tended to become institutional and mechanical, but the word "job" here suggests condemnation of a stronger sort.

[16] Presumably the "Second Speech on Foote's Resolution," which was later famous as the "Reply to Hayne." During April and May, Emerson had had Webster much in his mind as both a political and an intellectual hero. Journal entries group him with Shakespeare, Michaelangelo, and Mirabeau and pair him with Newton.

[17] *Observations on the Growth of the Mind* (1826) by Sampson Reed, a druggist by trade but a theologian by training, who was one of the most influential of American Swedenborgians. His influence on Emerson began in 1821 with an oration, "Genius," which he delivered at the Harvard Commencement of that year.

I need not tell you, my dear Sir, what pleasure a letter from you would give me when you have a few moments to spare to so remote a friend. If any word in my letter should provoke you to a reply I shall rejoice in my sauciness. I am spending the summer in the country,[18] but my address is "Boston, care of Barnard, Adams, & Co." Care of O. Rich London. Please to make my affectionate respects to Mrs Carlyle whose kindness I shall always gratefully remember. I depend upon her intercession to insure your writing to me. May God grant you both his best blessing.   Your friend,   R. Waldo Emerson

5. Great Cheyne Row, Chelsea, London,
12th August, 1834—

My Dear Sir,

Some two weeks ago I received your kind gift from Fraser. To say that it was welcome would be saying little: is it not as a voice of affectionate remembrance, coming from beyond the Ocean waters, first decisively announcing for me that a whole New Continent *exists,* that I too have part and lot there! "Not till we can think that here and there one is thinking of us, one is loving us, does this waste Earth become a peopled Garden." [1] Among the figures I can recollect as visiting our Nithsdale Hermitage, all like *Apparitions* now, bringing with them airs from Heaven or else blasts from the other region, there is perhaps not one of a more undoubtedly *supernal* character than yourself: so pure and still, with intent so charitable; and then vanishing too so soon into the azure Inane, as an Apparition should! Never has your Address in my Notebook met my eye but with a friendly influence. Judge if I am glad to know that there, in Infinite Space, you still hold by me.

I have read in both your Books, at leisure times; and now nearly finished the smaller one. He is a faithful thinker that Swedenborgian Druggist of yours, with really deep Ideas, who makes me too pause and

---

[18] Emerson and his mother were living in a boardinghouse in Newton, Massachusetts, a village so quiet that, as he wrote to his brother William on May 26, "nothing but the heavenly bodies is seen to move unless it be perhaps a few thrushes & the cows" (*Let RWE,* I, 411).

[1] A free translation from *Wilhelm Meisters Lehrjahre,* VII, 5. In his first letter to Joseph Neuberg, December 21, 1839, Carlyle made a similar use of this passage: "as our Goethe's Theresa says, 'first makes the waste empty world into a peopled garden for me!'" (NLS, MS 551).

think, were it only to consider what manner of man *he* must be, and what manner of thing, after all, Swedenborgianism must be.² "Thro' the smallest window, look well and you can look out into the Infinite." ³ Webster also I can recognise: a sufficient, effectual man; whom one must wish well to, and prophecy well of. The sound of him is nowise poetic-rhythmic; it is clear, one-toned, you might say metallic, yet distinct, significant not without melody. In his face above all I discern that "indignation," which if it do not make "verses," ⁴ makes *useful* way in the world. The higher such a man rises the better pleased I shall be. And so here, looking over the water, let me repeat once more what I believe is already dimly the sentiment of all Englishmen, Cisoceanic and Transoceanic, that we and you are *not* two countries, and cannot for the life of us be; but only two *parishes* of one country, with such wholesome parish hospitalities, and dirty temporary parish feuds; as we see, both of which brave parishes *vivant! vivant!* And among the glories of *both* be Yankee-doodle-doo, and the Felling of the Western Forest, proudly remembered; and for the rest, by way of parish-constable, let each cheerfully take such George Washington or George Guelph ⁵ as it can get, and bless Heaven! I am weary of hearing it said, "We love the Americans," "we wish well" &c &c: what in God's name should we do else?

You thank me for Teufelsdröckh: how much more ought I to thank you for your hearty, genuine tho' extravagant acknowledgement of it! Blessed is the voice that amid dispiritment stupidity and contradiction proclaims to us: *Euge!* Nothing ever was more ungenial than the soil this poor Teufelsdröckhish seedcorn has been thrown on here; none cries, Good speed to it; the sorriest nettle or hemlock seed, one would think, had been more welcome. For indeed our British periodical crit-

---

² In "Count Cagliostro," published in *Fraser's Magazine* in August, 1833, Carlyle had catalogued Swedenborgians with such quacks as Mesmerists and Illuminati. Later he confessed in a letter to J. J. G. Wilkinson that he had thought Swedenborg "an amiable but inane visionary. . . . But I have been rebuked already; a little book, by one Sampson Reed, of Boston, in New England, which some friend sent hither, taught me that a Swedenborgian may have thoughts of the calmest kind on the deepest things; that in short, I did *not* know Swedenborg, and ought to know him." This letter, which was quoted in the *New Jerusalem Magazine*, XIII (August, 1840), 576, "caused," Wilkinson wrote, an English reprint of *The Growth of the Mind*.

³ Cf. *Sartor Resartus*, bk. I, ch. xi (*Works TC*, I, 57).   ⁴ Juvenal, *Satires*, I, 79.

⁵ The house of Hanover is descended from the Guelphs.

ics, and especially the public of Fraser's Magazine (which I believe I have now done with) exceed all speech; require not even contempt, only oblivion.[6] Poor Teufelsdröckh! Creature of mischance, miscalculation, and thousandfold obstruction! Here nevertheless he is as you see; has struggled across the Stygian marshes, and now, as a stitched Pamphlet "for Friends," [7] cannot be *burnt,* or lost—before his time. I send you one copy for your own behoof; three others you yourself can perhaps find fit readers for: as you spoke in the plural number, I thought there might be three; more would rather surprise me. From the British side of the water, I have met simply *one* intelligent response; clear, true, tho' almost enthusiastic as your own: my British Friend too is utterly a stranger, whose very name I know not, who did not print, but only write and to an *unknown* third party.[8] Shall I say then: "In the mouth of *two* witnesses"? [9] In any case, God be thanked, I am done with it, can wash my hands of it, and send it forth; sure that the Devil will get his full share of it, and not a whit *more,* clutch as he may. But as for you, my Transoceanic Brothers, read this earnestly, for it *was* earnestly meant and written, and contains no *voluntary* falsehood of mine. For the rest if you dislike it, say that I wrote it four years ago, and could not now so write it, and on the whole (as Fritz the Only [10] said) "will do better another time."—With regard to style and so forth, what you call your "saucy" objections are not only most intelligible to me, but welcome and instructive. You say well that I take up that attitude because I have no known public, am *alone* under the Heavens, speaking into friendly or unfriendly space; add only that I will not defend such attitude, that I call it questionable, tentative, and only the best that I in these mad times could conveniently hit upon. For you are to know, my view is that now at last we have lived to see all manner of Poetics and Rhetorics and Sermonics, and one may say generally all manner of *Pulpits* for addressing man-

[6] Perhaps an echo of Goethe's phrase, "Nichtachtung, ja Verachtung." See below, C.11.11.45.

[7] The title page said, "Reprinted for Friends from Fraser's Magazine." There were fifty-eight copies

[8] "A letter from some nameless Irishman in Cork to another here (Fraser read it to me without names)": Carlyle's diary for July 26, 1834, quoted in Froude, II, 359. The Irishman was a priest named O'Shea, whom Carlyle was to meet during his Irish journey of 1849 (Norton, *Correspondence of Carlyle and Emerson,* I, 21).

[9] Matt. 18: 16.

[10] Frederick the Great. See *Sartor Resartus,* bk. II, ch. 1 (*Works TC,* I, 65).

kind from, as good as broken and abolished: alas, yes; if you have any earnest meaning, which demands to be not only listened to but *believed* and *done,* you cannot (at least I cannot) utter it *there,* but the sound sticks in my throat, as when a Solemnity were *felt* to have become a Mummery; and so one leaves the pasteboard coulisses, and three unities, and Blairs lectures,[11] quite behind; and feels only that there is *nothing sacred,* then, but the *Speech of Man* to believing Men! [12] *This,* come what will, was, is and forever must be *sacred;* and will one day doubtless anew environ itself with fit modes, with Solemnities that are *not* Mummeries. Meanwhile, however, is it not pitiable? For tho' Teufelsdröckh exclaims: "Pulpit! canst thou not *make* a pulpit, by simply *inverting the nearest tub*"; [13] yet alas he does not sufficiently reflect that it is still only a *tub,* that the most inspired utterance will come from *it,* inconceivable, misconceivable to the million; questionable (not of *ascertained* significance) even to the few. Pity us therefore; and with your just shake of the head join a sympathetic even a hopeful smile. Since I saw you, I have been trying, am still trying, other methods, and shall surely get nearer the truth, as I honestly strive for it. Meanwhile I know no method of much consequence, except that of *believing,* of being sincere: from *Homer* and the *Bible* down to the poorest Burns's *Song* I find no other *Art* that promises to be perennial.

But now quitting theoretics, let me explain, what you long to know, how it is that I date from London. Yes, my friend, it is even so: Craigenputtock now stands solitary in the wilderness, with none but an old woman and foolish grouse-destroyers in it; [14] And we for the last ten weeks, after a fierce universal disruption, are here with our household-gods. Censure not; I came to London for the best of all

---

[11] Hugh Blair's *Lectures on Rhetoric and Belles Lettres* (1783) was studied by Emerson at Harvard (*Let RWE,* I, 78) and doubtless by Carlyle at Edinburgh.

[12] Compare Emerson's dictum in "Self-Reliance": "Nothing is at last sacred but the integrity of your own mind" (*Works,* II, 50).

[13] Teufelsdröckh, in this case especially, seems to be Carlyle himself. On December 17, 1841, he wrote to his mother with respect to a proposed professorship at the University of Edinburgh: "I can make a ten times better 'Professorship' for myself wheresoever on either side of the ocean I choose to turn up the bottom of a tub, and say that I will speak from it" (NLS, MS 520).

[14] House and grounds brought an annual rent of £20 (*Letters 1826–1836,* p. 445). For Carlyle's feeling about a grouse-destroying aristocracy, see *Past and Present,* bk. III, ch. 8.

reasons: To seek bread and work. So it literally stands; and so do I literally stand with the hugest gloomiest Future before me, which in all sane moments I goodhumouredly defy. A strange element this; and I is good as an Alien in it. I care not for Radicalism, for Toryism, for Church, Tithes or the "Confusion" of Useful Knowledge: [15] much as I can speak and hear, I am alone, alone. My brave Father, now victorious from his toil, was wont to pray in evening worship: "Might we say, we are not alone, for God is with us!" Amen! Amen!

I brought a *Ms.* with me of another curious sort; entitled the *Diamond Necklace:* perhaps it will be printed soon, as an Article or even as a separate Booklet; a *queer* production, which you shall see. Finally I am busy constantly studying with my whole might for a Book on the *French Revolution.* It is part of my creed that the only Poetry is History, could we tell it right. This truth (if it prove one) I have not yet got to the limitations of; and shall in no way except by *trying* it in practice. The story of the Necklace was the first attempt at an experiment.

My sheet is nearly done; and I have still to complain of you for telling me nothing of yourself except that you are in the country. Believe that I want to know much and all. My wife too remembers you with unmixed friendliness; bids me send you her kindest wishes. Understand too that your old Bed stands in a new room here, and the old welcome at the door. Surely we shall see you in London one day. Or who knows but Mahomet may go to the Mountain? It occasionally rises like a mad prophetic dream in me that I might end in the Western Woods!

From Germany I get Letters, Messages, and even visits; but now no tidings, no influences, of moment. Goethe's Posthumous Works are all published; and Radicalism (poor hungry, yet inevitable Radicalism!) is the order of the day. The like, and even more, from France Gustave d'Eichthal (did you hear?) has gone over to Greece, and become some kind of Manager under King Otho.[16]

[15] "Our zeal for popularizing . . . is to be seen on every side . . . our *Societies for the Diffusion of Useful Knowledge* with their sixpenny treatises": Carlyle to Goethe in *Correspondence between Goethe and Carlyle,* ed. Charles Eliot Norton (London, 1887), p. 169.

[16] D'Eichthal spent twenty months in Greece as director of the Bureau of Political Economy.

Continue to love me, you and my other friends; and as Packets sail so swiftly [17] let me know it frequently. All good be with you!

Most faithfully,   T. Carlyle

Coleridge, as you doubtless hear, is gone. How great a Possibility, how small a realized Result! They are delivering Orations about him, and emitting other kinds of froth, *ut mos est.* What hurt can it do?

Concord, Mass.   20 November 1834

My dear Sir,

Your letter, which I received last week, made a bright light in a solitary & saddened place. I had quite recently received the news of the death of a brother in the island of Porto Rico, whose loss to me will be a life-long sorrow.[1] As he passes out of sight, come to me visible as well as spiritual tokens of a fraternal friendliness which by its own law, transcends the tedious barriers of Custom & nation, & opens its way to the heart. This is a true consolation, & I thanked my jealous Δαιμων for the godsend so significantly timed. It, for the moment, realizes the hope to which I have clung with both hands, through each disappointment, that I might converse with a man whose ear of faith was not stopped, and whose argument I could not predict.[2] May I use the word, "I thank my God whenever I call you to remembrance." [3]

I receive with great pleasure the wonderful Professor now that first the decent limbs of Osiris are collected.[4] We greet him well to Cape Cod & Boston Bay. The rigid laws of matter prohibit that the soul imprisoned within the strait edges of these types should add one syllable thereto, or we had adjured the Sage by every name of venera-

---

[17] Emerson's return voyage in 1834 took thirty-two days (Rusk, *Life,* p. 197), but the crossing was sometimes made in two weeks: see below, C.8.18.41.

[1] Edward Bliss Emerson, two years younger than Waldo, died of tuberculosis on October 1, 1834 (Rusk, *Life,* p. 206).

[2] Compare this passage from "Self-Reliance": "what a blind-man's buff is this game of conformity. If I know your sect I anticipate your argument" (*Works,* II, 54).

[3] Cf. Phil. 1: 3.

[4] A reader unfamiliar with Emerson might interpret this strange sentence as a learned and ribald joke: the only part of the body of Osiris which Isis could not collect was, by New England standards, indecent (Plutarch, "Isis and Osiris," in *Moralia,* V, 47). But probably "decent" is used here in its archaic sense of "comely."

tion to take possession by so much as a Salve! of his Western World, but he remained inexorable for any new communications.

I feel like congratulating you upon the cold welcome which, you say, Teufelsdroch has met. As it is not earthly happy, it is marked of a high sacred sort. I like it a great deal better than ever, & before it was all published, I had eaten nearly all my words of objection. But do not think it shall lack a present popularity. That it should not be known seems possible, for if a memoir from Laplace had been thrown into that muckheap of Frasers Magazine, who would be the wiser? But this has too much wit & imagination not to strike a class who would not care for it as a faithful Mirror of this very Hour. But you know the proverb "To be fortunate, be not too wise." [5] The great men of the day are on a plane so low as to be thoroughly intelligible to the vulgar. Nevertheless, as God maketh the world forevermore, whatever the devils may seem to do, so the thoughts of the best minds always become the last opinion of Society. Truth is ever born in a manger, but is compensated by living till it has all souls for its Kingdom. Far far better seems to me the unpopularity of this Philosophical Poem (shall I call it?) than the adulation that followed your eminent friend Goethe. With him I am becoming better acquainted, but mine must be a qualified admiration. It is a singular piece of good nature in you to apotheosize him. I cannot but regard it as his misfortune with conspicuous bad influence on his genius,—that velvet life he led. What incongruity for genius whose fit ornaments & reliefs are poverty & hatred, to repose fifty years in chairs of state; & what pity that his Duke did not cut off his head to save him from the mean end (forgive) of retiring from the municipal incense "to arrange tastefully his gifts & medals." [6] Then the Puritan in me accepts no apology for bad morals in such as *he*. We can tolerate vice in a splendid nature whilst that nature is battling with the brute majority in defence of some human principle. The sympathy his manhood & his misfortunes call out, adopts even his faults, but genius pampered—acknowledged—crowned

---

[5] In "Napoleon" Emerson wrote, "An Italian proverb, too well known, declares that 'if you would succeed, you must not be too good'" (*Works*, IV, 228).

[6] This seems to refer to the "Golden Jubilee" of 1825 in celebration of Goethe's fiftieth year in the service of Weimar. On this occasion Goethe received many gifts and at least one gold medal, and, according to Sarah Austin's *Characteristics of Goethe*, III, 105, "after his exalted guests had quitted him, he examined all his presents, and grouped and disposed them so as fully to enjoy their beauty."

—can only retain our sympathy by turning the same force once expended against outward enemies, now against inward, & carrying forward & planting the standard of Oromasdes so many leagues farther on into the envious Dark. Failing this, it loses its nature & becomes talent, according to the definition—more skill in attaining the vulgar ends. A certain wonderful friend of mine said, that "a false priest is the falsest of false things" [7] But what makes the priest? A cassock? O Diogenes! [8] or, the power (& thence the call) to teach man's duties as they flow from the Superhuman. Is not he who perceives & proclaims the superhumanities, he who has once intelligently pronounced the words "Self Renouncement" "Invisible Leader," "Heavenly Powers of Sorrow" & so on, forever the liege of the same? [9]

Then to write luxuriously is not the same thing as to live so, but a new & worse offence. It implies an intellectual defect also, the not perceiving that the present corrupt condition of human nature (which condition this harlot muse helps to perpetuate) is a temporary or superficial state. The good word lasts forever: the impure word can only buoy itself in the gross gas that now envelopes us, & will sink altogether to ground as that works itself clear in the everlasting effort of God. May I not call it temporary? for when I ascend into the pure region of truth, (or, under my undermost garment, as Epictetus & Teufelsdroch would say,) [10] I see that to abide inviolate though all men fall away from it; yea though the whole generation of Adam should be healed as a sore off the face of the creation. So, my friend, live Socrates & Milton, those stanch puritans, forevermore! Strange is it to me that you should not yet sympathize (yet so you said) with Socrates, so ironical, so true, & who "tramped in the mire with wooden shoes whenever they would force him into the clouds." [11] I seem to see him offering the hand to you across the ages which sometime you will grasp.

[7] *Sartor Resartus,* in *Works TC,* I, 172.   [8] Diogenes Teufelsdröckh, that is.

[9] Here Emerson seems to be referring to Goethe. "Self-Renouncement" suggests "Die Entsagenden," which is the subtitle of *Wilhelm Meisters Wanderjahre,* and "Invisible Leader" appears in the *Lehrjahre:* "Ohne den Beistand meines treuen unsichtbaren Führers hätte es mir übel geraten können" (*Goethes Sämtliche Werke,* XVIII, 131). Cf. *Journals,* III, 313–15.

[10] The phrase seems to come from neither Epictetus nor Teufelsdröck. In *Nature* Emerson was to write, "Unity . . . lies under the undermost garment of Nature," (*Works RWE,* I, 44) without reference to either philosopher.

[11] In a lecture given in Boston on November 19, 1835, Emerson attributed this sentence to Madame de Staël, without mentioning Socrates (*The Early Lectures of*

I am glad you like Sampson Reed & that he has inspired some curiosity respecting his church. Swedenborgianism, if you should be fortunate in your first meetings, has many points of attraction for you: for instance this article "The Poetry of the Old Church is the reality of the New"; [12] which is to be literally understood, for they esteem, in common with all the Trismegisti; [13] the Natural World as strictly the symbol or exponent of the Spiritual, & part for part; the animals to be incarnations of certain affections; & scarce a popular expression esteemed figurative, but they affirm to be the simplest statement of fact. Then is their whole theory of social relations—both in & out of the body—most philosophical, & tho' at variance with the popular theology, selfevident. It is only when they come to their descriptive theism, if I may say so, & then to their drollest heaven, & to some autocratic not moral decrees of God that the mythus loses me. In general, too, they receive the fable instead of the moral of their Aesop. They are to me however deeply interesting as a sect which I think must contribute more than all other sects to the new faith which must arise from out of all.

You express a desire to know something of myself. Account me "a drop in the ocean seeking another drop," [14] or God-ward, striving to keep so true a sphericity as to receive the due ray from every point of the concave heaven. Since my return home, I have been left very much at leisure. It were long to tell all my speculations upon my profession & my doings thereon; but, possessing my liberty, I am determined to keep it at the risk of uselessness, (which risk God can very well abide,) until such duties offer themslves as I can with integrity discharge. One thing I believe,—that, Utterance is place enough: & should I attain through any inward revelation to a more clear perception of my as-

---

Ralph Waldo Emerson, ed. Stephen E. Whicher and Robert E. Spiller, I, 263–64). The editors of that lecture discovered the source of the quotation to be a review of Madame de Staël's *Oeuvres Inédites* in the *Edinburgh Review* for October, 1821 (XXXVI, 61). I have been unable to find the sentence in the works of Madame de Staël.

[12] Paraphrased from Reed's essay "Self-Love Essential Evil," *New Jerusalem Magazine*, IV (May, 1831), 342 (Kenneth W. Cameron, *Emerson the Essayist*, I, 290).

[13] In his journal for June 26, 1838, Emerson listed the following as Trismegisti: "Moses, Zoroaster, Pythagoras, Heraclitus, Socrates, Jesus, Confucius, St. Augustine, Giordano Bruno, Spinoza, Swedenborg, Synesius, Plotinus" (*Journals*, IV, 498).

[14] This was evidently a familiar quotation (cf. Whitman's line, "Out of the rolling ocean the crowd came a drop gently to me"), but I have been unable to find it.

signed task, I shall embrace it with joy & praise. I shall not esteem it a low place, for instance, if I could strengthen your hands by true expressions of the pleasure & hope which your writings communicate to me & to some of my countrymen. Yet the best poem of the poet is his own mind & more even than in any of the works I rejoice in the promise of the workman.—Now I am only reading & musing & when I have any news to tell of myself you shall hear them.

Now as to the welcome hint that you might come to America, it shall be to me a joyful hope. Come & found a new Academy that shall be church & school & parnassus, as a true Poet's house should be. I dare not say that wit has better chance here than in England of winning world-wages, but it can always live, and it can scarce find competition. Indeed, indeed, you shall have the continent to yourself, were it only as Crusoe was King. If you cared to read literary lectures, our people have vast curiosity & the apparatus is very easy to set agoing. Such "pulpit" as you pleased to erect would at least find no hindrance in the building. A friend of mine & of yours remarked, when I expressed the wish that you would come here, "that people were not here as in England sacramented to organized schools of opinion, but were a far more convertible audience." If at all you can think of coming here, I would send you any & all particulars of information with cheerfullest speed.

I have written a very long letter, yet have said nothing of much that I would say upon chapters of the Sartor. I must keep that, & the thoughts I had upon "poetry in history," [15] for another letter, or (might it be!) for a dialogue face to face. Let me not fail of the Diamond Necklace. I found three greedy receivers of Teufelsdroch,[16] who also radiate its light. For the sake of your knowing what manner of men you move I send you two pieces writ by one of them, Frederic Henry Hedge, the article on Swedenborg & that on Phrenology.[17] And

[15] See above, C.8.12.34.

[16] One was his aunt by marriage, Mrs. Samuel Ripley; another was the Rev. F. H. Hedge, who in *The Christian Examiner* for July, 1834, had written a very favorable review of Carlyle's *Life of Schiller* (see Dall, *Transcendentalism in New England*); the third was Miss Lydia Jackson, who was soon to become Emerson's second wife (see Holmes, *Ralph Waldo Emerson*, p. 70).

[17] *The Christian Examiner*, XV (November, 1833), 193–218, and XVII (November, 1834), 249–69: both articles are levelheaded and skeptical. The first Emerson had thought one of "the best pieces that have appeared in the Examiner" (*Let RWE*, I, 402).

as you like Sampson Reed, here are two more of his papers.[18] *Do* read them. And since you study French History, do not fail to look at our Yankee portrait of Lafayette.[19] Present my best remembrances to Mrs Carlyle,—whom that stern & blessed solitude has armed & sublimed out of all reach of the littleness & unreason of London. If I thought we could win her to the American shore, I would send her the story of those godly women, the contemporaries of John Knox's daughter [20] who came out hither to enjoy the worship of God amidst wild men & wild beasts.   Your friend & servant,   R. Waldo Emerson.

[18] One of these was probably "'Self-Love Essential Evil." See above, n. 12.

[19] Probably Edward Everett's *Eulogy on Lafayette, Delivered in Faneuil Hall* . . . *September 6, 1934.* The first draft of this letter has "pray take our Yankee portrait of Lafayette."

[20] Jane Carlyle was descended from the daughter of John Knox.

1835

5. Cheyne Row Chelsea, London

3d Feby, 1835

My Dear Sir,

I owe you a speedy answer as well as a grateful one; for, in spite of the swift ships of the Americans, our communings pass too slowly. Your letter, written in November, did not reach me till a few days ago; your Books or Papers have not yet come,—tho' the ever-punctual Rich, I can hope, will now soon get them for me. He showed me his *waybill* or invoice, and the consignment of these friendly effects "to another gentleman," and undertook with an air of great fidelity to bring all to a right bearing. On the whole, as the Atlantic is so broad and deep, ought we not rather to esteem it a beneficent miracle that messages can arrive at all; that a little slip of paper will skim over all these weltering floods, and other inextricable confusions; and come at last, in the hand of the Twopenny Postman,[1] safe to your lurking-place, like green leaf in the bill of Noah's Dove? Let us be grateful for mercies; let us use them while they are granted us. Time was when "they that feared the Lord spake *often* one to another."[2] A friendly thought is the purest gift that man can afford to man. "Speech" also, they say, "is cheerfuller than light itself."[3]

The date of your letter gives me unhappily no idea but that of Space and Time. As you know my whereabout, will you throw a little light on your own: I can imagine Boston, and have often seen the musket vollies on Bunker Hill; but in this new spot there is nothing for me save sky and earth, the chance of retirement, peace and winter seclusion. Alas, I can too well fancy one other thing: the bereavement

---

[1] From 1801 to 1839, letters could be sent from one part of London to another for twopence each. And see below, C.6.27.35.

[2] Mal. 3: 16.

[3] On April 18, 1834, Carlyle had written to Leigh Hunt: "Is not Speech defined to be cheerfuller than light, and the eldest daughter of Heaven?" (Conway, *Thomas Carlyle*, p. 205).

you allude to, the sorrow that will so long be painful before it can become merely sad and sacred. Brothers, especially in these days, are much to us: had one no Brother, one could hardly understand what it was to have a Friend; they are the Friends whom Nature chose for us; Society and Fortune, as things now go, are scarcely compatible with Friendship, and contrive to get along, miserably enough, without it. Yet sorrow not above measure for him that is gone. He is, in very deed and truth, with God,—*where* you and I both are. What a thin film it is that divides the Living from the Dead! In still nights, as Jean Paul says, "the limbs of my Buried Ones touched cold on my soul, and drove away its blots, as dead hands heal eruptions of the skin." [4]— Let us turn back into Life.

That you sit there bethinking yourself, and have yet taken no course of activity, and can without inward or outward hurt so sit, is on the whole rather pleasing news to me. It is a great truth which you say that Providence can well afford to have one sit: another great truth which you feel without saying it is that a course wherein clear faith cannot go with you may be worse than none; if clear faith go never so slightly against it, then it *is* certainly worse than none. To speak with perhaps ill-bred candour, I like as well to fancy you *not* preaching to Unitarians, a Gospel after their heart. I will say farther that you are the only man I ever met with of that persuasion whom I could un-obstructedly like. The others that I have seen were all a kind of half-way-house characters, who, I thought, should, if they had not wanted courage, have ended in Unbelief; in "faint possible Theism," [5] which I like considerably worse than Atheism. Such, I could not but feel, deserve the fate they find here; the bat-fate: to be killed among the rats as a bird, among the birds as a rat. I know your Channing a little; I have met with our Fox; [6] but find my opinion only confirmed by

[4] J. P. F. Richter, *The Life of Quintus Fixlein,* in Carlyle's *German Romance* (*Works TC,* XXII, 331). The day after Emerson received this letter he wrote in his journal: " 'The limbs of my buried ones,' etc. I dislike the bad taste of almost every-thing I have read of Jean Paul; this scrap for instance: Shakspear never said these hard artificial things" (*Journals,* III, 473).

[5] Seven years before, in an interpretation of Kant, Carlyle had written: "Should Understanding attempt to prove the existence of God, it ends . . . in Atheism, or a faint possible Theism" ("State of German Literature" [*Works TC,* XXVI, 82]).

[6] W. E. Channing was in Great Britain during the summer of 1822 (*Memoir of William Ellery Channing,* II, 228), but it is unlikely that Carlyle "knew" more than his published works. W. J. Fox was already a person of considerable public

these. You can pardon me this heresy? Nay who knows but it is doubts of the like kind in your own mind that keep you for a time inactive even now? For the rest, that you *have* liberty to choose by your own will merely, is a great blessing, too rare for those that could use it so well; nay often it is difficult to use. But till *ill health* of body or of mind warns you that the moving not the sitting posture is essential, *sit* still, contented in conscience; understanding well that no man, that God only knows *what* we are working, and will show it one day; that such and such a one who filled the whole Earth with his hammering and trowelling and would not let men pass for his rubbish, turns out to have built of mere coagulated froth, and vanishes with his edifice, traceless, silently or amid hootings illimitable; while again that other still man, by the word of his mouth, by the very look of his face, was scattering influences, as *seeds* are scattered—"to be found flourishing as a banyan-grove after a thousand years." [7] I beg your pardon for all this preaching, if it be superfluous: impute it to no miserable motive.

Your objections to Goethe are very natural, and even bring you nearer me: nevertheless I am by no means sure that it were not your wisdom, at this moment to set about learning the German Language with a view towards studying *him* mainly! I do not assert this; but the truth of it would not surprise me. Believe me, it is impossible you can be more a Puritan than I; nay I often feel as if I were far too much so: but John Knox himself could he have seen the peaceable impregnable *fidelity* of that man's mind, and how to him also Duty was *infinite,* Knox would have passed on, wondering, not reproaching. But I will tell you in a word why I like Goethe: his is the only *healthy* mind, of any extent, that I have discovered in Europe for long generations; it was he that first convincingly proclaimed to me (convincingly, for I saw it done): Behold, even in this scandalous sceptico-Epicurean generation, when all is gone but Hunger and Cant, it is still possible that Man be a Man! For which last Evangel, the confirmation and rehabilitation of all other Evangels whatsoever, how can I be too grateful?

---

importance, as a writer, as a leader in the reform movement, and as a preacher whose eloquence was said, by Hazlitt, to surpass that of Edward Irving. Carlyle had a slight personal acquaintance with Fox through Mill; in August, 1834, there had been a moment of bitterness and embarrassment between Carlyle and Mill as a result of Mill's appointing, or seeming to appoint, Fox to the *London Review* editorship which Carlyle had hoped for (Neff, *Carlyle,* p. 159).

[7] *Sartor Resartus* (*Works TC,* I, 31).

On the whole, I suspect you yet know only Goethe the Heathen (Ethnic); but you will know Goethe the Christian by and by, and like that one far better. Rich showed me a Compilation in green cloth boards that you had beckoned across the water: pray read the fourth volume of that,[8] and let a man of your clearness of feeling say, whether that was a Parasite or a Prophet.—And then as to "misery" and the other dark ground on which you love to see genius paint itself,—alas, consider whether misery is not *ill health* too; also whether good fortune is not worse to bear than bad; and on the whole whether the glorious serene Summer is not greater than the wildest hurricane,— as Light, the Naturalists say, is stronger a thousand times than Lightning. And so I appeal to Philip sober; [9]—and indeed have hardly said as much about Goethe since I saw you, for nothing reigns here but twilight delusion (falser for the time than midnight darkness) on that subject, and I feel that the most suffer nothing thereby, having properly nothing or little to do with such a matter: but with you, who are not "seeking recipes for happiness," [10] but something far higher, it is not so, and *therefore* I have spoken and appealed; and hope the new curiosity, if I have awakened any, will do you no mischief.

But now as to myself; for you will grumble at a sheet of speculation sent so far: I am here still, as Rob Roy was on Glasgow Bridge, *"byding tryste";* [11] busy extremely with work that will not profit me at all in some senses; suffering rather in health and nerves; and still with nothing like dawn on any quarter of my horizon. The *Diamond Necklace* has not been printed, but will be, were this *French Revolution* out; which latter, however, drags itself along in a way that would fill your benevolent heart with pity. I am for three small volumes now, and have one done. It is the dreadfullest labour (with these nerves, this liver) I ever undertook; all is so inaccurate, superficial, vague, in

[8] Volume IV of Carlyle's *German Romance* (1827) was his translation of *Wilhelm Meisters Wanderjahre.* His *Wilhelm Meister's Apprenticeship* had been published in 1824.

[9] Nine years later in his essay "New England Reformers" Emerson made full use of the "Philip sober" anecdote: "You remember the story of the poor woman who importuned King Philip of Macedon to grant her justice, which Philip refused: the woman exclaimed, 'I appeal:' the king, astonished, asked to whom she appealed: the woman replied, 'From Philip drunk to Philip sober'" (*Works,* III, 270). The classical source is Valerius Maximus, bk. VI, ch. 2.

[10] This looks like what might be called a self-quotation, but I do not recognize it.

[11] Scott, *Rob Roy,* ch. 21.

the numberless Books I consult; and without accuracy at least, what other good is possible? Add to this that I have no hope about the thing, except only that I *shall be done with it:* I can reasonably expect nothing from any considerable class here, but at *best* to be scolded and reproached; perhaps to be left standing "on my own basis," [12] without note or comment of any kind,—save from the Bookseller, who will lose his printing. The hope I have however is sure: if life is lent me, I shall be *done with* the business; I will write this "history of Sansculottism," the notablest phenomenon I meet with since the time of the Crusades or earlier; after which my part in it is played. As for the future, I heed it little when so busy; but it often seems to me, as if one thing were becoming indisputable: that I must seek another craft than literature for these years that may remain to me. Surely, I often say, if ever man had a finger-of-Providence shown him, thou hast it; literature will neither yield thee bread, nor a stomach to digest bread with: quit it in God's name, shouldst thou take spade and mattock instead. The truth is, I believe literature to be as good as dead and gone in all parts of Europe at this moment, and nothing but hungry Revolt and Radicalism appointed us for perhaps three generations; I do not see how a man can honestly live by writing, in another dialect than that, in England at least; so that if you determine on not living dishonestly, it will behove you to look several things full in the face, and ascertain what is what with some distinctness. I suffer also terribly from the solitary existence I have all along had; it is becoming a kind of passion with me, to feel myself among my brothers. And then, How? Alas, I care not a doit for Radicalism, nay I feel it to be a wretched necessity, unfit for me; Conservatism being not unfit only but false for me: yet these two are the grand Categories under which all English spiritual activity that so much as thinks remuneration possible must range itself. I look around accordingly on a most wonderful vortex of things; and pray to God only that as my day is so my strength may be.[13] What will come out of it is wholly uncertain: for I have possibilities too; the possibilities of London are far from exhausted as yet: I have a brave Brother, who invites me to come and be quiet with him in Rome;[14] a brave friend (known to you) who opens the door of a new western

---

[12] In his essay on Burns (*Works TC,* XXVI, 297) and in *Sartor Resartus* (*Works TC,* I, 21) Carlyle had used the phrase without quotation marks in the sense of *alone* or *independently.* Perhaps the present appearance is a self-quotation.

[13] Cf. Deut. 33: 25.

[14] John Carlyle was at this time traveling physician to the Countess of Clare.

world,—and so we will stand considering and consulting, at least till the Book be over. Are all these things interesting to you? I know they are.

As for America and Lecturing, it is a thing I do sometimes turn over, but never yet with any seriousness. What your friend says of the people being more persuadable, so far as having no Tithe-controversy &c &c will go, I can most readily understand it. But apart from that, I should rather fancy America mainly a new Commercial England, with a fuller pantry: little more or little less. The same unquenchable, almost frightfully unresting spirit of endeavour, directed (woe is me!) to the making of money, or money's worth, namely food finer and finer, and gigmanic renown higher and higher: nay must not your gigmanity be a *purse*-gigmanity,[15] some half-shade worse than a purse-and-pedigree one? Or perhaps it is not a whit worse; only tougher, more substantial; on the whole better? At all events ours is fast becoming identical with it; for the pedigree ingredient is as near as may be gone: *gagnez de l'argent, et ne vous faites pas pendre,* this is very nearly the whole Law, first Table and Second. So that you see when I set foot on American land it will be on no utopia; but on a *Conditional* piece of ground, where some things are to be expected and other things not.— I may say, on the other hand, that lecturing (or I would rather it were *Speaking*) is a thing I have always had some hankering after: it seems to me I could really *Swim* in that element, were I once thrown into it: that in fact it would develope several things in me, which struggle violently for developement. The great want I have towards such an enterprise is one you may guess at: want of a *rubric,* of a title to name my speech by. Could any one but appoint me Lecturing Professor of Teufelsdrockh's science: "Things in General"! To discourse of Poets and Poetry in the Hazlitt style, or talk stuff about the Spirit of the Age,[16] were most unedifying: one knows not what to call himself. However, there is no doubt that were the child born it *might* be christened: wherefore I will really request you to take the business into your consideration, and give me in the most rigorous sober manner you can

[15] Carlyle was delighted by this dialogue from the trial of the famous murderer Thurtell: "*Q.* What sort of person was Mr. Weare? *A.* He was always a respectable person. *Q.* What do you mean by respectable? *A.* He kept a gig." He quoted the passage in a footnote to his 1830 article on Richter and for a long time salted his prose with such derivatives as "gigmanic" and "gigmanity."

[16] In 1818 Hazlitt delivered *Lectures on the English Poets;* in 1825 he published *The Spirit of the Age: or Contemporary Portraits.*

some scheme of it: How *many* Discourses; what Towns; the probable
Expenses, the probable net Income, the Time &c &c, all that you can
suppose a man wholly ignorant might want to know about it. America
I should like well enough to visit; much as I should another part of
my native country: it is as you see distinctly possible that such a thing
might be; we will keep it hanging to solace ourselves with it, till the
time decide.

Have I involved you in double postage by this loquacity? Or what
is your American rule: [17] I did not intend it when I began; but today
my confusion of head is very great, and words must be multiplied with
only a given quantity of meaning.

My wife, who is just gone out to spend the day with a certain "celebrated Mrs Austin" (called also the "celebrated Translatress of Puckler
Muskau") [18] charged me very specially to send you her love, her good
wishes and thanks: I assure you there is no hypocricy in that. She votes
often for taking the Transatlantic scheme into contemplation; declares
farther that my Book and Books must and will indisputably prosper
(at some future era), and takes the world beside me,—as a good wife
and daughter of John Knox should.—Speaking of "celebrated" persons
here, let me mention that I have learned by stern experience, as children do with fire, to keep in general quite out of the way of celebrated
persons, more especially celebrated women. This Mrs. Austin who is
half ruined by celebrity (of a kind) is the only woman I have seen not
wholly ruined by it. Men, strong men I have seen die of it; or go mad
by it.[19] *Good* fortune is far worse than bad!—Will you write with all
dispatch my dear Sir; fancy me a fellow wayfarer, who cordially bids
you God-Speed, and would fain keep in sight of you, within sound of
you.—Yours with great sincerity,   T. Carlyle.[20]

---

[17] See below, C.6.27.35.

[18] Sarah Austin, wife of the Utilitarian jurist John Austin, was one of the
Carlyles' oldest and closest London friends. In 1832 she had published a translation of Prince Hermann Pückler-Muskau's *Briefe eines Verstorbenen*, a scandalous
and exceedingly popular account of fashionable life in England during the Twen-
ties. See Pückler-Muskau, *A Regency Visitor*, ed. E. M. Butler.

[19] Probably Carlyle had in mind his boyhood friend Edward Irving who had died
on December 7, 1834, after a sensational and erratic career in the ministry. In an
obituary article for *Fraser's Magazine*, Carlyle wrote, "Applause! madness is in
thee, and death; thy end is Bedlam and the Grave" (*Works TC* XXVIII, 322).

[20] On the outside fold of this letter there is, besides the address, this inscription
in Carlyle's hand: "With a parcel care of S. Burdett."

Boston   11 March 1835

Mr Thomas Carlyle
My dear Sir:

I have much pleasure in making you acquainted with Mr Henry
Barnard [1] of Hartford, Conn., who has been induced by his interest in
yr writings to seek an introduction to you. I am happy in rendering
Mr Barnard the same good office M. D'Eichthal rendered me. I trust
he will be as fortunate in finding you at home.

Your friend & servant   R. Waldo Emerson

Concord, 12 March, 1835.[1]

My Dear Sir,—I am glad of the opportunity of Mr. Barnard's visit to
say health and peace be with you. I esteem it the best sign that has
shone in my little section of space for many days, that some thirty or
more intelligent persons understand and highly appreciate the *Sartor*.
Dr. Channing sent to me for it the other day, and I have since heard
that he had read it with great interest.[2] As soon as I go into town I
shall see him and measure his love. I know his genius does not and
cannot engage your attention much. He possesses the mysterious en-
dowment of natural eloquence, whose effect, however intense, is
limited, of course, to personal communication. I can see myself that
his writings, without his voice, may be meagre and feeble. But please
love his catholicism, that at his age can relish the *Sartor*, born and
inveterated as he is in old books. Moreover, he lay awake all night,
he told my friend last week, because he had learned in the evening
that some young men proposed to issue a journal, to be called *The
Transcendentalist,* as the organ of a spiritual philosophy.[3] So much
for our gossip of to-day.

[1] Henry Barnard was a recent graduate of the Yale Law School. The manuscript
of this letter owned by the RWEMA is in another hand than Emerson's.

[1] This is Norton's text. The manuscript owned by the RWEMA is a rough draft.

[2] The RWEMA owns an undated letter from Dr. Channing which invites Emerson
and his brother to tea and asks: "Have you Carlisle's Sartor resartus? I should be
pleased to see it."

[3] Except for this letter and Emerson's letter of April 30, 1835, I find no reference
to the projected journal. Perhaps the young men learned that within a few months
the first number of *The Western Messenger* would be published in Cincinnati.

But my errand is yet to tell. Some friends here are very desirous that
Mr. Fraser should send out to a bookseller here fifty or a hundred
copies of the *Sartor*. So many we want very much; they would be sold
at once. If we knew that two or three hundred would be taken up,
we should reprint it now. But we think it better to satisfy the known
inquirers for the book first, and when they have extended the demand
for it, then to reproduce it, a naturalized Yankee. The lovers of
Teufelsdröckh here are sufficiently enthusiastic. I am an icicle to them.
They think England must be blind and deaf if the Professor makes no
more impression there than yet appears. I, with the most affectionate
wishes for Thomas Carlyle's fame, am mainly bent on securing the
medicinal virtues of his book for my young neighbors. The good
people think he overpraises Goethe. There I give him up to their
wrath. But I bid them mark his unsleeping moral sentiment; that every
other moralist occasionally nods, becomes complaisant and traditional;
but this man is without interval on the side of equity and humanity!
I am grieved for you, O wise friend, that you cannot put in your own
contemptuous disclaimer of such puritanical pleas as are set up for
you; but each creature and Levite must do after his kind.

Yet do not imagine that I will hurt you in this unseen domain of
yours by any Boswellism. Every suffrage you get here is fairly your
own. Nobody is coaxed to admire you, and you have won friends
whom I should be proud to show you, and honorable women not a
few. And cannot you renew and confirm your suggestion touching your
appearance in this continent? Ah, if I could give your intimation the
binding force of an oracular word!—in a few months, please God, at
most, I shall have wife, house, and home wherewith and wherein to
return your former hospitality.[4] And if I could draw my prophet and
his prophetess to brighten and immortalize my lodge, and make it the
window through which for a summer you should look out on a field
which Columbus and Berkeley[5] and Lafayette did not scorn to sow,
my sun should shine clearer and life would promise something better
than peace. There is a part of ethics, or in Schleiermacher's distribution it might be physics,[6] which possesses all attraction for me; to wit,

[4] On January 30, 1835, Emerson had become engaged to be married to Lydia Jackson (Rusk, *Life*, p. 211).

[5] George Berkeley, not yet a bishop, came to Newport, Rhode Island, in 1729 and
remained for two and a half years while waiting for the government to establish
a college in the Bermudas which would plant arts and learning in America.

[6] On December 14, 1834, Emerson had written in his journal: "In Boston, Hedge

the compensations of the Universe, the equality and the coexistence of action and reaction, that all prayers are granted, that every debt is paid. And the skill with which the great All maketh clean work as it goes along, leaves no rag, consumes its smoke,—will I hope make a chapter in your thesis.

I intimated above that we aspire to have a work on the First Philosophy in Boston. I hope, or wish rather. Those that are forward in it debate upon the name.[7] I doubt not in the least its reception if the material that should fill it existed. Through the thickest understanding will the reason throw itself instantly into relation with the truth that is its object, whenever that appears. But how seldom is the pure loadstone produced! Faith and love are apt to be spasmodic in the best minds. Men live on the brink of mysteries and harmonies into which yet they never enter, and with their hand on the door-latch they die outside.[8] Always excepting my wonderful Professor,[9] who among the living has thrown any memorable truths into circulation? So live and rejoice and work, my friend, and God you aid, for the profit of many more than your mortal eyes shall see. Especially seek with recruited and never-tired vision to bring back yet higher and truer report from your Mount of Communion of the Spirit that dwells there and creates all. Have you received a letter from me with a pamphlet sent in December?[10] Fail not, I beg of you, to remember me to Mrs. Carlyle.

Can you not have some *Sartors* sent? Hilliard, Gray, & Co. are the best publishers in Boston. Or Mr. Rich has connections with Burdett in Boston.   Yours with respect and affection,

R. Waldo Emerson

---

read me good things out of Schleiermacher concerning the twofold divisions of study; 1. Physics, or that which is; 2. Ethics, or that which should be" (*Journals,* III, 393).

[7] By "work" Emerson means the magazine mentioned above; among the names debated was *The Spiritual Inquirer* (E.4.30.35); by "First Philosophy" he means, approximately, transcendentalism. In one of his notebooks for 1833 is this sentence: "The *first* Philosophy, that of mind, is the science of what *is,* in distinction from what *appears*" (Journals, III, 235).

[8] Compare this passage from Emerson's "The Poet": "The fate of the poor shepherd, who, blinded and lost in the snowstorm perishes in a drift within a few feet of his cottage door, is an emblem of the state of man. On the brink of the waters of life and truth, we are miserably dying" (*Works,* III, 33).

[9] I.e., Professor Teufelsdröckh.

[10] Emerson refers here, presumably, to his letter of November 20.

Concord, 30 April, 1835.[1]

My Dear Sir,—I received your letter of the 3d of February on the
20th instant, and am sorry that hitherto we have not been able to
command a more mercantile promptitude in the transmission of these
light sheets. If desire of a letter before it arrived, or gladness when it
came, could speed its journey, I should have it the day it was written.
But, being come, it makes me sad and glad by turns. I admire at the
alleged state of your English reading public without comprehending
it, and with a hoping scepticism touching the facts. I hear my Prophet
deplore, as his predecessors did, the deaf ear and the gross heart of
his people, and threaten to shut his lips; but, happily, this he cannot
do, any more than could they. The word of the Lord *will* be spoken.
But I shall not much grieve that the English people and you are not
of the same mind if that apathy or antipathy can by any means be
the occasion of your visiting America. The hope of this is so pleasant
to me, that I have thought of little else for the week past, and having
conferred with some friends on the matter, I shall try, in obedience
to your request, to give you a statement of our capabilities, without
indulging my *penchant* for the favorable side.

Your picture of America is faithful enough: yet Boston contains
some genuine taste for literature, and a good deal of traditional
reverence for it. For a few years past, we have had, every winter, several courses of lectures, scientific, political, miscellaneous, and even
some purely literary, which were well attended. Some lectures on
Shakespeare were crowded; and even I found much indulgence in
reading, last winter, some Biographical Lectures, which were meant
for theories or portraits of Luther, Michelangelo, Milton, George
Fox, Burke. These courses are really given under the auspices of Societies, as "Natural History Society," "Mechanics' Institutes," "Diffusion of Useful Knowledge," &c., &c., and the fee to the lecturer is
inconsiderable, usually $20 for each lecture. But in a few instances
individuals have undertaken courses of lectures, and have been well
paid. Dr. Spurzheim[2] received probably $3,000 in the few months

---

[1] This is Norton's text. The RWEMA owns what is described, in a notation in
Emerson's hand, as a "Copy of letter to T. Carlyle forwarded 8 May 1835," but is
clearly, however, a rough draft rather than a copy: it contains a blank space after
"with a population of" and it omits much that appears in Norton's version.

[2] Johann Christoph Spurzheim, German phrenologist, died of typhus in Boston in
1832, shortly after the beginning of his first American lecture tour.

that he lived here. Mr. Silliman, a Professor of Yale College, has lately received something more than that for a course of fifteen or sixteen lectures on Geology.[3] Private projects of this sort are, however, always attended with a degree of uncertainty. The favor of my townsmen is often sudden and spasmodic, and Mr. Silliman, who has had more success than ever any before him, might not find a handful of hearers another winter. But it is the opinion of many friends whose judgment I value, that a person of so many claims upon the ear and imagination of our fashionable populace as the "author of the *Life of Schiller,*" "the reviewer of *Burns's Life,*" the live "contributor to the *Edinburgh* and *Foreign* Reviews," nay, the "worshipful Teufelsdröckh," the "personal friend of Goethe," would, for at least one season, batter down opposition, and command all ears on whatever topic pleased him, and that, quite independently of the merit of his lectures, merely for so many names' sake.

But the subject, you say, does not yet define itself. Whilst it is "gathering to a god,"[4] we who wait will only say, that we know enough here of Goethe and Schiller to have some interest in German literature. A respectable German here, Dr. Follen, has given lectures to a good class upon Schiller.[5] I am quite sure that Goethe's name would now stimulate the curiosity of scores of persons. On English literature, a much larger class would have some preparedness. But whatever topics you might choose, I need not say you must leave under them scope for your narrative and pictorial powers; yes, and space to let out all the length of all the reins of your eloquence of moral sentiment. What "Lay Sermons" might you not preach! or methinks "Lectures on Europe" were a sea big enough for you to swim in. The only condition our adolescent ear insists upon is, that the English as it is spoken by the unlearned shall be the bridge between our teacher and our tympanum.

Income and Expenses.—All our lectures are usually delivered in the same hall,[6] built for the purpose. It will hold 1,200 persons; 900 are

[3] Benjamin Silliman was professor of chemistry and mineralogy at Yale from 1802 to 1853. He was one of the most successful of the popular lecturers on scientific subjects.

[4] I have not been able to identify this quotation.

[5] Charles Follen, German revolutionary and refugee, was at this time professor of German literature in Harvard College. In 1833 he had written the preface to the first American edition of Carlyle's *Schiller,* with which Emerson was evidently not familiar.

[6] The Masonic Temple on Tremont Street.

thought a large assembly. The expenses of rent, lights, doorkeeper, &c. for this hall, would be $12 each lecture. The price of $3 is the least that might be demanded for a single ticket of admission to the course,—perhaps $4; $5 for a ticket admitting a gentleman and lady. So let us suppose we have 900 persons paying $3 each, or $2,700. If it should happen, as did in Prof. Silliman's case, that many more than 900 tickets were sold, it would be easy to give the course in the day *and* in the evening, an expedient sometimes practised to divide an audience, and because it is a great convenience to many to choose their time. If the lectures succeed in Boston, their success is insured at Salem, a town thirteen miles off, with a population of 15,000. They might, perhaps, be repeated at Cambridge, three miles from Boston, and probably at Philadelphia, thirty-six hours distant. At New York anything literary has hitherto had no favor. The lectures might be fifteen or sixteen in number, of about an hour each. They might be delivered, one or two in each week. And if they met with sudden success, it would be easy to carry on the course simultaneously at Salem, and Cambridge, and in the city. They must be delivered in the winter.

Another plan suggested in addition to this. A gentleman here is giving a course of lectures on English literature to a private class of ladies, at $10 to each subscriber. There is no doubt, were you so disposed, you might turn to account any writings in the bottom of your portfolio, by reading lectures to such a class, or, still better, by speaking.

Expense of Living.—You may travel in this country for $4 to $4.50 a day. You may board in Boston in a "gigmanic" style for $8 per week, including all domestic expenses. Eight dollars per week is the board paid by the permanent residents at the Tremont House,— probably the best hotel in North America. There, and at the best hotels in New York, the lodger for a few days pays at the rate of of $1.50 per day. Twice eight dollars would provide a gentleman and lady with board, chamber, and private parlor, at a fashionable boarding-house. In the country, of course, the expenses are two thirds less. These are rates of expense where economy is not studied. I think the Liverpool and New York packets demand $150 of the passenger, and their accommodations are perfect. (N.B.—I set down all sums in dollars. You may commonly reckon a pound sterling worth $4.80.)

"The man is certain of success," say those I talk with, "for one winter, but not afterwards." That supposes no extraordinary merit in the lectures, and only regards you in your leonine aspect. However, it was suggested that, if Mr. C. would undertake a Journal of which we have talked much, but which we have never yet produced, he would do us great service, and we feel some confidence that it could be made to secure him a support. It is that project which I mentioned to you in a letter by Mr. Barnard,—a book to be called *The Transcendentalist,* or *The Spiritual Inquirer,* or the like, and of which F. H. Hedge was to be editor. Those who are most interested in it designed to make gratuitous contributions to its pages, until its success could be assured. Hedge is just leaving our neighborhood to be settled as a minister two hundred and fifty miles off, in Maine,[7] and entreats that you will edit the journal. He will write, and I please myself with thinking I shall be able to write under such auspices. Then you might (though I know not the laws respecting literary property) collect some of your own writings and reprint them here. I think the *Sartor* would now be sure of a sale. Your *Life of Schiller,* and *Wilhelm Meister,* have been long reprinted here. At worst, if you wholly disliked us, and preferred Old England to New, you can judge of the suggestion of a knowing man, that you might see Niagara, get a new stock of health, and pay all your expenses by printing in England a book of travels in America.

I wish you to know that we do not depend for your *éclat* on your being already known to rich men here. You are not. Nothing has ever been published here designating you by name.[8] But Dr. Channing reads and respects you. That is a fact of importance to our project. Several clergymen, Messrs. Frothingham, Ripley, Francis,[9] all of them scholars and Spiritualists, (some of them, unluckily, called Unitarian,) love you dearly, and will work heartily in your behalf. Mr. Frothing-ham, a worthy and accomplished man, more like Erasmus than Luther, said to me on parting, the other day, "You cannot express in terms

[7] Frederic Henry Hedge was minister of the Unitarian church in Bangor, Maine, from 1835 to 1850.

[8] Carlyle's name was known, however, to the many American readers of British periodicals: see above, Introduction, p. 11.

[9] Nathaniel Frothingham, George Ripley, and Convers Francis were all Unitarian ministers; all were soon to be members of the "Transcendental Club" (Rusk, *Life,* pp. 243–44).

too extravagant my desire that he should come." George Ripley, having heard, through your letter to me, that nobody in England had responded to the *Sartor,* had secretly written you a most reverential letter, which, by dint of coaxing, he read to me, though he said there was but one step from the sublime to the ridiculous. I prayed him, though I thought the letter did him no justice, save to his heart, to send you it or another; and he says he will. He is a very able young man, even if his letter should not show it.[10] He said he could, and would, bring many persons to hear you, and you should be sure of his utmost aid. Dr. Bradford,[11] a medical man, is of good courage. Mr. Loring,[12] a lawyer, said, "Invite Mr. and Mrs. Carlyle to spend a couple of months at my house," (I assured him I was too selfish for that,) "and if our people," he said, "cannot find out his worth, I will subscribe, with others, to make him whole of any expense he shall incur in coming." Hedge promised more than he ought. There are several persons beside, known to me, who feel a warm interest in this thing. Mr. Furness, a popular and excellent minister in Philadelphia,[13] at whose house Harriet Martineau was spending a few days, I learned the other day "was feeding Miss Martineau with the *Sartor.*" And here some of the best women I know are warm friends of yours, and are much of Mrs. Carlyle's opinion when she says, Your books shall prosper.

On the other hand, I make no doubt you shall be sure of some opposition. Andrews Norton, one of our best heads, once a theological professor, and a destroying critic, lives upon a rich estate at Cambridge, and frigidly excludes the Diderot paper from a *Select Journal* edited by him,[14] with the remark, "Another paper of the Teufelsdröckh School." The University perhaps, and much that is conservative in literature and religion, I apprehend, will give you its cordial

[10] See Slater, "George Ripley and Thomas Carlyle," *PMLA,* LXVII (June, 1952), 341–49.

[11] Gamaliel Bradford was a physician and the superintendent of the Massachusetts General Hospital.

[12] Ellis Gray Loring had been a classmate of Emerson's at the Boston Latin School. He was one of the twelve founders of the New England Anti-Slavery Society.

[13] William Henry Furness was also a friend of Emerson's from Latin School days. Their correspondence was published as *Records of a Lifelong Friendship.*

[14] Norton was in 1833 and 1834 one of the editors of *The Select Journal of Foreign Periodical Literature.*

opposition, and what eccentricity can be collected from the Obituary Notice on Goethe, or from the *Sartor,* shall be mustered to demolish you. Nor yet do I feel quite certain of this. If we get a good tide with us, we shall sweep away the whole inertia, which is the whole force of these gentlemen, except Norton. That you do not like the Unitarians will never hurt you at all, if possibly you do like the Calvinists. If you have any friendly relations to your native Church, fail not to bring a letter from a Scottish Calvinist to a Calvinist here, and your fortune is made. But that were too good to happen.

Since things are so, can you not, my dear sir, finish your new work and cross the great water in September or October, and try the experiment of a winter in America? I cannot but think that if we do not make out a case strong enough to make you build your house, at least you should pitch your tent among us. The country is, as you say, worth visiting, and to give much pleasure to a few persons will be some inducement to you. I am afraid to press this matter. To me, as you can divine, it would be an unspeakable comfort; and the more, that I hope before that time so far to settle my own affairs as to have a wife and a house to receive you. Tell Mrs. Carlyle, with my affectionate regards, that some friends whom she does not yet know do hope with me to have her company for the next winter at our house, and shall not cease to hope it until you come.

I have many things to say upon the topics of your letter, but my letter is already so immeasurably long, it must stop. Long as it is, I regret I have not more facts. Dr. Channing is in New York, or I think, despite your negligence of him, I should have visited him on account of his interest in you. Could you see him you would like him. I shall write you immediately on learning anything new bearing on this business. I intended to have despatched this letter a day or two sooner, that it might go by the packet of the 1st of May from New York. Now it will go by that of the 8th, and ought to reach you in thirty days. Send me your thoughts upon it as soon as you can. I *jalouse* of that new book. I fear its success may mar my project.

Yours affectionately, R. Waldo Emerson.

5. Cheyne Row   Chelsea, London
13th May, 1835

Thanks, my kind friend, for the news you again send me. Good news, good new friends; nothing that is not good comes to me across these waters. As if the "golden west," seen by Poets, were no longer a mere optical phenomenon, but growing a reality, and coining itself into solid blessings! To me it seems very strange; as indeed generally this whole Existence here below more and more does.

We have seen your Barnard: a most modest, intelligent, compact, hopeful-looking man; who will not revisit you without conquests from his Expedition hither. We expect to see much more of him; to instruct him, to learn of him: especially about that real-imaginary locality of "Concord," where a kindly-speaking voice lives incarnated, there is much to learn.

That you will take to yourself a wife is the cheerfullest tidings you could send us. It is, in no wise, meet for man to be alone; [1] and indeed the beneficent Heavens, in creating Eve, did mercifully guard against that. May it prove blessed, this new arrangement! I delight to prophecy for you peaceful days in it; peaceful, not idle; filled rather with that best activity which is the stillest. To the future or perhaps at this hour actual Mrs Emerson, will you offer true wishes from two British Friends; who have not seen her with their eyes, but whose thoughts need not be strangers to the Home she will make for you. Nay, you add the most chivalrous summons: which who knows but one day we may actually stir ourselves to obey! It may hover for the present among the gentlest of our daydreams; mild-lustrous; an impossible possibility. May all go well with you, my worthy Country-man, Kinsman, and brother Man!

This so astonishing reception of Teufelsdrockh in your New England circle seems to me not only astonishing, but questionable; *not* however, to be quarreled with. I may say: If the New England cup is dangerously sweet, there are here in Old England whole antiseptic floods of good *hop*-decoction; therein let it mingle; work wholesomely towards what clear benefit it can. Your young ones too, as all exaggeration is transient, and exaggerated love almost itself a blessing, will get thro' it without damage.—As for Fraser, however, the idea of

[1] Cf. Gen. 2: 18.

a New Edition is frightful to him; or rather, ludicrous, unimaginable. Of him no man has inquired for a *Sartor:* in his whole wonderful world of Tory Pamphleteers, Conservative Younger-brothers, Regent-Street Loungers, Crockford Gamblers,[2] Irish Jesuits, drunken Reporters, and miscellaneous unclean persons (whom nitre and much soap will not wash clean), not a soul has expressed the smallest wish that way. He shrieks at the idea. Accordingly I realized these four copies from, all he will surrender; and can do no more. Take them with my blessing. I beg you will present one to the honourablest of those "honourable women"; say to her that her (unknown) image as she reads shall be to me a bright faultless vision, textured out of mere sunbeams; to be loved and worshipped: the best of all Transatlantic women! Do at any rate, in a more business-like style, offer my respectful regards to Dr Channing, whom certainly I could not count on for a reader, or other than a grieved condemnatory one; for I reckoned tolerance had its limits. His own faithful long-continued striving towards what is Best I knew and honoured: that he will let me go my own way thitherward, with a God-speed from him, is surely a new honour to us both.—Finally, on behalf of the British world (which is not all contained in Fraser's shop) I should tell you that various persons, some of them in a dialect not to be doubted of, have privately expressed their recognition of this poor Rhapsody, the best the poor Clothes-Professor could produce in the circumstances: nay, I have Scottish Presbyterian Elders who read, and thank. So true is what you say about the aptitude of all natural hearts for receiving what is from the heart spoken to them. As face answereth to face! Brother, if thou wish me to believe, do thou thyself believe first: this is as true as that of the *flere* and *dolendum;*[3] perhaps truer. Wherefore, putting all things together, cannot I feel that I have washed *my* hands of this business in a quite tolerable manner? Let a man be thankful; and on the whole *go* along, while he has strength left to go.

This Boston *Transcendentalist*, whatever the fate or merit of it prove to be, is surely an interesting symptom. There must be things not dreamt of, over in that Transoceanic Parish! I shall cordially wish

[2] Crockford's, a club in St. James's Street, was described in Baedeker's *London* of 1898 as "notorious for its high play under the Regency."

[3] "Si vis me flere, dolendum est/Primum ipsi tibi": Horace, *Ars Poetica*, XI, 102–3.

well to this thing; and hail it as the sure forerunner of things better. The Visible becomes the Bestial when it rests not on the Invisible. Innumerable tumults of Metaphysic must be struggled thro' (whole generations perishing by the way), and at last Transcendentalism evolve itself (if I construe aright), as the *Euthanasia* of Metaphysic altogether. May it be sure, may it be speedy! Thou shalt open thy *eyes,* O Son of Adam; thou shalt *look,* and not forever jargon about *laws* of Optics and the making of spectacles! For myself, I rejoice very much that I seem to be flinging aside innumerable sets of spectacles (could I but *lay* them aside,—with gentleness!) and hope one day actually to see a thing or two. Man *lives* by Belief (as it was well written of old); [4] by Logic he can only at best long to live. Oh I am dreadfully afflicted with Logic here, and wish often (in my haste) that I had the besom of destruction [5] to lay to it for a little!

> "Why? and Wherefore?—God wot simply Therefore!
> Ask not Why; 'tis Sith thou hast to care for." [6]

Since I wrote last to you (which seems some three months ago), there has a great mischance befallen me: the saddest, I think, of the Kind called Accidents I ever had to front. By dint of continual endeavour for many weary weeks, I had got the first volume of that miserable French Revolution rather handsomely finished: from amid infinite contradictions I felt as if my head were fairly above water, and I could go on writing my poor Book, defying the Devil and the World; with a certain degree of assurance, and even of joy. A Friend borrowed this volume of Manuscript, a Kind Friend but a careless one; to write notes on it, which he was well qualified to do. One evening about two months ago, he came in on us, "distraction (literally) in his aspect": [7] the Manuscript, left carelessly out, had been torn up as waste paper, and all but three or four tatters was clean gone! I could not complain, or the poor man (. . . . .) [8] seemed as if

---

[4] Cf. Rom. 1: 17; and *Heroes and Hero-Worship* (*Works TC*, V, 2–3).

[5] Isa. 14: 23.   [6] These lines seem very Carlylean: perhaps they are original.

[7] *Hamlet,* act II, scene ii, line 581.

[8] The words between Carlyle's parentheses here have been inked over so effectively that they are illegible even under ultraviolet and infrared light. There seem to be, however, two sentences of four or five words each. The first of these begins with a *D* and ends with a question mark; the second begins with an *M* which is followed, I believe, by an *i* and ends with an underscored word. I think it likely that Carlyle identified "the poor man" as John Stuart Mill, Emerson's India House

he would have shot himself: we had to gather ourselves together, and show a smooth front to it; which happily tho difficult was not impossible to do. I began again at the beginning; to such a wretched paralyzing torpedo of a task as my hand never found to do; at which I have worn myself these two months to the hue of saffron, to the humour of incipient desperation; and now four days ago, perceiving well that I was like a man swimming in an element that grew ever rarer, till at last it became vacuum (think of that!), I with a new effort of self-denial, sealed up all the paper-fragments, and said to myself: In this mood thou makest *no* way, writest *nothing* that requires not to be erased again; lay it by for one complete week! And so it lies, under lock and key: I have digested the whole misery; I say, If thou canst *never* write this thing: why then never do write it: God's Universe will go along *better* without it. My belief in a Special Providence grows yearly stronger, unsubduable, impregnable: however, you see all the mad increase of entanglement I have got to strive with, and will pity me in it. Bodily exhaustion (and "Diana in the shape of Bile") [9] I will at least try to exclude from the controversy. By God's blessing, perhaps the Book shall yet be written; but I find it will not do, by sheer direct force; only by gentler side-methods. I have much else to write too: I feel often, as if with one year of health and peace I could write something considerable;—the image of which sails dim and great thro' my head. Which year of health and peace God, if He see meet, will give me yet; or withhold from me, as shall be for the best.

I have dwelt and swum now for about a year in this World-Mahlstrom of London; with much pain, which however has given me many thoughts, more than a counterbalance for that. Hitherto there is no outlook, but confusion darkness, innumerable things against which a man must "set his face like a flint." [10] Madness rules the world, as it has generally done: one cannot, unhappily, without loss, say to it, Rule then; and yet must say it.—However, in two months more I

---

acquaintance of 1833, and then decided to keep Mill's secret. He did not, so far as I know, disclose Mill's name to anyone except members of his own family. Thirteen years later Emerson told the story to some English friends without mentioning Mill (January Searle, *Emerson, His Life and Writings,* p. 47).

[9] An allusion, not quite accurate, to *Hudibras,* I, ii, 781–84: see Norton's note in *Early Letters of Thomas Carlyle,* I, 242.

[10] Isa. 50: 7.

expect my good Brother from Italy (a brave fellow, who is a great comfort to me): we are then for Scotland to gather a little health, to consider ourselves a little. I must have this Book done before anything else will prosper with me.

Your American Pamphlets got to hand only a few *days* ago; worthy old Rich had them not originally; seemed since to have been oblivious, out of Town, perhaps unwell. I called one day, and unearthed them. Those papers you marked I have read. Genuine endeavour; which may the Heavens forward!—In this poor Country all is swallowed up in the barren Chaos of Politics: Ministries tumbled out, Ministries tumbled in; all things (a fearful substratum of "Ignorance and Hunger" [11] weltering and heaving under them) apparently in rapid progress towards—the melting pot. There will be news from England by and by: many things have reached their term; Destiny "with lame foot" [12] has overtaken them, and there will be a reckoning. Oh blessed are you where, what jargonning soever there be at Washington, the poor man (*un*governed can govern himself) shoulders his axe, and walks into the western woods,—sure of a nourishing Earth and an overarching Sky! It is verily the Door of Hope to distracted Europe; which otherwise I should see crumbling down into blackness of darkness.[13]—That too shall be for good.

I wish I had anything to send you besides these four poor pamphlets; but I fear there is nothing going. Our Ex-Chancellor has been promulgating triticalities (significant as novelties, when *he* with his wig and lordhood utters them) against the Aristocracy; whereat the upper circle are terribly scandalized.[14] In Literature, except a promised or obtained (but to me still unknown) volume of Wordsworth,[15] nothing nameworthy doing.—Did I tell you that I *saw* Wordsworth this winter? Twice, at considerable length; with almost no disappointment. He is a *natural* man (which means whole immensities here and now); flows like a natural well yielding mere wholesomeness,—tho' as

[11] Here Carlyle quotes, it would seem, from his own essay "Characteristics" (*Works TC*, XXVIII, 20).

[12] Cf. Horace, *Odes* III, ii, 32.   [13] Jude 13.

[14] Brougham, who had been lord chancellor from 1830 to 1834, had just published a pamphlet entitled *Thoughts upon the Aristocracy of England*.

[15] Presumably *Yarrow Revisited, and Other Poems*. Carlyle read most of the volume on Sunday, May 24, in Kensington Gardens, but he liked only "A Wren's Nest" (Froude, *Thomas Carlyle: Life in London*, I, 47).

it would not but seem to me, in *small* quantity, and astonishingly *diluted*. Franker utterance of mere garrulities and even platitudes I never heard from any man;—at least never, whom I could *honour* for uttering them. I am thankful for Wordsworth; as in great darkness and perpetual *skyrockets* and coruscations, one were, for the smallest clear-burning farthing candle.—Southey also I saw; a far *cleverer* man in speech; yet a considerably smaller man. Shovelhatted; the shovel-hat is grown to him: one must take him as he is.

The second leaf is done: I must not venture on another. God bless you, my worthy Friend; you and her who is to be yours! My wife bids me send heartiest wishes and regards from her too across the Sea. Perhaps we shall all meet one another some day—if not Here, then Yonder!—Faithfully always,   T. Carlyle

Chelsea, London, 27th June, 1835—

My Dear Friend,

Your very kind Letter has been in my hand, these four weeks; the subject of much meditation, which has not yet cleared itself into anything like a definite practical issue. Indeed, the conditions of the case are still not wholly before me: for if the American side of it, thanks to your perspicuous minuteness, is now tolerably plain, the European side continues dubious, too dim for a decision. So much in my own position here is vague, not to be measured; then there is a Brother, coming home to me from Italy, almost daily expected now; whose ulterior resolutions cannot but be influential on mine, for we are Brothers in the old good sense, and have one heart and one interest and object, and even one purse; and Jack is a *good man,* for whom I daily thank Heaven, as for one of its principal mercies. He is Travelling Physician to the Countess of Clare; well entreated by her and hers; but I think, weary of that inane element of "the English Abroad," and as good as determined to have done with it; to seek *work* (he sees not well how), if possible, *with* wages; but even almost *without,* or with the lowest endurable, if need be. Work *and* wages: the two prime necessities of man! It is pity they should ever be disjoined; yet of the two if one *must,* in this mad Earth, be dispensed with, it is really wise to say at all hazards, Be it the wages then. This Brother (if the Heavens have been kind to me) must be in Paris one of these days; then here speedily; and "the House must resolve itself into a committee"—of ways and means.—Add to all this that I myself have been and am one of the stupidest living men; in one of my vacant interlunar [1] conditions; unfit for deciding on anything: were I to give you my actual *view* of the case it were a view such as Satan had from the pavilion of the Anarch old. Alas, it is all too like chaos: confusion of dense and rare: I also know what it is to drop *plumb:* fluttering my pennons vain,[2]—for a series of weeks!

One point only is clear: that you, my Friend, are very friendly to me; that New England is as much my country and home as Old England. Very singular and very pleasant it is to me to feel as if I had a *house of my own* in that far country: so many leagues and geographical degrees of wild-weltering "unfruitful brine," [3] and then the hospitable hearth and the smiles of brethren a-waiting one there! What with railways, steamships, printing-presses, it has surely become a most *monstrous* "tissue" this life of ours; if evil and confusion in the one Hemisphere, then good and order in the other, a man knows not how: and so it rustles forth, immeasurable, from "that roaring Loom of Time," [4]—miraculous ever as of old!—To Ralph Waldo Emerson, however, and those that love me as he, be thanks always; and a sure place in the sanctuary of the mind. Long shall we remember that Autumn Sunday that landed him (out of Infinite Space) on the Craigenputtock wilderness, *not* to leave us as he found us. My Wife says, whatever I decide on, I cannot thank you too heartily;—which really is very sound doctrine. I write to tell you so much; and that you shall hear from me again when there is more to tell.

It does seem next to certain to me that I could preach a very considerable quantity of things from that Boston Pulpit, such as it is,—were I once fairly started. If so, what an unspeakable relief were it too! Of the whole mountain of miseries one grumbles at in this life, the central and parent one, as I often say, is that you cannot utter yourself. The poor soul sits struggling, impatient, longing vehemently out towards all corners of the Universe, and cannot get its hest delivered, not even so far as the voice might do it. Imprisoned, en-

---

[1] *Samson Agonistes,* I, 68.   [2] Cf. *Paradise Lost,* II, 932–88.
[3] Probably a translation of a phrase from *The Iliad,* book I, line 316.
[4] *Faust,* act I, scene 1, line 156: "am sausenden Webstuhl der Zeit."

chanted, like the Arabian Prince with half his body marble: [5] it is really bad work. Then comes bodily sickness, to act and react, and double the imbroglio. Till at last, I suppose, one does rise, like Eliphaz the Temanite; [6] states that his inner man is bursting (as if filled with carbonic acid and new wine); that by the favour of Heaven he *will* speak a word or two: would it were come so far,—if it be ever to come!

On the whole I think the odds are that I shall some time or other get over to you; but that for this winter I ought not to go. My London expedition is not decided hitherto; I have begun various relations and arrangements, which it were questionable to cut short so soon. That beggarly Book, were there nothing else, hampers me every way. To fling it once for all into the fire were perhaps the best; yet I grudge to do that. To finish it, on the other hand, is denied me for the present, or even so much as to work at it. What am I to do? When my Brother arrives, we go all back to Scotland for some weeks; there, in seclusion, with such calmness as I can find or create, the plan for the winter must be settled. You shall hear from me then; let us hope, something more reasonable than I can write at present. For about a month, I have gone to and fro utterly idle: understand that, and I need explain no more. The wearied machine refused to be urged any farther; after long spasmodic struggling comes collapse. The burning of that wretched Manuscript has really been a sore business for me. Nevertheless that too shall clear itself, and prove a *favour* of the Upper Powers: *tomorrow* to fresh fields and pastures new! [7] This monstrous London has taught me several things during the past year; for if its wisdom be of the most *un*instructive ever heard of by that name of wisdom, its Folly abounds with lessons,—which one ought to learn. I feel (with my burnt manuscript) as if defeated in this campaign; defeated, yet not altogether disgraced. As the great Fritz [8] said, when the battle had gone against him: "Another time we will do better."

As to Literature, Politics, and the whole multiplex aspect of existence here, expect me not to say one word. We are a singular people, in a singular condition. Not many nights ago, in one of those phe-

[5] In "The Tale of the Fisherman and the Jinni." See *The Book of the Thousand Nights and a Night,* trans. Burton (London, 1893), I, 63.

[6] Job 4: 2: "Who can withhold himself from speaking?"

[7] The last line of "Lycidas," misquoted as usual.   [8] Frederick the Great.

nomenal assemblages named routs, whither we had gone to see the countenance of O'Connel and Company (the Tail was a Peacock's tail, with blonde-muslin women and heroic Parliamentary men), one of the company, a "distinguished female" (as we call them) informed my wife that "O'Connell was the master-spirit of this age." [9] If so, then for what we have received let us be thankful,—and enjoy it *without* criticism.—It often painfully seems to me as if much were coming fast to a crisis here; as if the crown-wheel had given way, and the whole horologe were rushing rapidly down, down, to its end! Wreckage is swift; rebuilding is slow and distant. Happily another than we has charge of it.

My new American Friends have come, and gone. Barnard went off northward some [fort]night ago; furnished with such guidance and furtherance as I could give him. Professor Longfellow went about the same time; to Sweden, then to Berlin and Germany: we saw him twice or thrice and his ladies, with great pleasure; [10] as one sees worthy souls from a far country, who cannot abide with you, who throw you a kind of greeting as they pass. I inquired considerably about Concord and a certain man there; one of the fair pilgrims told me several comfortable things.—By the bye, how very good you are, in regard to this of Unitarianism! I declare I am ashamed of my intolerance:— and yet you have ceased to be a Teacher of theirs, have you not? I mean to address you this time by the secular title of Esquire; as if I liked you better so. [11] But truly, in black clothes or in white, by this style or by that, the man himself can never be other than welcome to

[9] Cf. *Julius Caesar,* act III, scene i, line 163. Daniel O'Connell was at this time in a position of great power in a parliament almost equally divided between Whigs and Tories.

[10] Longfellow, like Barnard, came with a letter of introduction from Emerson. According to F. B. Sanborn (*Ralph Waldo Emerson,* p. 83), Longfellow found Emerson waiting for him with the letter aboard the steamer from Portland to Boston, "sitting inside a coil of rope, with his hat pulled over his eyes." Emerson said "that he had lately been sending his friend some American literature. 'I suppose you sent him Irving,' said Longfellow. 'No,' said Emerson, 'Mr. Irving is only a word-catcher.'" Seven years later, when American visitors were less of a novelty in Cheyne Row, Longfellow came again, and Carlyle wrote next day to James Aitken: "We had another American last night, called Longfellow, 'Professor Longfellow,'—Professor *Dull*fellow I rather found him, and was glad enough to see him go" (NLS, MS 511, October 11, 1842).

[11] This decision was well timed. On March 4 Emerson had asked Lydia Jackson: "Please never write my name with that prefix *Rev.*" (*Let RWE,* I, 441).

me. You will further allow me to fancy that you are now wedded; and offer our united congratulations and kindest good wishes to that new fair Friend of ours, whom one day we shall surely know more of,—if the Fates smile.

My sheet is ending, and I must not burden you with double postage, for such stuff as this. By dint of some inquiry I have learnt the law of the American Letter-carrying; and I now mention it for our mutual benefit. There are from New York to London three packets monthly (on the 1st, on the 10th, on the 20th); the masters of these carry Letters gratis for all men; and put the same into the Post-Office; there are some pence charged on the score of "ship-letter" there, and after that, the regular postage of the country, if the letter has to go farther. I put this, for example, into a place called North & South American Coffee-house in the City here, and pay two-pence for it, and it flies. Doubtless there is some similar receiving-house with its "leather bag" somewhere in New York, and fixed days (probably the *same* as our days) for emptying, or rather for tying and despatching said leather bag: if you deal with the London Packets (so long as I am here) in preference to the Liverpool ones, it will all be well. As for the *next* Letter (if you write as I hope you may before hearing from me again), pray direct it "Care of John Mill Esq. India House, London"; and he will forward it directly, should I even be still absent in the North.—Now will you write; and pray write something about *yourself.* We both love you here, and send you all good prayers. *Vale faveque!*—Yours ever, T. Carlyle

Concord, 7 October, 1835.[1]

My dear friend,

Please God, I will never again sit six weeks of this short life, over a letter of yours, without attempting a reply. I received, in August, your letter of June, &, just then, hearing that a lady—a little lady with a mighty heart, Mrs Child,—was about to visit England, (invited thither, for work's sake, by the African or Abolition society,) & that she begged an introduction to you, I used the occasion to say, the godsend was come, & that I would acknowledge it particularly, as soon

[1] The MS of this letter is in the Berg Collection of the New York Public Library. The RWEMA owns the MS of a rough draft.

as three tasks, then impending, were ended. I have now learned, that *Mr* Child was detained, for some weeks, in New York, & did not sail.[2] Last night, I received your letter written in May with the copies of the Sartor, which, by a strange oversight, have been lying weeks, probably, months, in the Custom House. On such provocation, I can sit still no longer.

My three tasks were, a literary Address; a historical Discourse, on the 200th anniversary of the incorporation of my town here; (my first adventure in print which I shall send you.) the third, my marriage, now happily consummated;[3] all three, from the least to the greatest, trod so fast upon each other's heel, as to leave me, who am a slow awkward workman, no interstice big enough for a letter that should convey any information. Now congratulate me, my friend, as indeed you have already done, that I live with my wife, in my *own* house, waiting on the great Providence. The house is not large, but convenient, & very *elastic*. The more hearts, (specially great hearts,) it holds, the better it looks & feels. I have not yet had so much leisure but that the fact of having ample space to spread my books & blotted papers, is still gratifying. So know, now, that your house in America waits for you, and that my wife is dressing a chamber for Mrs Carlyle. If virtue & friendship have not yet become fables, do believe we keep your face for the living type. I am very glad to hear of the Brother you describe so well: I have one too, & know what it is to have presence in two places. Charles C. E. is a lawyer now settled, say, rather, abiding in this room, &, as I believe, no better lord Hamlet ever was. He is our doctor on all questions of taste manners or action.[4] And one of the pure pleasures I promise myself, in the coming months, is, to make you two gentlemen know each other.

I could cry at the disaster that has befallen you in the loss of the book. Charles says the only thing that "friend" could do, on such an

---

[2] Lydia Maria Child, a novelist turned abolitionist, was the sister of Carlyle's admirer Convers Francis. Her husband, David Lee Child, a lawyer, did go abroad in 1836, to study the Belgian beet-sugar industry, but Mrs. Child seems not to have accompanied him (MS letter from LMC to Carlyle, 4.7.38, owned by the National Library of Scotland).

[3] In August Emerson delivered a literary address in Boston entitled "The Best Mode of Inspiring a Correct Taste in English Literature"; on September 12 he delivered his historical discourse in Concord; on September 14, in Plymouth, he married Lydia Jackson (Rusk, *Life*, pp, 222, 223, 238).

[4] Cf. *Hamlet,* act III, scene i, lines 159–61.

occasion, was, to shoot himself, & wishes to know if he have done so. Such mischance might well quicken your curiosity to know what oversight there is of us, & I greet you well on your faith & the resolution issuing out of it. You have certainly found a right manly consolation, & can afford to faint & rest, a month or two, on the laurels of such endeavors I trust, ere this, you have recollected the entire creation out of the secret cells, where, under the smiles of every muse, it first took life. When you are weary, believe, that you who stimulate virtuous young men, do not write a line in vain. And, whatever betides us in the inexorable Future, what is better than to have awaked in many men the sweet sense of beauty & to have added to the courage of virtue? So do not, as you will not, let the imps from all the fens of weariness & apathy, have a minute too much. To die of feeding the fires of others, were sweet; since it were not death, but self multiplication. And yet, I like not the sound of what I have said, I who hold an orthodox substantial personal immortality.

This morning, in happiest time, I have a letter from George Ripley, who tells me you have written him, & that you say pretty confidently, you will come over the water next summer.[5] Io paean. He tells me also that Alexander Everett (brother of Edward) has sent you the North American Review in which Mr E had written a friendly notice of the Sartor, adding a private letter.[6] I am delighted; for this

[5] Ripley's letter is printed in *Let RWE*, I, 432–33. What Carlyle actually wrote was: "You are likely to see my worthy Emerson. Pray tell him that he has still no chance to be forgotten here. We hope he is wedded before this time & as happy as he ought to be. He & I had some correspondence about my coming to Boston this very winter. I have written him, (if I remember) two letters about it; the last full of mere uncertainty, but promising another so soon as there came any clearness. Will you tell him that it seems to be as good as settled, that I shall *not* get across this winter, and fully likelier than ever that I shall next winter. The medical brother of whom I wrote to him is still at Geneva only, all in uncertainty; I meanwhile had to make up my mind to reccommence my poor *burnt manuscript* (of which E. knows enough;) you can add that before you read this to him the burnt ashes have again grown *leaves* after a sort; that the ugliest task ever set me is got done. Whereupon I determine that the Book of the French Revolution shall be written *out* before I leave it. Almost two volumes to do; & no prospect whatever to be counted on but that of getting delivered from them! However, it may be long before the Upper Powers set one down with *tools* for another such task: having begun it, let us end it; and then—?"

[6] Alexander Everett was the editor of the *North American Review;* his friendly but superficial notice of *Sartor* (XLI, [October, 1835], 454–82) was largely concerned with a mock-serious argument that Teufelsdröckh was fictitious. See below, C.4.29.36.

man represents a clique to which I am a stranger, & which I supposed might not love you. It must be you shall succeed, when Saul prophesies.[7] I only tremble to see all *my* importance quite at an end: now that doctors of divinity [8] & the solemn review itself break silence to praise you, I lose my plume as your harbinger.

I shall immediately send your book to Dr Channing. Miss Martineau is with him, at Newport. I have seen her lately twice. She knows a young man, named Reeve,[9] I believe, to whom you have done great service. I was quite taken with the sweet tempered sensible lady, but what a pitiable life she leads!—in a procession endless of company. But what of this? I beg of you to hold fast your purpose: tis as good a plot as ever was laid, & though I regret the delay, as a year is a large fraction of adult life, yet I believe every month will mend your chance of a good hearing. You shall be sure of an audience in Boston, & of readers if you will write. I could add some fresh testimonies of affection to those you know. Yet I fear you contrast us a little too favorably with Europe. I wish my country a better comprehension of its felicity. But I read your forebodings concerning England with some domestic application.

Government here too has come to be a trade & is managed solely on commercial principles. A man plunges into politics to make his fortune & only cares that the world should last *his* day. We have had in different parts of the country mobs & moblike legislation & even judicature,[10] which betrayed an almost Godless state of Society. So that I begin to think that, even here, we must look upon our Associations & institutions as crutches that may soon be plucked away from

[7] I Sam. 10: 12.

[8] Perhaps Emerson had in mind the passage in Ripley's letter which said that F. H. Hedge—a divine though not a doctor of divinity—was considering an American edition of *Sartor Resartus*.

[9] Henry Reeve, a nephew of Carlyle's friend Sarah Austin, had studied under Schelling at Munich and had a wide acquaintance with continental men of letters; in 1832 Carlyle had written him a letter of introduction to Goethe (Laughton, *Memoirs of the Life and Correspondence of Henry Reeve, C. B., D. C. L.*, I, 26). Harriet Martineau had told Emerson in August that she considered Reeve, along with Mill, one of the four "ablest young men in England" (*Journals*, III, 542).

[10] Emerson seems to refer here to the mob violence which, during the past year and a half, in both the North and the South, had been directed against Negroes and abolitionists (Kull, *A Short Chronology of American History*, pp. 104–5); he may also have in mind the legislative and judicial persecution of Prudence Crandall.

us & revisit & examine our principles to see what will abide by us in every hour. There are books & papers & public lecturing too, in this country, that I could recommend as medicine, to any gentleman who finds the love of life too strong in him.

But the more refractory the marble is, the more durable shall the beauty be, you shall hew out of it; and a man or a god may find work in America. Let me have early & particular information of your western movements, & indeed, of any & all that concern you. I will not keep this tardy letter for the pamphlet soon to creep from our village press, but will send that after. Lidian E. sends her particular thanks for your gift [11] & friendliest wishes to you & yours.

R. Waldo Emerson.

[11] There is a tradition in the Emerson family that this gift was the sconce which now hangs in the house in Concord.

1836

Concord, Mass. 8 April, 1836.

My dear friend,

I am concerned at not hearing from you. I have written you two letters one in October, one in November, I believe, since I had any tidings of you.[1] Your last letter is dated 29 June '35. I have counted all the chances of delay & miscarriage of letters and still am anxious, lest you are ill, or have forgotten us. I have looked at the advertising sheet of the booksellers, but it promises nothing of the history. I thought I had made the happiest truce with sorrow in having the promise of your coming—I was to take possession of a new kingdom of virtue & friendship Let not the new wine mourn.[2] Speak to me out of the wide silence. Many friends inquire of me concerning you, and you must write some word immediately on receipt of this sheet.

With it goes our American reprint of the Sartor.[3] Five hundred copies only [4] make the edition, at $1.00 a copy. About 150 copies are subscribed for. How it will be received, I know not. I am not very sanguine, for I often hear or read somewhat concerning its repulsive style. Certainly, I tell them, it is very odd. Yet I read a chapter lately with great pleasure. I send you also with Dr. Channing's regards & good wishes a copy of his little work, lately published, on our great local question of Slavery.[5]

You must have written me since July. I have reckoned upon your projected visit the ensuing summer or autumn, and have conjectured the starlike influences of a new spiritual element. Especially Lectures. My own experiments for one or two winters & the readiness with which

---

[1] I know no record other than this of a letter written in November. Norton suggests that Emerson had in mind his letter of October 7 and the one which he wrote in August for Mrs. Child.

[2] Cf. Matt. 9: 14–17.   [3] See above, Introduction, pp. 16–17.

[4] The word "are" was crossed out by Emerson.

[5] The booklet *Slavery*, published late in 1835, a moderate work which the abolitionists found unsatisfactory.

you embrace the work, have led me to think much & to expect much
from this mode of addressing men. In New England, the Lyceum, as
we call it, is already a great institution. Beside the more elaborate
courses of lectures in the cities, every country town has its weekly
evening meeting, called a Lyceum, and every professional man in the
place is called upon, in the course of the winter, to entertain his fellow
citizens with a discourse on whatsoever topic.—The topics are miscellaneous as heart can wish. But in Boston, Lowell, Salem, courses are
given by individuals. I see not why this is not the most flexible of all
organs of opinion; from its popularity & from its newness permitting
you to say what you think, without any shackles of prescription. The
pulpit in our age certainly gives forth an obstructed and uncertain
sound,[6] and the faith of those in it, if men of genius, may differ so
much from that of those under it, as to embarrass the conscience of
the speaker, because so much is attributed to him from the fact of
standing there. In the Lyceum, nothing is presupposed. The orator
is only responsible for what his lips articulate. Then what scope it
allows! You may handle every member & relation of humanity. What
could Homer, Socrates, or St Paul say that can not be said here? The
audience is of all classes, and its character will be determined always
by the name of the lecturer. Why may you not give the reins to your
wit, your pathos, your philosophy,—and become that good despot which
the virtuous orator is?

Another thing. I am persuaded that if a man speak well he shall
find this a well rewarded work in New England. I have written this
year ten lectures; [7] I had written as many, last year.[. . .]for reading
both these & those at pla[ces] whither I was invited, I have received
this last[. . .]about 350 dollars. Had I, in lieu of receiving a lecturer's fee, myself advertised that I would deliver these in certain
places, these receipts would have been greatly increased.[8] I insert all
this, because my prayers for you in this country are quite of a commercial spirit. If you lose no dollar by us, I shall joyfully trust your
genius & virtue for your satisfaction on all other points.

[6] Cf. I Cor. 14: 8.

[7] The ten lectures of the past season were concerned with English literature; they
were given first to the Society for the Diffusion of Useful Knowledge, in Boston
(Rusk, *Life,* p. 238).

[8] At this point the rough draft has: "Indeed I am just now invited to go & spend
a fortnight at Salem and read a course to some subscribers on liberal terms."

I cannot remember that there are any other mouthpieces that are specially vital at this time except criticism and parliamentary debate. I think this of ours would possess in the hands of a great genius great advantages over both. But what avail my commendations of the form, until I know that the man is alive and well? If you love them that love you, write me straightway of your welfare. My wife desires to add to mine her friendliest greetings to Mrs. Carlyle, & to yourself.

Yours affectionately, R. Waldo Emerson.

I ought to say that Le Barron Russell a worthy young man who studies Engineering did cause the republication of Teufelsdrock.[9] I trust you shall yet see a better American Review of it than the North American

5. Cheyne Row, Chelsea, London,
29th April 1836—

My Dear Emerson,

Barnard is returning across the water, and must not go back without a flying salutation for you. These many weeks I have had your Letter [1] by me; these many weeks I have felt always that it deserved and demanded a grateful answer; and, alas, also that I could give it none. It is impossible for you to figure what mood I am in. One sole thought, that Book! That weary Book! occupies me continually: wreck and confusion of all kinds goes tumbling and falling around me, within me; but to wreck and growth, to confusion and order, to the world at large I turn a deaf ear; and have life only for this one thing,—which also in general I feel to be one of the pitifullest that ever man went about possessed with. Have compassion for me! It is really very miserable: but it will end. Some months more, and it is *ended;* and I am done with French Revolution, and with Revolution and Revolt in general; and look once more, with free eyes, over this Earth, where are other things than mean internecine work of that kind: things fitter for me, under the bright Sun, on this green Mother's-bosom (tho' the Devil does dwell in it)! For the present really, it is like a Nessus' shirt, burning you into madness, this wretched Enterprise; nay it is also like a kind of Panoply, rendering you invulnerable insensible to all *other* mischiefs.

[9] See above, Introduction, pp. 16–17.   [1] That of October 7, 1835.

I got the fatal First Volume finished (in the miserablest way, after great efforts) in October last; my head was all in a whirl; I flew to Scotland and my Mother for a month of rest. Rest is nowhere for the son of Adam.[2] All looked so "spectral" to me in my old-familiar Birthland; Hades itself could not have seemed stranger; Annandale also was part of the Kingdom of TIME. Since November I have worked again as I could; a second volume got wrapt up and sealed out of my sight within the last three days. There is but a Third now: one pull more, and *then!* It seems to me, I will fly into some obscurest cranny of the world, and lie silent there for a twelvemonth. The mind is weary, the body is very sick; a little black speck dances to and fro in the left eye (part of the *retina* protesting against the liver, and striking work): I cannot help it; it must flutter and dance there, like a signal of distress, unanswered till I be done. My familiar friends tell me farther that the Book is all wrong, style cramp &c &c: my friends, I answer, you are very right; but this also, Heaven be my witness, I cannot help.—In such sort do I live here; all this I had to write you, if I wrote at all.

For the rest I cannot say that this huge blind monster of a City is without some sort of charm for me. It leaves one alone, to go his own road unmolested. Deep in your soul you take up your protest against it, defy it, and even despise it; but need not divide yourself from it for that. Worthy individuals are glad to hear your thought, if it have any sincerity; they do not exasperate themselves or you about it; they have not even time for such a thing. Nay in stupidity itself on a scale of this magnitude, there is an impressiveness, almost a sublimity; one thinks how, in the words of Schiller, "the very gods fight against it in vain"; [3] how it lies on its unfathomable foundations there, inert yet peptic, nay eupeptic, and is a *Fact* in the world, let theory object as it will. Brown-stout, in quantities that would float a seventy-four, goes down the throats of men; and the roaring flood of Life pours on;— over which Philosophy and Theory are but a poor shriek of remonstrance, which oftenest were wiser perhaps to hold its peace. I grow daily to honour Facts more and more; and Theory less and less. A Fact it seems to me is a great thing; a Sentence printed if not by God,

[2] Cf. Deut. 32: 8.

[3] "Mit der Dummheit kämpfen Götter selbst vergebens": Schiller, *Die Jungfrau von Orleans,* act III, scene vi. In his *Life of Schiller* Carlyle had translated the line: "Stupidity can baffle the very gods" (*Works TC,* XXV, 164).

then at least by the Devil;—neither Jeremy Bentham nor Lytton Bulwer had a hand in *that*.

There are two or three of the best souls here I have known for long: I feel less alone with them; and yet one is alone: a stranger and a pilgrim.[4] These friends expect mainly that the Church of England is not dead but asleep;[5] that the leather coaches with their gilt pannels can be peopled again with a living Aristocracy, instead of the simulacra of such. I must altogether hold my peace to this; as I do to much. Coleridge is the Father of all these.[6] *Ay de mi!* [7]

But to look across the "divine salt-sea." [8] A letter reached me, some two months ago, from Mobile, Alabama; the writer, a kind friend of mine, signs himself James Freeman Clarke: I have mislaid, not lost his Letter; and do not at present know his permanent address (for he seemed to be only on a visit at Mobile); but you doubtless do know it. Will you therefore take or even find an opportunity to tell this good Friend that it is not the wreckage of the Liverpool ship he wrote by, nor insensibility on my part that prevents his hearing direct from me; that I see him, and love him in this Letter; and hope we shall meet one day under the Sun,—shall live under it at any rate with many a kind thought towards one another.[9]—The North American Review you spoke of never came (I mean, tha[t] Copy of it, with the

---

[4] Heb. 11: 13.   [5] Cf. Luke 8: 52.

[6] John Sterling, who had come to live in London during the autumn of 1835, was surely one of these friends: "Sterling seemed much engrossed in matters theological . . . talked often about Church, Christianity Anglican and other . . . all in the Coleridge dialect"; another was probably "The Rev. Mr. Dunn, a venerable and amiable Irish gentleman"; a third was perhaps Frederick Denison Maurice (Carlyle, *The Life of John Sterling*, II, 3; *Works TC*, XI, 123).

[7] Alexander Carlyle in *New Letters and Memorials of Jane Carlyle* (II, 23), says that *ay de mi* and its Latin equivalent *eheu* appeared frequently in Carlyle's speech.

[8] A translation, presumably Carlyle's own, of the last two words in line 153 of book III of the *Odyssey*. The idea of divinity, not usual in English renderings of this phrase, may come from the translation of Johann Heinrich Voss, which Carlyle had recently been reading or thinking about (see below, n. 10): "die heilige Salzflut" was Voss's version.

[9] Clarke, at this time a Unitarian minister in Louisville, Ky., was just about to undertake the editorship of *The Western Messenger*. On March 28, 1836, he wrote to Margaret Fuller: "When I was in Mobile, I saw a leathern bag hanging in a certain place, marked thus: 'Letter-bag; Ship Sarah sails tomorrow for Liverpool.' I went home instantly, and wrote a letter to Thomas Carlyle, returned, and dropped it in the bag, and am now waiting the result. Do you think *Teufelsdröckh* will take any notice of it, or will he mistake me for a gigman?" (*Autobiography, Diary, and Correspondence*, ed. E. E. Hale, p. 115).

Note in it); but another Copy became rather public here,—to the [amuse]ment of some. I read the Article myself: surely this Reviewer, who does not want in[. . .]otherwise, is an original: Either a *thrice*-plied quiz (Sartor's "Editor" a *twice*-plied one); or else opening on you a grandeur of still Dulness, rarely to be met with on Earth.

My friend! I must end here. Forgive me till I get done with this Book. Can you have the generosity to write, *without* an answer? Well, if you can*not*, I will answer. Do not forget me. My love and my Wife's to your good Lady to your Brother and all friends. Tell me what you do; what your world does. As for my world, take this (which I rendered from the German Voss, a tough old-Teutonic fellow) for the best I can say of it:

"As journeys this Earth, her eye on a Sun, thro' the heavenly spaces;
And radiant in azure, or Sun-less, swallowed in tempests,
Falters not, alters not; journeying equal, sunlit or stormgirt:
So thou, Son of Earth, who hast Force, Goal and Time, go still onwards." [10]

Adieu, my dear friend!—Believe me ever,[11]

Concord, Massachusetts, 17 September, 1836 [1]
My Dear Friend,—I hope you do not measure my love by the tardiness of my messages. I have few pleasures like that of receiving your kind and eloquent letters. I should be most impatient of the long interval between one and another, but that they savor always of Eternity, and promise me a friendship and friendly inspiration not reckoned or ended by days or years. Your last letter, dated in April, found me a mourner, as did your first. I have lost out of this world my brother Charles,[2] of whom I have spoken to you,—the friend and companion of many years, the inmate of my house, a man of a beautiful genius,

---

[10] Lines 70–74 of Johann Heinrich Voss's "Weihe" to his translation of *Homer's Werke* (I, ix): "Wie, von der Sonne geführt, hinwallt die Beleberin Erde;/ Jetzt in Sturm und Gewölk, und jetzt in ätherischer Klarheit/ Strebet sie fort, und erfreuet mit Licht und Wärme die Völker:/ Also streb', o Genoss, durch Freud' und Schmerz auf der Laufbahn,/ Nicht abwankend vom Ziel, mit getrost ausharrendem Eifer."

[11] The signature has been cut off.

[1] Norton's text. The RWEMA owns the MS of a rough draft.

[2] Charles Chauncy Emerson, five years younger than Ralph Waldo Emerson, died May 9, 1836, of tuberculosis (Rusk, *Life*, p. 230). Shortly before the onset of his final illness he had received a letter from James Walker, editor of *The Christian Examiner*, asking him to write a review of *Sartor Resartus* (MS, April 15, 1836, owned by RWEMA).

born to speak well, and whose conversation for these last years has treated every grave question of humanity, and has been my daily bread. I have put so much dependence on his gifts that we made but one man together; for I needed never to do what he could do by noble nature much better than I. He was to have been married in this month, and at the time of his sickness and sudden death I was adding apartments to my house for his permanent accommodation. I wish that you could have known him. At twenty-seven years the best life is only preparation. He built his foundation so large that it needed the full age of man to make evident the plan and proportions of his character. He postponed always a particular to a final and absolute success, so that his life was a silent appeal to the great and generous. But some time I shall see you and speak of him.

We want but two or three friends, but these we cannot do without, and they serve us in every thought we think. I find now I must hold faster the remaining jewels of my social belt. And of you I think much and anxiously since Mrs. Channing,[3] amidst her delight at what she calls the happiest hour of her absence, in her acquaintance with you and your family, expresses much uneasiness respecting your untempered devotion to study. I am the more disturbed by her fears, because your letters avow a self-devotion to your work, and I know there is no gentle dulness in your temperament to counteract the mischief. I fear Nature has not inlaid fat earth enough into your texture to keep the ethereal blade from whetting it through. I write to implore you to be careful of your health. You are the property of all whom you rejoice in heart and soul, and you must not deal with your body as your own. O my friend, if you would come here and let me nurse you and pasture you in my nook of this long continent, I will thank God and you therefor morning and evening, and doubt not to give you, in a quarter of a year, sound eyes, round cheeks, and joyful spirits. My wife has been lately an invalid,[4] but she loves you thoroughly, and hardly stores a barrel of flour or lays her new carpet without some

[3] Susan Higginson Channing, mother of William Henry Channing, who had been traveling in Europe with her son. She made at least two visits to the Carlyles. "They are, certainly," she wrote to a friend, "the most interesting couple I ever saw, and live in a style of the most charming, primitive simplicity. It was worth crossing the Atlantic to see such people" (O. B. Frothingham, *Memoir of William Henry Channing*, p. 123).

[4] In place of "has . . . invalid," the first draft reads "is now a feeble dyspeptic." Lidian Emerson was in the last month of pregnancy (Rusk, *Life*, p. 231).

hopeful reference to Mrs. Carlyle. And in good earnest, why cannot you come here forthwith, and deliver in lectures to the solid men of Boston the *History of the French Revolution* before it is published,— or at least whilst it is publishing in England, and before it is published here. There is no doubt of the perfect success of such a course now that the *five hundred copies of the Sartor are all sold,* and read with great delight by many persons.

This I suggest if you too must feel the vulgar necessity of *doing;* but if you will be governed by your friend, you shall come into the meadows, and rest and talk with your friend in my country pasture. If you will come here like a noble brother, you shall have your solid day undisturbed, except at the hours of eating and walking; and as I will abstain from you myself, so I will defend you from others. I entreat Mrs. Carlyle, with my affectionate remembrances, to second me in this proposition, and not suffer the wayward man to think that in these space-destroying days a prayer from Boston, Massachusetts, is any less worthy of serious and prompt granting than one from Edinburgh or Oxford.

I send you a little book I have just now published, as an entering wedge, I hope, for something more worthy and significant.[5] This is only a naming of topics on which I would gladly speak and gladlier hear. I am mortified to learn the ill fate of my former packet containing the *Sartor* and Dr. Channing's work.[6] My mercantile friend is vexed, for he says accurate orders were given to send it as a packet, not as a letter. I shall endeavor before despatching this sheet to obtain another copy of our American edition.

I wish I could come to you instead of sending this sheet of paper. I think I should persuade you to get into a ship this Autumn, quit all study for a time, and follow the setting sun. I have many, many things to learn of you. How melancholy to think how much we need confession! [. . . . .][7] Yet the great truths are always at hand, and all the tragedy of individual life is separated how thinly from that universal

[5] *Nature* had been published on the 9th or 10th of September (*Let RWE,* II, 37).

[6] The fourth sentence of this letter indicates that a Carlyle letter of the spring has been lost and explains the absence from Carlyle's letter of November 5, 1836, of any proper comment on the American *Sartor.* In view of the date of Charles's death, the missing letter must have been written late in April. The ill fate of the *Sartor* package would seem to be that it was mailed at letter rate and was so expensive that Carlyle, not knowing what it contained, refused to accept it from the postman.

[7] "Some words appear to be lost here" (Norton's note).

nature which obliterates all ranks, all evils, all individualities. How little of you is in your *will!* Above your will how intimately are you related to all of us! In God we meet. Therein we *are,* thence we descend upon Time and these infinitesimal facts of Christendom, and Trade, and England Old and New. Make the soul now drunk with a sleep, and we overleap at a bound the obstructions, the griefs, the mistakes, of years, and the air we breathe is so vital that the Past serves to contribute nothing to the result.

I read Goethe, and now lately the posthumous volumes, with a great interest. A friend of mine who studies his life with care would gladly know what records there are of his first ten years after his settlement at Weimar, and what Books there are in Germany about him beside what Mrs. Austin [8] has collected and Heine. Can you tell me?

Write me of your health, or else come.

Yours ever,   R. W. Emerson.

P. S.—I learn that an acquaintance is going to England, so send the packet by him.

Chelsea, London, 5th November, 1836

My dear Friend,

You are very good to write to me, in my silence, in the mood you must be in. My silence you may well judge is not forgetfulness; it is a forced silence; which this kind Letter *unforces* into words. I write the day after your letter comes, lest the morrow bring forth something new to hinder me.

What a bereavement, my Friend, is this that has overtaken you! Such a Brother, with such a Life opening round him, like a blooming garden where he was to labour and gather, all vanished suddenly like frostwork, and hidden from your eye! It is a loss, a sore loss; which God had appointed you. I do not tell you not to mourn: I mourn with you; and could wish all mourners the spirit you have, in this sorrow. O I know it well. Often enough in this noisy Inanity of a vision where *we* still linger, I say to myself, Perhaps thy Buried Ones [1] are not

---

[8] The "celebrated Mrs. Austin" (see above, C.2.3.35, n. 18) had published in 1833 *Characteristics of Goethe from the German of Falk, Von Müller, and Others;* the book by Heine was probably *Die Romantische Schule,* published early in 1836 and generally disliked for its irreverence.

[1] J. P. F. Richter. See above, C.2.3.35, n. 4.

far from thee, are with thee; they are in Eternity, which is a Now and HERE! And yet Nature will have her right; Memory would feel desecrated if she could forget. Many times, in the crowded din of the Living, some sight, some features of a face will recal to you the Loved Face; and in these turmoiling streets you see the little silent Church-yard, the green grave that lies there so silent,—inexpressibly *wae*. O perhaps we shall all meet YONDER, and the tears be wiped from all eyes.[2] One thing is no Perhaps: surely we *shall* all meet, *if* it be the will of the Maker of us. If it be not His will,—then is it not better so? Silence,—since in these days we have no Speech! Eye hath not seen; nor ear heard, in any day.—[3]

You inquire so earnestly about my welfare; hold open still the hos-pitable door for me. Truly *Concord,* which I have sought out on the Map, seems worthy of its name: no dissonance comes to me from that side; but grief itself has acquired a harmony: in joy or grief a voice says to me, Behold there is one that loves thee; in thy loneliness, in thy darkness, see how a hospitable candle shines from far over seas, how a friendly heart watches! It is very good, and precious for me.

As for my health, be under no apprehension. I am always sick; I am sicker and worse, body and mind, a little, for the present; but it has no deep significance: it is *weariness* merely; and now by the bounty of Heaven, I am as it were within sight of land. In two months more, this unblessed Book will be *finished;* at Newyearday we begin printing: before the end of March, the thing is out, and I am a free man! Few happinesses I have ever known will equal that, as it seems to me. And yet I ought not to call the poor Book unblessed: no, it has girdled me round like a panoply these two years; kept me invulnerable, indiffer-ent, to innumerable things. The poorest man in London has perhaps been one of the freest: the roaring press of gigs and gigmen, with their gold blazonry and fierce gig-wheels have little incommoded him; they going their way, he going his.—As for the results of the Book, I can rationally promise myself, on the economical, pecuniary or otherwise worldly side, simply *zero.* It is a Book contradicting all rules of For-mulism, that have not a Reality within them, which so few have;—terrifying, the more quietly the worse, internecine war with Quacks high and low. My good Brother, who was with me out of Italy in summer, declared himself shocked, and almost terrorstruck: "Jack," I

[2] Rev. 1: 17.   [3] I Cor. 2: 9.

answered, "innumerable men give their lives cheerfully to defend Falsehoods and Half-Falsehoods; why should not one writer give his life cheerfully to say, in plain Scotch-English, in the hearing of God and Man, To me they seem false and half-false? At all events, thou seest, I cannot help it. It is the nature of the beast." So that, on the whole, I suppose there is no more unpromotable unappointable man now living in England than I. Literature also, the miscellaneous place of refuge, seems done here, unless you will take the Devil's wages for it; which one does not incline to do. A *disjectum membrum;* [4] cut off from relations with men? Verily so; and now forty years of age; and extremely dyspeptical: a hopeless-looking man. Yet full of what I call desperate-hope! One does verily stand on the Earth, a Star-dome encompassing one; seemingly accoutred and enlisted and sent to battle, with rations good, indifferent or bad,—what can one do but in the name of Odin, Tuiskone,[5] Hertha, Horsa and all Saxon and Hebrew Gods, fight it out?—This surely is very idle talk.

As to the Book, I do say seriously that it is a wild savage ruleless very bad Book; which even you will not be able to like; much less any other man. Yet it contains strange things; sincerities drawn out of the heart of a man very strangely situated; reverent of nothing but what is reverable in all ages and places: so we will print it, and be done with it;—and try a new turn next time.—What I am to do, were the thing done, you see therefore, is most uncertain. How gladly would I run to Concord! And if I were there, be sure the do-nothing arrangement is the only conceivable one for me. That my sick existence subside again, this is the first condition; that quiet vision be restored me. It is frightful what an impatience I have got for many kinds of fellow-creatures. Their jargon really hurts me like the shrieking of inarticulate creatures that ought to be articulate. There is no resource but to say: Brother, thou surely art not hateful; thou art loveable, at lowest pitiable;—alas, in my case, thou art dreadfully wearisome, unedifying: go thy ways, with my blessing. There are hardly three people among these two millions, whom I care much to exchange[. . .]with, in the humour I have. Nevertheless, at bottom, it is not my purpose to quit London

[4] Originally a reference to Horace, *Satires,* I, 4, 62, the phrase *disjecta membra* had wide currency in eighteenth-century English.

[5] Tacitus, in his *Germania,* paragraph 3, mentions the god Tuisto as the founder of the German race. In Jacob Grimm's *Deutsche Mythologie* (I, 161), the name is spelled *Tuisco.*

finally, till I have as it were *seen it out*. In the very hugeness of the monstrous City, contradiction cancelling contradiction, one finds a sort of composure for oneself that is not to be met with elsewhere perhaps in the world: people tolerate you, were it only that they have not time to trouble themselves with you. Some individuals even love me here; there are one or two whom I have even learned to love,—tho', for the present, cross circumstances have snatched them out of my orbit again mostly.[6] Wherefore, if you ask me, What I am to do? the answer is clear so far, "Rest myself a while"; and all farther is as dark as chaos. Now for resting, taking that by itself, my Brother who has gone back to Rome with some thoughts of settling as a Physician there, presses me to come thither, and rest in Rome. On the other hand, a certain John Sterling (the best man I have found in these regions) has been driven to Bourdeaux lately for his health; he will have it that I must come to him, and walk thro' the South of France to Dauphine, Avignon and over the Alps next spring! Thirdly my Mother will have me return to Annandale, and lie quiet in her little habitation;—which I incline to think were the wisest course of all. And lastly from over the Atlantic comes my good Emerson's voice—we will settle nothing, except that all shall remain unsettled. *Die Zukunft decket Schmerzen und Glücke.*[7]

I ought to say however that about Newyearday I will send you an Article on *Mirabeau,* which they have printed here (for a thing called the *London Review*); and some kind of Note to escort it. I think Pamphlets travel as Letters in New England, provided you leave the *ends* of them open: if I be mistaken, pray instruct Messrs Barnard to *refuse* the thing, for it has small value. The *Diamond Necklace* is to be printed also, in *Fraser;* inconceivable hawking that poor Paper has had; till now Fraser takes it—for £50, not being able to get it for nothing. The *Mirabeau* was written at the passionate request of John Mill, and likewise for *needful* lucre. I think it is the first shilling of money I have earned by my craft these four years: where the money I have lived on has come from while I sat here scribbling gratis, amazes me to think; yet surely it has come (for I *am* still here), and Heaven only to thank for it,—which is a great fact. As for Mill's *London Review* (for he is quasi-editor), I do not recommend it to you. Hide-

---

[6] John Sterling, for one.

[7] From Goethe's "Loge," *Sämtliche Werke,* II, 231. In *Past and Present* (*Works TC,* X, 237) Carlyle translated these lines as "The Future hides in it/Gladness and Sorrow."

bound Radicalism; a to me well nigh insupportable thing! Open it not: a breath as of Sahara, and the Infinite Sterile, comes from any page of it. A young Radical Baronet [8] has laid out £3000 on getting the world instructed in *that* manner: it is very curious to see.—Alas, the bottom of the sheet! Take my hurried but kindest thanks for the prospect of your *second* Teufelsdk: the first too is now in my possession; Brother John went to the Post-Office, and worked it out for a ten shillings. It is a beautiful little Book; and a Preface to it such as no kindest friend could have improved.[9] Thank my kind Editor very heartily from me.

My wife was in Scotland in summer, driven thither by ill health; she is stronger since her return, tho' not yet strong; she sends over to Concord her kindest wishes. If I fly to the Alps or the Ocean, her Mother & she must keep one another company, we think, till there be better news of me. You are to thank Dr Channing also for his valued gift. I read the Discourse, and other friends of his read it, with great estimation; but the *end* of that black question lies beyond my ken. I— suppose, as usual, Might and Right will have to make themselves synonymous in some way. CANST and SHALT if they are *very* well understood, mean the same thing under this Sun of ours. Adieu my dear Emerson, *Gehab' Dich wohl!* Many affectionate regards to the Lady Wife: it is far within the verge of Probabilities that I shall see her face and eat of her bread, one day. But she must not get sick! It is a dreadful thing sickness; really a thing which I begin frequently to think *criminal*—at least in myself. Nay, in myself it really *is* criminal; wherefore I determine to be well, one day. Good be with you and yours!

T. Carlyle

As to Goethe and your Friend: I know not anything out of G's own works (which have many notices in them) that treats specially of those ten years. Doubtless your Friend knows Jördens's Lexicon (which dates all the writings, for one thing), the Conversations Lexicon Supplement, & such like. There is an essay by one Schubarth which has reputa-

---

[8] Sir William Molesworth, although only twenty-six years of age, had been a member of parliament since 1832. At Cambridge he had been a friend of Carlyle's former pupil Charles Buller; in London he was closely associated with the Mills. He purchased *The Westminster Review* in 1836 in order to merge it with *The London Review*.

[9] See above, Introduction, p. 17.

tion; but it is critical and ethical mainly. The Letters to Zelter, the L. to Schiller will do nothing for those years, but are essential to see. Perhaps in some late Nr of the *Zeitgenossen* there may be something? Blackguard *Heine* is worth very little; *Mentzel* is duller, decenter, not much wiser.[10] A very curious Book is Eckermann's *Conversations with G.*— just published—No room more!

[10] K. H. Jördens compiled a *Lexikon deutscher Dichter und Prosaisten* (1806–11). The *Konversations-Lexikon* was an important German encyclopedia; Carlyle probably refers to two supplementary volumes which appeared in 1809 and 1811. K. C. Schubarth published *Zur Beurtheilung Goethe's mit Beziehung auf verwandte Literatur und Kunst* in 1817, and *Über Goethe's Faust* in 1830. Wolfgang Menzel in *Die deutsche Literatur* (1836) made a strong attack on Goethe. The *Zeitgenossen* was a Leipzig magazine which specialized in contemporary biography.

1837

5. Cheyne Row, Chelsea, London,
13th February, 1837

My dear Emerson,

You had promise of a Letter to be despatched you about Newyear's-day; which promise I was myself in a condition to fulfil at the time set, but delayed it, owing to delays of Printers and certain "Articles" that were to go with it. Six weeks have not yet entirely brought up these laggard animals: however, I will delay no longer for them. Nay it seems the Articles, were they never so ready, cannot go with the Letter; but must fare round by Liverpool or Portsmouth in a separate conveyance. We will leave them to the bounty of Time.

Your little Book and the copy of *Teufelsdröckh* came safely; soon after I had written. The *Teufelsdröckh* I instantaneously despatched to Hamburg, to a Scottish Merchant there, to whom there is an allusion in the Book; who used to be my *Speditor* (one of the politest extant tho' totally a stranger) in my missions and packages to and from Weimar.[1] The other, former Copy, more specially yours, had already been, as I think I told you, delivered out of durance, and got itself placed in the Bookshelf, as *the* Teufelsdröckh. George Ripley tells me, you are printing another edition; much good may it do you![2] There is now also a kind of whisper and whimper rising *here* about printing one. I said to myself once, when Bookseller Fraser shrieked so loud at a certain message you sent[3] him, "Perhaps after all they *will* print this

---

[1] On December 2, 1836, Carlyle wrote to his brother John: "I had a very kind letter from Emerson the American lately: he has lost an excellent younger Brother very suddenly, but takes it in a most gentle devout manner. A little Book of his called *Nature* (really of fine spirit, and insight here and there) has come since; with a new copy of *Teufelk*. The Edition of T. it seems is sold off. This copy I despatched instantly to Hamburg; to a certain Mr Parish who used to be my speditor to Goethe" (NLS, MS 523). The allusion to Parish appears in bk. I, ch. 11, of *Sartor* (*Works TC*, I, 59).

[2] Ripley had written a second letter to Carlyle on December 29, 1836: see above, E.4.30.35, n. 9.

[3] See above, C.5.13.35.

poor rag of a thing into a Book, after I am dead it may be,—if so seem good to them. *Either* way!"—As it is, we leave the poor orphan to its destiny, all the more cheerfully. Ripley says farther he has sent me a critique of it by a better hand than the *North American:* I expect it, but have not got it yet. The *North American* seems to say that *he* too sent me one. It never came to hand, nor any hint of it,—except I think once before thro' you. It was not at all an unfriendly review; but had an opacity of matter-of-fact in it that filled one with amazement. Since the Irish Bishop who said "there were some things in *Gulliver,* on which he for one would keep his belief *suspended,*" [4]—nothing equal to it, on that side, has come athwart me. However, he *has* made out that Teufelsdröckh is, in all human probability, a fictitious character; which is always something, for an Inquirer into Truth.—Will you, finally, thank Friend Ripley in my name, till I have time to write to him and thank him.

Your little azure-coloured *Nature* gave me true satisfaction. I read it, and then lent it about to all my acquaintance that had a sense for such things; from whom a similar verdict always came back. You say it is the first chapter of something greater. I call it rather the Foundation and Ground-plan on which you may build whatsoever of great and true has been given you to build. It is the true Apocalypse this when the "open secret" [5] becomes revealed to a man. I rejoice much in the glad serenity of soul with which you look out on this wondrous Dwelling-place of yours and mine,—with an ear for the for the *"Ewigen Melodien,"* [6] which pipe in the winds round us, and utter themselves forth in all sounds and sights and things: *not* to be written down by gamut-machinery; but which all right writing is a kind of attempt to write down. You will see what the years will bring you. It is not one of your smallest qualities in my mind, that you *can* wait so quietly and let the years do their hest. He that cannot keep himself quiet is of a morbid nature; and the thing he yields us will be like him in that, whatever else it be.—Miss Martineau [7] (for I have seen her since I

---

[4] Swift wrote to Pope from Dublin on November 27, 1726: "A Bishop here said that book was full of improbable lies, and for his part, he hardly believed a word of it" (*Correspondence of Jonathan Swift, D.D.,* ed. F. E. Ball, III, 366).

[5] This is Carlyle's translation of Goethe's phrase "das öffentliche Geheimnis": see Slater, "Goethe, Carlyle, and the Open Secret," *Anglia,* LXXVII (1958), 422–26.

[6] Goethe, *Faust,* part II, act III (*Goethes Werke,* V, 355).

[7] In Carlyle's letter to his brother John of December 2, 1836, there is this sketch of Harriet Martineau: "a strange visitor called here one day: Miss Martineau, the

wrote) tells me you are "the only man in America," who has quietly set himself down on a competency to follow his own path, and do the work his own will prescribes for him. Pity that you were the only one! But be one, nevertheless; be the first, and there will come a second and a third. It is a poor country where all men are sold to Mammon, and can make nothing but Railways and Bursts of Parliamentary Eloquence! And yet your New England here too has the upper hand of our Old England, of our Old Europe: we too are *sold* to Mammon, soul, body and spirit; but (mark that, I pray you, with double pity) Mammon will not *pay* us,—we are "Two Million three hundred thousand in Ireland that have not potatoes enough"! [8] I declare, in History I find nothing more tragical. I find also that it will alter; that for me as one it has altered. Me Mammon will pay or not as he finds convenient; buy me he will not.—In fine, I say, sit still at Concord, with such spirit as you are of; under the blessed skyey influences, with an open sense, with the great Book of Existence open round you: we shall see whether you too get not something blessed to read us from it.

The Paper is declining fast, and all is yet speculation. Along with these two "Articles" (to be sent by Liverpool; there are two of them, *D. Necklace* and *Mirabeau*),[9] you will very probably get some stray Proofsheet—of the unutterable *French Revolution!* It is actually at Press; *two* Printers working at separate Volumes of it,—tho' still too slo[wly.] In not many weeks, my hands will be washed of it! You, I hope, can have litt[le con]ception of the feeling with which I wrote the last word of it, one night in early January, when the clock was striking ten, and our frugal Scotch supper coming in! I did not cry; nor I did not pray: but could have done both. No such *spell* shall get itself fixed

---

Poetess Political Economist! She is not half so ill-favoured as they represented her; indeed not ill-favoured at all; but a rather interesting woman: very shrewd, and very good; of the Unitarian friend-of-humanity species. She is deaf as a Post, but carries an ear trumpet, and manages quite handsomely. She has been to America, you know; and is now winnowing out the fruit of her harvest there" (NLS, MS 523).

[8] In chapter VI of the last book of *The French Revolution (Works TC*, IV, 312) Carlyle wrote: "But what if History somewhere on this Planet were to hear of a Nation, the third soul of whom had not, for thirty weeks each year, as many third-rate potatoes as would sustain him"; and referred in a footnote to the Report of the Irish Poor-Law Commission, 1836.

[9] "The Diamond Necklace," written at Craigenputtock, was published in *Fraser's Magazine* for January and February, 1837; "Mirabeau" was published in *The London and Westminster Review* for January, 1837.

on me for some while to come! A beggarly Distortion; that will please
no mortal, not even myself; of which I know not whether the fire
were not after all the due place! And yet I ought not to say so: there
is a great blessing in a man's doing what he utterly can, in the case he
is in. Perhaps great quantities of dross are burnt out of me by this
calcination I have had; perhaps I shall be far quieter and healthier of
mind and body than I have ever been since boyhood. The world, tho'
no man had ever less empire in it, seems to me a thing lying *under* my
feet; a mean imbroglio, which I never more shall fear, or court, or
disturb myself with: welcome and welcome to go wholly *its own way;*
I wholly clear for going mine.—Thro' the summer months I am somewhere or other, to *rest* myself, in the deepest possible sleep. The residue
is vague as the wind;—unheeded as the wind. *Some* way it will turn
out that a poor well-meaning Son of Adam has bread growing for him
too, better or worse: *any* way; or even *no* way, if that be it,—I shall be
content. There is a scheme here among Friends for my Lecturing in a
thing they call Royal Institution, but it will not do there, I think.[10]
The instant two or three are gathered together [11] under any terms, who
want to learn something I can teach them,—then, we will, most readily,
as Burns says, "loose our tinkler jaw," [12] but not I think till then; were
the Institution even Imperial. America has faded considerably into the
background of late: indeed, to say truth, whenever I think of myself
in America, it is as in the Backwoods, with a rifle in my hand; God's
sky over my head, and this accursed Lazarhouse of quacks and blockheads, and sin and misery (now near a head) lying all behind me forever more. A thing, you see, which is and can be at bottom but a
day-dream! To rest thro the summer: that is my only fixed wisdom; a
resolution taken; only the place where uncertain.—What a pity this
poor sheet is done! I had innumerable things to tell you about people
whom I have seen, about books,—Miss Harriet Martineau, Mrs Butler,[13] Southey; Influenza, Parliament, Literature and the Life of Man
—the whole of which must lie over till next time. Write to me; do not

[10] The course was conceived and organized by Harriet Martineau and Jane Wilson.
When they found the Royal Institution unavailable, they engaged a ballroom
called Willis's Rooms (Wilson, *Carlyle on Cromwell and Others*, p. 4).

[11] Matt. 18: 20.

[12] Cf. the Burns fragment sometimes called "The American War," which begins
"When Guildford good our pilot stood."

[13] Fanny Kemble.

forget me. My Wife, who is sitting by me, in very poor health (this long while) sends "Kindest remembrances"—"compliments" she expressly does not send. Good be with you always, my dear Friend!

T. Carlyle

We send our felicitation to the Mother and little Boy; which latter you had better tell us the name of.

Concord, Mass
31 March 1837 [1]

My dear friend,

Last night, I said I would write to you forthwith. This morning, I received your letter of 13 February, & *with it*, the Diamond Necklace, the Mirabeau, & the olive leaf of a proofsheet. I write out the sum of my debt as the best acknowledgement I can make. I had already received, about New-Year's day, the preceding letter. It came in the midst of my washbowl-storm of a Course of Lectures on the Philosophy of History.[2] For all these gifts & pledges—thanks. Over the finished History, joy & evergreen laurels. I embrace you with all my heart. I solace myself with the noble nature God has given you, & in you, to me, & to all.

I had read the Diamond Necklace three weeks ago, at the Boston Atheneum, & the Mirabeau I had just read when my copy came. But the Proofsheet was virgin gold. The Mirabeau, I forbode, is to establish your Kingdom in England. That is genuine thunder, which, nobody that wears ears, can affect to mistake for the rumbling of cart wheels. I please myself with thinking that my Angelo has blocked a Colossus which may stand in the public square to defy all competitors. To be sure, that is its least merit—that nobody can do the like—yet is it a gag to Cerberus. Its better merit is, that it inspires self-trust, by teaching the immense resources that are in human nature; so I sent it to be read by a brave man who is poor & decried.[3] The doctrine is indeed

---

[1] R. L. Rusk argues convincingly that this letter should have been dated April 1 (*Let RWE*, II, 63).

[2] These lectures were given weekly at the Masonic Temple in Boston from December 8 to March 2 (*Let RWE*, II, 48).

[3] Alcott, at whom "all the little dogs" were barking because of his recent *Conversations with Children on the Gospels*. On March 24 Emerson had written him: "go read the paper on Mirabeau by Carlyle in the new Westminster Review. It is

true & grand which you preach as by cannonade, that God made a man, and it were as well to stand by & see what is in him, &, if he act ever from his impulses, believe that he has his own checks, & however extravagant, will keep his orbit, & return from far; a faith that draws confirmation from the sempiternal ignorance & stationariness of society, & the sempiternal growth of all the individuals.

The Diamond Necklace I read with joy, whilst I read with my own eyes. When I read with English or New English eyes, my joy is marred by the roaring of the opposition. I doubt not, the exact story is there told as it fell out; & told for the first time; but the eye of your readers, as you will easily guess, will be bewildered by the multitude of brilliant-coloured hieroglyphics whereby the meaning is conveyed. And for the Gig,—the Gig,—it is fairly worn out, & such a cloud-compeller must mock that particular symbol no more.[4]

I thought as I read this piece that your strange genius was the instant fruit of your London. It is the aroma of Babylon. Such as the great metropolis, such is this style: so vast, enormous, related to all the world, & so endless in details. I think you see as pictures every street, church, parliament-house, barrack, baker's shop, mutton-stall, forge, wharf, & ship, and whatever stands, creeps, rolls, or swims thereabouts, & make all your own. Hence your encyclopediacal allusion to all knowables, & the virtues & vices of your panoramic pages. Well, it is your own; and it is English; and every word stands for somewhat; and it cheers & fortifies me. And what more can a man ask of his writing fellow-man? Why, all things; inasmuch as a good mind creates wants at every stroke.

The proofsheet rhymes well with Mirabeau, and has abated my fears from your own & your brother's account of the new book. I greet it well. Auspicious Babe, be born! The first good of the book is that it makes you free & as I anxiously hope makes your body sound. A possible good is that it will cause me to see your face. But I seemed to read in Mirabeau, what you intimate in your letter, that you will not come westward. Old England is to find you out, & then the New will have no charm. For me, it will be the worse; for you, not. A man, a few

---

all thunder & admonishes us of the might that in us lies, even in depression & under the frowns of the incapable" (*Let RWE*, II, 62).

[4] Mill also had objected to the "gig" passages when he was considering *The Diamond Necklace* for publication in his *London Review* (Carlyle, *Letters to . . . Mill*, p. 123). After 1837, except for a single passage in *Past and Present*, the gig disappeared from Carlyle's work.

men, cannot be to you (with your ministering eyes,) that which you should travel far to find. Moreover I observe that America looks, to those who come hither, as unromantic & unexciting as the Dutch canals. I see plainly that our society, for the most part, is as bigoted to the *respectabilities* of religion & education as yours; that there is no more appetite for a revelation here than elsewhere; and the educated class are, of course, less fair-minded than others. Yet in the moments when my eyes are open, I see that here are rich materials for the philosopher & poet, &, what is more to your purpose as an artist, that we have had in these parts no one philosopher or poet to put a sickle to the prairie wheat. I have really never believed that you would do us that crowning grace of coming hither, yet if God should be kinder to us than our belief, I meant & mean to hold you fast in my little meadows on the Musketaquid (now Concord) river, and show you (as in this country we can anywhere) an America in miniature in the April or November town meeting.[5] Therein should you conveniently study & master the whole of our hemispherical politics reduced to a nutshell, & have a new version of Oxenstiern's little-wit,[6] and yet be consoled by seeing that here the farmers patient as their bulls of head-boards—provided for them in relation to distant national objects, by kind editors of newspapers,—do yet their will & a good will in their own parish. If a wise man would pass by New York & be content to sit still in this village a few months, he should get a thorough native knowledge which no foreigner has yet acquired. So I leave you with God, & if any oracle in the great Delphos should say "Go," why fly to us instantly. Come & spend a year with me, & see if I cannot respect your retirements.

I must love you for your interest in me & my way of life, and the more that we only look for good-nature in the creative class. They pay the tax of grandeur, & attracted irresistibly to make, their living is usually weak & hapless. But you are companionable—God has made

[5] In his *Historical Discourse at Concord*, September, 1835, Emerson had written: "In a town-meeting, the great secret of political science was uncovered, and the problem solved, how to give every individual his fair weight in the government, without any disorder from numbers. In a town-meeting, the roots of society were reached" (*Works RWE*, XI, 46–47).

[6] The seventeenth-century Swedish chancellor, Axel Oxenstjerna, is said to have asked his son: "Do you not know . . . with what little wisdom the world is governed?" (Carl Hallendorff and Adolf Schück, *History of Sweden* [Stockholm, 1938], p. 218).

you man as well as Poet—that I lament the 3000 miles of mountainous water. Burns might have added a better verse to his poem, importing that one might write Iliads & Hamlets, & yet come short of truth by infinity, as every written word must; but "the man's the Gowd for a' that." And I heartily thank the Lady for her goodwill. Please God she may be already well. We all grieve to know of her ill health. People who have seen her, never stop with *Mr* Carlyle, but count him thrice blest in her. My wife believes in nothing for her but the American Voyage. I shall never cease to expect you both until you come. My boy is five months old, he is called Waldo, a lovely wonder, that made the Universe look friendlier to me.

My wife, one of your best lovers, sends her affectionate regards to Mrs Carlyle & says that she takes exception in your letters only to that sentence that she would go to Scotland if you came here. Wifey beseeches her to come & possess her new-dressed chamber. Do not cease to write whenever you can spare me an hour. A man named Bronson Alcott is great & one of the jewels we have to show you. Goodbye.

R. W. Emerson

The second edition of *Sartor* is out and sells well.[7] I learned the other day that 25 copies of it were ordered for England.[8] It was very amiable of you,—that word about it in Mirabeau.[9]

5. Cheyne Row, Chelsea, London,
1st June 1837—

My dear Friend,

A word must go to Concord in answer to your last kind word. It reached me that word of yours on the morning of a most unspeakable day; the day when I half dead with fret agitation and exasperation was to address extempore an audience of London quality people on the subject of German Literature! The heart's wish of me was that I might

---

[7] On May 30, 1837, Carlyle wrote to his brother John: "I had a flaming Letter from Emerson in America in laud of the Mirabeau &c; second edition of *Dreck*, & what not: 'goot worts Master Slender, goot worts' " (NLS, MS 523).

[8] Harriet Martineau had taken twenty-five copies of the American *Sartor* with her when she returned to England in August, 1836. After she had sold those, she ordered twenty-five more (Martineau, *Autobiography*, ed. M. W. Chapman, I, 289).

[9] "This refers to Carlyle's introducing, in his paper on *Mirabeau*, a citation from *Sartor*, with the words, 'We quote from a New-England Book' " (Norton's note).

be left in deepest oblivion, wrapt in blankets and silence, not speaking, not spoken to, for a twelvemonth to come. My Printers had only let me go, out of their Treadmill, the day before. However, all that is over now; and I am still here alive to write to you, and hope for better days.

Almost a month ago there went a copy of a Book called *French Revolution* with your address on it over to Red-Lion Square, and thence, as old Rich declared himself now *emeritus,* back to one Kennet (I think) near Covent Garden, who professes to correspond with Hilliard & Company, Boston, and undertook the service. The Book is not gone yet, I understand; but Kennet engages that it shall leave Liverpool infallibly on the fifth of June. I wish you a happy reading of it therefore: it is the only copy of my sending that has crossed the water. Ill printed (there are many errors, one or two gross ones); ill written, ill thought! But in fine it *is* off my hands; that is a fact worth all others. As to its reception here or elsewhere, I anticipate nothing or little. Gabble, gabble, the astonishment of the dull public brain is likely to be considerable, and its ejaculations unedifying. We will let it go its way. Beat this thing, I say always, under thy dull hoofs, O dull Public; trample it and tumble it into all sinks and kennels; if thou canst kill it, kill it in God's name: if thou canst not kill it, why then thou wilt not.

By the bye speaking of dull Publics, I ought to say that I have seen a Review of myself in the *Christian Examiner* [1] (I think that is it, of Boston); the author of which, if you know him, I desire you to thank on my part. For if a dull million is good, then withal a seeing unit or two is also good. This man images back a beautiful idealized Clothes-Philosopher, very satisfactory to look upon; in whose beatified features I did verily detect more similitude to what I myself meant to be than in any or all the other criticisms I have yet seen written of me. That a man see himself reflected from the soul of his brother man in this brotherly improved way: there surely is one of the most legitimate joys of existence. Friend Ripley took the trouble to send me this Review, in which I detected an Article of his own; there came also some Discourses of his much to be approved of; a Newspaper passage-of-fence with a Philistine of yours, and a set of Essays on Progress-of-the-species

---

[1] N. L. Frothingham, "Sartor Resartus," *Christian Examiner,* XXI (September, 1836), 74–84.

and such like by a man whom I grieved to see confusing himself with that.[2] Progress of the species is a thing I can get no good of at all. These Books, which Miss Martineau has borrowed from me, did not arrive till three weeks ago or less. I pray you to thank Ripley for them very kindly; which at present I still have not time to do. He seems to me a good man, with good aims; with considerable natural health of mind, wherein all goodness is likely to grow better, all clearness to grow clearer. Miss Martineau laments that he does not fling himself, or not with the due impetuosity, into the Black Controversy; a thing lamentable in the extreme when one considers what a world this is, and how perfect it would be could Mungo once get his stupid case rectified, and eat his squash as a stupid *Apprentice* instead of stupid *Slave!*

Miss Martineau's Book on America [3] is out, here and with you. I have read it for the good Authoress's sake, whom I love much. She is one of the strangest phenomena to me. A genuine little Poetess, buckramed, swathed like a mummy, into Socinean and Political-Economy formulas, and yet verily alive in the inside of that! "God has given a Prophet to every People in its own speech," say the Arabs.[4] Even the English Unitarians were one day to have their Poet, and the best that could be said for them too was to be said. I admire this good lady's integrity, sincerity; her quick sharp discernment to the depth it goes: her love also is great; nay in fact it is too great: [the] host of illustrious obscure mortals whom she produces on you, of Preachers, Pamph-[leteers,] Anti-slavers, Able Editors, and other Atlases bearing (unknown to us) the world on their shoulder, is absolutely more than enough. What they say to her Book here I do not well know. I fancy the general reception will be good, and even brilliant. I saw Mrs

[2] No article appeared under Ripley's signature in the September *Christian Examiner,* but in the November issue he published a review of James Martineau's *Rationale of Religious Enquiry* initialed "G. R." His *Discourses on the Philosophy of Religion* were published in Boston in 1836. The "passage of fence" was an exchange of letters with Andrews Norton published in the Boston *Daily Advertiser* (O. B. Frothingham, *George Ripley,* p. 96).

[3] *Society in America.* On August 8, Emerson wrote in his journal, "I have read Miss Martineau's first volume with great pleasure" (*Journals,* IV, 267).

[4] Ten years before, Carlyle had read in a letter from Goethe: "Der Koran sagt: 'Gott had jedem Volke einen Propheten gegeben in seiner eignen Sprache' " (Goethe, *Correspondence between Goethe and Carlyle,* ed. Charles Eliot Norton, p. 18). The relevant passage in the Koran (Surah XIV, verse 4) is different enough in wording to suggest that Carlyle is here quoting Goethe.

Butler [5] last night, "in an ocean of blonde and broadcloth," one of those oceans common at present. *Ach Gott!* They are not of Persons these soirees but of Cloth Figures.

I mean to retreat into Scotland very soon, to repose myself as I intended. My Wife continues here with her Mother; here at least till the weather grow too hot or a journey to join me seem otherwise advisable for her. She is gathering strength, but continues still weak enough. I rest myself "on the sunny side of hedges" [6] in native Annandale, one of the obscurest regions; no man shall speak to me, I will speak to no man, but have dialogues yonder with the old dumb crags, of the most unfathomable sort. Once rested I think of returning to London for another season. Several things are beginning which I ought to see end before taking up my staff again. In this enormous chaos the very multitude of conflicting perversions produces something more like a *calm* than you can elsewhere meet with. Men let you alone, which is an immense thing: they do it even because they have no time to meddle with you. London or else the Back-woods, of America or Craigenputtock! We shall see.

I still beg the comfort of hearing from you. I am sick of soul and body but not incurable; the loving word of a Waldo Emerson is as balm to me, medicinal now more than ever. My Wife earnestly joins me in love to the Concord Household. May a blessing be in it, on one and all! I do nowise give up the idea of sojourning there one time yet. On the contrary it seems almost certain that I shall. Good be with you. Yours always. T. Carlyle

Concord, 13 September, 1837

My dear friend,

Such a gift as the French Revolution demanded a speedier acknowledgement. But you mountaineers that can scale Andes before breakfast for an airing, have no measures for the performance of lowlanders &

[5] Fanny Kemble, presumably: she was in London at this time and had called on Carlyle in February (*Wilson, Carlyle to "The French Revolution,"* p. 413).

[6] This may be an echo of the Carlyles' household-talk: in a letter of March 4, 1837, Jane Carlyle expressed a desire "to lie about the roots of hedges" (*Letters and Memorials,* ed. Froude, I, 55). Or it may refer to a saying which Emerson was even less likely to have heard: Carlyle wrote to his wife on July 11, 1858, "I ought to *drag* my thoughts, as poor old Graham used to say, 'round to the sunny side of the hills' " (NLS, MS 615).

valetudinarians. I am ashamed to think & will not tell what little things have kept me silent.

The "French Revolution" did not reach me until three weeks ago, having had at least two long pauses by the way, as I find, since landing. Between many visits received & some literary haranguing done, I have read two volumes & half the third: and I think you a very good giant; disporting yourself with an original & vast ambition of fun; pleasure & peace not being strong enough for you, you choose to suck pain also, & teach fever & famine to dance & sing. I think you have written a wonderful book which will last a very long time. I see that you have created a history, which the world will own to be such. You have recognized the existence of other persons than officers & of other relations than civism. You have broken away from all books, & written a mind. It is a brave experiment & the success is great. We have men in your story & not names merely; always men, though I may doubt sometimes whether I have the historic men. We have great facts—and selected facts—truly set down. We have always the co-presence of Humanity along with the imperfect damaged individuals. The soul's right of Wonder is still left to us; and we have righteous praise & doom awarded, assuredly without cant: yes comfort your self on that particular, O ungodliest divine man! Thou cantest never. Finally, we have not—a dull word. Never was there a style so rapid as yours—which no reader can outrun; and so it is for the most intelligent. I suppose nothing will astonish more than the audacious wit of cheerfulness which no tragedy & no magnitude of events can overpower or daunt. Henry VIII loved a Man,[1] and I see with joy my bard always equal to the crisis he re-presents. And so I thank you for your labor, and feel that your cotemporaries ought to say, All hail, Brother! live forever; not only in the great Soul which thou largely inhalest, but also as a named person in this thy definite deed.

I will tell you more of the book when I have once got it at focal distance—if that can ever be, and muster my objections when I am sure of their ground. I insist, of course, that it might be more simple, less Gothically efflorescent. You will say no rules for the illumination of windows can apply to the aurora borealis. However, I find refreshment when every now & then a special fact slips into the narrative couched in sharp business like terms. This character-drawing in the

---

[1] The first draft has here, "I love a Man."

book is certainly admirable; the lines are ploughed furrows; but there was cake & ale before, though thou be virtuous.[2] Clarendon surely drew sharp outlines for me in Falkland, Hampden, & the rest, without defiance or skyvaulting.[3] I wish I could talk with you face to face for one day & know what your uttermost frankness would say concerning the book.

I feel assured of its good reception in this Country. I learned last Saturday that in all eleven hundred & sixty six copies of Sartor have been sold. I have told the publisher of that book that he must not print the History until some space has been given to people to import British copies. I have ordered Hilliard, Gray, & Co. to import twenty copies as an experiment. At the present very high rate of exchange which makes a shilling worth 30 cents, they think with freight & duties, the book would be too costly here for sale, but we confide in a speedy fall of exchange—then my books shall come. I am ashamed that you should educate our young men & that we should pirate your books. One day we will have a better law, or perhaps—you will make our law yours.

I had your letter long before your book. Very good work you have done in your lifetime, & very generously you adorn & cheer this pilgrimage of mine by your love. I find my highest prayer granted in calling a just & wise man my friend. Your profuse benefaction of genius in so few years m[akes] me feel very poor & useless. I see that I must go o[n &] trust to you & to all the brave for some longer time, hoping yet to prove one day my truth & love. There are in this country so few scholars, that the services of each studious person are needed to do what he can for the circulation of thoughts, to the end of making some counterweight to the money force [4] & to give such food as he may to the nigh starving Youth. So I religiously read lectures every winter, & at other times whenever summoned. Last year, "the Philosophy of History," twelve lectures; and now I meditate a course on what I call "Ethics." I peddle out all the wit I can gather from Time or from Nature, and am pained at heart to see how thankfully that little is received.

Write to me, good friend, tell me if you went to Scotland,—what you do, & will do, tell me that your wife is strong & well again as when I saw her at Craigenputtock. I desire to be affectionately remembered

---

[2] *Twelfth Night*, act II, scene iii, line 125.

[3] Emerson had been reading Clarendon in August (*Journals*, IV, 264).

[4] The first draft has here, "counterweight to the mass of flesh."

to her. Tell me when you will come hither. I called together a little club a week ago who spent a day with me counting fifteen souls—each one of whom warmly loves you.[5] So if the French Revolution does not convert the "dull public" of your native Nineveh,[6] I see not but you must shake their dust from your shoes & cross the Atlantic to a New England.   Yours in love & honor,   R. Waldo Emerson.

May I trouble you with a commission when you are in the City. You mention being at the shop of Rich in Red Lion Square. Will you say to him that he sent me some books two or three years ago without any account of prices annexed. I wrote him once myself,—once through S. Burdett, bookseller; & since through C. P. Curtis, Esq. who professes to be his attorney, in Boston,—three times—to ask for this account. No answer has ever come. I wish he would send me the account, that I may settle it. If he persist in his self-denying contumacy, I think you may immortalise him as bookseller of the Gods.

I shall send you an Oration presently delivered before a literary society here which is now being printed.[7] Gladly I hear of the Carlyle*t* so they say—in the new Westminster.[8]

Concord, 2 November, 1837.

My dear Sir,

I have much pleasure in introducing to your acquaintance my friend Charles Sumner, Esq. a gentleman much known & valued in our community for his attainments in the science & literature of the Law. Mr Sumner has a particular claim on your regard from the warm interest he has taken in your writings.[1] I hope he finds you well.
                    Your friend & servant,   R. Waldo Emerson.
Thomas Carlyle, Esq.

[5] On September 1, the day after he delivered his Phi Beta Kappa Address, Emerson was host to the group of scholars and ministers which was variously called Hedge's Club and the Transcendental Club (*Journals*, IV, 289).

[6] "That great city, wherein are more than sixscore thousand persons that cannot discern between their right hand and their left" (Jonah 4: 11).

[7] *An Oration, Delivered before the Phi Beta Kappa Society, at Cambridge, August 31, 1837.*

[8] "Parliamentary History of the French Revolution," *London and Westminster Review*, XXVII (April, 1837), 233–47.

[1] In 1830, when he was only nineteen, Sumner had copied out passages from Carlyle's essay on Burns (Pierce, *Memoir and Letters of Charles Sumner*, I, 50).

Concord, 2 November, 1837[1]

My dear Friend,—Mr. Charles Sumner, a lawyer of high standing for his age, and editor or one editor of a journal called *The Jurist,* and withal a lover of your writings, tells me he is going to Paris and thence to London, and sets out in a few days. I cannot, of course, resist his request for a letter to you, nor let pass the occasion of a greeting. Health, Joy, and Peace be with you! I hope you sit still yet, and do not hastily meditate new labors. Phidias need not be always tinkering. Sit still like an Egyptian.[2] Somebody told me the other day that your friends here might have made a sum for the author by publishing *Sartor* themselves, instead of leaving it with a bookseller.[3] Instantly I wondered why I had never such a thought before, and went straight to Boston, and have made a bargain with a bookseller to print the *French Revolution.* It is to be printed in two volumes of the size of our American *Sartor,* one thousand copies, the estimate making the cost of the book say (in dollars and cents) $1.18 a copy, and the price $2.50. The bookseller contracts with me to sell the book at a commission of twenty per cent on that selling price, allowing me however to take at cost as many copies as I can find subscribers for. There is yet, I believe, no other copy in the country than mine: so I gave him the first volume, and the printing is begun. I shall take care that your friends here shall know my contract with the bookseller, and so shall give me their names. Then, if so good a book can have a tolerable sale, (almost contrary to the nature of a good book, I know,) I shall sustain with great glee the new relation of being your banker and attorney. They have had the wit in the London *Examiner,* I find, to praise at last; and I mean that our public shall have the entire benefit of that page. The *Westminster* they can read themselves.[4] The printers think they can get the book out by Christmas. So it must be long before I can tell you what cheer. Meantime do you tell me, I entreat

[1] This is Norton's text.   [2] Cf. Isa. 30: 7.

[3] Elizabeth Peabody. See *Let RWE,* II, 101.

[4] Leigh Hunt's *Examiner* for September 17, 1837, described *The French Revolution* as "one of the few books of our time that is likely to live for some generations beyond it . . . a book of unquestionable originality and genius." John Stuart Mill wrote in *The London and Westminster Review* for July, 1837 (XXVII, 17): "No work of greater genius, either historical or poetical, has been produced in this country for many years."

you, what speed it has had at home. The best, I hope, with the wise and good withal.

I have nothing to tell you and no thoughts. I have promised a course of Lectures for December, and am far from knowing what I am to say; but the way to make sure of fighting into the new continent is to burn your ships. The "tender ears," as George Fox said,[5] of young men are always an effectual call to me ignorant to speak. I find myself so much more and freer on the platform of the lecture-room than in the pulpit, that I shall not much more use the last; and do now only in a little country chapel at the request of simple men to whom I sustain no other relation than that of preacher.[6] But I preach in the Lecture-Room and then it tells, for there is no prescription. You may laugh, weep, reason, sing, sneer, or pray, according to your genius. It is the new pulpit, and very much in vogue with my northern countrymen. This winter, in Boston, we shall have more than ever: two or three every night of the week. When will you come and redeem your pledge? The day before yesterday my little boy was a year old,—no, the day before that,— and I cannot tell you what delight and what study I find in this little bud of God, which I heartily desire you also should see. Good, wise, kind friend, I shall see you one day. Let me hear, when you can write, that Mrs. Carlyle is well again.   R. Waldo Emerson

                                        Chelsea, London, 8th December, 1837
My dear Emerson,

How long it is since you last heard of me I do not very accurately know; but it is too long. A very long, ugly, inert and unproductive chapter of my own history seems to have past since then. Whenever I delay writing, be sure matters go not well with me; and do you in that case write to me were it again and over again,—unweariable in pity.

I did go to Scotand, for almost three months; leaving my Wife here with her Mother. The poor wife had fallen so weak that she gave me real terror in the spring time, and made the Doctor look very grave

---

[5] Fox made frequent use of "tender" in the sense which the *NED* defines as "susceptible to moral or spiritual influence." See, for example, his *Journal,* ed. John L. Nickalls, p. 10.

[6] For the past two years Emerson had preached with some regularity in the neighboring village of East Lexington. He gave up that pulpit in February, 1838 (*Let RWE,* II, 6, 113).

indeed: she continued too weak for travelling: I was worn out as I had never in my life been. So on the longest day of June, I got back to my Mother's cottage; threw myself down, I may say, into what we may call the "frightfullest *magnetic sleep*," [1] and lay their avoiding the intercourse of men. Most wearisome had their gabble become; almost unearthly. But indeed all was unearthly in that humour. The gushing of my native brooks, the *sough* of the old solitary woods, the great roar of old native Solway (billowing fresh out of your Atlantic, drawn by the Moon): all this was a kind of unearthly music to me; I cannot tell you how unearthly. It did not bring me to rest; yet *towards* rest I do think: at all events, the time had come when I behoved to quit it again. I have been here since September: evidently another little "chapter" or paragraph, *not* altogether inert, is getting forward. But I must not speak of these things. How can I speak of them on a miserable scrap of blue paper? [2] Looking into your kind eyes with my eyes, I could speak: not here. Pity me, my friend, my brother; yet hope well of me: if I can (in all senses) rightly *hold my peace*, I think much will yet be well with me. SILENCE is the great thing I worship at present; almost the sole tenant of my Pantheon. Let a man know rightly how to hold his peace. I love to repeat to myself, "Silence is of Eternity."—Ah me, I think how I could rejoice to quit these jarring discords and jargonings of Babel; and go far, far away! I do believe if I had the smallest competence of money to get "food and warmth" [3] with, I would shake the mud of London from my feet, and go and bury myself in some green place, and never print any syllable more. Perhaps it is better as it is.

But quitting this, we will actually speak (under favour of "Silence") one very small thing; a pleasant piece of news. There is a man here called John Sterling (*Reverend* John of the Church of England too), whom I love better than anybody I have met with, since a certain skymessenger alighted to me at Craigenputtock, and vanished in the Blue again. This Sterling has written; but what is far better he has lived,

---

[1] Hypnosis. Carlyle evidently considered the phrase new enough to deserve quotation marks: see below, at close of this letter. *Magnetic* in the sense of *hypnotic* is as old as Mesmer, but the *NED* lists nothing similar to "magnetic sleep" before Dickens's "magnetic slumber" of *Nicholas Nickleby* (1838).

[2] Carlyle was not writing on blue stationery; presumably he used *blue* here as a colloquial expression of disapproval: see C.3.16.38 and the *NED*.

[3] *Sartor Resartus* (*Works TC*, I, 141).

he is alive. Across several unsuitable wrappages, of Church-of-England-ism and others, my heart loves the man. He is one, and the best of a small class extant here, who nigh drowning in a black wreck of In-fidelity (lighted up by some glare of Radicalism only, now growing *dim* too) and about to perish, saved themselves into a Coleridgian Shovelhattedness,—or determination to preach; to preach peace; were it only the spent *echo* of a peace once preached. He is still only about thirty; young; and I think will shed the shovelhat yet perhaps. Do you ever read *Blackwood?* This John Sterling is the "New Contributor" whom Wilson makes such a rout about, in the November and prior month: "Crystals from a Cavern" &c,—which it is well worth your while to see.[4] Well, and what then, cry you?—Why then, this John Sterling has fallen overhead in love with a certain Waldo Emerson; that is all. He saw the little book *Nature* here; and, across a whole *silva silvarum* of prejudices, discerned what was in it; took it to his heart,—and indeed into his pocket, and has carried it off to Madeira with him; whither unhappily (tho' now with good hope and expec-tation) the Doctors have ordered him. This is the small piece of pleas-ant news, that two sky-messengers (such they were both of them to me) have met and recognized each other; and by God's blessing there shall one day be a trio of us: call you that nothing?

And so now by a direct transition I am got to the "Oration." My friend! you know not what you have done for me there. It was long decades of years that I had heard nothing but the infinite jangling and jabbering and inarticulate twittering and screeching, and my soul had sunk down sorrowful, and said there is no articulate speaking then any more, and thou art solitary among stranger-creatures?—and lo, out of the West, comes a clear utterance, clearly recognisable as a *m[an's]* voice, and I *have* a kinsman and brother: God be thanked for it! I coul[d have] *wept* to read that speech; the clear high melody of it went tingling thro' my heart; I said to my wife "There, woman!" She read; and returned and charges me to return for answer, "that there had been nothing met with like it since Schiller went silent." My brave

<hr />

[4] In the October issue of *Blackwood's Edinburgh Magazine* (XLII, 562–72) there were twenty-five poems by the "New Contributor," one of which was editorially introduced as "superior to any of Shelley's." In November there were twenty pages more. "Crystals from a Cavern" was a collection of prose aphorisms and meditations published in the issue for July (XLII, 39–43).

Emerson! And all this has been lying silent, quite tranquil in him, these seven years, and the "vociferous platitude" [5] dinning his ears on all sides, and he quietly answering no word; and a whole world of Thought has silently built itself in these calm depths, and the day being come, says quite softly, as if it were a common thing, "Yes, I *am* here too."—Miss Martineau tells me, "some say it is inspired, some say it is mad." Exactly so; no *say* could be suitabler. But for you, my dear friend, I say and pray heartily: May God grant you strength, for you have a *fearful* work to do! Fearful I call it; and yet it is great, and the greatest. O for God's sake *keep yourself still quiet.* Do not hasten to write; you cannot be too slow about it. Give no ear to any man's praise or censure; know that that is *not* it: on the one side is as Heaven if you have strength to keep silent, and climb unseen; yet on the other side, yawning always at one's right-hand and one's left, is the frightfullest Abyss and Pandemonium! See Fenimore Cooper,—poor Cooper, he is *down in it;* and had a climbing faculty too.[6] Be steady, be quiet, be in *no* haste; and God speed you well! My space is done.

And so adieu, for this time. You must write soon again. My copy of the *Oration* has never come: how is this? I could dispose of a dozen well.[7]—They say I am to lecture again in Spring, *Ay de mi!* The "Book" is babbled about sufficiently in several dialects. Fraser wants to print my scattered Reviews and Articles; a pregnant sign. Teufelsdröckh to precede. The man "screamed" once at the name of it in a very musical manner. He shall not print a line, unless he give me *money* for it more or less. I have had enough of printing for one while, —thrown into "magnetic sleep" by it! Farewell my brother.

—T. Carlyle

O. Rich, it seems, is in Spain. His representative assured me some weeks since, that the Account was now sent.—There is an Article on Sir W. Scott: shocking; invitissima Minerva! [8]

Miss Martineau charges me to send kind remembrances to you and

---

[5] Carlyle used this phrase without quotation marks in a letter to Sterling of June 7, 1837 (Froude, *Thomas Carlyle: Life in London,* I, 93).

[6] The English newspapers had recently carried accounts of Cooper's quarrel with the people of Cooperstown (*Quarterly Review,* LIX [October, 1837], 344).

[7] The copy he read was Harriet Martineau's (Carlyle, *Letters to Mill,* p. 211).

[8] Cf. Cicero *De Officiis* I. xxxi. 110. On December 12 Carlyle wrote to his brother John: "I have been 'sharp' on Scott, but 'mannerly'; condemnatory, commiseratory, not irreverent. I wrote in great chagrin and plague" (*New Letters,* I, 101).

your Lady: her words were kinder than I have room for here.—Can you not, in defect or delay of Letter, send me a Massachusetts News-paper? I think it costs little or almost nothing now; and I shall know your hand.[9]

[9] On June 10, 1838, Emerson asked his brother in New York to drop "a couple of printed papers," which Emerson had sent down from Boston, "into the *London* letterbag of the first ship" (*Let RWE,* II, 136). See C.6.27.35 (last paragraph) for "the law of the American Letter-carrying."

1838

Concord, 9 February, 1838.

My dear friend.

It is ten days now—ten cold days—that your last letter has kept my heart warm & I have not been able to write before. I have just finished —Wednesday evening—a course of lectures which I ambitiously baptised "Human Culture" & read once a week to the curious in Boston. I could write nothing else the while, for weariness of the week's stated scribbling. Now, I am free as a wood-bird, & can take up the pen without fretting or fear. Your letter should & nearly did make me jump for joy—fine things about our poor speech at Cambridge—fine things from CARLYLE—scarcely could we maintain a decorous gravity on the occasion. And then news of a friend, who is also Carlyle's friend. What has life better to offer than such tidings? You may suppose I went directly & got me Blackwood, & read the prose & the verse of John Sterling, and saw that my man had a head & a heart, & spent an hour or two very happily in spelling his biography out of his own hand;—a species of palmistry in which I have a perfect reliance. I found many incidents grave & gay & beautiful, & have determined to love him very much.[1] In this romancing of the gentle affections we are children evermore. We forget the age of life, the barriers so thin yet so adamantean of space & circumstance—& I have had the rarest poems selfsinging in my head of brave men that work & conspire in a perfect intelligence across seas & conditions—& meet at last. I heartily pray that the Sea & its vineyards may cheer with warm medicinal breath a Voyager so kind & noble.

For the Oration,—I am so elated with your goodwill that I begin to fear your heart has betrayed your head this time & so the praise is not good on Parnassus but only in friendship. I sent it diffidently (I did

[1] On first reading, Emerson did not think highly of Sterling's work; even "after sleeping" he would merely say that it was "the poetry and prose of a thinking & virtuous man if it be not musical" (*Let RWE*, II, 106).

send it through bookselling Munroe)[2] to you & was not a little surprised by your generous commendations. Yet here, it interested young
men a good deal for an academical performance and an edition of 500
was disposed of in a month. A new edition is now printing, & I will
send you some copies presently to give to any body who you think will
read.

I have a little budget of news myself. I hope you had my letter—
sent by young Sumner—saying that we meant to print the French Revolution here for the author's benefit. It was published on the 25th
December. It is published at my risk, the booksellers agreeing to let
me have at cost all the copies I can get subscriptions for. All the rest
they are to sell & to have 20 per cent on the retail price for their
commission. The selling price of the book is $2.50. the cost of a copy
$1.26 the bookseller's commission .50 cents; so that T. C. only gains
76 cents on each copy they sell. But we have 200 subscribers & in each
copy they buy you have 1.26 except in cases where the distant residence
of subscribers makes a cost of freight. You ought to have three or four
quarters of a dollar more on each copy but we put the lowest price on
the book in terror of the Philistines & to secure its accessibleness to the
economical public. We printed 1000 copies: of these, five hundred are
already sold—in six weeks;—& Brown the bookseller[3] talks, as I think,
much too modestly, of getting rid of the whole edition in one year.
I say six months. The printing, &c. is to be paid & a settlement made in
six months from the day of publication; and I hope that settlement
will be the final one. And I confide in sending y[ou] seven hundred
dollars at least as a certificate that you have so many readers in the
West. Yet, I own, I shake a little at the thought of the booksellers account. Whenever I have seen that species of document, it was strange
how the hopefullest ideal dwindled away to a dwarfish actual. But you
may be assured I shall on this occasion summon to the bargain all the
Yankee in my constitution & multiply & divide like a lion.

The book has the best success with the best. Young men say, it is the
only history they have ever read. The middle aged & the old shake
their heads & cannot make anything of it. In short it has the success of

---

[2] James Munroe and Company of Boston published the *Oration*. To make sure
that Carlyle would see it, Emerson had sent him another copy through Sumner in
November (*Let RWE*, II, 103).

[3] The American publishers of *The French Revolution* were Charles C. Little and
James Brown.

a book which as people have not fashioned has to fashion the people. It will take some time to win all but it wins & will win. I sent a notice of it to the Christian Examiner, but the Editor sent it all back to me except the first & last paragraphs—those he printed.[4] And the Editor of the North American declined giving a place to a paper from another friend of yours. But we shall see. I am glad you are to print your Miscellanies, but forgive our Transatlantic effrontery, we are beforehand of you & we are already selecting a couple of volumes from the same & shall print them on the same plan as the History, & hope so to turn a penny for our friend again. I surely should not do this without consulting you as to the selection but that I had no choice. If I waited the bookseller would have done it himself & carried off the profit. I sent you (to Kennett) a copy of the French Rev. I regret exceedingly the printers blunder about the numbering the Books in the Volumes,[5] but he had warranted me a literal, punctual reprint of the copy without its leaving his office & I trusted him. I am told there are many errors. I am going to see for myself. I have filled my paper & not yet said a word of how many things. You tell me how ill was Mrs. C. & you do not tell me that she is well again. But I see plainly I must take speedily another sheet. I love you always.   R. W. Emerson

Boston, 12 March, 1838.

My dear friend,

Here in a bookseller's shop,[1] I have secured a stool & corner to say a swift benison. Mr Bancroft told me that the presence of English Lord Gosford [2] in town would give me a safe conveyance of pamphlets to you so I send some Orations of which you said so kind & cheering words. Give them to any one who will read them. I have written names

---

[4] *Christian Examiner*, XXIII (January, 1838), 386–87; published in *Uncollected Writings of Ralph Waldo Emerson*, pp. 26–27. It is an expansion and in part a repetition of Emerson's comments of September 13, 1837.

[5] Each volume of this two-volume edition contains ten books numbered from I to X without regard to Carlyle's original division into three volumes containing respectively seven, six, and seven chapters.

[1] Emerson was in Boston "to read a lecture on Peace" (*Journals*, IV, 409).

[2] George Bancroft was at this time Collector of Customs in Boston. The earl of Gosford, governor of Upper Canada during the recent rebellion, was waiting in Boston, at the Tremont House, for a British frigate which had been sent to take him home (Boston *Courier*, March 8, 1838).

in three. You have I hope got the letter sent nearly a month ago giving account of our reprint of the French Revolution & have received a copy of the same. I learn from the bookseller today that 650 copies are sold & the book continues to sell. So I hope that our settlement at the end of six months will be final or nearly so.

I had nearly closed my agreement the other day with a publisher for the emission of "Carlyles Miscellanies," when just in the last hour comes word from E. G. Loring that he has an authentic catalogue from the Bard himself.[3] Now, I have that, & could wish Loring had communicated his plan to me at first, or that I had had wit enough to have undertaken this matter long ago & conferred with you. I designed nothing for you or your friends; but merely a lucrative book for our daily market that would have yielded a pecuniary compensation to you, such as we are all bound to make & to have bought our Socrates a cloak. Loring contemplated something quite difffferent a "Complete Works" &c; & now clamors for the same thing, & I do not know but I shall have to gratify him & others at the risk of injury to this my vulgar hope of dollars; that innate idea of the American mind. This I shall settle in a few days No copyright can be secured here for an English book unless it contain original matter. But my moments are going, & I can only promise to write you quickly, at home & at leisure, for I have just been reading the History again, with many many thoughts, and I revere, wonder at, & love you.   R. Waldo Emerson

Chelsea, London, 16th March, 1838—

My dear Emerson,

Your letter thro' Sumner was sent by him from Paris about a month ago; the man himself has not yet made his appearance, or been heard of in these parts: [1] he shall be very welcome to me, arrive when he will. The February letter came yesterday, by direct conveyance from Dartmouth. I answer it today rather than tomorrow; I may not for long have a day freer than this. *Fronte capillata, post est occasio calva:* [2] true either in Latin or in English!

[3] See above, Introduction, p. 21.

[1] Sumner did not arrive in England till May 31, 1838. He heard Carlyle lecture in June but did not find time to call on him until December 1 (Pierce, *Memoir and Letters of Charles Sumner*, I, 318; II, 22).

[2] Cato, *Disticha*, II, 26.

You send me good news, as usual. You have been very brisk and helpful in this business of the *Revolution* Book, and I give you many thanks and commendations. It will be a very brave day when cash actually reaches me, no matter what the number of the coins, whether seven or seven hundred, out of Yankee-land; and strange enough, what is not unlikely, if it be the *first* cash I realize for that piece of work,— Angle-land continuing still *in*solvent to me! Well; it is a wide mother-land we have here, or are getting to have, from Bass's Straits all round to Columbia River, already almost circling the Globe: it must be hard with a man if somewhere or other he find not some one or other to take his part, and stand by him a little! Blessings on you my brother: nay your work is already twice blessed.—I believe after all, with the aid of my Scotch thrift, I shall not be absolutely thrown into the streets here, or reduced to borrow, and become the slave of somebody, for a morsel of bread. Thank God, no! Nay of late I begin entirely to despise that whole matter, so as I never hitherto despised it: "Thou beggarliest Spectre of Beggary that hast chased me ever since I was man, come on then, in the Devil's name, let us see what is in thee! Will the Soul of a Man, with Eternity within a few years of it, quail before *thee?*" Better, however, is my good pious Mother's version of it, "They cannot take God's Providence from thee; thou hast never wanted yet."

But to go on with business; and the republication of books in that Transoceanic England, New and improved Edition of England. In January last, if I recollect right, Miss Martineau in the name of a certain Mr Loring applied to me for a correct list of all my fugitive Papers; the said Mr Loring meaning to publish them for my behoof. This list she, not without solicitation, for I had small hope in it, did at last obtain, and send, coupled with a request from me that you should be consulted in the matter. Now it appears you had of yourself previously determined on something of the same sort, and probably are far on with the printing of your Two *select* volumes. I confess myself greatly better pleased with it on *that* footing than on another. Who Mr Loring may be I know not with any certainty at first hand; but who Waldo Emerson is I do know; and more than one god from the machine is not necessary. I pray you, thank Mr Loring for his goodness towards me (his intents are evidently charitable and not wicked); but consider yourself as in nowise bound at all by that blotted Paper he has; but do the best you can for me; consulting with him or not taking any counsel just as you see to be fittest on the spot. And so Heaven prosper you, both in your "aroused Yankee" state, and in all others;— and let us for the present consider that we have enough about Books and Guineas. I must add however that Fraser and I have yet made no bargain. We found on computing, that there would be five good volumes, including *Teufel^k;* for an edition of 750 I demanded £50 a volume, and Fraser refused: the poor man then fell dangerously ill, and there could not be a word farther said on the subject; till very lately, when it again became possible, but has not yet been put in practise. All the world cries out, Why *do you* publish with Fraser? "Because my soul is sick of Booksellers, and of trade, and deception, and 'need and greed' altogether; and this poor Fraser, not worse than the rest of them, has in some sort grown less hideous to me by custom." I fancy however, either Fraser will publish these things before long; or some Samaritan here will take me to some bolder brother of the trade that will. Great Samuel Johnson assisted at the beginning of Bibliopoly; [3] small Thomas Carlyle assists at the ending of it: both are sorrowful seasons for a man. For the rest, people here continue to receive that *Revolution* very much as you say they do *there:* I am right well quit of it; and the elderly gentlemen on both sides of the water may take comfort, they will not soon have to suffer the like again. But really England is wonderfully changed within these ten years;—the old gentlemen all shrunk into nooks, some of them even voting with the young.—The American ill-printed 2½ dollars copy shall, for Emerson's sake, be welcomest to me of all. Kennett will send it when it comes.

The *Oration* did arrive, with my name on it, one snowy night in January. It[. . .]to Madeira, probably there now. I can dispose of a score of copies to good advantage. Friend Sterling has done the best of all his things in the current *Blackwood,* "Crystals from a Cavern"; which see. He writes kind things of you from Madeira, in expectation of the speech. I will gratify him with your message; he is to be here in May; better, we hope, and in the way towards safety. Miss Martineau has given you a luminous section in her *new* Book about

---

[3] "The Bookseller-System, during its peculiar century, the whole of the eighteenth, did carry us handsomely along; and many good Works it has left us, and many good Men it maintained: . . . it is now expiring by PUFFERY, as the Patronage-System did by FLATTERY" ("Boswell's Life of Johnson," *Works TC,* XXVIII, 101).

America; you are one of the American "originals," [4]—the good Harriett! And now I have but one thing to add and to repeat: Be quiet,
be quiet! The fire that is in one's own stomach is enough, without
foreign bellows to blow it ever and anon. My whole heart shudders
at the thrice-wretched self-combustion in which I see all manner of
poor paper-lanterns go up, the wind of "popularity" puffing at them,
and nothing left ere long but ashes and sooty wreck. It is sad, most sad.
I shun all such persons and circles, as much as possible; and pray the
gods to make me a bricklayer's hodbearer rather. O the "cabriolets,
neat-flies," and blue twaddlers of both sexes therein, that drive many a
poor Mrs Rigmarole to the Devil! [5]—As for me, I continue doing as
nearly nothing as I can manage. I decline all invitations of society
that are declinable: a London rout is one of the maddest things under the moon; a London dinner makes me sicker for a week, and I
say often, It is better to be even dull than to be witty, better to be
silent than to speak.

Curious: your Course of Lectures "on Human Culture" seems to
be on the very subject I am to discourse upon here in May coming;
but I am to call it "on the History of Literature," and *speak* it, not
write it. While you read this, I shall be in the agonies! Ah me, often
when I think of the matter, how my one sole wish is to be left to
hold my tongue, and by what bayonets of Necessity clapt to my back
I am driven into that Lecture-room and in what mood, and ordered
to speak or die, I feel as if my only utterance should be a flood of
tears and blubbering! But that clearly, will not do. Then again I
think it is perhaps better so; who knows? At all events we will try
what is in this Lecturing in London. If something, well; if nothing,
why also well. But I do want to get out of these coils for a time. My
Brother is to be home again in May; if he go back to Italy, if our

---

[4] *Retrospect of Western Travel.* Emerson appeared in a chapter entitled "Originals" along with W. L. Garrison, Father Taylor ("a second homely Jeremy Taylor"),
Noah Worcester, and some anonymous eccentrics. "He is yet in the prime of life.
Great things are expected from him, and great things, it seems, he cannot but do,
if he have life and health. . . . He is a thinker and a scholar. He has modestly
and silently withdrawn himself from the perturbations and conflicts of the crowd
of men, without declining any of the business of life, or repressing any of his human
sympathies. . . . I could give anecdotes; but I have been his guest, and I restrain
myself" (II, 204–5).

[5] "This sentence is a variation on one at the beginning of the article on Scott"
(Norton's note).

Lecturing proved productive, why might we not all set off thitherward for the winter coming? There is a dream to that effect. It would
suit my wife too: she was alarmingly weak this time twelvemonth;
and I can only yet tell you that she is stronger, not strong: she has
not ventured out, except at midday and rarely then, since Autumn
last; she sits here patiently waiting summer, and charges me to send
you her love.—America also always lies in the background: I do believe, if I live long, I shall get to Concord one day. Your wife must
love me. If the little Boy be a well-behaved fellow, he shall ride on
my back yet: if not, tell him I will have nothing to do with him, the
riotous little imp that he is. And so God bless you always, my dear
friend!—Your affectionate   T. Carlyle

                                            Concord, 10 May, 1838.
My dear friend,
    Yesterday I had your letter of March. It quickens my purpose (al-
ways all but ripe) to write to you. If it had come earlier, I should
have been confirmed in my original purpose of publishing "Select
Miscellanies of T. C." As it is, we are far on in the printing of the
two first volumes (to make 900 pp.) of the papers as they stand in
your list. And, now I find, we shall only get as far as the 17th or 18th
article. I regret it, because this book will not embrace those papers
I chiefly desire to provide people with; and it may be some time, in
these years of bankruptcy & famine, before we shall think it prudent
to publish two volumes more. But Loring is a good man & thinks
that many desire to see the sources of Nile.[1] I, for my part, fancy that
to meet the taste of the readers we should publish *from the last,* backwards, beginning with the paper on Scott, which has had the best
reception ever known. Carlyleism is becoming so fashionable that the
most austere Seniors are glad to qualify their reprobation by ap-
plauding this review. I have agreed with the bookseller publishing the
Miscellanies, that he is to guarantee to you on every copy he sells,
$1.00; and you are to have the total profit on every copy subscribed

    [1] Emerson wrote in "New England Reformers": "Caesar, just before the battle of
Pharsalia, discourses with the Egyptian priest concerning the fountains of the Nile,
and offers to quit the army, the empire, and Cleopatra, if he will show him those
mysterious sources" (Emerson, *Works,* II, 274). The story comes from Lucan's *De
Bello Civili,* bk. X.

for. The retail price to be $2.50; the cost of the work is not yet precisely ascertained. The work will probably appear in six or seven weeks. We print 1000 copies. So whenever it is sold, you shall have 1000 dollars.

The French Revolution continues to find friends & purchasers. It has gone to New Orleans, to Nashville, to Vicksburg. I have not been in Boston lately, but have determined that nearly or quite 800 copies should be gone. On the 1 July I shall make up accounts with the booksellers, & I hope to make you the most favorable returns. I shall use the advice of Barnard, Adams, & Co in regard to remittances.

When you publish your next book I think you must send it out to me in sheets, & let us print it here contemporaneously with the English Edition. The eclat of so new a book would help the sale very much. But a better device would be, that you should embark in the Victoria steamer, & come in a fortnight to New York, & in 24 hours more, to Concord. Your study armchair, fireplace & bed long vacant auguring expect you. Then you shall revise your proofs & dictate wit & learning to the New World. Think of it in good earnest. In aid of your friendliest purpose, I will set down some of the facts. I occupy or *improve,* as we Yankees say, two acres only of God's earth, on which is my house, my kitchen-garden, my orchard of thirty young trees, my empty barn. My house is now a very good one for comfort, & abounding in room. Besides my house, I have, I believe, $22 000. whose income in ordinary years is 6 per cent. I have no other tithe or glebe except the income of my winter lectures which was last winter 800 dollars. Well, with this income, here at home, I am a rich man. I stay at home and go abroad at my own instance. I have food, warmth,[2] leisure, books, friends. Go away from home,—I am rich no longer. I never have a dollar to spend on a fancy. As no wise man, I suppose ever was rich in the sense of *freedom to spend,* because of the inundation of claims, so neither am I, who am not wise. But at home I am rich,—rich enough for ten brothers. My wife Lidian is an incarnation of Christianity,—I call her Asia[3]—& keeps my philosophy from Antinomianism. My mother—whitest, mildest, most conserva-

---

[2] See above, C.12.8.37, n. 3.

[3] "In general," says F. I. Carpenter, the continent of Asia meant to Emerson "the passive, the religious, the contemplative . . . the land where only the elemental questions of life are important" (*Emerson and Asia,* p. 32).

tive of ladies, whose only exception to her universal preference of old things is her son; my boy, a piece of love & sunshine, well worth my watching from morning to night; these & three domestic women who cook & sew & run for us, make all my household. Here I sit & read & write with very little system & as far as regards composition with the most fragmentary result: paragraphs incompressible each sentence an infinitely repellent particle. In summer with the aid of a neighbor, I manage my garden; & a week ago I set out on the west side of my house forty young pine trees to protect me or my son from the wind of January. The ornament of the place is the occasional presence of some ten or twelve persons good & wise who visit us in the course of the year.—But my story is too long already. God grant that you will come & bring that blessed wife, whose protracted illness we heartily grieve to learn, & whom a voyage & my wifes & my mothers nursing would in less than a twelvemonth restore to blooming health. My wife sends to her this message; "Come, & I will be to you a sister." What have you to do with Italy? Your genius tendeth to the New, to the West. Come & live with me a year, & if you do not like New England well enough to stay, one of these years (when the History has passed its ten editions & been translated into as many languages) I will come & dwell with you.

I gladly hear what you say of Sterling. I am foolish enough to be delighted with being an object of kindness to a man I have never seen & who has not seen me. I have not yet got the Blackwood for March, which I long to see, but the other three papers I have read with great satisfaction. They lie here on my table. But he must get well.

As to Miss Martineau I know not well what to say. Meaning to do me a signal kindness (& a kindness quite out of all measure of justice) she does me a great annoyance—to take away from me my privacy & thrust me before my time, (if ever there be a time) into the arena of the gladiators, to be stared at. I was ashamed to read, & am ashamed to remember. Yet as you see her, I would not be wanting in gratitude to a gifted & generous lady who so liberally transfigures our demerits. So you shall tell her, if you please, that I read all her book with pleasure but that part, & if ever I shall travel west or south, I think she has furnished me with the eyes.—Farewell, dear wise man. I think your poverty honorable above the common brightness of that thorn crown of the great. It earns you the love of men & the praises of a thousand years. Yet I hope the angelical Beldame all-helping all-hated has given you her last lessons & finding you so striding a proficient will dismiss you to a hundred editions & the adoration of the booksellers.

R. W. Emerson

I have never heard from Rich who you wrote had sent his account to me. Let him direct to me at Concord.

A young engineer in Cambridge by name McKean volunteers his services in correcting the proofs of the Miscellanies & he has your Errata.[4]—for love of the reading. . . .[5] Shall we have anthracite coal or wood in your chamber? My old mother is glad you are coming.

Chelsea, London, 15th June, 1838

My dear Emerson,

Our correspondence has fallen into a ravelled state; which would doubtless clear itself could I afford to wait for your next Letter, probably tumbling over the Atlantic brine about this very moment: but I cannot afford to wait, I must write straightway. Your answer to *this* will bring matters round again. I have had two irregular Notes of your writing, or perhaps three; two dated *March*, one by Mr Bancroft's Parcel, bringing twelve *Orations* withal; then some ten days later, just in this very time, another Note by Mr Sumner, whom I have not yet succeeded in seeing, tho' I have attempted it, and hope soon to do it. The Letter he forwarded me from Paris was acknowledged already, I think. And now if the Atlantic will but float me in safe that other promised Letter!

I got your American *French Revolution* a good while ago. It seems to me a very pretty Book indeed, wonderfully so for the money; neither does it seem what we can call *incorrectly* printed so far as I have seen; compared with the last *Sartor* it is correctness itself. Many thanks to you, my Friend, and much good may it do us all! Should there be any more reprinting, I will request you to rectify at least the three following errors, copied out of the English text indeed; nay mark them in your own New English Copy, whether there be reprinting or not: Vol. I. p. 81 last paragraph, *for* September *read* August;

---

[4] Henry Swasey McKean was a Harvard graduate of the class of 1828. He had presumably been given the errata by Loring.

[5] This ellipsis appears in the manuscript.

vol. II. p 344, first line, *for* book of prayer *read* look of prayer; p. 357, *for* blank *read* black (2nd paragraph, "all black"). And so *basta*. And let us be well content about this F. R. on both sides of the water, yours as well as mine.

"Too many cooks!" the Proverb says: it is pity if this new apparition of a Mr Loring should spoil the broth. But I calculate you will adjust it well and smoothly between you, some way or other. How you shall adjust it, or have adjusted it, is what I am practically anxious now to learn. For you are to understand that our English Edition has come to depend partly on yours. After long higgling with the foolish Fraser, I have quitted him, quite quietly, and given "Saunders and Otley, Conduit Street," the privilege of printing a small edition of *Teufelsdröckh* (500 copies), with a prospect of the "Miscellaneous Writings" soon following. Saunders and Otley are at least more reputable persons, they are useful to me also in the business of Lecturing. *Teufelsᵏ* is at Press, to be out very soon; I will send you a correct copy, the only one in America I fancy. The enterprise here too is on the "half-profits" plan, which I compute generally to mean equal partition of the oyster-*shells* and a net result of *zero*. But the thing will be economically useful to me otherwise; as a publication of the "Miscellaneous" also would be; which latter however I confess myself extremely unwilling to undertake the trouble of for *nothing*. To me they are grown or fast growing *obsolete,* these Miscellanies, for most part; if money lie not in them, what does lie for me? Now it strikes me you will infallibly edit these things at least as well as I, and are doing it at any rate; your printing too would seem to be cheaper than ours: I said to Saunders and Otley, Why not have 200 or 300 of this American Edition struck off with "London: Saunders & Otley Conduit Street" on the title-page, and sent over hither in sheets at what price they have cost my friends yonder? Saunders of course threw cold water on this project, but was obliged to admit that there would be some profit in it, and that for me it would be far easier. The grand profit for me is that people would understand better what I mean, and come better about me if I lectured again, which seems the only way of getting any wages at all for me here at present. Pray meditate my project if it be not already too late, hear what your Booksellers say about it, and understand that I will not in any case set to printing till I hear from you in answer to this.

How my sheet is filling, with dull talk about mere economics! I must still add that the *Lecturing* I talked of, last time, is verily over now; and well over. The superfine people listened to the rough utterance with patience, with favour, increasing to the last. I sent you a Newspaper once, to indicate that it was in progress. I know not yet what the money-result is; but I suppose it will enable us to exist here thriftily another year; not without hope of at worst doing the like again when the time comes. It is a great novelty in my lot; felt as a very considerable blessing; and really it has arrived, if it have arrived, in *due* time, for I had begun to get quite impatient of the other method. Poverty and Youth may do; Poverty and Age go badly together.—For the rest, I feel fretted to fiddlestrings; m[y] head and heart all heated, sick,—ah me! The question as ever is: Rest. But then where? My Brother invites us to come to Rome for the winter; my poor sick Wife might perhaps profit by it; as for me, Natty Leather-stocking's Lodge in the Western Wood, I think, were welcomer still. I have a great mind too to run off and see my Mother, by the new railways. What we shall do, whether not stay quietly here, must remain uncertain for a week or two. Write you always hither, till you hear otherwise.

The Orations were right welcome; my *Madeira* one, returned thence with Sterling, was circulating over the West of England. Sterling and Harriet stretched out the right hand with wreathed smiles.[1] I have read, a second or third time. Robert Southey has got a copy, for his own behoof and that of *Lake*land: if he keep his word as to *me,* he may do as much for you or more. Copies are at Cambridge, among the Oxonians too; I have with stingy discretion distributed all my copies but two. Old Rogers, a grim old Dilettante, full of sardonic sense, was heard saying, "It is German Poetry given out in American Prose." Friend Emerson ought to be content:—and has now above all things, as I said, to *be in no haste.* Slow fire does make sweet malt [2]: how true, how true! Also his next work ought to be a *concrete* thing; not *theory* any longer but *deed?* Let him "live it," as he says; that is the way to come to "painting of it." [3] Geometry and the art of design

---

[1] Milton, "L'Allegro," line 28.

[2] As "soft fire makes sweet malt" this proverb is cited seventeen times in Maurice Tilley's *A Dictionary of the Proverbs in England in the 16th and 17th Centuries* (Ann Arbor, 1950), p. 216.

[3] In the *Oration* Emerson had written: "When the artist has exhausted his ma-

being once well over, take the brush, and *andar con Dios!*—Mrs Child has sent me a Book *Philothea*,[4] and a most magnanimous epistle. I have answered as I could. The Book is beautiful, but of a *hectic* beauty, to me not pleasant, even fatal-looking. Such things grow not in the ground, on Mother Earth's honest bosom, but in hothouses,— Sentimental-Calvinist fire traceable underneath! Bancroft also is of the hothouse partly: I have a Note to send him by Sumner; [5] do you thank him meanwhile, and say nothing about *hothouses!* But, on the whole, men ought in New England too to "swallow their formulas"; [6] there is no freedom till then: yet hitherto I find only one man there who seems fairly on the way towards that, or arrived at that. Good speed to *him*. I had to send my wife's love: she is not dangerously ill, but always feeble, and has to struggle to keep erect; the summer always improves her, and this summer too. Adieu, dear Friend; may Good always be with you and yours.   T. Carlyle

                                             Boston   30 July 1838
My dear Sir,
     I am in town today to get what money the booksellers will relinquish from their faithful gripe & have succeeded now in obtaining a first instalment however small. I enclose to you a bill of exchange for fifty pounds sterling, which costs here exactly $242.22 the rate of exchange being 9 per cent. I shall not today trouble you with any account, for

---

terials, when the fancy no longer paints, when thoughts are no longer apprehended and books are a weariness,—he has always the resource *to live* (*Works*, I, 99).

[4] *Philothea* (1836) was a novel about Periclean Greece. On April 7, 1838, Mrs. Child (see above, E.10.7.35, n. 2) wrote Carlyle from Boston that during the preceding summer, "in a remote country town," she had slept with *Sartor Resartus* under her pillow, so "that with the morning light, I might refresh myself from its pages." She thanked him for "that unrhymed, unmeasured *poem* called the French Revolution . . . assuredly . . . a glorious work of art," and she urged him to come to America and lecture to the intellectually undernourished who "go about with mouths wide open, like young ravens seeking food." (NLS, MS 1796).

[5] Bancroft evidently included a volume or two of his *History of the United States* in the "parcel" with the twelve "Orations." A letter of thanks and criticism from Carlyle to Bancroft is published in Howe's *Life and Letters of George Bancroft*, I, 225.

[6] "This was the saying of the old Marquis de Mirabeau concerning his son, *Il a humé toutes les formules,* and is used as a text by Carlyle in his article on Mirabeau" (Norton's note).

my letter must be quickly ready to go by the steam Packet. An exact account has been rendered to me which though its present [1] balance in our favor is less than I expected yet as far as I understand it, agrees well with all that has been promised: at least [2] the balance in our favor when the edition is sold which the booksellers assure me will undoubtedly be done within a year from the publication, must be $760.00, and what more Heaven & the subscribers may grant. I shall follow this letter & bill by a duplicate of the bill in the next packet.

The "Miscellanies" is published in two volumes a copy of which goes to you immediately. Munroe tells me that 250 copies of it are already sold. Writing in a bookshop, my dear friend, I have no power to say aught than that I am heartily & always yours.

R. Waldo Emerson

Concord, 6 August, 1838

My dear friend,

The swift ships are slow when they carry our letters. Your letter dated 15 June arrived here last Friday 3 August. That day I was in Boston, & I have only now got the information necessary to answer it. You have probably already learned from my letter sent by the Royal William [1] (enclosing a bill of Exchange for £50) that our two first volumes of the Miscellanies are published. I have sent you a copy. The edition consists of 1000 copies. Of these 500 are bound, 500 remain in sheets. The title pages, of course, are all printed alike; but the publishers assure me, that new title pages can be struck off at a trifling expense, with the imprint of Saunders & Otley. The cost of a copy in sheets or "folded" (if that means somewhat more?) is .89 cents; & bound, is, $1.15 cents. The retail price is $2.50 a copy; & the author's profit $1.00; & the bookseller's, .35 cents, per copy, according to my understanding of the written contract.

Here I believe you have all the material facts. I think there is no doubt that the book will sell very well here. But if for the reasons you suggest, you wish any part of it you can have it as soon as ships can bring your will. When you see your copy, you will perceive that we

---

[1] The word "footing" was crossed out by Emerson.

[2] The words "it cannot" were crossed out by Emerson.

[1] Emerson's letter of July 30 had been superscribed: "Pr Steam Ship Royal Wm."

have printed half the matter. I should presently begin to print the remainder inclusive of the Article on Lockharts Scott in two more volumes—but now I think I shall wait until I hear from you. Of those books we will print a larger edition say 1250 or 1500 if you want a part of it in London. For I feel confident now that our public here is one thousand strong. Write me therefore *by the steampacket* your wishes.

I am sure you will like our edition. It has been most carefully corrected by two young gentlemen who successively volunteered their services, (the second when the first was called away), & who residing in Cambridge, where the book was printed, could easilier oversee it. They are, Henry S. McKean, an engineer, & Charles Stearns Wheeler, a Divinity Student,[2]—working both for love of you. To one other gentleman I have brought you in debt, Rev. Convers Francis, (brother of Mrs Child) who supplied from his library all the numbers of the Foreign Review from which we printed the work. We could not have done without his books, & he is a noblehearted man who rejoices in you. I have sent to all three, copies of the work as from you & I shall be glad if you will remember to sanction this expressly in your next letter.

Thanks for the letter: thanks for your friendliest seeking of friends for the poor oration. Poor little pamphlet to have gone so far & so high! I am ashamed. I shall however send you a couple more of the thin gentry presently, maugre all your hopes & cautions. I have written & read a kind of Sermon to the senior class of our Cambridge Theological School a fortnight ago; [3] and an address to the Literary Societies of Dartmouth College; [4] for though I hate American pleniloquence, I cannot easily say *No* to young men who bid me speak also. And both these are now in press. The first, I hear is very offensive. I will now try to hold my tongue until next winter.

But I am asked continually when you will come to Boston. Your

[2] Wheeler, a Harvard College roommate of Henry Thoreau, had been during the past year a student in the Harvard Divinity School (Eidson, *Charles Stearns Wheeler,* pp. 10, 16).
[3] The Divinity School Address was delivered on July 15 (Rusk, *Life,* p. 268).
[4] The Dartmouth College Address, later known as *Literary Ethics,* was delivered on July 24. Emerson asked that his ten-dollar fee be spent on books for the college library; among those that the students bought were Carlyle's *Miscellanies (Let RWE,* II, 144n).

lectures are boldly & joyfully expected by brave young men. So do not forget us: and if ever the scale beam trembles, I beseech you, let the love of me decide for America. I will not dare to teaze you on a matter of so many relations, & so important, and especially as I have written out, I believe, my requests, in a letter sent two or three months ago,—but I must see you somewhere, somehow, may it please God! I grieve to hear no better news of your wife. I hoped she was sound & strong ere this & can only hope still. My wife & I send her our hearty love.

　　　　　　　　　　Yours affectionately.　　　　R. W. Emerson.
P. S. at the request of our mutual friend RWE I enclose seconds of Exchange for 50£ to serve in case of need.

　　　　　　　　　　Respectfully　　　　　　　　A Adams [5]
Boston Aug 7. 1838

　　　　　　　　Scotsbrig, Ecclefechan (Annandale, Scotland)
　　　　　　　　　　　　　　　　　　25th Septr 1838
My dear Emerson,

　There cannot any right answer be written you here and now; yet I must write, such answer as I can. You said, "by steam-ship"; and it strikes me with a kind of remorse, on this my first day of leisure and composure, that I have delayed so long. For you must know, this is my Mother's house,—a place to me unutterable as Hades and the Land of Spectres were; likewise that my Brother is just home from Italy, and on the wing thitherward or somewhither swiftly again; in a word, that all is confusion and flutter with me here,—fit only for *silence!* My Wife sent me off hitherward, very sickly and unhappy, out of the London dust, several weeks ago; I lingered in Fifeshire, I was in Edinburgh, in Roxburghshire; have some calls to Cumberland, which I believe I must refuse; and prepare to creep homeward again, refreshed in health, but with a head and heart all seething and tumbling (as the wont is,

　　[5] Abel Adams, of the firm of Barnard and Adams, was a former parishioner of Emerson's and his business adviser (Emerson, *Journals*, X, 431). A second or third of exchange was, according to *The Century Dictionary*, the "second or third of a set of bills of exchange drawn in duplicate or triplicate . . . any one of which being accepted, the others are void." Perhaps by "seconds" Adams means that he has drawn the bill in triplicate: Emerson's letter of October 17 mentions a "third" letter of the summer of 1838, "sent . . . by another channel, enclosing a duplicate of the bill of Exchange."

in such cases), and averse to *pens* beyond all earthly implements. But my Brother is off for Dumfries this morning; you before all others deserve an hour of my solitude. I will abide by business; one *must* write about that.

Your Bill and duplicate of a Bill for £50, with the two letters that accompanied them, you are to know then, did duly arrive at Chelsea; and the larger Letter (of the 6th August) was forwarded to me hither some two weeks ago. I had also, long before that, one of the friendliest of letters from you with a clear and most inviting description of the Concord Household, its inmates and appurtenances; and the announcement, evidently authentic, that an apartment and heart's welcome was ready there for my Wife and me; that we were to come quickly, and stay for a twelvemonth. Surely no man has such friends as I. We ought to say, May the Heavens give us thankful hearts! For in truth there are blessings which do, like sun-gleams in wild weather, make this rough life beautiful with rainbows here and there. Indicating, I suppose, that there *is* a Sun, and general Heart of Goodness, behind all that;—for which, as I say again, let us be thankful evermore.

My Wife says she received your American Bill of so many pounds sterling for the Revolution Book, with a "pathetic feeling," which brought "tears" to her eyes.[1] From beyond the waters there is a hand held out; beyond the waters too live brothers. I would only the Book were an Epic, a *Dante* or undying thing, that New England might boast in aftertimes of this feat of hers, and put stupid poundless and penniless Old England to the blush about it! But after all, that is no matter; the feebler the well-meant Book is, the more "pathetic" is the whole transaction: and so we will go on, fuller than ever of "desperate hope" [2] (if you know what that is), with a feeling one would not give and could not get for several money-bags; and say or think, Long live true friends and Emersons,—and (in Scotch phrase) "May ne'er waur be amang us"!—I will buy something permanent, I think, out of this £50, and call it either *Ebenezer or Yankee-doodle-doo.* May good be repaid you manifold, my Kind Brother; may good be ever with you, my Kind Friends all!

[1] Cf. *Letters and Memorials,* I, 75.

[2] Here Carlyle seems to be quoting himself. He wrote to Sterling on December 25, 1837, about "the thing I used to call 'desperate hope'" (Froude, *Thomas Carlyle: Life in London,* I, 105). Also, see above, C.11.5.36.

But now as to this edition of the Miscellanies (poor things), I really think my Wife is wisest, who says I ought to leave you altogether to your own resources with it, America having an art of making money out of my Books, which England is unfortunately altogether without.[3] Besides till I once *see* the Two Volumes now under way, and can let a Bookseller see them, there could no bargain be made on the subject. We will let it rest there, therefore. Go on with your second Two Volumes as if there were no England extant, according to your own good judgement. When I get to London, I will consult some of the blockheads, with the Book in my hand: if we do want 200 copies, you can give us them with a trifling loss. It is possible they may make some better proposal about an Edition here: that depends on the fate of *Sartor* here, at present trying itself; which I have not in the least ascertained. For the present, thank as is meet all friends in your world that have interested themselves for me. Alas, I have nothing to give them but thanks. Henry Macklean, Charles Wheeler, Convers Francis: these Names shall, if it please Heaven, become Persons for me, one day. Well!—But I will say nothing more. That too is of the things on which all Words are poor to Silence. Good to the Good and Kind!—

A Letter from me must have crossed that *descriptive* Concord one, on the ocean, I think. Our correspondence is now standing on its feet. I well write to you again, whether I hear from you or not, so soon as my hand finds its cunning a[gain] in London,—so soon as I can see there what is to be done or said. All goes decidedly better, I think. My Wife was and is much healthier than last year, than in any late year. I myself get visibly quieter: my preternatural *Meditations in Hades* apropos of this Annandale of mine are calm compared with those of last year. By another Course of Lectures I have a fair prospect of living for another season; nay people call it a "new profession" I have devised for myself, and say I may live by it as many years as I like. This too is partly the fruit of my poor Book; one should not say that it was worth nothing to me even in money. Last year I fancied my audience mainly the readers of it; drawn round me, in spite of many things, by force of it. Let us be content. I have Jesuits, Sweden-borgians, old Quakeresses, *omne cum Proteus* [4]—God help me, no man ever had so confused a public!—I salute you my dear Friend and your

[3] Cf. *Letters and Memorials*, I, 79.   [4] Horace, *Odes*, I, ii, 7.

hospitable circle. May blessings be on your kind household, on your kind hearts. T. Carlyle.

A copy of the English *Teufelsdröckh* has lain with your name on it these two months in Chelsea; waiting an opportunity. It is worth nothing to you: a dingy ill-managed edition; but correct or nearly correct as to printing; it is right that such should be in your hands in case of need. The New England Pamphlets will be greedily expected. More than one inquires of me, Has that Emerson of yours written nothing else? And I have lent them the little Book *Nature* till it is nearly thumbed to pieces. Sterling is gone to Italy for the winter since I left town; swift as a flash! I cannot teach him the great art of *sitting still;* his fine qualities are really like to waste for want of that.

I read your paragraph to Miss Martineau; she received it, as she was bound, with a good grace. But I doubt, I doubt, O Ralph Waldo Emerson, thou hast not been sufficiently ecstatic about her—thou, graceless exception, confirmatory of a rule! In truth there *are* bores, of the first and of all lower magnitudes. Patience and shuffle the cards.⁵—

Concord, 17 October, 1838.

My dear friend,

I am quite uneasy that I do not hear from you. On the 21 July, I wrote to you & enclosed a remittance of £50 by a bill of exchange on Baring & Brothers, drawn by Chandler, Howard, & Co. which was sent in the steamer *Royal William* ˣ On the 2 August, I received your letter of inquiry respecting our edition of the *Miscellanies,* & wrote a few days later in reply; that we could send you out two or three hundred copies of our two first volumes, in sheets, at 89 cents per copy of two vols., & the small additional price of the new title-page. I said also that I would wait until I heard from you before commencing the printing of the two last volumes of the Miscellanies, and, if you desired it, would print any number of copies, with a title-page for London. This letter went in a steamer, the *Great Western* ˣ probably,

---

⁵ *Don Quixote,* bk. II, ch. xxxiii.

ˣ Perhaps I misremember the names. The first shd be last. [R. W. E.] Cf. Mark

—about the 10 or 12 Augt. I have heard nothing from you since. I trust my letters have not miscarried. (A third was sent also by another channel, enclosing a duplicate of the bill of Exchange.) With more fervency, I trust that all goes well in the house of my friend;—and I suppose that you are absent on some salutary errand of repairs & recreation. Use, I pray you, your earliest hour in certifying me of the facts.

One word more in regard to business. I believe I expressed some surprise, in the July letter, that the book sellers should have no greater balance for us, at this settlement. I have since studied the account better, & see that we shall not be disappointed in the year of obtaining at least the sum first promised, $760.00; but the whole expense of the edition is paid out of the copies first sold, & our profits depend on the last sales. The edition is almost gone, & you shall have an account at the end of the year.

In a letter within a twelvemonth I have urged you to pay us a visit in America, & in Concord. I have believed that you would come, one day, & do believe it. But if, on your part, you have been generous & affectionate enough to your friends here—or curious enough concerning our society to wish to come, I think you must postpone, for the present, the satisfaction of your friendship & your curiosity. At this moment, I would not have you here, on any account. The publication of my "Address to the Divinity College," (copies of which I sent you) has been the occasion of an outcry in all our leading local newspapers against my "infidelity," "pantheism," & "atheism." The writers warn all & sundry against me, & against whatever is supposed to be related to my connexion of opinion, &c; against Transcendentalism, Goethe & Carlyle.[1] I am heartily sorry to see this last aspect of the storm in our washbowl. For, as Carlyle is nowise guilty, & has unpopularities of his own, I do not wish to embroil him in my parish-differences. You were getting to be a great favorite with us all here, and are daily a greater, with the American public, but just now, *in Boston,* where I am known

---

10:31. Emerson remembered the names of the ships correctly but not the dates of the letters—Ed.

[1] Andrews Norton's anonymous article "The New School in Literature and Religion," in the Boston *Daily Advertiser* of August 27, 1838, was a sharp and effective attack on Transcendentalism with particular attention to Emerson and "that hyper-Germanized Englishman, Carlyle."

as your editor, I fear you lose by the association. Now it is indispensable to your right influence here, that you should never come before our people as one of a clique, but as a detached, that is, universally associated man; so I am happy, as I could not have thought, that you have not yet yielded yourself to my entreaties. Let us wait a little until this foolish clam[or] be overblown. My position is fortunately such as to put me quite out of the reach of any real inconvenience from the panic strikers or the panic struck; &, indeed, so far as this uneasiness is a necessary result of mere inaction of mind, it seems very clear to me that, if I live, my neighbors must look for a great many more shocks, & perhaps harder to bear. The article on German Religious Writers in the last Foreign Q. R. suits our meridian as well as yours; as is plainly signified by the circumstance that our newspapers copy into their columns the opening tirade *& no more*.[2] Who wrote that paper? And who wrote the paper on Montaigne in the Westminster? [3] I read with great satisfaction the Poems & Thoughts of Archaeus in Blackwood: "The Sexton's daughter" is a beautiful poem: and I recognize in them all, *the* Soul, with joy & love.[4] Tell me of the author's health & welfare; or will not he love me so much as to write me a letter with his own hand?—And tell me of yourself,—what task of love & wisdom the muses impose: & what happiness the good God sends to you & yours. I hope your wife has not forgotten me.

Yours affectionately,   R. W. Emerson

The Miscellanies Vols I & II are a popular book. About 500 copies have been sold. The second article on Jean Paul works with might on the inner man of young men. I hate to write you letters on business & facts like this. There are so few Friends that I think some time I

---

[2] *The Foreign Quarterly Review*, XXI (July, 1838), 247–83. The first three paragraphs of this article, which was primarily concerned with the works of J. H. Jung-Stilling, made a strong statement of the popular feeling about German mysticism and skepticism, but they were followed by a respectful treatment of German evangelicalism and a final argument that German theology and philosophy must be worth examining. The Boston *Courier* of September 24, 1838, reprinted the first three paragraphs without comment.

[3] "Montaigne and His Writings," *London and Westminister Review*, XXIX (August, 1838), 321–52. The author was John Sterling.

[4] John Sterling, writing as "Archaeus," had a long poem, "The Sexton's Daughter," in the July issue and some prose "Thoughts and Images" in the August issue. He was nowhere identified.

shall meet you nearer, for I love you more than is fit to say. W. H. Channing has written a Critique on you, which I suppose he has sent you in the Boston Review.[5]

5. Cheyne Row, Chelsea, London
7th Novr, 1838

My dear Friend,

It is all right; all your Letters with their inclosures have arrived in due succession: the last, inquiring after the fate of the others, came this morning. I was in Scotland, as you partly conjecture; I wrote to you already (tho' not without blameable delay), from my Mother's house in Annandale, a confused scrawl, which I hope has already got to hand, and quieted your kind anxieties: I am as well as usual in health, my Wife better than usual; nothing is amiss, except my negligence and indolence, which has put you to this superfluous solicitude on my account. However, I have an additional Letter by it; you must pardon me, you must not grudge me that undeserved pleasure, the reward of *evil*-doing. I may well *say*, you are a blessing to me on this Earth; no Letter comes from you with other than good tidings,—or can come while you live there to love me.

The Bill was thrust duly into Baring's brass slit "for acceptance," on my return hither some three weeks ago; and will, no doubt, were the days of grace run, come out in the shape of Fifty Pounds Sterling: a very curious product indeed. Do you know what I think of doing with it? *Dyspepsia,* my constant attendant in London, is incapable of help in my case by any medicine of appliance except one only, Riding on Horseback. With a good horse to whirl me over the world for two hours daily, I used to keep myself supportably well. Here, the maintenance of a Horse far transcends my means; yet it seems hard I should not for one little while be in a kind of approximate health in this Babylon where I have my bread to seek: it is like swimming with a millstone round your neck,—ah me! In brief, I am about half resolved to buy myself a sharp little nag with twenty of these Transatlantic Pounds, and ride him till the other thirty be eaten: I will call the creature "Yankee," and kind thoughts of those far away shall be with

---

[5] "Carlyle's French Revolution," *Boston Quarterly Review,* I (October, 1838), 407–17.

me every time I mount him. Will not that do? My wife says, it is the best plan I have had for years, and strongly urges it on. My kind friends!

As to those copies of the *Carlyle Miscellanies,* I unfortunately still can say nothing, except what was said in the former (Scotch) letter, that you must proceed in the business with an eye to America and not to us. My Booksellers Saunders and Ottley have no money for me, no definite offer in money to make for those 200 copies, of which you seem likely to make money if we simply leave them alone. I have asked these Booksellers, I have asked Fraser too: What will you *give me in ready money* for 250 copies of that book, sell it afterwards as you can? They answer always, we must see it first. Now the copy long ago sent me has never come to hand; I have asked for it of Kennet, but without success; I have nothing for it but to wait the winds and chances. Meanwhile S. and Otley want forsooth a "Sketches of German Literature" in three volumes; then a "Miscellanies in three volumes": that is *their* plan of publishing an English edition; and the outlook they hold out for me is certain trouble in this matter, and recompense entirely uncertain. I think on the whole it is extremely likely I shall apply to you for 250 copies (that is their favourite number) of these 4 volumes (nay if it be of any moment, you can bind me down to it *now,* and take it for sure): but I cannot yet send you the title-page; no bookseller purchasing till "we see it first." But after all will it suit America to print an *unequal* number of your two pairs of volumes? Do not the two together make the work? On the whole, consider that I shall in all likelihood want 250 copies, and consider it certain if that will serve the enterprise: we must leave it here today. I will stir in it now however, and take no rest till in one way or other you do get a titlepage from me, or some definite deliverance on the matter. O Athenians what a trouble I *give,* having *got* your applauses! [1]

Kennet the Bookseller gave me yesterday (on my way to "the City" with that Brother of mine the Italian Doctor who is here at present and a great lover of yours) ten copies of your Dartmouth oration: we read it over dinner in a chophouse in Bucklersbury, amid the clatter of some fifty stand of knives and forks; and a second time more leisurely at Chelsea here. A right brave Speech; announcing, in its own

---

[1] In the essay "Voltaire" Carlyle had attributed to Alexander the exclamation: "O Athenians, what toil do I undergo to please you!" (*Works TC,* XXVI, 437).

way, with emphasis of full conviction, to all whom it may concern, that great forgotten truth, *Man is still Man.* May it awaken a pulsation under the ribs of Death! I believe the time is come for such a Gospel. They must speak it out who have it,—with what audience there may be. I have given away two copies this morning; I will take care of the rest. Go on, and speed.—And now where is the heterodox Divinity one; which awakens such "tempest in a washbowl"; b[rings] Goethe, Transcendentalism and Carlyle into question, and on the whole evinces "what dif[ference] New England also makes between *Pan*theism and *Pot*-theism"? I long to see that; I expect to congratulate you on that too. Meanwhile we will let the washbowl storm itself out; and Emerson at Concord shall recognise it for a washbowl storming, and hold on his way. As to my share in it, grieve not for half an instant. Pantheism, Pottheism, Mydoxy, Thydoxy are nothing at all to me, a weariness the whole jargon, which I avoid speaking of, decline listening to: *Live,* for God's sake, with what Faith thou couldst get; leave off *speaking* about Faith! Thou knowest it not. Be *silent,* do not speak.—As to you, my friend, you are even to go on, giving still harder shocks if need be; and should I come into censure by means of you, there or here, think that I am proud of my company; that, as the boy Hazlitt said after hearing Coleridge, "I will go with that man"; [2] or as our wild Burns has it: "Wi' sic as he where'er he be/ May I be saved or damned!" [3]— Oime! what a foolish goose of a world this is. If it were not here and there an articulate-speaking man, one would be all-too lonely.

This is nothing at all like the Letter I meant to write you; but I will write again I trust in few days, and the first paragraph shall if possible hold all the business. I have much to tell you—which perhaps is as well not written. O that I did see you face to face! But the time shall come, if Heaven will. Why not *you* come over, since I cannot? There is a room here, there is welcome here, and two friends always. It must be done one way or the other.

I will take care of your messages to Sterling. He is in Florence; *he* was the Author of *Montaigne.* The F. Q. Reviewer of *Strauss* I take to be one Blackie [4] an Advocate in Edin^r, a frothy, semi-confused dis-

[2] This is in the spirit but not in the words of Hazlitt's "My First Acquaintance with Poets," which had been reprinted in *Literary Remains* in 1836.

[3] "Epitaph for Gavin Hamilton, Esq."

[4] John Stuart Blackie had in recent years contributed many articles on German literature to *Blackwood's* and *The Foreign Quarterly Review;* this was a review

ciple of mine and other men's; I guess this, but I have not read the Article: the man Blackie is from Aberdeen, has been roaming over Europe, and carries more sail than ballast. Brother John, spoken of above, is knocking at the door even now; he is for Italy again we expect in few days, on a better appointment: know that you have a third friend in him under this roof,—a man who quarrels with me all day in a small way, and loves me with the whole soul of him. My wife demanded to have "room for one line." What she is to write I know not, except it be what she has said, holding up the pamphlet, "Is it not a noble thing? None of them all but he" &c &c. I will write again without delay when the stray volumes arrive; before that if they linger. Commend me to all the kind household of Concord: wife mother and son.   Ever yours   T. Carlyle

"Forgotten you"? O no indeed! If there were nothing else to re-member you by, I should never forget the Visitor, who years ago in the Desart descend on us, out of the clouds, as it were, and made one day there look like enchantment for us, and left me weeping that it was only *one* day. When I think of America, it is of you—neither Harriet Martineau nor any one else succeeds in giving me a more extended idea of it. When I wish to see America it is still you—and those that are yours—I read all that you write with an interest which I feel in no other writing but my Husband's—or it were nearer the truth to say there is no other writing of living men but yours and his that I *can* read—God Bless you and Weib und Kind—Surely I shall some day see you all.   Your affectionate   Jane Carlyle

Chelsea, London, 15th November, 1838—

Dear Emerson,

Hardly above a week ago, I wrote to you in immediate answer to some friendly inquiries produced by negligence of mine: the Letter is probably tumbling on the salt waves at this hour, in the belly of the Great Western; or perhaps it may be still on firm land waiting, in which case this will go along with it. I had written before out of

<hr />

of D. F. Strauss's *Das Leben Jesu* in the issue of October, 1838. But Emerson had asked about another article (see above, E.10.17.38, n. 3), and he was misled by Carlyle's reply into thinking that Blackie was the author of that (*Let RWE*, II, 179).

Scotland, a Letter of mere acknowledgement and postponement; you must have received that before now, I imagine. Our small piece of business is now become articulate, and I will despatch it in a paragraph. Pity my stupidity that I did not put the thing on this footing long ago! It never struck me till the other day that tho' no copy of our "Miscellanies" would turn up for inspection here, and no Bookseller would bargain for a thing unseen, I myself might bargain, and leave *their* hesitations resting on their own basis. In fine I have rejected all their schemes of printing "Miscellaneous Works" here, printing "Sketches of German Literature," or printing anything whatever on the "half-profits system," which is like toilsomely scattering seed into the sea; and I settled yesterday with Fraser to give him the American sheets, and let them sell *themselves,* on clear principles, or remain unsold if they like. I find it infinitely the best plan, and to all appearance the profitablest as to money that could have been desired for me.[1]

What you have to do therefore is to get 250 copies (*in sheets*) of the whole Four Volumes so soon as the second two are printed, and have them with the proper titlepage sent off hither to Fraser's address; the sooner the better. The American titlepage, instead of "Boston:" &c at the bottom, will require to bear, in three lines: "London:/ James Fraser, 215 Regent Street/ 1839/." Fraser is anxious that you should not spell him with a *z;* your man can look on the Magazine, and beware. I suppose also you should print *labels* for the backs of the four volumes, to be used by the *half*-binder; they do the books in that way here now: but if it occasion any difficulty, never mind this; it was not spoken of to Fraser, and is my own conjecture merely; the thing can be managed in various other ways. Two hundred and fifty copies, then, of the entire book: there is nothing else to be attended to that you do not understand as well as I. Fraser will announce it in his Magazine; the eager select public will wait. Probably there is no chance before the middle of March or so? Do not hurry yourselves, or at all change your rate for *us:* but so soon as the work is ready in the course of Nature, the earliest conveyance to the Port of London will bring a little cargo, which one will welcome with a strange feeling! I declare myself delighted with the plan; an altogether romantic kind of plan,

---

[1] "I have fixed with Fraser to sell for *my* behoof 250 copies of it; I count on gaining pretty certainly £200 by the job": Carlyle to his mother, November 28, 1838 (*New Letters*, I, 145).

of romance and reality: fancy me riding on *"Yankee"* withal, at the time, and considering what a curious world this is, that bakes bread for one beyond the great ocean-stream, and how a poor man is not left after all to be trodden into the gutters, tho' the fight went sore against him, and he saw no backing anywhere. *Allah akbar,* God is great; no saying truer than that.—And so now, by the blessing of Heaven, we will talk no more of business this day.

My employments, my outlooks, condition and history here, were a long chapter; on which I could like so well to talk with you face to face; but as for writing of them, it is a mere mockery. In these four years, so full of pain and toil, I seem to have lived four decades. By degrees, the creature gets accustomed to its element; the salamander learns to live in fire, and be of the same temperature with it. Ah me! I feel as if grown old; innumerable things are become weary, flat, stale and unprofitable.[2] And yet perhaps I am not old, only wearied, and there is a stroke or two of work in me yet. For the rest, the fret and agitation of this Babylon wears me down: it is the most unspeakable life; of sunbeams and miry clay; a contradiction which no head can reconcile. Pain and poverty are not wholesome; but praise and flattery along with them are poison: God deliver us from that; it carries madness in the very breath of it! On the whole, I say to myself, what thing is then so good as *rest?* A sad case it is, and a frequent one in my circle, to be entirely cherubic, *all* face and wings. "Mes enfans," said a French gentleman to the cherubs in the Picture, "Mes enfans, asseyez-vous."— "Monseigneur," answer they "il n'y a pas de quoi!"[3] I rejoice rather in laziness; proving that I *can* sit.—But, after all, ought I not to be thankful! I positively can in some sort exist here for the while; a thing I had been for many years ambitious of to no purpose. I shall have to lecture again in spring, Heaven knows on what; it will be a wretched fever for me; but once thro' it, there will be board wages for another

---

[2] Cf. *Hamlet,* act I, scene ii, line 129.

[3] This joke, the origin of which I do not know, was so familiar even sixty years later that Henry James could expect his readers to catch a fragmentary allusion to it. In chapter IV of *The Turn of the Screw* he wrote, with reference to Miles and Flora: "They were like the cherubs of the anecdote, who had—morally, at any rate—nothing to whack!" Balzac, in one of the *Contes Drolatiques,* "Les Bons Propos des Religieuses de Poissy," offers a version in which the exchange of invitation and reply is between God and the angels. Theodor Reik, at the beginning of his book *Of Love and Lust,* quotes the cherub-archbishop version, attributing it to Montaigne, where, however, I have been unable to find it.

year. The wild Ishmael can hunt in *this* desart too, it would seem. I say, I will be thankful; and wait quietly what farther is to come, or whether anything farther. But indeed, to speak candidly, I do feel sometimes as if another Book were growing in me,—tho' I almost tremble to think of it. Not for *this* winter, O no! I will write an Article merely, or some such thing, and read trash if better be not. This I do believe is my horoscope for the next season: an Article on something, about New-Years day (the Westminster Editor,[4] a goodnatured admiring swan-goose from the North Country, will not let me rest); then Lectures; then—what? I am for some practical subject too; none of your pictures in the air, or *aesthetisches Zeug* (as Müllner's wife called it, Müllner of the "Midnight *Blade*"):[5] nay I cannot get up the steam on any such hest; it is extremely irksome as well as pointless at present. In the next Westminster Review therefore if you see a small scrub of a Paper signed "S.P.," on one Varnhagen a German,[6] say that it is by "Simon Pure," or by "Scissars and Paste," or even by "Soaped Pig"— whom no man shall catch! Truly it is a secret which you must not mention: I was driven to it by the swan-goose above-mentioned, not Mill but another. Let this [suf]fice for my winter's history: may the summer be more productive.

As for Concord and New England, alas my Friend I should but deface your Idyllion . . . an ugly contradiction, did I come in such mood as mine is. I am older in years than you; but in Humour I am older by centuries. What a hope is in that ever-young heart; cheerful, healthful as the morning! And as for me, you have no conception what a crabbed sulky piece of sorrow and dyspepsia I am grown; and growing, if I do not draw bridle. Let me gather heart a little! I have not forgotten Concord of the West; no, it lies always beautiful in the blue of the horizon, afar off and yet attainable; it is a great possession to

[4] John Robertson: see below, C.2.8.39, and Packe, *The Life of John Stuart Mill,* p. 211.

[5] "Midnight Blade" is a playful mistranslation: in "German Playwrights" (*Works TC*, XXVI, 391) Carlyle had rendered the title as "Midnight Paper." The *Mitternachtsblatt* was edited from 1826 to 1829 by the dramatist Adolph Müllner. The day after Müllner's death his widow said to his friend and biographer Schütz that everything would have gone well with her husband if he had not got that aesthetic stuff into his head (Schütz, *Müllner's Leben, Charakter und Geist,* p. 53).

[6] "Varnhagen von Ense's Memoirs," a review of memoirs and other works by the German soldier and statesman K. A. Varnhagen von Ense, published in *The London and Westmister Review,* XXXII (December, 1838), 60–84.

me, should it even never be attained. But I have got to consider lately
that it is you who are coming hither first. That is the right way, is
it not? New England is becoming more than ever part of Old England;
why, you are nearer to us now than Yorkshire was a hundred years
ago; this is literally a fact: you can come *without* making your will.
It is one of my calculations that all Englishmen from all zones and
hemispheres will, for a good while yet, resort occasionally to the
Mother-Babel, and see a thing or two there. Come if you dare; I said
there was a room, houseroom and heartroom, constantly waiting you
here; and you shall see blockheads by the million. *Pickwick* himself
shall be visible; innocent young Dickens, reserved for a questionable
fate. The great Wordsworth shall talk till you yourself pronounce him
to be a bore.[7] Southey's complexion is still healthy mahogany-brown,
with a fleece of white hair, and eyes that seem running at full gallop.
Leigh Hunt, "man of genius in the shape of a Cockney," is my near
neighbour, full of quips and cranks,[8] with goodhumour and no com-
mon-sense. Old Rogers with his pale head, white, bare, and cold as
snow, will look on you with those large blue eyes, cruel, sorrowful, and
that sardonic shelf-chin.—This is the man, O Rogers, that wrote the
German Poetry in American Prose; consider him well!—But whither
am I running? My sheet is done!

My Brother John returns again almost immediately to Italy. He has
got appointed Travelling Doctor to a certain Duke of Buccleuch, the
chief of our Scotch Dukes: an excellent position for him as far as
externals go. His departure will leave me lonelier; but I must reckon
it for the best: especially I must begin working. Harriet Martineau is
coming hither this evening; with beautiful enthusiasm for the Blacks
and others. She is writing a Novel: the first American book proved
generally rather wearisome, the second not so; we have since been
taught (not I) "How to observe." [9] Suppose you and I promulgate a
treatise next, "How to *see*"? The old plan was, to have a pair of eyes
first of all, and then to open them and endeavour with your whole
strength to *look*. The good Harriett! But "God," as the Arabs say,

[7] On March 21, 1837, Carlyle wrote to his brother John: "Wordsworth is in Town;
but I declined going near him: one is too sick and busy for *blethers* of that sort"
(NLS, MS 523).

[8] See Milton, "L'Allegro," line 27.

[9] Title of a book by Harriet Martineau on "manners and morals," published in
1838.

"has given to every people a Prophet (or Poet) in its own speech": [10] and behold now Unitarian mechanical Formalism was to have its Poetess too; and stragglings of genius were to spring up even thro' that like grass thro' a Macadam highway!—Adieu, my Friend. I wait still for your heterodox speech; and love you always.   T. Carlyle

An English *Sartor* goes off for you this day; thro' Kennet, to C. C. Little & J. Brown of Boston; the likeliest conveyance. It is correctly printed, and that is all. Its fate here (the fate of the publication I mean) remains unknown; "unknown and unimportant." [11]

Chelsea, London, 2nd December, 1838—

My dear Emerson,

Almost the very day after my last Letter went off, the long-expected two volumes of "Miscellanies" arrived. The heterodox pamphlet has never yet come to hand. I am now to write to you again about that "Miscellany" concern: the fourth letter, I do believe; but it is confirmatory of the foregoing three, and will be the last, we may hope.

Fraser is charmed with the look of your two volumes; declares them unsurpassable by art of his; and wishes (what is the main part of this message) that you would send his cargo in the *bound* state, bound and lettered as these are, with the sole difference that the leaves be *not* cut, or shaved on the sides, our English fashion being to have them *rough*. He is impatient that the Book were here; desires farther that it be sent to the Port of London rather than another Port, and that it be packed in *boxes* "to keep the corners of the volumes safe,"—all which I doubt not the Packers and Shippers of New England have dexterity enough to manage for the best, without desire of his. If you have printed off nothing yet, I will desire for my own behoof that Two hundred and *sixty* be the number sent; I find I shall need some ten to give away: if your first sheet is printed off, let the number stand as it was. It would be an improvement if you could print our titlepages on paper a little stronger; that would stand *ink*, I mean: the fly-leaves in the same, if you have such paper convenient; if not, not. Farther as to the matter of the titlepage, it seems to me your Printer might give

---

[10] See above, C.6.1.37, n. 4.

[11] Possibly a translation of a phrase from Euripides' *Iphigenia at Aulis*, line 16.

a bolder and broader type to the words "Critical and Miscellaneous," and add after "Essays" with a colon (:), the line "Collected and Republished," with a colon also; then the "By" &c. "In Four Volumes./ Vol I" &c I mean that we want in general a little more ink and decisiveness: shew your man the titlepage of the English "F. Revolution," or look at it yourself, and you will know. R. W. E.'s "Advertisement," [1] friendly and good, as all his dealings are to me ward, will of course be suppressed in the English copies. I see not that with propriety I can say anything by way of substitute: silence and the New England *imprint* will tell the story as eloquently as there is need.

For the rest you must tell Mr Loring, and all men who had a hand in it along with you, that I am altogether right well pleased with this edition, and find it far beyond my expectation. To my two young Friends Henry S. McKean (be so good as write these names more indisputably for me) and Charles Stearns Wheeler, in particular, I will beg you to express emphatically my gratitude; they have stood by me with right faithfulness, and made the correctest printing; a *great* service: had I known that there were such eyes and heads acting in behalf of me then, I would have scraped out the Editorial blotches too (notes of admiration, dashes, "we thinks" &c &c. common in Jeffrey's time in the Edin^r Review) and London misprints; which are almost the only deformities that remain now. It is *extremely* correct printing wherever I have looked, and many things are silently amended; [2] it is the most fundamental service of all. I have not the other *Articles* by me at present; I think they are of themselves a little more correct; at all events there are nothing but *misprints* to deal with;—the Editors, by this time, had got bound up to let me alone. In the "Life of Scott" fourth page of it (p. 296 of our edition), there is a sentence to be deleted. "It will tell us, say they, little new and nothing pleasing to know": out with this, for it is nonsense, and was marked for erasure in the *Ms.* I daresay. I know with certainty no more at present.

Fraser is to sell the 4 volumes at 2 guineas here. On studying accurately your program of the American mercantile method, I stood

---

[1] See above, Introduction, p. 22.

[2] Cf. this sentence from Johnson's "Preface to Shakespeare": "These corruptions I have often silently rectified" (*Selections from Samuel Johnson*, ed. R. W. Chapman, p. 259).

amazed to contrast it with our English one. The Bookseller here admits that he could by diligent bargaining get up such a book for something like the same cost or a *little* more; but the "laws of the trade" deduct from the very front of the selling-price—how much think you?—*forty per cent* and odd, where your man has only fifteen, for the mere act of vending! To cover all, they charge that enormous price. (A man, while I stood consulting with Fraser, came in, and asked for "Carlyle's Revolution"; they shewed it him, he asked the price; and exclaimed, "Guinea and a half! I can get it from A[meri]ca for nine shillings!" and indignantly went his way;—not without reason) [There] are "laws of the trade," which ought to be *repealed;* which I will take the li[berty] of contravening to all lengths by all opportunities—if I had but the power! But if this joint-stock American plan prosper, it will answer rarely. Fraser's first "French Revolution" for instance will be done, he calculates, about New Years day; and a second edition wanted; mine to do with what I like. If you in America wanted more also—? I leave you to think of this.—And now enough, enough!

My Brother went from us last Tuesday; ought to be in Paris yesterday. I am yet writing nothing; feel forsaken, sad, sick, not unhappy. In general Death seems beautiful to me; sweet and great. But Life also is beautiful, is great and divine, were it never to be joyful any more. I read Books, my Wife sewing by me, with the light of a sinumbra,[3] in a little apartment made snug against the winter; and am happiest when all men leave me alone, or nearly all—tho' many men love me rather, ungrateful that I am. My present book is *Horace Walpole;* I get endless stuff out of it; epic, tragic, lyrical, didactic: all *in*articulate indeed. An old blind schoolmaster in Annan used to ask with endless anxiety when a new scholar was offered him, "But are ye sure *he's not a Dunce?*" It is really the one thing needful in a man; for indeed (if we will candidly understand it) *all* else is presupposed in that. Horace Walpole is no dunce, not a fibre of him is duncish.—Your Friend Sumner was here yesterday, a good while, for the first time: an ingenious cultivated courteous man; a little sensitive or so, and with no

[3] An oil lamp with a ground glass globe, designed to give a shadowless and diffused light. "We have got a most beautiful Lamp (of the *Sinumbra* kind)," wrote Carlyle to his mother on September 12, 1834, ". . . and sit by it nightly over our needle-work & papers, really most cheerfully illuminated, at no great cost" (NLS, MS 511). On February 15, 1838, he reported to his mother: ". . . by aid of paper-stuffing . . . and shutting of folding-doors, I have made myself a very snug place" (NLS, MS 520).

other fault that I discerned. He borrowed my copy of your Dartmouth business, and bound himself to return with it soon. Some approve of that here, some condemn: my wife and another lady call it better even than the former, I not so good. And now the Heterodox, the Heterodox, where is that? Adieu my dear friend. Commend me to the Concord Household, to the little Boy, to his Grandmother and Mother and Father; we must all meet some day,—or *some no-day* then (as it shall please God)! My Wife heartily greets you all.

Ever yours   T. Carlyle

I sent your book, message and address to Sterling; he is in Florence or Rome. Read the Article *Simonides* by him in the *London & Westr:* [4] brilliant prose, translations—wooden? His signature is £ (Pounds *Sterling!*).—*Now* you are to write *soon?* I always forgot to tell you, there came long since two packages evidently in your hand, marked "One Printed Sheet," and "the Newspaper"; for which the Postman demanded about 15 shillings: *rejected*. After considerable correspondence the Newspaper was again offered me at *ten pence;* the *sheet* unattainable altogether: "No," even at tenpence. The fact is, it was wrong wrapt that Newspaper. Leave it open at the ends, and try me again, once. I think it will come almost gratis. Steam and iron are making all the Planet into one Village—A Mr Dwight wrote to me about the dedicating of some German translations: *Yes.* What are they or he? [5]— Your *Sartor* is off thro' Kennet. Could you send me two copies of the American *Life of Schiller,* if the thing is fit for making a present of, and easy to be got? If not, do not mind it at all.—Addio!

[4] A review of a new edition of the works of Simonides by F. G. Schneidewin, in *The London and Westminster Review*, XXXII (December, 1838), 99–136.

[5] John Sullivan Dwight was a young Unitarian minister who had recently taken Emerson's place in the church at East Lexington. His volume of translations was part of George Ripley's *Specimens of Foreign Standard Literature;* it was entitled *Select Minor Poems translated from the German of Goethe and Schiller with Notes,* and it was dedicated "To Thomas Carlyle, as a slight token of admiration and gratitude." Dwight's letter of October, 1838, and Carlyle's friendly and courteous answer are printed in George Willis Cooke's *John Sullivan Dwight,* pp. 22–26.

1839

Concord, 13 Jany 1839

My dear friend,

I am not now in any Condition to write a letter having neither the facts from the booksellers which you would know touching our future plans; nor yet a satisfactory account balanced & settled of our past dealings; &, lastly, no time to write what I would say,—as my poor lectures are in full course & absorb all my wits; but as the Royal William will not wait,—& as I have a hundred pounds to send on account of the sales of the French Revolution I must steal a few minutes to send my salutations. I have received all your four good letters: and you are a good & generous man to write so many. Two came on the 2d & 3d January & the last on the 9th. If the bookselling Munroe had answered me yesterday as he ought I should be able to satisfy you as to the time when to expect our cargo of Miscellanies. The 3d & 4th vols are now printing: tis a fortnight since we begun. You shall have 250 copies. I am not quite sure you can have more & bound & *entitled* & directed as you desire at least according to the best ability of our printer, as far as the typography is concerned, and we will speed the work as fast as we can. but as we have but a single copy of Fraser's magazine we do not get on rapidly. The *French Revolution* was all sold more than a month since. We should be glad of more copies but the bookseller thinks not of enough copies to justify a new edition yet. I should not be surprised however to see that some bold brother of the trade had undertaken it. Now what does your question point at in reference to your new edition? [asking "if we want more?"] [1] Could you send us out a part of your edition at American prices, & at the same time to your advantage? I wish I knew the precise answer to this question—then perhaps I could keep all pirates out of our bay.

I shall convey in two days your message to Stearns Wheeler who is

[1] These are Emerson's brackets.

now busy in correcting the new volumes, He is now Greek Tutor in Harvard College. Kindest thanks to Jane Carlyle for her generous remembrances which I will study to deserve. Has the heterodoxy arrived in Chelsea & quite destroyed us even in the Charity of our friend? I am sorry to have worried you so often about the summer letter. Now am I your debtor four times. The parish commotion too has long ago subsided here & my Course of Lectures on "Human Life" finds a full attendance.—I wait for the coming of the Westminster which has not quite yet arrived here though I have seen the London advertisement. It sounds prosperously in my ear what you say of Dr Carlyle's appointments. I was once very near the man in Rome but did not see him. I will atone as soon as I can for this truncated epistle. You must answer it immediately so far as to acknowledge the receipt of the enclosed bill of exchange: and soon I will send you the long promised *account* of the Fr. Rev. & also such moral account of the same as is over due.

Yours affectionately   R. W. Emerson

Chelsea, London, 8th Feby, 1839—

My dear Friend,

Your welcome little Letter, with the astonishing inclosure, arrived safe four days ago; right welcome, as all your Letters are, and bringing as these usually do the best news I get here. The miraculous draught of Paper [1] I have just sent to a sure hand in Liverpool, there to be till in due time it have ripened into a crop of a hundred gold sovereigns! On this subject, which gives room for so many thoughts, there is little that can be said, that were not an impertinence more or less. The matter grows serious to me, enjoins me to be silent and reflect. I will say at any rate, there never came money into my hands I was so proud of; the promise of a blessing looks from the face of it; nay it *will* be *twice* blessed. So I will ejaculate, with the Arabs, *"Allah akbar!"* and walk silent by the shore of the many-sounding Babel-tumult,[2] meditating on much. Thanks to the mysterious all-bounteous Guide of men, and to you my true Brother, far over the sea!—For the rest, I shewed

---

[1] Cf. the caption to Luke 5 and verses 4 and 9.

[2] In a letter to Forster of October 7, 1860 (MS owned by the Victoria and Albert Museum) this phrase appears more fully as "walking gloomy by the shore of the many-sounding sea." It would seem to be a translation, Carlyle's own, of part of lines 34 and 35 of book I of *The Iliad*. See also below, C.2.21.41.

Fraser this Nehemiah document,[3] and said I hoped he would blush very deep;—which indeed the poor creature did, till I was absolutely sorry for him.

But now first as to this question, What I mean? You must know poor Fraser, a punctual but most pusillanimous mortal, has been talking louder and louder lately of a "second edition" here; whereupon, as labour-wages are not higher here than with you, and printing-work, if well bargained for, ought to be about the same price, it struck me that, as in the case of the *Miscellanies,* so here inversely the supply of both the New and the Old England might be profitably combined. Whether aught can come of this, now that it is got close upon us, I yet know not. Fraser has only 75 copies left; but when these will be done his prophecy comprehends not—"surely within the year!" For the present I have set him to ascertain, and will otherwise ascertain for myself, what the exact cost of *stereotyping* the book were, in the same letter and style as yours; it is not so much more than printing, they tell me: I should then have done with it forever and a day. You on your side, and we on ours might have as many copies as were wanted for all time coming. This is, in these very days, under inquisition; but there are many points to be settled before the issue. I have not yet succeeded in finding a Bookseller of any fitness, but am waiting for one always. And even had I found such a one, I mean an energetic Seller that would sell on other terms than forty per cent. for his trouble, it were still a question whether one ought to venture on such a speculation: "quitting the old highways," as I say "in indignation at the excessive tolls, with hope that you will arrive cheaper in the steeple-chase way!" It *is* clear however that said highways are of the corduroy sort, said tolls an anomaly that must be remedied soon; and also that in all England there is no Book in a likelier case to adventure it with than this same,—which did not sell at all for two months, as I hear, which all Booksellers got terrified for, and which has crept along mainly by its own gravitation ever since. We will consider well, we shall see. You can understand that such a thing, for your market too, is in agitation; if any pirate step in before us in the meanwhile, we cannot help it.

Thanks again for your swift attention to the *Miscellanies;* poor Fraser is in great haste to see them; hoping for his forty-per-cent division of the spoil. If you have not yet got to the very end with your

[3] Perhaps a reference to the offering of first-fruits: Neh. 10: 35–36.

printing, I will add a few errata; if they come too late, never mind; they are of small moment: *Diamond Necklace* (page 24, of the separate Copy; of the Magazine I know not what page) delete the Note about "the Palais Royal Garden" at the bottom of the page;—I think I have since discovered that the date of that is wrong, and it can be dispensed with there. *Walter Scott*, p. 296 I pointed out one error already, a line to be deleted; p. 300, just after "beatified ghost-condition" occurs a short sentence "Let it be so": that is an editorial superfoetation, pray delete that; again, p. 335 last line but one, *rondo* (in the Note about Giotto) instead of *tondo* (it *was* t, and the editorial broadhoof changed it into r): [4] p. 343, just before the extract from Scott's Diary, "a hint (from Byron's Ravenna)," *read* "on hint."—I will not add a word more; but leave myself with my faithful correctors, to whom be all furtherance. Out upon it! My paper once more is all but done, and not a syllable of sense said.—

This foggy Babylon tumbles along as it was wont; and, as for my particular case, uses me not worse but better than of old. Nay there are many in it that have a real friendliness for me. For example, the other night, a massive portmanteau of Books, sent according to my written list, from the Cambridge University Library, from certain friends there whom I have never seen; [5] a gratifying arrival. For we have no Library here, from which we can borrow books home; and are only in these weeks striving to get one: [6] think of that! The worst is the sore tear and wear of this huge roaring Niagara of things on such a poor excitable set of nerves as mine. The velocity of all things, of the very word you hear on the streets, is at railway rate: joy itself is unenjoyable, to be avoided like pain; there is no wish one has so pressing as for quiet. Ah me, I often swear I will be *buried* at least in free breezy Scotland, out of this insane hubbub, where Fate tethers me [in life!] If Fate always tether me;—but if ever the smallest competence of worldly means be mine, I[. . .]fly this whirlpool as I

[4] Wheeler was understandably confused by this correction. "I cannot make out for the life of me," he wrote to Emerson on April 12, 1839, "whether we are to print the word tondo or rondo. I should think, were it not for the parenthesis, that rondo was the right word; but if rondo is right, how was the editor a 'broadhoof' for changing the wrong *t* to the right *r?*" (MS owned by the RWEMA).

[5] This library loan was arranged by a Cambridge alumnus, Douglas Heath, who was a "zealous reader" of Carlyle and an occasional visitor at Cheyne Row (*New Letters*, I, 149).

[6] See Frederick Harrison, ed., *Carlyle and the London Library*.

would the Lake of *Malebolge*,[7] and only visit it now and then! Yet
[. . .]it is the proper place after all, seeing all places are *im*proper:
who knows? Meanwhile I[. . .]a most dyspeptic solitary self-shrouded
life; consuming, if possible in silence, my considerable daily allotment
of pain; glad when any strength is left in me for working, which is the
only use I can see in myself,—too rare a case of late. The ground of
my existence is black as Death; too black, when all *void* too: but at
times there paint themselves on it pictures of gold and rainbow and
lightning; all the brighter for the black ground, I suppose. Withal I
am very much of a fool.—Some people will have me write on *Cromwell*
which I have been talking about. I do read on that and English subjects, finding that I know nothing and that nobody knows anything
of that: but whether anything will come of it remains to be seen. Mill
the Westminster friend is gone in bad health to the Continent, and
has left a rude Aberdeen Longear,[8] a great admirer of mine too, with
whom I conjecture I cannot act at all: so goodbye to that. The wisest
of all, I do believe, were that I bought my nag *Yankee,* and set to
galloping about the elevated places here! A certain Mr Coollidge (?),[9]
a Boston man of clear iron visage and character, came down to me the
other day with Sumner; he left a newspaper fragment, containing "the
Socinian Pope's denunciation of Emerson." [10] The thing denounced
had not then arrived, tho' often asked for at Kennet's; it did not arrive
till yesterday, but had lain buried in bales of I know not what. We
have read it only once, and are not yet at the bottom of it. Meanwhile,
as I judge, the Socinian "tempest in a washbowl" is all according to
nature, and will be profitable to you, not hurtful. A man is called to
let his light shine before men; [11] but he ought to understand better
and better what medium it is thro', what retinas it falls on: wherefore

[7] A place in Dante's Hell: *Inferno,* XVIII, 1.

[8] John Robertson (see Packe, *Life of John Stuart Mill,* pp. 211–12). And see above,
C.11.15.38.

[9] Norton identifies this visitor as "the late Mr. Joseph Coolidge." There was a
Boston merchant of this name 1798–1879) who in 1825 married the granddaughter
of Thomas Jefferson and to whom Jefferson gave the desk on which the Declaration
of Independence had been written (Jefferson, *Writings,* ed. A. E. Bergh, XVIII,
334, 349).

[10] This must have been Andrews Norton's Boston *Daily Advertiser* article of
August 27, 1838, which denounced both the Divinity School Address and the influence of Carlyle.

[11] Cf. Matt. 5: 16.

look *there*. I find in this as in the two other Speeches that noblest self-assertion, and believing originality, which is like sacred fire, the beginning of whatsoever is to flame and work; and for young men especially one sees not what could be more vivifying. Speak therefore, while you feel called to do it, and when you feel called. But for yourself, my friend, I prophecy it will not do always, a faculty is in you for a *sort* of speech which is itself *action,* an artistic sort. You *tell* us with piercing emphasis that man's soul is great; *shew* us a great soul of a man, in some work symbolic of such: this is the seal of such a message, and you will feel by and by that you are called to this. I long to see some concrete thing, some Event, Man's Life, American Forest, or piece of Creation, which this Emerson loves and wonders at, well *Emerson-ized:* depictured by Emerson, filled with the life of Emerson, and cast forth from him then to live by itself. If these Orations baulk me of this, how profitable soever they be for others, I will not love them.— And yet what am I saying? How do I know what is good for *you,* what authentically makes your own heart glad to work in it? I speak from *without,* the friendliest voice must speak from without; and a man's ultimate motivation comes only from *within.* Forgive me, and love me, and write soon. *À Dieu!*   T. Carlyle

My Wife, very proud of your salutation, sends a *sick* return of greeting. After a winter of unusual strength, she took cold the other day, and coughs again; tho' she will not call it serious yet. One likes none of these things. She has a brisk heart and a stout, but too weak a frame for this rough life of mine. I will not get sad about it.—One of the strangest things about these New England orations is a fact I have heard but not yet seen, that a certain W. Gladstone, an Oxford crack scholar, Tory M. P. and devout Churchman of great talent and hope, has contrived to insert a piece of you (first orat^n it must be) in a work of his on "Church and State," [12] which makes some figure at present! I know him for a solid serious silent-minded man; but how with his Coleridge shovel-hattism he has contrived to relate himself to *you,* there is the mystery. True men of all creeds, it *would* seem are brothers—

To write soon!

[12] Gladstone quoted four sentences from the Phi Beta Kappa oration and referred to the Dartmouth College oration (*The State in its Relations with the Church,* pp. 130, 25).

Concord, March 15, 1839.

My dear friend, I will spare you my apologies for not writing they are
so many. You have been very generous; I very promising and dilatory.
I desired to send you an Account of the sales of the "History," thinking that the details might be more intelligible to you than to me, &
might give you some insight into literary & social as well as bibliopolical relations. But many details of this account will not yet settle
themselves into sure facts, but do dance & mystify me, as one green
in legers. Bookseller says 991 copies came from Binder, 9 remaining
imperfect, & so not bound. But in all my reckonings of the particulars
of distribution, I make either more or less than 991 copies. And some
of my accounts are with private individuals at a distance & they have
their uncertainties & misrememberings also. But the facts will soon
show themselves, & I count confidently on a small balance against the
world to your credit.

The Miscellanies go forward too slowly, at about the rate of 72
pages a week, as I understand. Of the Fraser Articles, & of some others,
we have but a single copy, (such are the tough limits of some English
immortalities & editorial renowns,) but we expect the end of the printing in six weeks. The two first volumes, with title pages, are gone to
the binder,—260 copies,—with strait directions; & I presume will go
to sea very soon. We shall send the two last volumes by a later ship.
You will pay nothing for the books we send, except freight. We shall
deduct the cost of the books from the credit side of your account here.
We print of the second series 1250 copies, with the intention of printing a second edition of the first series, of 500, if we see fit hereafter
to supply the place of the emigrating portion of the first. You express
some surprise at the cheapness of our work. The publishers, I believe,
generally get more profits. They grumbled a little at the face of the
account on the 1 Jany: so, in the new contract for the new volumes,
I have allowed them 9 cents more on each copy sold by them. So that
you should receive 91 cents on a copy instead of $1.00. When the 260
copies of our two first vols. are gone to you, I think they will not have
but about 100 copies more to sell.

Your books are read. I hear, I think, more gratitude expressed for
the Miscellanies, than for the History. Young men at all our Colleges
study them in closets, & the Copernican is eradicating the Ptolemaic

lore. I have frequent & cordial testimonies to the good working of the leaven, & continual inquiry whether the man will come hither? *Speriamo.*

I was a fool to tell you once, you must not come: if I did tell you so. I knew better at the time, & did steadily believe, as far as I was concerned, that no polemical mud, however much was thrown, could by any possibility stick to me; for I was purely an observer; had not the smallest personal or *partial* interest; & merely spoke to the question as a historian; and I knew, whoever could see me, must see that. But, at the moment, the little pamphlet made much stir, & exclamation in the Newspapers; and the whole thousand copies were bought up. The ill wind has blown over. I advertised, as usual, my winter Course of Lectures, & it prospered very well. Ten lectures: I Doctrine of the Soul. II Home. III The School. IV Love. V. Genius. VI The Protest. VII Tragedy. VIII Comedy. IX Duty. X Demonology. I designed to add two more, but my lungs played me false with unseasonable inflammations so I discoursed no more on "Human Life." [1] Now I am well again.—But as I said, as I could not hurt myself, it was foolish to flatter myself that I could mix your cause with mine, & hurt you. Nothing is more certain than that you shall have all our ears, whenever you wish for them, & free from that partial position which I deprecated. Yet I cannot regret my letter which procured me so affectionate & magnanimous a reply.

Thanks too for your friendliest invitation. But I have a new reason why I should not come to England,—a blessed babe, named Ellen, almost three weeks old, a little fair soft lump of contented humanity, incessantly sleeping, & with an air of incurious security, that says, she has come to stay, has come to be loved,—which has nothing mean, & quite piques me.

Yet how gladly should I be near you for a time. The months & years make me more desirous of an unlimited conversation with you; & one day, I think, the God will grant it, after whatever way is best. I am lately taken with the Onyx Ring; which seemed to me full of knowledge, & good bold true drawing. Very saucy, was it not? in John Sterling to paint Collins; & what intrepid iconoclasm in this new Alci-

[1] The lectures were given weekly, except for two postponements, from December 5 to February 20. The "inflammation" seems to have been bronchitis (*Let RWE*, II, 177*n*, 184).

biades to break in among your Lares & disfigure your sacred Hermes himself in Walsingham. To me, a profane man, it was good sport to see the Olympic lover of Frederica, Lili, & so forth, lampooned. And by Alcibiades too, over whom the wrath of Pericles must pause & brood ere it falls.[2] I delight in this Sterling, but now that I know him better, I shall no longer expect him to write to me.

I wish I could talk with you on the grave questions graver than all literature which the trifles of each day open. Our doing seems to be a gaudy screen or popinjay to divert the eye from our no-doing. I wish too you could know my friends here. A man named Bronson Alcott is a majestic soul with whom conversation is possible. He is capable of truth, & gives me the same glad astonishment that he should exist which the World does. As I hear not yet of your reception of the Bill of Exchange which went by the Royal William in Jany I enclose the duplicate. And now all success to the Lectures of April or May! A new Kingdom with new extravagances of power & splendor,—I know. Unless you can keep your own secret better in Rahel &c[3] you must not give it me to keep. The London Sartor arrived in my hands 5 March, dated 15 Nov. So long is the way from Kennett to Little & Co. The book is welcome & awakens a sort of nepotism in me—my brother's child.[4]   R. W. Emerson.

I rejoice in the good accounts you give me of your household; in your wife's health; in your brother's position; my wife wishes to be affectionately remembered to you & yours. And the lady must continue to love her *old* Transatlantic friend.

[2] *The Onyx Ring*, published in *Blackwood's Magazine* for November and December, 1838, and January, 1839, is a sentimental *roman à clef* in which Carlyle appears as the hermit Collins and Goethe as a heartless Poet and Seducer called Walsingham. The story of Alcibiades' iconoclasm Emerson knew from Plutarch; he had been reminded of it by his recent reading of Landor's *Pericles and Aspasia* (*Complete Works of Walter Savage Landor*, ed. T. Earle Welby, X, 165).

[3] Emerson refers here to the article "Varnhagen von Ense's Memoirs" (*The London and Westminster Review*, XXXII, 60–84), which was concerned only in part with Varnhagen von Ense's wife, Rahel. Emerson's mistake is perhaps explained by the fact that a week earlier his friend Elizabeth Hoar had been "reading a fine book Rahel von Ense" (*Let RWE*, II, 192).

[4] A. H. Everett's review of *Sartor* was included in the first English edition among "Testimonies of Authors." The first draft of this letter has, after "my brother's child": "I read for the first time in it the critique of the N. A. Reviewer. O wise Bottom O agile buffalo & sweet Midas: do not lose thy sleep to listen with thy long ears again. And neither let me hear that snore again. Let us part in peace."

Concord, 19 March, 1839.[1]

My dear Friend,—Only last Saturday I despatched a letter to you containing a duplicate of the bill of exchange sent in January, and all the facts I knew of our books; and now comes to me a note from Wheeler, at Cambridge, saying that the printers, on reckoning up their amount of copy, find that nowise can they make 450 pages per volume, as they have promised, for these two last of the *Miscellanies*. They end the third volume with page 390, and they have not but 350 or less pages for the fourth. They ask, What shall be done? Nothing is known to me but to give them *Rahel*, though I grudge it, for I vastly prefer to end with *Scott*. *Rahel*, I fancy, cost you no night and no morning, but was writ in that gentle after-dinner hour so friendly to good digestion. Stearns Wheeler dreams that it is possible to draw at this eleventh hour some possible manuscript out of the unedited treasures of Teufelsdröckh's cabinets. If the manuscripts were ready, all fairly copied out by foreseeing scribes in your sanctuary at Chelsea, the good goblin of steam would—with the least waiting, perhaps a few days—bring the packet to our types in time. I have little hope, almost none, from a sally so desperate on possible portfolios; but neither will I be wanting to my sanguine co-editor, your good friend. So I told him I would give you as instant notice as Mr. Rogers [2] at the Merchants' Exchange Bar can contrive, and tell you plainly that we shall proceed to print *Rahel* when we come so far on; and with that paper end; unless we shall receive some contrary word from you. And if we can obtain any manuscript from you before we have actually bound our book, we will cancel our last sheets and insert it. And so may the friendly Heaven grant a speedy passage to my letter and to yours! I fear the possibility of our success is still further reduced by the season of the year, as the Lectures must shortly be on foot. Well, the best speed to them also. When I think of you as speaking and not writing them, I remember Luther's words, "He that can speak well, the same is a man." [3]

I hope you liked John Dwight's translations of Goethe, and his

---

[1] This is Norton's text.

[2] *Stimpson's Boston Directory* for 1839 lists a Sargent Rogers at "foreign let. office, City H." Ten years earlier, *Stimpson's* had given his address as "bar room, Merchants Hall."

[3] "Wer wol reden kann, der ist ein man," *D. Martin Luthers Werke* (Weimar, 1916), *Tischreden* IV, 126. Emerson probably found the sentence in Henry Bell's translation, *Colloquia Mensalia* (London, 1791), p. 462.

notes. He is a good, susceptible, yearning soul, not so apt to create as to receive with the freest allowance, but I like his books very much.

Do think to say in a letter whether you received *from me* a copy of our edition of your *French Revolution.* I ordered a copy sent to you,—probably wrote your name in it,—but it does not appear in the bookseller's account.   Farewell.   R. W. Emerson.

Chelsea, London, 13th April, 1839—

My dear Emerson,

Has anything gone wrong with you? How is it that you do not write to me? These three or four weeks, I know not whether *duly* or not so long, I have been in daily hope of some sign from you; but none comes; not even a Newspaper,—open at the ends. The German Translator Mr Dwight mentioned, at the end of a Letter I had not long ago, that you had given a brilliant course of Lectures at Boston, but had been obliged to *intermit it on account of illness.* Bad news indeed, that latter clause; at the same time, it was thrown in so cursorily I would not let myself be much alarmed; and since that, various New England friends have assured me here that there was nothing of great moment in it, that the business was all well over now, and you safe at Concord again. Yet how is it that I do not hear? I will tell you my guess is that those Boston Carlylean *"Miscellanies"* are to blame. The Printer is slack and lazy as Printers are; and you do not wish to write till you can send some news of him? I will hope and believe that only this is it, till I hear worse.

I sent you a Dumfries Newspaper the other week, for a sign of my existence and anxiety. A certain Mr Ellis of Boston is this day packing up a very small memorial of me to your Wife; a poor Print rolled about a bit of wood: let her receive it graciously in defect of better. It comes under your address. Nay properly it is my Wife's memorial to your Wife. It is to be hung up in the Concord drawing room. The two Households, divided by wide seas, are to understand always that they are united nevertheless.[1]

---

[1] This was a print of Guido Reni's *Aurora,* on which Carlyle had written, "Will the lady of Concord hang this Italian sun-chariot in her drawing-room and, seeing it, think of a household which has good reason to remember hers?" (*Journals,* V, 217n).

My special cause for writing this day rather than another is the old story, book business. You have brought that upon yourself, my friend; and must do the best you can with it. After all, why should not Letters be on business too? Many a kind thought, uniting man with man, in gratitude and helpfulness, is founded on business. The speaker at Dartmouth College seems to think it ought to be so.[2] Nor do I dissent. —But the case is this. Fraser and I are just about bargaining for a second edition of the *Revolution*. He will print 1500 for the English Market, in a somewhat closer style, and sell them here at 24 shillings a copy. His first edition is all gone but some handful; and the man is in haste, and has taken into a mood of hope,—for he is weak and aguish, alternating from hot to cold; otherwise, I find, a very accurate creature, and deals in his unjust trade as justly as any other will. He has settled with me; his half-profits amount to some £130, which by charging me for every presentation copy he cuts down to somewhere about £110; *not* the lion's share in the gross produce, yet a great share compared with an expectancy no higher than *zero!* We continue on the same system for this second adventure; I cannot go hawking about in search of new terms; I might go farther and fare worse. And now comes your part of the affair; in which I would fain have had your counsel; but must ask your help, proceeding with my own light alone. After Fraser's 1500 are printed off, the types remain standing, and I for my own behoof throw off 500 more, designed for your market. Whether 500 are too many or too few I can only guess: if too many we can retain them here and turn them to account; if too few there is no remedy. At all events, costing me only the paper and press-work, there is surely no Pirate in the union that can *undersell* us! Nay, it seems they have a drawback on our taxed paper, sufficient or nearly so to land the cargo at Boston without more charge. You see therefore how it is. Can you find me a Bookseller, as for yourself; he and you can fix what price the ware will carry when you see it. Meanwhile I must have his title page; I must have his directions (if any be needed); nay, for that matter, you might write a Preface if you liked,—tho I see not what you have to say, and recommend silence rather! The book is to be in three volumes duodecimo, and we will take care it be fit to shew its face in your market. A few errors of the press; and one correction (about the sinking of the *Vengeur*,

[2] Possibly; but the Phi Beta Kappa orator came closer to saying so.

which I find lately to be an indisputable falsehood); [3] these are all the changes. We are to have done printing, Fraser predicts, "in two months;"—say two and a half! I suppose you decipher the matter out of this plastering and smearing; and will do what is needful in it. "Great inquiry" is made for the *Miscellanies,* Fraser says; tho he suspects it may perhaps be but one or two men inquiring *often,*—the dog!

I am again upon the threshold of extempore lecturing: on "the Revolu[tions] of Modern Europe"; Protestantism, 2 lectures; Puritanism 2; French Revolution 2. I almost regret that I had undertaken the thing this year at all; for I am no longer driven by Poverty as heretofore, nay I am richer than I have been for ten years; and have a kind of prospect, for the first time this great while, of being allowed to subsist in this world for the future: a great blessing, perhaps the greatest, when it comes as a novelty! However, I thought it right to keep this Lecture business open, come what might. I care less about it than I did; it is not agony, and wretched trembling to the marrow of the bone, as it was the last two times. I believe, in spite of all my perpetual indigestions and nervous woes, I am actually getting into better health; the weary heart of me is quieter; I wait in silence for the new chapter, feeling merely that we are at the end of one period here. I count it *two* in my autobiography: we shall see what the *third* is; third there be. But I am in small haste for a third. How true is that of the old Prophets, "The *word of the Lord* came unto" such and such a one! [4] When it does not come, both Prophet and Prosaist ought to be thankful (after a sort), and rigorously hold their tongue.— Lord Durham's people have come over with golden reports of the Americans, and their brotherly feelings. One Arthur Buller [5] preaches to me, with emphasis, on a quite personal topic till one explodes in laughter to hear him, the good soul: that I, namely, am the most esteemed &c, and ought to go over and Lecture in all great towns of

[3] A final paragraph added to chapter VI of book V. Carlyle published a fuller correction, with documents, in "The Sinking of the Vengeur," *Fraser's Magazine,* XX (July, 1839), 76–84.

[4] Jer. 25: 3; Hos. 1: 1.

[5] Arthur Buller had accompanied Lord Durham on his mission to Canada in 1838. On this same day, Carlyle reported more fully to his mother what Buller had said: ". . . how I am 'the most popular author in America at present,' how this man said, how that man said;—in a word, how I must go out to America and lecture, 'and make a fortune in six months'!" (NLS, MS 511).

the union, and make &c &c! I really do begin to think of it in this interregnum that I am in. But there my Lectures must be written; but there I must become a *hawker,—ach Gott!*

The people are beginning to quote you here: *tant pis pour eux!* I have found you in two Cambridge books.[6] A certain Mr Richd M. Mylnes [7] M. P. a beautiful little Tory dilettante poet and politician whom I love much, applied to me for *Nature* (the others he has) that he might write upon it. Somebody has stolen Nature from me, or many have thumbed it to pieces; I could not find a copy. Send me one, the first chance you have. And see Miss Martineau in the last West^r Review: [8]—these things you are old enough to stand? They are even of benefit? Emerson is not without a select public, the root of a select public on this side of the water too.—Popular Sumner is off to Italy, the most popular of men,—inoffensive, like a worn sixpence that has no physiognomy left. We preferred Coolidge to him in this circle; a square-cut iron man, yet with clear symptoms of a heart in him. Your people will come more and more to their national Babylon, will they not, by the steamer?—Adieu my dear friend. My Wife joins me in all good prayers for you and yours.

Thomas Carlyle

Chelsea, London, 17th April, 1839

Dear Friend,

Some four days ago I wrote you a long Letter, rather expressive of anxiety about you; it will probably come to hand along with this. I had heard vaguely that you were unwell, and wondered why you did not write. Happily that point is as good as settled now, even by your silence about it. I have, half an hour ago, received your Concord Letter of the 19th of March; the Letter you speak of there as "written last Saturday" has not yet made its appearance, but may be looked for now shortly: as there is no mention here of any mischance, except

---

[6] One of these was perhaps *The New Cratylus* by J. W. Donaldson, in which *The American Scholar*, the work "of an able American writer," was quoted to support the opinion that "the better a man is educated professionally the less he is a man" (p. 6).

[7] Richard Monckton Milnes.

[8] Harriet Martineau in *The London and Westminster Review*, XXXII (April, 1839), 261–81, had words of praise for the Dartmouth oration.

the shortcoming of Printers' copy, I infer that all else is in a tolerably correct state; I wait patiently for the "last Saturday" tidings, and will answer as to the matter of copy, in good heart, without loss of a moment.

There is nothing of the manuscript sort in Teufelsdröckh's repositories that would suit you well; nothing at all in a completed state, except a long rigmarole dissertation (in a crabbed sardonic vein) about the early History of the Teutonic Kindred, wriggling itself along not in the best style thro' Proverb lore, and I know not what, till it end (if my memory serve) in a Kind of Essay on the *Minnesingers*. It was written almost ten years ago, and never contented me well. It formed part of a lucklessly projected "History of German Literature," subsequent portions of which, the *Nibelungen* and *Reinecke Fox,* you have already printed.[1] The unfortunate *"Cabinet Library* Editor," or whatever his title was, broke down; and I let him off,—without paying me; and this alone remains of the misventure; a thing not fit for you, nor indeed at bottom for anybody, tho' I have never burnt it *yet*.[2] My other manuscripts are scratchings and scrawlings,—children's INfant souls weeping, because they never could be born, but were left there whimpering *in limine primo!* [3]

On this side therefore is no help. Nevertheless, it seems to me, otherwise there is. *Varnhagen* may be printed I think without offense, since there is need of it: if that will make up your fourth volume to a due size, why not? It is the last faint murmur one gives in Periodical Literature, and may indicate the approach of silence and slumber. I know no errors of the Press in *Varnhagen:* there is one thing about Jean Paul F. Richter's *want* of humour in his *speech,* which somehow I could like to have the opportunity of uttering a

---

[1] Carlyle's essay on German literature of the fourteenth and fifteenth centuries was published in *The Foreign Quarterly Review* for October, 1831, as a review of a new edition of *Reinecke der Fuchs.* There and in most editions of the *Miscellanies* it was entitled "Early German Literature."

[2] Dionysius Lardner, who had planned to publish Carlyle's *History of German Literature* in two volumes of his *Cabinet Library,* was obliged to discontinue that series in 1832, and Carlyle could never find another publisher. In 1880 Max Müller wrote to Froude that the work was only "a curious fragment showing the state of knowledge of German literature at the time" (Wilson, *Carlyle to "The French Revolution",* pp. 266, 195). It was finally published, with scholarly introduction and notes by Hill Shine, in 1951.

[3] Vergil, *Aeneid,* XI, 423. Also, see above, Introduction, p. 83.

word on, tho' *what* word I see not very well. My notion is partly that V. overstates the thing, taking a Berlin *propos de salon* for a scientifically accurate record; and partly farther that the defect (if any) was *creditable* to Jean Paul, indicating that he talked from the abundance of the heart, not burning himself off in miserable perpetual sputter like a Town-wit, but speaking what he had to say, were it dull were it not dull,—for his own satisfaction first of all! If you in a line or two could express at the right point something of that sort, it were well; yet on the whole, if not, then is almost no matter. Let the whole stand there, as the commencement of slumber and stertorous breathing! [4]

Varnhagen himself will not bring up your fourth volume to the right size; hardly beyond 380 pages, I should think; yet what more can be done! Do you remember Fraser's Magazine for October 1832, and a Translation there, with Notes, of a thing called Goethe's *Mährchen?* It is by me; I regard it as a most remarkable piece, well worthy of perusal, especially by all readers of mine. The printing of your third volume will of course be finished before this Letter arrive; nevertheless I have a plan: that you (as might be done I suppose, by cancelling and reprinting the concluding leaf or leaves) append the said Translated Tale, in a smaller type, to that volume. It is 21 or 22 pages of Fraser, and will perhaps bring yours up to the mark. Nay indeed there are two other little Translations from Goethe which I reckon good, tho' of far less interest than the *Mährchen;* I think they are in the *Frasers* almost immediately preceding; one of them is called *Fragment from Goethe* (if I remember); in his *Works* it is "*Novelle*"; it treats of a visit of some princely household to a strange mountain ruin or castle, and the catastrophe is the escape of a shewlion from its booth in the neighbouring Market-Town. I have not the thing here,—alas, sinner that I am, it now strikes me that the "*two* other things," are this *one* thing, which my treacherous memory is making into two! This however you will find in the Number immediately, or not far from immediately, preceding that of the *Mährchen;* along with which, in the same type with whi[ch,] it would give us letter-press enough. It ought to stand *before* the *Mährchen:* read it, and say whether it is worthy or not worthy. Will this *Appendix* do, then? I should really rather *like* the *Mährchen* to be printed; and

[4] The whole did stand, without footnote or editorial parenthesis.

had thoughts of putting at the end of the English *Sartor*. The other I care not for, intrinsically, but think it very beautiful in its kind.— Some rubbish of my own, in small quantity, exists here and there in *Fraser;* one story, entitled *Cruthers and Jonson,* was written sixteen years ago, and printed somewhere early (probably the 2nd year) in that rubbish-heap, with several gross errors of the press (ma*r*es for maces was one!): it is the first thing I wrote or among the very first;— otherwise a thing to be kept rather secret, except from the like of you! This or any other of the "original" immaturities I will *not* recommend as an Appendix; I hope the *Mährchen,* or the *Mährchen*² and *Novella*¹ will suffice. But on the whole, to thee, O Friend, and thy judgement and decision without appeal I leave it altogether. Say Yes, say No; do what seemeth good to thee.—Nay now, writing with the speed of light, another consideration strikes me: why should vol. 3d be interfered with if it is finished? Why will not this *Appendix* do, these *Appendices,* to hang to the skirts of Vol. 4 as well? Perhaps better! The *Mährchen* in any case closing the rear. I leave it all to Emerson and Stearns Wheeler, my more than kind Editors: E. knows it better than I, be his decision irrevocable.

This Letter is far too long, but I *had not time* to make it shorter.— I got *your* F. Revn, and have seen no other: my name is on it in your hand. I received Dwight's Book, liked it, and have answered him: a good youth, of the kind you describe; no English man, to my knowledge, has yet uttered as much sense about Goethe and German things. I go this day to settle with Fraser about Printers and a second edition of the Revⁿ Book,—as specified in the other Letter: 500 copies for America, which are to cost he computes about 2/7, and *your* Bookseller will bind them, and defy Piracy. My Lectures come on, this day two weeks: O Heaven! *I* cannot "speak"; I can only gasp and writhe and stutter, a spectacle to gods and fashionables,—being forced to it by want of money. In five weeks I shall be free, and then—! Shall it be Switzerland, shall it be Scotland, nay shall it be America and Concord?   Ever your affectionate   —T. Carlyle

All love from both of us to the Mother and Boy. My wife is better than usual; rejoices in the promise of summer now at last visible after a spring like Greenland. Scarcity, discontent, fast ripening towards desperation, extends far and wide among our working people. God help them! In man as yet is small help. There will be work yet, before that account is liquidated; a generation or two of work! Miss Martineau is gone to Switzerland, after emitting *"Deerwood, a Novel."* [5] How do you like it? people ask. To which there are various answers returnable, but few so good as none. Ah me! Lady Bulwer too has written a Novel, in satire of her Husband.[6] I saw the Husband not long since; one of the wretchedest Phantasms, it seemed to me, I had yet fallen in with—many, many as they are here.

The £100 Bill came, in due time, in perfect order; and will be payable one of these days. I forget dates; but had well calculated that before the 19th of March this piece of news and my gratitude for it had reached you.

Boston, 20 April, 1839

My dear friend,

Learning here in town that letters may go today to the Great Western, I seize the hour to communicate a bookseller's message. I told Brown of C. C. Little & Co, that you think of stereotyping the History. He says that he can make it profitable to himself & to you to use your plates here, in this manner [which he desires may be kept secret here, & I suppose with you also] [1] You are to get your plates made & proved then you are to send them out here, to him, having first insured them in London, & he is to pay you a price for every copy he prints from them. As soon as he has printed a supply for our market,—& we want, he says, 500 copies now,—he will send them back to you. I told him I thought he had better fix the price per copy to be paid by him & I would send it out to you as his offer; He is willing to do so, but not today. It was only this morning I informed him of your plan. I think in a fortnight I shall need to write again—probably to introduce to you my countrywoman Miss Sedgwick,[2] the writer of affectionate New

---

[5] *Deerbrook. A Novel.* Carlyle made a fuller comment in a letter to his brother John: "She has published a Novel, very ligneous, very trivial-didactic, in fact very absurd for most part; and is well content with it" (Thomas Carlyle, *New Letters*, I, 159).

[6] Rosina Bulwer-Lytton's *Cheveley, or the Man of Honour.*

[1] Emerson's brackets.

[2] Catherine Maria Sedgwick. Her most recent novels had been *Clarence; or A Tale of Our Own Times* (1830) and *The Linwoods; or, "Sixty Years Since" in America* (1835).

England tales, & the like,—who is about to go to Europe, for a year or more,—I will then get somewhat definite from Brown as to rates & prices. Brown thought you might better send the plates here *first*, as we are in immediate want of copies; & afterwards print with them in London. He is quite sure that it would be more profitable to print them in this manner, than to try to import & sell here the *books* after being manufactured in London.

On the 30 April we shall ship at New York the two first volumes of the Miscellanies, 260 copies. In four weeks, the two second volumes will be finished, unless we wait for something to be added by yourself, agreeably to a suggestion of Wheeler's & mine. Two copies of Schiller's Life will go in the same box. We send them to the port of London. When these are gone only 100 copies remain unsold of the $D/$ [3] first volumes (Misc.)

Brown said it was important that the plates should be proved correct at London by striking off impressions before they were sent hither. This is the whole of my present message. I shall have somewhat presently to reply to your last letter received three weeks since. And may health & peace dwell with you & yours.   R. W. Emerson

                                        Concord, 25 April, 1839 [1]

My dear friend,

Behold my account! [2] A very simple thing, is it not! a very mouse, after such months, almost years, of promise! Despise it not, however; for such is my extreme dulness at figures & statements that this nothing has been a fear to me, a long time—how to extract it from the bookseller's promiscuous account with me, & from obscure records of my own. You see that it promises yet to pay you between 60 & 70 dollars more, if Mr Fuller, (a gentleman of Providence, who procured many subscriptions for us there) & Mr Owen (who owes us also for

[3] This symbol presumably means 1,000 (see above, E.8.6.38), but I have been unable to determine the significance of the virgule.

[1] This letter was delivered by Miss Sedgwick (E.4.28.39). On June 19, 1839, Carlyle wrote to his mother: "I have had repeated Letters from Emerson lately; all going right there; 'celebrated Americans' coming hither &c &c. Yesterday Jane and I went to call for a 'celebrated Miss Sedgewick' from that country who had brought a letter to us: a very good woman I believe; she was out when we called" (NLS MS 520).

[2] Plate II reproduces this account.

copies *subscribed* for) will pay us our demand. They have both been lately reminded of their delinquency. Herrick & Noyes, you will see credited for 8 copies, 18.00. They are booksellers who supplied 8 subscribers, & charged us $2.00 for their trouble & some alleged damage to a copy. One copy you will see is sold to Ann Pomeroy for $3.00. This lady bought the copy of me, & preferred sending me 3.00 to sending 2.50 for so good a book. You will notice one or two other variations in the price, in each of which I aimed to use a friend's discretion. Add lastly, that you must revise all my figures, as I am a hopeless blunderer, & quite lately made a brilliant mistake in regard to the amount of 9 multiplied by 12.

Have I asked you whether you received from me a copy of the History? I designated a copy to go, & the bookseller's boy thinks he sent one, but there is none charged in their account.

The account of the *Miscellanies* does not prosper quite so well. J. Munroe, & Co. to whom I gave the publishing of this book, because they thought themselves a little ill used when Little & Brown were preferred in the publication of the History, (J. M. & Co having made really the better offer, whilst Little's looked better)—are not so rich nor so extensively connected a house as Little's. They credit me nothing for a copy until six months after they have sold it. And make me pay a large part of my notes to the printer, whilst Little & Brown contrived to make the book pay them. This comes of making a sharp bargain & trying to earn a thousand dollars instead of seven or eight hundred. In J. M. & Co's account, rendered 1 Apr. and which includes the charge of 260 copies sent to James Fraser at $2.15 = $559.00, the result is, "Balance due J. M. & Co $278.49," although they have sold 811 copies on commission, & 79 to subscribers. I growl at this & growl. They endeavor to make me understand that the balance is all to be the other side on the 1 July. Yes; but as we have printed a larger edition of the new books, I foresee that we shall want all the profits of that day to bear the expenses of the new. Yet the men though shrewd I believe honest; and I doubt not the book will pay its promise in the end. Only we must content ourselves, perhaps for many months, with having secured our 260 copies out of the lion's teeth, as our present share. Little & Brown have failed to send me this day, after two applications, their offer in regard to the stereotyping the history. In a few days, if it seems worth sending, I will send it.

Thanks for your too friendly & generous expectations from my wit. Alas my friend, I can do no such gay thing as you say. I do not belong to the poets, but only to a low department of literature, the reporters; suburban men. But in God we are all great all rich & each entitled to say, all is mine. I hope the advancing season has restored health to your wife, and if benedictions will help her, tell her, we send them on every west wind. My wife & babes are well.   R. W. E.

I regret that when I asked you to send a paper for our book, if paper you had, I did not say, shun Kennett; his loitering is like the loitering of Rich. Longman, I believe, has a new correspondence with Little & Co. that promises despatch. Or if Wiley & Putnam, who are Yankees, send to their house at New York, my brother, William Emerson, Esq. 60 Wall Street, New York would forward anything to me, if we have occasion hereafter to interchange pacquets.

                                        Concord   26 April 1839
My dear Sir,
    My friend Rev. Chandler Robbins [1] of Boston, who is also an active literary friend of yours, desires an opportunity of seeing you. Mr Robbins is intimately acquainted with the literay & religious aspects of New England, for some years past, & can tell you the state of your own grafts in this plantation. On this account as well as on account of his own merits, I am happy in introducing him to you.
                    Your affectionate servant   R. Waldo Emerson.
T. Carlyle Esq.

                                        Concord, 28 April, 1829 [1]
My dear friend,
    I received last night C. C. Little, & Co's proposition in reference to

----

[1] Robbins was Emerson's successor at the Second Church in Boston (Rusk, *Life*, p. 199).

[1] The MS of this letter is owned by the Berg Collection of the New York Public Library. The date 1829 is written clearly and boldly. That was the year of Emerson's marriage to Ellen Tucker. On February 25, 1839, the day after the birth of his second child, Emerson wrote in his journal: "Lidian, who magnanimously makes my gods her gods, calls the babe Ellen. I can hardly ask more for thee, my babe, than that name implies" (*Journals*, V, 167).

the stereotyping the History. Their offer is based on my statement that you proposed to print the Book in two volumes similar to ours. They say "We should be willing to pay three hundred dollars for the use of plates for striking off 500 copies of the two volumes, with the farther agreement, that, if we wished to strike off another 500 in nine months after the publication of the first 500, we should have liberty to do so, paying the same again; that is, another $300 for the privilege of printing another 500 copies. The plates to be furnished us ready for use, & free of expense." They add, "Should Mr. Carlyle send the plates to this country he should be particular to ship them to *this port direct.*"

I am no judge of the liberality of this offer, as I know nothing of the expense of the plates. The men, Little & Brown, are fair in their dealings, & the most respectable bookselling firm in Boston. When you have considered the matter, I hope you will send me as early an answer as you can. For as we have no protection from pirates, we must use speed.

I ought to have added to my account & statement sent by Miss Sedgwick one explanation. You will find in the account a credit of 13.75 agreed on with Little & Co. as compensation for lost subscribers. We had a little book, kept in their bookshop, into which were transferred the names of subscribers, from all lists which were returned from various places. These names amounted to 200, more or less. When we came to settle the account, this book could not be found. They expressed much regret, & made much vain searching. Their Account with me recorded only 134 copies delivered to subscribers. Thus, a large number, say 66, had been sold by them to our subscribers, & our half dollar on each copy put in their pocket as commission. Expressly contrary to treaty! With some ado I mustered 55 names of subscribers known to me as such, not recorded on their books as having received copies, & demanded $27.50. They replied, that they also had claims; that they had sent the books to distant subscribers in various states, and had charged no freight, (with one or two exceptions where the books went alone,); that other booksellers had, no doubt, in many cases, sold the copies to subscribers for which I claimed the half dollar; & lastly, which is indeed the moving reason, that they had sent 20 copies up the Mississippi to a bookseller (in Vicksburg, I think,) who had made them no return. On these grounds they proposed that they should pay half my demand, & so compromise. They said however that if I insisted, they would pay the whole. I was so glad to close the affair with mutual goodwill, that I said with the unjust steward,[2] Write $13.75. So are we all pleased at your expense. πλέον ἥμισυ πάντος [3] I think I will not give you any more historiettes: they take too much room: but as I write, this time, only on business, you are welcome to this from your friend   R. W. E.

Concord, Mass. 15 May, 1839

My dear friend,

   Last Saturday, 11th instant, I had your two letters of 13 & 17 April. Before now, you must have one or two notes of mine touching the stereotype plates: a proposition superseded by your new plan. I have also despatched one or two sheets, lately, containing accounts. Now for the new matter. I was in Boston yesterday & saw Brown, the bookseller. He accedes gladly to the project of 500 American Copies of the History. He says, that the duty is the same on books in sheets, & books in boards; & desires, therefore, that the books may come out *bound*. You bind yours in cloth? Put up his in the same style as those for your market, only a little more strongly than is the custom with London books, as it will only cost a little more. He would be glad also to have his name added in the title page—(London: published by J. Fraser; and Boston: by C. C. Little & James Brown 112 Washington St.) or is not this the right way? He only said, he should like to have his name added. He threatens to charge me 20 per cent. commission. If, as he computes from your hint of 2/7, the work costs you, say, 70 cents per copy, unbound; he reckons it at a dollar, when bound; then, 75 cents duty, in Boston,—1.75. He thinks, we cannot set a higher price on it than $3.50, *because* we sold our former edition for $2.50. On that price, his commissions would be .70 cents; and $1.05 per copy, will to you. If when we see the book, we venture to put a higher price on it, your remainder shall be more. I confess, when I set this forth on paper, it looks as bad as your English trade,—this barefaced 20 per cent; but their plea is, we guarantee the sales, we advertise, we pay you when it is sold, though we give our customers 6 months credit. I have made no final bargain with the man & perhaps before the books arrive I shall be better advised & may get better terms from

[2] Luke 16: 1–8.   [3] See Hesiod, *Works and Days*, line 40.

him. Meantime, give me the best advice you can; & despatch the books with all speed, & if you send 600, I think, we will sell them.

I went to the Athenaeum & procured the Frasers', and will print the Novelle & the Mährchen at the end of the Fourth Volume, which has been loitering under *one* workman for a week or two past, awaiting this arrival. Now we will finish at once. Cruthers & Jonson, I read gladly. It is indispensable to such as would see the fountains of Nile;[1] but I incline to what seems your opinion, that it will be better in the *final* edition of your Works, than in this present First Collection of them. I believe I could find more matter now of yours if we should be pinched again. The Cat-Raphael?[2] and Mirabeau & Macaulay?[3] Stearns Wheeler is very faithful in his loving labor—has taken a world of pains with the sweetest smile. We are very fortunate in having him to friend.—For the Miscellanies once more the two boxes containing 260 copies of the first series went to sea in the St. James Captain Sebor addressed to Mr Fraser. (I hope rightly addressed; yet I saw a memorandum at Munroe's, in which he was named *John* Fraser.)

Arthur Buller has my hearty thanks for his good & true witnessing. And now that our old advice is endorsed by John Bull himself, you will believe & come. Nothing can be better. As soon as the lectures are over, let the trunks be packed. Only my wife & my blessed sister dear—Elizabeth Hoar, betrothed in better times to my brother Charles;—my wife & this lovely nun do say, that Mrs Carlyle must come hither also; that it will make her strong, & lengthen her days on the earth, & cheer theirs also. Come, & make a home with me; & let us make a truth that is better than dreams. From this farmhouse of mine, you shall sally forth as God shall invite you, & "lecture in the great cities."[4] You shall do it by proclamation of your own, or by the mediation of a Committee, which will readily be found. Wife, Mother, & sister shall nurse thy wife meantime, & you shall bring your re-

[1] Cf. Lucan, *De Bello Civico*, bk. X, lines 191–92.

[2] *The Foreign Review and Continental Miscellany*, II (1828), 236–40, had carried under the title "The Cat-Raphael" a review of a book about a Swiss painter named Gottfried Mind, who specialized in "Katzengruppen" and was known as "der Katzenrafael." The style of the article is not un-Carlylean.

[3] In *Fraser's Magazine* for May, 1833 (VII, 508–26), there is a satirical debate entitled "Mirabeau v. Macaulay" with "Notes and Comments by Morgan Rattler," which is rather in the fashion of Carlyle.

[4] See above C.4.13.39.

publican laurels home so fast that she shall not sigh for the Old
England. Eyes here do sparkle at the very thought. And my little
placid Musketaquid river looked gayer today in the sun. In very sooth
& love, my friend, I shall look for you in August. If aught that we
know not must forbid your wife at present, you will still come. In
October, you shall lecture in Boston; in November in N. York; in
December in Philadelphia; in January in Washington. I can show
you three or four great natures, as yet unsung by Harriet Martineau
or Anna Jameson,[5] that content the heart & provoke the mind. And
for yourself, you shall be as cynical & headstrong and fantastical as you
can be.

I rejoice in what you say of better health & better prospects. I was
glad to hear of Milnes, whose Poems [6] already lay on my table, when
your letter came. Since the little Nature book is not quite dead, I
have sent you a few copies and wish you would offer one to Mr Milnes
with my respects. I hope before a great while, I may have somewhat
better to send him. I am ashamed that my little books should be
"quoted" as you say. My affectionate salutations to Mrs Carlyle who
is to sanction & enforce all I have written on the Migration. In the
prospect of your coming, I feel it to be foolish to write. I have very
much to say to you. But now only Good Bye.   R. W. Emerson

                               Chelsea, London, 29th May, 1839—
My dear Emerson,

Your Letter, dated Boston 20th April, has been here for some two
weeks. Miss Sedgwick, whom it taught us to expect in "about a fortnight," has yet given no note of herself, but shall be right welcome
whenever she appears. Miss Martineau's absence (she is in Switzerland this summer) will probably be a loss to the fair Pilgrim;—which
of course the rest of us ought to exert ourselves to make good.

Your Bookseller's Proposition as to the stereotype edition of the
F. R. will already have become void for you by intelligence arrived
before this at Concord. I gave up the stereotype speculation, the plan
of printing at my own expense at all; the estimates indicated too

---

[5] Mrs. Jameson's *Winter Studies and Summer Rambles in Canada* was also concerned with America and Americans.

[6] Presumably *Poems of Many Years.*

much cost: it would have been a throwing of all the money I had yet
got out of this Book, and more, anew into the melting-pot,—with
bookseller alchymists to manage the projection (at a *minimum* charge
of 42 per cent) I myself understanding nothing of it. The comfort
is that by this new method with Fraser I cannot lose; the past is safe,
and for the future also the poor man is like to do something. My
satisfaction from your news, however, is that 500 copies are actually
wanted for the American market; precisely the number now, by
guess, getting ready for that. I, along with this letter, despatch you a
perfect sheet of the new edition, by way of specimen; the 500 New-
England and 1500 Old-England copies are printed *so*. There are to
be, it is computed, 47 sheets; to make three volumes, which Fraser will
sell here at 24/; some 7 shillings cheaper than the former. His estimate of cost has risen a little, by some change of paper and figure;
I find these 500 copies, as they leave the Printer's warehouses, unbound, 47 sheets each, will cost me 3/6 each, or within a penny or so
of that. It is said there is some kind of drawback on our taxed paper,
which will perhaps carry the commodity over to Boston or nearly so.
Between 3 and 4 shillings, prime cost; that is the best guess we can
make.

Now, my friend, the thing I want you to do is to present this specimen sheet to a Bookseller, and make a bargain with him, and send
me his name to put on the title-page. Such a task is rather shameful
on my part, I fear;—but how can I help it? You yourself opened this
American silver-vein for me; hitherto America has paid me in the
proportion of 3, while England paid only 2. On the whole, however,
if you cannot do any good, bargaining, pray give it up, and I will
keep the 500 copies here, and, putting the English title-page on them,
let them go into Fraser's general stock and sell as they can.—As to the
Miscellanies, Fraser will not start selling till all the four volumes are
here. He requests greatly that your Binder would take pains to bind
the two last volumes *exactly like* the first two. The first two ought to
be near our shores by this time; the last two will follow as they can:
it seems to be little matter whether they arrive in what is called "the
season," or not.

My Lectures are happily over ten days ago; with "success" enough,
as it is called; the only *valuable* part of which is some £200, gained
with great pain, but also with great brevity:—economical respite for

another solar year! The people were boundlessly tolerant; my agitation beforehand was less this year, my remorse afterwards proportionably greater. There was but one moderately good Lecture, the last,—on Sansculottism, to an audience mostly Tory, and rustling with the beautifulest quality silks! Two things I find: first that I *ought to have had a horse;* I had only three incidental rides or gallops, hired rides; my horse *Yankee* is never yet purchased, but it shall be, for I cannot live, except in great pain, without a horse. It was sweet beyond measure to escape out of the dust-whirlpool here, and *fly,* in solitude, thro' the ocean of verdure and splendour, as far as Harrow and back again; and one's nerves were *clear* next day, and words lying in one like water in a well. But the *second* thing I found was, that extempore speaking,[1] especially in the way of Lecture is an *art* or craft, and requires an apprenticeship, which I have neve[r] served. Repeatedly it has come into my head that I should go to America, [this] very Fall, and belecture you from North to South till I learn it! Such a thing do[es] lie in the bottom-scenes, should hard come to hard; and looks pleasant enough.—On the whole, I say sometimes, I must either begin a Book, or do it. Books are the lasting thing; Lectures are like corn ground into flour; there are loaves for today, but no wheat harvests for next year. Rudiments of a new Book (thank Heaven!) do sometimes disclose themselves in me. *Festinare lente.* It ought to be better than F. Rev^n; I mean better written. The greater part of that Book, as I read proofsheets of it in these weeks, does nothing but *disgust* me. And yet it was, as nearly as was good, the utmost that lay in me. I should not like to be nearer killed with any other Book!—Books too are a triviality. Life alone is great; with its infinite spaces, its everlasting times, with its Death, with its Heaven and its Hell. Ah me!

Wordsworth is here at present; a garrulous, rather watery, not wearisome old man. There is a freshness as of woods and mountain breezes in him; one says of him: Thou art not great, but thou are genuine; well speed *thou.* Sterling is home from Italy, recovered in health, indeed very well could he but *sit still.* He is for Cifton [2] near

---

[1] Emerson wrote in his journal on September 18, 1839: "How trifling to insist on *ex tempore* speech, or spontaneous conversation, and decry the written poem or dissertation, or the debating club. A man's deep conviction lies too far down in nature to be much affected by these trifles. Do what you can your genius will speak from you, and mine from me" (*Journals,* V, 257).

[2] Clifton.

Bristol, for the next three months. I hear him speak of some sonnet or other he means to address to you: as for me he knows well that I call his verses timbertoned, without true melody either in thought, phrase or sound. The good John! Did you ever see such a vacant turnip-lantern as that Walsingham Goethe? Iconoclast Collins strikes his wooden shoe thro' him, and passes on, saying almost nothing.— My space is done!

I greet the little *Maidkin,* and bid her welcome to this unutterable world. Commend her, poor little thing, to her little Brother, to her Mother and Father;—Nature, I suppose, has sent her strong letters of recommendation, without our help, to them all.—Where I shall be, in six weeks, is not very certain; likeliest in Scotland, whither our whole household, servant and all, is pressingly invited, where they have provided horses and gigs. Letters sent hither will still find me, or lie waiting for me, safe; but perhaps the speediest address will be "care of Fraser 15 Regent Street." My Brother wants me to the Tyrol and Vienna, but I think I shall not go. Adieu, dear friend. It is a great treasure to me that I have you in this world. My Wife salutes you all.—Yours ever and ever   T. Carlyle

Chelsea, London, 24th June, 1839—

Dear Friend,

Two Letters from you were brought hither by Miss Sedgwick last week. The series of post Letters is a little embroiled in my head; but I have a conviction that all hitherto due have arrived; that up to the date of my last despatch (a *Proofsheet* and a Letter) which ought to be getting into your hands in these very days, our correspondence is clear. That Letter and Proofsheet, two separate pieces, were sent to Liverpool some three weeks ago, to be despatched by the first conveyance thence; as I say, they are probably in Boston about this time. The Proofsheet was one of the Forty-seven such, which the new F. Rev^n is to consist of: with this, as with a correct sample, you were to act upon some Boston Bookseller, and make a bargain for me,—or at least report that none was to be made. A bad bargain will content me now, my hopes are not at all high.

For the present, I am to announce on the part of Bookseller Fraser that the First Portion of our celebrated "Miscellanies" have been hovering about on these coasts for several weeks, have lain safe "in the River" for some two weeks, and ought at last to be safe in Fraser's shop today or else tomorrow. I will ask there, and verify, before this Letter go. The reason of these "two weeks in the river" is that the packages were addressed *"John* Fraser, London" and the people had tried all the Frasers in London before they attempted the right individual, *James,* of 215 Regent Street. Of course, the like mistake in the second case will be avoided. A Letter, put ashore at Falmouth, and properly addressed, but without any *signature,* had first of all announced that the thing was at the door; and so with this "John Fraser" it has been knocking ever since, finding difficult admission. In the present instance such delay has done no ill, for Fraser will not sell till the Second Portion come; and with this the mistake will be avoided. What has shocked poor James much more is a circumstance which your Boston Booksellers have no power to avoid: the "enormousness" of the charges in our Post here! He sends me the account of them last Saturday, with eyes—such as drew Priam's curtains: [1] £31 and odd silver, whereof £28 as duty on Books at £5 per cwt. is charged by the rapacious Customhouse alone! What help, O James? I answer: we cannot bombard the British Customhouse, and sack it, and explode it; we must yield, and pay it the money; thankful for what is still left.— On the whole, one has to learn by trying. This notable finance-expedient, of printing in the one country what is to be sold in the other, did not take vandalic customhouses into view, which nevertheless do seem to exist. We must persist in it for the present reciprocal pair of times, having started in it for these: but on future occasions always, we can ask the past; and *see* whether it be not better to let each side of the water stand on its own basis. As for your "accounts," my Friend, I find them clear as day, verifiable to the uttermost farthing. You are a good man to conquer your horror of arithmetic; and, like hydrophobic Peter of Russia [2] making himself a sailor, become an Accountant for my sake. But now will you forgive me if I never do verify this same account, or look at it more in this world except as a memento of affection, its arithmetical ciphers so many hierograms, really *sacred* to me! A reflexion I cannot but make is that at bottom this money was all yours; not a penny of it belonged to me by

[1] Cf. *Henry IV, Part II,* act I, scene i, line 70.
[2] Peter suffered from convulsions but not, so far as I can discover, from a fear of water.

any law except that of helpful Friendship. I feel as if I could not examine it without a kind of crime. For the rest, you may rejoice to think that, thanks to you and the Books, and to Heaven over all, I am for the present no longer poor; but have a reasonable prospect of existing, which, as I calculate, is literally the *most* that money can do for a man. Not for these twelve years, never since I had a house to maintain with money, have I had as much money in my possession as even now. *Allah kerim!* We will hope all that is good on that side. And herewith enough of *it*.

You tell me you are but "a reporter": I like you for thinking so. And *you* will never know that it is *not true,* till you have tried. Meanwhile, far be it from me to urge you to a trial before your time come. Ah, it will come and soon enough; much better perhaps if it never came! A man has *"such* a baptism to be baptised withal,'' no easy baptism; and is "straitened till it be accomplished." ³ As for me I honour peace before all things; the silence of a great soul is to me greater than anything it will ever say, it ever can say. Be tranquil, my friend; utter no word till you cannot help it;—and think yourself a "reporter," till you find (not with any great joy) that you are not altogether that!

We have not yet seen Miss Sedgwick: your Letters with her card were sent hither by post; we went up next day, but she was out; no meeting could be arranged earlier than tomorrow evening when we look for her here.⁴ Her reception, I have no doubt, will be abundantly flattering in this England. American Notabilities are daily becoming notabler a[mong] us; the ties of the two Parishes, Mother and Daughter, getting closer and closer knit. Indissoluble ties:—I reckon that this huge smoky Wen ⁵ may, for some centuries yet, be the best Mycale for our Saxon *Panionium,* a yearly meeting-place of "All the Saxons," from beyond the Atlantic, from the Antipodes or wherever the restless wanderers dwell and toil. After centuries, if

³ Cf. Luke 12: 50.

⁴ Miss Sedgwick went to "a six o'clock family tea . . . at Carlyle's" and heard "an interesting account of his first acquaintance with E—n. He was living with his wife in a most secluded part of Scotland. They had no neighbors, no communication with the world. . . . One day a stranger came to them—a young American—and 'he seemed to them an angel.' They spoke of him as if they had never lost their first impression of his celestial nature" (*Letters from Abroad to Kindred at Home,* I, 92).

⁵ "The Wen" was Cobbett's name for London. See, for example, his *Rural Rides.*

Boston, if New York have become the most convenient *"All-Saxon-dom,"* we will right cheerfully go thither to hold such festival, and leave the Wen.—Not many days ago I saw at breakfast the notablest of all your Notabilities Daniel Webster.[6] He is a magnificent specimen; you might say to all the world, This is your Yankee Englishman, such limbs *we* make in Yankeeland! As a Logic-fencer, Advocate, or Parliamentary Hercules, one would incline to back him at first sight against all the extant world. The tanned complexion, that amorphous crag-like face; the dull black eyes under their precipice of brows, like dull anthracite furnaces, needing only to be *blown;* the mastiff-mouth, accurately closed:—I have not traced as much of *silent Berserkir-rage,* that I remember of, in any other man. "I guess I should not like to be *your* nigger!"[7]—Webster is not loquacious, but he is pertinent, conclusive; a dignified, perfectly bred man, tho' not English in breeding: a man worthy of the best reception from us; and meeting such, I understand. He did not speak much with me that morning, but seemed not at all to dislike me: I meditate whether it is fit or not fit that I should seek out his residence, and leave *my* card too, before I go? Probably not; for the man is political, seemingly altogether; has been at the Queen's levee &c &c: it is simply as a mastiff-mouthed *man* that he is interesting to me, and not otherwise at all.

In about seven days hence we go to Scotland till the July heats be over. That is our resolution after all. Our address there, probably till the end of August, is "Templand, Thornhill, Dumfries N. B."— the residence of my Mother-in-law, within a day's drive of my Mother's. Any Letter of yours sent by the old constant address (Cheyne Row, Chelsea) will still find me there; but the other, for that time, will be a day or two shorter. We all go, servant and all. I am bent on writing *something;* but have no faith that I shall be able. I *must* try. There is a thing of mine in Fraser for *July,* of no account, about the "sinking of the *Vengeur"* as you will see. The F. R[n] printing is not to stop; two thirds of it are done, at this present rate it ought to finish,

---

[6] On June 19, 1839, Carlyle wrote to his mother: "A much more famous man called Webster is here too at present: I breakfasted when he was with various English notabilities yesterday . . . a large, grim, *tauchy* man; as dangerous a looking fellow to quarrel with, either in argument or by handgrips, as I have met with lately" (NLS, MS 520).

[7] In a letter to Sterling written five days earlier, Carlyle used this sentence without quotation marks (*Letters to Mill,* p. 220).

and the whole be ready within three weeks hence. A Letter will be here from you about that time, I think: I will print no titlepage for the 500 till it do come. "Published by *Fraser and* Little" would, I suppose be unobjectionable,—tho' Fraser is the most nervous of creatures: but why put *him* in it at all; since these 500 copies are wholly Little's and yours?—Adieu my Friend. Our blessings are with you and your house. My Wife grows better with the hot weather; I always worse.—Yours ever—   T. Carlyle.

I say not a word about America or Lecturing, at present; because I mean to consider it intently in Scotland, and then to decide. My Brother is to be at Ischl (not far from Salzburg) during summer: he was anxious to have me there, and I to have gone; but—but—Adieu.

Fraser's shop. Books not yet come, but known to be safe, and expected *soon.* Nay the dextrous Fraser has argued away £15 of the duty, he says! All is right therefore. N. B. he says, you are to send me the 2nd Portion *in sheets,* the weight will be less. This if it be still time. —*Basta.*   T. C.

Concord, 4 July, 1839.[1]

I hear to-night, O excellent man! that, unless I send a letter to Boston to-morrow with the peep of day, it will miss the Liverpool steamer, which sails earlier than I dreamed of. O foolish Steamer! I am not ready to write. The facts are not yet ripe, though on the turn of the blush. Couldst not wait a little? Hurry is for slaves;—and Aristotle, if I rightly remember only that little from my college lesson, affirmed that the high-minded man never walked fast.[2] O foolish Steamer! wait but a week, and we will style thee Megalopsyche, and hang thee by the Argo in the stars.[3] Meantime I will not deny the dear and admirable man the fragments of intelligence I have. Be it known unto you then, Thomas Carlyle, that I received yesterday

---

[1] This is Norton's text. On July 28, 1839, Carlyle wrote from Templand to his brother John: "In F's packet yesterday came an Emerson Letter: all right in America; first portion of the Miscellanies done" (NLS, MS 523).

[2] "Signs of *Good Moral Character* are—a slow gait; a slow way of speaking with a breath-like and weak voice" (Aristotle, *Physiognomica*, III, *Works* [Oxford, 1913], VI, 808a).

[3] After Jason's return from Colchis, Athena transformed his ship the *Argo* into a constellation.

morning your letter by the "Liverpool" with great contentment of
heart and mind, in all respects, saving that the American Hegira, so
often predicted on your side and prayed on ours, is treated with a
most unbecoming levity and oblivion; and, moreover, that you do
not seem to have received all the letters I seem to have sent. With
the letter came the proof-sheet safe, and shall be presently exhibited
to Little and Brown. You must have already the result of our first
colloquy on that matter. I can now bring the thing nearer to certainty. But you must print their names as before advised on the title-
page.

Nearly four weeks ago Ellis sent me the noble Italian print for my
wife.[4] She is in Boston at this time, and I believe will be glad that I
have written without her aid or word this time, for she was so deeply
pleased with the gift that she said she never could write to you. It
came timely to me at least. It is a right morning thought, full of
health and flowing genius, and I rejoice in it. It is fitly framed and
to-morrow is to be hung in the parlor.

Our Munroe's press, you must believe, was of Aristotle's category
of the high-minded and slow. Chiding would do no good. They still
said, "We have but one copy, and so but one hand at work"! At last,
on the 1st of July, the book appeared in the market, but does not
come from the binder fast enough to supply the instant demand; and
therefore your two hundred and sixty copies cannot part from New
York until the 20th of July. They will be on board the London
packet which sails on that day. The publisher has his instructions to
bind the volumes to match the old ones. Our year since the publication of the Vols. I and II. is just complete, and I have set the man on
the account, but doubt if I get it before twelve or fourteen days. All
the edition is gone except forty copies, he told me; and asked me if
I would not begin to print a small edition of this First Series, five
hundred, as we have five hundred of the new Series too many, with
that view. But I am now so old a fox that I suspend majestically my
answer until I have his account. For on the 21st of July I am to pay
$462 for the paper of this new book: and by and by the printer's bill,
—whose amount I do not yet know; and it is better to be "slow and
high-minded" a little more, since we have been so much, and not go
deeper into these men's debt until we have tasted somewhat of their

[4] See above, C.4.13.39, n. 1.

credit. We are to get, as you know, by contract, near a thousand dollars from these first two volumes; yet a month ago I was forced to
borrow two hundred dollars for you on interest, such advances had
the account required. But the coming account will enlighten us all.

I am very happy in the "success" of the London lectures. I have
no word to add to-night, only that Sterling is not timber-toned, that I
love his poetry, that I admire his prose with reservations here and
there. What he knows he writes manly and well. Now and then he
puts a pasteboard man; but all our readers here take *Blackwood*
for his sake, and lately seek him in vain. I am getting on with some
studies of mine prosperously for me, have got three essays nearly done,
and who knows but in the autumn I shall have a book? Meantime
my little boy and maid, my mother and wife, are well, and the two
ladies send to you and yours affectionate regards,—they would fain
say urgent invitations. My mother sends to-night, my wife always.

I shall send you presently a copy of a translation published here
of Eckermann, by Margaret Fuller, a friend of mine and of yours,
for the sake of its preface mainly.[5] She is a most accomplished lady,
and her culture belongs rather to Europe than to America. Good bye.

R. W. Emerson.

Concord, 8 July, 1839.[1]

My dear sir,

Mr Francis Bowen[2] of Harvard University desires an opportunity
of conversing with you, as he passes through London. Mr Bowen leaves
our Cambridge, where he has taught the metaphysics, to prosecute
his studies in France & Germany.

Yours affectionately,   R. W. Emerson.

To Carlyle, Esq.

[5] " 'Conversations with Goethe. Translated from the German of Eckermann. By
S. M. Fuller.' Boston, 1839. This was the fourth volume in the series of 'Specimens
of Foreign Standard Literature,' edited by George Ripley. The book has a characteristic preface by Miss Fuller, in which she speaks of Carlyle as 'the only competent critic' of Goethe" (Norton's note).

[1] The MS of this letter is owned by the Berg Collection of the New York Public
Library. It shows no evidence of having gone through the mails.

[2] Bowen, two years before, had written in *The Christian Examiner* one of the
most hostile reviews that Emerson's *Nature* received (Rusk, *Life*, p. 242).

Concord, 8 August, 1839.[1]

Dear Friend

This day came the letter dated 24. June, with "steam packet" written by you on the outside, but no paddles wheeled it through the sea. It is 45 days old & too old to do its errand even had it come twenty days sooner—so far as printer & bookbinder are concerned. I am truly grieved for the mischance of the *John* Fraser & will duly lecture the sinning bookseller. I noticed the misnomer in a letter of his New York correspondent &, I believe, mentioned to you in a letter my fear of such a mischance. I am more sorry for the costliness of this adventure to you though in a gracious Nota Bene you cut down the fine one half. The new books tardily printed were tardily bound & tardily put to sea on the packet ship Ontario which left New York for London on the 1 August.—At least this was the promise of Munroe & Co. as I stood over the boxes in which they were packing them in the latter days of July. I hope they have not gone to *John* again, but you must keep an eye to both names. I can only hope also that your bookseller shall find the bindings perfectly matched. When I charged my men on this head, they replied, that all the foregone books were of one colour, blue,—& so there could be no doubt in binding the new; but since, they tell me that the binder has corrected them by showing his list of two or three colours, & has accordingly bound the new, the same number of the same colour. I dare scarcely hope they will prove right, but the binder said he would warrant them to the amount of the cost of retransportation.

In regard to the new "French Revolution," I hope you are not waiting still for a name. I received your proofsheet & showed it immediately to Brown, but I did not write you anew because I considered my first message on the subject our final answer to wit, that "C. C. Little & James Brown; Boston," would receive it on its arrival at that port & would then sell it on a commission not exceeding 20 per cent on whatever retail [2] price I with their advice should fix for the book. So I begged you to print their name. If this is still debateable, I suppose it of no important to them that the London publisher's

---

[1] The MS of this letter is owned by Mr. John Cooley.

[2] Emerson here crossed out the word "sale" and wrote in "retail."

name is prefixed, if he have any scruples. I hope to get the book sold, however, for a smaller commission than above named. You must not convict your London booksellers on the evidence of Munroe & Co.'s commission. They were very eager to have the book of Miscellanies out of Little & Co.'s hands to whom they feared it would go, & offered cheap terms. I thought it a grand bargain, but it has not proved so good as I thought. They have called upon me to pay the printing & the paper, (which Little & Co did not, in their book,) have credited me with no dollar until six months after a copy was sold, & now on 1 July, a year after the book was published & when only 40 copies remained unsold, we are in debt to them $104.31. As soon as I had paid all the dollars in my pocket, I borrowed more, and as the paper used in printing vols 3 & 4 is paid for, I shall have one of these days, I doubt not, an astonishing item of interest to charge you with in my accounts.

When I complained to these men of these inconveniences, & showed them Little & Co's Account, they showed me the difference of commission allowed to Little, & the fact of near 200 subscribers paying for *that* book on delivery; & really one would think, who had overheard the conversation, that J. M. & Co had done me the greatest favor in thus publishing, & thus putting me in debt, for they entrench themselves in their ciphering & shoot at me with volleys of figures. I am ashamed to write thus tediously but I wish to advertise you that I shall send you presently an abstract which at my desire they drew up of the cost & the profits of the book. Though you refuse my Leger, I am sure theirs will contain the accurate particulars.

I cannot tell you how glad I am that you have seen my brave senator, & seen him as I see him. All my days I have wished that he should go to England & never more than when I listened two or three times to debates [in] the house of Commons. We send out usually mean [per]sons as public agents, mere partisans, for whom I can only hope that no man with eyes will meet them, and now those thirsty eyes, those portrait-eating portrait-painting eyes of thine, those fatal perceptions have fallen full on the great forehead which I followed about, all my young days, from court house to senate chamber, from caucus to street. He has his own sins, no doubt; is no saint, is a prodigal. He has drunk this rum of Party, too, so long, that his strong head is soaked sometimes even like the soft sponges, but the "man's a man for a' that." [3] Better, he is a great boy, as wilful as non-chalant & good humored. But you must hear him speak,—not a show speech, which he never does well,—but *with cause*. He can strike a stroke like a smith. I owe to him a hundred fine hours & two or three moments of Eloquence. His voice in a great house is admirable. I am sorry if you decided not to visit him. He loves a *man*,[4] too. I do not know him, but my brother Edward read law with him, & loved him, & afterwards in sick & unfortunate days received the steadiest kindness from him.—Well, I am glad you are to think in earnest in Scotland of our cis-Atlantic claims. We shall have more rights over the wise & brave, I believe, before many years or months. We shall have more men & a better cause than has yet moved on our stagnant waters. I think our Church so called must presently vanish. There is an uni-versal timidity conformity in age; [5] and, on the other hand, the most resolute realism in the young. The man Alcott bides his time. I have a young poet in this village named Thoreau, who writes the truest verses.[6] I pine to show you my treasures; and tell Mrs. Carlyle we have women who deserve to know her. R. W. Emerson

The Yankees read & study the new volumes of "Miscellanies" even more than the old. The "Saml Johnson" & "Scott" are great favorites. Stearns Wheeler corrected proofs affectionately to the last. Truth & Health be with you alway!

Scotsbrig, Ecclefechan, 4th Sept^r, 1839—
Dear Emerson,

A cheerful and right welcome Letter of yours, dated 4th July, reached me here, duly forwarded, some three weeks ago; I delayed answering till there could some definite statement, as to bales of literature shipped or landed, or other matter of business forwarded a stage, be made. I am here, with my Wife, rusticating again, these two months; amid diluvian rains, chartism, teetotalism, deficient

---

[3] Cf. Burns's "Is there for honest poverty."   [4] See above, E.9.13.37.

[5] The MS is difficult to read here: Norton transcribed this phrase as "and rage."

[6] A week before, Emerson had written in his journal: "Last night came to me a beautiful poem from Henry Thoreau, 'Sympathy.' The purest strain, and the loftiest, I think, that has yet pealed from this unpoetic American forest" (*Journals*, V, 241).

harvest, and general complaint and confusion; which not being able to mend, all that I can do is to heed them as little as possible. "What care I for the house? I am only a lodger." [1] On the whole, I have sat under the wing of Saint Swithin; uncheery, sluggish, murky, as the wettest of his Days; [2]—hoping always nevertheless that blue sky, figurative and real, does exist, and will demonstrate itself by and by. I have been the stupidest and laziest of men. I could not write even to you, till some palpable call told me I must.

Yesternight however there arrives a despatch from Fraser, apprising me that the American *Miscellanies,* second cargo, are announced from Portsmouth, and "will probably be in the River tomorrow;" where accordingly they in all likelihood now are, a fair landing and good welcome to them! Fraser "knows not whether they are bound or not;" but will soon know. The first cargo, of which I have a specimen here, contented him extremely; only there was one fatality, the cloth of the binding was multiplex, party-coloured, some sets done in green, others in red, blue, perhaps skyblue! Now if the second cargo were *not* multiplex, party-coloured, nay multiplex *in exact accordance with the first,* as seemed almost impossible—?—Alas, in that case, one could not well predict the issue!—Seriously, it is a most handsome Book you have made; and I have nothing to return but thanks and again thanks. By the bye if you do print a small second edition of the First Portion, I might have had a small set of *errata* ready: but *where are they!* The Book only came into my hand *here* a few days ago; and I have been whipt from post to pillar without will of my own, without energy to form a will! The only glaring error I recollect at this moment is one somewhere in the second article on *Jean Paul:* "Osion" (I think, or some such thing) instead of "Orson": it is not an original American error, but copied from the English; if the Printer get his eye upon it, let him rectify; if not, not, I *deserve* to have it stand against me there. Fraser's joy, should the Books prove either unbound, or multiplex in the right way, will be great and unalloyed; he calculates on selling all the copies very soon. He has begun reprinting Goethe's *Wilhelm Meister* too, the *Apprenticeship* and *Travels* under one; and hopes to remunerate himself for that by and by: whether

[1] Cf. Seneca, *Epistulae Morales* (Loeb Classical Library), III, 391.

[2] According to legend, rain on St. Swithin's Day, July 15, means rain for the forty days that follow.

there will then remain any small peculium for me is but uncertain; meanwhile I correct the press nothing doubting. One of these I call my best translation, the other my worst; I have read that latter, the *Apprenticeship,* again in these weeks; not without surprise, disappointment, nay aversion here and there, yet on the whole with ever new esteem. I find I can pardon *all* things in a man except purblindness, falseness of vision,—for indeed does not that presuppose every other kind of falseness?

But let me hasten to say that the *F. Revolution,* 500 strong, for the New England market, is also, as Fraser advises, "to go to sea in three days." It is bound in red cloth, gilt; a pretty book, James says; which he will sell for 25 shillings here:—nay the London brotherhood have "subscribed" for 180 at once, which he considers great work. I directed him to consign to Little and Brown in Boston, the *property* of the thing *yours,* with such phraseology and formalities as they use in those cases. I paid him for it yesterday (to save discount) £95; that is the whole cost to me, 20 or 30 pounds more than was once calculated on. Do the best with it you can, my friend; and never mind the result. If the thing fail, as is likely enough, we will simply quit that transport trade, and say experience must be *paid for.* The titlepage was "Boston: Charles C. Little and James Brown," then, in a second line and smaller type, "London: James Fraser;" to which arrangement James made not the slightest objection, or indeed rather seemed to like it.—So much for trade matters: is it not *enough?* I declare I blush sometimes, and wonder where the good Emerson gets all his patience. We shall be thro' the affair one day, and find something better to speak about than dollars and pounds. And yet, as you will say, why not even of dollars? Ah, there are leaden-worded [bills] of exchange I have seen which have had an almost sacred character to me! *Pauca verba.*[3]

Doubt not your new utterances are eagerly waited for here; above all things the "Book" is what I want to see. You might have told me what it was about. We shall see by and by. A man that has discerned somewhat, and knows it for himself, let him speak it out, and thank Heaven. I pray that they do not confuse you by their praises; their blame will do no harm at all. Praise is sweet to all men; and yet alas, alas, if the light of one's own heart go out, bedimmed with poor vapours and sickly false glitterings and flashings, what profit is it!

[3] *Love's Labour's Lost,* act IV, scene ii, line 171.

Happier in darkness, in all manner of mere outward darkness, misfortune and neglect, "so that *thou canst endure*," [4]—which however one cannot—to *all* lengths. God speed you, my Brother. I hope all good things of you; and wonder whether like Phoebus Apollo you are destined to be a youth forever.—Sterling will be right glad to hear your praises; not unmerited, for he is a man among millions that John of mine, tho' his perpetual-mobility wears me out at times. Did he ever write to you? His latest speculation was that he should and would; but I fancy it is among the clouds again. I hear from him the other day, out of Welsh villages where he passed his boyhood, &c, all in a flow of "lyrical recognition," [5] hope, faith and sanguine unrest; I have even some thoughts of returning by Bristol (in a week or so, that must be), and seeing him. The dog has been reviewing me, he says, and it is coming out in the next *Westminster!* He hates terribly my doctrine of *"Silence."* As to America and lecturing I cannot in this torpid condition venture to say one word. Really it is not impossible even for this winter; and yet lecturing is a thing I shall never grow to like; still less lionizing Martineau-ing: *Ach Gott!* My Wife sends a thousand regards; *she* will never get across the ocean, you must come to her; she was almost *dead,* crossing from Liverpool hither, and declares she will never go to sea for any purpose whatsoever again. Never till next time! My good old Mother is here, my Brother John (home with his Duke from Italy); all send blessings and affection to you and yours. Adieu till I get to London.   Yours ever   T. Carlyle

Chelsea, London, 8 Decr, 1839—

My dear Emerson,

What a time since we have written to one another! Was it you that defalcated? Alas, I fear it was myself; I have had a feeling these nine or ten weeks that you were expecting to hear from me; that I absolutely could not write. Your kind gift of Fuller's Eckermann was handed in to our Hackney Coach, in Regent Street, as we wended homewards from the railway and Scotland, on perhaps the 8th of September last; a welcome memorial of distant friends and doings: nay perhaps there was a Letter two weeks prior to that:—I am a great sinner! But the truth is, I could not write; and now I can, and do it.

---

[4] Cf. Exod. 18: 23.   [5] I have not been able to identify this quotation.

Our sojourn in Scotland was stagnant, sad; but tranquil, *well let alone,*—an indispensable blessing to a poor creature fretted to fiddle-strings, as I grow to be in this Babylon, take it as I will. We had eight weeks of desolate rain; with about eight days bright as diamonds inter-calated in that black monotony of bad weather. The old Hills are the same; the old streams go gushing along as in past years, in past ages; but he that looks on them is no longer the same: and the old Friends, where are they? I walk silent thro' my old haunts in that country; sunk usually in inexpressible reflexions, in an immeasurable chaos of musings and mopings that cannot be reflected or articulated. The only work I had on hand was one that would not prosper with me: an Article for the *Quarterly Review* on the state of the Working Classes here. The thoughts were familiar to me, old, many years old; but the utterance of them, in what spoken dialect to utter them! The *Quar-terly Review* was not an eligible vehicle, and yet the eligiblest; of Whigs, abandoned to Dilettantism and withered sceptical convention-ality, there was no hope at all; the *London-and-Westminster* Radicals, wedded to their Benthamee formulas, and tremulous at their own shadows, expressly rejected my proposal many months ago: [1] Tories alone remained; Tories I often think have more stuff in them in spite of their blindness than any other class we have;—Walter Scott's *sym-pathy* with his fellow creatures, what is it compared with Sydney Smith's, with a Poor Law Commissioner's! Well: this thing would not prosper with me in Scotland at all; nor here at all, where nevertheless I had to persist writing; writing and burning, and cursing my destiny, and then again writing. Finally the thing came out, as an Essay on *Chartism;* was shown to Lockhart, according to agreement; [2] was praised by him, but was also found unsuitable by him; suitable to explode a whole fleet of Quarterlies into skyrockets in these times! And now Fraser publishes it himself, with some additions, as a little volume; and it will go forth in a week or two on its own footing; and England will see what she has to say to it, whether something or nothing; and one man, as usual, is right glad that *he* has nothing more to do with it. This is the reason why I could not write. I mean to send

[1] Mill did wish to "publish it in his *final* Number as a kind of final shout," but Carlyle decided that his article should not go down with the magazine (*New Let-ters of Thomas Carlyle,* I, 176).

[2] Lockhart and Carlyle had reached a tentative agreement in May about *"an article on the Working Classes"* (ibid., 161).

you the Proofsheets of this thing, to do with as you see cause; there will be but some five or six, I think. It is probable my New England brothers may approve some portions of it; may be curious to see it reprinted: you ought to say Yes or No in regard to that. I think I will send all the sheets together; or at farthest, at two times.

Fraser, when we returned hither, had already received his *Miscellanies;* had about despatched his 500 *French-Revolutions,* "insured" and so forth, consigned I suppose to your protection and the proper Bookseller's; probably they have got over from New York into your neighbourhood before now. Much good may they do you! The *Miscellanies,* with their variegated binding, proved to be in perfect order; and are now all sold; with much regret from poor James that we had not a thousand more of them! This thousand he now sets about providing, by his own industry, poor man; I am revising the American copy in these days; the Printer is to proceed forthwith. I admire the good Stearns Wheeler as I proceed; I write to him my thanks by this post, and send him by Kennet a copy of Goethe's *Meister* for symbol of acknowledgment.[3] Another copy goes off for you, to the care of Little and Company. Fraser has got it out two weeks ago; a respectable enough book, now that the version is corrected somewhat. Tell me whether you dislike it less; what you do think of it? By the bye, have you not learned to read German now? I rather think you have. It is three months well spent, if ever months were, for a thinking Englishman of this age.—I hope Kennet will use more despatch than he sometimes does. Thank Heaven for these Boston steamers they project! May the Nereids and Poseidon favour them! They will bring us a thousand miles nearer, at one step; by and by we shall be of one parish after all.

During Autumn I speculated often about a Hegira into New England this very year: but alas! my horror of *Lecturing* continues great; and what else is there for me to do there? These several years I have had no wish so pressing as to hold my peace. I begin again to feel some use in articulate speech; perhaps I shall one day have something that I *want* to utter even in your side of the water. We shall see. Patience, and shuffle the cards.[4]—I saw no more of Webster; did not even learn well where he was; till lately I noticed in the Newspapers

[3] These volumes, which are still owned by the Wheeler family, are inscribed "Mr. Stearns Wheeler [from] T. C. London, Dec. 1839" (Eidson, *Charles Stearns Wheeler,* p. 106).

[4] See above, C.9.25.38, n. 5.

that he had gone hom[e a]gain. A certain Mr Brown [5] (I think) brought me a letter from you, not long since; I forw[arded] him to Cambridge and Scotland: a modest inoffensive man. He said he had never personally met with Emerson. My Wife recalled to him the story of the Scotch Traveller on the top of Vesuvius: "Never saw so beautiful a scene in the world!"—"Nor I," replied a stranger standing there, "except once; on the top of Dunmiot in the Ochil Hills in Scotland." —"Good Heavens! That is a part of my Estate, and I was never there! I will go thither." Yes, do!—We have seen no other transoceanic that I remember. We expect your *Book* soon! We know the subject of your winter Lectures too; at least Miss Martineau thinks she does, and makes us think so. Heaven speed the work—Heaven send my good Emerson a clear utterance, in all right ways, of the nobleness that dwells in him. He knows what silence means; let him know speech also, in its season: the two are like canvas and pigment, like darkness and light-image painted thereon; the one is essential to the other, not possible without the other.

Poor Miss Martineau is in Newcastle-on-Tyne this winter; sick, painfully not dangerously; with a surgical brother-in-law.[6] Her meagre didacticalities afflict me no more; but also her blithe friendly presence cheers me no more. We wish she were back. This silence, I calculate, forced silence will do her much good. If I were a legislator, I would order every man, once a week or so, to lock his lips together, and utter no vocable at all for four-and-twenty hours: it would do him an immense benefit, poor fellow. Such racket, and cackle of mere hearsay and sincere-cant grows at last entirely deafening, enough to drive one mad,—like the voice of mere infinite rookeries answering your voice! Silence, silence!—Sterling sent you a Letter from Clifton, which I set under way here, having added the address.[7] He is not well again, the good Sterling; talks of Madeira this season again: but I hope otherwise. You of course read his sublime "article"? [8] I tell him it was— a thing *un*tellable!

Mr Southey has fallen, it seems, into a mournful condition: oblivion,

---

[5] See below, C.1.6.40 and E.8.30.40.   [6] See below, C.2.21.41, n. 3.

[7] This was the letter of September 30, 1838. See Sterling, *A Correspondence between John Sterling and Ralph Waldo Emerson*, ed. E. W. Emerson, p. 25.

[8] See below, E.12.12.39, n. 1. To Sterling, Carlyle wrote: "Mill says it is the best thing you ever wrote; and, truly, so should I, if you had not shut my mouth" (Froude *Thomas Carlyle: Life in London*, I, 145).

mute hebetation, loss of all faculty. He suffered greatly, nursing his former wife in her insanity, for years till her relief by death; suffered, worked, and made no moan; the brunt of the task over, he sank into collapse in the hands of a new wife he had just wedded. What a lot for him; for her especially! The most excitable, but most methodic man I have ever seen. Τέλος! that is a word that awaits us all.—I have my brother here at present; tho' talking of Lisbon with his Buccleuchs. My Wife seems better than of late winters. I actually had a Horse,[9] nay actually have it, tho' it is gone to the country till the mud abate again! It did me perceptible good; I mean to try it farther. I am no longer so desperately *poor* as I have been for twelve years back: sentence of starvation or beggary seems revoked at last, a blessedness really very considerable. Thanks, thanks! We send a thousand regards to the two little ones, to the two mothers. *Valete nostrum memores.*[10]

T. Carlyle

Concord, 12 December, 1839.

My dear friend,

Not until 29 November did the 500 Copies of the French Revolution arrive in Boston Fraser unhappily sent them to New York whence they came not without long delays. They came in in perfectly good order, not in the pretty red, you told us of, but in a sober green;— not so handsome & saleable a *back*, our booksellers said, as their own; but in every other respect a good book. The duties at the New York Custom House on these and a quantity of other books sent by Fraser, amounted to $400.36 whereof, I understand, the Fr. Rev. pays for its share $243.00. No bill has been brought us for freight, so we conclude that you have paid it. I confided the book very much to the conscience & discretion of Little & Brown, and after some ciphering they settle to sell it at $3.75 per copy, wherefrom you are to get the cost of the book and (say) $1.10 per copy, profit, and no more.[1] The booksellers eat the rest. The book is rather too dear for our market of cheap manufactures, and therefore we are obliged to give the booksellers a good

---

[9] Not "Yankee" but "Citoyenne," a gift from John Marshall, a linen manufacturer of Leeds (Wilson, *Carlyle on Cromwell and Others*, p. 71).

[10] Juvenal, *Satire* III, 318.

[1] The word "After" at the beginning of this sentence was crossed out by Emerson.

per centage to get it off at all: for we stand in daily danger of a cheap edition from some rival neighbor. I hope to give you good news of its sale soon, although I have been assured today that no book sells, the times are so bad. Brown had disposed of 50 or 60 copies to the trade, & 12 at retail. He doubted not to sell them all in six months. Before I leave these books let me say at Brown's instance that he wishes Fraser to send him an invoice of the *other books* sent, & instructions; having received nothing of the sort. He proposes to draw on Fraser for the amount of the duties on *them*.

Of the Miscellanies, something is to be said. My second edition of the Vols 1 & 2, is printing, & they have finished the first volume. On the 1 January J. Munroe & Co are to render me a six months' account of their sales, which I hope will meet the payment of about $600. due about that time for printing vols III & IV. If not, we shall make the Fr. Rev. pay the debts of its elder brother. Our account may get a little complex, but we are very sure of an ultimate liquidation and a good profit.

Several persons have asked me to get some copies of the German Romance sent over here for sale. Last week a gentleman desired me to say he wanted *four* copies and today I have been charged to procure another. I think if you will send me by Little & Brown through Longman, *six* copies, we can find an immediate market.

It gives me great joy to write to my friend once more, slow as you may think me to use the privilege. For a good while I dared believe you were coming hither, & why should I write?—and now for weeks I have been absorbed in my foolish lectures, of which only two are yet delivered & ended. There should be eight more—Subject, The Present Age.—Out of these follies I remember you with glad heart. Lately I had Sterling's letter, which, since I have read his Article on You, I am determined to answer speedily.[2] I delighted in the spirit of that Paper, loving you so well & accusing you so conscientiously. What does he at Clifton? If you communicate with him tell him I thank him for his letter and hold him dear. I am very happy lately in adding one or two new friends to my little circle; and you may be sure every friend of mine is a friend of yours. So when you come here, you shall

[2] Emerson received Sterling's letter on November 6; he answered it on May 29 (*Journals*, V, 313, 406). Sterling's article "On the Writings of Thomas Carlyle," appeared in *The London and Westminster Review*, XXXIII (1839), 1–68.

not be lonely. A new person is always to me a great event, & will not let me sleep.—I believe I was not wise to volunteer myself to this fever fit of Lecturing again. I ought to have written instead in silence & serenity. Yet I work better under this base necessity and then I have a certain delight (base also?) in speaking to a multitude. But my joy in friends, those *sacred* people, is my consolation for the mishaps of this adventure and they for the most part come to me from this *publication* of myself.—After ten or twelve weeks I think I shall address myself earnestly to writing, and give some form to my formless scripture.

I beg you will write to me and tell me what you do, and give me good news of your wife & your brother. Can they not see the necessity of your coming to look after your American interests? My wife & mother love both you & them.—A young man of New York told me the other day he was about getting you an invitation from an Association in that city to give them a course of Lectures on such terms as would at least make you whole in the expenses of coming thither. We could easily do that in Boston. R W Emerson

What manner of person is Heraud? [3] Do you read Landor, or know him, O seeing man? Fare well!

[3] J. A. Heraud, formerly an assistant editor of *Fraser's Magazine,* was at this time editor of *The Monthly Magazine,* and had recently written a letter to Bronson Alcott in praise of his much-abused *Records of a School* (Emerson, *Journals,* V, 322).

1840

Chelsea, London, 6 Jany, 1840—

My dear Emerson,

It is you, I surely think, that are in my debt now; nevertheless I must fling you another word: may it cross one from you coming hither—as near the *Lizard Point* as it likes!

Some four sheets making a Pamphlet called *Chartism* addressed to you at Concord are, I suppose, snorting along thro' the waters this morning, part of the Cargo of the *British Queen*. At least I gave them to Mr Brown (your unseen friend) about ten days ago, who promised to dispose of them; the *British Queen,* he said, was the earliest chance. The Pamphlet itself (or rather Booklet, for Fraser has gilt it &c, and asks five shillings for it as a Book) is out since then;[1] radicals and others yelping considerably in a discordant manner about it: I have nothing other to say to *you* about it than what I said last time, that the sheets were *yours* to do with as you saw good,—to burn if you reckoned that fittest. It is not entirely a Political Pamphlet; nay there are one or two things in it which my American Friends specially may like: but the interests discussed are altogether English, and cannot be considered as likely to concern *New*-Englishmen very much. However, it will probably be itself in your hand, before this sheet, and you will have determined what is fit.

A copy of *Wilhelm Meister,* two copies, one for Stearns Wheeler, are probably in some of the "Line Ships" at this time too: good voyage to them! The F. Revolutions were all shipped, insured &c; they have, I will suppose, arrived safe, as we shall hear by and by. What freightages, landings and embarkments! For only two days ago I sent you off thro' Kennett, another Book: John Sterling's Poems, which he has collected into a volume. Poor John has overworked himself again, or the climate without fault on his side has proved too hard for him: he sails

[1] *Chartism* was published late in December, 1839 (Dyer, *Bibliography of . . . Carlyle's Writings,* p. 52).

for Madeira again next week! His Doctors tell me there is no intrinsic danger; but they judge the measure safe as one of precaution. It is very mortifying: he had nestled himself down at Clifton, thinking he might now hope to continue there; and lo he has to fly again.—Did you get his Letter? The address to him now will be, for three months to come, *"Edward* Sterling Esq, South Place, Knightsbridge, London," his Father's designation.

Farther I must not omit to say that Richard Monckton Mylnes purposes, thro' the strength of Heaven, to *review* you! In the next No of the *London and Westminster* the courageous youth will do this feat, if they let him. Nay *he* has already done it, the Paper being actually written: he employed me last week in negociating with the Editor about it; and their answer was, "Send us the Paper, it promises very well." We shall see whether it comes out or not; keeping silence till then. Mylnes is a *Tory* Member of Parliament; think of that! For the rest, he describes his religion in these terms, "I *profess* to be a *Crypto-*Catholic." Conceive the man! A most bland-smiling, semi-quizzical, affectionate, highbred, Italianized little man of 5 feet 1, who has long olive-blond hair, a dimple, next to [no] chin, and flings his arm round your neck when he addresses you [in pub]lic [2] society! Let us hear now what *he* will say of the American *Vates.*

Fraser the Bookseller was here few minutes ago about those everlasting *Miscellanies,* which he has hardly got to Press yet; which he pleads amazingly to have made into *six* volumes by adding *Chartism* and the things in German Romance. I have got all the Book read over; punctuation corrected &c &c, and mean to wash *my* hands of it as far as possible henceforth. I am doing little or nothing. When comes the Emerson *Book?* At all events, the Emerson Letter!—Good be ever with you, my friend!—Your affectionate,   T. Carlyle [3]

Chelsea, London, 17th Jany, 1840—

Dear Emerson,

Your letter of the 12th December, greatly to my satisfaction, has arrived; the struggling steamship in spite of all hurricanes has brought

[2] Conjectural. The MS is torn here and immediately above.

[3] The last paragraph of this letter was cut off, and is now owned by the Yale University Library.

it safe across the waters to me. I find it good to write you a word in return straightway; tho' I think there are already two or perhaps even three messages of mine to you flying about unacknowledged somewhere under the moon; nay the last of them perhaps may go by the same packet as this,—having been forwarded, as this will be, to *Liverpool,* after the *British Queen* sailed from London.

Your account of the *F. Revolution* packages, and prognosis of what Little and Brown will do with them is altogether as it should be. I apprised Fraser instantly of *his* invoiceless Books &c; he answers that order has been taken in that long since, "instructions" sent, and I conclude, arrangements for *bills* least of all forgotten. I mentioned what share of the duty was his; and that your men meant to draw on him for it. That is all right.—As to the *F. Revolution* I agree with your Booksellers altogether about it; the American Edition actually pleases myself better for looking at; nor do I know that this new English one has much superiority for use: it is despicably printed, I fear, so far as false spellings, and other slovenlinesses can go: Fraser "finds the people like it"; *credat Iudaeus;* [1]—as for me, I have told him I will not *print any more* with that man but with some other man. Curious enough: the price Little & B. have fixed upon was the price I remember guessing at beforehand, and the result they propose to realize for me corresponds closely with my prophecy too. Thanks, a thousand thanks for all the trouble you never grudge to take. We shall get ourselves handsomely out of this export and import speculation; and know, taught at a rather *cheap* rate, not to embark in the like again.

There went off a *W. Meister* for you, and a letter to announce it, several weeks ago; that was message first. Your travelling neighbour Brown took charge of a Pamphlet named *Chartism,* to be put into the British Queen's Letter-bag (where I hope, and doubt not, he did put it, tho' I have seen nothing of him since); that and a letter in reference to it was message second. Thirdly I sent off a volume of Poems by Sterling, likewise announced in that letter. And now this that I actually write is the fourth (it turns out to be) and last of all the messages. Let us take arithmetic along with us in all things.—Of *Chartism* I have nothing farther to say, except that Fraser is striking off another 1000 copies to be called 2nd edition; and that the people accuse me

---

[1] "Credat Judaeus Apella non ego": Horace, *Satires,* book I, Satire 5, line 100.

not of being an incendiary and speculative sansculotte threatening to become practical, but of being a Tory,—thank Heaven. The *Miscellanies* are at press, at *two* presses; to be out, as Hope asseverates, in March: five volumes, without *Chartism;* with Hoffman and Tieck from German Romance, stuck in somewhere as Appendix; with some other trifles stuck in elsewhere, chiefly as Appendix; and no essential change from the Boston edition. Fraser, "overwhelmed with business," does not yet send me his net-result of those 250 copies sold off some time ago; as soon as he does, you shall hear of it for your satisfaction.—As to *German Romance,* tell my friends that it has been out of print these ten years; procurable, of late not without difficulty, only in the Old-Book shops. The comfort is that the *best* part of it stands in the new *W. Meister:* Fraser & I had some thought of adding *Tieck's* and *Richter's* parts, had they suited for a volume; the rest *may* without detriment to anybody perish.

Such press-correctings and arrangings waste my time here, not in [the] agreeablest way. I begin, tho' in as sulky a state of health as ever, to look again towards some new kind of work. I have often thought of Cromwell and Puritans; but do not see how the subject can be presented still alive. A subject dead is not worth presenting. Meanwhile I read rubbish of Books; Eichhorn,[2] Grimm &c; very considerable rubbish, one grain in the cartload worth pocketing. It is pity I have no appetite for lecturing! Many applications have been made to me here; —none more touching to me than one, the day before yesterday, by a fine innocent-looking Scotch lad, in the name of himself and certain other Booksellers' shopmen eastward in the city! I cannot get them out of my head. Poor fellows! they have nobody to say an honest word to them, in this articulate-speaking world, and they apply to *me*.—For you, good friend, I account you luckier; I do verily: lecture there what innumerable things you have got to say on "The Present Age";—yet withal do not forget to *write* either, for that is the lasting plan after all. I have a curious Note sent me for inspection the other day; it is addressed to a Scotch Mr Erskine [3] (famed among the saints here) by

[2] Probably J. G. Eichhorn, German theologian and biblical scholar.

[3] Thomas Erskine of Linlethan, a rich lawyer, author of *Remarks on the Internal Evidence for Revealed Religion*. In the Berg Collection of the New York Public Library there is a copy of Emerson's Dartmouth *Oration* inscribed on the front cover "Rev. John Sterling/With the respects of/ R.W.E." and "Thomas Erskine Esq/ *meo periculo*/ T.C."

a Madame Necker, Madame de Staël's Kinswoman, to whom he the said Mr E. had lent your first Pamphlet at Geneva. She regards you with a certain love, yet a *shuddering* love. She says, *"Cela sent l'Ameri-cain qui après avoir abattu les forets à coup de hache, croit qu' on doit de meme conquérir le monde intellectuel"!* What R. M. Mylnes will say of you we hope also to see.—I know both Heraud and Landor; but, alas, what room is here! Another sheet with less of "arithmetic" in it will soon be allowed me. Adieu dear friend.

Yours ever & ever   T. Carlyle

                                        New York   18 March 1840

My dear friend,

I have just seen the steamer "British Queen" enter this harbor from sea, and here lies the "Great Western" to sail tomorrow. I will not resist hints so broad upon my long procrastinations. You shall have at least a tardy acknowledgment that I received in January your letter of December, which I should have answered at once, had it not found me absorbed in writing foolish lectures which were then at high tide. I had written you a little earlier, tidings of the receipt of your "Fr. Revolution." Your letter was very welcome, as all your letters are. I have since seen tidings of the "Essay on Chartism," in an English Periodical, but have not yet got my proofsheets. They are probably still rolling somewhere outside of this port; for all our packet ships have had the longest passages; only one has come in for many a week. We will be as patient as we can.

I am here on a visit to my brother, who is a lawyer in this city, and lives at Staten Island, at a distance of half an hour's sail. The City has such immense natural advantages, & such capabilities of boundless growth, & such varied & ever increasing accommodations & appliances for eye & ear, for memory & wit, for locomotion & lavation, & all manner of delectation,—that I see that the poor fellows that live here, do get some compensation for the sale of their souls. And how they multiply! They estimate the population today at 350,000, and forty years ago, it is said, there were but 20,000. But I always seem to suffer from loss of faith on entering cities. They are great conspiracies; the parties are all masquers who have taken mutual oaths of silence, not to betray each others secret, & each to keep the others madness in countenance. You can scarce drive any craft here that does not seem a subornation of the treason. I believe in the spade and an acre of good ground. Whoso cuts a straight path to his own bread, by the help of God in the sun & rain & sprouting of the grain, seems to me an *universal* workman. He solves the problem of life not for one but for all men of sound body. I wish I may one day send you word, or better, show you the fact that I live by my hands without loss of memory or of hope.[1] And yet I am of such a puny constitution, as far as concerns bodily labor, that perhaps I never shall. We will see.

Did I tell you that we hope shortly to send you some American verses & prose of good intent? My vivacious friend Margaret Fuller is to edit a journal, whose first number she promises for 1 July next, which I think will be written with a good will if written at all. I saw some poetical fragments which charmed me,—if only the writer consents to give them to the public.[2]

I believe I have yet little to tell you of myself. I ended in the middle of February my ten lectures on the Present Age. They are attended by from 450 to 500 people, and the young people are so attentive & out of the hall ask me so many questions, that I assume all the airs of Age & sapience. I am very happy in the sympathy & society of from six to a dozen persons who teach me to hope & expect everything from my Countrymen. We shall have many Richmonds in the field, presently.[3] I turn my face homeward tomorrow, & this summer I mean to resume my endeavor to make some presentable book of Essays out of my mountain of manuscript, were it only for the sake of clearance. I left my wife, & boy, & girl,—the softest & gracefullest little maiden alive, creeping like a turtle with head erect all about the house,—well at home a week ago. The boy has two deep blue wells for eyes, into which I gladly peer when I am tired. Ellen, they say, has no such depth of orb, but I believe I love her better than ever I did the boy. I brought

---

[1] See below, E.4.21.40. Although Alcott did not move to Concord until late March or early April, he had undoubtedly discussed with Emerson his plan to live by his hands.

[2] The work of William Ellery Channing the younger, to whom Emerson had written on January 30, 1840, ". . . a number of your poems . . . I have read & still read with great delight. I have seen no verses written in America that have such inward music, or that seem to me such authentic inspiration" (*Let RWE*, II, 252). Emerson published a dozen of the poems in the second number of *The Dial* (October, 1840) with introductory praise for their bold and unconventional imagery.

[3] Cf. *Richard III*, act V, scene iv, line 11.

my mother with me here to spend the summer with William E. and his wife & ruddy boy of four years. All these persons love & honor you in proportion to their knowledge & years. My letter will find you I suppose meditating new lectures for your London disciples. May love & truth inspire them. I can see easily that my predictions are coming to pass & that having waited until your Fame was in the flood tide we shall not now see you at all on western shores. Our saintly Dr Tuckerman,[4] I am told, had a letter within a year from Lord Bryon's daughter *informing* the good man of the appearance of a certain wonderful genius in London named Thomas Carlyle, and all his astonishing workings on her own & her friends' brains—and him the very monster whom the Doctor had been honoring with his best dread & consternation these five years. But do come in one of Mr Cunard's ships as soon as the booksellers have made you rich. If they fail to do so come & read lectures which the Yankees will pay for. Give my love & hope & perpetual remembrance to your wife,—& my wife's also, who bears her in her kindest heart & who resolves every now & then, to write to her that she may thank her for the beautiful Guido.

You told me to send you no more accounts. But I certainly shall, as our financial relations are grown more complex & I wish at least to relieve myself of this unwonted burden of booksellers accts. & long delays, by sharing them. I have had one of their Estimates by me a year, waiting to send. Farewell.   R.W.E.

Chelsea, London, 1 April, 1840—

My dear Emerson,

A Letter has been due to you from me, if not by palpable law of reciprocity, yet by other law and right, for some week or two. I meant to write so soon as Fraser and I had got a settlement effected. The travelling Sumner being about to return into your neighbourhood, I gladly accept his offer to take a message to you. I wish I had anything beyond a dull Letter to send! But unless, as my wife suggests, I go and get you a D'Orsay[1] *Portrait* of myself, I see not what there is!

[4] Presumably the Unitarian minister Joseph Tuckerman (1778–1840) who had preached in England in 1834.

[1] Count Alfred D'Orsay, French dandy, a favorite of fashionable London, was a gifted amateur painter. See below, E.6.29.45.

Do you read German or not? I now and then fall in with a curious German volume, not perhaps so easily accessible in the Western world. Tell me. Or do you ever mean to learn it? I decidedly wish you would. —As to the D'Orsay Portrait, it is a real curiosity: Count D'Orsay the emperor of European Dandies pourtraying the Prophet of spiritual Sanscullotism! He came rolling down hither one day, many months ago, in his sun-chariot, to the bedazzlement of all bystanders; found me in dusty grey-plaid dressing-gown, grim as the spirit of Presbyterianism (my Wife said), and contrived to get along well enough with me. I found him a man worth talking to, once and away; a man of decided natural gifts, every utterance of his containing in it a wild caricature *likeness* of some object or other; a dashing man, who might, some twenty years sooner born, have become one of Bonaparte's Marshals, and *is* alas,—Count D'Orsay! The Portrait he dashed off in some twenty minutes (I was dining there, to meet Landor); we have not chanced to meet together since, and *I* refuse to undergo any more eight-o'clock dinners for such an object.—Now if I do not send you the Portrait, after all?

Fraser's account of the *Miscellanies* stood legibly extended over large spaces of paper, and was in several senses amazing to look upon. I trouble *you* only with the result. Two hundred and forty-eight copies (for there were some one or two "imperfect"): all these he had sold, at 2 guineas each; and sold swiftly, for I recollect in December or perhaps November he told me he was "holding back," not to run entirely out. Well, of the £500 and odds so realized for these Books, the portion that belonged to me was £239;—the £261 had been the expense of handing the ware over the counter, and drawing in the coin for it! "Rules of the Trade"; it is a Trade, one would surmise, in which the Devil has a large interest. However, not to spend an instant, polluting one's eyesight with that side of it,—let me feel joyfully, with thanks to Heaven and America, that I do receive such a sum in the shape of wages, by decidedly the noblest method in which wages could come to a man. Without friendship, without Ralph Waldo Emerson, there had been no sixpense of *that* money here. Thanks and again thanks. This Earth is not an unmingled ball of Mud, after all. Sunbeams visit it;—mud *and* sunbeams are the stuff it has from of old consisted of.—I hasten away from the Ledger, with the mere good-news that James is altogether content with the "progress" of all these

Books, including even the well-abused Chartism Book. We are just on the point of finishing our English reprint of the *Miscellanies;* of which I hope to send you a copy before long.

And now why do not *you* write to me? Your Lectures must be done long ago. Or are you perhaps writing a Book? I shall be right glad to hear of that; and withal to hear that you do *not* hurry yourself, but strive with deliberate energy to produce what in you is best. Certainly, I think, a right Book does lie in the man! It is to be remembered also always that the true *value* is determined by what we *do not* write! There is nothing truer than that now all but forgotten truth; it is eternally true. He whom it concerns can consider it.—You have doubtless seen Milnes's review of you. I know not that you will find it to strike direct upon the secret of *Emerson,* to hit the nail on the head, anywhere at all; I rather think not. But it is gently, not unlovingly done;—and lays the first plank of a kind of pulpit for you here and throughout all Saxondom: a thing rather to be thankful for. It on the whole surpassed my expectations. Milnes tells me he is sending you a copy and a Note,[2] by Sumner. He is really a pretty little robin-redbreast of a man.

You asked me about Landor and Heraud. Before my paper entirely vanishes, let me put down a word about them. Heraud is a loquacious scribacious little man, of middle age, of parboiled greasy aspect, whom Leigh Hunt describes as "wavering in the most astonishing manner between being Something and Nothing." To me he is chiefly remarkable as being still, with his entirely enormous vanity and very small stock of faculty,—out of Bedlam. He picked up a notion or two from Coleridge many years ago; and has ever since been rattling them in his head, like peas in an empty bladder, and calling on the world to "List the Music of the Spheres." [3] He escapes *assassination,* as I calculate, chiefly by being the cheerfullest, best-natured little creature extant. You cannot kill him, he laughs so sofly, even when he is like killing you. John Mill said: "I forgive him freely for interpreting the Universe, now when I find he cannot pronounce the *h*'s." Really this is no caricature; you have not seen the match of Heraud in your days. I mentioned to him once that Novalis had said, "The highest problem

---

[2] Carlyle had himself suggested this courtesy to Milnes (T. W. Reid, *The Life, Letters, and Friendships of Richard Monckton Milnes,* I, 240).

[3] Cf. *Twelfth Night,* act III, scene i, line 122.

of Authorship is the writing of a Bible." [4]—"That is precisely what I am doing!" answered the aspiring, unaspirating.—Of Landor I have not got much benefit either. We met first, some four years ago, on Cheyne Walk here: a tall broad burly man, with grey hair, and large fierce-rolling eyes; of the most restless impetuous vivacity not to be held in by the most perfect breeding,—expressing itself in high-coloured superlatives, indeed in reckless exaggeration, now and then in a dry sharp laugh not of sport but of mockery; a wild man, whom no extent of culture had been able to tame! His intellectual faculty seemed to me to be weak in proportion to his violence of temper: the judgement he gives about anything is more apt to be wrong than right, —as the inward whirlwind shows him this side or the other of the object; and *sides* of an object are all that he sees. He is not an original man; in most cases, one but sighs over the spectacle of commonplace torn to rags. I find him painful as a writer; like a soul ever promising to take wing into the Aether, yet never doing it, ever splashing web-footed in the terrene mud, and only splashing the worse the more he strives! Two new tragedies of his that I read lately are the fatallest stuff I have seen for long: not an ingot; ah no, a distracted coil of wire-drawings saleable in no market. Poor Landor has left his Wife (who is said to be fool) in Italy, with his children, who would not quit her; but it seems he has honestly surrendered all his money to her, except a bare annuity for furnished lodgings; and now lives at Bath, a solitary sexagenarian, in that manner. He visits London in May; but says always it would kill him soon: alas, I can well believe that! They say he has a kind heart; nor does it seem unlikely: a perfectly honest heart, free and fearless, dwelling amid such hallucinations, excitations, tempestuous confusions, I can see he has. Enough of him! Me he likes well enough, more thanks to him; but two hours of such speech as his leave me giddy and undone. I have seen some other Lions, and Lion's-*providers;* [5] but consider them a worthless species.—When will you write, then? Consider my frightful outlook with a Course of Lectures to give "On Heroes and Hero-Worship"—from Odin to Rob[t] Burns! My wife salutes you all. Good be in the Concord Household!—

Yours ever,   T. Carlyle

[4] A slightly different translation of this sentence from *Die Christenheit oder Europa* appears in Carlyle's "Novalis" (*Works TC,* XXVII, 43).

[5] "A popular name for the jackal" (*The Century Dictionary*).

Concord, 21 April 1840 [1]

My dear Friend,

Three weeks ago I received a letter from you following another in the week before which I should have immediately acknowledged but that I was then promised a private opportunity for the 25 April by which time I promised myself to send you sheets of accounts. I had also written you from New York about the middle of March. But now I suppose Mr Grinnèll,—a hospitable, humane, modest gentleman in Providence, Rhode Island; a merchant, much beloved by all his townspeople, & though no scholar yet very fond of silently listening to such, —is packing his trunk to go to England. He offered to carry any letters for me & as at his house during my visit to Providence [2] I was eagerly catechised by all comers concerning Thomas Carlyle, I thought it behoved me to offer him for his brethren, sisters, & companions' sake, the joy of seeing the living face of that wonderful man. Let him see thy face & pass on his way. I who cannot see it nor hear the voice that comes forth of it, must even betake me to this paper to repay the best I can the love of the Scottish man & in the hope to deserve more.

Your letter announces Wilhelm Meister, Sterlings Poems, & Chartism. I am very rich or am to be. But Kennett is no Mercury. Wilhelm & Sterling have not yet made their appearance, though diligently inquired after by Stearns Wheeler & me. Little & Brown now correspond with Longman, not with Kennett. But they will come soon, perhaps are already arrived.

"Chartism" arrived at Concord by mail not until one of the last days of March though dated by you, I think, 21 December. I returned home 3 April, & found it waiting. All that is therein said, is well & strongly said, and as the words are barbed & feathered the memory of men cannot choose but carry them whithersoever men go. And yet I thought the book itself instructed me to look for more. We seemed to have a right to an answer less concise to a question so grave & humane & put with energy & eloquence. I mean that whatever prob-

---

[1] The manuscript of this letter is owned by the Yale University Library.

[2] Emerson had been in Providence during the second half of March to deliver his course of lectures on "Human Life"; George Grinnell was a dealer in paints and hardware (*Let RWE*, II, 266n, 289n). See below, E.4.22.40.

abilities or possibilities of solution occurred should have been opened to us in some detail. But now it stands as a preliminary word & you will one day, when the fact itself is riper, write the second lesson; or those whom you have instructed will. I read the book twice hastily through & sent it directly to press fearing to be forestalled, for the London book was in Boston already. Little & Brown are to print it. Their estimate is—

Printing page for page with the copy	63.35
Paper	44.
Binding	90.
	$197.35

Costing say 20 cents per copy for 1000 copies bound. The book to sell for 50 cents: The Booksellers' commission 20 percent on the Retail price. The Author's profit, 15 cents per copy. They intend, if a cheap edition is published,—no unlikely event,—to stitch the book as pamphlet & sell it at 38 cents. I expect it from the press in a few days.[3] I shall not on this sheet break into the other accounts as I am expecting hourly from Munroe's clerk an entire Account of R. W. E. with T. C. of which I have furnished him with all the facts I had, & he is to write it out in the manner of his craft. I did not give it to him until I had made some unsuccessful experiments myself.

I am here at work now for a fortnight to spin some single cord out of my thousand and one strands of every color & texture that lie ravelled around me in old snarls. We need to be possessed with a mountainous conviction of the value of our advice to our contemporaries if we will take such pains to find what that is. But no, it is the pleasure of the spinning that betrays poor spinners into the loss of so much good time. I shall work with the more diligence on this book-to-be of mine that you inform me again & again that my penny tracts are still extant, nay, that, beside friendly men, learned & poetic men read & even review them. I am like Scholasticus of the Greek Primer who was ashamed to bring out so small a dead child before such grand people. Pygmalion shall try if he cannot fashion a better, certainly a bigger.—I am sad to hear that Sterling sails again for his health. I am ungrateful not to have written to him as his letter was very welcome

[3] The book was published April 29 (*Let RWE*, II, 279n).

to me I will not promise again until I do it. I received a note last week forwarded by Mr Hume from New York & instantly replied to greet the good messenger to our Babylonian city, & sent him letters to a few friends of mine there. But my brother writes me that he had left New York for Washington when he went to seek him at his lodgings. I hope he will come northward presently & let us see his face.[4]

22 April. Last evening came to me the promised account drawn up by Munroe's clerk Chapman. I have studied it with more zeal than success. An Account seems an ingenious way of burying facts: it asks wit equal to his who hid them to find them. I am far as yet from being master of this statement, yet as I have promised it so long, I will send it now, & study a copy of it at my leisure. It is intended to begin where the last account I sent you, viz, of "Fr. Revolution," ended, with a balance of $9.53 in your favor. You will see that of the 1 & 2 Miscellanies, they have counted from my list seventeen Copies given. I believe they have added one by misake. I count 16; of these, six were to editors; three, to friends who helped us by loan of books or correcting of the proofs; & the rest to persons whom I fancied had commanding claims on you or me. I believe, in the former Account, H. Fuller was charged with 16 copies "Fr. Rev." not paid. In this he is credited with payment for 10;—3 he returned to Little & Co. who account for them; and for 3 copies more, he yet promises to render a return. I send you also a paper which Munroe drew up a long time ago by way of satisfying me that as far as Vols 1 & 2 were concerned, the result had accorded with the promise that you should have $1000. profit from the edition. We prosper marvellously on paper, but the realized benefit loiters. Will you now set some friend of yours in Fraser's shop at work on this paper, & see if this statement is true & transparent. I trust the Munroe firm,—chiefly Nichols, the clerical partner,—and yet it is a duty to understand one's own affair. When I ask at each six months' reckoning, Why we should always be in debt to them? they still remind me of new & newer printing, & promise correspondent profits at last. By sending you this account, I make it

---

[4] The forwarded note was from Carlyle; it introduced Alexander Hume as "a respectable Scottish man . . . a lover of literature & a worker therein." Emerson sent notes introducing Hume to his brother William, to Orville Dewey, and to William Cullen Bryant (*Let RWE*, II, 278–79).

entirely an affair between you & them. You will have all the facts which any of us know. I am only concerned as having advanced the sums which are charged in the account for the payment of paper & printing, and which promise to liquidate themselves soon, for Munroe declares he shall have $550. to pay me in a few days. For the benefit of all parties, bid your clerk sift them. One word more and I have done with this matter which shall not be weary if it comes to good.— the account of the London 500 "Fr. Rev^n." is not yet six months old & so does not come in. Neither does that of the 2d edit 1 & 2 Miscellanies, for the same reason. They will come in due time.

I have very good hope that my friend Margaret Fuller's Journal,— after many false baptisms now saying it will be called The Dial, & which is to appear in July,—will give you a better knowledge of our young people than any you have had. I will see that it goes to you when the sun first shines on its face. You asked me if I read German, & I forget if I have answered. I have contrived to read almost every volume of Goethe, and I have 55 but I have read nothing else: but I have not now looked even into Goethe for a long time. There is no great need that I should discourse to you on books, least of all on *his* books; but in a lecture on Literature in my course last winter, I blurted all my nonsense on that subject, & who knows but Margaret Fuller may be glad to print it & send it to you! [5] I know not.

A. Bronson Alcott who is a great man if he cannot write well, has come to Concord with his wife & three children & taken a cottage & an acre of ground to get his living by the help of God & his own spade. I see that some of the Education people in England have a school called "Alcott House," after my friend. At home here, he is despised & rejected of men [6] as much as was ever Pestalozzi.[7] But the creature thinks & talks, & I am glad & proud of my neighbor. He is interested more than need is in the Editor Heraud. So do not fail to tell me of him. Of Landor, I would gladly know your knowledge. And now I think I will release your eyes.   Yours always,   R. W. E.

[5] This lecture became the article "Thoughts on Modern Literature" in *The Dial* for October, 1840; it was reprinted in Emerson's *Works*, XII, 309–36. See below, C.12.9.40.

[6] Isa. 53: 3.

[7] Alcott and his English admirers were followers of the Swiss educator Pestalozzi (Odell Shepard, *Pedlar's Progress: the Life of Bronson Alcott*, pp. 84–85).

Concord, 22 April, 1840 [1]

My dear friend,—Mr George Grinnell a merchant much beloved in the city of Providence in Rhode Island where he resides, is about to sail for England on errands connected with his trade. I avail myself the more willingly of Mr Grinnell's offer to carry letters to you that I shall so bring him to see you face to face, which he desires.

Yours ever, R. W. Emerson

Concord, 22 April, 1840.[1]

My dear friend,

There is a lady now in England whom I wish you to see, & who I wish may see you. Her name is Jane Tuckerman; her father's name Gustavus Tuckerman, a merchant in Boston, Mass.; her grandfather's name is John Francis, in Birmingham, England. She sailed from New York the 1 April. She is in delicate health, & her friends have hoped that a voyage & a visit would restore her. She is very well worth seeing & hearing on her own account, being a lovely person, the dear friend of very good friends, and the sweetest of singers. I know it will gratify her very much to see & know you & your great man; & if she should be in London for any time, you must not fail to do her that grace. Miss Martineau, if she is in London again, will certainly know of her movements; & I have just written a note of introduction to you to be sent to Miss Tuckerman. If you see her, be sure to make her sing Xarifa to you, one of Lockhart's Spanish ballads [2] I believe. If you do not love that I should send you so many visitors—I cannot help it that you are yourself and also Thomas Carlyle's wife. But in the case

[1] A manuscript copy of this letter which was made by Carlyle's amanuensis Frederick Martin is owned by the National Library of Scotland (MS 2884); the present text is transcribed from that copy. Another copy, almost identical, is owned by the RWEMA.

[1] This is Rusk's text. "MS owned by the Preussische Staatsbibliothek; ph in CUL. For Jane Frances Tuckerman, see *The New England Historical & Genealogical Register*, V (1851), 160. For her singing, cf. the letter of Sept 9, 1839. 'G. Tuckerman' and 'Miss Tuckerman, of Boston' are listed in *The Evening Post*, New York, Apr. 1, 1840, as passengers on the 'Oxford' for Liverpool" (Rusk's note).

[2] "Xarifa is the heroine in 'The Bridal of Andalla,' *Ancient Spanish Ballads*, tr. J. G. Lockhart, Edinburgh and London, 1823, pp. 129–131" (Rusk's note).

of Miss Tuckerman I have no fear of your reproaches. Let her bring
back word that your health is confirmed. My wife greets you well &
almost my babes.   Your old friend.   R. W. Emerson.

Mrs Jane Carlyle.

                                        Concord, 30 June, 1840.[1]

My dear Carlyle,—Since I wrote a couple of letters to you,—I know
not exactly when, but in near succession many weeks ago,—there has
come to me *Wilhelm Meister* in three volumes, goodly to see, good to
read,—indeed quite irresistible; for though I thought I knew it all, I
began at the beginning and read to the end of the *Apprenticeship,*
and no doubt shall despatch the *Travels,* on the earliest holiday. My
conclusions and inferences therefrom I will spare you now, since I
appended them to a piece I had been copying fairly for Margaret
Fuller's *Dial,*—"Thoughts on Modern Literature," and which is the
substance of a lecture in my last winter's course. But I learn that my
paper is crowded out of the first Number, and is not to appear until
October. I will not reckon the accidents that threaten the ghost of an
article through three months of pre-existence! Meantime, I rest your
glad debtor for the good book. With it came Sterling's *Poems,* which,
in the interim, I have acknowledged in a letter to him. Sumner has
since brought me a gay letter from yourself, concerning, in part,
Landor and Heraud; in which as I know justice is not done to the
one I suppose it is not done to the other. But Heraud I give up freely
to your tender mercies: I have no wish to save him. Landor can be
shorn of all that is false and foolish, and yet leave a great deal for
me to admire. Many years ago I have read a hundred fine memorable
things in the *Imaginary Conversations,* though I know well the faults
of that book, and the *Pericles and Aspasia* within two years has given
me delight. I was introduced to the man Landor when I was in Florence, and he was very kind to me in answering a multitude of questions. His speech, I remember, was below his writing. I love the rich
variety of his mind, his proud taste, his penetrating glances, and the
poetic loftiness of his sentiment, which rises now and then to the
meridian, though with the flight, I own, rather of a rocket than an
orb, and terminated sometimes by a sudden tumble. I suspect you of

[1] This is Norton's text. The RWEMA owns a rough draft.

very short and dashing reading in his books; and yet I should think you would like him,—both of you such glorious haters of cant. Forgive me, I have put you two together twenty times in my thought as the only writers who have the old briskness and vivacity. But you must leave me to my bad taste and my perverse and whimsical combinations.

I have written to Mr. Milnes who sent me by Sumner a copy of his article with a note. I addressed my letter to him at "London,"—no more. Will it ever reach him? I told him that if I should print more he would find me worse than ever with my rash, unwhipped generalization.[2] For my journals, which I dot here at home day by day, are full of disjointed dreams, audacities, unsystematic irresponsible lampoons of systems, and all manner of rambling reveries, the poor drupes and berries I find in my basket after endless and aimless rambles in woods and pastures. I ask constantly of all men whether life may not be poetic as well as stupid?

I shall try and persuade Mr. Calvert,[3] who has sent to me for a letter to you, to find room in his trunk for a poor lithograph portrait of our Concord "Battle-field," [4] so called, and village, that you may see the faint effigy of the fields and houses in which we walk and love you. The view includes my Grandfather's house (under the trees near the Monument), in which I lived for a time until I married and bought my present house, which is not in the scope of this drawing. I will roll up two of them, and, as Sterling seems to be more nomadic than you, I beg you will send him also this particle of foreign parts.

With this, or presently after it, I shall send a copy of the *Dial.* It is not yet much; indeed, though no copy has come to me, I know it is far short of what it should be, for they have suffered puffs and dulness to creep in for the sake of the complement of pages; but it is better

[2] Emerson's letter to Milnes of May 30, 1840, was more explicit and Emersonian than this sentence suggests. "Will you forgive me," he asked, "if I say that I hope to win your assent to bolder and broader generalizations? . . . I have no expectation of any good to result from social arguments, which are only mirrors and reverberations of a few individuals. The hope of man resides in the private heart" (T. Wemyss Reid, *Life of . . . Milnes,* I, 241).

[3] George Henry Calvert, journalist and man of letters, had been a student with Emerson at Harvard College and with Emerson's brother William at Göttingen. He had written the first American book on phrenology and had made a verse translation of Schiller's *Don Karlos.*

[4] Emerson sent two prints to his brother William in New York with the request that Calvert carry them to Carlyle. "Carlyle," he said, "has such a passion for exact informn that I know the thing will be welcome to him" (*Let RWE,* II, 307).

than anything we had; and I have some poetry communicated to me for the next number which I wish Sterling and Milnes to see. In this number what say you to the *Elegy* written by a youth who grew up in this town and lives near me,—Henry Thoreau? A criticism on Persius is his also. From the papers of my brother Charles, I gave them the fragments on Homer, Shakespeare, Burke: and my brother Edward wrote the little *Farewell*, when last he left his home. The Address of the Editors to the Readers is all the prose that is mine, and whether they have printed a few verses for me I do not know.[5] I am daily expecting an account for you from Little and Brown. They promised it at this time. It will speedily follow this sheet, if it do not accompany it. But I am determined, if I can, to send one letter which is not on business. Send me some word of the Lectures. I have yet seen only the initial notices. Surely you will send me some time the D'Orsay portrait. Sumner thinks Mrs. Carlyle was very well when he saw her last, which makes me glad.—I wish you both to love me, as I am affectionately

Yours,   R. W. Emerson.

Chelsea, London, 2 July, 1840—

My dear Emerson,

Surely I am a sinful man to neglect so long making any acknowledgement of the benevolent and beneficent Arithmetic you sent me! It is many weeks, perhaps it is months since the worthy citizen, your Host as I understood you in some of your Northern states,[1]—stept in here, one mild evening, with his mild honest face and manners; presented me your Bookseller Accounts; talked for half an hour, and then went his way into France. Much has come and gone since then; Letters of yours, beautiful Disciples of yours:—I pray you forgive me! I have been lecturing, I have been sick; I have been beaten about in all ways. Nay, at bottom, it was only three days ago that I got the *Bibliopoliana* back from Fraser; to whom, as you recommended, I, totally inadequate like yourself to understand such things, had straightway handed them for examination. I always put off writing till Fraser should have

[5] The first number did contain two poems by Emerson, "The Problem" and "To ****," later entitled "To Eva." Thoreau's poem was called not "Elegy" but "Sympathy."

[1] George Grinnell. See E.4.22.40, n. 1.

spoken. I did not urge him, or he would have spoken any day: there is my sin.

Fraser declares the Accounts to be made out in the most beautiful manner; intelligible to any human capacity; correct, so far as he sees, and promising to yield by and by a beautiful return of money. A precious crop, which we must not cut in the blade; mere time will ripen it into yellow nutritive ears yet. So he thinks. The only point on which I heard him make any criticism was on what he called, if I remember, "the number of copies *delivered*"—that is to say, delivered by the Printer and Binder as actually available for sale. The edition being of a thousand, there have only 984 come bodily forth; 16 are "waste." Our Printers, it appears, are in the habit of adding 1 for every 50 beforehand, whereby the *waste* is usually made good and more; so that in 1000 there will usually be some dozen called "author's copies" over and above. Fraser supposes your Printers have a different custom. That is all. The rest is apparently every-way *right;* is to be received with faith; with faith, charity, and even hope,—and packed into the bottom of one's drawer, never to be looked at more except on the outside, as a memorial of one of the best and helpfullest of men! In that capacity it shall lie there.

My Lectures were in May, about *Great Men.* The misery of it was hardly equal to that of former years, yet still was very hateful. I had got to a certain feeling of superiority over my audience; as if I had something to tell them, and would tell it them. At times I felt as if I could, in the end, learn to speak. The beautiful people listened with boundless tolerance, eager attention. I meant to tell them, among other things, that man was still alive, Nature not dead or like to die; that all true men continued true to this hour, Odin himself true, and the Grand Lama of Thibet himself not wholly a lie. The Lecture on Mahomet ("the Hero as Prophet") astonished my worthy friends beyond measure. It seems then this Mahomet was not a quack? Not a bit of him! That he is a better Christian, with his "bastard Christianity," than most of us shovel-hatted? I guess than almost any of you! Not so much as Oliver Cromwell ("the Hero as King") would I allow to have been a Quack. All quacks I asserted to be and to have been Nothing, *chaff* that would not grow: my poor Mahomet was "wheat with barn sweepings"; Nature had tolerantly hidden the barn-sweepings; and as to the *wheat,* behold she had said Yes to it and it was growing!—On the whole, I fear I did little but confuse my esteemed audience: I was amazed, after all their reading of me, to be understood so ill;—gratified nevertheless to see how the rudest *speech* of a man's heart goes into men's hearts, and is the welcomest thing there. Withal I regretted that I had not six months of preaching, whereby to learn to preach, and explain things fully! In the fire of the moment I had all but decided on setting out for America this autumn, and preaching far and wide like a very lion there. Quit your paper formulas, my brethren,—equivalent to old wooden idols, *undivine* as they: in the name of God, understand that you are alive, and that God is alive! Did the Upholsterer make this Universe? Were you created by the Tailor? I tell you, and conjure you to believe me literally, No, a thousand times No! Thus did I mean to preach, on "Heroes, Hero-worship and the Heroic," in America too. Alas, the fire of determination died away again: [2] all that I did resolve upon was to write these Lectures down, and in *some* way promulgate them farther. Two of them accordingly are actually written; the Third to be begun on Monday: it is my chief work here, ever since the end of May. Whether I go to preach them a second time extempore in America rests once more with the Destinies. It is a shame to talk so much about a thing, and have it still hang *in nubibus:* . . . I was, and perhaps am, really nearer doing it than I had ever before been. [A] month or two now, I suppose, will bring us back to the old nonentity again. Is there at bottom, in the world or out of it anything one would like so well, with one's whole heart *well*, as PEACE? Is lecturing and noise the way to get at that? Popular Lecturer! Popular writer! If they would undertake in Chancery, or Heaven's Chancery, to make a wise man Mahomet Second and Greater, "Mahomet of Saxondom," not reviewed only, but worshipped for twelve centuries by all Bulldom, Yankeedoodledom, Felondom New Zealand, under the Tropics and in part of Flanders,—would he not rather answer: Thank you; but in a few years I shall be dead, twelve centuries will have become Eternity; part of Flanders-Immensity—we will sit still here if you please, and consider what quieter thing we can do! Enough of this.

---

[2] That Carlyle was indeed playing seriously with the idea of an American tour may be seen in a letter to his mother of May 20, 1840: "I tell [Jane] that when I go to lecture in America, she shall not go with me; there is no use in having two persons made miserable by it [*i.e.*, the lecturing] instead of one!" (NLS, MS 520).

Richard Milnes had a Letter from you, one morning lately, when I met him at old Rogers's. He is brisk as ever; his kindly *Dilettantism* looking sometimes as if it would grow a [so]rt of Earnest by and by. He has a new volume of Poems out: I advised him to try Prose; he admitted that Poetry would not be generally read again in these ages, —but pleaded "it was so convenient for veiling commonplace!" The honest little heart.—We did not know what to make of the bright Miss Tuckermann [3] here; she fell in love with my wife,—the *contrary,* I doubt, with me: my hard realism jarred upon her beautiful rosepink dreams. Is not all that very morbid; unworthy of the Children of Odin, not to speak of Luther, Knox and the other brave? I can do nothing with vapours, but wish them *condensed.* Kennett had a copy of the English *Miscellanies* for you, a good many weeks ago: indeed it was just a day or two *before* your advice to try Green henceforth. Has the *Meister* ever arrived? I received a Controversial Volume from Mr Ripley: pray thank him very kindly. Somebody borrowed the Book from me; I have not yet read it. I did read a Pamphlet which seems now to have been made part of it. Norton surely is a chimera; but what has the whole business they are jarring about become? [4] As healthy *worshipping* Paganism is to Seneca and Company so is healthy worshipping Christianity to—*I* had rather not work the sum! —Send me some swift news of yourself dear Emerson. We salute you and yours, in all heartiness of brotherhood.

Yours ever & always   —T. Carlyle

Concord, 30 August, 1840.[1]

My dear Carlyle,

I fear, nay, I know that when I wrote last to you about the 1 July, I promised to follow my sheet immediately with a bookseller's account. The bookseller did presently after render his account, but on

---

[3] On July 21, 1840, Emerson wrote to Margaret Fuller: "A new letter from Carlyle who would seem to be too old to see Jane Tuckerman clearly" (*Let RWE,* II, 317). And on August 17 he wrote to Caroline Sturgis: "At Jamaica Plains I saw Jane Tuckerman's letter to you with great content. Mr. Carlyle can not be forgiven" (MS owned by the RWEMA).

[4] Ripley, *Letters to Andrews Norton on "The Latest Form of Infidelity."* This second passage at arms was occasioned by Norton's attack on Emerson's Divinity School Address.

[1] The MS of this letter is owned by the Berg Collection of the New York Public Library.

its face appeared the fact,—which with many and by me unanswerable reasons they supported,—that the balance thereon credited to you, was not payable until the 1 October. The account is footed, "Nett sales of "Fr. Revolution" to 1 July 1840 due Oct. 1—$249.77" Let us hope then that we shall get not only a new page of statement but also some small payment in money a month hence. Having no better story to tell, I told nothing.

But I will not let the second of the Cunard Boats leave Boston without a word to you. Since I wrote by Calvert, came your letter describing your lectures & their success: very welcome news; for a good London newspaper, which I had consulted, promised reports, but gave none. I have heard so oft of your projected trip to America, that my ear would now be dull & my faith cold, but that I wish it so much. My friend, your audience still waits for you here willing & eager, & greatly larger no doubt than it would have been when the matter was first debated. Our community begin to stand in some terror of Transcendentalism, and the Dial, poor little thing, whose first number contains scarce anything considerable or even visible, is just now honoured by attacks from almost every newspaper & magazine; which at least betrays the irritability & the instincts of the good public. But they would hardly be able to fasten on so huge a man as you are, any party badge. We must all hear you for ourselves. But beside my own hunger to see & know you, and to hear you speak at ease & at large under my own roof, I have a growing desire to present you to three or four friends, & them to you. Almost all my life has been passed alone. Within three or four years I have been drawing nearer to a few men & women whose love gives me in these days more happiness than I can write of. How gladly I would bring your Jovial light upon this friendly constellation, & make you too know my distant riches! We have our own problems to solve also & a good deal of movement & tendency emerging into sight every day in church & state, in social modes, & in letters. I sometimes fancy our cipher is larger & easier to read than that of your English society. You will naturally ask me if I try my hand at the history of all this,— I who have leisure and write? No, not in the near & practical way which they seem to invite. I incline to write philosophy, poetry, possibility,—anything but history. And yet this phantom of the next age limns himself sometimes so large & plain that every feature is apprehensible, & challenges a painter. I can brag little of my diligence or achievement this summer. I dot evermore in my endless journal, a line on every unknowable in nature; but the arrangement loiters long, & I get a brick kiln instead of a house.—Consider, however, that all summer I see a good deal of company,—so near as my fields are to the city. But next winter I think to omit lectures, & write more faithfully. Hope for me that I shall get a book ready to send you by New Years Day.

Sumner came to see me the other day. I was glad to learn all the little that he knew of you & yours. I do not wonder you set so lightly by my talkative countryman. He has bro't nothing home but names, dates, & surfaces. At Cambridge last week I saw Brown, for the first time.[2] I had little opportunity to learn what he knew. Mr. Hume has never yet shown his face here. He sent me his Poems from New York, & then went South, & I know no more of him.[3]

My Mother & Wife send you kind regards & best wishes,—to you & to all your house. Tell your wife that I hate to hear that she cannot sail the seas. Perhaps now she is stronger she will be a better sailor. For the sake of America, will she not try the trip to Leith again? It is only twelve days from Liverpool to Boston. Love & truth & power abide with you always!   R. W. E.

                                         Chelsea, London, 26 Septr, 1840—
My dear Emerson,

Two Letters of yours are here, the latest of them for above a week: [1] I am a great sinner not to have answered sooner. My way of life has been a thing of petty confusions, uncertainties; I did not till a short while ago see any definite highway, thro' the multitude of bye-lanes that opened out on me, even for the next few months. Partly I was busy; partly too, as my wont is, I was half asleep:—perhaps you do not know the *combination* of these two predicables in one and the same unfortunate human subject! Seeing my course now for a little, I must speak.

According to your prognosis, it becomes at length manifest that I

<hr>

[2] See above, C.12.8.39.

[3] Hume was the editor of *Scottish Songs* (London, 1835), and *English Songs and Ballads* (London, 1838). Probably he sent Emerson both volumes (*Let RWE*, II, 296n).

[1] On September 17, 1840, Carlyle wrote to his brother John: "I had a letter from Emerson yesterday: some little cash coming from the Yankee F. Revn" (NLS, MS 523).

do *not* go to America for the present. Alas, no! It was but a dream of the fancy; projected, like the French shoemaker's fairy shoes, "in a moment of enthusiasm." [2] The nervous flutter of May Lecturing has subsided into stagnancy; into the feeling that, of all things in the world, public speaking is the hatefullest for me; that I ought devoutly to thank Heaven there is no absolute compulsion laid on me at present to speak! My notion in general was but an absurd one: I fancied I might go across the sea; open my lips wide; go raging and lecturing over the Union like a very lion (too like a frothy mountebank) for several months;—till I had gained, say a thousand pounds; therewith to retire to some small quiet cottage by the shore of the sea, at least three hundred miles from this, and sit silent there for ten years to come, or forever and a day perhaps! That was my poor little daydream;—*in*capable of being realized. It appears, I have to stay here, in this brick Babylon; tugging at my chains, which will not break for me: the less I *tug* the better. Ah me! On the whole, I have written down my last course of lectures, and shall probably print them; and you, with the aid of proof-sheets, may again print them; that will be the easiest way of lecturing to America! It is truly very weak to speak about that matter so often and long, that matter of coming to you; and never to come. *Frey ist das Herz,* as Goethe says, *doch ist der Fuss gebunden.*[3] After innumerable projects, and invitations towards all the four winds, for this summer, I have ended about a week ago by—simply going nowhither, not even to see my dear aged Mother, but sitting still here under the autumn sky such as I have it; in these vacant streets I am lonelier than elsewhere, have more chance for composure than elsewhere! With Sterne's starling I repeat to myself, "I can't get out." [4]—Well, hang it, stay *in* then; and let people alone of it!

I have parted with my horse; after an experiment of seven or eight months, most assiduously prosecuted, I came to the conclusion, that tho' it did me *some* good, there was not *enough* of good to warrant such equestrianism: so I plunged out, into green England, in the end of July, for a whole week of riding, an *explosion* of riding, therewith to end the business, and send off my poor quadruped for sale.

---

[2] I have not been able to identify this quotation or the French shoemaker.

[3] An inaccurate recollection of a line from Goethe's poem, "An Lord Byron," *Sämtliche Werke,* III, 11) "Nicht ist der Geist, doch ist der Fuss gebunden."

[4] *A Sentimental Journey* (Everyman's Library), p. 76.

I rode over Surrey,—with a leather valise behind me and a mackintosh before; very singular to see: over Sussex, down to Pevensey where the Norman Bastard landed; I saw Julius Hare [5] (whose "Guesses at truth" you perhaps know) saw Saint Dunstan's stithy and hammer, at Mayfield, and the very tongs with which he took the Devil by the nose;—finally I got home again, a right wearied man; sent my horse off to be sold, as I say; and finished the writing of my Lectures on Heroes. This is all the rustication I have had, or am like to have. I am now over head and ears in *Cromwellean* Books; studying, for perhaps the fourth time in my life, to see if it be possible to get any credible face to face acquaintance with our English Puritan period; or whether it must be left forever a mere hearsay and echo to one? Books equal in dulness were at no epoch of the world penned by unassisted man. Nevertheless, courage! I have got, within the last twelvemonth, actually, as it were, to *see* that this Cromwell was one of the greatest souls ever born of the English Kin; a great amorphous semi-articulate Baresark; very interesting to me. I grope in the dark vacuity of Baxters, Neales; [6] thankful for here a glimpse and there a glimpse. This is to be my reading for some time.

The *Dial N⁰ I* came duly: of course I read it with interest; it is an [ut]terance of what is purest, youngest in your land; pure, ethereal as the voices of the Morning! And yet—you know me—for me it is *too* ethereal, speculative, theoretic: all theory becomes more and more confessedly inadequate, untrue, unsatisfactory, almost a kind of mockery to me! I will have all things condense themselves, take shape and body, if they are to have my sympathy. I have a *body* myself; in the brown leaf, sport of the autumn winds, I find what mocks all prophesyings, even Hebrew ones,—Royal Societies, and Scientific Associations eating venison at Glasgow, not once reckoned in! Nevertheless go on with this, my Brothers. The world has many most strange utterances of a prophetic nature in it at the present time; and this surely is well worth listening to among the rest.[7] Do you know Eng-

---

[5] Rector of Herstmonceaux in Sussex: John Sterling had served under him as curate (Carlyle, *Works TC*, XI, 96).

[6] On September 19 Carlyle had written to Sterling that he was reading *"Baxter's Life"* (Thomas Carlyle, *New Letters*, I, 213); probably he meant the autobiographical *Reliquiae Baxterianae* of 1696. The "Neales" were probably Daniel Neal, author of a *History of the Puritans* (1732).

[7] Emerson wrote to Margaret Fuller on October 20: "I have yesterday a letter

lish Puseyism? Good Heaven, in the whole circle of History is there the parallel of that,—a true worship rising at this hour of the day for Bands and the Shovel-hat. Distraction surely, incipience of the "final deliration," [8] enters upon the poor old English Formulism that has called itself for some two centuries a Church. No likelier symptom of its being soon about to leave the world has come to light in my time. As if King Macready should *quit* Covent-Garden, go down to St.-Stephen's, and insist on saying, *Le roi le veut!* [9]—I read last night the wonderfullest article to that effect, in the shape of a criticism on myself, in the *Quarterly Review*. It seems to be by one Sewell, [10] an Oxford doctor of note, one of the chief men among the Pusey-and-Newman corporation. A good man, and with good notions, whom I have noted for some years back. He finds me a worthy fellow; "true, most true," [11]—except where I part from Puseyism, and reckon the shovel-hat to be an old bit of felt; then I am false, most false. As the Turks say, *Allah akbar!*

I forget altogether what I said of Landor; but I hope I did not put him in the Heraud category: a cockney windbag is one thing; a scholar and bred man, tho' incontinent, explosive, half-true, is another. He has not been in town, this year; Milnes describes him as *eating* greatly at Bath, and perhaps even cooking! Milnes did get your letter: I told you? Sterling has the Concord landscape; mine is to go upon the wall here, and remind me of many things. Sterling is busy writing; he is to make Falmouth do, this winter, and try to dispense with Italy. He cannot away with my doctrine of *Silence;* the good John. My Wife has been better than usual all summer; she begins to shiver again as winter draws nigh. Adieu, dear E. Good be with you and yours. I must be far gone when I cease to love you. "The stars are above us, the graves are under us." [12] Adieu.   T. Carlyle

---

from Carlyle who . . . faintly praises The Dial Number I" (*Let RWE,* II, 349).

[8] "Characteristics," *Works TC,* XXVIII, 21

[9] "Le Roy le veult" is the Norman-French formula by which the British king gives assent to the wishes of Parliament (Courtenay Ilbert, *Parliament: Its History, Constitution and Practice,* pp. 75–76).

[10] William Sewall, professor of moral philosophy at Oxford and until 1841 a leader of the Oxford Movement. His article on Carlyle appeared in the *Quarterly Review,* LXVI (1840), 446–503.

[11] Possibly a Shakespearean echo. Cf. *Othello,* act I, scene iii, line 79; and *Winter's Tale,* act V, scene i, line 12.

[12] Goethe, "Symbolum," in *Sämtliche Werke,* II, 231.

Thomas Carlyle in a/c with **R. W. Emerson**

Dr.		Cr.
1840		
April	To balance as per last a/c	685.73
July 29	" Cash for Paper to finish 2d ed. Miscell	28.12
Sept.	" " " Printing — do. — do.	481.34
	" " " Binding 175 copies do.	45.70
	" " " Folding 1 " "	.10
	" " " Little & Co. for sundries, viz: —¼% exch. on 200.36 to New York	.50
	Printing, Paper & Binding Chartism	148.82
	duties on French Revolutn	256.35
	Interest	9.57
		$1656.23
1840		
Oct. 1.	To balance brought down	$502.62

Cr.		
1840		
Oct. 1.	By Sales of 1&2 Misc. 1st ed. J.M.&Co	45.50
	" " " " 2d ed. "	71.36
	" " " 3&4 " 1st "	360.94
	" " " 187 Fr. Revolun C.C.L. & Co. "	523.60
	" " " 491 Chartism @ .31 "	152.21
	" balance to new a/c	502.62

Concord, Oct. 30, 1840

My dear friend, My hope is that you may live until this creeping booksellers' balance [1] shall incline at last to your side. My rude ciphering based on the last Account of this kind which I sent you in April from J. Munroe & Co. had convinced me that I was to be in debt to you at this time 40 pounds or more; so that I actually bought £40.[2] the day before the Caledonia sailed, to send you: but on giving my new accounts to J. M. & Co to bring the statement up to this time, they astonished me with the abovewritten result. I professed absolute incredulity but Nichols laboured to show me the rise & progress of all my blunders. Please to send the account with the last to your Fraser & have it sifted. That I paid a few weeks since, $481.34; & again $28.12, for printing & paper respectively, is true.— C. C. Little & Co acknowledge the sale of 82 more copies of the London Edit. "French Revolution" since the 187 copies of 1 July. but these they do not get paid for until 1 Jany, & we it seems must wait as long. We will see if the New Year's Day will bring us more pence. I received by the Acadia a letter from you which I acknowledge now, lest I should not answer it more at large on another sheet, which I think to do. If you do not despair of American book-sellers send the new proof of the Lectures when they are in type to me by John Green 121 Newgate St (I believe); to the care of J. Munroe, & Co. He sends a box to Munroe by every steamer. I sent a *Dial. No II* for you, to Green. Kennett, I hear, has failed. I hope he did not give his creditors my "Miscellanies," which you told me were there. I shall be glad if you will draw Cromwell, though, if I should choose, it would be Carlyle. You will not feel that you have done your work until those devouring eyes & that portraying hand have achieved England in the Nineteenth Century. Perhaps you cannot do it until you have made your American visit. I assure you the view of Britain is excellent from New England.—We are all a little wild here with numberless projects of social reform. Not a reading man but has a draft of a new Community in his waistcoat pocket. I am gently mad myself, and am

---

[1] The account on p. 282 is not in Emerson's hand.

[2] On October 14 Emerson had written to Abel Adams for "a bill of exchange on London worth about $210. or $220. to be paid to Thomas Carlyle" (*Let RWE*, II, 346).

resolved to live cleanly. George Ripley is talking up a colony of agri-
culturists & scholars with whom he threatens to take the field & the
book. One man renounces the use of animal food; & another of coin;
& another of domestic hired service; & another of the state; [3] and on
the whole we have a commendable share of reason & hope. I am
ashamed to tell you, though it seems most due, anything of my own
studies they seem so desultory idle & unproductive. I still hope to print
a book of Essays this winter, but it cannot be very large. I write myself
into letters, the last few months, to three or four dear & beautiful
persons my country-men & women here.[4] I lit my candle at both ends,
but will now be colder & scholastic. I mean to write no lectures this
winter. I hear gladly of your wife's better health: and a letter of Jane
Tuckerman's which I saw, gave the happiest tidings of her. We do not
despair of seeing her yet in Concord, since it is now but twelve & a
half days to you. I had a letter from Sterling, which I will answer. In
all love & good hope for you & yours,

                    your affectionate   R. W. Emerson

P. S. I see that this Account is but an abstract & can not tell you
much. I find in his full acct with me he writes that of Vols I & II 1st
Edit

Cr.	23 copies sold & not paid are charged to me	49.65
	43 copies sold are credited	92.45
	1 subscn not paid credited	2.50

Vols I & II 2d Edit 1 copy to C. S. Wheeler	
charged to me	2.06
28 copies on hand	57.68
90 do sold not paid	185.40
cash pd bindg 175 copies	45.70

| Cr. | By 175 copies | 360.50 |

| Vols III & IV | |
| Dr.   To 98 copies on hand | 201.88 |

---

[3] Alcott had been a vegetarian since 1835; early in 1843 he was to be arrested for
refusal to pay his town tax (Alcott, *Journals,* ed. Odell Shepard, pp. 115, 150). Edward Palmer, an occasional guest in Emerson's house, had got along without money
since 1837 (Emerson, *Journals,* V, 87). And Emerson, although he never renounced
domestic hired service, made a bold but unsuccessful attempt in the spring of 1841
to have his servants eat their meals with the family (*Let RWE,* II, 389).

[4] During the summer, Emerson had been, for him, closely involved in the private
affairs of Margaret Fuller and two of her friends, Caroline Sturgis and the "beautiful" Anna Barker (*Let RWE,* II, 303–43).

	192	sold not pd.	395.52
	3	subscribers	7.50
Cr.	By 235	copies sold not pd.	484.10
	4	to subscribers	10
	229	on hand	471.74

Chelsea, 9 Dec^r, 1840—

Dear Emerson,

My answer, on this occasion, has been delayed above two weeks, by a rigorous searching investigation into the procedure of the hapless Book-conveyer Kennet, in reference to that copy of the Miscellanies. I was deceived by hopes of a conclusive response from day to day; not till yesterday did any come. My first step, taken long ago, was to address a new copy of the Book, not to you luckless man, but to *Lydia* Emerson the fortunate wife; this copy Green now has lying by him, waiting for the January steamer (we sail only *once* a month in this season); before the New Year has got out of infancy the Lady will be graciously pleased to make a few inches of room on her bookshelves for this celebrated performance. And now as to Kennet, take the brief outcome of some dozen visitations, judicial interrogatories, searches of documents and other piercing work on the part of methodic Fraser, attended with demurrers, pleadings, false denial, false affirmings on the part of innocent chaotic Kennet: namely that the said Kennet, so urged, did in the end of last week, fish up from his repositories your very identical Book directed to Munroe's care, duly booked, and engaged for, in May last, but left to repose itself in the Covent-Garden crypts ever since without disturbance from gods or man! Fraser has brought back the Book, and you have lost it;—and the Library of my native village in Scotland is to get it; and not Kennett any more in this world, but Green ever henceforth is to be our Book Carrier. There is a history. Green, it seems, addresses also to Munroe; but the thing, I suppose, will now shift for itself without watching.

As to the bibliopolic accounts, my Friend!—we will trust them with a faith known only in the purer ages of Roman Catholicism,—when Papacy had indeed become a Dubiety, but was not yet a Quackery and Falsehood, was a thing *as* true as it could manage to be! That really may be the fact of this too. In any case what signifies it much? Money were still useful; but it is not now so indispensable. Booksellers by their knavery or their fidelity cannot kill us or cure us. Of the truth of Waldo Emerson's heart to me, there is, God be thanked for it, no doubt at all.

My Hero-Lectures lie still in Manuscript. Fraser offers no amount of cash adequate to be an outward motive; and inwardly there is as yet none altogether clear, tho' I rather feel of late as if it were clearing. To fly in the teeth of English Puseyism, and risk such shrill welcome as I am pretty sure of, is questionable: yet at bottom why not? Dost thou not as entirely reject this new Distraction of a Puseyism as man can reject a thing; and couldst utterly abjure it, and even abhor it,— were the *shadow* of a cobweb ever likely to become momentous, the cobweb itself being *beheaded,* with axe and block on Tower Hill, two centuries ago? [1] I think it were as well to *tell* Puseyism that it has something of good, but also much of bad and even worst. We shall see. If I bruit the thing, we shall surely take in America again; either by stereotype or in some other way. Fear not that!—Do you attend at all to this new *Laudism* of ours? It spreads far and wide among our Clergy in these days; a most notable symptom, very cheering to me many ways; whether or not one of the fatallest our poor Church of England has ever exhibited, and betokening swifter ruin to it than any other, I do not inquire.[2] Thank God, men do discover at least that there is still a God present in their affairs, and must be, or their affairs are of the Devil, naught, and worthy of being sent to the Devil! This once given I find that all is given; daily History, in Kingdom and in Parish, is an *experimentum crucis* to shew what *is* the Devil's and what not. But on the whole are we not the *formallest* people ever created under this Sun? Cased and overgrown with Formulas, like very lobsters with their shells, from birth upwards; so that in the man we see only his breeches, and believe and swear that wherever a pair of old breeches are there is a man! I declare I could both laugh and cry.

[1] In a letter to Thomas Spedding, November 9, 1840, Carlyle referred to the "shadow namely, of the right reverend Father Archbishop Laud, who, little more than a cobweb even while living, had the head cut off him near two hundred years ago" (Wilson, *Carlyle on Cromwell and Others,* p. 114).

[2] In a letter to Sterling which is printed in Froude, *Thomas Carlyle: Life in London,* I, 165, Carlyle wrote: "The Church of England stood long upon her tithes and her decencies; but now she takes to shouting in the market-place, 'My tithes are nothing, my decencies are nothing; I am either miraculous celestial or else nothing.' It is to me the fatallest symptom of speedy change she ever exhibited. What an alternative!"

These poor good men, merciful, zealous, with many sympathies and thoughts, there do they vehemently appeal to me, *Et tu Brute?* Brother, wilt thou too insist on the breeches being old; not ply a needle among us here?—To the naked Caliban, gigantic, for whom such breeches would not be a glove, who is stalking and groping there in search of *new* breeches and accoutrements, sure to get them, a[nd] to tread into nonentity whoever hinders him in the search,—they are blind a[s if] they had no eyes. Sartorial men; ninth-parts of a man:—enough of them.

The second N⁰ of the *Dial* has also arrived some days ago. I like it decidedly better than the first; in fact it is right well worth being put on paper, and sent circulating;—I find only as before that it is still too much of a *soul* for circulating as it should. I wish you could in future contrive to mark at the end of each Article who writes it, or give me some general key for knowing. I recognise Emerson readily; the rest are οι πολλοι for most part.[3] But it is all good and very good as a *soul;* wants only a body, which want means a great deal! Your Paper on Literature [4] is incomparably the worthiest thing hitherto; a thing I read with delight. Speak out, my brave Emerson; there are many good men that listen! Even what you say of Goethe gratifies me; it is one of the few things yet spoken of him from personal insight, the sole kind of things that should be spoken! You call him *actual* not *ideal;* there is truth in that too; and yet at bottom is not the whole truth rather this: The actual well-seen *is* the ideal? The *actual,* what really is and exists: the past, the present, the future no less, do all lie there! Ah yes, one day you will find that this sunny-looking, courtly Goethe held veiled in him a Prophetic sorrow deep as Dante's,—all the nobler to me and to you, that he could so hold it. I believe this; no man can *see* as he sees, that has not suffered and striven as man seldom did.—Apropos of *this,* Have you got Miss Martineau's *Hour and Man!* [5] How curious it were to have the real History of the Negro Toussaint; and his *black* Sansculottism in Saint-Domingo; the most atrocious form Sansculottism could or can assume. This of a "black Wilberforce-Washington," as Sterling calls it, is decidedly something.

---

[3] Emerson had sent a list of authors with Carlyle's copy of the first number (MS owned by RWEMA).

[4] See above, E.4.21.40, n. 5.

[5] A novel, recently published, about Toussaint L'Ouverture.

—Adieu, dear Emerson: time presses, paper is done. Commend me to your good Wife, your good Mother, and love me as well as you can. Peace and health under clear winter skies be with you all.

T. Carlyle

My Wife rebukes me sharply that I have "forgot her love!" She is much better this winter than of old.

Having mentioned Sterling I should say that he is at Torquay (Devonshire) for the winter, meditating new publication of Poems. I work still in Cromwellism; all but desperate of any feasible issue worth naming. I "enjoy bad health" too,—considerably.

1841

Chelsea, London, 21 Feby, 1841—

Dear Mrs Emerson,

Your Husband's Letter shall have answer when some moment of leisure is granted me; he will wait till then, and must. But the beautiful utterance which you send over to me; [1] melodious as the voice of flutes, of Æolean Harps borne on the rude wind so *far*,—this must have answer, some word or growl of answer, be there leisure or none! The Acadia, it seems, is to return from Liverpool the day after tomorrow I shove my paper-whirlpools aside for a little, and grumble in pleased response.

You are an enthusiast; make Arabian Nights out of dull foggy London Days; with your beautiful female imagination, shape burnished copper Castles out of London Fog! It is very beautiful of you;—nay it is not foolish either, it is wise. I have a guess what of truth there may be in that; and you the fair Alchymist, are you not all the richer and better that you know the *essential* gold, and will not have it called pewter or spletter,[2] tho in the shops it *is* only such? I honour such Alchymy, and love it; and have myself done something in that kind. Long may the talent abide with you; long may I abide to have it exercised on me!

Except the Annandale Farm where my good Mother still lives, there is no House in all this world which I should be gladder to see than the one at Concord. It seems to stand as only over the hill, in the next parish to me, familiar from boyhood. Alas, and wide waste Atlantics roll between; and I cannot walk over of an evening!—I never give up the hope of getting thither some time. Were I a little richer, were I a little healthier; were I this and that—!—One has no Fortunatus' "Time-annihilating" or even "Space-annihilating Hat"; it were a thing worth having in this world.

My Wife unites with me in all kindest acknowledgements: she is

---

[1] These letters are missing.   [2] Presumably *spelter* misspelled.

getting stronger these last two years; but is still such a *sailor* as the Island hardly parallels: had she the *Space-annihilating Hat,* she too were soon with you.

Your message shall reach Miss Martineau; my Dame will send it in her first Letter. The good Harriett is not well; [3] but keeps a very courageous heart. She lives by the shore of the beautiful blue Northumbrian Sea; a "many-sounding" [4] solitude which I often envy her. She writes unweariedly, has many friends visiting her. You saw her *Toussaint L'ouverture:* how she has made such a beautiful "black Washington" (or "Washington-Christ-Macready" as I have heard some call it, of a rough-handed, hardheaded, semi-articulate gabbling Negro; and of the horriblest phasis that "Sansculottism" *can* exhibit, of a *Black* Sansculottism, a musical Opera or Oratorio in pink stockings! It is very beautiful. Beautiful as a child's heart,—and in so shrewd a head as that. She is now writing express Children's-Tales, which I calculate I shall find more perfect.

Some ten days ago there went from me to Liverpool, per[haps] there will arrive at Concord by this very Acadia, a bundle of Printed Sheets directed to your Husband: pray apprise the man of that. They are sheets of a volume called *Lectures on Heroes;* the Concord Hero gets them without direction or advice of any kind. I have got some four sheets more ready for him here; shall perhaps send them too, along with this. Some four *again* more will complete the thing. I know not what he will make of it;—perhaps wry faces at it?

Adieu, dear Mrs Emerson. We salute you from this house. May all good which the Heavens grant to a kind heart, and the good which they never *refuse* to one such, abide with you always. I commend myself to your and Emerson's good Mother, to the mischievous Boys and all the Household. Peace and fair spring-weather be there!

Yours with great regard,   T. Carlyle

[3] For the past year and a half, Harriet Martineau had been an invalid, confined to her bed and sofa by an obscure illness which she attributed to "a tumour . . . of a kind which usually originates in mental suffering" (*Autobiography,* I, 442). She remained for five years, as she wrote in the first of a series of articles on Mesmerism, "a prisoner from illness. My recovery now, by means of mesmeric treatment alone, has given me the most thorough knowledge possible that Mesmerism is true" (*The Athenaeum,* Nov. 23, 1844, p. 1070).

[4] See above, C.2.8.39, n. 2.

Concord, 28 February 1841

My dear Carlyle,

Behold Mr George Nichols's [1] new digest & exegesis of his October accounts. The letter seems to me the most intelligible of the two papers, but I have long been that man's victim, semiannually, & never dare to make head against his figures. You are a brave man, & out of the ring of his enchantments, & withal have magicians of your own who can give spell for spell, & read his incantations backward. I entreat you to set them on the work, and convict his figures if you can. He has really taken pains, & is quite proud of his establishment of his accounts. In a month it will be April, & he will have a new one to render. Little & Brown also in April promise a payment on "French Revolution,"—and I suppose something is due from Chartism. We will hope that a bill of exchange will yet cross from us to you, before our booksellers fail.

I hoped before this to have reached my last proofsheet, but shall have two or three more yet. In a fortnight or three weeks, my little raft will be afloat.[2] Expect nothing more of my powers of construction, no shipbuilding, no clipper, smack, nor skiff even, only boards & logs tied together. I read to some Mechanics' Apprentices a long lecture on Reform, one evening, a little while ago.[3] They asked me to print it, but Margaret Fuller asked it also, & I preferred the Dial, which shall have the dubious sermon & I will send it to you in that.—You see the bookseller *reverendizes* me notwithstanding your laudable perseverance to adorn me with profane titles, on the one hand, & the growing habit of the majority of my correspondents to clip my name of all titles, on the other. I desire that you & your wife will keep your kindness for   R. W. Emerson

[1] The clerical partner of James Munroe: see above, E.4.21.40, and *Stimpson's Boston Directory* for 1836.

[2] Emerson's first volume of essays went to press on January 1, 1841; on March 19 he mailed a copy to Carlyle (*Journals*, V, 506, 519-20).

[3] "Man the Reformer," read before the Mechanics' Apprentices Library Association in Boston on January 25 (*Works, I*, 225).

Boston, 30 April, 1841

My dear Carlyle,

Above [1] you have a bill of exchange for one hundred pounds sterling drawn by T. W. Ward & Co. on the Messrs Barings payable at sight. Let us hope it is but the first of a long series. I have vainly endeavored to get your account to be rendered by Munroe & Co to the date of 1 April. It was conditionally promised for the day of the last steamer (15 Apr). It is not ready for that which sails tomorrow & carries this. Little & Co. acknowledge a debt of $607.90 due to you 1 April & just now paid me: and regret that their sales have been so slow which they attribute to the dulness of all trade among us for the last two years. You shall have the particulars of their account from Munroes statement of the a/c between you & me. Munroe & Co have a long apology for not rendering their own account their bookkeeper left them at a critical moment they were without one six weeks—&c—but they add, if we could give you it, to what use, since we should be utterly unable to make you any payment at this time?—To what use, surely? I am too much used to similar statements from our booksellers & others in the last few years to be much surprised; nor do I doubt their readiness or their power to pay all their debts at last, but a great deal of mutual concession & accomodation has been the familiar report of our trades-men now for a good while—a vice which they are all fain to lay at the doors of the Government whilst it belongs in the first instance no doubt to the rashness of the individual traders. These men I believe to be prudent honest & solvent, & that we shall get all our debt from them at last. They are not reckoned as rich as Little & Brown. By the next steamer they *think they can* promise to have their account ready.—I am sorry to find that we have been driven from the market by the New York Pirates in the affaire of the Six Lectures. The book was received from London & for sale in New York & Boston before my last sheets arrived by the Columbia. Appleton in N. Y. braved us & printed it & furthermore told us that he intends to print in future everything of yours that shall be printed in London complaining in rude terms of the monopoly your publishers have exercised & the small commissions they allow to the Trade &c &c. Munroe showed me the letter which certainly was not an amiable one. In this distress then I

[1] The bill of exchange was evidently written just above the heading of this letter.

beg you when you have more Histories & Lectures to print to have the Ms copied by a scrivener before you print at home & send it out to me & I will keep all Appletons & Corsairs whatsoever out of the lists. Not only these men made a book (of which by the bye Munroe sends you by this steamer a copy, which you will find at John Green's, Newgate Street) but the New York newspapers print the book in chapters & you circulate for six cents per newspaper at the corners of all streets in N. Y. & Boston: gaining in fame what you lose in coin.— The book is a good book & goes to make men brave & happy. I bear glad witness to its cheering & arming quality. I have put into Munroe's box which goes to Green, a *Dial No IV* also which I could heartily wish were a better book [2]—But Margaret Fuller, who is a noble woman, is not in sufficiently vigorous health to do this editing work as she would & should, & there is no other who can & will.

Yours affectionately   R. W. Emerson

Chelsea, London, 8 May, 1841—

My dear Emerson,

Your last Letter found me on the southern border of Yorkshire; [1] whither Richard Milnes had persuaded me with him, for the time they call "Easter Holidays" here. I was to shake off the remnants of an ugly *Influenza* which still hung about me; my little portmanteau, unexpectedly driven in again by perverse accidents, had stood packed, its cowardly owner, the worst of all travellers, standing dubious the while, for two weeks or more; Milnes offering to take me as under his cloak, I went with Milnes. The mild, cordial, tho' somewhat dilettante nature of the man distinguishes him for me among men, as men go. For ten days I rode or sauntered among Yorkshire fields and knolls; the sight of the young spring, new to me these seven years, was beautiful,

---

[2] Four days later Emerson told his Aunt Mary that Number IV of *The Dial* interested him so little that he had not yet succeeded in reading it (*Let RWE*, II, 398).

[1] This letter is missing. Carlyle had been at Fryston, the house of Milnes's father, near Wakefield and Leeds (Wilson, *Carlyle to "The French Revolution,"* p. 134). On April 17 he wrote to his wife: "I have this moment enclosed Emerson's Letter in a *twopenny* cover for Fraser (your cover was overweight), and directed James to send off the missing sheets as soon as possible: I do not suppose any great benefit will ever come to us from that New-England reprint, especially as there is already a robber in the field; but we must do the best we can for it, the rather as that is so easily done" (NLS, MS 610).

or better than beauty. Solitude itself, the great Silence of the Earth was as balm to this weary sick heart of mine; not Dragons of Wantley (so they call Lord Wharncliff, the wooden Tory man),[2] not babbling itinerant Barrister people, fox-hunting Aristocracy, nor Yeomanry Captains cultivating milk-white moustachios, nor the perpetual racket, and "dinner at 8 o'clock," could altogether countervail the fact that green Earth was around one and unadulterated sky overhead, and the voice of waters and birds,—not the foolish speech of Cockneys at *all* times! —On the last morning as Richard and I drove off towards the railway, your Letter came in, just in time; and Richard, who loves you well, hearing from whom it was, asked with such an air to see it that I could not refuse him. We parted at the "station," [3] flying each his several way on the wings of steam; and have not yet met again. I went over to Leeds, staid two days with its steeple-chimnies and smoke-volcano still in view; [4] then hurried over to native Annandale, to see my aged excellent Mother yet again in this world while she is spared to me. My birthland is always as the Cave of Trophonius [5] to me; I return from it, with a haste to which the speed of Steam is slow,—with no smile on my face; avoiding all speech with men! It is not yet eight-and-forty hours since I got back; your Letter is among the first I answer, even with a line; your new Book—But we will not yet speak of that.

For first I have to say that from Leeds without any loitering I wrote Fraser about the defective "first six sheets"; [6] by whom, as I learned shortly after, they were straightway made up in the due post-office figure; despatched to Liverpool, and then "shipped in the *Cato* for Boston on the 22d of April";—*quod bonum sit.*[7] I cannot conjecture what has become of the *other* set; for they, and all the sheets of the Book were duly sent off, in swift succession, by conveyances

[2] On April 14, 1841, Carlyle had written to his wife: "The 'Dragon of Wantley' is Lord Wharncliff, so nicknamed hereabouts; a solemn old Tory Lord . . . innocent, wooden-limited, a very good old Dragon" (NLS, MS 610).

[3] This usage was still new; in 1838 *The Times* had been similarly cautious (*NED*).

[4] After leaving Fryston, Carlyle stayed at another country house, that of the Spring Rices; from the windows of his room the chimneys of Leeds were visible (Froude, *Thomas Carlyle: Life in London*, I, 182).

[5] An oracular cave in Boeotia so awesome that no one who visited it ever smiled again.

[6] Evidently a phrase from the missing letter.

[7] Cf. Livy, I, 17, 10: "Quod bonum, faustum, felixque sit."

which fair juges reckoned safe. Probably *they* have now arrived, before Fraser's? If they have not, if Fraser's too have not, and there is still somewhat wanting,—then let it and them wander forever and ever in the ocean brine, let the New York pirate work his will, and my brave Emerson free himself from such sorry trouble; for which I would again apologize, were not apologies a new trouble to him! Nay, probably he feels it a luxury to help in any way his brother over here; in which case why should I grudge it him? Is not the man worthy to help, —one of those rare men that *are* worthy? As for the antecedent Bookseller's Account, to me dim as hieroglyphics, James Fraser did look it over, with his sharp trade-eyes; declared it, if I remember, to be all correct according to bibliopolic tables of the Law,—except (now I bethink me) that of one Book (I no longer know, or almost never knew, which Book) there were more copies marked printed than were accounted for as either sold or unsold in the statement,—an error which your man will by and by rectify of himself; or else we will denounce it, specify it with details! And now enough of Book*sellers,* the ignoble blockheads; let me speak a moment about Books, about one Book.

My friend, I *thank* you for this volume of yours; not for the copy alone which you send to me, but for writing and printing such a Book. *Euge!* say I, from afar. The voice of one crying [in] the desert; [8] —it is once more the voice of a *man.* Ah me, I fel[t as] if in the wide world there were still but this one voice that responded intelligently to my own; as if the rest were all hearsays, melodious or unmelodious echoes; as if this alone were true and alive. My blessing on you, good Ralph Waldo! I read the Book all yesterday; my wife scarcely yet done with telling me her news. It has rebuked me, it has aroused and comforted me. Objections of all kinds I might make, how many objections to superficies and detail, to a dialect of thought and speech as yet imperfect enough, a hundredfold too narrow for the Infinitude it strives to speak: but what were all that? It *is* an Infinitude, the real vision and belief of one, seen face to face: a "voice of the heart of Nature" [9] is here once more. This is the one fact for me, which absorbs all others whatsoever. Persist, persist; you have much to say and to

[8] Cf. Mark 1: 3.

[9] In Lecture III of *Heroes and Hero-Worship* Carlyle had said: ". . . the heart of Nature [is] everywhere music" (*Works TC*, V, 84).

do. These voices of yours which I liken to *un*embodied souls, and censure sometimes for having no body,—how *can* they have a body? They are light-rays darting upwards in the East; they will yet *make* much and much to have a body! You are a new era, my man, in your new huge country: God give you strength, and speaking and silent faculty, to do such a work as seems possible now for you! and if the Devil will be pleased to set all the Popularities *against* you and evermore against you,—perhaps that is of all things the very kindest any *Angel* could do.

Of myself I have nothing good to report. Years of sick idleness and barrenness have grown wearisome to me. I do nothing. I waver and hover, and painfully speculate even now, as to health, and where I shall spend the summer out of London! I am a very poor fellow;—but hope to grow better by and by. Then this *alluvies* of foul lazy stuff that has long swum over me may perhaps yield the better harvest. *Esperons!* —Hail to all of you from both of us.

Yours ever   T. Carlyle

Chelsea, London, 21 May, 1841—

My dear Emerson,

About a week ago I wrote to you, after too long a silence. Since that, there has another Letter come, with a Draught of one hundred pounds in it, and other comfortable items not pecuniary; a line in acknowledgement of the money is again very clearly among my duties. Yesterday, on my first expedition up to Town, I gave the Paper to Fraser; who is to present the result to me in the shape of cash tomorrow. Thanks, and again thanks. This £100, I think, nearly clears off for me the outlay of the second *F. Revolution;* an ill-printed, ill-conditioned publication, the prime cost of which, once all lying saved from the Atlantic whirlpools and hard and fast in my own hand, it was not perhaps well-done to venture thitherward again. To the new trouble of my friends withal! We will now let the rest of the game play itself out as it can; and my friends, and my one friend, must not take more trouble than their own kind feelings towards me will reward.

The Books, the *Dial* N⁰ 4, and Appleton's pirated *Lectures,* are still expected from Green. In a day or two he will send them: if not, we will jog him into wakefulness, and remind him of the *Parcels De-livery Company,* which carries luggage of all kinds, like mere letters, many times a day, over all corners of our Babylon. In this, in the universal British *Penny Post,* and a thing or two of that sort, men begin to take advantage of their crowded ever-whirling condition in these days, which brings such enormous disadvantages along with it *un*sought for.—Bibliopolist Appleton does not seem to be a "Hero,"—except after his own fashion. He is one of those of whom the Scotch say, *"Thou* wouldst do little for God if the Devil were dead!" The Devil is unhappily dead, in that international bibliopolic province, and little hope of his reviving for some time; whereupon this is what Squire Appleton does. My respects to him: even in the Bedouin de-partment I like to see a complete man, a clear decisive Bedouin.—For the rest, there is one man who ought to be apprised that I can now stand robbery a little better; that I am no longer so very poor as I once was. In Fraser himself there do now lie vestiges of money! I feel it a great relief to see, for a year or two at least, the despicable bugbear of Beggary driven out of my sight; for *which* small mercy, at any rate, be the Heavens thanked. Fraser himself for these two edi-tions, 1000 copies each, of the *Lectures* and *Sartor,* pays me down on the nail £150; consider that miracle! Of the other Books which he is selling on a joint-stock basis, the poor man likewise promises some-thing, tho' as yet ever since New-yearsday I cannot learn what, owing to a grievous sickness of his,—for which otherwise I cannot but be sorry, poor Fraser within the Cockney limits being really a worthy, accurate and rather friendly creature. So you see me here provided with bread and water, for a season,—it is but for a season one needs either water or bread,—and rejoice with me accordingly. It is the one useful, nay I will say the one *innoxious,* result of all this trumpeting, reviewing, and dinner-invitationing; from which I feel it indispensa-ble to withdraw myself more and more resolutely, and altogether count it as a thing not there. Solitude is what I long and pray for. In the babble of men my own soul goes all to babble: like soil you were forever *screening,* tumbling over with shovels and riddles; in *which* soil no fruit can grow! My trust in Heaven is, I shall yet get away "to some cottage by the sea-shore"; [1] far enough from all the mad and

---

[1] Apparently a self-quotation: see C.9.26.40, where it appears without quotation marks.

mad-making things that dance round me here, which I shall then look on only as a theatrical phantasmagory, with an eye only to the *meaning* that lies hidden in it. You, friend Emerson, are to be a Farmer, you say, and di[g] Earth for your living? Well; I envy you that as much as any other [of] your blessednesses. Meanwhile I sit shrunk together here, in a small *dressing-closet,* aloft in the back part of the house, excluding all cackle and cockneys; and, looking out over the similitude of a May grove (with little brick in it, and only the minarets of West-minster and gilt cross of St Pauls visible in the distance, and the enormous roar of London softened into an enormous hum), endeavour to await what will betide. I am busy with Luther in one *Marheinecke's* very long-winded Book.[2] I think of innumerable things; steal out westward at sunset among the Kensington lanes; would this *May* weather last, I might be as well here as in any attainable place. But June comes; the rabid dogs get muzzles; all is brown-parched, dusty, suffocating, desperate, and I shall have to run! Enough of all that. On my paper there comes, or promises to come, as yet simply nothing at all. Patience;—and yet who can be patient?—

Had you the happiness to see yourself not long ago, in *Fraser's Magazine,* classed *nominatim* by an emphatic earnest man,[3] not with-out a kind of splayfooted strength and sincerity,—among the chief Heresiarchs of the world? Perfectly right. Fraser was very anxious to know what I thought of the Paper,—"by an entirely unknown man in the country." I counselled, "that there was something in him, which he ought to improve by holding his peace for the next five years."—

Adieu, dear Emerson; there is not a scrap more of paper. All copies of your *Essays* are out at use; with what result we shall perhaps see. As for me I love the Book and man, and their noble rustic herohood and manhood:—one voice as of a living man amid such jabberings of galvanised corpses: *Ach Gott!*—Yours evermore   T. Carlyle

---

[2] Philip Konrad Marheineke was a German philosopher and divine. The book was probably his *Geschichte der deutschen Reformation* (1816) and was probably the gift of Carlyle's friend Varnhagen von Ense (Carlyle, *New Letters,* I, 230).

[3] "Religious Authority the Principle of Social Organization," *Fraser's Magazine,* XXIII (February, 1841), 129–48, classes "the confused but passionate harangues of Emerson in America" with Goethe's *Wilhelm Meister* and Schleiermacher's *Reden über Religion* as aiming at an unchristian apotheosis of man.

Concord, 30 May, 1841.

My dear friend,

In my letter written to you on the 1st May (& enclosing a bill of exchange of £100 sterling which, I hope, arrived safely) I believe I promised to send you by the next steamer an account for April. But the false tardy Munroe & Co did not send it me until one day too late. Here it is, as they render it, compiled from Little & Brown's statement & their own. I have never yet heard whether you have received their "Analysis" or explanation of the last abstract they drew up of the mutual claims between the great houses of T.C. & R.W.E. & I am impatient to know whether you have caused it to be examined, & whether it was satisfactory. This new one is based on that, & if that was incorrect, this must be also.—I am daily looking for some letter from you, which is perhaps near at hand. If you have not written, write me exactly & immediately, on this subject, I entreat you.—You will see that in this sheet I am charged with a debt to you of $184.29. I shall tomorrow morning pay to Mr James Brown (of Little & Brown) who should be the bearer of this letter, $185.00, which sum he will pay you in its equivalent of English coin. I give Mr Brown an introductory letter to you, and you must not let slip the opportunity to make the man explain his own accounts, if any darkness hang on them. In due time, perhaps, we can send you Munroe or Nichols also, & so all your factors shall render direct account of themselves to you. I believe I shall also make Brown the bearer of a little book written some time since by a young friend of mine in a very peculiar frame of mind—thought by most persons to be mad—and of the publication of which I took the charge. Mr Very requested me to send you a copy.[1] —I had a letter from Sterling, lately, which rejoiced me in all but the dark picture it gave of his health. I earnestly wish good news of him. When you see him, show him these poems, & ask him if they have not a grandeur?

When I wrote last, I believe all the sheets of the Six Lectures had not come to me. They all arrived safely, although the last package not until our American pirated copy was just out of press in New

---

[1] *Essays and Poems,* by Jones Very (Boston, 1839); the publishers were C. C. Little and J. Brown. Carlyle was soon to see Emerson's review of this volume in *The Dial* for July, 1841.

York. My private reading was not less happy for this robbery whereby the eager public were supplied. Odin was all new to me; & Mahomet, for the most part, & it was all good to read, abounding in truth & nobleness. Yet, as I read these pages, I dream that your audience in London are less prepared to hear, than is our New England one. I judge only from the tone. I think I know many persons here who accept thoughts of this vein so readily now, that, if you were speaking on this shore, you would not feel that emphasis you use, to be necessary. I have been feeble & almost sick during all the spring, & have been in Boston but once or twice, & know nothing of the reception the book meets from the Catholic Carlylian Church. One reader & friend of yours dwells now in my house—and, as I hope, for a twelve-month to come,—Henry Thoreau,—a poet whom you may one day be proud of—a noble manly youth full of melodies & inventions. We work together day by day in my garden, & I grow well & strong.[2] My mother, my wife, my boy & girl, are all in usual health & according to their several ability salute you & yours. Do not cease to tell me of the health of your wife & of the learned & friendly physician.

Yours,   R. W. Emerson

I conclude to copy Brown's a/c also, & enclose the original.

Concord, 30 May, 1841

My dear Sir,

It gives me pleasure to introduce to you Mr James Brown of the firm of C. C. Little & James Brown, of Boston, whose name is already known to you as your American publishers. Mr Brown is & has long been in great esteem with our literary community both as a principal partner in our best bookselling house, and for his own merits as a worthy & honorable man. As Mr B. kindly takes the charge of a private package for you, I hope you will both find leisure to look into your account with him, & make it a little plainer than I have succeeded in doing. I doubt not, Mr Brown will be obliged to you for an introduction to Mr Fraser.

Your affectionate Servant,   R. W. Emerson.

T. Carlyle, Esq.

[2] On April 22, 1841, Emerson wrote to Margaret Fuller: "Henry Thoreau is coming to live with me & work with me in the garden & teach me to graft apples (*Let RWE*, II, 394). On April 26, Thoreau began his journal entry, "At R.W.E.'s" (*Journal*, I, 253).

Chelsea, London, 25 June, 1841—

Dear Emerson,

Now that there begins again to be some program possible of my future motions for some time, I hastily despatch you some needful outline of the same.

After infinite confused uncertainty, I learn yesternight that there has been a kind of country-house got for us, at a place called Annan, on the north shore of the Solway Frith, in my native county of Dumfries. You passed thro' the little Burgh, I suppose, in your way homeward from Craigenputtock: it stands about midway, on the great road, between Dumfries and Carlisle. It is the place where I got my schooling;—consider what a *preter*natural significance such a scene has now got for me! It is within eight miles of my aged Mother's dwelling place; within riding distance, in fact, of almost all the Kindred I have in the world.—The house, which is built since my time, and was never yet seen by me, is said to be a reasonable kind of house. We get it for a small sum in proportion to its value (thanks to kind accident); the 300 miles of travel, very hateful to me, will at least entirely obliterate all traces of *this* Dust-Babel; the place too being naturally almost ugly, as far as a green leafy place in sight of sea and mountains can be so nicknamed, the whole gang of picturesque Tourists, Cockney friends of Nature &c &c, who penetrate now by steam, in shoals every autumn, into the very center of the Scotch Highlands,—will be safe over the horizon! In short, we are all bound thitherward in few days; must cobble up some kind of gypsey establishment; and bless Heaven for solitude, for the sight of green fields, heathy moors; for a silent sky over one's head, and air to breathe which does *not* consist of coal-smoke, finely powdered flint, and other beautiful *etceteras* of that kind among others! God knows I have need enough to be left altogether alone for some considerable while (for*ever*, as it at present seems to me), to get my inner world, and my poor bodily nerves, both all torn to pieces, set in order a little again! After much vain reluctance therefore; disregarding many considerations,—disregarding *finance* in the front of these,—I am off; and calculate on staying till I am heavily *sated* with country, till at least the last gleam of summer weather has departed. My way of life has all along hitherto been a resolute *staying at home:* I find now however that I *must* alter my habits, cost what it may; that I cannot live all the year round in Lon-

don, under pain of dying or going rabid;—that I must, in fact, learn
to travel, as others do, and be hanged to me! Wherefore, in brief, my
Friend, our address for the next two or three months is "Newington
Lodge, Annan, Scotland,"—where a Letter from Emerson will be a
right pleasant visitor! *Faustum sit*.[1]

My second piece of news, not less interesting I hope, is that *Emerson's Essays*, the Book so-called, is to be reprinted here; nay, I think,
is even now at press,—in the hands of that invaluable Printer, Robson,
who did the *Miscellanies*. Fraser undertakes it, "on *half-profits*"; T.
Carlyle writing a Preface,—which accordingly he did (in rather sullen
humour,—not with you!) last night and the foregoing days.[2] Robson
will stand by the text to the very utmost; and I also am to read the
Proof-sheets. The edition is of 750; which Fraser thinks he will sell.
With what joy shall I then sack up the small £10 sterling perhaps of
"Half-profits" and remit them to the man Emerson; saying: There,
man! Tit for [tat] the reciprocity *not* all on one side!— —I ought to
say, moreover, that this was a volunteer scheme of Fraser's; the risk
is all his, the origin of it was with him: I advised him to have it reviewed, as being a really noteworthy Book; "write you a Preface,"
said he, "and I will reprint it";—to which, after due delay and meditation, I consented. Let me add only, on this subject, the story of a
certain Rio,[3] a French Breton, with long, distracted, black hair. He
found your Book at Richard Milnes's, a borrowed copy, and could not
borrow it; whereupon he appeals passionately to me; carries off my
wife's copy, this distracted Rio; and is to "read it *four* times" during
this current autumn, at Quimperle in his native Celtdom! The man
withal is a *Catholic,* eats fish on friday;—and a great lion here when
he visits us; one of the *naivest* men in the world: concerning whom
nevertheless, among fashionables, there is a controversy, "Whether he
is an Angel, or partially a Windbag and *Humbug?*" Such is the lot
of loveliness in the world! A *truer* man I never saw; how *wind*less,
how windy, I will not compute at present. Me he likes greatly (in

[1] See above, C.5.8.41, n. 7.

[2] The preface is dated 11 August 1841. It praises Emerson for his retirement into
"rustic obscurity," and for his possession of such Carlylean virtues as Silence and
Belief, but it has little to say of his "literary talent" and it finds that "the utterance
is abrupt, fitful."

[3] Alexis-François Rio, a critic and historian of painting, had written *Essai sur
l'histoire de l'esprit humain dans l'antiquité* (1828–30) and the first two volumes of
De l'art chrétien (1841).

spite of my unspeakable contempt for his fish on friday); likes,—but withal is apt to *bore*.

Enough, dear Emerson; and more than enough for a day so hurried. Our Island is all in a ferment electioneering: Tories to come in;— perhaps not to come in; at all events not to stay long, without alter- ing their figure much! I sometimes ask myself rather earnestly, What is the duty of a Citizen? To be, as I have been hitherto, a pacific *Alien?* That is the *easiest,* with my humour!—Our brave Dame here, just rallying for the *remove,* sends loving salutations. Good be with you all always. Adieu, dear E.   T. Carlyle

Appleton's Book of *Hero-Worship* has come; for which pray thank Mr Munroe for me: it is smart on the surface; but printed altogether scandalously!—

Concord, 31 July, 1841.[1]

My dear Carlyle,—Eight days ago—when I had gone to Nantasket Beach, to sit by the sea and inhale its air and refresh this puny body of mine—came to me your letter, all bounteous as all your letters are, generous to a fault, generous to the shaming of me, cold, fas- tidious, ebbing person that I am. Already in a former letter you had said too much good of my poor little arid book,—which is as sand to my eyes,—and now in this you tell me it shall be printed in London, and graced with a preface from the man of men. I can only say that I heartily wish the book were better, and I must try and deserve so much favor from the kind gods by a bolder and truer living in the months to come; such as may perchance one day relax and invigorate this cramp hand of mine, and teach it to draw some grand and adequate strokes, which other men may find their own account and not their good-nature in repeating. Yet I think I shall never be killed by my ambition. I behold my failures and shortcomings there in writing, wherein it would give me much joy to thrive, with an equanimity which my worst enemy might be glad to see. And yet it is not that I am occupied with better things. One could well leave to others the record, who was absorbed in the life. But I have done nothing. I think the branch of the "tree of life" [2] which headed to a

---

[1] This is Norton's text.

[2] Probably a reference to Igdrasil, the Norse "tree of existence," which Carlyle had treated in the first lecture of *Heroes and Hero-Worship,* although the quoted phrase is from Genesis 3: 22.

bud in me, curtailed me somehow of a drop or two of sap, and so
dwarfed all my florets and drupes. Yet as I tell you I am very easy in
my mind, and never dream of suicide. My whole philosophy—which
is very real—teaches acquiescence and optimism. Only when I see
how much work is to be done, what room for a poet—for any spiritualist—in this great, intelligent, sensual, and avaricious America, I lament
my fumbling fingers and stammering tongue. I have sometimes fancied
I was to catch sympathetic activity from contact with noble persons;
that you would come and see me; that I should form stricter habits
of love and conversation with some men and women here who are
already dear to me,—and at some rate get off the numb palsy, and
feel the new blood sting and tingle in my fingers' ends. Well, sure I
am that the right word will be spoken though I cut out my tongue.
Thanks, too, to your munificent Fraser for his liberal intention to
divide the profits of the *Essays*. I wish, for the encouragement of such
a bookseller, there were to be profits to divide. But I have no faith in
your public for their heed to a *mere* book like mine. There are things
I should like to say to them, in a lecture-room or in a "steeple house," [3]
if I were there. Seven hundred and fifty copies! Ah no!

And so my dear brother has quitted the roaring city, and gone back
in peace to his own land,—not the man he left it, but richer every
way, chiefly in the sense of having done something valiantly and well,
which the land, and the lands, and all that wide elastic English race
in all their dispersion, will know and thank him for. The holy gifts
of nature and solitude be showered upon you! Do you not believe
that the fields and woods have their proper virtue, and that there are
good and great things which will not be spoken in the city? I give
you joy in your new and rightful home, and the same greetings to
Jane Carlyle! with thanks and hopes and loves to you both.

R. W. Emerson.

As usual at this season of the year, I, incorrigible spouting Yankee,
am writing an oration to deliver to the boys in one of our little
country colleges, nine days hence. [4] You will say I do not deserve the
aid of any Muse. O but if you knew how natural it is to me to run
to these places! Besides, I always am lured on by the hope of saying

[3] A Quaker phrase for "church."

[4] *The Method of Nature. An Oration Delivered before the Society of the Adelphi,
in Waterville College, Maine, August 11, 1841.*

something which shall stick by the good boys. I hope Brown did not fail to find you, with thirty-eight sovereigns (I believe) which he should carry you.

Newby, Annan, Scotland, 18 Aug^t, 1841—

My dear Emerson,

Two days ago your Letter, direct from Liverpool, reached me here; only fifteen days after date on the other side of the Ocean: one of the swiftest messengers that have yet come from you. Steamers have been known to come, they say, in nine days. By and by we shall visibly be, what I always say we virtually are, members of neighbouring Parishes; paying continual visits to one another. What is to hinder huge London from being to universal Saxondom what small Mycale was to the tribes of Greece,—a place to hold your Παν-Ιωνιον in? A meeting of *All the English* ought to be as good as one of All the Ionians; and as Homeric "equal ships" [1] are to Bristol Steamers, so, or somewhat so, may New York and New Holland be to Ephesus and Crete, with their distances, relations, and etceteras!—Few things on this Earth look to me greater than the Future of that Family of Men.—

It is some two months since I got into this region; my Wife followed me with her maid and equipments some five weeks ago. Newington Lodge, when I came to inspect it with eyes, proved to be too tough an undertaking: upholsterers, expense and confusion—the Cynic snarled, "Give me a whole Tub rather! I want nothing but shelter from the elements, and to be let alone of all men." After a little groping, this little furnished Cottage, close by the beach of the Solway Frith, was got hold of: here we have been, in absolute seclusion, for a month,—no company but the corn-fields and the everlasting sands and brine; mountains, and thousand-voiced memories on all hands, sending their regards to one, from the distance. Daily (sometimes even nightly!) I have swashed about in the sea; I have been perfectly idle, at least inarticulate; I fancy I feel myself considerably sounder of body and of mind. Deeply do I agree with you in the great unfathomable meaning of a colloquy with the dumb Ocean, with the dumb Earth, and their eloquence! A Legislator would prescribe some weeks of this annually as a religious duty for all mortals, if he

---

[1] A translation of the last two words in line 306 of book I of *The Iliad*.

could. A Legislator will prescribe it for himself, since he can! You too have been at Nantasket; my Friend, this great rough purple sea-flood that roars under my little garret-window here, this too comes from Nantasket and farther,—swung hitherward by the Moon and the Sun.—It cannot be said that I feel "happy" here, which means joyful;—as far as possible from that. The Cave of Trophonius [2] could not be grimmer for one, than this old Land of Graves. But it is a sadness worth any hundred "happinesses." *N'en parlons plus.* By the way, have you ever clearly remarked withal what a despicable function "view-hunting" is. Analogous to "philanthropy," "pleasures of virtue" &c, &c. I for my part, in these singular circumstances, often find an honestly ugly country the preferable one. Black eternal peat-bog, or these waste-howling sands with mews and sea-gulls: you meet at least no Cockney to exclaim, "How charming it is!"—

One of the last things I did in London was to pocket Bookseller Brown's £38: a very honest-looking man, that Brown; whom I was sorry I could not manage to welcome better. You asked in that Letter about some other item of business,—Monro's or Brown's Account to acknowledge?—something or other that I was to *do:* I only remember vaguely that it seemed to me I had as good as done it. Your Letter is not here now, but at Chelsea.

Three sheets of the *Essays* lay waiting me at my Mother's, for correction; needing as good as none. The type and shape is the same as [that] of late *Lectures on Heroes.* Robson the Printer, who is a very punctual intelligent man, a scholar withal, undertook to be himself the corrector of the other sheets: I hope you will find them "exactly conformable to the text, *minus* mere typographical blunders and the more salient American spellings (labor for labour &c)." The Book is perhaps just getting itself subscribed in these very days. It should have been out before now: but poor Fraser is in the country, dangerously ill, which perhaps retards it a little; and the season, at any rate, is at the dullest. By the first conveyance I will send a certain Lady two copies of it. Little danger but the Edition will sell; Fraser knows his own trade well enough, and is as much a "desperado" as poor Attila Schmelzle was! [3] Poor James, I wish he were well again; but really at times I am very anxious about him.—The Book will

[2] See above, C.5.8.41, n. 5.

[3] The protagonist of *Schmelzle's Journey to Flaetz,* by Richter, which Carlyle had translated in *German Romance.*

sell; will be liked and disliked. Harriet Martineau, whom I saw in passing hitherward,[4] writes with her accustomed enthusiasm about it. Richard Milnes too is very warm. John Sterling scolds and kisses it (as the manner of the man is), and concludes by inquiring, whether there is any procurable likeness of Emerson?

—Good Heavens! Here came my Wife, all in tears, pointing out to me a poor ship, just tumbled over on a sandbank on the Cumberland Coast, men still said to be alive on it,—a Belfast steamer doing all it can to get in contact with it! Moments are precious (say the people on the beach), the flood runs ten miles an hour. Thank God, the steamer's boat is out: "eleven men," says a person with a glass, "are saved: it is an American timber-ship, coming up without a Pilot." And now,—in ten minutes more—there lies the melancholy mass alone among the waters, wreck boats all hastening towards it, like birds of prey; the poor Canadians all up and away towards Annan.—What an end for my letter; which nevertheless must end! Address to Chelsea next t[ime.] I can say no more.   Yours Ever   —T.C.

                                        Concord, 14 October, 1841 [1]
My dear Carlyle,

Mr Gambardella,[2] a native of Italy, whence his liberal political opinions drove him to this country some years ago desires to see you during his visit to England whither the love of painting and of pictures draws him. He pleases himself and his friends with the purpose —as far as in him lies,—of sending us back some day an effigy of yourself. Mr Gambardella who is only recently known to me is esteemed & beloved by good persons, my friends: and beyond our interest in him, you see, has contrived to give us all a personal interest in his acquaintance with you.

                    Yours affectionately,   R. W. Emerson.

[4] See below, E.10.30.41, n. 4.

[1] The MS of this letter is in the Berg Collection of the New York Public Library. On the back there are in Carlyle's hand three paragraphs of an early version of "Baillie the Covenanter," much reworked and crossed out.

[2] "Spiridione Gambardella was born at Naples. He was a refugee from Italy, having escaped, the story was, on board an American man-of-war. He had been educated as a public singer, but he had a facile genius, and turned readily to painting as a means of livelihood. He painted some excellent portraits in Boston, between 1835 and 1840, among them one of Dr. Channing . . ." (Norton's note to E.11.14.41).

Concord, 30 October, 1841.

My dear Carlyle,

I was in Boston yesterday & found at Munroe's your promised pacquet of the two London Books! They are very handsome,—that for my wife is beautiful—and I am not so old or so cold but that I can feel the hope & the pleasure that lie in this gift. It seems I am to speak in England—great England—fortified by the good word of one whose word is fame.[1] Well it is a lasting joy to be indebted to the wise & generous; and I am well contented that my little boat should swim, whilst it can, beside your great galleys. Nor will I allow my discontent with the great faults of the book—which the rich English dress cannot hide,—to spoil my joy in this fine little romance of friendship & hope. I am determined—so help me all muses! to send you something better another day.

But no more printing for me at present. I have just decided to go to Boston once more, with a course of lectures, which I will perhaps baptise "On the Times," by way of making once again the experiment whether I cannot—not only speak the truth, but speak it truly, or, *in proportion.* I fancy, I need more than another to *speak,* with such a formidable tendency to the lapidary style. I build my house of boulders: somebody asked me "if I built of medals?" [2] Besides I am always haunted with brave dreams of what might be accomplished in the lecture room—so free & so unpretending a platform,—a Delos not yet made fast [3]—I imagine an eloquence of infinite variety—rich as conversation can be, with anecdote, joke, tragedy, epics & pindarics, argument & confession. I should love myself wonderfully better if I could arm myself to go, as you go, with the word in the heart & not in a paper.

When I was in Boston I saw the booksellers, the children of Tantalus,—no—but they who trust in them are. This time, Little & Brown render as their credit account to T. C. $366.00 (I think it was)

---

[1] The absence here of any direct comment on the preface gives support to the rumor which Everett heard in November, 1842, that Emerson "did not like the patronizing strain of Carlyle's preface to his volume of essays" (Frothingham, *Edward Everett,* p. 212).

[2] Margaret Fuller: see *Let RWE,* II, 455n.

[3] Delos drifted about the Aegean until it was made fast by Zeus to serve as a birthplace for Apollo.

payable in three months from 1 October. They had sold all the London "French Revolutions" but fifteen copies. May we all live until 1 October! J. Munroe & Co acknowledge about $180.00 due and now rightfully payable to T. C., but, unhappily, not yet paid. By the help of brokers, I will send that sum more or less in some English Currency, by the next steamship, which sails in about a fortnight, and will address it, as you last bade me, to *Chelsea*.

What news, my dear friend, from your study? What designs ripened or executed? What thoughts? What hopes? You can say nothing of yourself that will not greatly interest us all. Harriet Martineau, whose sicknesses may it please God to heal! wrote me a kind, cheerful letter, and the most agreeable notice of your health & spirit on a visit at her house.[4] My little boy is five years old today and almost old enough to send you his love. With kindest greetings to Jane Carlyle, I am your & her friend R. W. E.

Concord   14 November 1841

My dear Carlyle,

Above you have a bill of exchange for forty pounds sterling with which sum you must credit the Munroe account. The bill I must not fail to notice is drawn by a lover of yours who expresses great satisfaction in doing us this courtesy: and courtesy I must think it when he gives me a bill *on sight* whilst of all other merchants I have got only

---

[4] Harriet Martineau wrote to Emerson on August 8, 1841: "Carlyle was here the other day, & is about to come again, with his wife (who grows upon me continually.) They write that *their* sea, on the Solway, is like coffee grounds. *Mine* is clear as a mountain brook, & stretches over to Denmark; so that I think they will come, & stay some time. He was, the other day, like a transformed man. Every feature was changed & every action. He has always before been the most miserable person I have ever known,—pricked & pierced with suffering,—suffering of which no one knows the cause, for which no sufficient cause is apparent. The tenderest & most patient sympathy can hardly endure his complaints, so unintermitting as they are. —so habitual have his groans become. But the other day, he was *gay*. His laugh was loosened,—his countenance relaxed, & he ran about like a school boy. And he was as tender as if I was dying. It was one of the happiest days I ever passed" (MS owned by RWEMA). Carlyle and his wife did stop to visit the invalid on their way south in September (Froude, *Thomas Carlyle: Life in London*, I, 189), and Carlyle wrote to his mother from Tynemouth: "Poor Miss Martineau seems to me far worse than when I came up in June; much weaker, & with a *false* kind of excitement in her manner. The sight of her gives me real sorrow: nor am I sure that our staying here is calculated to do her any good" (NLS, MS 511).

one payable at some remote day. Sam Ward is a beautiful & noble youth of a most subtle & magnetic nature, made for an artist, a painter, & in his art has made admirable sketches, but his criticism, I fancy was too keen for his poetry (shall I say?); he sacrificed to Despair, & threw away his pencil. For the present, he buys & sells.[1] I wrote you some sort of letter a fortnight ago, promising to send a paper like this. The hour when this should be dispatched finds me by chance very busy with little affairs. I sent you by an Italian Signor Gambardella,—who took a letter to you with good intent to persuade you to sit to him for your portrait,—a "Dial," & some copies of an Oration I printed lately. If you should have any opportunity to send one of them to Harriet Martineau, my debts to her are great, and I wish to acknowledge her abounding kindness by a letter, as I must. I am now in the rage of preparation for my Lectures "on the Times," which begin in a fortnight. There shall be eight, but I cannot yet accurately divide the topics. If it were eighty, I could better. In fear lest this sheet should not safely & timely reach its man, I must now write some duplicate.   Farewell, dear friend,   R. W. Emerson.

                                        Chelsea, 19 Nov[r], 1841—
Dear Emerson,
   Since that going down of the American Timber-ship on one of the banks of the Solway under my window, I do not remember that you have heard a word of me. I only added that the men were all saved, and the beach all in agitation, certain women not far from hysteria; —and then ended. I did design to send you some announcement of our return hither; but fear there is no chance that I did it! About ten days ago the Signor Gambardella arrived with a Note and Books from you: and here now is your Letter of October 30th; which, arriving at a moment when I have a little leisure, draws forth an answer almost instantly.
   The Signor Gambardella, whom we are to see a second time tonight or tomorrow, amuses and interests us not a little. His face is the very

---

[1] Samuel Gray Ward, twenty-four years of age, a close friend of Margaret Fuller and a contributor to *The Dial*, was working with his father in the American agency of Baring, the British banking firm (Cooke, *An Historical and Biographical Introduction to Accompany "The Dial"*, II, 254).

image of the classic God Pan's; with horns and cloven feet we feel that
he would make a perfect woodgod;—really some of Poussin's Satyrs
are almost portraits of this brave Gambardella. I will warrant him a
right glowing man of Southern-Italian vitality, full of laughter, wild
insight, caricature, and every sort of energy and joyous savagery: a
most profitable element to get introduced (in moderate quantity), I
should say, into the general current of your Puritan blood over in
New England there! Gambardella has behaved with magnanimity in
that matter of the Portrait: I have already sat, to men in the like
case, some four times, and G. knows it is a dreadful weariness; I directed him, accordingly, to my last Painter one Lawrence [1] a man of
real parts, whom I wished G. to know,—and whom I wished to know
G. withal, that he might tell me whether there was any probability
of a *good* picture by him in case one did decide on encountering the
weariness. Well; G. returns with a magnanimous report that Lawrence's picture far transcends any capability of his; that whoever in
America or elsewhere will have a likeness of the said individual must
apply to Lawrence not to Gambardella,—which latter artist heroically
throws down his brush, and says, Be it far from me! The brave
Gambardella: if I can get him this night to dilate a little farther on
his Visit to the *Community of Shakers*,[2] and the things he saw and felt
there, it will be a most true benefit to me. Inextinguishable laughter
seemed to me to be in Gambardella's vision of that Phenomenon,—
the sight and the seer: but we broke out too loud all at once, and he
was afraid to continue.— —Alas, there is almost no laughter going
in the world at present. True laughter is as rare as any other truth,—
the sham of it frequent and detestable like all other shams. I know
nothing wholesomer; but it is rarer even than Christmas, which comes
but once a year, and does always come once.

Your satisfactions, and reflexions, at sight of your English Book are
such as I too am very thankful for. I understand them well. May worse
guest never visit the Drawing-room at Concord than that bound Book.
Tell the good Wife to be rejoiced in it: she has all the pleasure;—to
her poor Husband it will be increase of pain withal: nay let us call it

---

[1] Samuel Laurence had done an oil portrait of Carlyle in 1838 and crayon sketches
in 1838 and 1841. For Carlyle in another mood about the oil, see below, C.2.16.45.

[2] Probably the community at Harvard, Massachusetts, which was one of the sights
of the Concord neighborhood.

increase of valiant labour and endeavour; no evil for a man, if he
be fit for it! A man must learn to digest praise too and not be poisoned
with it: some of it *is* wholesome to the system under certain circumstances; the most of it a healthy system will learn by-and-by to throw
into the slop-bason, harmlessly, without any *trial* to digest it. A
thinker, I take it, in the long-run finds that essentially he must ever
be and continue *alone;*—alone: "silent, rest over him the stars, and
under him the graves!" [3] The clatter of the world, be it a friendly be
it a hostile world, shall not intermeddle with him much.—The Book
of Essays, however, does decidedly "speak [in] England," in its way,
in these months; and even makes what one may call a kind of appropriate "sensation" here. Reviews of it are many, in all notes of the
gamut;—of small value mostly; as you might see by the two Newspaper specimens I sent you (Did you get these two Newspapers?) The
worst enemy admits that there are piercing radiances of perverse insight in it; the highest friends, some few, go to a very high point indeed. Newspapers are busy with extracts;—much complaining that it
is "abstruse," neological, hard to get the meaning of. All which is very
proper. Still better,—tho' poor Fraser, alas, is dead (poor Fraser!) [4]
and no help could come from industries of the Bookshop, and Books
indeed it seems were never selling worse than of late months,—I learn
that the "sale of the Essays goes very steadily forward," and will wind
itself handsomely up in due time, we may believe! So Emerson henceforth has a real Public in Old England as well as New. And finally my
Friend, do *not* disturb yourself about turning *better* &c &c; write as it
is given you, and not till it be given you, and never mind it a whit.

The new *Adelphi* piece [5] seems to me, as a piece of composition,
the best *written* of them all. People cry over it: "Whitherward? What,
What?" In fact I do again desiderate some *concretion* of these beautiful *abstracta*. It seems to me they will never be right otherwise; that
otherwise they are but as prophecies yet, not fulfilments.

The *Dial* too, it is all spirit-like, aeriform, aurora-borealis like. Will
no *angel* body himself out of that; no stalwart Yankee *man,* with

[3] Goethe, "Symbolum"; see above, C.9.26.40, n. 11.

[4] James Fraser died October 2, 1841. On October 5 Carlyle wrote to his sister
Jean: ". . . it is a mournful and a solemn thing for me, this loss of him in middle
course; I think he could only be some five and thirty; he was an innocent-hearted,
gleg, accurate little man. Ah me!" (NLS, MS 511).

[5] *The Method of Nature;* see above, E.7.31.41, n. 4.

colour in the cheeks of him, and a coat on his back! These things I *say:* and yet, very true, you alone can decide what practical meaning is in them. Write you always, *as it is given you,* be it in the solid, in the aeriform, or whatsoever way. There is no other rule given among men.—I have sent the criticism on Landor [6] to an Editorial Friend of L's, by whom I expect it will be put into the Newspapers here for the benefit of Walter Savage; he is not often so well praised among us, and deserves a little good praise. (*Turn back*) [7]

You propose again to send me monies,—surprising man! I am glad also to hear that that beggarly misprinted F. R[n] is nearly out among you. I only hope farther your Booksellers will have an eye on that rascal Appleton, and not let *him* reprint, and deface, if more copies of the Book turn out to be wanted. Adieu, dear E. Good speed to you at Boston, and in all true things. I hope to write soon again.

Yours ever   T. Carlyle

Chelsea, 6 Dec[r], 1841—

Dear Emerson,

Tho' I wrote to you very lately, and am in great haste today, I must lose no time in announcing that the Letter with the £40 draught came to hand some mornings ago; and now, this same morning, a second Letter round by Dumfriesshire, which had been sent as a duplicate, or substitute in case of accident, for the former. It is all right, my friend: Samuel Ward's paper has got itself changed into forty gold sovereigns, and lies here waiting us; thanks, many thanks! Sums of that kind come always upon me like manna out of the sky; surely they, more emphatically than any others, are the gift of Heaven. Let us receive, use, and be thankful. I am not so poor now at all; Heaven be praised: indeed I do not know, now and then when I reflect on it, whether being *rich* were not a considerably harder problem. With the wealth of Rothschild what farther good thing could one get,— if not perhaps some hut to live in, under free skies, in the country, with a horse to ride and have a little less pain on! *Angulus ille ridet!* [1]

---

[6] An essay by Emerson in *The Dial,* II (October, 1841), 262–71.

[7] The last paragraph of this letter is written upside down above the heading.

[1] An allusion to Horace, *Odes,* II, vi, 13: "Ille terrarum mihi praeter omnis/ Angulus ridet."

—I will add, for practical purposes in the future, that it is in general of little or no moment whether an American Bill be at sight or after a great many days; that the paper can wait as conveniently here as the cash can,—if your New-England House and Baring of Old England will forbear bankruptcy in the mean while. By the bye, will you tell me some time or other in *what* American funds it is that your funded money, you once gave me note of, now lies? I too am a creditor to America,—State of Illinois or some such State: 1000 dollars of mine, which some years ago I had no use for, now lies there, paying I suppose for canals, in a very obstructed condition! My Brother here is continually telling me that I shall lose it all,—which is not so bad; but lose it all by my own unreason,—which is very bad. It struck me I would ask where Emerson's money lies, and lay mine there too, let it live or perish as it likes! [2]

Your *Adelphi* went straightway off to Miss Martineau with a message. Richard Milnes has another; John Sterling is to have a third,— had certain other parties seen it first.[3] For the man Emerson is become a person to be seen in these times. I also gave a Morning-Chronicle Editor your brave eulogy on Landor, with instructions that it were well worth publishing there, for Landor's and others' sake. Landor deserves more praise than he gets at present; the world too, what is far more, should hear of him oftener than it does. A brave man after his kind,—tho' considerably "flamed on from the Hell beneath." [4] He speaks notable things; and at lowest and worst has the faculty too of holding his peace.

The "Lectures on the Times," are even now in progress? Good speed to the Speaker, to the Speech. Your Country is luckier than most at this time; it has still real Preaching; the tongue of man is not, whensoever it begins wagging, entirely sure to emit babblement, twaddlement, sincere-cant, and other noises which awaken the passionate wish for silence! That must alter everywhere: the human tongue

[2] In 1838 Carlyle and his brother John had bought $1,000 worth of Illinois stock at 6 percent interest (ALS, TC to John, December 26, 1838, owned by NLS, MS 523). During the twenties and thirties, all but seven of the American states had borrowed heavily abroad, especially in England, to finance programs of internal improvement (Faulkner, *American Economic History*, p. 324).

[3] This should probably read: ". . . had not certain other parties. . . ." At any rate, John Forster had the oration and was to forward it to Sterling (Carlyle, *New Letters*, I, 243).

[4] I have been unable to identify this quotation.

is no wooden watchman's-rattle or other *obsolete* implement; it continues forever new and useful, nay indispensable.

As for me and my doings—*Ay de mi!* [5]

[5] The rest of this letter, probably just the close and the signature, has been cut off.

1842

New York, 28 Feb. 1842

My dear friend,

I enclose a Bill of Exchange for fortyeight pounds sterling payable by Baring Brothers Co after sixty days from 25 Feb.

This sum is part of a payment from Little & Brown on account of sales of your London "French Revolution" and of "Chartism." As another part of their payment they asked me if they might not draw on the Estate of James Fraser for a balance due from his house to them & pay you so. I, perhaps unwisely, consented to make the proffer to you with the distinct stipulation, however, that if it should not prove perfectly agreeable to you & exactly as available as another form of money, you should instantly return it to me & they shall pay me the amount $41.57, or £8.12.5 in cash. My mercantile friend Abel Adams did not admire my wisdom in accepting this bill of Little & Brown so I told them I should probably bring it back to them and if there is a shadow of inconvenience in it, you will send it back to me by the next steamer. For they have no claims on us. I decide not to inclose the Little & Brown bill in this sheet, but to let it accompany this letter in the same packet.

I grieve to hear that you have bought any of our wretched Southern stocks. In New England all southern and southwestern debt is usually regarded as hopeless, unless the debtor is personally known. Massachusetts stock is in the best credit of any public stock. Ward told me that it would be safest for you to *keep* your Illinois stock, although he could say nothing very good of it.

Our city banks in Boston are in better credit than the Banks in any other city here, yet one in which a large part of my own property is invested, has failed, for the two last half years, to pay any dividend,[1] & I am a poor man until next April, when, I hope, it will not fail me

[1] The delinquency of the City Bank had sent Emerson to New York to deliver his course of lectures "On the Times" (*Let RWE*, III, 14).

again. If you wish to invest money here, my friend Abel Adams, who is the principal partner in one of our best houses, Barnard, Adams, & Co. will know how to give you the best assistance & action the case admits.

My dear friend, you should have had this letter & these messages by the last steamer, but when it sailed my son a perfect little boy of five years and three months had ended his earthly life.[2] You can never sympathize with me; you can never know how much of me such a young child can take away. A few weeks ago I accounted myself a very rich man, and now the poorest of all. What would it avail to tell you anecdotes of a sweet & wonderful boy, such as we solace & sadden ourselves with at home every morning & every evening? From a perfect health & as happy a life & as happy influences as ever child enjoyed, he was hurried out of my arms in three short days by *Scarlatina*.—We have two babes yet,—one girl of three years, & one girl of three months & a week, but a promise like that Boy's I shall never see.

How often I have pleased myself that one day I should send to you, this Morningstar [3] of mine, & stay at home so gladly behind such a representative! I dare not fathom the Invisible & Untold to inquire what relations to my Departed ones I yet sustain. Lidian, the poor Lidian, moans at home by day & by night. You too will grieve for us, afar.

I believe I have two letters from you since I wrote last. I shall write again soon, for Bronson Alcott will probably go to London in about a month,[4] & him I shall surely send to you hoping to atone by his great nature for many smaller ones that have craved to see you. Give me early advice of receiving these Bills of Exchange.

Tell Jane Carlyle our sorrowing story with much love, and with all good hope for her health & happiness. Tell us, when you write, with as much particularity as you can, how it stands with you, & all your household; with the Doctor, and the friends; what you do, & propose to do, & whether you will yet come to America, one good day?

Yours with love   R. Waldo Emerson

[2] Waldo died on the evening of January 27 (*Let RWE*, III, 6).

[3] On the day after the boy's death Emerson wrote to Mary Moody Emerson: "He adorned the world for me like a morning star" (*Let RWE*, III, 7).

[4] About two weeks earlier Emerson had offered to raise four or five hundred dollars for an "Alcott-Voyage-fund"; eventually he had to contribute most of the money himself. Alcott did not sail until May 8. See F. B. Sanborn and William T. Harris, *Amos Bronson Alcott: His Life and Philosophy*, I, 329.

Templand, Thornhill, Dumfries, Scotland
28 March, 1842

My Dear Friend,

This is heavy news that you send me; the heaviest outward bereavement that can befall a man has overtaken you. Your calm tone of deep quiet sorrow, coming in on the rear of poor trivial worldly business, all punctually dispatched and recorded too, as if the Higher and Highest had not been busy with you, tells me a sad tale. What can we say in these cases? There is nothing to be said,—nothing but what the wild son of Ishmael, and every thinking heart, from of old have learned to say: God is great! He is terrible and stern; but we know also He is good. "Though He slay me yet will I trust in Him." [1] Your bright little Boy, chief of your possessions here below, is rapt away from you; but of very truth *he* is with God, even as we that yet live are,—and surely in the way that was *best* for him and for you and for all of us. —Poor Lidian Emerson, poor Mother! To her I have no word. Such poignant unspeakable grief, I believe, visits no creature as that of a Mother bereft of her child. The poor sparrow in the bush affects one with pity, mourning for its young; how much more the human soul of one's Friend! I cannot bid her be of comfort; for there is as yet no comfort. May good Influences watch over her, bring her some assuagement. As the Hebrew David said, "We shall go to him, he will not return to us." [2]

I also am here in a house rendered vacant and sacred by Death. A sore calamity has fallen on us,—or rather has fallen on my poor Wife (for what am I but like a spectator in comparison): she has lost unexpectedly her good Mother, her sole surviving Parent, and almost only relative of much value that was left to her. The manner too was almost tragic. We had heard of illness here, but only of commonplace illness, and had no alarm. The Doctor himself, specially applied to, made answer as if there was no danger: his poor Patient, in whose character the like of that intimately lay, had rigorously charged him to do so: her poor Daughter was far off, confined to her room by illness of her own; why alarm her, make her wretched? The danger itself did seem over; the Doctor accordingly obeyed. Our first intimation of alarm was despatched on the very day which proved the final one. My poor Wife

[1] Job 13: 15.   [2] Cf. II Sam. 12: 23.

casting sickness behind her got instantly ready, set off by the first railway train: travelling all night, on the morrow morning at her uncle's
door in Liverpool she is met by tidings that all is already ended. She
broke down there; she is now home again at Chelsea, a cheery amiable
younger Jane Welsh,[3] to nurse her: the tone of her Letters is still full of
disconsolateness. I had to proceed hither, and have to stay here till this
establishment can be abolished, and all the sad wrecks of it in some
seemly manner swept away. It is above three weeks that I have been
here; not till eight days ago could I so much as manage to command
solitude, to be left altogether alone. I lead a strange life; full of sadness,
of solemnity, not without a kind of blessedness. I say it is right and
fitting that one be left entirely alone now and then,—alone with one's
own griefs and sins, with the mysterious ancient Earth round one, the
everlasting Heaven over one, and what one can make of these. Poor
rustic businesses, subletting of Farms, disposal of houses, household
goods: these strangely intervene, like matter upon spirit, every day;—
wholesome this too perhaps. It is many years since I have stood so in
close contact face to face with the reality of Earth, with its haggard
ugliness, its divine beauty, its depths of Death and of Life. Yesterday,
one of the stillest Sundays, I sat long by the side of the swift river
Nith; sauntered among woods all vocal only with rooks and pairing
birds. The hills are often white with snow-powder, black brief spring
tempests rush fiercely down from them, and then again the sky looks
forth with a pal[e] pure brightness,—like Eternity from behind Time.
The *sky*, when one thinks of it is *always* blue, pure changeless azure;
rains and tempests are only for the little dwellings where men abide.
Let us think of this too. Think of this, thou sorrowing Mother! Thy
Boy has escaped many showers.

In some three weeks I shall probably be back at Chelsea. Write thitherward as soon as you have opportunity; I will write again before long,
even if I do not hear from you. The monies &c are all safe here as you
describe: if Fraser's Executor make any demur, your Bookseller shall
soon hear of it.

I had begun to write some Book on Cromwell: I have often begun,
but know not how to set about it; the most unutterable of all subjects
I ever felt much meaning to lie in. There is risk yet that, with the loss
of still farther labour, I may have to abandon it;—and then the great

[3] A cousin.

dumb Oliver may lie unspoken for ever: gathered to the mighty *Silent* of the Earth; for, I think, there will hardly ever live another man that will believe in him and his Puritanism as I do. To *him* small matter.

Adieu, my good kind Friend, ever dear to me, dearer now in sorrow. My Wife when she hears of your affliction will send a true thought over to you also. The poor Lidian!—John Sterling is driven off again, setting out I think this very day for Gibraltar Malta and Naples.[4] Farewell, and better days to us.—Your affectionate   T. Carlyle

Concord, 31 March, 1842
My dear Carlyle,

I wrote you a letter from my brothers office in New York nearly a month ago to tell you how hardly it had fared with me here at home, that the eye of my home was plucked out when that little innocent boy departed in his beauty & perfection from my sight. Well I have come back hither to my work & my play, but he comes not back, and I must simply suffer it. Doubtless the day will come which will resolve this, as every thing gets resolved, into light, but not yet.

I write now to tell you of a piece of life. I wish you to know that there is shortly coming to you a man by the name of Bronson Alcott. If you have heard his name before, forget what you have heard. Especially if you have ever read anything to which this name was attached, be sure to forget that: and, inasmuch as in you lies, permit this stranger when he arrives at your gate to make a new & primary impression. I do not wish to bespeak any courtesies or good or bad opinion concerning him. You may love him, or hate him, or apathetically pass by him, as your genius shall dictate: Only I entreat this, that you do not let him go quite out of your reach until you are sure you have seen him & know for certain the nature of the man. And so I leave contentedly my pilgrim to his fate.

I should tell you that my friend Margaret Fuller who has edited our little Dial with such dubious approbation on the part of you & other men has suddenly decided a few days ago that she will edit it no more. The second volume was just closing; shall it live for a third year? You should know that if its interior & spiritual life has been ill fed, its out-

---

[4] This was Sterling's fifth and last attempt to escape tuberculosis by a change of climate (*Works TC*, XI, 224).

ward & bibliopolic [1] existence has been worse managed. Its publishers failed, its short list of subscribers became shorter, and it has never paid its laborious editor, who has been very generous of her time & labor, the smallest remuneration. Unhappily to me to me alone could the question be put whether the little aspiring starveling should be reprieved for another year. I had not the cruelty to kill it and so must answer with my own proper care & nursing for its new life. Perhaps it is a great folly in me who have little adroitness in turning off work to assume this sure vexation, but the Dial has certain charms to me as an opportunity, which I grudge to destroy. Lately at New York I found it to be to a certain class of men & women, though few, an object of tenderness & religion.[2] You cannot believe it?

Mr Lee [3] who brings you this letter is the son of one of the best men in Massachusetts, a man whose name is a proverb among merchants for his probity for his sense & his information. The son, who bears his father's name, is a favorite among all the young people for his sense & spirit, and has lived always with good people.

I have read at New York six out of eight lectures *on the Times* which I read this winter in Boston. I found a very intelligent & friendly audience The penny papers *reported* my lectures, somewhat to my chagrin when I tried to read them; many persons came & talked with me, and I felt when I came away that New York is open to me henceforward whenever my Boston parish is not large enough. This summer I must try to set in order a few more chapters from these rambling lectures, one on "the Poet" & one on "Character" at least. And now will you not tell me what you read & write? Is it Cromwell still? For I supposed from the Westminster piece [4] that the laborer must be in that quarter.

I send herewith a new Dial no viii and the last of this dispensation. I hope you have received every number. They have all been sent in order. I have written no line in this Number. I send a letter for Ster-

---

[1] Cf. "an outward and visible sign of an inward and spiritual grace," the definition of *sacrament* in the Anglican catechism.

[2] Henry James had the magazine on his table, and Albert Brisbane was eager to contribute a Fourierist article to it (*Let RWE*, III, 30, 33).

[3] See below, E.3.31.42 (2). Henry Lee, Jr., a Harvard graduate of 1836, was one of the founders of the American Bell Telephone Company (New-York *Daily Tribune*, November 26, 1898, p. 11).

[4] This was "Baillie the Covenanter," which appeared in *The Westminster Review* for January, 1842.

ling [5] as I do not know whether his address is still at Falmouth. Is he now a preacher? By the Acadia you should have received a letter of Exchange on the Barings & another on James Fraser's Estate.

With constant good hope for yourself & for your wife I am your friend
                                                              R. W. Emerson.

                                        Concord, 31 March, 1842 [1]
My dear Carlyle,

The bearer Mr Henry Lee, Jr. a graduate a few years since at our Cambridge, and now a merchant in Boston desires to see your face. If you wish to learn any thing of that good city, I could not refer you to a more frank or well informed gentleman.
                        Yours ever,   R. W. Emerson.

                                        Concord, 1 July, 1842—
My dear Carlyle,

I have lately received from our slow friends James Munroe & Co $246. on account of their sales of the Miscellanies—and I enclose a bill of Exchange for £51. which cost $\frac{246.50}{100}$ dollars. It is a long time since I sent you any sketch of the Account itself, & indeed a long time since it was *posted*, as the booksellers say; but I will find a time & a clerk also for this.

I have had no word from you for a long space—You wrote me a letter from Scotland after the death of your wifes mother, and full of pity for me also; and since, I have heard nothing. I confide that all has gone well & prosperously with you; that the iron Puritan is emerging from the Past, in shape & stature as he lived; and you are recruited by sympathy & content with your picture; and that the sure repairs of time & love & active duty have brought peace to the orphan daughter's

---

[5] In this enclosed letter to Sterling, Emerson wrote of Alcott: "Since Plato and Plotinus we have not had his like. I have written to Carlyle that he is coming, but have told him nothing about him. For I should like well to set Alcott before that sharp-eyed painter for his portrait, without prejudice of any kind" (Sterling, *Correspondence between John Sterling and Ralph Waldo Emerson*, p. 52).

[1] The MS of this letter is owned by the Berg Collection of the New York Public Library.

heart. My friend Alcott must also have visited you before this and you have seen whether any relation could subsist between men so differently excellent. His wife here has heard of his arrival on your coast—no more. I submitted to what seemed a necessity of petty literary patriotism—I know not what else to call it,—& took charge of our thankless little Dial, here, without subscribers enough to pay even a publisher, much less any laborer; it has no penny for editor or contributor,[1] nothing but abuse in the newspapers, or, at best, silence; but it serves as a sort of portfolio, to carry about a few poems or sentences which would otherwise be transcribed and circulated; and always we are waiting when somebody shall come & make it good—But I took it, as I said, & it took me, and a great deal of good time, to a small purpose. I am ashamed to compute how many hours & days these chores consume for me. I had it fully in my heart to write at large leisure in noble mornings opened by prayer or by readings of Plato or whomsoever else is dearest to the Morning Muse, a chapter on Poetry,[2]—for which all readings all studies are but preparation: but now it is July, & my chapter is in rudest beginnings. Yet when I go out of doors in the summer night, & see how high the stars are, I am persuaded that there is time enough, here or somewhere, for all that I must do; and the good world manifests very little impatience. Stearns Wheeler the Cambridge tutor, a good Grecian, and the editor, you will remember, of your American Editions, is going to London in August, probably, & on to Heidelberg, &c. He means, I believe, to spend two years in Germany, and will come to see you on his way; a man whose too facile & good-natured manners do some injustice to his virtues, to his great industry & real knowledge. He has been corresponding with your Tennyson & editing his poems here.[3] My mother, my wife, my two little

---

[1] *The Dial* had about three hundred subscribers and there was reason to believe that it might earn a net profit of about fifty dollars a year (Rusk, *Life*, p. 295).

[2] This became the first essay of the second series.

[3] Late in 1840 Wheeler had sent Tennyson an offer to edit his poems for Little and Brown. Tennyson, persuaded by this letter that the time had come for a new edition (". . . when I was wavering before, your letter has decided me"), prepared the two-volume *Poems* of 1842 and sent it on its publication to Wheeler, who had it brought out by Ticknor and Company in Boston. On June 11, 1842, when the book was already in the press, Wheeler asked Emerson "to be good enough to furnish a page or two of Preface; telling our good Public who Alfred Tennyson is," but the poems appeared without any such introduction (Eidson, *Charles Stearns Wheeler*, pp. 39–42).

girls are well: the youngest, Edith, is the comfort of my days; Peace &
Love be with you, with you both, & all that is yours!

R. W. Emerson

In our present ignorance of Mr Alcotts address I advised his wife to
write *to your Care,* as he was also charged to keep you informed of his
place. You may therefore receive letters for him with this.

Chelsea, London, 19 July, 1842—

My dear Emerson,

Lest Opportunity again escape me, I will take her, this time, by the
forelock, and write while the matter is still hot. You have been too long
without hearing of me; far longer, at least, than I meant. Here is a
second Letter from you, besides various intermediate Notes by the
hands of Friends, since that Templand Letter of mine: the Letter
arrived yesterday; my answer shall get under way today.

First under the head of business let it be authenticated that the
Letter inclosed a Draft for £51; a new unexpected munificence out of
America; which is ever and anon dropping gifts upon me,—to be received, as indeed they partly are, like manna dropped out of the sky;
the gift of unseen Divinities! The last money I got from you changed
itself in the usual soft manner from dollars into Sovereigns, and was
what they call "all right,"—all except the little Bill (of £8 and odds, I
think) drawn on Fraser's Executors by Brown (Little & Brown?) ; which
Bill the said Executors having refused for I know not what reason,
I returned it to Brown with note of the dishonour done it, and so the
sum still stands on his Books in our favour. Fraser's people are not now
my Booksellers, except in the matter of your *Essays* and a second edition of *Sartor;* the other Books I got transferred to a certain pair of
people named "Chapman and Hall, 186. Strand"; which operation, tho'
(I understand) it was transacted with great and vehement reluctance
on the part of the Fraser people, yet it produced no *quarrel* between
them and me, and they still forward parcels &c and are full of civility
when I see them:—so that whether this had any effect or none in their
treatment of Brown and his Bill I never knew; nor indeed, having as
you explained it no concern with B's and their affairs, did I ever
happen to inquire. I avoid all Booksellers; see them rarely, the blockheads; study never to think of them at all. Booksales, reputation, profit

&c &c: all this at present is really of the nature of an encumbrance to me; which I study, not without success, to sweep almost altogether out of my head. One good is still possible to me in Life, one only: to screw a little more work out of myself, my miserable despicable yet living, acting, and so far imperial and celestial *Self;* and this, God knows, is difficulty enough without any foreign one!

You ask after *Cromwell:* ask not of him; he is like to drive me mad. There he lies, shining *clear* enough to me, nay glowing, or painfully *burning;* but far down; sunk under two hundred years of Cant, Oblivion, Unbelief and Triviality of every kind: thro' all which, and to the top of all which, what mortal industry or energy will avail to raise him! A thousand times I have rued that my poor activity ever took that direction. The likelihood still is that I may abandon the task undone. I have bored thro' the dreariest mountains of rubbish; I have visited Naseby Field,[1] and how many other unintelligible fields and places; I have &c &c:—alas, what a talent have I for getting into the Impossible! Meanwhile my studies still proceed; I even take a gowlish kind of pleasure in raking through these old bone-houses and burial-aisles now; I have the strangest fellowship with that huge genius of DEATH (universal president there), and catch sometimes, thro' some chink or other, glimpses into blessed *ulterior* regions,—blessed, but as yet altogether *silent.* There is no use in writing of things past, unless they can be made in fact things present: not yesterday at all, but simply today and what it holds of fulfillment and of promises is *ours:* the dead ought to bury their dead, ought they not? In short, I am very unfortunate, and deserve your prayers—in a quiet kind of way! If you lose tidings of me altogether, and never hear of me more,—consider simply that I have gone to my natal element, that the Mud Nymphs have sucked me in; as they have done several in their time!

Sterling was here about the time your Letters to him came: your American reprint of his pieces was naturally gratifying him much.[2] He seems getting yearly more restless; necessitated to find an outlet for

[1] Carlyle stopped at Rugby on his way south from Scotland in May to visit Naseby Field with Dr. Thomas Arnold (Froude, *Thomas Carlyle: Life in London,* I, 217).

[2] In April Rufus Griswold of Philadelphia had published a pirated edition of Sterling's poems (*Let RWE,* III, 16n), but Carlyle probably refers to the long-projected and never-completed edition of A. L. Russell, an iron manufacturer of Plymouth (Sterling, *Correspondence of Sterling and Emerson,* pp. 39 ff., and *Let RWE,* VI, 572).

himself, unable as yet to do it well. I think he will now write Review Articles for a while; which craft is really perhaps the one he is fittest for hitherto. I love Sterling: a radiant creature; but very restless; incapable either of rest or of effectual motion: aurora borealis and sheet lightning; which if it could but *concentrate* itself, as I [. . .] always —!—We had much talk; but on the whole, even his talk is [not] much better for me than silence at present. *Me Miserum!* [3]

Directly about the time of Sterling's departure came Alcott, some two weeks after I had heard of his arrival on these shores. He has been twice here, at considerable length; the second time, all night. He is a genial, innocent, simple-hearted man, of much natural intelligence and goodness, with an air of rusticity, veracity, and dignity withal, which in many ways appeals to one. The good Alcot, with his long lean face and figure, with his grey worn temples and mild radiant eyes; all bent on saving the world by a return to acorns and the golden age; he comes before one like a kind of venerable Don Quixote, whom nobody can even laugh at without loving! I could like much to speak with him, were it not that there is no keeping of him from his one topic long together; and my hopeless unbelief in that, and indeed in the whole scope of his present *sally* into modern existence (as little better than one of Quixote's), evidently gives him pain. We differ, so far as I can yet compute, from the very centre. His aim is, it would seem, to *be* something, and become a universal blessing thereby; my fixed longgrowing conviction is that a man had better not attempt to *be* anything, but struggle with the whole soul of him to *do* something; on "vegetable diet," or what diet and conditions soever he can suitablest come at, and make safe truce and armed neutrality with the world by means of: then, having cleared a little free space for himself, let him *work,* in God's name, say I: then let him live on vegetables, and *be* happy and godlike, says Brownson; an enterprise terribly infested with latent Demons (vanity &c), and in brief, as I believe, *in*competent to Adam's children in this Earth! I do not want another Simon Stylites, however cunning his *pillar* may be. In short, I will speak no more with Alcot about his vegetables (if I can possibly avoid it), but question him on Emerson, on New England, on a thousand things on which his tidings are well worth hearing. The disease of Puritanism was *Antinomi-*

---

[3] Horace, *Epistles,* I, vii, 92–93: "'Pol, me miserum, patrone vocares,/ Si velles,' inquit, 'verum mihi ponere nomen!'"

anism;—very strange, does that still affect the *ghost* of Puritanism?—
(turn back) [4]

My poor Wife is still weak, overshadowed with sorrow: her loss is great, the loss almost as of the widow's mite; for except her good mother she had almost no kindred left; and as for *friends*—they are not rife in this world.—God be thanked withal they are not entirely non-extant! Have I not a Friend, and Friends, tho' they too are in sorrow? Good be with you all.   T. Carlyle

Mr Alcott's two Letters were forwarded yesterday; not indeed to his address, for I do not know that; but to a man who lives in the close neighborhood & knows and will find him.

By far the valuablest thing that Alcot brought me was the newspaper report of Emerson's last Lectures in New York. Really a right wholesome thing; radiant, fresh as the morning: a thing worth reading; which accordingly I clipped from the Newspaper, and have in a state of assiduous circulation to the comfort of many.—I cannot bid you quit the *Dial;* tho' it too, alas, is *Antinomian* somewhat! *Perge, perge,* nevertheless.—And so *now* an end.   T.C.

                            Chelsea, London, 29 August, 1842—
My dear Emerson,

This morning your new Letter, of the 15th August,[1] has arrived; exactly one fortnight old: thanks to the gods and steam-demons! I already, perhaps six weeks ago, answered your former Letter,—acknowledging the manna-gift of the £51, and other things; nor do I think the Letter can have been lost, for I remember putting it into the Post-Office myself. Today I am on the eve of an expedition into Suffolk, and full of petty business: however, I will throw you one word,—were it only to lighten my own heart a little. You are a kind friend to me, and a precious;—and when I mourn over the impotence of Human Speech, and how each of us, speak or write as he will, has to stand *dumb,* cased up in his own unutterabilities, before his unutterable Brother, I feel

---

[4] The rest of this letter is written in the margins. For Alcott's opinion of Carlyle and his account of his visits to Cheyne Row, see Shepard, *Pedlar's Progress,* pp. 316–17).

[1] This letter is missing. On the day of its arrival Carlyle sent it on to his wife in Suffolk (TC to Jane [8.29.42] NLS, MS 611).

always as if Emerson were the man I could soonest *try* to speak with, —were I within reach of him! Well; we must be content. A pen is a pen, and worth something; tho' it expresses about as much of a *man's* meaning perhaps as the stamping of a hoof will express of a horse's meaning; a very poor expression indeed!

Your bibliopolic advice about Cromwell or my next Book shall be carefully attended, if I live ever to write another Book! But I have again got down into primeval Night; and live alone and mute with the *Manes,* as you say; uncertain whether I shall ever more see day. I am partly ashamed of myself; but cannot help it. One of my grand difficulties I suspect to be that I cannot write *two Books at once;* cannot be in the seventeenth century and in the nineteenth at one and the same moment; a feat which excels even that of the Irishman's *bird:* "Nobody but a bird can be in two places at once!" For my heart is sick and sore in behalf of my own poor generation; nay I feel withal as if the one hope of help for it consisted in the possibility of new Cromwells and new Puritans: thus do the two centuries stand related to me, the seventeenth *worthless* except precisely in so far as it can be made the *nineteenth;* and yet let anybody *try* that enterprise! Heaven help me.—I believe at least that I ought *to hold my tongue;* more especially at present.

Thanks for asking me to write you a word in the *Dial.* Had such a purpose struck me long ago, there have been things passing thro' my head,—march-marching as they ever do, in long-drawn scandalous Falstaff-regiments (a man ashamed to be seen passing thro' Coventry with such a set!) [2]—some one of which, snatched out of the ragged rank, and dressed and drilled a little, might perhaps fitly have been saved from Chaos and sent to the *Dial.* In future we shall be on the outlook. I love your Dial, and yet it is with a kind of shudder. You seem to me in danger of dividing yourselves from the Fact of this present universe, in which alone ugly as it is can I find any anchorage, and soaring away after Ideas, Beliefs, Revelations and such like,—into perilous altitudes as I think; beyond the curve of perpetual frost, for one thing! I know not how to utter what impression you give me; take the above as some stamping of the fore-hoof. Surely I could wish you *returned* into your own poor nineteenth century, its follies and maladies, its blind or half-blind but gigantic toilings, its laughter and its

[2] Cf. *Henry IV, Part I,* act IV, scene ii, lines 10–50.

tears, and trying to evolve in some measure the hidden Godlike that lies
in *it;*—that seems to me the kind of feat for literary men. Alas, it is so
easy to screw oneself up into high and ever higher altitudes of Transcendentalism, and see nothing under one but the everlasting snows of
Himmalayah, the Earth shrinking to a Planet, and the indigo firma-
ment sowing itself with daylight stars; easy for *you*, for me: but whither
does it lead? I dread always, to inanity and mere injuring of the lungs!
—"Stamp, stamp, stamp!"—Well, I do believe, for one thing, a man
has no right to say to his own generation, turning quite away from it,
"Be damned!" It is the whole Past and the whole Future, this same
cotton-spinning, dollar-hunting, canting and shrieking, very wretched
generation of ours. Come back into it, I tell you;—and so for the
present will "stamp" no more.

The good Alcott and I have prospered, I am afraid, almost as ill as
it was possible for two honest men kindly affected towards one another
to do. How much he understands about me I know not; but what, how
much or how little I understand about him, he knows still less. The
third time we met, little Browning *Paracelsus* was here,[3] a neat dainty
little fellow, speaking in the Cockney quiz-dialect; to whom poor
Alcott's vegetable-diet concern was as ridiculous as it could be to most.
They did not prosper together; I walked up to town with them, and
still no prosperity: Browning at length went away; and then the exasperated Sage did speak, and when we two came to part, answered my,
"When shall I see you again?" by a solemn "Never, I guess!" It was
really too ridiculous: however, there was no help; and I have not seen
him again; nor, as I never could learn his address, does any remedy
seem possible. He is a rustic man; ignorant of the life-methods of civilized men, which civilized men have adopted that they may not be

---

[3] In a letter dated September 31, 1842, Browning wrote to his friend Alfred
Domett: "Carlyle I saw some weeks since: a crazy or sound asleep—not dreaming
—American was with him—a special friend of Emerson's—and talked! I have since
heard, to my solace, that my outrageous laughters have made him ponder seriously
of the hopelessness of England—which he would convert to something or other"
(Browning, *Robert Browning and Alfred Domett,* ed. F. G. Kenyon, p. 46). Another
account of the meeting appears in a letter from Carlyle to Sterling of July 28, 1842
(NLS, MS 531): "Alcot came to me again the other day; little Paracelsus Browning, a
dainty Leigh-Huntish kind of fellow, with much ingenuity, vivacity and Cockney
gracefulness, happened to be here; and answered his solemn drawling recommendations of vegetable diet with light Cockney banter and logic; whereupon Alcot, at
parting, told me 'he would never come to me again!' "

intolerable to one another; nor apparently has he the faintest notion to learn them. I told him, "All this thing that we saw around us (head of St. James's Street, with Piccadilly, with England) "had been existing now for a matter of two thousand years, not on his behalf at all, but on its own only, and had never heard of him till yesterday: why would he get angry that it did not all at once turn round and shape itself according to his image!" In vain: the excellence of the vegetable philosophy, and conquest of the world by a return to acorns and the primeval innocence, seemed so indubitable, that he did think it at least deserved a serious consideration from the oldest St James's Street and Piccadilly: —Ah me!

If there be still time, which I doubt there is not, I wish you would tell this good man that my whole heart is kindly affected to him; that I do esteem his Potatoe-gospel a mere imbecillity which *cannot* be discussed in this busy world at this time of day;—but that he ought really to come back to me! That I shall rejoice to see him again; and not bore him, if I can help it, if he will avoid boring me.—His Letters, of which there came three this morning, I always put in a track which I know attains him, among some connexions he has at Richmond.— —Adieu, my friend; I must not add a word more. My Wife out on a visit; it is to bring her back that I am now setting forth for Suffolk.[4] I hope to see Ely too, and St Ives and Huntingdon, and various Cromwelliana. My blessings on the Concord Household now and always. Commend me expressly to your Wife and your Mother. Farewell, dear friend.

T. Carlyle

Concord, 15 October, 1842

My dear Carlyle,

I am in your debt for at least two letters since I sent you any word. I should be well content to receive one of these stringent epistles of bark & steel & mellow wine with every day's post, but as there is no hope that more will be sent without my writing to signify that these have come, I hereby certify that I love you well and prize all your mes-

[4] Jane Carlyle was staying with the Bullers, in whose house Carlyle had once been a tutor, at the rectory of their youngest son Reginald—near Bury St. Edmunds (Carlyle, *Letters and Memorials*, I, 114)

sages. I read with special interest what you say of these English studies and I doubt not the Book is in steady progress again. We shall see what change the changed position of the author will make in the book. The first History expected its public; the second is written to an expecting people. The tone of the first was proud,—to defiance: we will see if applauses have mitigated the master's temper. This time he has a hero, and we shall have a sort of standard to try by the hero who fights, the hero who writes. Well; may grand & friendly spirits assist the work in all hours; may impulses & presences from that profound world which makes & embraces the whole of humanity, keep your feet on the Mount of Vision which commands the Centuries, & the book shall be an indispensable Benefit to men, which is the surest fame. Let me know all that can be told of your progress in it. You shall see in the last *Dial* a certain shadow or mask of yours, "another Richmond," [1] who has read your lectures & profited thereby. Alcott sent me the paper from London, but I do not know the name of the writer.

As for Alcott, you have discharged your conscience of him manfully & knightly: I absolve you well. But I am vexed that he should have been mad about diet, & with you. It is a new thing with him, this eating better than his neighbors, & I could heartily wish he had either not come to it, or had gotten through it, before he saw you; for it has excluded his proper topics, and inflamed the man, who was gentle & intellectual, to be sore & tedious. His latest letters from London give me little pleasure, and although very happy at first, I think he soon ceased to derive any benefit from his excursion. He is a great man & was made for what is greatest, but I now fear that he has already touched what best he can, & through his more than a prophet's egotism, and the absence of all useful reconciling talents, will bring nothing to pass, & be but a voice in the wilderness. As you do not seem to have seen in him his pure & noble intellect, I fear that it lies under some new & denser clouds.[2]

[1] Cf. *Richard III*, act V, scene iv, line 11. This "Richmond" was Alcott's English disciple Charles Lane; his article "Cromwell" appeared in *The Dial*, III (October, 1842), 258–64.

[2] Carlyle thought this "a very sensible Letter about poor Alcott: 'a man of egoism more than a prophet's!'" ALS to John Carlyle, 11.23.42 (NLS, MS 524). In the first draft of Emerson's letter the last sentence of paragraph two reads as follows: "But until I see him I have not settled it whether it is he or you that is guilty of your failure to see his nobility."

For the Dial & its sins, I have no defence to set up. We write as we can, and we know very little about it. If the direction of these speculations is to be deplored, it is yet a fact for literary history, that all the bright boys & girls in New England, quite ignorant of each other, take the world so, & come & make confession to fathers & mothers,— the boys that they do not wish to go into trade, the girls that [they] [3] do not like morning calls & evening parties. They are all religious, but hate the churches: they reject all the ways of living of other men, but have none to offer in their stead.[4] Perhaps, one of these days, a great Yankee shall come, who will easily do the unknown deed.

The booksellers have sent me accounts lately, but—I know not why —no money. Little & Brown, from January to July, had sold very few books. I inquired of them concerning the bill of exchange on Fraser's Estate, which you mention, and they said it had not been returned to them, but only some information, as I think, demanded by Fraser's administrator, which they had sent, & as they heard nothing again, they suppose that it is allowed & paid to you. Inform me on this matter. Munroe & Co. allow some credits, but charge more debits—for binding, &c. and also allege few sales in the hard times. I have got a good friend of yours, a banking man, to promise that he will sift all the accounts & see if the booksellers have kept their promises. But I have never yet got all the paper in readiness for him . . .[5] I am looking to see if I have matter for new lectures, having left behind me last spring some half promises in New York. If you can remember it tell me who writes about Loyola & Xavier in the Edinburgh.[6] Sterling's papers—if he is near you,—are all in Mr Russell's hands. I played my part of Fadladeen with great rigor and sent my results to Russell,[7] but have not now written to J.S.   Yours   R.W.E.

[3] This word, accidentally omitted, appears in the first draft.

[4] In the first draft this paragraph ends thus: "We are all religious but hate our churches. We are sure society is wrong in its trades & professions but we are in the dark what we ought to do. A great reconciling Yankee will come presently & do the deed now unknown."

[5] Thus in the manuscript.

[6] The leading article in the July, 1842, issue of *The Edinburgh Review* was a review of the *Exercitia Spiritualia* of Ignatius Loyola.

[7] Fadladeen is the "Great Nazir or Chamberlain of the Harem" in Moore's *Lalla Rookh*, a dull and finicky critic of the tales in verse which are told to the princess: Emerson had evidently selected the material which was to go into Russell's edition.

Chelsea, London, 17 Nov^r, 1842—

My dear Emerson

Your Letter finds me here today; busied with many things, but not likely to be soon more at leisure; wherefore I may as well give myself the pleasure of answering it on the spot. The Fraser Bill by Brown and Little has come all right; the Dumfries Banker apprises me lately that he has got the cash into his hands. Pray do not pester yourself with these Bookseller unintelligibilities: I suppose their accounts are all reasonably correct, the cheating, such as it is, done according to rule: what signifies it at any rate? I am no longer in any vital want of money; alas, the want that presses far heavier on me is a want of faculty, a want of *sense;* and the feeling of that renders one comparatively very indifferent to money! I reflect many times that the wealth of the Indies, the fame of ten Shakespeares or ten Mahomets, would at bottom do me no good at all. Let us leave these poor slaves of the Ingot and slaves of the Lamp to their own courses,—within a *certain* extent of halter!

What you say of Alcott seems to me altogether just. He is a man who has got into the Highest intellectual region,—if that be the Highest (tho' in that too there are many stages), wherein a man can believe and discover for himself, without need of help from any other, and even in opposition to all others: but I consider him entirely unlikely to accomplish anything considerable, except some kind of crabbed, semiperverse, tho' still manful existence of his own; which indeed is no despicable thing. His "more than prophetic egoism"—alas, yes! It is of such material that Thebaid Eremites,[1] Sect-founders, and all manner of crossgrained fanatical monstrosities have fashioned themselves,—in very *high,* and in the highest regions, for that matter. Sect-founder withal are a class I do not like. No truly great man, from Jesus Christ downwards, as I often say, ever founded a Sect,—I mean wilfully intended founding one. What a view must a man have of this Universe, who thinks *"he* can swallow it all,"[2] who is not doubly and trebly happy that he can keep it from swallowing him! On the whole, I sometimes hope we have now done with Fanatics and Agonistic Posturemakers in this poor world: it will be an immense improvement on the

---

[1] According to *The Catholic Encyclopedia,* "the eremitical life was introduced into the Lower Thebaid by St. Anthony" in the third century.

[2] Cf. *The French Revolution,* bk. II, ch. vii (*Works TC,* II, 54).

Past; and the "New Ideas," as Alcott calls them, will prosper greatly the better on that account! The old gloomy Gothic Cathedrals were good; but the great blue Dome that hangs over all is better than any Cologne one.—On the whole, do not tell the good Acott a word of all this; but let him love me as he can, and live on vegetables in peace; as I, living *partly* on vegetables, will continue to love him!

The best thing Alcot did while he staid among us was to circulate some copies of your *Man the Reformer.* I did not get a copy; I applied for one, so soon as I knew the right fountain; but Alcott, I think, was already gone. And now mark,—for this I think is a novelty, if you do not already know it: Certain Radicals have reprinted your Essay in Lancashire, and it is freely circulating there, and here, as a cheap pamphlet, with excellent acceptance so far as I discern. Various Newspaper reviews of it have come athwart me: all favourable, but all too shallow for sending to you. I myself consider it a *truly excellent* utterance; one of the best words you have ever spoken. Speak many more such. And whosoever will distort them into any "vegetable" or other crotchet,—let it be at his own peril; for the word itself is *true;* and will have to make itself a *fact* therefore; tho' not a distracted *abortive* fact, I hope! Words of that kind are not born into Facts in *the seventh month;* well if they see the light full-grown (they and their adjuncts) in the *second century;* for old Time is a most deliberate breeder!—But to speak without figures, I have been very much delighted with the clearness, simplicity, quiet energy and veracity of this discourse; and also with the fact of its spontaneous appearance here among us. The prime mover of the Printing, I find is one Thomas Ballantyne, editor of a Manchester Newspaper, a very good cheery little fellow, once a Paisley weaver, as he informs me,—a great admirer of all worthy things.[3]— —My paper is so fast failing, let me tell you of the Writer on Loyola. He is a James Stephen, Head Under-Secretary of the Colonial Office,—that is to say, I believe, real governor of the British Col-

[3] G. W. Cooke's *A Bibliography of Ralph Waldo Emerson,* p. 73, lists an edition of *Man the Reformer* published by Abel Heywood in Manchester in 1843. On December 3, 1842, Thomas Ballantyne, editor of the Manchester *Guardian,* wrote to Emerson with much praise for last year's volume of essays from "all the devout admirers of T. Carlyle" and with even more praise for *Man the Reformer* because of its "practical utility" and intelligibility to all men. "T. Carlyle," he said, "a few days ago in stating that he had not a copy of *Man the Reforme*r (new English ed) to send you, said he thought I might as well send one myself, which I now take the liberty of doing" (MS owned by RWEMA).

onies, so far as they have any governing. He is of Wilberforce's creed, of Wilberforce's Kin; a man past middle age, yet still in full vigour; reckoned an enormous fellow for "despatch of business" &c, especially by Taylor (*van Artevelde*) and others who are with him or under him in Downing-street: [4] to me, tho' I like much in him, he has one heavy fault, he cannot, in speaking to you, let his head stand steady on his shoulders, but keeps it continually waggling,—as if making a yet better position for itself! In fact I regard the man as standing on the confines of Genius and Dilettantism,—a man of many really good qualities, and excellent at the despatch of business. There we will leave him.—A Mrs Lee of Brookline near you has made a pleasant book about Jean Paul, chiefly by excerpting.[5] I am sorry to find Gunderode and Co a decided weariness! [6]—Cromwell—Cromwell? Do not mention such a word, if you love me! And yet—Farewell, my Friend, tonight!

Yours ever   T. Carlyle

I will apprise Sterling before long: he is at Falmouth, and well; urging me much to start a Periodical here!

Gambardella promises to become a real Painter; there is a glow of real fire in the wild southern man: next to no *articulate* intellect or the like, but of *in*articulate much, or I mistake. He has tried to paint *me* for you; but cannot, he says!

---

[4] Stephen was related to the philanthropist and abolitionist William Wilberforce only by marriage: his stepmother was Wilberforce's sister; but he did grow up as a member of the "Clapham sect" of Anglican evangelicals. Henry Taylor, essayist and dramatist, held a responsible position under Stephen at the colonial office; he was best known for his historical drama *Philip Van Artevelde* of 1834.

[5] This was *The Life of Jean Paul Frederic Richter, Compiled from various Sources, Together with his Auto-Biography,* translated from the German, by Eliza Buckminster Lee. Emerson had read the book in October (*Let RWE,* III, 92), and it was to be reviewed in *The Dial* of January, 1843.

[6] This refers to an article by Margaret Fuller, "Bettine Brentano and Her Friend Günderode," in *The Dial* for January, 1842.

1843

Staten Island
New York, 26 Feby 1843

My dear Carlyle,

My friend & relative by marriage, Rev. Orville Dewey,[1] desires to visit you. It gives me pleasure to introduce to you a social & liberal man, who is dearly valued by the best Society in New York, where he is an Unitarian clergyman. You will find him well acquainted with the most noted of our people, as I believe he already is with many of the most eminent of yours.

Yours affectionately,   R. W. Emerson

T. Carlyle, Esq.

Chelsea, London, 11 March, 1843—

Dear Emerson,

I know not whose turn it is to write; tho' a suspicion has long attended me that it was yours, and above all an indisputable wish that you would do it: but this present is a cursory line, all on business,— and as usual all on business of my own.

I have finished a Book, and just set the Printer to it; one solid volume (rather bigger than one of the French-Revolution Volumes, as I compute): it is a somewhat fiery and questionable "Tract for the Times"; *not* by a Puseyite,[1] which the horrible aspect of things here

---

[1] Orville Dewey was the husband of Emerson's cousin Louisa Farnham (*Let RWE*, I, 52n). In a letter of sympathy, April 21, 1842, written from Europe after the death of Emerson's son Waldo, he had included a far-sighted request for an introduction to Carlyle "early in the spring of next year" (MS owned by RWEMA). In June of 1843 Carlyle wrote to a correspondent who was, I believe, the American agriculturist Henry Colman: "A Mr and Mrs Orville Dewey, from New York, send me down a Note from Emerson, with a request to know when they are to call,—but have omitted to add any address of their own! I wish you could find them, and bring them down with you on Monday evening,—or at least make known to them my embarrassment" (MS owned by the Historical Society of Pennsylvania).

[1] The last of the "Puseyite" *Tracts for the Times* had been published in 1841.

has forced from me;—I know not whether as preliminary to *Oliver* or not; but it had gradually grown to be the preliminary of anything possible for me: so there it is written; and I am a very sick, but withal a comparatively very free man. The Title of the thing is to be *Past and Present:* it is divided into Four Books, "Book I. Proem," "Book II. The Ancient Monk." "Book III. The Modern Worker;" and "Book IV. Horoscope." (or some such thing):—the size of it I guessed at above.

The practical business, accordingly, is: How to cut out that New-York scoundrel, who fancies that because there is no gallows it is permitted to steal? [2] I have a distinct desire to do that;—altogether apart from the money to be gained thereby. A friend's goodness ought not to frustrated by a scoundrel destitute of gallows.—You told me long since how to do the operation; and here, according to the best way I had of fitting your scheme into my materials, is my way of attempting it.

The Book will not be out here for six good weeks from this date; it could be kept back for a week or two longer, if that were indispensable: but I hope it may not. In three weeks, half of it will be printed; I, in the meanwhile, get a correct Ms. Copy of the latter half made ready: joining the printed sheets and this *Ms.,* your Bookseller will have a three-week start of any rival, if I instantly despatch the Parcel to him. Will this do? This with the announcement of the Title as given above. Pray write to me straightway, and say. Your answer will be here before we can publish; and the Packet of Proofsheets and Manuscript may go off whether there be word from you or none.—And so enough of *Past and Present.* And indeed enough of all things for my haste is excessive in these hours.

The last *Dial* came to me about three weeks ago *as a Post-Letter,* charged something like a guinea of postage, if I remember; so it had to be rejected, and I have not yet seen that No; but will when my leeway is once brought up a little again. The two preceding Nos were, to a marked extent, more like life than anything I had seen before of the *Dial.* There was not indeed anything, except the Emersonian Papers alone which I know by the first ring of them on the tympanum of the mind, that I properly speaking *liked;* but there was much that I did not dislike, and did half like; and I say, "*I fausto pede;* [3] that will decidedly do better!"—By the bye, it were as well if you kept rather a strict outlook on Alcott and his English *tail,*—I mean so far as we here

[2] Appleton: see above, E.4.30.41.　　　[3] Horace, *Epistles,* II, ii, 37.

have any business with it. Bottomless imbecils ought not be seen in company with R[alph] Waldo Emerson, who has already *men* listening to him on this side of the water. The "tail" has an individual or two of that genus,—and the rest is mainly yet undecided. For example, I knew old Greaves [4] myself; and can testify, if you will believe me, that few greater blockheads (if "blockhead" may mean "exasperated imbecil" and the ninth-part of a thinker) broke the world's bread in his day. Have a care of such! I say always to myself,—and to you, which you forgive me.

Adieu my dear Emerson. May a *good* Genius guide you; for you are *alone, alone;* and have a steep pilgrimage to make,—leading *high,* if you do not slip or stumble!

Ever your affectionate   T. Carlyle

Chelsea, 15 March, 1843—

My dear Emerson,

About four days ago I wrote to you about a new Book to be called *Past and Present.* I learn now that this Letter, which I will make "No. 2," can still go along with the former; and so, having made a variety of calculations and arrangements, I will now with all brevity (my haste being boundless) communicate to you the practical result of them.

Our next steamer for Boston will sail on the 1st of April. I have secured a Copyist for the second portion of *Past and Present,* who is to be ready with his work all done, in time for that conveyance; the Printer, a punctual man, undertakes on the other hand to be ready with his share of the operation: wherefore, in brief, you can instruct your Boston Bookseller to expect a Complete Copy of the work by that said steamer, so that his Printers may fall upon it, tooth and nail,— and overtake ours if they can; at all events, completely distance the New-Yorker, it is to be hoped.

This is the essential of "No 2." I will do what is in me to be punctual; and as my subordinates are steady people, I think we shall manage it. —Our Book, as I compute, may be still some four weeks, after the

---

[4] James Pierrepont Greaves, mystic, reformer, transcendentalist, Pestalozzian, vegetarian, was the teacher of Alcott's English friends Lane and Wright. He died at Alcott House, Surrey, in March, 1842. Carlyle was perhaps reminded of him by Lane's long biographical article in *The Dial* for October, 1842, and January, 1843.

April steamer goes, in a hidden nascent state. If a Letter of yours in answer to this arrived before Publication, as is possible, and informed us that another week or two of delay will be essential, that too can easily be granted.

I send no "Apologies": for they would but occupy my time and yours. I am very busy. Among my other operations I have undertaken to hear Lyell lecture on Geology,—a somewhat superfluous enterprise, at once wearisome and ineffectual; our Geologist being dreadfully *Neptunean* [1] in his qualities, I fear!—

John Sterling arrived yesterday, to see his Mother who is very poorly. I have not got eye on him yet, but shall attempt it today. Blessings and desert of blessings on you!

Yours ever   T. Carlyle

Chelsea, 1 April, 1843—

My dear Emerson,

Along with this Letter there will go from Liverpool, on the 4th, inst, the promised Parcel, complete copy of the Book called *Past and Present,* of which you already had two simultaneous announcements. The name of the Steam Packet, I understand, is *the Britannia.* I have addressed the Parcel to the care of "Messrs Little and Brown, Booksellers, Boston," with your name atop: I calculate, it will arrive safe enough.

About 100 pages of the *Ms.* copy have proved superfluous, the text being there also in a printed shape; I had misestimated the Printer's velocity; I was anxious too that there should be no failure as to time. The *Ms.* is very indifferent in that section of it; the damage therefore is smaller: your press-corrector can acquaint himself with the *hand* &c, by means of it. A poor young governess, confined to a horizontal posture, and many sad thoughts, by a disease of the spine, was our artist in that part of the business: her writing is none of the distinctest; but it was a work of charity to give it her.[1] I hope the thing is all as correct

---

[1] The Neptunists, of whom Lyell was not one (*Principles of Geology,* I, xii), believed in the exclusively aqueous origin of geological phenomena. Here Carlyle seems to be making a joke about watery discourse: on March 9, 1843, he had written to Sterling that as a lecturer Lyell was "clear, but of Kin to Neptune, I fear!" (*Letters to Mill, Sterling, and Browning,* p. 267).

[1] On March 24, 1843, Carlyle had written to his mother: "One of my chief copyists is a poor young woman who has been bedrid for almost a year, totally unable to

as I could make it. I do not bethink me of anything farther I have to add in the way of explanation.

In fact my prophecy rather is at present that Appleton the gibbetless thief at New York will beat us after all! Never mind if he do. To say truth, I myself shall almost be glad: there has been a botheration in this anxious arrangement of parts, correcting of scrawly manuscript copies of what you never wished to read more, and insane terror withal of having your own *Ms.* burnt or lost,—that has exceeded my computation. Not to speak of this trouble in which I involve you, my Friend; which, I truly declare, makes me ashamed! True, one *is* bound to resist the Devil in all shapes; if a man come to steal from you, you will put on what locks and padlocks are at hand, and not on the whole say, "Steal, then!" But if the locks prove insufficient, and the thief do break thro',— that side of the alternative also will suit you very well; and, with perhaps a faint prayer for gibbets when they are necessary, you will say to Appleton, next time, *"Macte virtute,* my man!"²

All is in a whirl with me today; no other topic but this very poor one can be entered upon.—I hope for a Letter from your own hand soon, and some news about still more interesting matters.

A young man, named Philips, I think, wrote to me from Nottinghamshire about two years ago, with a most absurd *manuscript,* in flagrant imitation of my *Chartism;* a thing to be or not to be "published," &c: I answered swiftly, "Not to be"; and the young man became silent. The other day there comes a new enthusiastic Letter from the same party, and a *printed* Paper this time, of very greatly improved quality,—and in flagrant imitation, this time, of Waldo Emerson! I wrote to the young man: *"Benissime,* Do as thou hast *said!"* for it is all about the greatness of the soul &c &c. Men are very strange. Thi[s] Philips seems to be of the schoolmaster profession; has really a sincere sound in him now;—and may perhaps be heard of again by and by.³

Adieu my Friend; I feel still as if, in several senses, you stood alone with me under the sky at present! ⁴

---

stir from the spot, with a disease in the backbone . . . poor thing, *she* is striving to write, or to sew, or to do anything she possibly can for herself, lying fixed on her back! The writing she makes is not good; but it is very pains-taking: how can I complain of it?" (Carlyle, *New Letters,* I, 288).

² Vergil, *Aeneid,* IX, 641.

³ George Searle Phillips, of Manchester, who was to become Emerson's friend and biographer (*Let RWE,* III, 452).

⁴ The signature of this letter has been cut off.

Concord, 29 April, 1843

My dear Carlyle,

It is a pleasure to set your name once more at the head of a sheet. It signifies how much gladness, how much wealth of being, that the good, wise, man-cheering, man-helping friend, though unseen, lives there yonder, just out of sight. Your star burns there just below our eastern horizon, & fills the lower & upper air with splendid & splendescent auroras. By some refraction which new lenses or else steamships shall operate, shall I not yet one day see again the disc of benign Phosphorus? It is a solid joy to me that whilst you work for all, you work for me & with me, even if I have little to write, & seldom write your name.

Since I last wrote to you, I found it needful, if only for the household's sake, to set some new lectures in order, & go to new congregations of men. I live so much alone, shrinking almost cowardly from the contact of worldly and public men, that I need more than others to quit home sometimes, & roll with the river of travellers, & live in hotels. I went to Baltimore, where I had an invitation, & read two lectures on New England. On my return, I stopped at Philadelphia, & my Course being now grown to four lectures, read them there. At New York, my snowball was larger, and I read five lectures on New England. 1, Religion; 2, Trade; 3 Genius, Manners, & customs. 4, Recent literary & spiritual influences from abroad. 5 [1] spiritual history.—Perhaps I have not quite done with them yet, but may make them the block of a new & somewhat larger structure for Boston, next winter. The newspaper reports of them in N. Y., were such offensive misstatements, that I could not send you, as I wished, a sketch.[2] Between my two speeches at Baltimore, I went to Washington, 37 miles, and spent four days. The two poles of an enormous political battery, galvanic coil on coil, self-increased by series on series of plates from Mexico to Canada, & from the sea westward to the Rocky Mountains, here meet & play, and make

[1] Emerson has crossed out the word "Domestic" here.

[2] Perhaps Emerson had in mind an account in the New-York *Daily Tribune* of February 22, 1843, which represented him as inviting mankind to dance, with Carlyle and other visionaries, at the foot of the rainbow, where "mortality and immortality shall be identical—and sin and holiness—and labor and rest—vulgarity and gentility—study and idleness—solitude and society—black and white, shall all become one great commingled homogeneous and heterogeneous spot of pure glorification forever."

the air electric & violent. Yet one feels how little, more than how much, man is represented there. I think, in the higher societies of the Universe, it will turn out, that the angels are molecules, as the devils were always Titans, since the dulness of the world needs such mountainous demonstration, & the virtue is so modest & concentrating.

But I must not delay to acknowledge the arrival of your Book. It came ten or eleven days ago, in the Britannia, *with* the *three* letters of different dates announcing it.—I have read the superfluous hundred pp. of Ms. and find it only too popular. Besides its abundance of brilliant points & proverbs, there is a deep steady tide taking in, either by hope or by fear, all the great classes of society,—and the philosophic minority also, by the powerful lights which are shed on the phenomenon. It is true contemporary history, which other books are not, and you have fairly set solid London city aloft afloat in bright mirage in the air. I quarrel only with the popular assumption, which is perhaps a condition of the Humour itself, that the state of society is a new state, and was not the same thing in the days of Rabelais, & of Aristophanes, as of Carlyle. Orators always allow something to masses, out of love to their own art, whilst austere philosophy will only know the particle. This were of no importance, if the historian did not so come to mix himself in some manner with his erring & grieving nations, and so saddens the picture: for health is always private & original, & its essence is in its unmixableness.—But this Book, with all its affluence of wit, of insight, & of daring hints, is born for a longevity which I will not now compute.—In one respect, as I hinted above, it is only too good, so sure of success, I mean, that you are no longer secure of any respect to your property in our freebooting America.

You must know that the cheap press has, within a few months, made a total change in our book markets. Every English book of any name or credit is instantly converted into a newspaper or coarse pamphlet, & hawked by a hundred boys in the streets of all our cities for 25, 18, or 12 cents. Dickens's "Notes" for 12 cents, Blackwood's Magazine for 18 cts., & so on. Three or four great New York & Philadelphia printing houses do this work, with hot competition. One prints Bulwer's novel yesterday, for 25 cents; and already in twenty four hours, another has a coarser edition of it for 18 cents, in all thoroughfares.—What to do with my sealed parcel of Mss & proofs? No bookseller would in these perilous circumstances offer a dollar for my precious parcel. I inquired of the lawyers whether I could not by a copyright protect my edition from piracy until an English copy arrived, & so secure a sale of a few weeks. They said, no; yet advised the taking a certificate of copyright, that we might try the case if we wished. After much consulting & balancing for a few hours, I decided to print, as heretofore, on our own account, an edition, but cheap, to make the temptation less, to retail at 75 cents. I print 1500 copies, & announce to the public that it is your edition, & all good men must buy this. I have written to the great Reprinters, namely to Park Benjamin, & to the Harpers, of New York, to request their forbearance; & have engaged Little & Brown to publish, because, I think, they have something more of weight with Booksellers, & are a little less likely to be invaded than Munroe. If we sell a thousand copies at 75 cents, it will only yield you about 200 dollars: if we should be invaded, we can then afford to sell the other 500 copies, at 25 cents, without loss. In thus doing, I involve you in some risk; but it was the best course that occurred.—Hitherto, the "Miscellanies" have not been reprinted in the cheap forms; and in the last year, J. M. & Co [3] have sold few copies; all books but the cheapest being unsold in the hard times; something has however accrued to your credit there. J. M. & Co. fear that if the new book is pirated at N. Y. & the pirate prospers, instantly the "Miscellanies" will be plundered. We will hope better or at least exult in that which remains to Wit & Worth unplunderable, yet infinitely communicable.[4]

I have hardly space left to say what I would concerning the Dial. I heartily hoped I had done with it when lately our poor good careless publishing Miss Peabody, who sent your number so wisely through the English post office, wrote me that its subscription would not pay its expenses (we all writing for love.) But certain friends are very unwilling it should die & I a little unwilling, though very unwilling to be the life of it, as editor. And now that you are safely through your book, & before the greater Sequel rushes to its conclusion, send me, I pray you, that short chapter which hovers yet in the limbo of contingency, in solid letters & points. Let it be, if that is readiest, a criticism on the Dial, and this too Elysian race, not blood, & yet not ichor.—Let Jane Carlyle be on

---

[3] James Munroe & Co.

[4] On May 21 Emerson wrote to a correspondent who had asked for a bit of Carlyle's manuscript that he thought *Past and Present* his best book (*Let RWE*, III, 175).

my part, &, watchful of his hours, urge the Poet in the golden one. I think to send you a duplicate of the last Number of the D. By Mr Mann who with his bride (sister of the above-mentioned Miss Peabody) is going to London & so to Prussia.[5] He is little known to me, but greatly valued as a philanthropist in this State. I must go to work a little more methodically this summer, and let some thing grow to a tree in my wide straggling shrubbery. With your letters came a letter from Sterling, who was too noble to allude to his books & mss. sent hither, & which Russell all this time has delayed to print; I know not why, but discouraged, I suppose, in these times by booksellers. I must know precisely, & write presently to J.S. Farewell!   R. W. Emerson.

My dear Carlyle,

Horace Mann, Esq. with his Lady, is taking his way through London to Germany, & has kindly charged himself with a parcel to you. Mr Mann is our State-Secretary of the Board of Education, and has the official oversight of public-school education in Massachusetts. Mr. M. has filled high public offices in the state, & has the esteem & confidence of many good men.   Yours ever,   R. W. Emerson

Concord, April 30, 1843.[1]

Concord, 15 August, 1843.

Thomas Carlyle, Esq.

My dear Carlyle,

Allow me to introduce to you Rev. Theodore Parker, who visits England on his way to the Continent. Mr Parker is a theologian eminent for his learning & his independence, & for his great power in persuading our people to adopt his opinions. I cannot let so good a Scholar go by you, without sending him to your door.[1]

                    Yours ever,   R. W. Emerson.

[5] Horace Mann, secretary of the Board of Education of Massachusetts, was married to Mary Peabody on the first of May. Late in that month he spent an evening with Carlyle and was pleased with "the genuine, boyish, unrestrained heartiness of his laugh" (Mann, *Life of Horace Mann*, p. 180).

[1] The MS is owned by Mr. Daniel Maggin.

[1] During the preceding year Theodore Parker had met strong opposition from Boston orthodoxy because of his volume of radical-unitarian essays, *A Discourse of Matters Pertaining to Religion*, and his translation of De Wette's *Einleitung in das Alte Testament*. He was about to sail for a year of travel in Europe.

27 August, 1843.[1]

Dear Emerson,—The bearer of this is Mr. Macready, our celebrated Actor, now on a journey to America, who wishes to know you. In the pauses of a feverish occupation which he strives honestly to make a noble one, this Artist, become once more a man, would like well to meet here and there a true American man.[2] He loves Heroes as few do; and can recognize them, you will find, whether they have on the *Cothurnus* or not. I recommend him to you; bid you forward him as you have opportunity, in this department of his pilgrimage.

Mr. Macready's deserts to the English Drama are notable here to all the world; but his dignified, generous, and every-way honorable deportment in private life is known fully, I believe, only to a few friends. I have often said, looking at him as a manager of great London theatres, "This Man, presiding over the unstablest, most chaotic province of English things, is the one public man among us who has dared to take his stand on what he understood to be *the truth,* and expect victory from that: he puts to shame our Bishops and Archbishops." It is literally so.

With continued kind wishes, yours as of old.   T. Carlyle.

Concord, 30 October, 1843.

My dear friend,

I seize the occasion of having this morsel of paper for twentyfive

[1] This is Norton's text.

[2] On August 21 Jane Carlyle had written to her husband, absent in Scotland: "I have something to ask on the part of Mrs. Macready: 'If you could give William any letters of introduction for America, it would be such a favour.' She cannot bear the idea of his 'going merely as a player, without private recommendations.' . . . The letters to America will be needed within ten days. To Emerson? Who is there else worth knowing in America?" (Carlyle, *Letters and Memorials,* I, 182). And Carlyle replied, ". . . I can think of nobody worth knowing but Emerson and perhaps Greig" (NLS, MS 611). To Macready Carlyle wrote on that same day that most of his American friends, except Emerson, "belong, alas, alas, to the species Bore. . . . Emerson's place is some sixteen miles from Boston. He is a man of small but competent fortune; of truly notable faculty and worth, one of the clearest, shrewdest, most simple-hearted and friendly of men,—in quiet but invincible opposition, as I conjecture, to the whole current of American things. There is no man in that country so well worth seeing, that I have heard of" (MS owned by the Berg Collection of the New York Public Library).

pounds sterling, from the booksellers to send you (and which fail not to find enclosed, as clerks say,) to inquire whether you still exist in Chelsea, London. and what is the reason that my generous correspondent has become dumb for weary months? I must go far back to resume my thread. I think in April last I received your Manuscript &c of the Book, which I forthwith proceeded to print, after some perplexing debate with the booksellers, as I fully informed you in my letter of April or beginning of May. Since that time, I have had no line or word from you, I must think that my letter did not reach you, or that you have written what has never come to me. I assure myself that no harm has befallen you, not only because you do not live in a corner & what chances in your dwelling will come at last to my ears, but because I have read with great pleasure the story of Dr. Francia,[1] which gave the best report of your health & vivacity.

I wrote you in April or May an account of the new state of things which the cheap press had wrought in our bookmarket & specially what difficulties it put in the way of our edition of Past & Present. For a few weeks I believed that the letters I had written to the principal New York & Phila booksellers, & *the preface* [2] had succeeded in repelling the pirates. But in the fourth or fifth week appeared a mean edition in N. York published by one Collyer (an unknown person & supposed to be a masque of some other bookseller) [3] sold for 12½ cents and of this wretched copy several thousand were sold, whilst our 75 cent edition went off slower. There was no remedy & we must be content that there was no expense from our edition, which before September had paid all its cost, & since that time has been earning a little, I believe. I am not fairly entitled to an account of the book from the publishers until 1 January.

[1] "Dr. Francia," Carlyle's high-spirited eulogy of the Paraguayan dictator, was published in *The Foreign Quarterly Review* for July, 1843.

[2] The preface was entitled "American Editor's Notice": "This book is printed from a private copy in manuscript, sent by the author to his friends in this country, and is published for his benefit. I hope this notice that the profits of the sale of this edition are secured to Mr. Carlyle will persuade every well disposed publisher to respect his property in his own book." It was signed "R. W. Emerson, Concord, Mass., May 1, 1843."

[3] The New York editions of 1843 and 1845 were published by W. H. Colyer. Doggett's *New York Business Directory* for those years lists William H. Colyer not as a publisher but as a printer.

For James Munroe & Co., I am sorry to find my accounts have fallen into some arrears. In their late semi annual reckonings, they have rendered smaller credits for the Miscellanies, which they imputed to the hard times, and always to the cheap press, which hurts the sale of all books of old prices. But in Jany 1842, J Munroe & Co. dissolved partnership by the departure of Nichols from the firm, & a new firm under the same name was formed by the union of a man by the name of Dennett [4] with J. M. The old firm then paid me some balance that had accrued, but it is only in the last week I discovered in the course of a correspondence with them for information on the a/cs, that they had then acknowledged a balance of $157 as ultimately due you from them for Miscellanies then sold but not then paid for (to them). I shall immediately demand the payment of that balance. They have also acknowledged & paid the sum of say $165. since accrued. Of this sum I send herewith $121.11 in the shape of the bill of exchange, & shall endeavour to send you the remainder and remainders presently. I have never yet done what I have tho't this & the last week seriously to do, namely, to charge the good & faithful E. P. Clark a man of accounts as he is a cashier in a Bank, with the total auditing, and analysing of these accounts of yours. My hesitation has grown from the imperfect materials which I have to offer him to make up so long a story. But he is a good man, & do you know it? a Carlylese of that intensity that I have often heard he has collected a sort of album of several volumes, containing illustrations of every kind, historical, critical, &c. to the Sartor.[5] I must go to Boston & challenge him. Once when I asked him, he seemed willing to assume it.

No more of accounts tonight. I send you by this ship a volume of translations from Dante by Dr Parsons of Boston a practising dentist & the son of a dentist.[6] It is his gift to you. Lately went Henry James to you with a letter from me. He is a fine companion from his intelligence valour & worth, and is & has been a very beneficent person, as I learn. He carried a volume of poems from my friend & nearest neigh-

---

[4] William H. Dennett appears in *Stimpson's Boston Directory* for 1843 as associated with James Munroe & Co.

[5] E. P. Clark, according to Stimpson, was then a cashier at The New England Bank. His album is owned by the Harvard College Library.

[6] *The First Ten Cantos of the Inferno of Dante Alghieri*, translated by Thomas William Parsons, were published in Boston in 1843. Emerson himself had recently translated the *Vita Nuova* (*Let RWE*, III, 183).

bor W. Ellery Channing,[7] whereof give me, I pray you, the best opinion you can. I am determined he shall be a poet & you must find him such. I have too many things to tell you to begin at the of this sheet which after all this waiting I have been compelled to scribble in a corner with Company waiting for me. Send me instant word of yourself if you love me & of those whom you love & so God keep you & yours

R. Waldo Emerson.

Chelsea, London, 31 Oct[r], 1843—

My dear Emerson,

It is a long weary time since I have had the satisfaction of the smallest dialogue with you. The blame is all my own; the reasons would be difficult to give,—alas, they are properly no-reasons, children not of *Something* but of mere Idleness, Confusion, Inaction, Inarticulation, of *Nothing* in short! Let us leave them then, and profit by the hour which yet is.

I ran away from London into Bristol and South Wales, when the heats grew violent, at the end of June. South Wales, North Wales, Lancashire, Scotland: I roved about everywhere seeking some Jacob's-pillow [1] on which to lay my head and dream of things heavenly;—yes that at bottom was my modest prayer, tho' I disguised it from myself: and the result was, I could find no pillow at all; but sank into ever meaner restlessness, blacker and blacker biliary gloom, and returned in the beginning of September thoroughly eclipsed and worn out, probably the weariest of all men living under the sky. Sure enough I have a fatal talent of converting all Nature into Preternaturalism for myself: a truly horrible Phantasm-Reality it is to me; what of heavenly radiances it has, blended in close neighborhood, in intimate union, with the hideousness of Death and Chaos,—a very ghastly business indeed! On the whole, it is better to hold one's peace about it.—I flung myself down on sofas here,—for my little Wife had trimmed up our little dwellingplace into quite glorious order in my absence, and I had only to lie down: there, in reading books, and other make-believe em-

---

[7] *Poems* by William Ellery Channing was published in Boston early in May. At about the same time Channing and his wife, the younger sister of Margaret Fuller, moved into the next house to Emerson's on the Cambridge Turnpike (*Let RWE*, III, 170n, 174n).

[1] Cf. Gen. 28: 11.

ployments, I could at least keep silence, which was an infinite relief. Nay gradually, as indeed I anticipated, the black vortexes and deluges have subsided; and now that it is past I begin to feel myself better for my travels after all. For one thing, articulate speech having returned to me,—you see what use I make of it.

On the table of the London Library, voted in by some unknown benefactor whom I found afterwards to be Richard Milnes, there lay one thing highly gratifying to me: the last two Numbers of the *Dial*. It is to be one of our Periodicals henceforth; the current Number lies on the table till the next arrive; then the former goes to the Binder; we have already, in a bound volume, all of it that Emerson has had the editing of. This is right. Nay in Edinburgh, and indeed wherever ingenuous inquisitive minds were met with, I have to report that the said Emerson could number a select and most loving public; select, and I should say fast growing: for good and indifferent reasons it may behove the man to assure himself of this. Farther, to the horror of poor Nickisson (Bookseller Fraser's successor), a certain scoundrel interloper here has reprinted *Emerson's Essays* on greyish paper to be sold at two shillings,[2]—distracting Nickisson with the fear of change! I was glad at this, if also angry: it indicates several things. Nickisson has taken his measures, will reduce the price of his remaining copies; indeed he informs me the best part of his edition was already sold, and he has even some colour of money due from England to Emerson thro' me! With pride enough will I transmit this mournful noble peculium: and after that, as I perceive, such chivalrous international doings must cease between us. *Past and Present*, some one told me, was in spite of all your precautions straightway sent forth in modest grey, and your benevolent speculation ruined. Here too, you see, it is the same. Such chivalries therefore are now impossible; for myself I say, "Well let them cease; thank God they once were, the memory of that can never cease with us!"—

In this last Number of the *Dial*, which by the bye your Bookseller never forwarded to me, I found one little Essay, a criticism on myself, —which, if it should do me mischief, may the gods forgive you for! It is considerably the most dangerous thing I have read for some years. A decided likeness of myself recognisable in it, as in the celestial mirror

---

[2] The book was published by W. Tweedie as *Twelve Essays* (Cooke, *Bibliography of Ralph Waldo Emerson*, p. 77).

of a friend's heart; but so enlarged, exaggerated, all *transfigured,*—the most delicious, the most dangerous thing! Well, I suppose I must try to assimilate it also, to turn it also to good, if I be able. Eulogies, dyslogies, in which one finds no features of one's own natural face, are easily dealt with; easily left unread, as stuff for lighting fires, such is the insipidity, the wearisome *non*entity of pabulum like that: but here is another sort of matter! "The beautifullest piece of criticism I have read for many a day," says every one that speaks of it. May the gods forgive you.—I have purchased a copy for three shillings, and sent it to my Mother: one of the *indubitablest* benefits I could think of in regard to it.[3]

There have been two friends of yours here in these very days: Dr Russell[4] just returning from Paris; Mr Parker, just bound thither. We have seen them rather oftener than common, Sterling being in town withal. They are the best figures of strangers we have had for a long time; possessions, both of them, to fall in with in this pilgrimage of Life. Russell carries friendliness in his eyes, a most courteous modest intelligent man; an English intelligence too, as I read, the best of it lying unspoken, not as a logic but as an instinct. Parker is a most hardy, compact, clever little fellow, full of decisive utterance, with humour and good-humour, whom I like much. They shine like suns, these two, amid multitudes of watery comets and tenebrific constellations, too sorrowful without such admixture on occasion!

As for myself, dear Emerson, you must ask me no questions till— alas, till I know not when! After four weary years of the most unreadable reading, the painfullest poking and delving, I have come at last to the conclusion that I *must* write a Book on Cromwell; that there is no rest for me till I do it. This point fixed, another is not less fixed hitherto, that a Book on Cromwell is *impossible*. Literally so: you would weep for me if you saw how, between these two adamantine certainties, I am whirled and tumbled. God only knows what will become of me in the business. Patience, Patience!

By the bye, do you know a "Massachusetts Historical Society," and a James Bowdoin, seemingly of Boston? In "Vol II. third series" of their

---

[3] Emerson's review of *Past and Present* appeared in *The Dial* for July, 1843. It was reprinted in his *Works*, XII, 379–91.

[4] Le Baron Russell, a student of engineering at the time of the American *Sartor*, was now a physician (*Let RWE*, III, 226; V, 171*n*).

"Collections" lately I met with a disappointment almost ludicrous. Bowdoin, in a kind of dancing embarrassed style, gives longwinded painfully minute account of certain precious volumes containing "Notes of the Long Parliament," which now stand in the New York Library; poises them in his assaying balance, speculates, prophesies, inquires concerning them: to me it was like news of the lost Decades of Livy: Good Heavens, it soon became manifest that these precious volumes are nothing whatever but a wretched broken old dead *Ms.* copy of part of our printed *Commons Journals!* printed since 1745, and known to all barbers! [5] If the Historical Society desired it, any Member of Parliament could procure them the whole stock, *Lords* and *Commons,* a wheelbarrowful or more, with no cost but the carriage. Every member has the right to demand a copy, and few do it, few will let such a mass cross their doorthreshold! This of Snowdoin's [6] is a platitude of some magnitude.— —Adieu, dear Emerson. Rest not, haste not; *you* have work to do. [7]

T. Carlyle

Chelsea, London, 17 Nov^r, 1843—

Dear Emerson,

About this time probably you will be reading a Letter I hurried off for you by Dr Russell in the last Steamer; and your friendly anxieties will partly be set at rest. Had I kept silence so very long? I knew it was a long while; but my vague remorse had kept no date! It behoves me now to write again without delay; to certify with all distinctness that I have safely received your Letter of the 30 Oct^r, safely the Bill for Twenty-five pounds contained it;—that you are a brave friendly man, of most serene beneficent way of life; and that I—God help me!—

By all means appoint this Mr Clark to the honorary office of account-keeper,—if he will accept it! By Parker's [1] list of questions from him, and by earlier reminiscences recalled on that occasion, I can discern that

[5] Carlyle included a note on this American blunder in Appendix No. 28 of later editions of *Cromwell.*

[6] During the summer, Carlyle had climbed Snowdon (Froude, *Thomas Carlyle: Life in London,* I, 338).

[7] Cf. Goethe's stanza from *Zahme Xenien II:* "Wie das Gestirn,/ Ohne Hast,/ Aber ohne Rast,/ Drehe sich jeder/ Um die eigene Last" (*Sämtliche Werke,* IV, 43). For the special significance of these lines to Carlyle, see *Correspondence between Goethe and Carlyle,* ed. Norton, pp. 291–95.

[1] Theodore Parker: see above E.8.15.43.

he is a man of lynx eyesight, of an all-investigating curiosity: if he will accept this sublime appointment, it will be the clearest case of elective affinity.[2] Accounts to you must be horrible; as they are to me: indeed I seldom read beyond the *last* line of them, if I can find the last; and one of the insupportabilities of Bookseller Accounts is that nobody but a wizard or regular adept in such matters, can tell where the last line, and final net result of the whole accursed babblement, is to be found! By all means solicit Clark;—at all events, do you give it up, I pray you, and let the Booksellers do their own wise way. It really is not material; let the poor fellows have length of halter. Every new Bill from America comes to me like a kind of heavenly miracle; a reaping where I never sowed, and did not expect to reap: the quantity of it is a thing I can never bring in question.—For your English account with Nickisson I can yet say nothing more; perhaps about Newyearsday the poor man will enable me to say something. I hear however that the Pirate has sold off, or nearly so, his two-shillings Edition of the *Essays,* and is preparing to print another; this, directly in the teeth of Cash and double-entry bookkeeping, I take to be good news.

James is a very good fellow, better and better as we see him more—something shy and skittish in the man; but a brave heart intrinsically, with sound earnest sense, with plenty of insight and even humour. He confirms an observation of mine, which indeed I find is hundreds of years old, that a stammering man is never a worthless one. Physiology can tell you why. It is an excess of delicacy, excess of sensibility to the presence of his fellow creature, that makes him stammer. Hammond L'Estrange says, "Who ever heard of a stammering man that was a fool?" [3] Really there is something in that.—James is now off to the Isle of Wight; will see Sterling at Ventnor there; see whether such an Isle or France will suit better for a winter residence.

W. E. Channing's Poems are also a kind gift from you. I have read the pieces *you had cut up for me:* worthy indeed of reading! That Poem *on Death* is the utterance of a valiant noble heart, which in rhyme or prose I shall expect sure news of by and by. But at bottom "Poetry" is a most suspicious affair for me at present! You cannot fancy the oceans of Twaddle that human creatures emit upon me in these

---

[2] The English translation of Goethe's novel *Die Wahlverwandschaften* was entitled *Elective Affinities.*

[3] Probably Hamon L'Estrange (1605–60), Royalist theologian and historian.

times; as if when the lines had a jingle in them, a Nothing could be Something, and the point were gained! It is becoming a horror to me, —as all speech without meaning more and more is. I said to Richard Milnes, "Now in honesty what is the use of putting your accusative *before* the verb, and otherwise entangling the syntax; if there really *is* an image of any object, thought, or thing within you, for God's sake let me have it the *shortest* way, and I will so cheerfully excuse the *omission* of the jingle at the ends: cannot I do without that!"—Milnes answered, "Ah, my dear fellow, it is because we have no thought, or almost none; a little thought goes a great way when you put it into rhyme!" [4] Let a man try to the very uttermost to *speak* what he means before *singing* is had recourse to. Singing, in our curt English speech, contrived expressly and almost exclusively for "despatch of business," is terribly difficult. Alfred Tennison, alone of our time, has proved it to be possible in some measure. If Channing will persist in melting such obdurate speech into musi[c] he shall have my true wishes,—my augury that it will take an enormou[s] *heat* from him!—Another Channing, whom I once saw here, sends me a Progress-of-the-Species Periodical from New York.[5] *Ach Gott!* These people and their affairs seem all "melting" rapidly enough, into thaw-slush or one knows not what. Considerable madness is visible in them. *Stare super antiquas vias:* [6] "No, they say, we cannot stand, or walk, or do any good whatever there; by God's blessing, we will fly,—will not you!—here goes!" And their *flight,* it is as the flight of the *un*winged,—of oxen endeavouring to fly with the "wings" of an ox! By such flying, universally practised, the "ancient ways" are really like to become very deep before long. In short, I am terribly sick of all that;—and wish it would stay at home at Fruitlands,[7] or where there is good pasture for it.— —My friend Emerson, alone of all voices out of America, has sphere-music in him for me,—alone of them all hitherto; and is a prophecy and sure dayspring in the East; immeasurably cheering to me. God long prosper him; keep

---

[4] See above, C.7.2.40.

[5] William Henry Channing was at this time editing a Fourierist magazine called *The Present;* its first number (September, 1843) began with Carlyle's translation, from *Past and Present,* of Goethe's "Symbolum."

[6] Cf. Jer. 6: 16 (Vulgate).

[7] In *The Dial,* IV (July, 1843), 135, under the title "Fruitlands" there were five paragraphs about the farm where Alcott and Charles Lane had begun their "effort to initiate a Family in harmony with the primitive instincts in man."

him duly apart from that bottomless hubbub, which is not at all cheering! And so ends my Litany for this day.

The Cromwell business, tho' I punch daily at it with all manner of levers remains immoveable as Ailsa Crag. Heaven alone knows what I shall do with it. I see and say to myself, It *is* heroical; Troy Town was probably not a more heroic business; and this belongs to thee, to thy own people,—must it be dead forever?—Perhaps yes,—and kill me too into the bargain. Really I think it very shocking that we run to Greece, to Italy, to &c &c, and leave all at home lying buried as a Nonentity. Were I absolute Sovereign and Chief Pontiff here, there should be a study of the old English ages first of all. I will pit Odin against any Jupiter of them; find Sea-Kings that would have given Jason a Rowland for his Oliver! We are, as you sometimes say, a book-ridden people, —a phantom-ridden people.— —All this small household is well; salutes you and yours with love old and new. Accept this hasty messenger; accept my friendliest farewell, dear Emerson.

Yours ever   T. Carlyle

Concord, 31 December, 1843

My dear friend,

I have had two good letters from you, and it is fully my turn to write, so you shall have a token on this latest day of the year. I rejoice in the good will you bear to so many friends of mine, especially Russell & James. It is no fault of mine,—if they will go to you you must thank yourself. Best when you are mutually contented. I wished lately I might serve Mr Macready, who sent me your letter—I called on him, & introduced him to Sam. G. Ward, my friend & the best man in the city, and, besides all his personal merits, a master of all the offices of hospitality. Ward was to keep himself informed of Macready's times, & bring me to him when there was opportunity. But he stayed but a few days in Boston, and, Ward said, was in very good hands, & promised to see us when he returns by & by. I saw him in Hamlet, but should much prefer to see him as Macready.[1]

---

[1] For a comment on this theatrical experience, see the passage beginning "I went last Tuesday to see Macready in *Hamlet*" in Whipple's "Some Recollections of Ralph Waldo Emerson," *Harper's New Monthly Magazine*, LXV (September, 1882), 580.

I must try to entice Mr M. out here into my pines & alder bushes. Just now, the moon is shining on snowdrifts, four, five, & six feet high, but, before his return, they will melt; and already this my not *native* but *ancestral* village, which I came to live in nearly ten years ago because it was the quietest of farming towns, and off the road, is found to lie on the directest line of road from Boston to Montreal, a railroad is a-building through our secretest woodlands, and, tomorrow morning, our people go to Boston in two hours instead of three, &, next June, in one. This petty revolution in our country matters [2] was very odious to me when it began, but it is hard to resist the joy of all one's neighbours, and I must be contented to be carted like a chattel in the cars & be glad to see the forest fall. This *rushing* on your journey is plainly a capital invention for our spacious America, but it is more dignified & manlike to walk barefoot.—But do you not see that we are getting to be neighbours? a day from London to Liverpool; twelve or eleven to Boston; and an hour to Concord: and you have owed me a visit these ten years.

I mean to send with your January Dial a copy of the Number for Sterling, as it contains a review of his tragedy & poems, by Margaret Fuller. I have not yet seen the article, and the lady affirms that it is very bad, as she was ill all the time she was writing; but I hope & believe better. She—Margaret Fuller, is an admirable person, whose writing gives feeble account of her. But I was to say that I shall send this Dial for J.S. to your care as I know not the way to the Isle of Wight.

Enclosed in this letter I send a bill of Exchange for thirtytwo pounds, 8 shillings, 2 pence payable by Baring & Co. It happens to represent an exact balance on Munroe's books and that slow mortal should have paid it before. I have not yet got to Clark, I who am a slow mortal, but have my eye fixed on him. Remember me & mine with kindest salutations to your wife & brother.

Ever yours,   R. W. Emerson

---

[2] Perhaps an allusion to *Hamlet,* act III, scene ii, line 123.

1844

Chelsea, 31 Jany, 1844—

Dear Emerson,—Some ten days ago came your Letter with a new Draft of £32 and odd money in it: all safe; the Draft now gone into the City to ripen into gold and silver, the Letter to be acknowledged by some hasty response now and here. America, I say to myself looking at these money drafts, is a strange place; the highest comes out of it and the lowest! Sydney Smith is singing dolefully about doleful American repudiation *"disowning* of the soft impeachment"; [1]—and here on the other hand is an American Man in virtue of whom America America [2] has become definable withal as a place from which fall heavenly manna-showers upon certain men, at certain seasons of history, when perhaps manna showers were not the unneedfullest things!—We will take the good and the evil, here as elsewhere, and heartily bless Heaven.

But now for the Draft at the top of this leaf. One Colman, a kind of Agricultural Missionary, much in vogue here at present, has given it me; [3] it is Emerson's, the net produce hitherto (all but 2 cents) of *Emerson's Essays.* I enclose * farther the Bookseller's hieroglyph papers; unintelligible as all such are; but sent over to you for scrutiny by the expert. I gather only that there are some 500 and odd of the dear-priced edition sold, some 200 and odd still to sell, which the bookseller says are (in spite of pirates) slowly selling;—and that the half profit upon the whole adventure up to this date has been £24.15.11 sterling,—equal,

[1] Cf. Sheridan, *The Rivals,* act V, scene iii. Late in 1843 Smith had publicly petitioned the United States Congress for the payment of a debt repudiated by the State of Pennsylvania (S. J. Reid, *A Sketch of the Life and Times of the Rev. Sydney Smith,* p. 378).

[2] This is an accidental repetition at the beginning of a new page.

[3] Henry Colman was a Unitarian minister who was studying agriculture in England. He had first come to visit Carlyle on May 27, 1843 (TC to John, 5.29.43, NLS, MS 512). Presumably the draft was written by him, on a Boston bank, and sold to Carlyle.

* I send them by a private hand rather; this by post. They will follow in a day or so, I suppose. [TC]

as I am taught, at 4.88 *dollars* per pound *sterling,* to 121.02 dollars; for
which, all but the cents, here is a draft on Boston, payable at sight.
Pray have yourself straightway *paid;* that if there be any mistake or
delay I may rectify it while time yet is.—I add, for the intelligence of
the Bookseller Papers, that Fraser with whom the bargain originally
stood was succeeded by Nickisson; these are the names of the parties.
And so dear Friend accept this munificent sum of money; and expect
a blessing with it if good wishes from the heart of man can give one.
So much for that.

Did you receive a Dumfries Newspaper with a criticism in it? The
author is one Gilfillan a young dissenting minister in Dundee; a person
of great talent, ingenuousness, enthusiasm and other virtue; whose
position as a Preacher of bare old Calvinism under penalty of death,
sometimes makes me tremble for him. He has written in that same
Newspaper about all the notablest men of his time; Godwin, Corn-Law
Elliot and I know not all whom: if he publish the Book, I will take care
to send it you. I saw the man for the first time last autumn at Dumfries;
as I said, his being a Calvinist Dissenting Minister, economically fixed,
and spiritually with such germinations in him, forces me to be very
reserved to him.[4]

John Sterling's Dial shall be forwarded to Ventnor in the Isle of
Wight, whenever it arrives. He was here, as probably I told you, about
two months ago, the old unresting brilliantly radiating man. He is now
much richer in money than he was, and poorer by the loss of a good
Mother and good Wife: [5] I understand he is building himself a brave
house, and also busy writing a poem. He flings *too* much "sheet-light-
ning" and unrest into me when we meet in these low moods of mine;
and yet one always longs for him back again: "no doing with him or
without him," the dog!

My thrice unfortunate Book on Cromwell,—it is a real descent to
Hades, to Golgotha and Chaos! I feel oftenest as if it were possibler to
die oneself than to bring it into life. Besides my health is in general
altogether despicable, my "spirits" equal to those of the ninth-part of
a dyspeptic tailor! One needs to be able to go on in all kinds of spirits,

---

[4] George Gilfillan. The book was published in 1845 under the title *A Gallery of
Literary Portraits.*

[5] Sterling's wife and his mother had died, within three days of each other, in
April, 1843 (Carlyle, *Works TC,* XI, 247).

in climate sunny or sunless, or it will never do. The Planet Earth, says Voss—take four hexameters from Voss:

> Journeys this Earth, her eye on a Sun, thro' the heavenly spaces;
> Joyous in radiance, or joyless by fits and swallowed in tempests;
> Falters not, alters not, equal advancing, home at the due hour:
> So thou, weatherproof, constant, may equal with day, March!— [6]

I have not a moment more tonight;—and besides am inclined to write unprofitables if I persist. Adieu my friend; all blessings be with you always.　　　　　Yours ever truly　　　　　T. Carlyle

Concord 29 February 1844

My dear Carlyle,

I received by the last steamer your letter, & its prefixed order for one hundred twenty one dollars, which order I sent to Ward, who turned it at once into money. Thanks, dear friend, for your care & activity which have brought me this pleasing & most unlooked for result. And I beg you if you know any family representative of Mr Fraser, to express my sense of obligation to that departed man. I feel a kindness not without some wonder for those goodnatured five hundred Englishmen who could buy & read my miscellany. I shall not fail to send them a new collection, which I hope they will like better. My faith in the Writers as an organic class, increases daily, and in the possibility to a faithful man of arriving at statements for which he shall not feel responsible, but which shall be parallel with nature. Yet without any effort I fancy I make progress also in the doctrine of Indifferency, and am certain & content that the truth can very well spare me, & have itself spoken by another without leaving it or me the worse. Enough if we have learned that music exists, that it is proper to us, and that we cannot go forth of it. Our pipes, however shrill & squeaking, certify this our faith in tune, and the eternal Amelioration may one day reach our ears & instruments. It is a poor second thought, this literary activity. Perhaps I am not made obnoxious to much suffering, but I have had happy hours enough in gazing from afar at the splendours of the Intellectual Law, to overpay me for any pains I know. Existence may go on to be better, &, if it have such insights, it never can be bad. You sometimes charge me with I know not what sky-blue sky-void idealism. As far as

---

[6] See above, C.4.29.36.

it is a partiality, I fear I may be more deeply infected than you think me. I have very joyful dreams which I cannot bring to paper, much less to any approach to practice, and I blame myself not at all for my reveries, but that they have not yet got possession of my house & barn. But I shall not lose my love for books.[1] I only worship Eternal Buddh in the retirements & intermissions of Brahma.[2]—But I must not egotize & generalize to the end of my sheet, as I have a message or two to declare.—I enclose a bill of exchange on the Barings for thirtysix pounds; which is the sum of two recent payments of Munroe & of Little & Brown, whereof I do not despair you shall yet have some account in booksellers figures. I have got so far with Clark, as to have his consent to audit the accounts when I shall get energy & time enough to compile them out of my ridiculous Journal. Munroe begs me to say what possibly I have already asked for him, that when the History of Cromwell is ready to be seen of men, you will have an entire copy of the manuscript taken & sent over to us. Then will he print a cheap edition such as no one will undersell, & secure such a share of profit to the author as the cheap press allows. Perhaps only 30 or 40 pounds would make it worth while to take the trouble. A valued friend of mine wishes to know who wrote (perhaps three years ago) a series of metaphysical articles in Blackwood on Consciousness. Can you remember & tell me? And now, I commend you to the good God, you and your history, and the true kind wife who is always good to the eager Yankees,[3] and am yours heartily.   R. W. Emerson

Chelsea, 3 April, 1844—

Dear Emerson,

   Till within five minutes of the limit of my time, I had forgotten that this was the third of the Month;[1] that I had a Letter to write acknowl-

---

[1] The first draft has "my love for the muse & her children."

[2] This sentence becomes clearer, though not less idiosyncratic, in the light of two passages from Emerson's journal: "Winter, Night, Sleep, are all the invasions of eternal Buddh . . . very fine names has it got to cover up its chaos withal, namely, trances, raptures, abandonment, ecstasy, all Buddh, naked Buddh"; and "Brahma, or the Soul" (*Journals*, VI, 382; IX, 56).

[3] Jane Carlyle did not always suffer the eager Yankees gladly. See her letter to John Welsh of November 28, 1843. And Carlyle himself wrote to his sister Jean, on April 18, 1844: "I am beginning to be plagued again with Yankees!" (NLS, MS 512).

[1] At this time the mail packets sailed for America on the fourth and the eighteenth of the month: see below, C.11.11.45.

edging even money! Take the acknowledgement, given in all haste, not without a gratitude that will last longer: the 36 pounds and odd shillings came safe in your Letter; a new unlooked-for Gift. America, I think, is like an amiable family teapot; you think it is all out long since, and lo, the valuable implement yields you another cup, and another! Many thanks to *you,* who are the heart of America to me.

Republishing for one's friend's sake, I find on consulting my Bookseller, is out here; we have Pirates waiting for any American thing of mark, as you have for every British: to the tender mercies of these, on both sides, I fancy the business must be committed. They do good too; as all does, even carrion: they send you *faster* abroad, if the world have any use for you;—oftenest it only thinks it has. Your *Essays,* the Pirated *Essays* make an ugly yellow tatter of a Pamphlet price ⅙; but the edition is all sold, I understand: and even Nickisson has not entirely ceased to sell. The same Pirate who pounced upon you made an attempt the other day on my poor *Life of Schiller,* but I put the due spoke in his wheel. They have sent me *Lowell's Poems;* they are bringing out *Jean Paul's Life* &c &c; the hungry *canaille.* It is strange that men should feel themselves so entirely at liberty to steal, simply because there is no gallows to hang them for doing it.—Your new Book will be eagerly waited for by that class of persons; and also by another class which is daily increasing here.

The only other thing I am "not to forget" is that of the *Essay on Consciousness* in *Blackwood.* The writer of those Papers is one Ferrier,[2] a Nephew of the Edinburgh Miss Ferrier who wrote *Marriage* and some other Novels; Nephew also of Professor Wilson (Christopher North), and married to one of his Daughters. A man of perhaps five-and-thirty; I remember him in boyhood, while he was boarded with an Annandale Clergyman; I have seen him since manhood, and liked him well: a solid, square visaged dark kind of man, more like your Theodore Parker than any mutual specimen I can recollect. He got the usual education of an Edinburgh Advocate; but found no practise at the Bar, nor sought any with due anxiety, I believe; addicted himself to logical meditations;—became, the other year, Professor of Universal History or some such thing in the Edinburgh University, and lectures

---

[2] "An Introduction to the Philosophy of Consciousness," by James Frederick Ferrier, was published serially in *Blackwood's Magazine* between February, 1838, and March, 1839.

with hardly any audience: a certain *young* public wanted *me* to be that Professor there,[3] but I knew better.—Is this enough about Ferrier?

I will not add another word; the time being *past,* irretrievable except by half-running!

Write us your Book; and be well and happy always![4]

                                        Concord, 19 June, 1844[1]

My dear Mrs Carlyle,

Mrs Lee of Boston, an old friend of my friends, (although my own opportunities of intercourse with her have been rare,) visits London, & desires to be acquainted with yourself & with your husband. Mrs Lee enjoys the distinguished esteem of the best society in our New England metropolis, wherein her social character & position have always given her a leading influence. In the last few years she has made herself known to a far larger circle by some little books which have had a wide popularity in this country & have been republished, I believe, in England, "Three Experiments in Living": "Lives of the Painters," & more recently, a "History of the Hugonots."[2] I pray you to lay your commands on our historian to lay down for an hour that busy pen, & accompany you on a visit to Mrs. Lee: and I shall assure myself at a later day to hear a good report of your health & peace.

                    Your affectionate servant,   R. W. Emerson
Mrs Jane Carlyle.

                                        Chelsea, 5 Augt, 1844—

Dear Emerson,

There had been a long time without direct news from you, till four days ago your Letter arrived.[1] This day I understand to be the ultimate

[3] Late in 1841 a group of students at Edinburgh University had asked Carlyle to be a candidate for a new chair in history; he declined (Froude, *Thomas Carlyle: Life in London,* I, 193 f.).

[4] The signature has been cut off.

[1] The MS of this letter is owned by the Berg Collection of the New York Public Library.

[2] This lady was Hannah Farnham Sawyer Lee; the three little books, whose titles Emerson remembered and spelled inaccurately, were *Three Experiments of Living* (1837), *Historical Sketches of Old Painters* (1838), and *The Huguenots in France and America* (1843).

[1] This letter, written presumably before July 10 (see below, n. 6), is missing.

limit of the American Mail,—yesterday, had it not been Sunday, would
have been the limit: I write a line therefore, tho' in very great haste.

Poor Sterling, even I now begin to fear, is in a very bad way. He had
two successive attacks of spitting of blood, some three months ago, or
more; the second attack of such violence, and his previous condition
then so weak, that the Doctor as good as gave up hope,—the poor
Patient himself had from the first given it up. Our poor Friend has had
so many attacks of that nature, and so rapidly always rallied from them,
I gave no ear to these sinister prognostics; but now that I see the summer influences passing over him without visible improvement and our
good weather looking towards a close without so much strength added
as will authorize even a new voyage to Madiera,—I too am at last joining in the general discouragement; all the sadder to me that I shut it
out so long. Sir James Clark, our best accredited Physician for such
diseases, declares that Life for certain months may linger, with great
pain; but that recovery is not to be expected. Great part of the lungs, it
appears, is totally unserviceable for respiration; from the remainder,
especially in times of coughing, it is with the greatest difficulty that
breath enough is obtained. Our poor Patient passes the night in a sitting position; cannot lie down: that fact sticks with me ever since I
heard it! He is very weak, very pale; still "writes a great deal daily";
but does not wish to see anybody; declines to "see even Carlyle," who
offered to go to him. His only Brother, Anthony Sterling, a hardy
soldier, lately withdrawn from the Army, and settled in this quarter,
whom we often communicate with, is about going down to the Isle of
Wight this week: he saw John four days ago, and brings nothing but
bad news,—of which indeed this removal of his to the neighbourhood
of the scene is a practical testimony. The old Father,[2] a widower for the
last two years, and very lonely and dispirited, seems getting feebler and
feebler: he was here yesterday; a pathetic kind of spectacle to us. Alas,
alas! But what can be said? I say Nothing; I have written only one Note
to Sterling: I feel it probably that I shall never see him more,—nor his
like again in this world. His disease, as I have from of old construed it,
is a burning of him up by his own fire. The restless vehemence of the
man, struggling in all ways these many years to find a legitimate outlet,
and finding except for transitory unsatisfactory corruscations none, has

[2] Edward Sterling, who had been during the thirties the chief editorial writer for
The Times.

undermined its Clay Prison in the weakest point (which proves to be the lungs), and will make outlet *there*. My poor Sterling! It is an old tragedy; and very stern whenever it repeats itself of new.— —

Today I get answer about Alfred Tennyson: all is right on that side. Moxon informs us that the Russell Books and Letter [3] arrived duly and were duly forwarded and safely received; nay farther that Tennyson is now in Town, and means to come and see me. Of this latter result I shall be very glad: Alfred is one of the few British or Foreign Figures (a not increasing Number, I think!) who are and remain beautiful to me; —a true human soul, or some authentic approximation thereto, to whom your own soul can say, Brother!—However, I doubt h[e] will not come; he often skips me, in these brief visits to Town; skips [every]-body indeed; being a man solitary and sad, as certain men are, dwelling in an element of gloom,—carrying a bit of Chaos about him, in short, which he is manufacturing into Cosmos!

Alfred is the son of a Lincolnshire Gentleman Farmer, I think; indeed you see in his verses that he is a native of "moated granges," [4] and green fat pastures, not of mountains and their torrents and storms. He had his breeding at Cambridge, as if for the Law, or Church; being master of a small annuity on his Father's decease, he preferred clubbing with his Mother and some Sisters, to live unpromoted and write Poems. In this way he lives still, now here now there; the family always within reach of London, never in it; he himself making rare and brief visits, lodging in some old comrade's rooms. I think he must be under forty, not much under it. One of the finest looking men in the world. A great shock of rough dusty-dark hair; bright-laughing hazel eyes; massive aquiline face, most massive yet most delicate, of sallow brown complexion, almost Indian-looking; clothes cynically loose, free-and-easy; —smokes infinite tobacco. His voice is musical metallic,—fit for loud laughter and piercing wail, and all that may lie between; speech and speculation free and plenteous: I do not meet, in these late decades, such company over a pipe!—We shall see what he will grow to. He is often unwell; very chaotic,—his way is thro' Chaos and the Bottomless and Pathless; not handy for making out many miles upon. [O Paper!] [5]

I trust there is now joy in place of pain in the House at Concord, and

---

[3] See below, E.9.1.44, n. 4. Perhaps Russell had become involved in a similar enterprise with Tennyson and Tennyson's publisher, Moxon.
[4] Cf. Tennyson's "Mariana."   [5] Carlyle's brackets.

a certain Mother grateful again to the Supreme Powers! [6] We are all in our customary health here, or nearly so; my Wife has been in Lancashire, among her kindred there, for a month lately: our swoln City is getting empty and still; we think of trying an autumn *here* this time.—Get your Book ready; there are readers ready for it! And be busy and victorious! **Ever yours** **T. Carlyle**

My "History" is frightful! If I live, it is like to be completed; but whether I shall live and not rather be buried alive, broken-hearted, in the Serbonian Quagmires of English Stupidity, and so sleep beside Cromwell, often seems uncertain. Erebus has no uglier, brutaller element. Let us say nothing of it. Let us do it, or leave it to the Devils. *Ay de mi!*

Boston, 1 September, 1844—

My dear Carlyle,

I have just heard that in an hour Mr Wilmer's mailbag [1] for London, by the Acadia, closes, and I will not lose the occasion of sending you a hasty line: though I had designed to write you from home on sundry matters, which now must wait. I send by this steamer some sheets, to the bookseller, John Chapman,[2]—proof sheets of my new book of Essays. Chapman wrote to me by the last steamer, urging me to send him some manuscript that had not yet been published in America, & he thought he could make an advantage from printing it, and even in some conditions, procure a copy-right; and he would publish for me on the plan of half-profits. The request was so timely, since I was not only printing a book, but also a pamphlet (an Address to citizens of some thirteen towns who celebrated in Concord the Negro Emancipation on 1 August last) [3] that I came to town yesterday, & hastened the printers, and have now sent him proofs of *all* the Address & of more than half

[6] On July 10, after a difficult pregnancy, Lidian Emerson gave birth to a son, Edward Waldo (Rusk, *Life,* p. 299).

[1] No Wilmer appears in *Stimpson's Boston Directory.*

[2] Chapman had recently become the English agent for *The Dial;* he was an admirer of Emerson's writings and was associated with what Carlyle called "Alcott's English tail." (See *Let RWE,* III, 265n; and see above, C.3.11. 43 (*Let RWE,* III, 265n).

[3] *Address Delivered in Concord on the Anniversary of the Emancipation of the Negroes in the British West Indies August 1, 1844.*

the book. If you can give Chapman any counsel, or save me from any nonsense, by enjoining on him careful correction, you shall.

I looked eagerly for a letter from you by the last steamer, to give me exact tidings of Sterling. None came: but I received a short note from Sterling himself, which intimated that he had but a few more days to live. It is gloomy news. I beg you will write me everything you can relate of him, by the next mail. If you can learn from his friends whether the pacquet of his manuscripts & printed papers returned by Russell [4] & sent by me through Harnden's Express to Ventnor, arrived safely, it would be a satisfaction.

Yours affectionately,   R. W. Emerson.

By the next or the following steamer, I shall have £25 or £30 to send from booksellers.

Chelsea, 29 September, 1844—

Dear Emerson,

There should a Letter have come for you by that Steamer; for I write one duly, and posted it in good time myself: I will hope therefore it was but some delay of some subaltern official, such as I am told occasionally chances, and that you got the Letter after all in a day or two. It would give you notice, more or less, up to its date, of all the points you had inquired about: there is now little to be added; except concerning the main point, That the catastrophe has arrived there, as we foresaw, and all is ended.

John Sterling died at his house in Ventnor on the night of Wednesday 18th September, about eleven o'clock; unexpectedly at last, and to appearances without pain. His Sister-in-law Mrs Maurice,[1] had gone down to him from this place about a week before; other friends were waiting as it were in view of him; but he wished generally to be alone, to continue to the last setting his house and his heart more and more in order for the Great Journey. For about a fortnight back he had ceased to have himself formally dressed; had sat only in his dressing-gown, but I believe was still daily wheeled into his Library, and sat very calmly sorting and working there. He sent me two Notes, and various messages, and gifts of little Keepsakes to my Wife and myself: the Notes

---

[4] Andrew L. Russell, a manufacturer of Plymouth, had undertaken in 1842 to bring out an American edition of Sterling's works, but in spite of pressure from Emerson he did nothing further about it (*Let RWE*, VI, 572).

[1] Sterling and his Cambridge friend F. D. Maurice married sisters.

were brief, stern and loving; altogether noble; never to be forgotten in this world. His Brother Anthony, who had been in the Isle of Wight within call for several weeks, had now come up to Town again; but, after about a week, decided that he would run down again, and look. He arrived on the Wednesday night, about nine o'clock; found no visible change; the brave Patient calm as ever, ready to speak as ever, —to say, in direct words which he would often do, or indirectly as his whole speech and conduct did, "God is Great." Anthony and he talked for a while, then took leave for the night; in few minutes more, Anthony was summoned to the bedside, and at 11 o'clock as I said the curtain dropt, and it was all ended.—*Euge!*

Whether the American Mss. had arrived I do not yet know, but probably shall before this Letter goes; for Anthony is to return hither on Sunday, and I will inquire. Our Friend is buried in Ventnor Churchyard; four big Elms overshadow the little spot; it is situated on the South-east side of that green Island, on the slope of steep hills (as I understand it) that look towards the Sun, and are close within sight and hearing of the Sea. There shall he rest and have fit lullaby, this brave one. He has died, as a man should; like an old Roman, yet with the Christian Bibles and all newest revelations present to him. He refused to see friends; men whom I think he loved as well as any, me for one when I obliquely proposed it, he refused. He was even a little stern on his nearest relatives when they came to him: Do I need your help to die? Phocion-like he seemed to feel degraded by physical decay; to feel that he ought to wrap his mantle round him, and say, "I come, Persephoneia; it is not I that linger!" [2]—His Sister-in-law, Anthony's Wife, probably about a month ago, while they were still in Wight, had begged that she might see him yet once; her husband would be there too, she engaged not to speak. Anthony had not yet persuaded him, when she, finding the door half open, went in: His pale changed countenance almost made her shriek; she stept forward silently, kissed his brow in silence; he burst into tears. Let us speak no more o[f] this.— —A great quantity of papers, I understand, are left for my [determ]ination; what is to be done with them I will sacredly endeavour to do.

[2] Diogenes Laertius, "Zeno," in *The Lives and Opinions of Eminent Philosophers* (Bohn's Classical Library), p. 270. See also Froude, *Thomas Carlyle: Life in London,* II, 355.

I have visited your Bookseller Chapman; seen the Proofsheets lying on his table; taken order that the reprint shall be well corrected,—indeed I am to read every sheet myself, and in that way get acquainted with it, before it go into stereotype. Chapman is a tall lank youth of five-and-twenty; full of goodwill, but of what other equipment time must yet try. By a little Book of his,[3] which I looked at some months ago, he seemed to me sunk very deep in the dust-hole of extinct Socinianism; a painful predicament for a man! He is not sure of saving much copyright for you; but he will do honestly what in that respect is doable; and he will print the Book correctly, and publish it decently, I saying *imprimatur* if occasion be,—and your ever-increasing little congregation here will do with the new word what they can. I add no more today; reserving a little nook for the answer I hope to get two days hence. Adieu my friend: it is silent Sunday; the populace not yet admitted to their beer-shops, till the respectabilities conclude their rubric-mummeries (a much more audacious feat than beer!); we have wet wind at North-east, and a sky somewhat of the dreariest:—Courage! a *little* way above it, reigns mere blue and sunshine eternally!

—T.C.

Wednesday, 2 Oct^r.—the Letter had to wait till today, and is still in time. Anthony Sterling, who is yet at Ventnor, apprises me this morning that according to his and the Governess's belief the Russell Mss. arrived duly, and were spoken of more than once by our Friend. —On Monday I received from this same Anthony a big packet by Post; it contains among other things all your Letters to John, wrapt up carefully, and addressed in his hand "Emerson's Letters, to be returned' thro' the hands of Carlyle": they shall go towards you next week, by Mr James, who is about returning. Among the other Papers was one containing seven stanzas of verse addressed "to T. Carlyle," 14 Sept^r; full of love and enthusiasm;—the Friday before his death: I was visiting the old City of Winchester that day, among the tombs of Canutes and eldest noble ones: you may judge how sacred the memory of those hours *now* is!

I have read your Slavery Address; this morning the first *half*-sheet, in Proof, of the Essays has come: perfectly correct, and right good reading.—Yours ever   T. Carlyle

[3] *Human Nature.*

Concord 30 Sept. 1844

My dear friend,

I enclose a bill of exchange for thirty pounds sterling which I procured in town today at 5.00 each pound, or $150.00; so high, it seems,
is the rate at present, higher, they said, than for years. It is good booksellers' money from Little & Brown, & James Munroe, & Co., in unequal proportions. If you wish for more accurate information & have
a great deal of patience, there is still hope that you may obtain it before
death; for I this day met E. P. Clark in Washington Street, and he reported some progress in auditing of accounts, and said that when presently his family should return to town for the winter, he would see to
the end of them, i.e. the accounts.

I received with great satisfaction your letter of July, which came by
a later steamer than it was written for, but gave me exact & solid information on what I most wished to know. May you live forever! &
may your reports of men & things be accessible to me whilst I live. Even
if, as now in Sterling's case, the news are the worst, or nearly so, yet let
whatever comes for knowledge be precise, for the direst tragedy that is
accurately true must share the blessing of the universe.—I have no later
tidings from Sterling, and must still look to you to tell me what you
can. I dread that the story should be short. May you have much good
to tell of him, & for many a day to come! The sketch you drew of Tennyson was right welcome, for he is an old favourite of mine,—I owned
his book before I saw your face;—though I love him with allowance.
O cherish him with love & praise, and draw from him whole books full
of new verses, yet. The only point on which you never give precise intelligence, is your own book: but you shall have your will in that; so
only you arrive on the shores of light at last, with your mystic freight
fished partly out of the seas of time, & partly out of the empyrean deeps.

I have much regretted a sudden note I wrote you just before the
steamer of 1 September sailed, entreating you to cumber yourself about
my proofsheets sent to the London bookseller. I heartily absolve you
from all such vexations. Nothing could be more inconsiderate. Mr
Chapman is undoubtedly amply competent to ordinary correction &
I much prefer to send you my little book in decent trim than in rags
& stains & deformities more than its own. I have just corrected & sent
to the steamer the last sheets for Mr Chapman who who is to find

English readers if he can. I shall ask Mr C. to send you a copy, for his edition will be more correct than mine. What can I tell you better? Why even this that this house rejoices in a brave boy, now near three months old. Edward we call him, & my wife calls him Edward Waldo. When shall I show him to you? And when shall I show you a pretty pasture & woodlot which I bought last week on the borders of a lake which is the chief ornament of this town called Walden Pond?[1] One of these days, if I should have any money, I may build me a cabin or a turret there high as the treetops and spend my nights as well as days in the midst of a beauty which never fades for me.

Yours with love,   R. W. Emerson

Chelsea, 3 Nov^r, 1844—

Dear Emerson,

By the clearest law I am bound to write you a word today, were my haste even greater than it is. The last American fleet or ship, about the middle of last month, brought me a Draft for Thirty Pounds; which I converted into ready cash, and have here,—and am now your grateful debtor for, as of old. There seems to be no end to those Boston Booksellers! I think the well is dry; and straightway it begins to run again. Thanks to you:—it is, I dare say, a thing you too are grateful for. We will recognize it among the good things of this rather indifferent world. —By the way, if that good Clarke *like* his business, let him go on with it; but if not, stop him, poor fellow! It is to me a matter of really small moment whether those Booksellers' accounts be ever audited in this world, or left over to the General Day of Audit. I myself shudder at the sight of such things; and make my bargain here so always as to have no trade with them, but to be *netto* from the first: why should I plague poor Clarke with them, if it be any plague to him? The Booksellers will never *know* but we examine them! The very terror of Clarke's name will be as the bark of chained mastiff,—and no need for actual biting! Have due pity on the man.

Your English volume of Essays, as Chapman probably informs you

---

[1] A "town" in New England may include several villages; Walden Pond lies two miles from the village of Concord. For an account of the turret that never was built there, see Raymond Adams, "Emerson's House at Walden," *The Thoreau Society Bulletin*, July, 1948.

by this Post, was advertised yesterday, "with a Preface from me." That is hardly accurate, that latter clause. My "Preface" consists only of a certificate that the Book is correctly printed, and sent forth by a Publisher of your appointment, whom therefore all readers of yours ought to regard accordingly. Nothing more.[1] There proves, I believe, no visible real vestige of a Copyright obtainable here; only Chapman asserts that he *has* obtained one, and that he will take all contraveners into Chancery,—which has a terrible sound; and indeed the Act he founds on is of so distracted inextricable a character, it may mean anything and all things, and no Serj't Talfourd whom we could consult durst take upon him to say that it meant almost anything whatever.[2] The sound of "Chancery," the stereotype character of this volume, and its cheap price, may perhaps deter pirates,—who are but a weak body in this country as yet. I judged it right to help in that; and impertinent, at this stage of affairs, to go any farther. The Book is very fairly printed, onward at least to the Essay *New England Politics,* where my "perfect-copy" of the sheets as yet stops.[3] I did not read any of the Proofs except two; finding it quite superfluous, and a sad waste of time to the hurried Chapman himself. I have found yet but one error, and that a very correctible one, "narvest" for "harvest";—no other that I recollect at present.

The work itself falling on me by driblets has not the right chance yet,—not till I get it in the bound state, and read it all at once,—to produce its due impression on me. But I will say already of it, It is a *sermon* to me, as all your other deliberate utterances are; a real *word,* which I feel to be such,—alas, almost or altogether the one such, in a world all full of jargons, hearsays, echoes, and vain noises, which cannot pass with me for *words!* This is a praise far beyond any "literary" one; literary praises are not worth repeating in comparison.—For the rest,

---

[1] The preface was dated October 25, 1844, London; it warned "*un*authorized reprinters, and adventurous spirits inclined to do a little in the pirate line . . . that *theft* in any sort is abhorrent to the mind of man."

[2] The English copyright law of 1842 was introduced into the House of Commons in 1837 by Thomas Talfourd, Serjeant-at-law. Carlyle may actually have consulted Talfourd. On October 4, 1844, he wrote to John Forster: "[Chapman] has heard that Sergt Talfourd is the oracle on all such matters; and in his despair the poor Chapman wishes me to go and ask the learned Sergt direct. For Emerson's sake I will cheerfully do it, if it be feasible" (MS owned by the Victoria and Albert Museum).

[3] The last essay in the volume is "New England Reformers."

I have to object still (what you will call objecting against the Law of Nature) that we find you a Speaker, indeed, but as it were a *Solilo-quizer* on the eternal mountain-tops only, in vast solitudes where men and their affairs lie all hushed in a very dim remoteness; and only *the man* and the stars and the earth are visible,—whom, so fine a fellow seems he, we could perpetually punch into, and say, "Why won't you come and help us then? We have terrible need of one man like you down among us! It is cold and vacant up there; nothing paintable but rainbows and emotions; come down and you shall do life-pictures, passions, facts,—which *transcend* all thought, a[nd] leave it stuttering and stammering!"—To which he answers that he won't[,] can't, and doesn't want to (as the Cockneys have it): and so I leave him, and say, "You Western Gymnosophist! Well, we can afford one man for that too. But—!"—By the bye I ought to say, the sentences are very *brief;* and did not, in my *sheet* reading, always entirely cohere for me. Pure gen-uine Saxon; strong and simple; of a clearness, of a beauty—But they did not, sometimes, rightly stick to their foregoers and their followers: the paragraph not as a beaten *ingot,* but as a beautiful square *bag of duck-shot* held together by canvas! I will try them again, with the Book deliberately before me.—There are also one or two utterances about "Jesus," "immortality," and so forth, which will produce wide-eyes here and there.[4] I do not say it was wrong to utter them; a man obeys his own Daemon in these cases as his Supreme Law. I daresay you are a little bored occasionally with "Jesus" &c, as I confess I myself am, when I discern what a beggarly Twaddle they have made of all that, what a greasy Cataplasm to lay to their own poltrooneries;—and an impatient person may exclaim with Voltaire, in serious moments: *"Au nom de Dieu, ne me parlez plus de cet homme-là!* I have had enough of him;—I tell you I am alive too!"—[5]

Well, I have scribbled at a great rate; regardless of Time's flight! My Wife thanks many times for M. Fuller's Book. I sent by Mr James a small Packet of *your* Letters—which will make you sad to look at them! Adieu, dear friend.   T. Carlyle

[4] Carlyle probably refers here to the treatment of "the popular doctrine of the im-mortality of the soul" in "Nature" and the cataloguing of Jesus with Pericles, Caesar, Michelangelo, and Washington in "Nominalist and Realist."

[5] Emerson translated this epigram, with curious insensitivity, in "Uses of Great Men": "I pray you, let me never hear that man's name again" (*Works,* IV, 27).

Concord, 31 December, 1844

My dear friend,

I have long owed you a letter & have much to acknowledge. Your two letters containing tidings the first of the mortal illness, & the second of the death of Sterling, I had no heart to answer. I had nothing to say. Alas, as in so many instances heretofore, I knew not what to think. Life is somewhat customary & usual; and death is the unusual & astonishing: it kills in so far the survivor also, when it ravishes from him friendship & the most notable & admirable qualities. That which we call faith seems somewhat stoical & selfish, if we use it as a retreat from the pangs this ravishment inflicts. I had never seen him, but I held him fast: now I see him not, but I can no longer hold him. Who can say what he yet is & will be to me? The most just & generous can best divine that. I have written in vain to James to visit me, or to send me tidings. He sent me, without any note, the parcel you confided to him, & has gone to Albany, or I know not whither.

I have your notes of the progress of my London printing, &, at last, the book itself. It was thoughtless in me to ask your attention to the book at all in the proof state: the printer might have been fully trusted with corrected printed pages before him. Nor should Chapman have taxed you for an advertisement: only, I doubt not he was glad of a chance to have business with you; and, of course, was too thankful for any *Preface*. Thanks to you for the kind thought of a "Notice," & for its friendly wit. You shall not do this thing again, if I should send you any more books. A preface from you is a sort of banner or oriflamme, a little too splendid for my occasion, & misleads. I fancy my readers to be a very quiet, plain, even obscure class,—men & women of some religious culture & aspirations, young, or else mystical, & by no means including the great literary & fashionable army which no man can count, who now read your books. If you introduce me, your readers & the literary papers try to read me, & with false expectations. I had rather hav[e] fewer readers & only such as belong to me.

I doubt not your stricture on the book as sometimes unconnected & inconsecutive is just. Your words are very gentle. I should describe it much more harshly. My knowledge of the defects of these things I write is all but sufficient to hinder me from writing at all. I am only a sort of lieutenant here in the deplorable absence of captains, & write the laws ill as thinking it a better homage than universal silence. You Londoners know little of the dignities & duties of country Lyceums But of what you say now & heretofore respecting the remoteness of my writing & thinking from real life, though I hear substantially the same criticism made by my countrymen, I do not know what it means. If I can at any time express the law & the ideal right, that should satisfy me without measuring the divergence from it of the last act of Congress. And though I sometimes accept a popular call, & preach on Temperance or the Abolition of slavery, as lately on the First of August,[1] I am sure to feel before I have done with it, what an intrusion it is into another sphere & so much loss of virtue in my own. Since I am not to see you from year to year is there never an Englishman who knows you well, who comes to America, & whom you can send to me to answer all my questions. Health & love & joy to you & yours! R. W. Emerson

[1] See above, E.9.1.44.

1845

My dear Carlyle,

Carey & Hart of Philadelphia,[1] booksellers, have lately proposed to buy the remainder of our Boston edition of your Miscellanies, or, to give you a *bonus* for sanctioning an edition of the same, which they propose to publish. On inquiry, I have found that only 13 entire sets of 4 volumes, remain to us unsold: whilst we have 226 copies of Vol III; and 243 copies of Vol IV, remaining. In replying to Mr Carey, I proposed, that, besides the proposed *bonus,* he should buy of me these odd volumes, which are not bound but folded, at 25 cents a volume, (Munroe having roughly computed the cost at 40 cents a volume,) But this he declines to do, and offers fifty pounds sterling for his *bonus.* I decided at once to accept his offer, thinking it a more favorable winding up of our account, than I could otherwise look for; as Mr Carey knows much better how to defend himself from pirates than I do. So I am to publish that his edition is edited with your concurrence. Our own remaining copies of entire sets I shall sell at once to Munroe, at a reduced price, and the odd volumes I think to dispose of by giving them a new & independent title-page. In the circumstances of the trade here, I think Mr Carey's offer a very liberal one, and he is reputed in his dealings eminently just and generous.

My friend William Furness [2] who has corresponded with me on Carey's behalf has added now another letter to say that Mr Carey wishes to procure a picture of Mr Carlyle to be engraved for this edition. "He understands there is a good head by Lawrence, and he wishes to employ some London artist to make a copy of it in oil or water colours, or in any way that will suffice for the engraver; and he proposes to apply to Mr Carlyle for permission through Inman the American

---

[1] Edward L. Carey and Abraham Hart were among the most enterprising of American publishers.

[2] A Unitarian minister of Philadelphia who had been a schoolfellow of Emerson's.

artist who is now in England." [3] Furness goes on to ask for my "good word" with you in furtherance of this design. Well, I heartily hope you will not resist so much good nature & true love; for Mr Furness & Mr Griswold [4] and others who compose a sort of advising committee to Mr Carey, are sincere lovers of yours. One more opportunity this crisis in our accounts will give to that truest of all Carlyleians, E. P. Clark, to make his report. I called at his house two nights ago, in Boston: he promised immediate attention, but quickly drew me aside to his "Illustrations of Carlyle," an endless train of books & portfolios & boxes of prints in which every precious word of that master is explained or confirmed. Affectionately yours, R. W. Emerson

Chelsea, 16 Feby, 1845—[1]

Dear Emerson,

By the last Packet which sailed on the 3^d of the month I forgot to write to you, tho' already in your debt one Letter; and here now has another Letter arived, which on the footing of mere business demands to be answered. I write straightway; not knowing how the Post-Office people will contrive the conveyance, or whether it can be sooner than by the next Steamship, but willing to give them a chance.

You have made another brave bargain for me with the Philadelphia people; to all which I can say nothing but *"Euge! Papae!"* It seems to me strange, in the present state of copyright, how my sanction or the contrary can be worth £50 to any American Bookseller; but so it is, to all appearance; let it be so, therefore, with thanks and surprise. The Messrs Carey and Lea distinguish themselves by the beauty of their Editions; a poor Author does not go abroad among his friends in dirty paper, full of misprints, under their guidance: this is as handsome an item of the business as any. As to the Portrait too, I will be as "amiable" as heart could wish; truly it will be worth my while to take a little pains that the kind Philadelphia Editors do once for all get a faithful Portrait of me, since they are about it, and so prevent counterfeits from getting into circulation. I will endeavour to do in that matter

[3] Henry Inman had been commissioned, by Edward L. Carey and others, to do portraits of Wordsworth and Macaulay.

[4] Carey and Hart were the publishers of Rufus Griswold's *The Poets and Poetry of America* (1842).

[1] MS owned by the Historical Society of Pennsylvania.

whatsoever they require of me; to the extent even of sitting two days for a Crayon Sketch such as may be engraved,—tho this new sacrifice of patience will not perhaps be needed as matters are. It stands thus: There is no Painter, of the numbers who have wasted my time and their own with trying, that has indicated any capability of catching a true likeness, but one Samuel Lawrence, a young Painter of real talent, not quite so young now, but still only struggling for complete mastership in the management of colours. He does Crayon Sketches in a way to please almost himself; but his oil paintings, at least till within a year or two, have indicated only a great faculty still crude in that particular. His oil portrait of me, which you speak of, is almost terrible to behold! It has the look of a *Jötun,* of a Scandinavian Demon, grim, sad as the Angel of Death;—and the colouring is so *brick*ish, the finishing so coarse, it reminds you withal of a flayed horse's-head:" *Dinna speak o't!"* But the preparatory Crayon-Sketch of this, still in existence, is admired by some judges: poor John Sterling bought it from the Painter, and it is now here in the hands of his Brother, who will readily allow any authorized person to take a drawing of it. Lawrence himself I imagine would be the fittest man to employ;—or your Mr Ingram, if he be here and a capable person: one or both of these might superintend the engraving of it here, and not part with the Plate till it were pronounced satisfactory. In short I am willing to do "anything in reason"! Only if a Portrait is to be, I confess I should rather avoid going abroad under the hands of bunglers, at least of bunglers sanctioned by myself. There is a Portrait of me in some miserable Farrago called *Spirit of the Age;* [2] a Farrago unknown to me, but a Portrait known, for poor Lawrence brought it down with sorrow in his face: it professes to be from his Painting; is a "Lais *without* the beauty" [3] (as Charles Lamb used to say); a flayed horse's-head without the spiritualism good or bad,—and simply figures in my mind as a detestability, which I had much rather never have seen. These poor Spirit-of-the-Age people applied to me; I described myself as "busy" &c, shoved them off me, and this monster of iniquity, resembling nothing in the Earth or under it, is the result. In short, I am willing, I am willing;—and so let us not waste another drop of ink upon it at present!—On the whole

[2] *A New Spirit of the Age,* biographical and critical sketches edited by Richard Horne.

[3] Lais was a hetaera of Corinth, famous for her beauty.

are not you a strange fellow? You apologize as if with real pain for "trouble" I had, or indeed am falsely supposed to have had, with Chapman here; and forthwith engage again in correspondences, in speculations, negociations, and I know not what, on my behoof! For shame, for shame! Nay you have done one very ingenious thing; set Clark upon the Boston Bookseller's Accounts: it is excellent;—Michael Scott setting the Devil to twist ropes of sand.[4] "There, my brave one; see if you don't find work there for a while!" I never think of this Clark without love and laughter. Once more, *Euge*.

Chapman is fast selling your Books here; striking off a new 500 from his stereotypes. You are wrong as to your Public in this country: it is a very pretty Public, extends pretty much I believe thro' all ranks, and is a growing one,—and a truly *aristocratic*, being of the bravest inquiring minds we have. All things are breaking up here, like Swedish Frosts in the end of March; a *gâchis épouvantable*. Deep, very serious, eternal instincts are at work; but as yet no serious *word* at all that I hear, except what reaches me from Concord at intervals. Forward, forward!— And you do not know what I mean by calling you "unpractical," "theoretic" &c? O *coeca corda!* [5] But I have no room for such a theme at present.

The reason why I tell you nothing about Cromwell is, alas, that there is nothing to be told. I am day and night, these long months and years, very miserable about it,—nigh broken hearted often. Such a scandalous accumulation of Human Stupidity in any form never lay before on such a subject. No history of it *can* be written to this wretched fleering, sneering, twaddling godforgetting generation: how can you explain Men to Apes by the Dead Sea? [6] And I am very sickly too, and my Wife is ill all this cold weather;—and I am sunk in the bowels of Chaos, and only some once in the three months or so see so much as a possibility of ever getting out! Cromwell's own *Letters and Speeches* I have gathered together, and washed clean from a thousand

---

[4] Such a feat is recorded in a footnote to *The Lay of the Last Minstrel,* II, xiv. Michael Scott had been "under the necessity of finding constant employment" for "a spirit."

[5] Cf. Lucretius, *De Rerum Natura,* II, 14.

[6] "The dwellers by the Dead Sea who were changed to apes are referred to in various places by Carlyle. He tells the story of the metamorphosis, which he got from the Introduction to Sales's Koran in *Past and Present,* Book III, Ch. 3" (Norton's note).

ordures; these I do sometimes think of bringing out in a legible shape, perhaps soon. Adieu, dear Friend; with blessings always,   T. Carlyle

Poor Sydney Smith is understood to be dying; "water on the chest", past hope of Doctors. Alas!—

Concord, June 29, 1845.[1]

My dear friend,

I grieve to think of my slackness in writing which suffers steamer after steamer to go without a letter. But I have still hoped before each of the late packets sailed, that I should have a message to send that would enforce a letter. I wrote you some time ago of Mr Carey's liberal proposition in relation to your Miscellanies. I wrote, of course, to Furness, through whom it was made to me, accepting the proposition, & I forwarded to Mr Carey a letter from me to be printed at the beginning of the book, signifying your good will to the edition, & acknowledging the justice & liberality of the publishers.[2] I have heard no more from them, and now a fortnight since, the newspaper announces the death of Mr Carey. He died very suddenly, though always an invalid, & extremely crippled. His death is very much regretted in the Philadelphia papers, where he bore the reputation of a most liberal patron of good & fine arts. I have not heard from Mr Furness, & have thought I should still expect a letter from him. I hope our correspondence will stand as a contract which Mr Carey's representatives will feel bound to execute. They had sent me a little earlier a copy of Mr Sartain's[3] engraving from their watercolor copy of Laurence's head of you. They were eager to have the engraving pronounced a good like-

---

[1] The MS owned by the RWEMA is an unsigned rough draft or copy.

[2] This letter was printed as the "Advertisement" to Critical and Miscellaneous Essays (Philadelphia, 1846):

Messrs. Carey & Hart,

Gentlemen:—I have to signify to his American readers, Mr Carlyle's concurrence in this new edition of his Essays, and his expressed satisfaction in the author's share of pecuniary benefit which your justice and liberality have secured to him in anticipation of the sale. With every hope for the success of your enterprise,

                    I am your obedient servant,   R. W. Emerson

Concord, June, 1845

[3] John Sartain was a prominent Philadelphia engraver; his reproduction of the Laurence watercolor was used as frontispiece for the Carey and Hart volume.

ness. I showed it to Sumner, & Russell, & Theodore Parker,—who have seen you long since I had, & they shook their heads unanimously & declared that D'Orsay's profile was much more like.[4] I creep along the roads & fields of this town as I have done from year to year. When my garden is shamefully overgrown with weeds, I pull up some of them. I prune my apples & pears. I have a few friends who gild many hours of the year. I sometimes write verses. I tell you with some un-willingness, as knowing your distaste for such things, that I have re-ceived so many applications from readers & printers for a volume of poems, that I have seriously taken in hand the collection, transcription, or scription of such a volume & may do the enormity before New Years day. Fear not, dear friend, you shall not have to read one line. Perhaps I shall send you an official copy, but I shall appeal to the tenderness of Jane Carlyle, and excuse your formidable self, for the benefit of us both. Where all writing is such a caricature of the subject, what sig-nifies whether the form is a little more or less ornate & luxurious. Meantime, I think to set a few heads before me as good texts for winter evening entertainments. I wrote a deal about Napoleon a few months ago, after reading a library of memoirs. Now I have Plato, Montaigne, & Swedenborg, and more in the clouds behind. What news of Naseby & Worcester.

Chelsea, 29 August, 1845—

Dear Emerson,

Your Letter, which had been very long expected, has been in my hand above a month now; and still no answer sent to it. I thought of answering straightway; but the day went by, days went by;—and at length I decided to wait till my insupportable Burden (the "Stupidity of Two Centuries" as I call it, which is a heavy load for one man!) were rolled off my shoulders, and I could resume the *habit* of writing Letters, which has almost left me for many months. By the unspeakable blessing of Heaven that consummation has now arrived, about four days ago I wrote my last word on *Cromwell's Letters and Speeches;* and one of the earliest uses I make of my recovered freedom is to

---

[4] Carlyle too was pleased with the fashionable D'Orsay portrait of 1839: "really very like," he wrote (Carlyle, *New Letters,* I, 162). It is very unlike the photographs of a few years later.

salute you again. The Book is nearly printed: two big volumes; about a half of it, I think, my own; the real utterances of the man Oliver Cromwell once more legible to earnest men. Legible really to an unexpected extent: for the Book took quite an unexpected figure in my hands; and is now a kind of Life of Oliver, the best that circumstances would permit me to do: whether either I or England shall be, in my time, fit for a better, remains submitted to the Destinies at present. I have tied up the whole Puritan Paper-Litter (considerable masses of it still unburnt) with tight strings, and hidden it at the bottom of my deepest repositories: there shall *it,* if Heaven please, lie dormant for a time and times. Such an element as I have been in, no human tongue can give account of. The disgust of my soul has been great; a really *pious* labour: worth very little when I have done it; but the best I could do; and that is quite enough. I feel the liveliest gratitude to the gods that I have got out of it alive. The Book is very dull, but it is actually legible: all the ingenious faculty I had, and ten times as much would have been useful there, has been employed in elucidation; in saying, and chiefly in forbearing to say,—in annihilating continents of brutal wreck and dung: Ach Gott!—But in fact you will see it by and by; and then form your own conclusions about it. They are going to publish it in October, I find: I tried hard to get you a complete copy of the sheets by this Steamer; but it proves to be flatly impossible;— perhaps luckily; for I think you would have been bothering yourself with some new Bookseller negociation about it; and that, as copyright and other matters now stand, is a thing I cannot recommend.—Enough of it now: only let all my silences and other shortcomings be explained thereby. I am now off for the North Country, for a snatch still at the small remnants of Summer, and a little free air and sunshine. I am really far from well, tho' I have been riding diligently for three months back, and doing what I could to help myself.

Very glad shall I be, my Friend, to have some new utterances from you either in verse or in prose! What you say about the vast *imperfection* of all modes of utterance is most true indeed. Let a man speak and sing, and do, and sputter and gesticulate as he may,—the meaning of him is most ineffectually shewn forth, poor fellow; rather *indicated* as if by straggling symbols, than *spoken* or visually expressed! Poor fellow! So the great rule is, That he *have* a good manful meaning, and then that he take what "mode of utterance" is honestly the readiest for him.—I wish you would take an American Hero, one whom you really love; and give us a History of him,—make an artistic bronze statue (in good *words*) of his Life and him! I do indeed.—But speak of what you will, you are welcome to me. Once more I say, No other voice in this wide waste world seems to my sad ear to be *speaking* at all at present. The more is the pity for us.

I forbid you to plague yourself any farther with these Philadelphia or other Booksellers. If you could hinder them to promulgate any copy of that frightful picture by Lawrence, or indeed any picture at all, I had rather stand as a shadow than as a falsity in the minds of my American friends: but this too we are prepared to encounter. And as for the money of these men,—if they will pay it, good and welcome; if they will not pay it, let them keep it with what blessing there may be in it! I have your noble offices in that and in other such matters already unforgettably sure to me; and, in real part, that is almost exactly the whole of valuable that could exist for me in the affair. Adieu, dear Friend. Write to me again; I will write again at more leisure.

Yours always   T. Carlyle

Concord, Sept. 15, 1845

My dear friend,

I have seen Furness of Philadelphia, who was, last week, in Boston, and inquired of him what account I should send you of the new Philadelphia Edition. "Has not Mr Carey paid you?" he said.—No. "Then has he not paid Carlyle directly?"—No, as I believe, or I should have heard of it.—Furness replied, that the promised £50 were sure, & that the debt would have been settled before this time if Mr Carey had lived. So as this is no longer a Three blind Calenders' business of Arabian Nights,[1] I shall rest secure. I have doubted whether the bad name which Philadelphia has gotten in these times would not have disquieted you in this long delay. If you have ever heard directly from Carey & Hart, you will inform me. I am to read to a society in Boston [2] presently some lectures,—on Plato, or the philosopher; Swedenborg, or the Mystic; Montaigne, or the Skeptic; Shakespeare, or the Poet;

---

[1] In Lane's translation the calenders appear as the Three Royal Mendicants. Emerson's allusion does not seem particularly apt.

[2] The Boston Lyceum (*Let RWE*, III, 300).

Napoleon, or the man of the world;—if I dare, and much lecturing makes us incorrigibly rash. Perhaps before I end it, my list will be longer, and the measure of presumption overflowed. I may take names less reverend than some of these—but six lectures I have promised. I find this obligation usually a good spur to the sides of that dull horse I have charge of. But many of its advantages must be regarded at a long distance.—I have heard nothing from you for a long time—so may your writing prosper the more! I wish to hear, however, concerning you & your house & your studies, when there is little to tell. The steamers come so fast—to exchange cards would not be nothing. My Wife & children & my mother are well Peace & love to your household! [3]

R. W. Emerson

Concord, 30 September, 1845

My dear friend,

I had hardly sent away my letter by the last steamer, when yours full of good news arrived. I greet you heartily on the achievement of your task, and the new days of freedom obtained and deserved. Happiest, first, that you can work, which seems the privilege of the great, and then also, that thereby you can come at the sweetness of victory & rest. Yes, flee to the country, ride, run, leap, sit, spread yourself at large, & in all ways celebrate the immense benevolence of the Universe towards you; and never complain again of dyspepsia, crosses, or the folly of men: for in giving you this potent concentration, what has been withholden? I am glad with all men that a new book is made, that the gentle creation as well as the grosser goes ever on. Another month will bring it to me, and I shall know the secrets of these late silent years. Welcome the child of my friend! Why should I regret that I see you not, when you are forced thus intimately to discover yourself beyond the intimacy of conversation.

But you should have sent me out the sheets by the last steamer, or a Ms copy of the book. I do not know but Munroe would have printed it at once, & defied the penny press. And slow Time might have brought in his hands a most modest reward.

I wrote you the other day the little I had to say on affairs. Clark the

---

[3] On October 1, 1845, Carlyle wrote to his wife: "Emerson's Letter is hardly worth sending: however, here it is. I had already as it were answered it" (NLS, MS 612).

financial conscience has never yet made any report, though often he promised. Half the year he lives o[ut] of Boston, and unless I go to his bank, I never see his face. I think he will not die till he have disburthened himself of this piece of arithmetic. I pray you to send me my copy of this book at the earliest hour, and to offer my glad congratulations to Jane Carlyle, on an occasion, I am sure, of great peace & relief to her spirit.　　　　And so Farewell.　　　　R. W. Emerson

Concord, 30 October, 1845.

My dear friend,

In a multitude of petty matters and just escaped from a company of friends, I have only leisure to say that I have received a letter from Mr A. Hart of Philadelphia, Mr Edward L. Carey's surviving partner, requesting me to inform you, that your draft on Messrs Brown Shipley & Co, Liverpool, at four months sight, for Fifty Pounds sterling, will be duly honoured. Will you, on obtaining the "acceptance" of the draft from these parties, write immediately to A. Hart, Esq. of Carey & Hart 126 Chestnut Street, Philadelphia, informing him of the receipt in so far. William H. Furness's good offices have not failed us in any step of this affair. You have been very heedless of us & of your own interest in not sending us a complete copy of the "Book" in advance of the publication. As it is, I look for it with great expectation.

Ever yours　　　　R. W. Emerson

Chelsea, 11 Nov^r, 1845—

My dear Emerson,

I have had two Letters from you since I wrote any; the latest of them was lying here for me when I returned, about three weeks ago; the other I had received in Scotland: it was only the last that demanded a special answer;—which, alas, I meant faithfully to give it, but did not succeed! With meet despatch I made the Bookseller get ready for you a Copy of the unpublished *Cromwell* Book; hardly complete as yet, it was nevertheless put together, and even some kind of odious rudiments of a *Portrait* were bound up with it; and the Packet inscribed with your address was put into Wiley and Putnam's hands in time for the Mail Steamer;—and I hope has duly arrived? If it have not, pray set the Booksellers a-hunting. Wiley and Putnam was the carrier's name; this is all the indication I can give, but this, I hope, if indeed any prove needful, will be enough. One may hope you have the Book already in your hands, a fortnight before this reaches you, a month before any other Copy can reach America. In which case the Parcel, *without* any Letter, must have seemed a little enigmatic to you! The reason was this: I miscounted the day of the month, unlucky that I was. Sitting down one morning with full purpose to write at large, and all my tools round me, I discover that it is no longer the *third* of November; that it is already the *fourth,* and the American Mail-Packet has already lifted anchor! Irrevocable, irremediable! Nothing remained but to wait for the 18th;—and now, as you see, to take Time by the forelock,—*queue,* as we all know, he has none.

My visit to Scotland was wholesome for me, tho' full of sadness, as the like always is. Thirty Years mows away a Generation of Men. The old Hills the old Brooks and Houses are still there; but the Population has marched away, almost all; it is not there any more. I cannot enter into light talk with the survivors and successors; I withdraw into silence, and converse with the old dumb crags rather, in a melancholy and abstruse manner.—Thank God, my good old Mother is still there; old and frail, but still young of heart; as young and strong *there,* I think, as ever. It is beautiful to see affection survive where all else is submitting to decay; the altar with its sacred fire still burning when the outer walls are all slowly crumbling; material Fate saying, *"They are mine"*!—I read some insignificant Books; smoked a great deal of tobacco; and went moping about among the hills and hollow water-courses, somewhat like a shade in Hades. The Gospel which this World of Fact does preach to one differs considerably from the sugary twaddle one gets the offer of in Exeter-Hall [1] and other Spouting-places! Of which, in fact, I am getting more and more weary; sometimes really impatient. It seems to me the reign of Cant and Spoonyism has about lasted long enough. Alas, in many respects, in this England I too often feel myself sorrowfully in a "minority of one"; [2]—if in the whole world, it amounts to a minority of *two,* that is something! These words of Goethe often come into my mind, *"Verachtung ja Nicht-achtung."* [3]

---

[1] London headquarters of the Evangelical wing of the Church of England.

[2] In *Heroes and Hero-Worship* Carlyle had said that every new opinion is at first a "minority of one" (*Works TC,* V, 61).

[3] Cf. *Dichtung und Wahrheit* (*Werke,* XXII, 53).

Lancashire, with its Titanic Industries, with its smoke and dirt, and brutal stupor to all but money and the five mechanical Powers, did not excite much admiration in me; considerably less, I think than ever! Patience, and shuffle the cards!— [4]

The Book on Cromwell is not to come out till the 22d of this month. For many weeks it has been a real weariness to me; my hope, always disappointed, that *now* is the last time I shall have any trade with it. Even since I began writing, there has been an Engraver here,[5] requiring new indoctrination,—poor fellow! Nay in about ten days it *must* be over: let us not complain. I feel it well to be worth *nothing*, except for the little fractions or intermittent fits of pious industry there really were in it; and my one wish is that the human species would be pleased to take it off my hands, and honestly let me hear no more about it! If it please Heaven, I will rest a while still, and then try something better.

In three days hence, my Wife and I are off to the Hampshire coast for a winter visit to kind friends there, if in such a place it will prosper long with us. The climate there is greatly better than ours; they are excellent people, well affected to us; and can be lived with, tho' of high temper and ways! They are the Lord-Ashburtons, in fact; more properly the younger stratum of that house; partly a kind of American people,—who know Waldo Emerson, among other fine things, very well! [6] I think we are to stay some three weeks: the bustle of moving is already begun

You promise us a new Book soon? Let it *be* soon, then. There are many persons here that will welcome it now. To one man here it is ever as an *articulate voice* amid the infinite cackling and cawing. That remains my best definition of the effect it has on me. Adieu, my Friend. Good be with you and your Household always.

Vale   —T.C.

[4] See above, C.9.25.38, n. 5.

[5] The frontispiece of the book was an engraving of a portrait of Cromwell.

[6] William Bingham Baring, a member of the powerful banking family of that name, was the eldest son of the first Lord Ashburton and of Anne Louisa Bingham of Philadelphia; he was at this time paymaster-general in Peel's administration. His wife, Harriet, was the daughter of the Earl of Sandwich.

Concord, 15 Dec. 1845.

My dear Carlyle,

I have just received this evening, half an hour ago, your new book; a beautiful book to the eye and, I am well assured, satisfying & rejoicing.

I wish it found me in better humour But observe my date. I first heard of this parcel by your letter of 11 Nov. which came by the Cambria, a week or more ago, and announced that the book had come by the steamer leaving Liverpool 4 Novr. thro' the hands of Wiley & Putnam. I wrote instantly to these men at New York, and enclosed my letter to Horace Greeley there, editor of the N. Y. Tribune, the great Whig paper, telling him the facts & bidding him receive the book of W. & P. & print it himself, & give you the best share of profit he could. This, because there was no time for the slower presses of Munroe,— the book being in N. Y. & the next steamer to be looked for so soon. Greeley went to W. &. P., & wrote me that "they decline delivering the book as they were reprinting it, having bought it in London of Chapman & Hall, & would deliver my copy as soon as they could safely do so." This was cool enough, I thought; & I wrote immediately to my brother William in N. Y., a lawyer, to go & demand my copy, & take such steps as to make his demand effectual. Now, before I have yet heard from him, they have got far enough on with their printing, it seems, to render up my book, & it comes with the civilest letter, saying, that not possibly can any blame attach to Mr Putnam, their agent in London, but if any wrong has been done to Mr Carlyle, the blame must attach to Chapman & Hall, his publishers, by whom this course of their printing the book, [& withholding mine] [1] was authorized. Meantime they have got a double edition forward in N. Y. one cheap 12 mo [2] the other 8vo & dearer; [3] and, of course, will possess the American market. I am not in possession of their entire statement, for they refer to a letter which they have written to me, but which I have not received.—

---

[1] These are Emerson's brackets.

[2] "Advertised in the New-York *Daily Tribune,* Dec. 16, 1845, as Nos. 39 and 40 of *Wiley and Putnam's Library of Choice Reading,* at fifty cents each, published on that day" (Rusk's note in *Let RWE,* III, 318).

[3] "*Oliver Cromwell's Letters and Speeches: with Elucidations by Thomas Carlyle,* 2 vols., New York, Wiley & Putnam, 1845" (Rusk's note).

I shall bethink myself how to prevent these men in future from withholding parcels addressed to my name; And I beg you will not again employ them as carriers. Little & Brown in Boston, & also J. Munroe & Co—best, are in correspondence with John Chapman in Newgate Street.—I dare not tell you what is my topic for this week's lecture on Thursday night.[4] The housemates are already deep in Cromwell, but I—Farewell.   Affectionately   R. W. Emerson

Not to disturb the sweet tone of this letter with any irrelevant strain I will ask if you received a letter saying that Mr Hart of Carey & Hart would honour your draft on certain bankers in Liverpool named?

[4] This was the lecture on Plato in the series called "Representative Men" (*Let RWE*, III, 306n, 318n).

1846

Chelsea, 3 Jany, 1846—

Dear Emerson,

I received your Letter by the last Packet three or four days ago: this is the last day of answering, the monthly Packet sails toward you again from Liverpool tomorrow morning; and I am in great pressure with many writings, elsewhither and thither: therefore I must be very brief. I have just written to Mr Hart of Philadelphia; his Draft (as I judge clearly by the Banker's speech and silence) is accepted, all right; and in fact, means *money* at this time: for which I have written to thank him heartily. Do you very heartily thank Mr Furness for me;—Furness and various friends, as Transatlantic matters now are, must accept a *silent* gratitude from me. The speech of men and American hero-worshippers is grown such a babblement: in very truth,—*silence* is the thing that chiefly has meaning—there or here. Another Letter was in answer to a certain New York Bookselling House, Homan and Ellis, 295. Broadway," if I read it right; [1] who, quite too late, made offer to me for an edition of the Cromwell Book,—plundered without "offer" by our vulpine friends *"Wily* and *Put-on-him!"* Of whom now a word.

My Friend, I am grieved to see your vexation; and, according to this Broadway offer just mentioned, it may be a loss of some £90 or £100, this trick of the Wilies: but otherwise it is not of any consequence at all,—nor, in that way either, is it properly of any consequence. I did, however, write instantly to Chapman and Hall, giving them a sight of your Letter, and requiring from them an instant distinct contradiction of the Wiley statement, "That Chapman and Hall had given liberty" &c. The answer to this comes out rather *in favour* of the Wiley and Putnam, whose procedures seemed very like highway robbery at first; wherefore it is right that I should put you in possession of it.

---

[1] On the back of Emerson's letter of October 30, 1845, Carlyle had written: "1 half the profits—10 percent on the retail price of the work. Messrs Homes & Ellis, Publishers—295 Broadway Nw York 15 Novr 1845." *Doggett's New York City Directory for 1846 and 1847* lists no publisher named either Homes or Homan.

Just before the sailing of the Novr Packet, the Book being now quite completed, and the engraving on the way towards completion, I hastily called on Chapman; wrote your name on a Sheet of Paper; and directed him to have a copy bound for you with that autograph in it; and to despatch the same by the Packet about to sail. Chapman suggested that "*un*bound, the Book would do as well *for reprinting*" I said hastily, "I do not wish to bother him with that; bind it!" Cursory words; which poor Chapman interpreted to mean that the American Edition of my Book was a thing thrown out into the streets, lying disowned there like a yellow cabbage-leaf,—which *he*, therefore, might pick up, and sell for a penny if he could in a private way! Accordingly he goes across to Wiley here, or Wiley comes across to him,—in short he gives Wiley another copy of the Book for his New York friends (with instruction that they need not *hasten* your copy of it;—which was rather a bold stroke of his,—but with no Authority, as he avers, to *retain* it when demanded); and for this service receives the reward of £10, and buttons the same into his pocket nothing doubting. Such is his Official Narrative, a very penitent Piece wherein he eagerly restores to me the buttoned £10, and really seems very sorry for himself, poor greedy creature. Nay I may as well inclose it for you, and then so far you will have the case before you.

In reply to that Note I have signified to Chapman how *he* commercially stood in selling that waste article, too rashly judged to be thrown into the street; that I did *not* throw it into the street, but into the hands of R. W. E. to do unbiassed his own friendly pleasure with it, —which pleasure, and the calculable results thereof, have now become very evident! For I enclose him the Homan & Ellis Letter, offering me (I think) "Half-profits, or the Tenth part of the retail-price at once," for an Edition: and I bid the poor man go over to his Wileys here, shew them these terms, say, These are my clear due from them: are they ready as honourable men to give me these? If *so*, it shall still be well: if *not*,—they may go to—a Certain Person, and it shall not be well!

Was not here a magnanimous proceeding; looking for grace from a graceless face? I despatched that Note, two days ago; expecting of course no answer but "Hum-m-ha!" but as yet I have not even got that; and it rejoices my mind to think that I have the dogs in a kind of fix! Enough of them: let us not waste another syllable upon them, now or henceforth, the wretched hungerstruck hyaenas that they are.

To my very great astonishment, the book *Cromwell* proves popular here; and there is to be another edition very soon. Edition, with improvements—for some 50 or so of new (not *all* insignificant) Letters have turned up, and I must try to do something rational with these;—with which painful operation I am again busy. It will make the two volumes about *equal* perhaps,—which will be one benefit! If any American possibility lie in this, I will take better care of it.— —Alas, I have not got one word with you yet! Tell me of your Lectures;—of all things

Ever yours   T. Carlyle

We returned from Hampshire exactly a week ago; never passed six so totally idle weeks in our lives.—Better in health a little? Perhaps.

Chelsea, 3 Feby, 1846—

Dear Emerson,

One word to you before the Packet sail;—on business of my own, once more; in such a state of *haste* as could hardly be greater. The Printers are upon me, and I have not a moment.

Contrary to all human expectation, this Book on Cromwell proves saleable to mankind here, and a Second Edition is now going forward with all speed. The publication of the First has brought out from their recesses a *new* heap of Cromwell Letters;—which have been a huge embarrassment to me; for they are highly unimportant for most part, and do not tend to alter or materially modify anything. Some Fifty or Sixty new Letters in all (many of them from Printed Books that had escaped me): the great majority, with others yet that may come in future time, I determine to print simply as an Appendix; but several too, I think about Twenty in all, are to be fitted into the Text, chiefly in the early part of the First Volume, as tending to bring some matters into greater clearness there. I am busy with that even now; sunk deep into the Dust-abysses again!—Of course I have made what provision I could for printing a Supplement &c to the possessors of the First Edition: but I find this Second will be the *Final* standing Edition of the Book; decidedly preferable to the First; not to be touched by me *again*, except on very good cause indeed. New Letters, except they expressly contradict me, shall go at once into the back apartment, or Appendix, in future.

The Printers have sent me some five or six sheets, they send me hitherto a sheet daily; but perhaps there are not above 3 or 2 in a perfect state: so I trouble you with none of them by this Packet. But by next Packet (3d of March), unless I hear to the contrary, I will send you all the Sheets that are ready; and so by the following Packets, till we are out of it;—that you, on the scene there, may do with them once for all whatsoever you like. If *nothing* can be done with them,—believe me I shall be very glad of that result. But if you can so much as oblige any honest Bookseller of your or my acquaintance by the gift of them, let it be done; let Pirates and ravenous Bipeds of Prey be excluded from participating: that of itself will a comfortable and a proper thing!— You are hereby authorized to promulgate in any way you please, That the Second Edition will be augmented, corrected, as aforesaid; and that Mr [Any Son of Adam you please to name] [1] is, so far as I have any voice in the matter, appointed by me, to the exclusion of all and sundry others on what pretext soever, to print and vend the same to my American Friends. And so it stand; and the sheets (probably near 30 in number) will be out with the March Packet:—and if nothing can come of it, I for one shall be very glad! The Book is to be in Three Volumes now; the first ends at p. 403 Vol I; the Third begins at p. 155 Vol II, of the present edition.

What are you doing? Write to me: how the Lectures went, how all things went and go!—We are over head and ears in Anti-Corn-Law here; the Aristocracy struck almost with a kind of horror at sight of that terrible Millocracy, rising like a huge hideous Frankenstein up in Lancashire,—seemingly with boundless ready-money in its pocket, and a very fierce humour in its stomach! To me it is as yet almost uglier than the Aristocracy; and I will not fire guns when this small victory is gained; I will recommend a day of Fasting rather, that such a victory required such gaining.

Adieu my Friend. Is it likely we shall meet in "Oregon," [2] think you? That would be a beautiful affair, on the part of the most enlightened Nation!   Yours ever   T. Carlyle

[1] These are Carlyle's brackets.

[2] Ever since the Presidential campaign of 1844, in which the Democrats had used the slogan "Fifty-four Forty or Fight," the American press and Congress had been full of war talk over the Oregon Territory. Bellicosity had been intensified in both Britain and America by the intransigence of Polk's Annual Message to Congress in 1845. On December 23, 1845, the American cabinet had gravely discussed "the probabilities of a war with Great Britain" (MacCormac, *James K. Polk*, p. 582 *et supra*).

Chelsea, 3 March, 1846—

Dear Emerson,

I must write you a word before this Packet go, tho' my haste is very great. I received your two Newspapers (price only twopence) ; by the same ship there came, and reached me some days later, a Letter from Mr Everett enclosing the *Cromwell* portions of the same printed-matter, clipt out by scissors; written, it appeared, by Mr Everett's nephew; [1] some of whose remarks, especially his wish that I might once be in New England, and see people "praying," amused me much! The Cotton Letter &c I have now got to the bottom of; Birch's Copy is in the Museum here,—a better edition than I had.[2] Of "Leverett" [3] and the other small American Documents— alas, I get cartloads of the like or beter tumbled down at my door, and my chief duty is to front them resolutely with a *shovel*. "Ten thousand tons" is but a small estimate for the quantity of loose and indurated Lumber I have had to send sounding, on each hand of me, down, down to the eternal deeps, never to trouble *me* more! The jingle of it, as it did at last get under way, and go down, was almost my one consolation in those unutterable operations.—I am again over head and ears; but shall be out soon: never to return more.

By this Packet, according to volunteer contract, there goes out by the favour of your Chapman a number of sheets, how many I do not exactly know, of the New Edition: Chapman First and Chapman Second (yours and mine) [4] have undertaken to manage the affair for this month and for the following months;—many thanks to them both for taking it out of my hands. What you are to do with the Article you already know. If no other customer present himself, can you signify to

[1] Edward Everett Hale, a young Unitarian minister of Worcester. The printed matter was a review of *Cromwell* from the Boston *Daily Advertiser* of January 21, 1846.

[2] Carlyle had published, from an earlier printed source, a letter of October 2, 1651, from Cromwell to John Cotton. The British Museum possessed a copy of the original made by the eighteenth-century historian Thomas Birch.

[3] In Appendix No. 28 of *Cromwell* Carlyle published a letter of April 3, 1655, to "Captain John Leverett, Commander of the Forts lately taken from the French in America," of which the original was in the possession of the Massachusetts Historical Society.

[4] Carlyle's Chapman was Edward, of the firm of Chapman and Hall (DNB); Emerson's was John, unrelated, who had been English agent for *The Dial* (Rusk, *Life*, p. 309).

Mr Hart of Philadelphia that the sheets are much at his service; his conduct on another occasion having given him right to such an acknowledgement from me? Or at any rate, *you* will want a new Copy of this Book; and can retain the sheets for that object.—Enough of them.

From Mr Everett I learn that your Boston Lectures have been attended with renown enough: when are the Lectures themselves to get to print? I read, last night, an Essay on you, by a kind of "Young Scotland" [5] as we might call it, in an Edinburgh Magazine; very fond of you, but shocked that you were Antichristian:—really not so bad. The stupidities of men go crossing one another; and miles down, at the bottom of all, there is a little veinlet of sense found running at last!—

If you see Mr Everett, will you thank him for his kind remembrance of me, till I find leisure (as I have vainly hoped today to do) to thank him more in form. A dignified compact kind of man; whom I remember with real pleasure.[6]

Jargon abounds in our Newspapers and Parl^t Houses at present;— with which "the present Editor," and indeed I think the Public at large, takes little concern, beyond the regret of being *bored* by it. The Corn-Laws are going very quietly the way of all deliriums; and then there will at least be one delirium less, and we shall start upon new ones.

Not a word more today, but my blessings and regards. Good be with you and yours always.

Ever your affectionate   T. Carlyle

Chelsea, 18 April, 1846—

Dear Emerson,

Your two Letters [1] have both come to hand, the last of them only

---

[5] An allusion to the Irish nationalist party which called itself Young Ireland.

[6] Everett, now president of Harvard College, had been the American minister in London from 1841 to 1845 and had had occasional social contact with Carlyle (P. R. Frothingham, *Edward Everett*, p. 248). On May 13, 1844, Carlyle wrote to his mother: "The other night we were with a great body of gaping Americans, men and women; I talked a good while with the American Ambassador, a really sensible wellbred man, and got thro' the business as smoothly as I could" (NLS, MS 512).

[1] These letters, the contents of which may be partly inferred from Carlyle's reply, are missing. On April 15 Carlyle sent the second one to his wife, who was at Addiscombe with the Ashburtons: "Here is a leaf slit from a Yankee Newspaper sent

three days ago. One word in answer before the Packet sail; one very hasty word, rather than none.

You have made the best of Bargains for me;[2] once again, with the freest contempt of trouble on my behalf; which I cannot sufficiently wonder at! Apparently it is a fixed-idea of yours that the Bibliopolic Genus shall not cheat me; and you are decided to make it good. Very well: let it be so, in as far as the Fates will.

Certainly I will conform in all points to this Wiley-and-Putnam Treaty, and faithfully observe the same. The London Wileys have not yet sent me any tidings; but when they do, I will say your terms on the other side of the sea are the Law to us, and it is a finished thing.—No sheets, I think, will go by this midmonth Packet, the Printer and Bookseller were bidden not mind that: but by the Packet of May 3d, I hope the Second Volume will go complete; and, if the Printers make speed, almost the whole remainder may go by the June one. There is to be a "Supplement to the First Edition," containing all the new matter that is *separable:* of this too the Wileys shall have their due Copy to reprint: it is what I could do to keep my faith with purchasers of the First Edition here; but, on the whole, there will be no emulating of the Second Edition except by a reprint of the whole of it; changes great and small have had to introduce themselves everywhere, as these New Letters were woven in.— —I hope before May 3d, I shall have ascertained whether it will not be the simplest way (as with my present light

---

Emerson; also a letter from Emerson; both of which will be worth reading. Send them on to my Mother, if you can get time; with order, if you care about it, to have them returned to you" (NLS, MS 512; the date is written in pencil in the hand of Alexander Carlyle).

[2] Emerson was engaged in finding a publisher for the second edition of *Cromwell.* His first plan was to out-pirate Wiley and Putnam, and he wrote for help to Horace Greeley, who replied on March 17, 1846: "I can do nothing in the matter of Cromwell. My partner is an old bookseller and a shrewd business man, and he has been looking about the City at my request, but gives it up. I enclose you Appleton's note, by which you will see what he recommends, but that is nothing. Wiley would just laugh at Colyer's getting out a complete edition ahead of him, wait till that was published, take the additional matter out of it, and print it forthwith; meantime not a hundred copies of Colyer's shabby edition would have sold—certainly not to any one that would want a good copy of the work. No—we are beaten in this business and the fault is Carlyle's own. He ought to have known better than to give any one authority to throw away the American market for his book. . . . The mischief is done, and the fault is not yours nor mine" (MS owned by RWEMA). For Emerson's final arrangements, see below, C.4.30.46.

it clearly appears) to give the sheets direct to the Wiley and Putnam here, and let *them* send them? In any case, the cargo shall come one way or other.

Furthermore,—yes, you shall have that sun-shadow, a Daguerrotype likeness, as the sun shall please to paint it: there has often been talk of getting me to that establishment, but I never yet could go. If it be possible, we will have this also ready for the 3d of May.[3] *Provided* you, as you promise, go and do likewise! A strange moment that, when I look upon your dead shadow again; instead of the living face, which remains unchanged within me, enveloped in beautiful clouds, and emerging now and then into strange clearness! Has your head grown greyish? On me are "grey hairs here and there,"—and I do "know it." I have lived half a century in this world, fifty years complete on the 4th of December last: that is a solemn fact for me! Few and evil have been the days of the years of thy servant,[4]—few for any good that was ever done in them. *Ay de mi!*

Within late weeks I have got my Horse again; go riding thro' the loud torrent of vehiculatory discords, till I get into the fields, into the green lanes; which is intrinsically a great medicine to me. Most comfortless riding it is, with a horse of such *kangaroo* disposition, till I do get to the sight of my old ever-young green-mantled Mother again; but for an hour there, it is a real blessing to me. I have company sometimes, but generally prefer solitude, and a dialogue with the trees and clouds. Alas, the speech of men, especially the witty-speech of men, is oftentimes afflictive to me: "in the wide Earth," I say sometimes with a sigh, "there is none but Emerson that responds to me with a voice wholly human!" All "Literature" too is become I cannot tell you how contemptible to me. On the whole one's blessedness is to do as Oliver: Work while the sun is up; work *well* as if Eternities depended on it; and then sleep,—if under the guano-mountains of Human Stupor, if handsomely *forgotten* all at once, that latter is the handsome thing! I have often thought what W. Shakspeare would say, were he to sit one night in a "Shakspeare Society," and listen to the empty twaddle and other long-eared melody about him there!—Adieu, my Friend. I fear I have forgotten many things: at all events I have forgotten the inexorable flight of the minutes, which are numbered out to me at present.   Ever yours   T. Carlyle

[3] Reproduced in Plate III.   [4] Cf. Gen. 47: 9.

I think I recognise the Inspector of Wild-Beasts, in the little Boston Newspaper you send! A small hatchet-faced grey-eyed goodhumoured Inspector, who came with a Translated Lafontaine, and took his survey not without satisfaction? Comfortable too how rapidly he fathomed the animal, having just poked him up a little.[4] Ach Gott! Man is forever interesting to man;—and all men, even Hatchet-faces, are *globular* and complete!

Chelsea, 30 April, 1846—

Dear Emerson,

Here is the *Photograph* going off for you by Bookseller Munroe of Boston; the Sheets of *Cromwell*, all the Second and part of the Last Volume, are to go direct to New York: both Parcels by the Putnam conveyance. For Putnam has been here since I wrote, making large confirmations of what you conveyed to me; and large Proposals of an ulterior scope,—which will involve you in new trouble for me. But it is trouble you will not grudge, inasmuch as it promises to have some issue of moment; at all events the negociation is laid entirely into your hands: therefore I must with all despatch explain to you the essentials of it, that you may know what Wiley *says* when he writes to you from New York.

Mr Putnam, really a very intelligent, modest, and reputable-looking little fellow, got at last to sight of me about a week ago;—explained with much earnestness how the whole origin of the *mistake* about the First Edition of *Cromwell* had lain with Chapman my own Bookseller (which in fact I had already perceived to be the case);[1] and farther

---

[4] The abolitionist Elizur Wright, just returned from a sojourn in England where he had peddled his *Fables of La Fontaine* from house to house, was now the editor and publisher of *The Weekly Chronotype*. For the issue of March 18, 1846, he wrote a vivid account of his visit to Carlyle: "It was my special desire to sound him on the subject of chattel slavery. And I did, to the bottom, easily. The result would have delighted John C. Calhoun. He thinks men ought to be thankful to get themselves governed, if it is only done in a strong and resolute way."

[1] See above, Introduction, pp. 26–27. On December 7, 1845, Carlyle had written to Chapman: "I find you have done an excusable but to me very unfortunate transaction. What I said, on the occasion referred to, which I well enough remember, was by no means an authorization of you to sell an edition of my Book in America or elsewhere; it was a mere private statement of my own private purpose not to trouble my friend Emerson with editing or bargaining for me, but to send him a copy of my Book so soon as it had become possible, and to leave him to do there-

set forth, what was much more important, that he and his Partner were, and had been, ready and desirous to *make good* said mistake, in the amplest most satisfactory manner,—by the ready method of paying me *now* ten percent on the selling-price of all the copies of Cromwell sent into the market by them; and had (as I knew already) covenanted with you to do so, in a clear, *bonâ-fide,* and to you satisfactory manner, in regard to that First Edition: in consequence of which you had made a bargain with them of like tenor in regard to the Second.[2] To all which I could only answer, that such conduct was that of men of honour, and would, in all manner of respects be satisfactory to me.— Wherefore the new sheets of *Cromwell* should now go by *his* Package direct to New York, and the other little Parcel for you he could send to Munroe:—that as one consequence? "Yes, surely," intimated he; but there were other consequences, of more moment behind that.

Namely that they wanted (the Wiley & Putnam house did) to publish certain other Books of mine, the List of which I do not now recollect; under similar conditions: viz that I was to certify in a line or two prefixable to each Book, that I had read it over in preparation for this Printer, and did authorize them to print and sell it;—in return for which ten per cent on the sale-price (and all manner of facilities volunteered to convince even Clark of Boston, the Lynx-eyed Friend now busy for me looking thro' millstones, that all was straight, and said ten percent actually paid on every copy sold): This was Putnam's offer, stated with all transparency, and in a way not to be misunderstood by either of us.

To which I answered that the terms seemed clear and square and every way good, and such as I could comply with heartily,—so far as I was at liberty, but not farther. Not farther: for example there was Hart of Philadelphia (I think the Wileys do not want the *Miscellanies*) there were Munroe, Little and Browne &c—in short there was R. W. Emerson, who knew in all ways how far I was free and not free, and who would take care of my integrity and interest at once, and do what was just and prudent; and to *him* I would refer the whole question, and

with according to his own friendly pleasure" (MS owned by the Pierpont Morgan Library).

[2] On May 3, 1846, Carlyle wrote to his brother John: "American Putnam has been here; a small, long-headed, thin-necked intelligent man, and very modest for a Yankee. He, after much apologetic preambling which he would not cut short, undertook at length with all clearness of statement to accept the Second Edition of Cromwell on the terms specified by Emerson" (NLS, MS 524).

whatever he engaged for, that and no other than that I would do. So that you see how it is, and what a coil you have again got into! Mr Putnam would have had some "Letter," some "exchange of Letters," to the effect above-stated: but I answered "It was better we did not write at all till the matter was clear and liquid with you, and then we could very swiftly write,—and act. I would apprise you how the matter stood, and expect your answer, and bid you covenant with Mr Wiley what you found good, prompt I to fulfil whatever *you* undertook for me." This *is* a true picture of the affair, the very truest I can write in haste; and so I leave it with you—*ach Gott!*

If your Photograph succeed as well as mine, I shall be almost tragically glad of it. This of me is far beyond all pictures; really very like: I got Laurence the Painter to go with me, and he would not let the people off till they had actually made a likeness. My Wife has got another, which she asserts to be much "more amiable-looking," and even liker! O my Friend, it is a strange Phantasmagory of a Fact, this huge tremendous World of ours, Life of ours!—Do you bethink you of Craigenputtock, and the still evening there? I could burst into tears, if I had that habit: but it is of no use The Cromwell business will be ended about the end of May,—I do hope!

You say not a word of your own Affairs: I have vaguely been taught to look for your Book shortly;—what of it? We are well, or tolerably well, and the summer is come: adieu.

Blessings on you and yours.   T.C.

Concord, 14 May, 1846

Dear friend

I daily expect the picture, & wonder—so long as I have wished it, I had never asked it before. I was in Boston the other day & went to the best reputed Daguerrotypist, but though I brought home three transcripts of my face, the housemates voted them rueful, supremely ridiculous, I must sit again, or, as true Elizabeth Hoar said, I must not sit again, not being of the right complexion which Daguerre & iodine delight in. I am minded to try once more, and if the sun will not take me, I must sit to a good crayon sketcher Mr Cheney,[1] & send you his draught.

[1] John Cheyney had been an engraver for Carey and Hart (*Let RWE*, III, 114*n*).

For Wiley & Putnam, I am glad if you like the bargain. It has this drawback it is nothing yet. Ever since they learned anything about an appendix, they have said we will not print till that comes. In the interim their book sells but not for you. Certainly by all means let the sheets be given to Putnam in London.

Good rides to you & the longest escapes from London streets! I too have a new plaything, the best I ever had—a woodlot. Last fall I bought a piece of more than forty acres on the border of a little lake half a mile wide & more, called Walden Pond—a place to which my feet have for years been accustomed to bring me once or twice in a week at all seasons. My lot to be sure is on the further side of the water, not so familiar to me as the nearer shore. Some of the wood is an old growth, but most of it has been cut off within twenty years & is growing thriftily. In these May days, when maples poplars oaks birches walnut & pine are in their spring glory, I go thither every afternoon, & cut with my hatchet an Indian path through the thicket all along the bold shore, & open the finest pictures. My two little girls know the road now though it is nearly two miles from my house & find their way to the spring at the foot of a pine grove & with some awe to the ruins of a village of shanties all overgrown with mullein which the Irish who built the railroad left behind them. At a good distance in from the shore the land rises to a rocky head, perhaps sixty feet above the water. Thereon I think to place a hut, perhaps it will have two stories & be a petty tower, looking out to Monadnoc & other New Hampshire Mountains. There I hope to go with book & pen when good hours come.[2] I shall think there, a fortnight might bring you from London to Walden Pond.—Life wears on, and do you say the grey hairs appear? Few can so well afford them. The black have not hung over a vacant brain as England & America know, nor white or black will it give itself any sabbath for many a day henceforward, as I believe. What have we to do with old age. Our existence looks to me more than ever initial. We have come to see the ground & look up materials & tools. The men who have any positive quality are a flying advance party for reconnoitering. We shall yet have a right work & kings for competitors. With ever affectionate remembrance to your wife, your friend

R. W. Emerson.

[2] See above, E.9.30.44, n. 1.

Concord   31 May 1846

My dear friend,

It is late at night & I have postponed writing not knowing but that my parcel would be ready to go—and now a public meeting & the speech of a rarely honest & eloquent man [1] have left me but a span of time for the morning's messenger.—The photograph came safely, to my thorough content.[2] I have what I have wished. This head is to me out of comparison more satisfying than any picture. I confirm my recollections & I make new observations: it is life to life. Thanks to the Sun! This artist remembers what every other forgets to report, & what I wish to know, the true sculpture of the features, the angles, the special organism, the rooting of the hair, the form & the placing of the head I am accustomed to expect of the English a securing of the essentials in their work, and the sun does that, & you have done it in this portrait, which gives me much to think & feel. I was instantly stirred to an emulation of your love & punctuality, and, last Monday, which was my forty third birthday, I went to a new Daguerrotypist, who took much pains to make his picture right. I brought home three shadows not agreeable to my own eyes. The machine has a bad effect on me. My wife protests against the imprints as slanderous. My friends say, they look ten years older, and, as I think, with the air of a decayed gentleman touched with his first paralysis.[3] However I got yesterday a trusty vote or two for sending one of them to you, on the ground that I am not likely to get a better. But it now seems probable that it will not get cased & into the hands of Harnden [4] in time for the steamer tomorrow It will then go by that of the 16th.

I am heartily glad that you are in direct communication with these really energetic booksellers Wiley & Putnam. I understood from Wiley's letter to me, weeks ago, that their ambition was not less than to have a monopoly of your books. I answered, It is very desireable for us too; saving always the rights of Mr Hart in Philadelphia.—I told him you had no interest in Munroe's "Sartor" which from the

---

[1] Perhaps the abolitionist Parker Pillsbury (see Emerson, *Journals*, VII, 201), but I have found no reference to such a meeting in the Concord *Freeman* or in the records of the Concord Lyceum.

[2] Reproduced in Plate III.

[3] There is fuller comment on this photograph in Emerson's *Journals*, VII, 196.

[4] An imprint on the outside of E.10.30.40 reads: "Forwarded from Harnden's Package Express & Foreign Letter Office No. 3 Court St Boston."

first was his own adventure, and Little & Brown had never reprinted Past & Present or Chartism. The "French Revolution," "Past & Present," "Chartism," & the "Sartor," I see no reason why they should not have. Munroe & L & B. have no real claims, & I will speak to them But there is one good particular in Putnams proffer to you, which Wiley has not established in his (first & last) agreement with me, namely, that you shall have an interest in what is already sold of their first Edition of Cromwell. By all means close with Putnam of the good mind, exempting only Hart's interest. I have no recent correspondence with Wiley & P. and I greatly prefer that they should deal directly with you. Yet it were best to leave an American reference open for audit & umpirage to the staunch E. P. Clark of the New England Bank.   Ever yours,   R. W. Emerson

Chelsea, 18 June, 1846—

Dear Emerson,

I have had two Letters of yours, the last of them (31st May) only two days, and have seen a third written to Wiley of New York. Yesterday Putnam was here, and we made our bargain, and are to have it signed this day at his shop: two copies, one of which I mean to insert along with this, and give up to your, or E. P. Clark's keeping. For, as you will see, I have appointed Clark my representative, economic plenipotentiary and factotum, if he will consent to act in that sublime capacity,—subject always to your advice, to your *controul* in all *ultra*-economic respects, of which you alone are cognizant of the circumstances or competent to give a judgement. Pray explain this with all lucidity to Mr Clark: and endeavour to impress upon him that it is (to all appearance) a real affair of business we are now engaged in; that I would have him satisfy his own sharp eyes (by such methods as he finds convenient and sufficient, by examination at New York or how he can) that the conditions of this bargain *are* fairly complied with by the New York Booksellers,—who promise "every facility for ascertaining *how many* copies are printed," &c &c; and profess to be of the integrity of Israelites indeed, in all respects whatever! If so, it may be really useful to us. And I would have Mr. Clark, if he will allow me to look upon him as my *man of business* in this affair, take reasonable pains, be at any reasonable expense &c (by himself or by deputy) to ascertain that it *is* so in very fact! In that case, if something come of it, we shall get the something and be thankful; if nothing come of it, we shall have the pleasure of caring nothing about it.—I have given Putnam two Books (*Heroes* [1] & *Sartor*) ready, corrected; the others I think will follow in the course of next month;—*F. Revolution* waits only for an *Index* which my man is now busy with. The *Cromwell*, Supplement and all, he has now got,—published two days ago, after sorrowful delays. Your Copy will be ready *this afternoon,*—too late, I fear, by just one day: it will lie, in that case, for a fortnight, and then come. Wiley will find that he has no resource but to reprint the Book; he will reprint the Supplement too, in justice to former purchasers; but this is the *final* form of the Book, this second edition; and to this all readers of it will come at last.

We expect the Daguerrotype by next Steamer; but you take good care not to prepossess us on its behalf! In fact, I believe, the only satisfactory course will be to get a Sketch done too; if you have any Painter that can manage it tolerably, pray set about that, as the true solution of the business—out of the two together we shall make a likeness for ourselves that will do. Let the Lady Wife be satisfied with it; *then* we shall pronounce it genuine!—

I envy you your forest-work, your summer umbrages, and clear silent lakes. The weather here is getting insupportable to us for heat. Indeed if rain do not come within two weeks, I believe we must wind up our affairs, and make for some shady place direct:—Scotland is perhaps likeliest; but nothing yet is fixed: you shall duly hear.— Directly after this, I set off for Putnam's in Waterloo Place; sign his papers there; stick one Copy under a Cover for you, and despatch.— Send me word about all that you are doing and thinking. Be busy, be still and happy.   Yours ever   T. Carlyle

Concord, 15 July, 1846.

My dear Carlyle,

I received by the last steamer your letter with the copy of the

[1] On this day Carlyle wrote the "imprimatur" which was printed in the Wiley and Putnam edition of *Heroes and Hero-Worship:* "This Book, 'Heroes and Hero-Worship,' I have read over and revised into a correct style for Messrs. Wiley and Putnam of New York, who are hereby authorized, they and they only, so far as I can authorize them, to print and vend the same in the United States."

Covenant with Wiley & Putnam, which seems unexceptionable. I like the English side of those men very well; that is, Putnam seems eager to stand well & rightly with his fellow men. Wiley at N. Y. it was, who provoked me, last winter, to write him an angry letter when he declared his intention to reprint our new matter without paying for it. When he thought better of it, & came to terms, I had not got so far as to be affectionate, and have never yet resumed the correspondence I had with him a year ago, about my own books. I hope you found my letter to them, tho' I do not remember which, properly cross. I believe I only enumerated difficulties. I have talked with Little & Brown about their editions of "Chartism," & "Past & Present;" they have no new sales of the books since they were printed on by the pirates, & say that the books lie still in their shelves, as also do a few copies of the *London & Boston* edition of "French Revolution." I prayed them immediately to dispose of these things, by auction, or at their trade sales, at whatever prices would sell them, and leave the market open for W. & P.; which they promise to do.

To Munroe I went, & learn that he has bought the stereotype plates of the N. Y. pirate edition of "Sartor," & means to print it immediately. He is willing to stop if W. & P. will buy of him the plates at their cost. I wrote so to them, but they say *no*. And I have not spoken again with Munroe. I was in town yesterday & carried the copy of the Covenant to E. P. Clark, & read him your message. His Bank occupies him entirely just now, for his President is gone to Europe, & Clark's duties are the more onerous. But finding that the new responsibilities delegated to him are light & tolerable, and, at any rate, involve no retrospection, he very cheerfully signified his readiness to serve you, & I graciously forbore all allusion to my heap of booksellers' accounts which he has had in keeping now—for years, I believe. He told me that he hopes at no distant day to have a house of his own,—(he & his wife are always at board) & whenever that happens, he intends to devote a chamber in it to his "Illustrations of Mr Carlyle's Writings," which, I believe, I have told you before, are a very large & extraordinary collection of prints, pictures, books, & manuscripts. I sent you the promised Daguerrotype with all unwillingness, by the steamer, I think of 16 June. On 1 August, Margaret Fuller goes to England & the Continent; & I shall not fail to write to you by her, and you must not fail to give a good & faithful interview to this wise, sincere, accomplished, & most entertaining of women. I wish to bespeak Jane Carlyle's friendliest ear to one of the noblest of women. We shall send you no other such.

I was lately inquired of again by an agent of a huge Boston society of young men whether Mr Carlyle would not come to America & read Lectures on some terms which they could propose. I advised them to make him an offer, and a better one than they had in view. Joy & Peace to you in your new freedom! R. W. E.

Chelsea, 17 July, 1846—

Dear Emerson,

Since I wrote last to you,—I think, with the Wiley-and-Putnam Covenant enclosed,—the Photograph, after some days of loitering at the Liverpool Custom-house, came safe to hand. Many thanks to you for this punctuality: this poor Shadow, it is all you could do at present in that matter! But it must not rest there, no. This Image is altogether unsatisfactory, illusive, and even in some measure tragical to me! First of all, it is a bad Photograph; no eyes discernible, at least one of the eyes not, except in rare favourable lights: then, alas, Time itself and Oblivion must have been busy. I could not at first, nor can I yet with perfect decisiveness, bring out any feature completely re-calling to me the old Emerson, that lighted on us from the Blue, at Craigenputtock, long ago,—eheu! Here is a genial, smiling energetic face, full of sunny strength, intelligence, integrity, good humour; but it lies imprisoned in baleful shades, as of the valley of Death; seems smiling on me as if in mockery, "Dost know me, friend? I am dead, thou seest, and distant, and forever hidden from thee;—I belong al-ready to the Eternities, and thou recognisest me not!" On the whole, it is the strangest feeling I have:—and practically the thing will be that you get us by the earliest opportunity some *living* pictorial sketch, chalk-drawing or the like, from a trustworthy hand; and send *it* hither to represent you. Out of the two I shall compile for myself a likeness by degrees: but as for this present, we cannot put up with it at all; to my Wife and me, and to sundry other parties far and near that have interest in it, there is no satisfaction in this. So there will be nothing for you but compliance, by the first fair chance you have: furthermore I bargain that the *Lady* Emerson have, within reasonable limits, a royal veto in the business (not absolute, if that threaten extinction to the enterprise, but absolute within the limits of possibility); and that she take our case in hand, and graciously consider what can and shall be done. That will answer, I think.

Of late weeks I have been either idle, or sunk in the sorrowfullest cobbling of old shoes again; sorrowfully reading over old Books for the Putnams and Chapmans, namely. It is really painful, looking in one's own old face; said "old face" no longer a thing extant now!— Happily I have at last finished it; the whole Lumber-troop with clothes duly brushed (F. *Revolution* has even got an Index too) [1] travels to New York in the Steamer that brings you this. *Quod faustum sit:*—or indeed I do not much care whether it be *faustum* or not; I grow to care about an astonishingly small number of things as times turn with me! Man, all men seem radically *dumb,* jabbering mere jargons, and noises from the teeth outwards; the inner meaning of them,—of them and of me, poor devils,—remaining shut, buried forever. If almost all Books were burnt (my own laid next the coal), I sometimes in my spleen feel as if it really would be better with us! Certainly could one generation of men be forced to live without rhetoric, babblement, hearsay, in short with the tongue well cut out of them altogether,—their fortunate successors would find a most improved world to start upon! For Cant does lie piled on us, high as the zenith; an Augean Stable with the poisonous confusion piled *so* high: which, simply if there once *could* be nothing *said,* would mostly dwindle like summer snow gradually about its business and leave us free to use our eyes again! When I see painful Professors of Greek, poring in their sumptuous Oxfords over dead *Greek* for a thousand years or more, and leaving live *English* all the while to develop itself under charge of Pickwicks and Sam Wellers, as if *it* were nothing and the other were all things: this, and the like of it everywhere, fills me with reflexions! Good Heavens, will the people not come out of their wretched Old-Clothes Monmouth-Streets, Hebrew and other; [2] but lie

---

[1] The index was made by an impoverished Aberdeen physician named Christie whom, two years before, Carlyle had employed as a secretary "six hours daily for £ a week . . . not quite so dear weekly as a horse" (letters from TC to John Carlyle, 10.2.44 and 6.30.46, NLS, MS 521 and MS 512).

[2] This Teufelsdröckhian passage refers to both the Hebraic element in Christianity and the district of London where Jewish merchants dealt in old clothes. See below, C.8.31.47.

there dying of the basest pestilence,—dying and as good as dead! On the whole, I am very weary of most "Literature":—and indeed in very sorrowful abstruse humour otherwise at present.

For remedy to which I am, in these very hours, preparing for a sally into the green country, and deep silence; I know not altogether how or whitherward as yet; only that I must tend towards Lancashire; towards Scotland at last. My Wife already waits me in Lancashire; went off, in rather poor case, much burnt by the hot town, some ten days ago; and does not yet report much improvement. I will write to you somewhere in my wanderings. The Address "Scotsbrig, Ecclefechan N. B." if you chance to write directly or soon after this arrives, will, likely, be the shortest: at any rate, that or "Cheyne Row" either, is always sure enough to find me in a day or two after trying.

By a kind of accident I have fallen considerably into American History in these days; and am even looking out for Am^n Geography to help me. Jared Sparks, Marshall &c are hickory and buckskin; but I do catch a credible trait of human life from them here and there; Michelet's genial champagne *froth*,—alas, I could find no fact in it that would stand handling; and so have broken down in the middle of *La France*, and run over to hickory and Jared for shelter!—Do you know Beriah Green? A body of Albany Newspapers represent to me the people quarrelling in my name, in a very vague manner, as to the propriety of being "governed"; and Beriah's is the only rational voice among them.[3] Farewell, dear Friend. Speedy news of you!

T. Carlyle

Concord, 31 July, 1846

My dear friend,

The new edition of Cromwell in its perfect form & in excellent dress, and the copy of the Appendix came munificently safe by the

---

[3] Green, an abolitionist and clergyman of Whitesboro, N. Y., had replied in the Albany *Patriot* to Elizur Wright's attack on Carlyle. The controversy was joined by William Goodell, and it was reported in full in *The Weekly Chronotype* of June 17, 1846. On June 30, 1846, Carlyle wrote to his brother John: "Today there came . . . four Yankee Newspapers (Albany, New York) with a wonderful controversy about me,—which Jane magnanimously declines to read a word of, really not unwisely I believe" (NLS, MS 512). On July 15, 1846, he wrote to his wife: "Nothing of the Letter Kind; only another Yankee Newspaper with further dreary controversy about the character of Carlyle,—which I have already disposed of" (NLS, MS 612).

last steamer. When thought is best, then is there most,—is a faith of which you alone among writing men at this day will give me experience. If it is the right frankincense & sandalwood, it is so good & heavenly to give me a basketful & not a pinch. I read proudly, a little at at time, & have not got through the new matter. But I think neither the new letters nor the Commentary could be spared. Wiley & Putnam shall do what they can, and we will see if New England will not come to reckon this the best chapter in her Pentateuch.

I send this letter by Margaret Fuller, of whose approach, I believe I wrote you some word. There is no foretelling how you visited & crowded English will like our few educated men or women, and in your learned populace my luminaries may easily be overlooked. But of all the travellers whom you have so kindly received from me, I think of none since Alcott went to England, whom I so much desired that you should see & like, as this dear old friend of mine. For two years now, I have scarcely seen her, as she has been at New York, engaged by Horace Greeley as a literary editor of his "Tribune" newspaper. This employment was made acceptable to her by good pay, great local & personal conveniences of all kinds, & unbounded confidence & respect from Greeley himself, & all other parties connected with this influential journal (of 30 000 subscribers, I believe). And Margaret F's work as critic of all new books, critic of the drama, of music, & good arts in New York, has been honourable to her. Still this employment is not satisfactory to me. She is full of all nobleness, and with the generosity native to her mind & character, appears to me an exotic in New England, a foreigner from some more sultry & expansive climate. She is, I suppose, the earliest reader & lover of Goethe, in this country, and nobody here knows him so well. Her love too of whatever is good in French & specially in Italian genius, give her the best title to travel. In short, she is our citizen of the world by quite special diploma. And I am heartily glad that she has an opportunity of going abroad, that pleases her. Mr Spring, a merchant of great moral merits, (and, as I am informed an assiduous reader of your books,) has grown rich, & resolves to see the world with his wife & son, & has wisely invited Miss Fuller to show it to him.[1] Now, in the first place, I wish you to see Margaret, when you are in special good

[1] Marcus Spring was a Fourierist and a friend of Horace Greeley (Wade, *Margaret Fuller*, p. 140).

humour, & have an hour of boundless leisure. And I entreat Jane Carlyle to abet & exalt & secure this satisfaction to me. I need not, & yet perhaps I need say, that M. F. is the safest of all possible persons who ever took pen in hand—Prince Metternich's closet not closer or half so honorable. In the next place; I should be glad if you can easily manage to show her the faces of Tennyson & of Browning. She has a sort of right to them both not only because she likes their poetry, but because she has made their merits widely known among our young people. And be it known to my friend Jane Carlyle, whom, if I cannot see, I delight to name, that her visiter is an immense favorite in the parlour as well as in the library, in all good houses where she is known. And so I commend her to you.

Yours affectionately,   R. W. Emerson

Boston, 1 August, 1846

Thomas Carlyle, Esq.
My dear Sir,

My friend Miss Fuller in company with Mr & Mrs Marcus Spring of New York, are leaving Boston, this day,[1] for England. I hope they may find you returned from your rustication, before they leave London for the Continent. I shall not think Miss Fuller has been in England, until she has seen you & Mrs Carlyle; and, since I cannot go to London myself, you must tell her every thing for me.

Farewell!   R. W. Emerson

Chelsea, 18 Dec^r, 1846—

Dear Emerson,—This is the 18th of the month, and it is a frightful length of time, I know not how long, since I wrote to you,—sinner that I am! Truly we are in no case for paying debts at present, being all sick more or less, from the hard cold weather, and in a state of great temporary puddle: but, as the adage says, "one should *own* debt, and crave days";—therefore accept a word from me, such as it may be.

---

[1] "The *Daily Evening Transcript* of Aug. 1, 1846, lists Margaret Fuller among the passengers on the 'Cambria,' which cleared that day for Liverpool" (Rusk's note in *Let RWE*, III, 341).

I went, as usual, to the North Country in the Autumn; passed some two extremely disconsolate months,—for all things distress a wretched thinskinned creature like me,—in that old region, which is at once an Earth and a Hades to me, an unutterable place, now that I have become mostly a *ghost* there! I saw Ireland too on my return,[1] saw black potatoe-fields, a ragged noisy population, that has long in a headlong baleful manner followed the *Devil's* leading, listened namely to blustering shallow-violent Impostors and Children of Darkness, saying, "Yes, we know *you,* you are Children of Light!"[2]—and so has fallen all out at elbows in body and in soul; and now having lost its *potatoes* is come as it were to a crisis; all its windy nonsense cracking suddenly to pieces under its feet: a very pregnant crisis indeed! A country cast suddenly into the meltingpot,—say into the Medea's-Cauldron; to be boiled into horrid *dissolution;* whether into new *youth,* into sound healthy life, or into eternal death and annihilation, one does not yet know![3] Daniel O'Connell stood bodily before me, in his green Mullaghmart Cap; haranguing his retinue of Dupeables: certainly the most *sordid* Humbug I have ever seen in this world; the emblem to me, he and his talk and the worship and credence it found, of all the miseries that can befal a Nation. I also conversed with Young Ireland in a confidential manner;[4] for Young Ireland, really meaning what it says is worth a little talk: the Heroism and Patriotism of a new generation; welling fresh and new from the breasts of Nature; and already poisoned by O'Connellism and the *Old* Irish atmosphere of bluster, falsity, fatuity, into one knows not what. Very sad to see. On the whole no man ought, for any cause, to speak *lies;* or have anything do with lies; but either hold his tongue, or speak a bit of the truth: that is the meaning of a *tongue,* people used to know!—Ireland was not the place to console my sorrows. I returned home very sad out of Ireland;—and indeed have remained one of the saddest, idlest, most useless of Adam's sons ever since; and do still remain so. I care not to *write* anything more,—so it seems to me at present. I am in my

---

[1] The best account of Carlyle's week in famine-stricken Ireland is his own reminiscence in *Letters and Memorials,* I, 275–77.

[2] I Thess. 5: 5.

[3] The story of Medea and her cauldron appears in Ovid's *Metamorphoses,* bk. VII, lines 279–349.

[4] O'Connell's *rapproachment* with the Whigs offended not only Carlyle but also the extremists among his followers who called themselves Young Ireland.

vacant interlunar cave [5] (I suppose that is the truth);—and I ought to wrap my mantle round me, and lie, if dark, *silent* also. But, alas, I have wasted almost all your poor sheet first!—

Miss Fuller came duly as you announced; was welcomed for your sake and her own. A high-soaring, clear, enthusiast soul; in whose speech there is much of all that one wants to find in speech. A sharp subtle intellect too; and less of that shoreless Asiastic dreaminess than I have sometimes met with in her writings. We liked one another very well, I think, and the Springs too were favourites. But, on the whole, it could not be concealed, least of all from the sharp female intellect, that this Carlyle was a dreadfully heterodox, not to say a dreadfully savage fellow, at heart; believing no syllable of all that Gospel of Fraternity, Benevolence, and *new* Heaven-on-Earth, preached forth by all manner of "advanced" creatures from George Sand to Elihu Burritt, in these days; that in fact the said Carlyle not only disbelieved all that, but treated it as poisonous cant,—*sweetness* of sugar-of-lead,— a detestable *phosphorescence* from the dead body of a Christianity, that would not admit itself to be dead, and lie buried with all its unspeakable putrescences, as a venerable dead one ought! Surely detestable enough.—To all which Margaret listened with much good nature; tho' of course with sad reflexions not a few.—She is coming back to us, she promises. Her dialect is very vernacular,—extremely exotic in the London climate. If she do not gravitate too irresistibly towards that class of New-Era people (which includes whatsoever we have of prurient, esurient, morbid, flimsy, and in fact pitiable and unprofitable, and is at a sad discount among men of sense), she may get into good tracks of inquiry and connexion here, and be very useful to herself and others. I could not shew her Alfred (he has been here since) nor Landor: but surely if I can I will,—that or a hundred times as much as that,—when she returns.[6]— —They tell me you are about collecting your Poems. Well; tho' I do not approve of rhyme at all; yet it is impossible Emerson in rhyme or prose can put down any thought that was in his heart but I should wish to get into mine. So

---

[5] *Samson Agonistes,* line 89.

[6] Carlyle wrote to his brother John on October 8, 1846: "Yesternight there came a bevy of Americans from Emerson; one Margaret Fuller the chief figure of them: a strange *lilting* lean old maid, not nearly such a bore as I expected: we are to see them again." A month later he wrote: "Last night, a weary tea with the American Margt Fuller and Mazzini,—not to be repeated!" (NLS, MS 524).

let me have the Book as fast as may be. And do others like it if you *will* take circumbendibuses for sound's sake! And excuse the Critic who seems to you so unmusical; and say, it is the nature of beast!— —Adieu, dear Friend: write to me, write to me.

Yours ever   T. Carlyle

1847

Concord, 31 January, 1847.

My dear Carlyle,

Your letter came with a blessing last week. I had already learned from Margaret Fuller at Paris that you had been very good & gentle to her;—brilliant & prevailing, of course, but, I inferred, had actually restrained the volleys & modulated the thunder, out of true courtesy & goodness of nature, which was worthy of all praise in a spoiled conqueror at this time of day. Especially, too, she expressed a true recognition & love of Jane Carlyle; and thus her visit proved a solid satisfaction; to me also, who think that few people have so well earned their pleasures as she.

She wrote me a long letter; she has been very happy in England, & her time & strength fully employed. Her description of you & your discourse, (which I read with lively curiosity also,) was the best I have had on that subject.[1]

I tried hard to write you by the December steamer to tell you how forward was my book of Poems: but a little affair makes me much writing. I chanced to have three or four items of business to despatch when the steamer was ready to go, & you escaped hearing of them. I am the trustee of Charles Lane, who came out here with Alcott & bought land, which, though sold, is not paid for.[2] Somebody or somebodies in Liverpool & Manchester have proposed once or twice, with

[1] Probably the letter printed in Emerson's *Memoirs of Margaret Fuller Ossoli*, pp. 184–88, which contains this report on Carlylean politics: "All Carlyle's talk, that evening, was a defence of mere force,—success the test of right;— and if people would not behave well, put collars round their necks;—find a hero, and let them be his slaves, &c." On March 25, 1847, Carlyle sent his sister Jean a clipping from an American newspaper: "It is a Yankee woman's doing (one Miss Fuller, a friend of Emerson's whom we saw here, rather a good woman): I remember I *was* somewhat hard upon her and certain crotchets of hers" (NLS, MS 512).

[2] This was the unfortunate Alcott Utopia, Fruitlands. Emerson sold it, for Lane, to another Utopian, Joseph Palmer, but was involved for a number of years in the collection of payments on the mortgage (*Let RWE*, III, 340n).

more or less specification, that I should come to those cities to lecture.[3] And who knows but I may come one day? Steam is strong, & Liverpool is near. I should find my account in the strong inducement of a new audience to finish pieces which have lain waiting with little hope for months or years. Ah then, if I dared, I should be well content to add some golden hours to my life in seeing you, now all full grown & acknowledged amidst your own people,—to hear & to speak is so little, yet so much! But life is dangerous & delicate. I should like to see your solid England. The map of Britain is good reading for me. Then I have a very ignorant love of pictures, and a curiosity about the Greek statues & stumps in the British Museum.[4] So beware of me, for on that distant day when I get ready, I shall come.

Long before this time you ought to have received from John Chapman a copy of "Emerson's Poems," so-called, which he was directed to send you Poor man! you need not open them. I know all you can say. I printed them not because I was deceived into a belief that they were poems, but because of the softness or hardness of heart of many friends here who have made it a point to have them collected.[5] Once having set out to print, I obeyed the solicitations of John Chapman of an ill-omened street in London [6] to send him the book in *manuscript,* for the better securing of copyright. In printing them here I have corrected the most unpardonable negligences, which negligences must be all stereotyped under his fair London covers & gilt paper to the eyes of any curious London reader; from which recollection I strive to turn away my eyes.

Little & Brown have just rendered me an account by which it appears that we are not quite so well off as was thought last summer, when they said, they had sold at auction the balance of your books which had been lying unsold. It seems now that the books supposed to be sold were not all taken & are returned to them; 100 Chartisms

---

[3] In the fall of 1846 Alexander Ireland, whom Emerson had known during his first visit in England, wrote from Manchester urging a lecture tour (*In Memoriam: Ralph Waldo Emerson,* p. 57).

[4] The first draft has here, in addition: "I should like to see the bookshops, the colleges, the churches, the castles in your land abounding in good names."

[5] Here the first draft has also this sentence: "I reckon myself a good beginning of a poet very urgent & decided in my bent and in some coming millenium I shall yet sing."

[6] Newgate Street.

6₃ Past & Presents. Yet we are to have some eighty three dollars, $83.68
which you shall probably have by the next steamer.

Yours affectionately,   R. W. Emerson

Concord, 24 February, 1847.

My dear Carlyle,

Mr Francis Cunningham of Milton, near Boston, who goes to England on his way to the Continent, asks an introduction to you, that
he may not go through London without seeing your face, though his
short stay there, & the invalid condition of a valued friend in his
party, should give him no second opportunity with you. Mr Cunningham is an amiable & accomplished man, who had part of his education
in Germany, & knew Bettine von Arnim, at Berlin, in his youth, and
has been a translator of Neander—I believe—for our students here.[1]
You will find him acquainted with our best people, & with your own
friends here.   Ever yours,   R. W. Emerson.

Concord   27 February 1847

My dear Carlyle,

I enclose a bill of Exchange for £17 sterling, payable on sight by
Harnden & Co, which cost here $85.00, & with which you will credit
the account of Little & Brown, as, I believe, I wrote you already.

I called, using this occasion—on E. P. Clark of the New England
Bank, the other day, to learn whether he had brought those ancient
accounts confided to him to any audition & result. No;—the Bank
President had been in Europe, crowding Clark with additional duties:
and now has given way to a new President who still leaves the duties
with him; & the intrinsic difficulties of a bookseller's account,—which,
it seems, are proverbial in Banking Houses;—And Nichols the sometime partner of Munroe had special labyrinths of his own.[1]—And
Clark listened readily to the first proposition of returning all the
papers to me—And here they are come faithfully back, without a

---

[1] Cunningham, a Unitarian clergyman (*Let RWE*, III, 374n), had been the translator of J. K. L. Gieseler's *Textbook of Ecclesiastical History* (Philadelphia, 1836);
J. A. W. Neander was another church historian.

[1] "*The Massachusetts Register* for 1846 names Philip Marett as president of the
New England Bank, while *Loring's Massachusetts Register* for 1847 lists Thomas
Lamb in that office, with Charles Nichols as paying teller" (Rusk's note).

single summary, note or figure, that I can discern of my analyst &
auditor after so many years!

I asked him if he had any report concerning your late books from
Wiley & Putnam? No; Nor any letter from Mr Carlyle ever on that
subject. That, I told him, I thought he should have. And I think you
had better clothe his hands & warm his heart with an express authority
to audit Wiley & Putnam's accounts with T. C. Write to him, I mean,
& ask him directly what you bade me ask him, to charge himself with
this friendly office. I am sure he would take it in the kindest part, and
as he would have the beginning of the account, would find nothing
burdensome. He is so much a man of business that he cannot move
in the matter without such an order; & it seems best, unless your direct
dealings with W. & P. in London, have shown you better ways.

You should be visited about the time of receiving this, by Mr Cunningham, an early college acquaintance of mine, though my junior,
an educated & travelled gentleman, who has begged an introduction
to you, whilst, he says he shall make the least demands on your time.
I believe his journeying now is mainly for the benefit of his wife's
sister Miss Forbes who is an invalid. Her brothers are great Canton
merchants at Boston, and the women excellent people.[2] I am sorry I
have neglected to inform myself, but Cunningham obviously wished
an introduction for himself only.

Margaret Fuller writes in good heart from Paris,[3] where she has a
great deal to learn, & only one serious impediment, that she cannot yet
speak French glibly enough for her rapid purposes. She says, she shall
not return to England for a year. My friend Thoreau has written &
printed in "Grahams Magazine" here an Article on Carlyle [4] which
he will send to you as soon as the second part appears in a next
number, & which you must not fail to read. You are yet to read a good
American book made by this Thoreau, & which is shortly to be printed,
he says.[5]   Your friend,   R. W. Emerson

[2] This was the Forbes family with which Emerson was to be connected by the
marriage of his daughter Edith.

[3] "Perhaps in one of her letters of Dec., 1846, or Jan., 1847, incompletely printed
in *Memoirs*, Boston, II, 188ff" (Rusk's note).

[4] " 'Thomas Carlyle and his Works,' *Graham's* for Mar. and Apr., 1847" (Rusk's
note).

[5] Thoreau's *Week on the Concord and Merrimack Rivers* did not appear until
1849.

Chelsea, London, 2 March, 1847—

Dear Emerson,

The Steamer goes tomorrow; I must, tho' in a very dim condition, have a little word for you conveyed by it. In the miscellaneous maw of that strange Steamer, shall lie among other things a friendly *word!*

Your very kind Letter lay waiting me here, some ten days ago; doubly welcome after so long a silence. We had been in Hampshire, with the Barings, where we were last year;—some four weeks or more; totally idle: our winter had been, and indeed still is, unusually severe; my Wife's health in consequence was sadly deranged; but this idleness, these Isle-of-Wight sea-breezes have brought matters well round again; so we cannot grudge the visit or the idleness, which otherwise too might have its uses. Alas, at this time, my normal state is to be altogether *idle;* to look out upon a very lonely universe, full of grim sorrow, full of splendour too; and not to know at all, for the moment, on what side I am to attack it again!—I read your Book of Poems, all faithfully, at Bay House (our Hampshire quarters); where the obstinate people,—with whom you are otherwise, in prose, a first favourite, —foolishly *refused* to let me read aloud; foolishly, for I would have made it mostly all plain by commentary:—so I had to read for myself; and can say, in spite of my hardheartedness, I did gain tho' under impediments a real satisfaction, and some tone of the Eternal Melodies[1] sounding, afar off, ever and anon, in my ear! This is fact; a truth in Natural History; from which you are welcome to draw inferences. A grand view of the Universe, everywhere the sound (unhappily, *far off,* as it were) of a valiant genuine Human Soul: this, even under rhyme, is a satisfaction worth some struggling for. But indeed you are very perverse; and thro' this perplexed *un*diaphanous element, you do not fall on me like radiant summer rainbows, like floods of sunlight, but with *thin* piercing radiances which affect me like the light of the *stars.* It is so: I wish you would become *concrete,* and write in prose the straightest way; but under any form I must put up with you; that is my lot.—Chapman's edition, as you probably know, is very beautiful. I believe there are enough of ardent silent seekers in England to buy up this edition from him, and resolutely study the same: as for the review multitude, they dare not exactly call it "unintelligible

[1] See above, C.2.13.37, n. 6.

moonshine," and so will probably hold their tongue. It is my fixed opinion that we are all at sea as to what is called Poetry, Art &c in these times; labouring under a dreadful incubus of *Tradition,* and mere "Cant heaped balefully on us up to the very Zenith," [2] as men in nearly all other provinces of their Life, except perhaps the railway province, do now labour and stagger;—in a word that Goethe-and-Schiller's *"Kunst"* has far more brotherhood with Pusey-and-Newman's *Shovelhattery,* and other of the like deplorable phenomena, than it is in the least aware of! I beg you take warning: I am more serious in this than you suppose. But no, you will not; you whistle lightly over my prophecies, and go your own stiffnecked road. Unfortunate man!—

I had read in the Newspapers, and even heard in speech from Manchester people, that you were certainly coming this very summer, to lecture among us: but now it seems, in your Letter, all postponed into the vague again. I do not personally know your Manchester negotiators, but I know in general that they are men of respectability, insight and activity; much connected with the lecturing department, which is a very growing one, especially in Lancashire, at present;— men likely, for the rest to *fulfil* whatsoever they may become engaged for to you. My own ignorant tho' confident guess, moreover, is, that you would, in all senses of the word, *succeed* there; I think, also rather confidently, we could promise you an audience of British Aristocracy in London here,—and of British commonalty all manner of audiences that you liked to stoop to. I heard an ignorant blockhead (or mainly so) called Elihu Burritt bow-wowing here, some months ago, to an audience of several thousands, in the City, one evening,—upon Universal Peace, or some other field of balderdash; which the poor people seemed very patient of.[3] In a word, I do not see what is to hinder you to come whenever *you* can resolve upon it. The adventure is perfectly promising: an adventure familiar to you withal; for Lecturing is with us fundamentally just what it is with you: Much prurient curiosity, with some ingenuous love of wisdom, an element of real reverence for the same: everywhere a perfect openness to any man speaking in any measure things manful. Come, therefore; gird yourself together, and come. With little or no peradventure, you will realize what your

---

[2] A self-quotation. See above, C.7.17.46.

[3] "The Learned Blacksmith" of New Britain, Conn., had gone to England in June, 1846, to found the League of Universal Brotherhood.

modest hope is, and more;—and I, for my share of it, shall see you once again under this sun! O Heavens, there *might* be some good in that! Nay, if you will travel like a private quiet person, who knows but I, the most unlocomotive of mortals, might be able to escort you up and down a little; to look at many a thing along with you, and even to open my long-closed heart and speak about the same?—There is a spare-room always in this House for you,—in this heart, in these two hearts, the like: bid me help in this enterprise, in all manner of ways where I can; and on the whole, get it rightly put together, and embark on it, and arrive!

The good Miss Fuller has painted us all *en beau,* and your smiling imagination has added new colours. We have not a triumphant life here; very far indeed from that, *ach Gott!*—as you shall see. But Margaret is an excellent soul: in real regard with both of us here. Since she went, I have been reading some of her Papers in a new Book we have got: [4] greatly superior to all I knew before; in fact the undeniable utterances (now first undeniable to me) of a true heroic mind; —altogether unique, so far as I know, among the Writing Women of this generation; rare enough too, God knows, among the Writing Men. She is very narrow, sometimes; but she is truly high: honour to Margaret, and more and more good-speed to her.—Adieu, dear Emerson. I am ever yours   T.C.

Chelsea, 18 March, 1847—

Dear Emerson,—

Yesterday morning, setting out to breakfast with Richard Milnes (Milnes's breakfast is a thing you will yet have to experience) I met, by the sunny shore of the Thames, a benevolent Son of Adam in blue coat & red collar, who thrust into my hand a Letter from you. A truly miraculous Son of Adam in red collar, in the sunny spring morning!— The Bill of Seventeen Pounds is already far on its way to Dumfries, there to be kneaded into gold by the due artists: today is American Post-day; and already, in huge hurry about many things, I am scribbling you some word of answer.

I have written, as you bade me, a long dull positive Letter to Mr Clark, which pray give to him when once you have read and sealed it:

[4] The British edition of her *Papers on Literature and Art.*

let me hope you will find the worthy man ready to undertake, and to proceed without further bother to either of us; or that failing him, you will find some other (the approximately best in your circle) to set about the work, as real *work,*—and so let us have our hands washed of it. Very possible (tho' I really have no cause to think it probable) the Wiley people may mean to pay me with large admixture of *chaff* among their wheat, very possible too there may be no way of preventing it: but to do the approximately *best* we can for preventing it,— this is a clear duty; this let us do, this by your help one good time; and *then* "with unspeakable composure," [1] leave the outcome to the gods! The outcome will not kill us, either way, *then,*—thanks to Heaven.

The night *before* Milnes's morning, I had furthermore seen your Manchester correspondent, Ireland,—an old Edin^h acquaintance too, as I found. A solid, dark, broad, rather heavy man; full of energy, and broad sagacity and practicality;—infinitely well affected to the man Emerson too. It was our clear opinion that you might come at any time with ample assurance of "succeeding," so far as wages went, and otherwise; that you ought to come, and must, and would,—as he, Ireland, would farther write to you. There is only one thing I have to add of my own, and beg you to bear in mind,—a date merely. *Videlicet,* that the time for lecturing to the London West-End, I was given everywhere to understand, is *from the latter end of April* (or say April altogether) *to the end of May:* this is a fixed statistic fact, all men told me: of this you are in all arrangements to keep mind. For it will actually do your heart good to look into the faces, and speak into minds, of really Aristocratic Persons,—being one yourself, you sinner, —and perhaps indeed this will be the greatest of all the *novelties* that await you in your voyage. Not to be seen, I believe, at least never seen by me in any perfection, except in London only. From April to the end of May; during those weeks you must be *here,* and free: remember that date. Will you come in Winter then, next Winter,—or when? Ireland professed to know you by the Photograph too; which I never yet can.—I wrote by last Packet: enough here. Your friend Cunningham has not presented himself; shall be right welcome when he does,— as all that in the least belong to you may well hope to be. Adieu. Our love to you all.   Ever Yours   T. Carlyle

[1] Here again, I think, Carlyle is quoting himself.

Concord, 1 April, 1847.

T. Carlyle, Esq.

My dear Carlyle,

A near neighbor & friend of mine, E. Rockwood Hoar,[1] Esq. a lawyer much distinguished in his profession, and recently a member of the Senate of Massachusetts, is commanded by his physician to leave off working, & to travel. He goes to England & to Europe, for a few months. I cannot deny him the pleasure of seeing you. And, as Mr Hoar is particularly desirous of seeing Cambridge or Oxford, or both, I wish you would give him the best advice you can in that direction.

Yours affectionately,   R. W. Emerson

Concord, 30 April, 1847.

My dear Carlyle,

I have two good letters from you, & until now you have had no acknowledgment. Especially I ought to have told you how much pleasure your noble invitation in March gave me. This pleasing dream of of going to England dances before me sometimes. It would be, I then fancy, that stimulation which my capricious, languid, & languescent study needs. At home, no man makes any proper demand on me, and the audience I address is a handful of men & women too widely scattered than that they can dictate to me that which they are justly entitled to say. Whether supercilious or respectful, they do not say anything that can be heard. Of course, I have only myself to please, and my work is slighted as soon as it has lost its first attraction. It is to be hoped, if one should cross the sea, that the terror of your English culture would scare the most desultory of Yankees into precision & fidelity: and perhaps I am not yet too old to be animated by what would have seemed to my youth a proud privilege. If you shall fright me into labour & concentration, I shall win my game; for I can well afford to pay any price to get my work well done. For the rest, I hesitate, of course, to rush rudely on persons that have been so long invisible angels to me. No reasonable man but must hold these bounds in awe:—I—much more,—who am of a solitary habit, from my child-

---

[1] The brother of Elizabeth Hoar (Rusk, *Life,* p. 294). See above, E.5.15.39.

hood until now.—I hear nothing again from Mr Ireland. So I will let the English Voyage hang as an afternoon rainbow in the East, and mind my apples & pears for the present.

You are to know that in these days I lay out a patch of orchard near my house, very much to the improvement as all the household affirms, of our homestead.[1] Though I have little skill in these things, and must borrow that of my neighbors, yet the works of the garden & orchard at this season are fascinating, & will eat up days & weeks, and a brave scholar should shun it like gambling, & take refuge in cities & hotels from these pernicious enchantments. For the present, I stay in the new orchard.

I gave Clark his letter sealed,[2] and I doubt not you will hear from him. Duyckinck, a literary man in New York, who advises Wiley & Putnam in their publishing enterprises,[3] wrote me lately, that they had $600. for you, from Cromwell. So may it be.

Yours,   R.W.E.

Chelsea 18 May, 1847—

Dear Emerson,—I have got a letter from Clark; undertaking to act as I desired, nay indicating that he has already begun in some measure

---

[1] Here the first draft reads: "I have been buying land again & again in the last two years, and now since the first day of April have been laying out an orchard near my house that in a year or two when the disposition of the ground is well completed you ought to see." For an account of Emerson's orchard see Rusk, *Life*, pp. 324–25.

[2] On March 18, 1847, Carlyle wrote to E. P. Clark, asking him to undertake, for *"due professional wages,"* the inspection of his accounts with Wiley and Putnam and the collection of his royalties: "Of Messrs W. & P.'s intention to keep these terms, as regular merchants and honourable men, I have no reason to entertain the slightest doubt. But it becomes important for me, as you will perceive,—apart even from the probably very considerable *pecuniary* interests involved in the business,— to ascertain for myself, with the completest possible assurance, that the terms *are* accurately kept; that no portion of the concern which is really mine in this matter be in any way huddled into twilight and confusion, but that it be all really seen into, managed, and made the best of,—as it beseems all the concerns of a reasonable man, in this exact world, to be" (MS owned by RWEMA).

[3] Evert Duyckinck was best known at this time as the editor of the New York *Literary World, a Journal of American and Foreign Literature, Science, and Art.* He was soon to begin editing for Wiley and Putnam a series of books entitled *Library of Choice Reading* (Putnam, *Memoirs,* I, 269–71).

to act. A short response of heartfelt satisfaction goes for him by this Packet; [1] and so, let us hope, for unlimited periods, this matter is set floating, on its own voyage under its own captain, and will trouble us no more.

My time is nearly up today; but I write a word to acknowledge your last Letter (30 April), and various other things. For example, you must tell Mr Thoreau (is that the exact name? for I have lent away the printed pages) that his Philadelphia Magazine with the *Lecture,* in two pieces, was faithfully delivered here, about a fortnight ago; and carefully read, as beseemed, with due entertainment and recognition. A vigorous Mr Thoreau,—who has formed himself a good deal upon one Emerson, but does not want abundant fire and stamina of his own;—recognises us, and various other things, in a most admiring greathearted manner; for which, as for *part* of the confused voice from the jury-box (not yet summed into a verdict, nor likely to be summed till Doomsday, nor needful to sum) the poor prisoner at the bar may justly express himself thankful!—In plain prose, I like Mr Thoreau very well; and hope yet to hear good and better news of him:—only let him not "turn to foolishness"; [2] which seems to me to be terribly easy, at present, both in New England and Old! May the Lord deliver us all from *Cant;* may the Lord, whatever else he do or forbear, teach us to look Facts honestly in the face, and to beware (with a kind of shudder) of smearing *them* over with our despicable and damnable palaver, into irrecognizability, and so *falsifying* the Lord's own Gospels to his unhappy blockheads of children, all staggering down to Gehenna and the everlasting Swine's-trough for *want* of Gospels—O Heaven, it is the most accursed sin of man; and done everywhere, at present, on the streets and high places, at noon-day! Very seriously I say, and pray as my chief orison, May the Lord deliver us from it.— —

About a week ago there came your neighbour Hoar; a solid, sensible, effectual-looking man, of whom I hope to see much more. So soon as possible I got him underway for Oxford, where I suppose he was, last week;—*both* Universities were too much for the limits of his time;

---

[1] The Houghton Library owns a letter from Carlyle to E. P. Clark, dated May 18, 1847, which begins: "I am delighted that you have formally undertaken this business of mine with the Wiley-and-Putnam people. I shall henceforth fling it altogether off *my* shoulders, and leave it very thankfully upon another man's. . . ."

[2] Cf. Ps. 85: 8 and II Sam. 15: 31.

so he preferred Oxford;—and now, this very day, I think, he was to set out for the Continent; not to return till the beginning of July, when he promises to call here again. There was something really pleasant to me in this Mr Hoar: and I had innumerable things to ask him about Concord, concerning which topic we had hardly got a word said when our first interview had to end. I sincerely hope he will not fail to keep his time in returning.

You do very well, my Friend, to plant orchards; and fair fruit shall they grow (if it please Heaven) for your grandchildren to pluck;—a beautiful occupation for the son of man, in all patriarchal and paternal times (which latter are patriarchal too)! But you are to understand withal that your coming hither to Lecture is taken as a settled point by all your friends here; and for my share I do not reckon upon the smallest doubt about the *essential* fact of it, simply on some calculation and adjustment about the circumstantials. Of Ireland, who I surmise is busy in the problem even now, you will hear by and by, probably in more definite terms: I did not see him again after my first notice of him to you; but there is no doubt concerning his determinations (for all manner of reasons) to get you to Lancashire, to England;—and in fact it is an adventure which I think you ought to contemplate as *fixed,*—say for this year and the beginning of next? Ireland will help you to fix the dates; and there is nothing else, I think, which should need fixing.—Unquestionably you would get an immense quantity of food for ideas, tho' perhaps not at all in the way you anticipate, in looking about among us: nay if you even thought us *stupid,* there is something in the godlike indifference with which London will accept and sanction even that verdict,—something highly instructive at least! And in short, for the truth must be told, London is properly *your* Mother City too,—verily you have about as much to do with it, in spite of Polk and Q. Victory,[3] as I had! And you ought to come and look at it, beyond doubt; and say to this Land, "Old Mother, how are you getting on at all?" To which the Mother will answer, "Thankee, young son, and you?"—in a way useful to both parties! That is truth

Adieu dear Emerson; good be with you always. Hoar gave me your *American* Poems: thanks. *Vale et me ama.*   T. Carlyle

[3] Queen Victoria, presumably.

Put that poor youth's sealed Note into the Post-Office. Your cover will not hold his Letter, or it would amuse you. An Orson [4] of Tennessee!

Concord, 2 June, 1847.

Dear Carlyle,

Rev. Frederic Henry Hedge [1] of Bangor in Maine, an old friend of mine, and a chief supporter of the cause of good letters in this country goes now to England France Germany, to Greece, & I know not where further; but first to England & to London. I have charged him to go & see you. I think I have sent a good many friends to you lately, but seldom any one who was on so many grounds entitled to know you as Mr Hedge. So I trust he will find you in an hour of happiest leisure.

Yours affectionately,   R. W. Emerson.

Concord   4 June 1847

Dear Carlyle,

I have just got your friendliest letter of May 18, with its varied news & new invitations. Really you are a dangerous Correspondent with your solid & urgent ways of speaking. No affairs & no studies of mine, I fear, will be able to make any head against these bribes. Well, I will adorn the brow of the coming months with this fine hope; then if the rich God at last refuses the jewel, no doubt he will give something better—to both of us.—But thinking on this project lately, I see one thing plainly, that I must not come to London as a lecturer. If the plan proceed, I will come & see you,—thankful to Heaven for that mercy,—should such a romance-looking reality come to pass,—I will come & see you & Jane Carlyle, and will hear what you have to say. You shall even show me, if you will, such other men & women as will suffer themselves to be seen & heard, asking for nothing again. Then

[4] Orson, in the late medieval tale *Valentine and Orson,* was brought up by a bear in the woods. Something of what Carlyle means here may be seen in a letter to David Aitken, dated February 22, 1841: "The other day [Dodds] sends me a most tumultuous boisterous explosion of a Letter: good in the heart of it, something almost like *genius* in the heart of it; but wild as the woods. Such an Orson will take terrible shaving and taming!" (MS owned by the University of Edinburgh).

[1] See below, E.6.4.47.

I will depart in peace, as I came. At Mr Ireland's "Institutes," [1] I will read lectures; and possibly in London too, if, when there, you looking with your clear eyes shall say that it is desired by persons who ought to be satisfied. But I wish such lecturing to be a mere contingency, & nowise a settled purpose. I had rather stay at home & forego the happiness of seeing you and the excitement of England than to have the smallest pains taken to collect an audience for me. So now we will leave this egg in the desart for the ostrich Time to hatch it or not.

It seems you are not tired of pale Americans, or will not own it. You have sent our Country-Senator where he wanted to go, and to the best hospitalities as we learn today directly from him. I cannot avoid sending you another of a different stamp. Henry Hedge is a recluse but catholic scholar in our remote Bangor, who reads German & smokes in his solitary study through nearly eight months of snow in the year, and deals out, every Sunday, his witty apothegms to the lumber-merchants & township-owners of Penobscot River, who have actually grown intelligent interpreters of his riddles by long hearkening after them. They have shown themselves very loving & generous lately, in making a quite munificent provision for his travelling. Hedge has a true & mellow heart under that arid temperament, & I hope you will like him.

I am well pleased that your booksellers are to pass under Clark's eye. He is the most amiable & the honestest of men. His Carlylism may be a little incongruous, but he enjoys it highly. He has lately suffered a great misfortune, which however has made him more known & prized. The President (Marett) [2] of the Bank of which he is Cashier, & who had been from youth Clark's intimate friend, (reckoned here a rich but a just man) went to Europe & left Clark acting President. Just before his return home, Clark discovered suspicious entries in his books, &, on investigation, a system of fraudulent practise on the part of this President reaching thro' seven years. Marett had come home; Clark went to him & opened the matter, assuring himself there must be yet some explanation.—There was none, and Clark went to the Directors, and showed them that they had been robbed of 64000

[1] Mechanics' Institutes, Athenaeums, etc., devoted to part-time adult education, had been established in most of the cities of Britain. By 1850 there were 610 Mechanics' Institutes with 102,000 members (Barnard, *A Short History of English Education*, p. 107).

[2] See above, E.2.27.47, n. 1.

dollars, by his friend & the most respectable of citizens. Marett paid the money & has gone to the South.

I have seen lately a Texan ardent & vigorous who assured me that Carlyle's writings were read with eagerness on the banks of the Colorado.[3] There was more to tell, but it is too late.

Ever yours,   R. W. Emerson

Concord, 31 July, 1847—

Dear Carlyle,

In my old age I am coming to see you. I have written this day, in answer to sundry letters brought me by the last steamer, from Mr Ireland & Mr Hudson of Leeds,[1] that I mean in good earnest to sail for Liverpool or for London about the 1 October; and I am disposing my astonished household—astonished at such a somerset of the sedentary master,—with that view. My brother William was here this week from New York; & will come again to carry my mother home with him for the winter; my wife & children three are combining for & against me; at all events, I am to have my visit. I pray you to cherish your good nature, your mercy—let your wife cherish it—that I may see, I indolent, this incredible worker, whose toil has been long since my pride & wonder,—that I may see him benign and unexacting—he shall not be at the crisis of some new labor—I shall not stay but an hour— what do I care for his fame? Ah how gladly I hoped once to see Sterling as mediator & amalgam, when my turn should come to see the Saxon Gods at home: Sterling, who had certain American qualities in his genius;—and now you send me his shade! I found at Munroe's shop the effigy, which, he said, Cunningham, whom I have not seen or heard from, had left there for me; a front face, & a profile, both—especially

---

[3] In a journal entry for May 15, Emerson mentioned a "Mr. Arrington of Texas" as one of thirteen guests gathered at his house to plan a new Transcendentalist magazine. This was probably Alfred W. Arrington, an ex-preacher, lawyer, and politician, recently come east from Texas, who published in 1847 a study of lynch law called *The Desperadoes of the South West*.

[1] James William Hudson of the Central Committee of the Yorkshire Union of Mechanics' Institutes had written from Leeds on June 29 in support of Ireland's invitation: "I can engage for the north and south of England that we should hail with delight the great transatlantic Essayist and our Lecture Halls would be crowded with men who have already learned to love and now only wait to *see* the American poet" (*Let RWE*, III, 407n).

the first—a very welcome satisfaction to my sad curiosity, the face very national, certainly, but how thoughtful & how friendly. What more belongs to this print—whether [you] are editing his books, or yourself drawing his lineaments, I know not.

I find my friends have laid out much work for me in Yorkshire & Lancashire. What part of it I shall do, I cannot yet tell. As soon as I know how to arrange my journey best, I shall write you again.

Yours affectionately,   R. W. Emerson

Rawdon, near Leeds, Yorkshire
31 Aug^t, 1847—

Dear Emerson,

Almost ever since your last Letter reached me, I have been wandering over the country, enveloped either in a restless whirl of locomotion, viewhunting &c, or sunk in the deepest torpor of total idleness and laziness—forgetting, and striving forget, that there was any world but that of dreams;—and tho' at intervals the reproachful remembrance has arisen sharply enough on me, that I ought, on all accounts high and low, to have written you an answer, never till today have I been able to take pen in hand, and actually begin that operation! Such is the naked fact. My Wife is with me; we leave no household behind us but a servant; the face of England, with its mad electioneerings, vacant tourist dilettanteings, with its shady woods, green-yellow harvest-fields and dingy mill-chimnies, so new and old, so beautiful and ugly, every way so *abstruse* and *un*speakable, invites to silence; the whole world, fruitful yet disgusting to this human soul of mine, invites me to silence; to sleep and dreams, and stagnant indifference, as if for the time one had *got* into the country of the Lotos-Eaters, and it made no matter what became of anything and all things. In good truth, it is a wearied man, at least a dreadfully slothful and slumberous man, eager for *sleep* in any quantity, that now addresses you! Be thankful for a few half-dreaming words, till we awake again.

As to your visit to us, there is but one thing to be said and repeated: that a prophet's chamber is ready for you in Chelsea, and a brotherly and sisterly welcome, on whatever day at whatever hour you arrive: this, which is all of the Practical that I can properly take charge of, is to be considered a given quantity always. With regard to Lecturing

&c, Ireland, with whom I suppose you to be in correspondence, seems to have awakened all this North Country into the fixed hope of hearing you,—and God knows they have need enough to hear a man with sense in his head;—it was just the other day I read in one of their Newspapers, "We understand that Mr Emerson the distinguished &c is certainly &c this winter," all in due Newspaper phrase, and I think they settled your arrival for "October" next. May it prove so! But on the whole there *is* no doubt of your coming; that is a great fact. And if so, I should say, Why not come at once, even as the Editor surmises? You will evidently do no other considerable enterprise till this voyage to England is achieved. Come, therefore;—and we shall see; we shall hear and speak! I do not know another man in all the world to whom I can *speak* with clear hope of getting adequate response from him: if I speak to you, it will be a breaking of my silence for the last time perhaps,—perhaps for the first time, on some points! *Allons.* I shall not always be so roadweary, lifeweary, sleepy and stony as at present. I can think there is yet another Book in me; "Exodus from Houndsditch" (I think it might be called), a pealing off of fetid *Jewhood* in every sense from myself and my poor bewildered brethren: [1] one other Book; and, if it were a right one, rest after that, the deeper the better, for evermore. Ach Gott!—

Hedge is one of the sturdiest little fellows I have come across for many a day. A face like a rock; a voice like a howitzer; only his honest kind grey eyes reassure you a little. We have met only once; but hope (mutually, I flatter myself) it may be often by and by. That hardy little fellow too, what has he to do with "Semitic tradition" and the "dusthole of extinct Socinianism," [2] George-Sand-ism, and the Twaddle of a thousand magazines? Thor and his Hammer, even, seem to me a little more respectable; at least, "My dear Sir, endeavor to clear your mind of Cant." [3] Oh, we are all *sunk,* much deeper than any of us imagines. And our worship of "beautiful sentiments" &c &c is as contemptible a form of long-ears as any other, perhaps the most so of any. It is in fact damnable.—We will say no more of it at present. Hedge came to me with tall lank Chapman at his side,—an innocent flail of

---

[1] See above, C.7.17.46, n. 2. [2] Self-quotations, perhaps.

[3] Carlyle's version of Johnson's injunction to Boswell, May 15, 1783: "My dear friend, clear your *mind* of cant. You may *talk* as other people do. . . . but don't *think* foolishly."

a creature, with considerable impetus in him: the two when they stood up together looked like a circle and tangent,—in more senses than one.

Jacobson, the Oxford Doctor,[4] who welcomed your Concord Senator in that City, writes to me that he has received (with blushes &c) some grand "Gift for his Child" from that Traveller; whom I am accordingly to thank, and blush to,—Jacobson not knowing his address at present. The "address" of course is still more unknown to *me* at present: but we shall know it, and the man it indicates, I hope, again before long. So much for that.

And now, dear Emerson, Adieu. Will your next Letter tell us the *When:* O my Friend!— —We are here with Quakers or Ex-Quakers rather;[5] a very curious people, "like water from the crystal well";[6] in a very curious country too, most beautiful and very ugly: but why write of it, or of anything more, while half asleep and lotos-eating! Adieu, my Friend; come soon, and let us meet again under this Sun.

Yours   T. Carlyle

Concord, 30 September 1847

My dear Carlyle,

The last steamer brought, as ever, good tidings from you, though certainly from a new *habitat,* at Leeds, or near it. If Leeds will only keep you a little in its precinct, I will search for you there; for it is one of the parishes in the diocese which Mr Ireland & his friends have carved out for me on the map of England.

I have taken a berth in the packet ship Washington Irving, which leaves Boston for Liverpool, next week, 5th October; having decided after a little demurring & advising, to follow my inclination in shunning the steamer. The owners will almost take oath that their ship cannot be out of a port twenty days. At Liverpool and Manchester, I shall take advice of Ireland & his officers of the "Institutes" and perhaps shall remain for some time in that region, if my courage & my head are equal to the work they offer me. I will write you what befals me in the strange city. Who knows but I may have adventures; —I who had never one;—as I have just had occasion to write to Mrs

---

[4] William Jacobson, who was next year to become Regius Professor of Divinity.

[5] William Edward Forster was at this time chiefly engaged in woolen manufacture.

[6] I think I have heard this phrase in a hymn, but I have been unable to find it.

Howitt, who inquired what mine were? [1] Well if I survive Liverpool and Manchester & Leeds, or rather my errands thither, I shall come some fine day to see you in your burly city, you in the centre of the world, and sun me a little in your British heart.—It seems a lively passage that I am entering in the old Dream World, and perhaps the slumbers are lighter & the morning is near. Softly, dear shadows, do not scatter yet! Knit your panorama close & well, till these rare figures just before me, draw near, and are greeted & known!—But there is no more time in this late night—& what need?—since I shall see you & yours so soon.   Ever yours   R. W. E.

Chelsea, 15 Oct[r], 1847—

My dear Emerson,

Your Letter from Concord, of the 31st of July, had arrived duly in London; been duly forwarded to my transient address at Buxton in Derbyshire,—and there, by the faithless Postmaster, *retained* among his lumber, instead of given to me when I called on him! We staid in Buxton only one day and night; two Newspapers, as I recollect, the Postmaster did deliver to me on my demand; but your Letter he, with scandalous carelessness, kept back, and left me to travel forward without: there accordingly it lay, week after week, for a month or more; and only by half accident, and the extraordinary diligence and accuracy of our Chelsea Postman, was it recovered at all, not many days ago, after my Wife's return hither. Consider what kind of fact this was and has been for us! For now, if all have gone right, you are approaching the coast of England; Chelsea and your fraternal House *hidden* under a disastrous cloud to you; and I know not so much as whitherward to write, and send you a word of solution. It is one of

---

[1] Mary Howitt, well known for her tales for children and her translations from Hans Christian Andersen, had been since the first of the year the editor of *Howitt's Journal*, a magazine which urged "the labouring classes, by means of temperance, self-education, and moral conduct, to be their own benefactor" (*Mary Howitt: An Autobiography* [Boston, 1889], II, 41-42). She had asked Emerson to send her information on his childhood and his private life which she would work into an article to coincide with his arrival in England (*Let RWE*, III, 417n). The magazine seems to have proved "a pecuniary failure" (Howitt, II, 43) before the article on Emerson could appear.

the most unpleasant mistakes that ever befel me. I have no resource but to inclose this Note to Mr Ireland, and charge him by the strongest adjurations to have it ready for you, the first thing, when you set foot upon our shores.[1]

Know then, my Friend, that in verity your Home while in England is *here;* and all other places whither work or amusement may call you, are but inns and temporary lodgings. I have returned hither a day or two ago, am free from any urgent calls or businesses of any kind; my Wife has your room all ready; [2]—and here surely, if anywhere in the wide Earth, there ought to be a brother's welcome and kind home waiting you! Yes, by Allah!—An "Express Train" leaves Liverpool every afternoon; and in some six hours, will set you down here: I know not what your engagements are; but I say to myself, why not come at once, and rest a little from your sea-changes,[3] before going farther? In six hours you can be out of the unstable waters, and sitting in your own room here: you shall not be bothered with talk till you repose; and you shall have plenty of it, hot and hot, when the appetite does arise in you. "N⁰ 5. Great Cheyne Row, Chelsea": come to the "London Terminus," from any side; say these magic words to any Cabman, and by night or by day you are a welcome apparition here,— foul befal us otherwise! This is the fact: what more can I say? I make my affidavit of the same; and require you, in the name of all Lares and Penates, and Household Gods ancient and modern which are sacred to men, to consider it and take brotherly account of it!—

Shall we hear of you, then, in a day or two; shall we not perhaps see you in a day or two! That depends on the winds and the chances; but our affection is independent of such. Adieu; *au revoir,* it now is! Come soon; come at once.　　Ever yours.　　　　　　　T. Carlyle

---

[1] Carlyle wrote to Ireland: "Pray do me the favour to contrive in some sure way that Emerson may get hold of that Note the instant he lands in England. I shall be permanently grieved otherwise; shall have failed in a clear duty (were it nothing more), which will never probably in my life offer itself again. Do not neglect I beg very much of you. And, on the whole, if you can, get Emerson put safe into the Express train, and shot up hither, as the first road he goes!" (Carlyle, *New Letters,* II, 49).

[2] Jane Carlyle had written to her husband a few days before his return: "I have been in a pretty mess with Emerson's bed, having some apprehensions he would arrive before it was up again. The quantity of sewing that lies in a lined chintz bed is something awfully grand!" (Carlyle, *Letters and Memorials,* I, 305).

[3] Cf. Shakespeare, *The Tempest,* act I, scene ii, line 396.

Manchester
Mrs Massey's, 2 Fenny Place, Fenny St.
Nov 5

Ah my dear friend! All these days have gone, and you have had no word from me, when the shuttles fly so swiftly in your English loom, and in so few hours we may have tidings of the best that live. At last, & only this day for the first *day*, I am stablished in my own lodgings on English ground, and have a fair parlour & chamber, into both of which the sun & moon shine, into which friendly people have already entered. Hitherto I have been the victim of trifles,—which is the fate & the chief objection to travelling. Days are absorbed in precious nothings But now that I am in some sort a citizen, of Manchester, & also of Liverpool, (for there also I am to enter on lodgings tomorrow, at *56 Stafford Street, Islington,*) perhaps the social heart of this English world will include me also in its strong & healthful circulations. I get the best letters from home by the last steamers & was much occupied in Liverpool yesterday in seeing Dr Nichol of Glasgow who was to sail in the Acadia & in giving him credentials to some Americans.[1] I find here a very kind reception from your friends, as they emphatically are, Ireland, Espinasse, Miss Jewsbury, Dr Hodgson, & a circle expanding on all sides outward, and Mrs Paulet at Liverpool.[2] I am learning there also to know friendly faces, and a certain Roscoe Club has complimented me with its privileges.[3] The oddest part of my new position

[1] John Pringle Nichol, Regius Professor of Astronomy at the University of Glasgow, was about to begin a lecture tour in the United States. Emerson wrote on his behalf to Longfellow and Parker (*Let RWE*, III, 433–34).

[2] Francis Espinasse was a journalist associated with Ireland. The novelist Geraldine Jewsbury, a close friend of Jane Carlyle, was until 1854 a resident of Manchester. W. B. Hodgson, LL.D., was principal of the Liverpool Mechanics' Institute. Elizabeth Paulet, wife of a Swiss merchant, was a friend of Geraldine Jewsbury. On November 22, 1847, Jane Carlyle wrote with reference to Miss Jewsbury, on whose current novel she had been reading proof: "Everything seems on the road to perdition! Here has that little good-for-nothing streamed off to Seaforth, for no more pressing object than to spend a day under the same roof with the Yankee-Seraph!" (letter to John Forster, MS owned by the Victoria and Albert Museum. The date is written in the hand of Alexander Carlyle; Carlyle himself had marked it only "Emerson's visit").

[3] Within the last two days Emerson had received a letter from Joseph Boult offering him the facilities of the Roscoe Club whenever he was in Liverpool: coffee room, news room, library, and gymnasium provided "Refined Social Intercourse and Rational Recreation" (MS owned by the RWEMA).

is my alarming *penny correspondence*,[4] which, what with welcomes, invitations to lecture, proffers of hospitality; suggestions from good Swedenborgists & others for my better guidance touching the titles of my discourses, &c, &c, all requiring answers, threaten to eat up a day like a cherry. In this fog & miscellany, & until the Heavenly sun shall give me one beam, will not you, friend & joy of many years send me a quiet line or two now & then to say that you still smoke your pipe in peace, side by side with wife & brother also well & smoking, or able to smoke. Now that I have in some measure calmed down the astonishment & consternation of seeing you dreams change into realities, I mean, at my next approximation or perihelion, to behold you with the most serene skeptical calmness So give my thanks & true affectionate remembrance to Jane Carlyle, & my regards also to Dr Carlyle, whose precise address, please also to send me.

Ever your lover,   R.W.E.

The address at the top of this note is the best for the present, as I mean to make this my centre.

Chelsea, 13 Nov^r, 1847—

Dear Emerson,

Your Book-parcels were faithfully sent off, directly after your departure: in regard to one of them I had a pleasant visit from the proprietor in person,—the young Swedenborgian Doctor, whom to my surprise I found quite an agreeable accomplished secular young gentleman, much given to "progress of the species" &c &c; from whom I suppose you have yourself heard.[1] The wandering umbrella, still short of an owner, hangs upon its peg here, without definite outlook. Of yourself there have come news, by your own Letters, and by various excerpts from Manchester Newspapers. *Glück zu!*—

This morning I received the Enclosed, and send it off to you without farther response. Mudie, if I mistake not, is some small Bookseller in the Russell-Square region; pray answer him, if you think him worthy of answer. A dim suspicion haunts me that perhaps *he* was the re-

---

[4] The prepaid penny post for domestic mail had been established since Emerson's first visit to England and had not yet been introduced into the United States.

[1] Probably Dr. J. J. G. Wilkinson, who was, as Emerson wrote in *English Traits* (*Works*, V, 250), "the editor of Swedenborg, the annotator of Fourier and the champion of Hahnemann."

publisher (or Pirate) of your first set of Essays: [2] but probably he regards this as a mere office of untutored friendship on his part. Or possibly I do the poor man wrong by misremembrance? Chapman could tell.

I am sunk deep here, in effete Manuscripts, in abstruse Meditations, in confusions old and new; sinking, as I may describe myself, thro' stratum after stratum of the Inane,—down to one knows not what depth! I unfortunately belong to the Opposition Party in many points, and am in a minority of one. To keep silence, therefore, is among the principal duties at present.

We had a call from Bancroft,[3] the other evening. A tough Yankee man; of many worthy qualities more tough than musical; among which it gratified me to find a certain small undercurrent of genial *humour,* or as it were *hidden laughter,* not noticed heretofore.

My Wife and all the rest of us are well; and do all salute you with our true wishes, and the hope to have you here again before long. Do not bother yourself with other than voluntary writing to me, while there is so much otherwise that you are obliged to write. If on any point you want advice, information, or other help that lies within the limits of my strength, command me, now and always. And so Good be with you; and a happy meeting to us soon again.

Yours ever truly,   T. Carlyle

Chelsea, 30 Nov^r, 1847

Dear Emerson,—Here is a word for you from Miss Fuller; [1] I send you the Cover also, tho' I think there is little or nothing in that. It contained another little Note for Mazzini; who is wandering in foreign parts, on paths unknown to me at present.[2] Pray send my regards to Miss Fuller, when you write.

We hear of you pretty often, and of your successes with the Northern populations. We hope for you in London again before long.—I am

---

[2] According to Cooke, the pirated edition of the first series of *Essays* was published by W. Tweedie. C. E. Mudie, however, soon to become the proprietor of one of the largest of English lending libraries, had published in 1844 *Man Thinking, an Oration.*

[3] Bancroft had been the American minister to Great Britain since September, 1846.

[1] See below, E.12.28.47.

[2] Margaret Fuller had met Mazzini at the Carlyles' house, where he had been for years a frequent visitor (Wade, *Margaret Fuller,* p. 189).

busy if at all, altogether *inarticulately* in these days. My respect for *silence,* my distrust of *Speech* seem to grow upon me. There is a time for both, says Solomon; [3] but we, in our poor generation, have forgotten one of the "times."

Here is a Mr Forster, of Rawden, or Bradford, in Yorkshire; our late host in the autumn time; who expects and longs to be yours when you come into those parts.

I am busy with William Conqueror's *Domesday Book* and with the commentaries of various blockheads on it:—Ah me!

All good be with you, and happy news from those dear to you.

Yours ever   T. Carlyle

2. Fenny Street; Higher
Broughton; Manchester
28 December

Dear Carlyle,

I am concerned to discover that Margaret Fuller in the letter which you forwarded prays me to ask you & Mrs Carlyle respecting the Count & Countess Pepoli,[1] who are in Rome for the winter, whether they would be good for her to know? That is pretty nearly the form of her question. As one third of the winter is gone, & one half will be, before her question can be answered, I fear, it will have lost some of its pertinence. Well, it will serve as a token to pass between *us,* which will please me, if it do not Margaret.—I have had nothing to send you tidings of. Yet I get the best accounts from home of wife & babes & friends. I am seeing this England more thoroughly than I had thought was possible to me. I find this lecturing a key which opens all doors. I have received everywhere the kindest hospitality from a great variety of persons. I see many intelligent & well informed persons, & some fine geniuses. I have every day a better opinion of the English, who are a very handsome & satisfactory race of men, and, in the point of material performance, altogether incomparable. I have made some vain attempts to end my lectures, but must go on a little longer. With kindest regards to the Lady Jane,

Your friend,   R.W.E.

Margaret F.'s address, if any thing is to be written, is, *Care of Maquay Pakenham, & Co. Rome.*

---

[3] Eccles. 3: 7.   [1] See below, C.12.30.47.

Chelsea, 30 Dec^r, 1847—

My dear Emerson,

We are very glad to see your handwriting again, and learn that you are well, and doing well. Our news of you hitherto, from the dim Lecture-element, had been satisfactory indeed, but vague. Go on, and prosper.

I do not much think Miss Fuller would do any great good with the Pepolis,—even if they are still in Rome, and not at Bologna as our advices here seemed to indicate. Madam Pepoli is an elderly Scotch Lady, of excellent commonplace vernacular qualities, hardly of more; the Count, some years younger, and a much airier man, is on all sides a beautiful *Dilettante,*—little suitable, I fear, to the serious mind that can recognise him as such! [1] However, if the people are still in Rome, Miss F. can easily try: Bid Miss F. present my Wife's compliments, or mine, or even *yours* (for they know all our domesticities here, and are very intimate, especially Madam with *My* Dame); upon which the acquaintance is at once made and can be continued if useful.

This morning, Richard Milnes writes to me for your Address; which I have sent. He is just returned out of Spain; home swiftly to "vote for the Jew Bill"; [2] is doing hospitalities at Woburn Abbey; and I suppose will be in Yorkshire (home, near Pontefract) before long. See him, if you have opportunity: a man very easy to *see* and get into flowing talk with; a man of much sharpness of faculty, well tempered by several inches of "Christian *fat*" [3] he has upon his ribs for covering. One of the idlest, cheeriest, most gifted of fat little men.

Tennyson has been here for three weeks; dining daily till he is near dead;—setting out a Poem withal. [4] He came in to us on Sunday evening last, and on the preceding Sunday: a truly interesting Son of Earth, and Son of Heaven,—who has almost lost his way, among the

---

[1] Count Carlo Pepoli (1796–1881), poet and revolutionary, had recently returned to Italy with his wife, the former Elizabeth Fergus, after ten years of political exile in London. He was soon to take part, like Margaret Fuller, in the revolution of 1848.

[2] A bill designed to mitigate the civil disabilities of Jews by changes in the wording of the parliamentary oath: it was passed by the commons but rejected by the lords (see article on Lionel Rothschild, in *Dictionary of National Biography*.) On January 17, 1848, Carlyle wrote to his wife: "[Milnes] is gone to Yorkshire; is bent to meet Emerson if he can, and to get W. E. Forster to be of the party" (NLS, MS 612).

[3] Perhaps a reference to *The Merchant of Venice*.   [4] *The Princess*.

will-o'wisps, I doubt; and may flounder ever deeper, over neck and nose at last, among the quagmires that abound! I like him well; but can do next to nothing for him. Milnes, with general cooperation, got him a Pension; and he has bread and tobacco: but that is a poor outfit for such a soul. He wants a *task;* and, alas, that of spinning rhymes, and naming it "Art" and "high Art" in a Time like ours, will never furnish him.

For myself I have been entirely *idle,*—I dare not even say, too abstrusely *occupied;* for I have merely been *looking* at the Chaos even, not by any means working in it. I have not even read a Book,—that I liked. All "Literature" has grown inexpressibly unsatisfactory to me. Better be silent than talk farther in this mood.

We are going off, on Saturday come a week, into Hampshire, to certain Friends you have heard me speak of. Our Address, till the beginning of February, is, "Hon. W. B. Baring/Alverstoke/Gosport/ Hants."—My Wife sends you many kind regards; remember us across the Ocean too;—and be well and busy till we meet

Yours ever   T. Carlyle

Last night there arrived Nº 1 of the *Massachusetts Review:* beautiful paper and print; and very promising otherwise. In the Introduction I well recognized the hand; in the first Article too,—not in any of the others.[5] *Faustum sit.*

---

[5] The first number of *The Massachusetts Quarterly Review,* intended to be the successor to *The Dial,* was dated December, 1847. The "Editors' Address" was written by Emerson; the first article, "The Mexican War," was by Theodore Parker; both were unsigned (Gohdes, *The Periodicals of American Transcendentalism,* p. 166).

1848

~

Dear Emerson,

We are delighted to hear of you again at first hand: our last traditions represented you at Edinburgh, and left the prospect of your return hither very vague. I have only time for one word tonight: to say that your room is standing vacant ever since you quitted it,—ready to be lighted up with all manner of physical and moral *fires* that the place will yield; and is in fact *your* room, and expects to be accounted such. I know not specially what your operations in this quarter are to be; but whatever they are, or the arrangements necessary for them, surely it is here that you must alight again in the big Babel, and deliberately adjust what farther is to be done. Write to us what day you are to arrive; and the rest is all already managed.

Jane has never yet got out since the cold took her; but she has at no time been so ill as is frequent with her in these winter disorders; she is now steadily improving, and we expect will come out with the sun and the green leaves,—as she usually does. I too caught an ugly cold, and, what is very uncommon with me, a kind of cough, while down in Hampshire; which, with other inarticulate matters, has kept me in a very mute abstruse condition all this while; so that, for many weeks past, I have properly had no history,—except such as trees in winter, and other merely passive objects may have. That is not an agreeable side of the page;—but I find it indissolubly attached to the other: no historical leaf with me but has them *both!* Reading does next to nothing for me at present; neither will thinking or even dreaming rightly prosper; of no province can I be quite master except of the *silent* one, in such a case. One feels there, at last, as if quite annihilated; and takes up arms again (the poor goose-quill is no great things of a weapon to arm with!) as if in a kind of sacred despair.

All people are in a sort of joy-dance over the new French Republic,[1]

---

[1] On March 4, Carlyle published in *The London Examiner* an essay on Louis

which has descended suddenly (or shall we say, *ascended,* alas?) out of the Immensities upon us; shewing once again that the righteous Gods do yet live and reign! It is long years since I have felt any such deep-seated pious satisfaction at a public event. Adieu: come soon; and warn us when.   Yours ever   T. Carlyle

Ambleside, 29 Feby. 1848

My dear Carlyle,

I am here in Miss Martineau's house, [1] and, having seen a great deal of England, and lately a good deal of Scotland, too, I am tomorrow to set forth again for Manchester, & presently for London. Yesterday, I saw Wordsworth for a good hour & a half, which he did not seem to grudge, for he talked freely & fast, &—bating his cramping Toryism & what belongs to it—wisely enough. He is in rude health, and though 77 years old, says he does not feel his age in any particular. Miss Martineau is in excellent health & spirits, though just now annoyed by the hesitations of Murray to publish her book,[2] but she confides infinitely in her book, which is the best fortune. But I please myself not a little that I shall in a few days see you again, and I will give you an account of my journey. I have heard almost nothing of your late weeks,—but that is my fault,—only I heard with sorrow that your wife had been ill, & could not go with you on your Christmas holidays. Now may her good days have come again! I say I have heard nothing of your late days; of your early days, of your genius, of your influence, I cease not to hear & to see continually, yea, often am called upon to resist the same with might & main. But I will not pester you with it now.—Miss Martineau, who is most happily placed here, & a model of housekeeping, sends kindest remembrances to you *both.*

Yours ever,   R. W. Emerson.

Philippe; it is reprinted in Shepherd's *Memoirs of the Life and Writings of Thomas Carlyle.*

[1] Two years before, Harriet Martineau had built a house in Westmorland not far from Wordsworth's Rydal Mount (Martineau, *Autobiography,* I, 503).

[2] *Eastern Life, Past and Present.* Its excursions into the dangerous field of comparative religion seemed to Murray, or so the story went, "a conspiracy against Moses" (Martineau, *Autobiography,* I, 552).

2 Fenny St. Manchester

2 March. Thursday

Dear Friend,

I hope to set forward today for London, & arrive there some time tonight. I am to go first to Chapman's house, where I shall lodge for a time. If it is too noisy, I shall move westward. But I hope you are to be at home tomorrow, for if I prosper, I shall come & beg a dinner with you,—it is not at 5 o'clock? I am sorry you have no better news to tell me of your health—your own & your wife's. Tell her I shall surely report you to Alcott, who will have his revenge. Thanks that you keep the door so wide open for me still. I shall always come in.

Ever yours, R. W. E.

Monday P M

19 June

Dear Carlyle,

Mrs Crowe of Edinburgh,[1] an excellent lady known to you & to many good people, wishes me to go to you with her. I tell her that I believe you relax the reins of labour as early as one hour after noon: and I propose 1 o'clock on Thursday for the invasion. If you are otherwise engaged, you must send me word. Otherwise, we shall come.

It was sad to hear no good news last evening from Jane Carlyle. I heartily hope, the night brought sleep, & the morning better health to her. Yours always, R. W. Emerson

Chelsea, 20 June, 1848—

Dear Emerson,

We shall be very glad to become acquainted with Mrs Crowe, of whom already by report we know many favourable things. Brown [1]

---

[1] Catherine Stevens Crowe, at whose house Emerson had met De Quincy (*Let RWE*, IV, 19).

---

[1] Samuel Brown, physician and chemist, with whom Emerson had stayed during his Edinburgh lectures (Rusk, *Life*, p. 338).

(of Portobello, Edinburgh) had given us intimation of her kind purposes towards Chelsea; and now on Thursday you (please the Pigs) [2] shall see the adventure achieved.—Two o'clock, not one, is the hour when labour ceases here,—if, alas, there be any "labour" so much as got begun; which latter is often enough the sad case. But at either hour we shall be ready for you.

I hope you penetrated the Armida Palace, and did your devoir to the sublime Duchess and her luncheon yesterday! [3] I cannot without a certain internal amusement (foreign enough to my present humour) represent to myself such a conjunction of opposite stars! But you carry a new image off with you, and are a gainer, you. *Allons.*

My Papers here are in a state of distraction, state of despair! I see not what is to become of them and me.

Yours ever truly   T. Carlyle

N. B. The Letter-Cover with a stamp *worked* into it, is already a *stamped cover;* and needs no new stamp, except the weight exceed half an ounce! How many additional pence, flung away in this manner, may you have given the Queen since you came among us!

———————————

My Wife arose without headache on Monday morning; but feels still a good deal beaten;—has not had "such a headache" for several years.

Chelsea, Friday [1] [June 23, 1848]

Dear Emerson,—I forgot to say, last night, that you are to *dine with us on Sunday;* that after our call on the Lady Harriet, we will take a stroll thro' the Park, look at the Sunday population, and find ourselves here at 5 o'clock for the above important object. Pray remember, therefore, and no excuse!

In haste Yours ever truly   T. Carlyle

[2] "If circumstances permit: a trivial rustic substitute for *please God*" (*The Century Dictionary*).

[3] Emerson had luncheon with the Duchess of Sutherland at Stafford House, "the best house in the kingdom," as he told Elizabeth Hoar, "the Queen's not excepted" (*Let RWE,* IV, 89). Armida is a character in *Jerusalem Delivered* who lures knights into a garden of indolence.

[1] See E.6.19.48. The date of this letter is Norton's conjecture; it seems likely enough, but I am unable to find any confirmation for it.

Monday Night [1] [July 3, 1848]

My dear Carlyle,

I did not succeed in getting to your house yesterday nor today, it
is but too evident: tomorrow I go to Windsor & Eton, with Mr
Kenyon; [2] &, Wednesday Morning, I mean to interrupt your works a
few moments with taking advice for Friday. and am till then, & always, Yours affectionately,   R.W.E.

Concord, October 2, 1848. [1]

My dear Carlyle,

Tis high time, no doubt, long since that you heard from me, and
if there were good news in America for you, you would be sure to
hear; All goes at heavy trot with us. In all the wide continent, I do
not hear of another village which holds as many readers as mine. But
fear not that I begin to fatigue you with our village, tho friends you
reck not of were eager to have tidings of you, & indeed had already
some strange ones which I shall not amuse you with. But I fell again
quickly into my obscure habits more fit for me than the fine things
I had seen. I made my best endeavour to to praise the rich Country
I had seen and its excellent energetic polished people. And it is very
easy for me to do so. England is the country of success, & success has a
great charm for me, more than for those I talk with at home. But

[1] "For the date, July 3 was the Monday preceding the visit to Windsor and Eton"
(Rusk's note).

[2] Probably John Kenyon, the poet and philanthropist. A year later Emerson included "John Kenyon, Esq." in a list of persons who were to receive copies of
Representative Men (*Journals*, VIII, 70).

[1] Evidently a fragment of a rough draft. The letter seems to have been mainly
concerned with Dr. John Carlyle's prose translation of *The Inferno* which Emerson
had brought home with him, complete except for two sheets, in August, and for
which he was attempting to find an American publisher. On October 4 he wrote
to his brother William, who had been negotiating with the Harpers: "Thanks,
hearty thanks for your persistent attention to the Dante. I wrote the Carlyles
yesterday & begged the Doctor to forward the remaining sheets immediately" (*Let
RWE*, IV, 116). Carlyle sent the letter to John on October 18: ". . . a word from
Emerson practically applying to you has arrived. . . . Emerson's report of Yankee
negociations need not distress you at all: perhaps it is but the *shortest* way, this
offer he has got, towards a result which in any case would have been essentially
the same. Get your Preface done; and be thankful that you do not need ever to
mind about 'sales' and remunerations either there or here" (NLS, MS 524).

they were obstinate to know if the English were superior to their possessions, and if the old religion warmed their hearts, & lifted a little the mountain of wealth. So I enumerated the list of brilliant persons I had seen, and the   But the question returned, Did you find kings & priests? Did you find sanctities & beauties that took away your memory, & sent you home a changed man, with new aims & with a discontent of your old pastures.

Chelsea, 6 Decr, 1848—

Dear Emerson,

We received your Letter duly, some time ago, with many welcomes; and have, as you see, been too remiss in answering it. Not from forgetfulness, if you will take my word; no, but from many causes, too complicated to articulate, and justly producing an indisposition to put pen to paper at all! Never was I more silent than in these very months; and with reason too, for the world at large, and my own share of it in small, are both getting more and more *un*speakable with any convenience! In health we of this household are about as well as usual;—and look across to the woods of Concord with more light than we had, realising for ourselves a most mild and friendly picture there. Perhaps it is quite as well that you are left alone of foreign interference, even of a Letter from Chelsea, till you get your huge bale of English reminiscences assorted a little. Nobody except me seems to have heard from you; at least the rest, in these parts, all plead destitution when I ask for news. What you saw and suffered and enjoyed here, will, if you had once got it properly warehoused, be new wealth to you for many years. Of one impression we fail not here: admiration of your pacific virtues, of gentle and noble tolerance, often *sorely* tried in this place! Forgive me my ferocities; you do not quite know what I suffer in these latitudes, or perhaps it would be even easier for you. Peace for me, in a Mother of Dead Dogs like this, there is not, was not, will not be,—till the battle itself end; which however is a sure outlook, and daily growing a nearer one.

You are to be burdened with a foolish bit of business for me again; do not grudge it, but do it since it has come in course! Here is the matter. About three years ago (I think in the end of 1845), Mr Hart, of the Bookselling Firm Carey & Hart in Philadelphia, sent me, as

you may remember, a Draft for £50 payable by some house in Liverpool; it was in return for liberty to print (without grumble from me)
the Book of Essays; and tho' an old *silent* friend in Philadelphia [1]
negociated the immediate details, you too I believe had a hand in the
affair, and were privy to it all along. Well, this Draft arrived; came
to me while I was at Alverstoke in Hampshire with Mr Baring (Hon.
W. Bingham Baring, now Lord Ashburton) probably about this very
season of the year: whether the Liverpool House had *accepted* I cannot now say; but their acceptance not being doubtful, the Paper
(payable probably in 60 days or so) was of course perfectly equivalent
to the sum marked on it; and accordingly Mr Baring, when I spoke
of negociating it, and inquired his advice, How? volunteered, as *my*
only Banker is a Scotch one at Dumfries, to give me at once in return
for it a Draft on *his* Bankers (the Drummonds, of Charing Cross here),
by whom the Paper would be duly managed without trouble to anybody, and the £50 at once paid me. And so undoubtedly the £50
was at once paid *me,* and I got it and spent it, and returned some
acknowledgement to Mr Hart for it; and had entirely forgotten it,
when about a year ago Mr Baring, surveying his Banker's account-
book, told me he could not find that item in it; was by me invited to
search farther, has searched farther, set his Bankers to search,—and
now, the other day, ascertains finally that there is no such payment
or transaction recorded in his favour,—and that, in brief, he must
have *lost* the Carey-and-Hart Draft for £50 payable by some Liverpool
House, and that it was never presented for payment, and consequently never paid! This he told me the other night; and I of course,
heartily vexed at this act of carelessness, engaged to inquire. The
things to be now done therefore are two: first to ascertain from Mr
Hart what the exact particulars of the Draft were (this will be tolerably easy, I suppose); and then secondly whether, supposing the money
were never demanded, it is now in the hands of the Philadelphia or
of the Liverpool House, or in whose hands,—in short, what is possible
for limited but honest human nature, pursuing correctness under impediments, still to do in the matter! Ascertain me these two things,
this one last thing, like a good fellow;—and I will let you lie quiet
for a very long time to come!—

Nay there is another practical question,—but it is from the female
side of the house to the female side,—and in fact concerns Indian

[1] W. H. Furness.

meal, upon which Mrs Emerson, or you, or the Miller of Concord (if he have any tincture of philosophy) are now to instruct us! The fact is, potatoes having vanished here, we are again, with motives large and small, trying to learn the use of Indian meal; and indeed do eat it daily to meat at dinner, tho' hitherto with considerable despair. Question *first* therefore: Is there by nature a *bitter* final taste, which makes the throat smart, and disheartens much the apprentice in Indian meal;—or is it accidental, and to be avoided? We surely anticipate the latter answer; but do not yet see how. At first we were taught the meal, all ground on your side of the water, had got fusty, *raw;* an effect we are well used to in oaten and other meals: but, last year, we had a bushel of it ground *here,* and the bitter taste was there as before (with the addition of much dirt and sand, our mill-stones I suppose being too soft);—whereupon we incline to surmise that there is perhaps, as in the case of oats, some pellicle or hull that ought to be *rejected* in making the meal? Pray ask some philosophic Miller if Mrs E. or you do not know;—and as a corollary this *second* question: what is the essential difference between *white* (or brown-grey-white) Indian Meal, and *yellow* (the kind we now have; beautiful as new guineas, but with an ineffaceable tastekin of *soot* in it)?—And question 3ᵈ, which includes all: How to cook *mush* rightly, at least without bitter? *Long*-continued boiling seems to help the bitterness, but does not cure it. Let some oracle speak! I tell all people, our staff of life is the Mississippi Valley henceforth;—and one of the truest benefactors were an American Minerva who could teach us to cook this meal; which our people, at present (I included) are unanimous in finding nigh uneatable, and loudly exclaimable against! Elihu Burritt had a string of recipes that went thro' all newspapers three years ago; but never sang there oracle of longer ears than that,—totally destitute of practical significance to any creature here!

And now enough of questioning. Alas, alas, I have a quite other batch of sad and saddest considerations,—on which I must not so much as enter at present! Death has been very busy in this little circle of ours, within the last few days. You remember Charles Buller, to whom I brought you over, that night, at the Barings' in Stanhope Street?[2] He died this day week, almost quite unexpectedly; a sore

[2] In a *Journal* entry for March (VII, 411) Emerson had written: "At Lady Harriet Baring's dinner, Carlyle and Milnes introduced me to Charles Buller, 'reckoned,' they said aloud, 'the cleverest man in England'—'until,' added Milnes—'until he

loss to all that knew him personally, and his gladdening sunny presence in many circles here; a sore loss to the political people too, for he was far the cleverest of all Whig men, and indeed the only genial soul one can remember in that department of things. We buried him yesterday; and now see what new thing has come. Lord Ashburton, who had left his mother well in Hampshire ten hours before, is summoned from poor Buller's funeral by telegraph; hurries back, finds his mother, whom he loved much, already dead! She was a Miss Bingham, I think, from Pennsylvania, perhaps from Philadelphia itself. You saw her; but the first sight by no means told one all or the best worth that was in that good Lady. We are quite bewildered by our own regrets and by the far painfuller sorrow of those closely related to these sudden sorrows. Of which let me be silent for the present;—and indeed of all things else, for *speech,* inadequate mockery of one's poor meaning, is quite a burden to me just now!

Neuberg comes hither sometimes; a welcome, wise kind of man.[3] Poor little Espinasse still toils cheerily at the oar; and various friends of yours are about us. Brother John did send thro' Chapman all the *Dante,*[4] which we calculate you have received long ago: he is now come to Town; doing a Preface &c, which also will be sent to you, and is just about publishing.—Helps, who has been alarmingly ill, and touring on the Rhine, since we were his guests, writes to me yesterday from Hampshire about sending you a new Book of his.[5] I instructed him How.

---

meddled with affairs.' For Buller was now Poor-Laws Commissioner, and had really postponed hitherto to make good the extraordinary expectation which his speeches in Parliament had created."

[3] Joseph Neuberg, a German businessman of Nottingham, had written Carlyle a letter of admiration in 1839 and received a graceful reply (NLS, MS 551). In 1848, as president of the Literary Department of the Nottingham Mechanics' Institute, he was Emerson's host in that city; Emerson, learning of his esteem for Carlyle, arranged a meeting between the two men ("Carlyle and Neuberg," *Macmillan's Magazine,* L [August, 1884], 280). On November 22, 1848, Neuberg sent Carlyle some genealogical data about Goethe entitled "Goethe's Grand-father *was* a tailor" (NLS, MS 551).

[4] When John Carlyle returned Emerson's letter of October 2, he wrote: "Please tell him when you write that I forwarded the last four sheets to John Chapman, with whom he lodged; and he engaged to send them in a package to his correspondents the Munroes, booksellers of Boston, as Emerson himself directed me to do. I have written to Chapman, and told him how they have been delayed; & I will punctually send the Preface &c as soon as they are printed. The four sheets were sent to Chapman in the first week of August" (NLS, MS 1775B).

[5] Arthur Helps, with whom Emerson and Carlyle had spent a rainy Sunday during

Adieu, dear Emerson; do not forget us, or forget to think as kindly as you can of us, while we continue in this world together!

Yours ever affectionately   T. Carlyle

Concord, Mass.
12 December 1848

Dr John Carlyle,
My dear Sir,

I had a letter from Mr Chapman, brought me lately by Dr Fisher, in which he expresses his fears that the remaining sheets of Dante did not reach me. They all did come to me, I think—very soon after I wrote to your brother a message for you.[1] They came, to my great satisfaction, wanting nothing but a title page, which did not come. I sent them immediately to Messrs Harper & Brothers, at New York; and soon after heard that all was nearly printed, but that they regretted that the title had not come; but they would supply themselves with that, from the first London Copy that came; which, too, they immediately expected. I have been weekly & daily looking for the appearance of the book, since; but it does not yet arrive.—It did not—I am sorry for it—occur to me, until after I had read Mr Chapman's letter, that I ought, immediately on receiving your last sheets, to have acknowledged them.—I have had no pleasure in my agency, since I found it had fallen on such evil times that a book so valuable was to be held so cheap. Did I tell you, you are to have nothing but American fame & ten copies? Will you send me instructions what to do with these ten?[2] Since the Election,[3] our people are in better spirits, and trade and, at last, book-trade will revive, it is believed.

---

their July trip to Stonehenge (Emerson, *Works*, V, 286), had just published the first volume of *Conquerors of the New World and Their Bondsmen*. On December 3, 1848, he wrote to Carlyle: "I should like to send Emerson a copy of 'the conquerors of the New World.' Not that anybody who reads the foreign intelligence in the *Times* (& I suppose they have a Times or something like it at Concord) can wish to be bothered with old historical affairs; but a gift is a gift. . . . Well, the upshot is, just tell me how to send anything to Emerson" (MS owned by the Victoria and Albert Museum).

[1] E.10.2.48.

[2] "John Carlyle wrote, Dec. 29, 1848, that he was content with the arrangement and asked that Emerson send the book to Parker, Longfellow, and Thomas Carlyle and dispose of the remaining copies as he thought best" (Rusk's note).

[3] "Of Taylor and Fillmore" (Rusk's note).

I doubt not, if we had had a few months to wait, we might have made some bargain for you.

I am staying diligently at home, putting my little farm & homestead in better order, but with nothing forward i[n] my library that I dare mention. I have read up & down in English history & topography, a little, lately, to verify & fix such memoranda as I brought home from my journeying last winter. With kindest regards to the household in Cheyne Row,

Your affectionate servant,   R. W. Emerson.

1849

Boston, 23 January 1849

My dear Carlyle,

Here in Boston for the day, though in no fit place for writing, you shall have, since the steamer goes tomorrow, a hasty answer to at least one of your questions. Furness writes me, under date [Philadelphia, 15 January.]—"I called on Mr Hart, this morning, & he turned to a copy of a letter addressed by him to you, under date Oct. 27, 1845, authorising Mr Carlyle to draw upon Brown, Shipley, & Co, Liverpool, for £50. He then showed me, in his account with Brown Shipley & Co., T. Carlyle's draft for £50, payable in April 1846, charged to Carey & Hart, as accepted, Dec. 2, 1845.[1] So the state of the case may be readily ascertained by asking the Liverpool house about it. They can tell, I suppose, to whom they paid the money." So far Furness; who hopes the best issue. Pray let me hear the result, and let it be, that the kindly Lord Ashburton recovers his money. You tell me heavy news of your friends, and of those who were friendly to me, for your sake. And I have found farther particulars concerning them in the newspapers. Buller I have known by name ever since he was in America with Lord Durham, and I well remember his face & figure at Mr Baring's. Even England cannot spare an accomplished man.

Since I had your letter, &, I believe, by the same steamer, your brother's Dante, complete within & without, has come to me, most welcome. I heartily thank him. Tis a most workmanlike book bearing every mark of honest value. I thank him for myself, & I thank him, in advance, for our people, who are sure to learn their debt to him, in the coming months & years. I sent the book, after short examination, the same day, to N. York, to the Harpers, lest their edition should come out without Prolegomena.[2] But they answered, the next day, that, they had already received directly the same matter:—yet have

---

[1] Furness's letter, as printed in *Records of a Lifelong Friendship*, gives the year as 1846. The brackets enclosing place and date are Emerson's.

[2] John Carlyle had written an extensive scholarly introduction to his translation.

not up to this time returned my book.—For the Indian corn,—I have been to see Dr Charles T. Jackson (my wife's brother, & our best chemist inventor of etherization,[3]) who tells me that the reason your meal is bitter, is, that all the corn sent to you from us is kiln dried here, usually at a heat of 300 degrees, which effectually kills the starch or diastase, (?), which would otherwise become sugar. The drying is thought necessary to prevent the corn from becoming musty in the contingency of a long voyage. He says, if it should go in the steamer, it would arrive sound without previous drying. I think, I will try that experiment shortly on a box or a barrel of our Concord maize; as Lidian Emerson confidently engages to send you accurate recipes for johnny-cake, mush, & hominy.

Why did you not send me word of Clough's hexameter poem, which I have now received & read with much joy.[4] But no, you will never forgive him his metres. He is a stout solid reliable man & friend,—I knew well; but this fine poem has taken me by surprise. I cannot find that your journals have yet discovered its existence. With kindest remembrances to Jane Carlyle, & new thanks to John Carlyle, your friend,   R. W. Emerson

Chelsea, 17 April, 1849—

Dear Emerson,

This is brought to you by Mr Humphrey Mildmay, a Nephew of Lord Ashburton's, a descendant and synonym of august old Puritan Regicides,[1]—and in fine a very amiable, ingenuous and ingenious young Gentleman;—who, in the interval between the university and Active Life, has come across, with your friend Mr Bates,[2] to look at America for a month or two. Pray give him welcome; encourage him in this good work; that others like him, more and more numerously, may run across and get acquainted with their big Cousins beyond seas,—which will be a useful process, I believe, both for the Cousins

[3] Dr. Jackson's claim to this honor was not undisputed.

[4] On his first reading of Clough's *Bothie of Tober-na-vuolich,* Emerson wrote in his journal: "And now Tennyson must look to his laurels"; on his second reading he wrote: " 'Tis a kind of new and better Carlyle" (*Journals,* VII, 560; VIII, 16).

[1] Sir Henry Mildmay was one of the judges of Charles I.

[2] Probably Joshua Bates, American-born banker, a partner in Baring Brothers and Company.

and them.—We are deep in the study of Indian meal here; and full of thoughts about you. Yours ever truly T. Carlyle

Chelsea, 19 April, 1849—
My dear Emerson,

Today is American Postday; and by every rule and law,—even if all laws but those of Cocker [1] were abolished from this universe,—a word from me is due to you! Twice I have heard since I spoke last: prompt response about the Philadelphia Bill; exact performance of your voluntary promise,—Indian Corn itself is now here for a week past.

Lord Ashburton has recovered his money; so he tells me, on inquiry, the other day; many thanks to you and the Pennsilvanian friends;—Furness in particular has had his hands full with that business; of which, let us hope, he has now heard the last. Still more interesting is the barrel of genuine Corn ears, or Indian Cobs of edible grain, from the Barn of Emerson himself! It came all safe and right, according to your charitable program; without cost or trouble to us of any kind; not without curious interest and satisfaction! The recipes contained in the precedent Letter, duly weighed by the competent jury of housewives (at least by my own Wife and Lady Ashburton) were judged to be of decided promise, reasonable-looking every one of them; and now that the stuff itself is come, I am happy to assure you that it forms a new epoch for us all in the Maize department: we find the grain *sweet,* among the sweetest, with a touch even of the taste of *nuts* in it, and profess with contrition that properly we have never tasted Indian Corn before. Millers, of due faculty (with Millstones of *iron*), being scarce in the Cockney region, and even cooks liable to err, the Ashburtons have on their resources undertaken the brunt of the problem: one of their own Surrey or Hampshire Millers is to grind the stuff, and their own cook, a Frenchman commander of a whole squadron, is to undertake the dressing according to the rules. Yesterday the Barrel went off to their country place in Surrey,—a small Bag of select ears being retained here, for our own private experimenting; and so by and by we shall see what comes of it.—I on my side have already drawn up a fit proclamation of the excellencies of

[1] Edward Cocker was a seventeenth-century arithmetician.

this invaluable corn, and admonition as to the benighted state of English eaters in regard to it;—to appear in Fraser's Magazine, or I know not where, very soon.[2] It is really a small contribution towards World-History, this small act of yours and ours: there is no doubt to me, now that I taste the real grain, but all Europe will henceforth have to relie more and more upon your western vallies and this article. How beautiful to think of lean tough Yankee settlers, tough as gutta-percha, with most *occult* unsubduable fire in their belly, steering over the Western Mountains, to annihilate the jungle, and bring bacon and corn out of it for the Posterity of Adam! The Pigs, in about a year, eat up all the rattle-snakes for miles round: a most judicious function on the part of the Pigs. Behind the Pigs comes Jonathan with his all-conquering ploughshare,—glory to him too! Oh, if we were not a set of cant-ridden blockheads, there is no *Myth* of Athens or Herakles equal to this *fact;*—which I suppose *will* find its real "Poets" some day or other; when once the Greek, Semitic and multifarious other Cobwebs are swept away a little! Well, we must wait.—For the rest, if this skilful Naturalist and you will make any more experiments on Indian Corn for us, might I not ask that you would try for a method of preserving *the meal* in a sound state for us? Oat-meal, which would spoil directly too, is preserved all year by kiln-drying the grain before it is ground,—parching it till it is almost *brown,* sometimes: the Scotch Highlanders, by intense parching, can keep their oatmeal good for a series of years. No miller here at present is likely to produce such beautiful meal as some of the American speci-mens I have seen:—if possible, we must learn to get the grain over in the shape of proper durable *meal.* At all events, let your Friend charitably make some inquiry into the process of millerage, the pos-sibilities of it for meeting our case;—and send us the result some day, on a separate bit of paper. With which let us end, for the present.

Alas, I have yet written nothing; am yet a long way off writing, I fear! Not for want of matter, perhaps, but for redundance of it; I feel as if I had the whole world to write yet, with the day fast bend-ing downwards on me, and didn't know where to begin,—in what manner to address the deep-sunk populations of the Theban Land.[3]

---

[2] "Indian Meal" appeared in *Fraser's Magazine* for May, 1849 (XXXIX, 561–63).

[3] Possibly a reference to the plague with which the Thebans are afflicted at the opening of *Oedipus Rex.*

Any way my Life is very *grim,* on these terms, and is like to be; God only knows what farther quantity of braying in the mortar this foolish clay of mine may yet need!—They are printing a 3ᵈ edition of Cromwell; that bothered me for some weeks, but now I am over with that, and the Printer wholly has it: a sorrowful, not now or ever a joyful thing to me, that. The *stupor* of my fellow blockheads, for centuries back, presses too heavy upon that,—as upon many things, O Heavens! People are about setting up some *Statue of Cromwell,* at St. Ives, or elsewhere: the King-Hudson Statue is never yet set up; and the King himself (as you may have heard) has been *discovered* swindling.[4] I advise all men *not* to erect a Statue for Cromwell just now.—Macaulay's History is also out, running thro' the fourth edition: did I tell you last time that I had read it,—with wonder and amazement?[5] Finally it seems likely Lord John Russell will shortly walk out (forever, it is hoped), and Sir R. Peel come in; to make what effort is in him towards delivering us from the *pedant* method of treating Ireland. The *beginning,* as I think, of salvation (if he can prosper a little) to England, and to all Europe as well. For they will all have to learn that man does need government, and that an able-bodied starving beggar is and remains (whatever Exeter Hall may say to it) a *Slave* destitute of a *Master;* of which facts England, and convulsed Europe, are fallen profoundly ignorant in these bad ages, and will plunge ever deeper till they rediscover the same. Alas, alas, the Future for us is not to be made of *butter,* as the Platforms prophesy; I think it will be harder than steel for some ages! No noble age was ever a soft one, nor ever will or can be.— —Your beautiful curious little discourse (report of a discourse) about the English was sent me by Neuberg; I thought it, in my private heart, one of the best words (for *hidden* genius lodged in it) I had ever heard; so sent it to the *Examiner,* from which it went to the *Times* and all the other Papers: an excellent sly little word.[6]—Clough has gone to Italy; I

---

[4] George Hudson, the "Railway King," a capitalist who until his downfall in 1849 was a popular hero. Carlyle used his story as an anti-democratic *exemplum* in "Hudson's Statue," one of the *Latter-Day Pamphlets,* published July 1, 1850.

[5] The first two volumes of Macaulay's *History of England from the Accession of James II* were published in 1849. Carlyle thought them "Flat: without a ray of genius" (Wilson, *Carlyle at his Zenith,* p. 83).

[6] In *The Examiner* for March 10, 1849, there appeared a lengthy account, reprinted from the New-York *Tribune,* of Emerson's December 27 lecture before the

have seen him twice,—could not manage his *hexameters,* tho' I like
the man himself, and hope much of him. "Infidelity" has broken out
in Oxford itself,—immense emotion in certain quarters in consequence, virulent outcries about a certain "Sterling Club," altogether
a *secular* society! [7] Adieu, dear Emerson; I had much more to say, but
there is no room. O forgive me, forgive me all trespasses,—and love
me what you can!   Yours ever   T. Carlyle

A nephew of Lord Ashburton's, a young Mr Mildmay (very good
young gent[n]), coming over with Bates by this same steamer, will deliver you a Note from me,—smile upon him.

Scotsbrig, Ecclefechan, N. B.

13 Aug[t], 1849—

Dear Emerson,—By all laws of human computation, I owe you a
Letter, and have owed, any time these seven weeks: let me now pay
a little, and explain. Your *second* Barrel of Indian Corn arrived also
perfectly fresh, and of admirable taste and quality; the very bag of
new-ground meal was perfect; and the "popped corn" d[o], when it
came to be discovered: with the whole of which admirable materials
such order was taken as promised to secure "the greatest happiness
to the greatest number"; [1] and due silent thanks were rendered to
the beneficence of the unwearied Sender:—but all this, you shall
observe, had to be done in the thick of a universal packing and
household bustle; I just on the wing for a "Tour in Ireland," my
Wife too contemplating a run to Scotland shortly after, there to meet
me on my return. All this was seven good weeks ago: I hope some-

---

Boston Mercantile Library Association; four days later it appeared in *The Times*
under the title "An American's Opinion of England." The lecture seems to have
been an early version of *English Traits,* with comments on the English land, climate, agriculture, industry, health, pluck, personal freedom, eccentricity, insularity,
arrogance, and materialism.

[7] For the "Sterling Club," a dinner and discussion group formed in 1838, see
Carlyle's *Life of John Sterling,* pt. II, ch. vi. Eleven years after its formation certain
clerical members of the group were attacked by religious periodicals for association
with unbelievers (Maurice, *The Life of Frederick Denison Maurice,* I, 516).

[1] Cf. Hutcheson, *An Inquiry into . . . Beauty and Virtue,* p. 177. Carlyle owned
a copy of this early essay in utilitarianism (*Illustrated Memorial Volume of the
Carlyle's House Purchase Fund Committee with Catalogue . . . ,* p. 76).

where in my Irish wayfaring to fling you off a Letter; but alas I reckoned there quite without my host (strict "host," called *Time*), finding nowhere half a minute left to me; and so now, having got home to my Mother, not to see my Wife yet for some days, it is my *earliest* leisure, after all, that I employ in this purpose. I have been terribly knocked about too,—jolted in Irish cars, bothered almost to madness with Irish balderdash, above all kept on dreadfully short allowance of sleep;—so that now first, when fairly down to rest, all aches and bruises begin to be fairly sensible; and my clearest feeling at this present is the uncomfortable one, that "I am not Caliban but a Cramp": [2] terribly cramped indeed, if I could tell you everything!

What the other results of this Irish Tour are to be for me I cannot yet in the least specify. For one thing, I seem to be farther from *speech* on any subject than ever: such masses of chaotic ruin everywhere fronted me, the general fruit of long-continued universal falsity and folly; and such mountains of delusion yet possessing all hearts and tongues: I could do little that was not even *noxious,* except *admire* in silence the general "Bankruptcy of Imposture" as one there finds and sees it come to pass, and think with infinite sorrow of the tribulations, futile wrestlings, tumults and disasters which yet await that unfortunate section of Adam's Posterity before any real improvement can take place among them. Alas, alas! The Gospels of Political Economy, of *Laissez-faire,* No-Government, Paradise to all Comers, and so many fatal Gospels,—generally, one may say, all the Gospels of this blessed "New Era,"—will first have to be tried, and found wanting. With a quantity of written and uttered Nonsense, and of suffered and inflicted Misery, which one sinks fairly dumb to estimate! A kind of comfort it is, however, to see that "Imposture" *has* fallen openly "bankrupt," here as everywhere else in our old world; that no dexterity of human tinkering, with all the Parliamentary Eloquence and Elective Franchises in nature, will ever set *it* on its feet again, to go many yards more; but that *its* goings and comings in this Earth have as good as ceased forever and ever! God is great; all Lies do now, as from the first, travel incessantly towards Chaos, and there at length lodge! In some parts of Ireland (the Western "insolvent unions," [3]

---

[2] "I am not Stephano, but a cramp": *Tempest,* act V, scene i, line 286.

[3] For purposes of Poor Law administration, two or more parishes were combined to form a "union."

some 27 of them in all), within a trifle of *one half* of the whole population are on Poor-Law rations (furnished by the British Government,
£1100 a week furnished here, £1300 there, £800 there); the houses
stand roofless, the lands unstocked, uncultivated, the landlords hidden
from bailifs, living sometimes "on the hares of their domain" [4]: such
a state of things was never witnessed under this sky before; and, one
would humbly expect, cannot last long!—What is to be done? asks
every one; incapable of *hearing* any answer, were there even one
ready for imparting to him. *"Blacklead* these 2 million idle beggars,"
I sometimes advised, "and sell them in Brazil as Niggers,—perhaps
Parliament, on sweet constraint, will allow you to advance them to be
Niggers!"— —In fact, the Emancipation Societies should send over a
deputation or two to look at these immortal Irish "Free men," the
ne-plus-ultra of their class: it would perhaps moderate the windpipe
of much eloquence one hears on that subject! Is not this the most illustrious of all "Ages"; making progress of the species at a grand rate
indeed? Peace be with it.

Waiting for me here, there was a letter from Miss Fuller in Rome,
written about a month ago; a dignified and interesting Letter; requesting help with Booksellers for some "History of the late Italian
revolution" she is about writing; and elegiacally recognising the worth
of Mazzini and other cognate persons and things. I instantly set about
doing what little seemed in my power towards this object,[5]—with what

---

[4] A phrase which Carlyle had heard in Ireland. In his *Reminiscences of my Irish
Journey in 1849*, p. 206, it appears as "living on the rabbits of their own park."

[5] On August 9 Carlyle sent the letter to Chapman with the following explanation
and recommendation: "Miss Margaret Fuller is an American Lady, of ripe years,
perhaps 40 and odd; deformed and lean in person, but full of ardent soul to the
finger-ends; enthusiastic, resolute, eloquent; writes really strikingly and well, with
a constant noble *fire* pervading all she says; style clear, brief and vivid; meaning
high and true, tho' occasionally somewhat airy and vague. The Books that I have
read of hers (which can be had at your Namesake's, I suppose) give me somewhat
the notion of a *spiritual Aurora Borealis.* She is a great ally of Emerson's, but
deeper in German and Foreign things than he; and indeed a much more vehement
and self-reliant, not to say dogmatic, autocratic and practically positive character.
She adores Mazzini; has lived in Rome, I think, these three years or more. Her
Book, I have little doubt, will be a striking thing in its way; and, as she will probably be *brief* withal, I do not consider it quite unlikely that you also might find
your account in it. But on that latter point, let me abstain from all shadow of
judgement. I give *you* the truest account I can of the Lady and her talent; and
bid you judge for yourself. She is, so far as I may note, *considerably* a higher-
minded and cleverer woman than any of the Lady Lions yet on your Books; and
if you and she could make any arrangement useful to both parties, I should be very

result is yet hidden,—and have written to the heroic Margaret: "more power to her elbow!" as the Irish say. She has a beautiful enthusiasm; and is perhaps in the right stage of insight for doing that piece of business well.—Of other persons or interests I will say nothing till a calmer opportunity; which surely cannot be very long in coming.

In four days I am to rejoin my wife; after which some bits of visits are to be paid in this North Country; necessary most of them, not likely to be profitable almost any. In perhaps a month I expect to be back in Chelsea; whither direct a word if you are still beneficent enough to think of such a Castaway!

Yours ever   T. Carlyle

I got Thoreau's Book; and meant well to read it, but have not yet succeeded, tho' it went with me thro' all Ireland: tell him so, please. Too Jean-Paulish, I found it hitherto.[6]

Concord, 28 Aug. 1849 [1]

My dear Doctor Carlyle,

I dare not count the steamers that have sailed since I proposed to send you the remainder of the broken message, of which Clarke carried a part.[2] The Harpers,—I think, directly after his departure,—sent me twelve more copies of Dante, which I made haste to present to good people here in your name, following in the distribution a mixed principle, for I gave to some because they were good Scholars, and to some because they were good talkers. They have gone for the most part to the best places, good seed to good soil, and I look for the best fruit.[3]

---

glad" (MS owned by the Pierpont Morgan Library). This history of a revolution in which the author had taken an active part was lost, in manuscript, in the ship-wreck of July, 1850, in which Margaret Fuller perished.

[6] A Week on the Concord and Merrimack Rivers has surely no stylistic similarity to the works of Richter; perhaps Carlyle meant that it was loose in structure. On September 18, 1848, he wrote to his wife: "I have read Thoreau's Book, which went with me in vain all over Ireland; a very fantastic yet not quite worthless Book" (NLS, MS 613).

[1] The MS of this letter to John Carlyle is owned by the Houghton Library.

[2] Probably James Freeman Clarke, who sailed from Boston for Liverpool on July 6 (Clarke: Autobiography, Diary, and Correspondence, p. 171).

[3] Emerson sent copies to Longfellow, Parker, S. G. Ward, J. E. Cabot, Mrs. S. A. Ripley, George P. Bradford, Thoreau, W. E. Channing, Alcott, J. S. Dwight, William Emerson, G. W. Hillard, E. P. Whipple, and Sarah Clarke (Typescript Journals, TU, p. 128). Longfellow thought the book "very good; as good as a prose translation can be" (Let RWE, IV, 158n).

I have the private report of a few witnesses in the most cordial acknowledgment of the merit of the translation, and honouring equally the capacity and the probity of the translator. For me, Mr. Bohn the bookseller has filled my head lately as a great benefactor of mankind, who, not to mention many other things, gives me Plato, in good English, cheap.[4] I cannot praise him enough. When I now read your Dante, slowly, at many sittings, from first to last, I said Heaven is wider than Mr. Bohn's bookshop, and here is another solid benefit to all who speak the English tongue. This good is done so privately and quietly, and yet it will prove the introduction of Dante to whole nations of men. I declare to you I am very well pleased with England in the 19th Century, giving such gifts. Come now, brave man, make the second, and the third step, in this labour, and, beside the noblest service done to English-speaking men, you enhance indefinitely the value of this first book, which gains so much in ceasing to be a fragment.[5] I doubt not, you will have your share of early readers, but the best will come slowly, and one at a time, and you will only hear from them accidentally. And, as you are not likely to meet as good a Dantean as yourself, you cannot choose, but must be magnanimous, and do the work on your own assurance that it is worth doing.

I am sorry that after two successive attempts to forward your brother's copy to Brantford, West Canada,[6] it has come back to me; the Expresses reporting that they have no Agencies in that direction. It is very easy to send to Canada East. I shall try another course before I give it up. With love to T. C. and J. C., and all benedictions

Yours   R. W. Emerson.

[4] Bohn's "Classical Library" had begun to appear in 1848.

[5] Although John Carlyle fully intended to translate the *Purgatorio* and the *Paradiso,* and worked at them for many years, he never completed his task.

[6] Alexander Carlyle, a farmer, had emigrated in 1843 (Carlyle, *New Letters,* I, 295).

1850

Chelsea, 19 July, 1850—

My dear Emerson, my Friend, my Friend,—You behold before you a remorseful man! It is well nigh a year now since I despatched some hurried rag of paper to you out of Scotland, indicating doubtless that I would speedily follow it with a longer Letter; and here, when grey Autum is at hand again, I have still written nothing to you, heard nothing from you! It is miserable to think of:—and yet it is a fact, and there is no denying of it; and so we must let it ly. If it please Heaven, the like shall not occur again. "Ohone Arooh!" as the Irish taught me to say, "Ohone Arooh!"

The fact is, my life has been black with care and toil,—labour above board and far worse labour below;—I have hardly had a heavier year (overloaded too with a kind of "health" which may be called frightful): to "burn my own smoke" in some measure, has really been all I was up to; and except on sheer immediate compulsion I have not written a word to any creature.—Yesternight I finished the last of these extraordinary *Pamphlets;*[1] am about running off some whither into the deserts, of Wales or Scotland, Scandinavia or still remoter deserts;—and my first signal of revived reminiscence is to you.

Nay I have not at any time forgotten you, be that justice done the unfortunate: and tho' I see well enough what a great deep cleft divides us, in our ways of practically looking at this world,—I see also (as probably you do yourself) where the rock-strata, miles deep, unite again; and the two poor souls are at one. Poor devils!—Nay if there were no point of agreement at all, and I were more intolerant of "ways of thinking" than I even am,—yet has not the man Emerson, from old years, been a Human Friend to me? Can I ever forget, or think otherwise than lovingly of the man Emerson?— —No more of this. Write to me in your first good hour; and say that there is still a brother-soul left to me alive in this world, and a kind thought surviving far over the sea!—

[1] "Jesuitism," the last of the *Latter-Day Pamphlets,* is dated "1st August, 1850."

Chapman, with due punctuality at the time of publication, sent me the *Representative Men;*[2] which I read in the becoming manner: you now get the Book offered you for a shilling, at all railway stations; and indeed I perceive the word "representative men" (as applied to the late tragic loss we have had in Sir R. Peel) has been adopted by the Able-Editors, and circulates thro' Newspapers as an appropriate household word. Which is some compensation to you for the piracy you suffer from the Typographic Letter-of-Marque men here. I found the Book a most finished clear and perfect set of *Engravings in the line manner;* portraitures full of *likeness,* and abounding in instruction and materials for reflexion to me: thanks always for such a Book; and Heaven send us many more of them. *Plato,* I think, tho' it is the most admired by many, did least for me: little save Socrates with his clogs and big ears remains alive with me from it. *Swedenborg* is excellent in *likeness;* excellent in many respects;—yet I said to myself, on reaching your general conclusion about the man and his struggles: "*Missed* the consummate flower and divine ultimate elixir of Philosophy, say you?[3] By Heaven, in clutching at *it,* and 'almost getting it,' he has tumbled into Bedlam,—which is a terrible *miss,* if it were never so *near!* A miss fully as good as a mile, I sh^d say!"— —In fact, I generally dissented a little about the *end* of all these Essays; which was notable, and not without instructive interest to me, as I had so lustily shouted "Hear, hear!" all the way from the beginning up to that stage.—On the whole, let us have another Book with your earliest convenience: that is the modest request one makes of you on shutting this.

I know not what I am now going to set about: the horrible barking of the universal dog-kennel (awakened by these *Pamph^ts*) must still itself again; my poor nerves must recover themselves a little:— I have much more to say; and by Heaven's blessing must try to get it said in some way, if I live.—Bostonian Prescott[4] is here, infinitely

---

[2] The book was published almost simultaneously in England and America. Carlyle received his copy on January 7 (Carlyle, *New Letters,* II, 85).

[3] This is not a quotation from Emerson's "Swedenborg."

[4] Carlyle had met Prescott in May at Sir Robert Peel's and in June at an elaborate aristocratic ball given by the Ashburtons (Froude, *Thomas Carlyle: Life in London,* I, 44, 48). On May 11, 1850, shortly before the first meeting, he wrote to his mother: "On Thursday night, I have to go and dine with Peel,—who has invited me, I guess, to meet a certain Yankee lion called Prescott (a man I can do nothing for) who is come over here. An indigestion is all I shall get by that. Heigho!" (NLS, MS 521).

lionised by a mob of gent^n; I have seen him in two places or three (but forbore speech): the Johnny-cake is good, the twopence worth of currants in it too are good;—but if you offer it as a bit of baked Ambrosia, *Ach Gott!*—

Adieu, dear Emerson, forgive & love me a little.

Yours ever   T. Carlyle.

Concord 5 August 1850

My dear friend, It is very ingenious in you, & the crown of your magnanimities,—when you have to shame me out of my numb-palsy, —to affect contrition for *your* shortcomings & promise goodness for the time to come. Who dares blame *you,* O much-enduring punctual-performing right-English Man? Who dares believe you have time to write letters to the idle,—you sinewy master workman, sweating from peep of day to the late stars, in the yards? Not I,—and now I write reluctantly. Why afflict you with the trifles that eat my days? "Patimur quisque suos Manes." [1] You are blameless to me, & full of unsleeping kindness. But I should not thank you so ill as to tax it too far. I read one thing with joy in your letter, the intimation of better health lately. Indeed I inferred so much from the sturdy tone of these wonderful "Pamphlets," all which I have duly read as they arrived. You have finished your task, you say, & you are already snuffing the air of new battlefields beyond.

I wish you great success in your crusade against the Times. It is very easy to see that as no less than Krishna sits beside Prince Ardjoon in the chariot,[2] so Destiny too writes many fiery sentences in these pamphlets. The vivid daguerrotype of the times, the next ages will thank you for; but the circling baulking Present refuses to be helped. We are all in one boat. The prophecy is only a part of the cargo, & for purposes of healing is helpless. The opium is too strong in the air than that words should make any impression on the dull tympana. Besides, the Age consists of its best men, & I do not wish them to believe their senses to that point as to get into a pretty fury with any windmills. The actors are to believe obstinately the newspapers, & that the world exists, but thinking men must trust their conviction

---

[1] "Not quite accurately quoted from Vergil, *Aeneid*, VI, 743" (Rusk's note).

[2] "In Emerson's favorite *Bhagavadgita*" (Rusk's note).

that right is as secure as the respirability of the air. And the Age has cost too much when the constant mood of the poet is jangled. We are beleaguered with contradictions, and the moment we preach, though we were archangels, things turn on their heel and leave us to fret alone. But there is no choice, & volcanoes must burn, as well as canaries sing. And, I believe, though I often dissented as I read, the main objection was, this ignoring of the benevolent necessity that rounds us all in. And the ignoring too of the general good intent that must be imputed to the worst of us poor oysters.

You will have heard our sad news of Margaret Fuller Marchesa Ossoli. She was drowned with her husband & child on the wreck of the ship Elizabeth on the 19 July, at 3 in the P. M. after sitting all day, from morning, in plain sight of the shore of Long Island, N. Y. . —I doubt you never saw in her what was inestimable here. But she died in happy hour for herself. Her health was much exhausted. Her marriage would have taken her away from us all, & there was a subsistence yet to be secured, & diminished powers, & old age.[3]

Tis so long since I have written, that I can recall some varieties in my monotony. I spent three weeks in New York in the spring. Then a letter from Cincinnati, signed by a hundred men, asking me to read lectures, drew me across the Alleganies, for the first time. Thence I went to the Mammoth Cave, in Kentucky, a grim hole in the earth, where I walked on rocks, & sailed on subterranean rivers, from the mouth nine measured miles under ground, & back again nine miles. The tramp took fourteen hours, & so I lost a day. Thence, down the Cumberland & Ohio rivers, & up the Missisippi, steaming up the river 5 days to Galena, crossed the prairies to the great Lakes, & to Niagara, & home.

Persist in your heroic good will to me. I am greatly comforted & relieved by this reopening of the channels, & shall proceed at once to write to several good men in England & Scotland who have the best

[3] Not surprisingly, Carlyle was displeased by the lessons in the theory and practise of optimism which this letter contained. On August 30 he wrote to his wife from Scotsbrig: "Emerson's Letter (come today from you) is worth little; you shall have it next time." The next day he said: "I keep Emerson's Letter till John have seen it: a word or two about poor Mt Fuller's death is all there is of any value in it." Finally, on September 2, he sent it to London: "Here comes Emerson's Letter too. An unsatisfactory Letter; promising me no result at all from my sore labours, and singing plainly a mild 'blessed (not accursed) are they that are at ease in Zion.' Of which I do not believe a syllable" (NLS, MS 613).

claims on me. Kindest remembrances to Jane Carlyle, of whom you say no word. And to your brother John.

Ever yours   R. W. E.

Chelsea, 14 Nov^r, 1850—

Dear Emerson,

You are often enough present to my thoughts; but yesterday there came a little incident which has brought you rather vividly upon the scene for me. A certain Mr "S. E. Ward" from Boston sends us, yesterday morning by post, a Note of yours addressed to Mazzini,[1] whom he cannot find; and indicates that he retains a similar one addressed to myself, and (in the most courteous, kindly and dignified manner, if Mercy prevent not) is about carrying it off with him again to America! To give Mercy a chance, I by the first opportunity get under way for Morley's Hôtel, the Address of Mr Ward; find there that Mr Ward, since morning, *has been* on the road towards Liverpool and America, and that the function of Mercy is quite extinct in this instance! My reflexions as I wandered home again were none of the pleasantest. Of this Mr Ward I had heard some tradition, as of an intelligent accomplished and superior man; such a man's acquaintance, of whatever complexion he be, is and was always a precious thing to me, well worth acquiring where possible; not to say that any friend of yours, whatever his qualities otherwise, carries with him an imperative key to all bolts and locks of mine, real or imaginary. In fact I felt punished;—and who knows, if the case were seen into, whether I deserve it? What "business" it was that deprived me of a call from Mr Ward, or of the possibility of calling on him, I know very well,—and Elizur Wright, the little dog, and others know![2] But the fact in that

---

[1] This was a request for information about the last six years of Margaret Fuller's life (*Let RWE*, IV, 232).

[2] In "The Present Time," the first of his *Latter-Day Pamphlets*, Carlyle had written of the American people: "They have begotten, with a rapidity beyond recorded example, Eighteen Millions of the greatest *bores* ever seen in this world before,—that hitherto is their feat in History!" Elizur Wright (see above, C.4.18.46) replied with a pamphlet entitled *Perforations in the "Latter-Day Pamphlets" by One of the "Eighteen Millions of Bores,"* which attacked Carlyle as ignorant and reactionary and concluded: ". . . we will take in good part the broad hint to make our calls shorter and less frequent at Cheyne Row." Almost twenty years later George Ripley hesitated to call on Carlyle because he remembered the "bores" episode (New-York *Daily Tribune*, August 25, 1869).

matter is very far different indeed from the superficial semblance; and I appeal to all the *gentlemen* that are in America for a candid interpretation of the same. "Eighteen million bores,"—good Heavens don't I know how many of that species we also have; and how, with us as with you, the difference between *them* and the Eighteen thousand noble-men and *non*-bores is immeasurable and inconceivable; and how, with us as with you, the *latter* small company, sons of the Empyrean, will have to fling the former huge one, sons of Mammon and Mud, into some kind of chains again, reduce them to some kind of silence again,—unless the old Mud-Demons are to rise and devour us all? Truly it is so I construe it: and if Elizur Wright and the Eighteen millions are well justified in their anger at me, E. S. Ward and the Eighteen thousand owe me thanks and new love. That is my decided opinion, in spite of you all! And so, along with Ward, probably in the same ship with him, there shall go my protest against the conduct of Ward; and the declaration that to the last I will protest! Which will wind up the matter (without any word of yours on it) at this time.— —³ For the rest, tho' Elizur sent me his Pamphlet, it is a fact that I have not read a word of it, nor shall ever read.⁴ My Wife read it; but I was away, with far other things in my head; and it was "lent to various persons" till it died!—Enough and ten times more than enough of all that. Let me on this last slip of paper give you some response to the Letter I got in Scotland, under the silence of the bright autumn sun, in my Mother's house, and read there.

You are bountiful abundantly in your reception of those L. D. Pamphlets; and right in all you say of them;—and yet withal you are not right, my Friend, but I am! Truly it does behove a man to know

³ Emerson's reaction to the episode may be seen in his letter to Ward of December 3, 1850: "I am, I think, quite compensated for your leaving Carlyle unvisited, by the fine vengeance of it, as you shall read in the letter he sends along with you" (*Let RWE*, IV, 236). Looking back on it from 1872, however, he was more charitable. On November 29 of that year he wrote to Ward from Florence: "I found in London, the other day, my old Carlyle, whose inimitable soliloquy rather than talking tis a pity you did not permit yourself to hear" (MS owned by the Harvard College Library).

⁴ Emerson himself had sent the pamphlet, or so Jane Carlyle thought from the handwriting in which it was addressed. "I vote for putting it in the fire . . ." she wrote to her husband on September 6; "it is illnatured of course—and *dully* so" (NLS, MS 613).

the immense resources of this universe, and, for the sake both of his peace and of his dignity, to possess his soul in patience,[5] and look nothing doubting (nothing wincing even, if that be his humour) upon all things. For it is most indubitable there is good in all;—and if you even see an Oliver Cromwell assassinated, it is certain you may get a cartload of turnips from his carcase. Ah me, and I suppose we had too much forgotten all this, or there had not been a man like you sent to shew it us so emphatically! Let us well remember it; and yet remember too that it is *not* good always, or ever, to be "at ease in Zion";[6] good often to be in fierce rage in Zion; and that the vile Pythons of this Mud-World do verily require to have sun-arrows shot into them, and redhot pokers struck thro' them, according to occasion: wo to the man that carries either of these weapons, and does not use it in their presence! Here, at this moment, a miserable Italian organ-grinder has struck up the *Marseillaise* under my window, for example: was the Marseillaise fought out on a bed of down, or is it worth nothing when fought? On those wretched *Pamphlets* I set no value at all, or even less than none: to me their one benefit is, my own heart is clear of them (a benefit *not* to be despised, I assure you!)—and in the Public, athwart this storm of curses, and emptyings of vessels of dishonour, I can already perceive that it is all well enough there too in reference to them; and the controversy of the Eighteen millions *versus* the Eighteen thousands, or Eighteen units, is going on very handsomely in that quarter of it, for aught I can see! And so, Peace to the brave that are departed; and, tomorrow to fresh fields and pastures new![7]—

I was in Wales, as well as Scotland, during Autumn time; lived three weeks within wind of St Germanus's old "College"[8] (1400 years of age or so) and also not far from *Merthyr Tydvil* Cyclops Hell, sootiest and horridest avatar of the Industrial Mammon I had ever anywhere seen;—went thro' the Severn Valley; at Bath stayed a night with Landor (a proud and high old man, who charged me with express remembrances for you); saw Tennyson too, in Cumberland, with his

---

[5] Cf. Luke 21: 19.

[6] Amos 6: 1. This seems to have been a phrase commonly applied to Emerson in the woeful house in Cheyne Row. See above, E.8.5.50, n. 3.

[7] See above, C.6.27.35, n. 7.

[8] Germanus, a fifth-century bishop and missionary, was said to have founded the college of Llancarvan, a few miles from Cowbridge, where Carlyle had stayed.

new Wife; and other beautiful recommendable and questionable things;—and was dreadfully tossed about, and torn almost to tatters by the manifold brambles of my way: and so at length am here, a much-lamed man indeed! Oh my Friend, have tolerance for me, have sympathy with me; you know not quite (I imagine) what a burden mine is, or perhaps you would find this duty, whh you always do, a little easier done! Be happy, be busy beside your still waters,[9] and think kindly of me there. My nerves, *health* I call them, are in a sad state of disorder: alas, that is nine-tenths of all the battle in this world. Courage, courage!—My Wife sends salutations to you and yours. Good be with you all always.

Your affect^e   T. Carlyle

[9] Ps. 23: 2.

1851

Chelsea, 8 July, 1851—

Dear Emerson,

Don't you still remember very well that there is such a man? I know you do, and will do. But it is a ruinously long while since we have heard a word from each other;—a state of matters that ought immediately to *cease*. It was your turn, I think, to write? It was somebody's turn! Nay I heard lately you complained of bad eyes; and were grown abstinent of writing. Pray contradict me this. I cannot do without some regard from you while we are both here. Spite of your many sins, you are among the most human of all the beings I now know in the world;—who are a very select set, and are growing ever more so, I can inform you!

In late months, feeling greatly broken and without heart for anything weighty, I have been upon a *Life of John Sterling;* which will not be good for much, but will as usual gratify me by taking itself off my hands: it was one of the things I felt a kind of obligation to do, and so am thankful to have done. Here is a patch of it lying by me, if you will look at a specimen. There are 400 or more pages (prophesies the Printer), a good many *Letters* and Excerpts in the latter portion of the volume. Already half printed, wholly written; but not to come out for a couple of months yet,—all trade being at a stand till this sublime "Crystal Palace" go its ways again.—And now since we are upon the business, I wish you w^d mention it to E. P. Clarke (is not that the name?) next time you go to Boston: if that friendly clear-eyed man have anything to say in reference to it and American book-sellers, let him say and do; he may have a Copy for anybody in about a month: if *he* have nothing to say, then let there be nothing anywhere said. For, mark O Philosopher, I expressly and with emphasis prohibit *you* at this stage of our history, and henceforth, unless I grow poor again. Indeed, indeed, the commercial mandate of the thing (Nature's little order on that behalf) being once fulfilled (by speaking to Clark), I do not care a snuff of tobacco how it goes, and will prefer, here as elsewhere, my night's rest to any amount of superfluous money.

This summer, as you may conjecture, has been very noisy with us, and productive of little,—the "Wind-dust-ry of all Nations" [1] involving everything in one inane tornado. The very shopkeepers complain that there is no trade. Such a sanhedrin of windy fools from all countries of the Globe were surely never gathered in one city before. But they will go their ways again, they surely will! One sits quiet in that faith;—nay looks abroad with a kind of pathetic grandfatherly feeling over this universal Children's Ball, which the British Nation in these extraordinary circumstances is giving itself! Silence above all, silence is very behoveful!—

I read lately a small old brown French duodecimo, which I mean to send you by the first chance there is. The writer is a Capitaine Bossu; the production a Journal of his experiences in "La Louisiana," "Oyo" (*Ohio*) and those regions, which looks very genuine, and has a strange interest to me, like some fractional *Odyssey* or. . . .[2] Only a hundred years ago, and the Mississippi has changed as never Valley did: in 1751, older and stranger, looked at from *its* present date, than Balbec or Nineveh! Say what we will, Jonathan is doing miracles (of a sort) under the sun in these times now passing.—Do you know *Bartram's Travels?* This is of the Seventies (1770) or so; treats of *Florida* chiefly, has a wondrous kind of floundering eloquence in it; and has also grown immeasurably *old*. All American libraries ought to provide themselves with that kind of Books; and keep them as a kind of future *biblical* article.—Finally on this head, can you tell me of any *good* Book on California? Good: I have read several bad. But that too is worthy of some wonder; that too, like the old Bucaniers, hungers and thirsts (in ingenuous minds) to have some true record and description given of it.

---

[1] The official title of the exhibition of 1851 was "The Great Exhibition of the Works of Industry of all Nations." On November 12, 1851, Carlyle wrote to J. S. Blackie about "the universal Saturnalia of Fools which we held last year under the title of 'Crystal Palace,' and 'Industry' (read Wind-dust-ry) of all Nations' " (NLS, MS 2622).

[2] Illegible to me. Norton prints "letter." The book was probably *Nouveaux voyages dans l'Amérique septentrionale* by N. Bossu (Amsterdam, 1777).

And poor Miss Fuller, was there any *Life* ever published of her; or is any competent hand engaged on it? Poor Margaret, I often remember her; and think how she is asleep now under the surges of the sea. Mazzini, as you perhaps know, is with us this summer; comes across once in the week or so, and tells me or at least my wife all his news. The Roman revolution has made a man of him,—quite brightened up ever since;—and the best friend *he* ever saw, I believe, was that same Quack-President of France, who relieved him while it was still time.[3]—My Brother is in Annandale, working hard over Dante at last; talks of coming up hither shortly. I am usually very ill and miserable in the *liver* regions; very *tough* otherwise,—tho' I have now got spectacles for small print in the twilight. *Eheu fugaces,*[4]—and yet why *Eheu?* In fact it is better to be silent.—Adieu, dear Emerson; I expect to get a great deal brisker by and by,—and in the first place to have a missive from Boston again. My wife sends you many regards. I am as ever,—affectionately yours   T. Carlyle

Concord, 28 July, 1851.

My dear Carlyle,

You must always thank me for silence, be it never so long, & must put on it the most generous interpretations. For I am too sure of your genius & goodness, & too glad that they shine steadily for all, to importune you to make assurance sure by a private beam very often. There is very little in this village to be said to you, &, with all my love of your letters, I think it the kind part to defend you from our imbecilities,—my own, & other men's. Besides, my eyes are bad, & prone to mutiny at any hint of white paper

And yet I owe you all my story, if story I have. I have been something of a traveller the last year, and went down the Ohio River to its mouth; walked nine miles into, & nine miles out of the Mammoth Cave, in Kentucky,—walked or sailed,—for we cross small underground streams,—and lost one day's light: then steamed up the Missisippi, five days, to Galena. In the upper Missisippi, you are always

---

[3] Carlyle meant, I think, that Louis Bonaparte's intervention in the Roman Revolution had saved Mazzini from having to put democracy into practise.

[4] Horace, *Odes*, II, xiv, 1: "Eheu fugaces, Postume, Postume, labuntur anni."

in a lake with many islands. "The Far West" is the right name for these verdant desarts. On all the shores, interminable silent forest. If you land, there is prairie behind prairie, forest behind forest, sites of nations, no nations. The raw bullion of nature, what we call "moral" value not yet stamped on it. But in a thousand miles the immense material values will show twenty or fifty Californias; that a good ciphering head will make one where he is. Thus at Pittsburgh, on the Ohio, the Iron City, whither, from want of railroads, few Yankees have penetrated, every acre of land has three or four bottoms, first of rich soil; then nine feet of bituminous coal; a little lower, fourteen feet of coal; then iron, or salt; salt springs with a valuable oil called petroleum, floating on their surface. Yet this acre sells for the price of any tillage acre in Massachusetts; and, in a year, the railroads will reach it, east & west.—I came home by the great northern lakes & Niagara.[1]

No books. a few lectures, each winter, I write & read. In the spring the abomination of our Fugitive Slave-Bill drove me to some writing & speechmaking, without hope of effect, but to clear my own skirts.[2] I am sorry I did not print, whilst it was yet time. I am now told the time will come again, more's the pity. Now, I am trying to make a sort of memoir of Margaret Fuller, or my part in one;—for Channing & Ward are to do theirs.[3] Without either beauty or genius, she had a certain wealth & generosity of nature which have left a kind of claim on our consciences to build her a cairn. And this reminds me that I am to write a note to Mazzini on this matter;[4] and, as you say you see him, you must charge yourself with delivering it. What we do must be ended by October.

You too are working for Sterling. It is right & kind. I learned so much from the N. Y. Tribune, and, a few days after, was on the point of writing to you, provoked by a foolish paragraph which appeared in Rufus Griswold's Journal (New York) purporting that R. W. E. possessed important letters of Sterling, without which Thomas Carlyle

---

[1] This account confuses two lecture tours in the West: Emerson did not go to the Mammoth Cave during the lecture season of 1850–51 (Rusk, *Life*, p. 382).

[2] Emerson wrote a speech which he called "The Fugitive Slave Law"; he read it first at Concord on May 3 (*Works*, XI, 177–214).

[3] Ward had, evidently, no part in the published *Memoirs*, which was the work of Emerson, William Henry Channing, and James Freeman Clarke.

[4] Emerson wrote this second note to Mazzini on July 29, 1851 (*Let RWE*, IV, 255).

could not write the Life!" [5] What scrap of hearsay about contents of Sterling's letters to me, or that I had letters, this paltry journalist swelled into this puffball,—I know not. He once came to my house, &, since that time, may have known Margaret Fuller in New York: but probably never saw any letter of Sterling's, or heard the contents of any. I have not read again Sterling's letters, which I keep as good Lares in a special niche, but I have no recollection of anything that would be valuable to you. For the American Public for the Book, I think it important that you should take the precise step of sending Phillips & Sampson the early copy, & at the earliest. I saw them, & also E. P. Clark, & put them in communication, & Clark is to write you at once.

Having got so far in my writing to you, I do not know but I shall gain heart, & write more letters over sea. You will think my sloth suicidal enough. So many men as I learned to value in your country, —so many as offered me opportunities of intercourse and I lose them all by silence. Arthur Helps is a chief benefactor of mine. I wrote him a letter by Ward,—who brought the letter back. I ought to thank John Carlyle, not only for me, but for a multitude of good men & women here who read his Inferno duly. W. E. Forster sent me his Penn Pamphlet: [6] I sent it to Bancroft, who liked it well, only he thought Forster might have made a still stronger case. Clough I prize at a high rate, the man & his poetry, but write not. Wilkinson [7] I thought a man of prodigious talent who somehow held it & so taught others to hold it cheap, as we do one of those bushelbasket memories which schoolboys & schoolgirls often show, & we stop their mouths lest they be troublesome with their alarming profusion. But there is no need

---

[5] "Among Sterling's most intimate correspondents was Ralph Waldo Emerson, and even Carlyle cannot write his life, we suspect, without having access to the extraordinary series of letters the poet sent to his American friend" (*The International Magazine of Literature, Art, and Science*, III [July 1, 1851], 465).

[6] *William Penn and Thomas B. Macaulay: Being Brief Observations on the Charges Made in Mr. Macaulay's History of England, Against the Character of William Penn* was published in Philadelphia in 1850. Emerson probably remembered at this point that, two years before, John Carlyle had seen the pamphlet in sheets and had asked Forster to send a copy to Concord (letter from JC to RWE, September 28, 1849, MS owned by RWEMA).

[7] Writing in *Representative Men* of a new edition of Swedenborg's scientific works, Emerson said: "The admirable preliminary discourses with which Mr. Wilkinson has enriched these volumes, throw all the contemporary philosophy of England into shade" (*Works*, IV, 111).

of beginning to count the long catalogue. Kindest, kindest remembrances to my benefactress also in your house, and health & strength & Victory to you!   Your affectionate   Waldo Emerson

Thomas Carlyle

Great Malvern, Worcestershire

25 Augt, 1851—

Dear Emerson,

Many thanks for your Letter, which found me here about a week ago, and gave a full solution to my bibliopolic difficulties. However sore your eyes, or however taciturn your mood, there is no delay of writing when any service is to be done by it! In fact you are very good to me, and always were, in all manner of ways; for which I do, as I ought, thank the Upper Powers and you. That truly has been and is one of the possessions of my life in this perverse epoch of the world.

No tidings have yet arrived from E. P. Clark himself; but I have settled the affair and despatched everything just as if he had written: namely I have sent off by John Chapman a Copy of the *Life of Sterling*, which is all printed and ready, but is not to appear till the first week of October; and by the same steamer, which left Liverpool 3 days ago for Boston direct, a Letter to the said E. P. Clark announcing the advent of such a Parcel, and emphatically authorizing him to make whatever bargain he finds—with Phps & Sampson or with any other Publisher or Publishers: the *Letter,* I understand, went in P. & Sampson's Parcel from Chapman, the *corpus delicti* itself, namely the *sheets* of the Book, went to a House called *Crosby & Nichols* or some such name: that was my Brother's management, who is now in Chelsea in our house, looking after *Dante* manuscripts &c, and who underwent these troubles for me in my absence. Along with the *sheets* was a poor little French Book for you,—Book of a poor naval *Mississippi* Frenchman, one "Bossu" I think; written only a century ago, yet which already seemed old as the Pyramids in reference to those strange fast-growing countries. I read it as a kind of defaced *romance;* very thin and lean, but all true, and very marvellous as such. Clark will give you that; and manage all the rest of the affair, I doubt not, with the due energy and success; to whom accordingly let us leave it with full faith of assurance.

It is above 3 weeks since my Wife and I left London (the Printer having done), and came hither with the purpose of a month of what is called "Water-cure"; for which this place, otherwise extremely pleasant and wholesome, has become celebrated of late years. Dr. Gully,[1] the pontiff of the business in our Island, warmly encouraged my purpose so soon as he heard of it; nay urgently offered at once that both of us should become his own guests till the experiment were tried: and here accordingly we are; I water-curing, assiduously walking on the sunny mountains, drinking of the clear wells, not to speak of wet wrappages, solitary sad *steepages,* and other singular procedures; my Wife not meddling for her own behoof, but only seeing me do it. These have been three of the idlest weeks I ever spent, and there is still one to come: after which we go northward to Lancashire, and across the Border where my good old Mother still expects me; and so, after some little visiting and dawdling hope to find ourselves home again before September end, and the inexpressible Glass Palace with its noisy inanity have taken itself quite away again. It was no increase of ill-health that drove me hither, rather the reverse; but I have long been minded to try this thing: and now I think the results will be,—*zero* pretty nearly, and one imagination the less. My long walks, my strenuous idleness have certainly done me good; nor has the "water" done me any *ill,* which perhaps is much to say of it. For the rest it is a strange quasi-monastic,—godless and yet *devotional,*—way of life whh human creatures have here; and useful to them beyond doubt. I foresee, this "Water-Cure," under better forms, will become the *Ramadhan* of the overworked unbelieving English in time coming; an institution they were dreadfully in want of this long while!—We had Twistleton [2] here (often speaking of you), who is off to America again,—will sail, I think, along with this Letter; a *semi*-articulate but solid-minded worthy man. We have other officials and other *Litterateurs* (T. B. Macaulay in his hired villa for one): but the mind rather shuns than seeks them; one finds solitary quasi-devotion preferable, and ἄριστον μὲν ὕδωρ as Pindar had it! [3]

Richard Milnes is married, about two weeks ago, and gone to Vienna for a jaunt. His Wife, a Miss Crewe (Lord Crewe's sister), about 40, pleasant intelligent and rather rich: that is the end of Richard's long

---

[1] J. M. Gully was the chief English advocate and practitioner of hydropathy.

[2] Edward Twisleton had been one of the original members of the Sterling Club. During October of 1851 he had some correspondence with Emerson about the school system of Massachusetts (*Let RWE*, IV, 261).

[3] *Olympian Odes,* I, 1.

first act. Alfred Tennyson, perhaps you heard, is gone to Italy with his Wife: their baby died or was dead-born; they found England wearisome: Alfred has been taken up on the top of the wave, and a good deal jumbled about since you were here. Item Thackeray; who is coming over to lecture to you: [4] a mad world, my Masters! [5]

Your Letter to Mazzini was duly despatched; and we hear from him that he will write to you, on the subject required, witht delay. Browning and his Wife, home from Florence, are both in London at present; mean to live in Paris henceforth for some time. They had seen something both of Margaret and her d'Ossoli, and appeared to have a true and lively interest in them; Brg spoke a long while to me, with emphasis, on the subject: I think it was I that had introduced poor Margaret to them. I said he ought to send these reminiscences to America, —that was the night before we left London, three weeks ago; his answer gave me the impression there had been some hindrance somewhere. Accordingly when your Letter, and Mazzini's reached me here, I *wrote* to Browning urgently on the subject: but he informs me that they *have* sent all their reminiscences, at the request of Mr Story; so that it is already all well.[6]—Dear Emerson, you see I am at the bottom of my paper. I will write to you again before long; we cannot let you lie fallow in that manner altogether. Have you got proper *spectacles* for your eyes? I have adopted that beautiful symbol of old age, and feel myself very venerable: take care of your eyes! Yours ever   T. Carlyle

[4] A letter which Harriet Martineau wrote to Emerson February 25, 1852, gives a memorable picture of Carlyle at a Thackeray lecture: "I saw the Carlyles a few months since;—just saw them, & O! dear! felt them too. They put me between them, at Thackeray's last lecture; & both got the fidgets. After the first half hour, C. looked at his watch, & held it across me, about once in two minutes; & he filled up the intervals with shaking himself, & drumming his elbow into my side. Such was the interview! They asked me to Chelsea, but my time in London was very short, & I cd not go" (MS owned by the RWEMA).

[5] This is the title of a play by Thomas Middleton.

[6] In the spring of 1847 Carlyle had given Margaret Fuller a letter of introduction to the Brownings (*Letters of Robert Browning*, p. 18). On August 22, 1851, Browning wrote Carlyle a full account of his part in the memoir: he and his wife, at the request of Mrs. William Wetmore Story, had put together their memories of the Ossolis and sent them, in a letter of April, 1851, to Mrs. Story "to use as might seem best" (*ibid.*, p. 33). That letter evidently went astray: see below, E.4.14.52.

1852

My dear Carlyle,

I have not grown so callous by my sulky habit, but that I know where my friends are, & who can help me, in time of need. And I have to crave your good offices today, &, in a matter relating once more to Margaret Fuller. Her mother, & her sister, Mrs W. E. Channing, who are neighbors of mine, have seen a paragraph in the London Athenaeum of February—,announcing that a lady in England holds certain manuscript journals, which Margaret left in trust with her, supposed to contain her travelling notes on England, &c.[1]

Mrs Fuller had once a letter from Margaret, mentioning the circumstances, & the lady's name, Miss Gillies; Margaret Gillies [2] she thinks, but she has destroyed the letter:—and she now requests me to aid her in conveying a note to this lady, asking that these MS.S be at once forwarded to Mrs Fuller. I enclose Mrs Fuller's note, praying you to give it

---

[1] "We have received permission to state that poor Margaret Fuller, on the eve of that visit to the Continent which was to prove so eventful and disastrous, left in the hands of a friend in London a sealed packet, containing, it is understood, the journals which she kept during her stay in England. Margaret Fuller—as they who saw her here all know—contemplated at that time a return to England at no very distant date;—and the deposit of these papers was accompanied by an injunction that the packet should then be restored with unbroken seal into her own hands. No provision was of course made for death:—and here we believe the lady in possession feels herself in a difficulty, out of which she does not clearly see her way. The papers are likely to be of great interest,—and were doubtless intended for publication; but the writer had peremptorily reserved the right of revision to herself, and forbidden the breaking of the seals, on a supposition which fate has now made impossible.—It seems to us, that the equity of the case under such circumstances demands only a reference to Margaret Fuller's heir, whoever that may be; and that with his or her concurrence, the lady to whom these manuscripts were intrusted—and who probably knows something of the author's feelings as to their contents—may very properly constitute herself literary executor to her unfortunate friend" (No. 1270, February 28, 1852, p. 254).

[2] Margaret Gillies was a miniaturist and watercolorist, best known for her portrait of Wordsworth.

an effectual direction. We think, Miss Gillies should not have waited for such an application.

You were so kind as to interest yourself, many months ago, to set Mazzini & Browning on writing their reminiscences for us. But we never heard from either of them. Lately I have learned by way of Sam. Longfellow, in Paris, brother of our poet Longfellow, that Browning assured him, that he did write & send a memoir to this Country,—to whom, I know not. It never arrived at the hands of the Fullers, nor of Story, Channing, or me;—though the book was delayed in the hope of such help. I hate that his paper should be lost.

The little French "Voyage" &c of Bossu, I got safely, & compared its pictures with my own, at the Mississippi, the Illinois, & Chicago. It is curious & true enough, no doubt, though its Indians are rather dim & vague, and "Messieurs Sauvages." Good Indians we have in Alexander Henry's "Travels in Canada," & in our modern Catlin, & the best Western America, perhaps, in F. A. Michaux "Voyage à l'ouest des Monts Alléghanys," & in Fremont. But it was California, I believe you asked about, and, after looking at Taylor, Parkman, & the rest,[3] I saw that the only course is to read them *all*, & every private letter that gets into the newspapers. So there was nothing to say.

I rejoiced with the rest of mankind in the "Life of Sterling," and now peace will be to his manes, down in this lower sphere. Yet I see well that I should have held to his opinion, in all those conferences where you have so quietly assumed the palms.[4] It is said here, that you work upon Frederick the Great?? However that be, health, strength, love, joy, & victory to you!   R. W. Emerson

Chelsea, 7 May, 1852—

Dear Emerson,

I was delighted at the sight of your hand again. My manifold sins against you, involuntary all of them I may well say, are often enough present to my sad thought; and a kind of remorse is mixed with the

---

[3] John S. Fremont's *Narrative of the Exploring Expedition to the Rocky Mountains* had appeared in 1845, Francis Parkman's *The Oregon Trail* in 1847, and Bayard Taylor's *Eldorado* in 1850; many editions of George Catlin's works on the Indians were available in both Great Britain and America.

[4] Emerson probably had in mind Carlyle's treatment of Coleridge and "this thrice-refined pabulum of transcendental moonshine" in Part I, chs. viii and ix.

other sorrow,—as if I could have *helped* growing to be, by aid of time and destiny, the grim Ishmaelite I am, and so shocking your serenity by my ferocities! I admit, you were like an angel to me, and absorbed in the beautifullest manner all thunderclouds into the depths of your immeasurable aether;—and it is indubitable I love you very well, and have long done, and mean to do. And on the whole you will have to rally yourself into some kind of Correspondence with me again; I believe you will find that also to be a commanded duty by and by! To me at any rate, I can say, it is a great want, and adds perceptibly to the sternness of these years: deep as is my dissent from your Gymnosophist view of Heaven and Earth,[1] I find an agreement that swallows up all conceivable dissents; in the whole world I hardly get, to my spoken human word, any other word of response which is authentically *human*. God help us, this is growing a very lonely place, this distracted dog-kennel of a world! And it is no joy to me to see it about to have its throat cut for its immeasurable devilries; that is not a pleasant process to be concerned in either more or less, considering above all how many centuries, bare and dismal all of them, it is like to take! Nevertheless *marchons,*—and swift too, if we have any speed, for the sun is sinking.

I flatter myself I have managed poor Miss Fuller's *Mss.* with good success. Miss Gillies, except almost by name, was not known to me, and my first inquiries after her were not quite prosperous; however in a couple of days I easily got a sure hand to convey to her Mrs Fuller's Note inclosed in a civil one of mine;[2] to which there came the answer here sent you (to be shewn to Mrs Fuller, by way of explaining Miss Gillies's sentiments and procedure in this business,—pray do not neglect that); and, in fine, by duly expediting matters I shall in few minutes have on the road a messenger to meet Miss Gillies at a given hour, and take delivery for me, with due "receipts" &c, of the *ipsissimum corpus* of the packet in question: and I hope to be able to tell you before the Post close (this being American Post-day) that it is actually

---

[1] In a letter to Harriet Taylor ten years before, Carlyle had used *gymnosophist* in a parallel construction with *hermit* and *monk* to indicate seclusion from and indifference to the world (*Letters . . . to . . . Mill . . . Sterling . . . and Browning,* p. 180).

[2] Carlyle wrote to Mill for Miss Gillies's address (*ibid.,* p. 183), and then, on May 3, 1852, enclosed Mrs. Fuller's note in a letter of his own which he sent to Miss Gillies by "Mr Woolner" (NLS, MS 1796), presumably Thomas Woolner, the Pre-Raphaelite sculptor, who had done a portrait-medallion of him the year before (Wilson, *Carlyle at his Zenith,* p. 341).

in my possession here,—nay I am not quite certain but I might manage to get it delivered to Chapman, and have it safely put on the road to America by the same steamer that goes today. This, however, owing to long distances and shortness of time, is by no means so certain: the rather as I am unable to stir in my own person, having the vilest dose of cold I can remember for many years back,—sad fruit of this withering east-wind, which is afflicting all Europe as well as me. Nay, on looking at my watch, I rather fear it is not now possible to get Chapman brought into play for this night: against next friday I shall engage to have the Packet, with due sureties and precautions, in his hand; and will write to you another Note then to that effect.

Poor Margaret, that is a strange tragedy that history of hers; and has many traits of the Heroic in it, tho' it is wild as the prophecy of a sybil. Such a predetermination to *eat* this big universe as her oyster or her egg, and to be absolute empress of all height and glory in it that her heart could conceive, I have not before seen in any human soul. Her "mountain *me*" [3] indeed:—but her courage too is high and clear, her chivalrous nobleness indeed is great; her veracity, in its deepest sense, *à toute épreuve.*—Your copy of the Book came to me at last (to my joy): I had already read it; there was considerable notice taken of it here; and *one* half-volume of it (and I grieve to say only one, written by a man called Emerson) [4] was completely approved by me and innumerable judges. The rest of the Book is not without considerable geniality and merits: but one wanted a clear concise Narrative beyond all other merits; and if you ask here (except in that half-volume) about any fact, you are answered (so to speak) not in words, but by a symbolic tune on the bagpipe, symbolic burst of wind-music from the brass band;—which is not the plan at all! [5]— —What can have become of Mazzini's Letter which he certainly did write and despatch to you is not easily conceivable. Still less in the case of Browning: for Browning & his Wife did also write; I myself in the end of last July having heard

[3] "Margaret occasionally let slip, with all the innocense imaginable, some phrase betraying the presence of a rather mountainous ME, in a way to surprise those who knew her good sense" (Emerson, *Memoirs of Margaret Fuller Ossoli*, I, 236).

[4] Emerson wrote or edited about half of the first volume of the *Memoirs.*

[5] "Margaret was a great creature; but you have no full biography of her yet. We want to know what time she got up in the morning and what sort of shoes and stockings she wore" (Carlyle, quoted by "Grace Greenwood" [Sarah Jane Clarke Lippincott] in *Haps and Mishaps of a Tour in Europe,* p. 49).

him talk kindly and well of poor Marg^t and her husband, took the liberty on your behalf of asking him to put something down on paper; and he informed me, then and repeatedly since, he had already done it, —at the request of Mrs Story, I think. His Address at present is "N° 138, Avenue des Champs Elysées, à Paris" if y^r American travellers still tho^t of inquiring.—Adieu, dear Emerson till next week.—Yours ever   T. Carlyle

Chelsea, 14 May, 1852—

Dear Emerson,

This day week, by our last steamer, there went tidings of my successful negociation on the Margaret-Fuller Packet of Papers; and, had my messenger returned fifteen minutes earlier than he did from the Gillies quarter, I w^d have despatched him express for John Chapman's in the Strand (the hour still permitting such an enterprise), and you had got the *ipsissimum corpus* of the Packet, and so had needed, with me at least, no farther correspondence on the subject. That being accidentally or providentially impossible, I engaged at least (by some hurried scrape of the pen somewhere on your Note) to send the Packet off "by next steamer,"—that is, by this which has now its anchor apeak; and which, alas, does *not* bring you the Packet, but only another set of papers and talking about it. Heaven send, the work do prove to be at least *worth* all the cry there has been upon it!—

I have the Packet * here safe, and will keep it so till we hear your decision on the subject: but the Misses Gillies, startled still farther by a Note in Mt Fullers hand, which till they tore off the outer cover (loose cover with their own address on it, and supposed to contain nothing more), they had never seen,—will in nowise consent to part altogether with this Packet so entrusted to them; and indeed appear to be pretty much convinced, in spite of all I can say and argue, that the Papers ought to be *burned* straightway, and act taken to that effect, and *so* the matter finished. By the Notes here sent, which are now *all* I ever got from Miss Gillies, you will perceive how they have got into the field of pious punctilio and "Pike's Cases of Conscience" [1]

---

* [Loose Package in brown paper, tied with string and sealed (by M. F.): dimensions 10 inches by 3 and by 7½; weight 3 lbs minus 1½ oz.]

[1] Samuel Pike's *Some Important Cases of Conscience* (1755–56) was a collection of lectures on ethical problems.

(so to speak), and are not likely ever to get quite out of it, except on pressure of gentle violence from the right quarter, if even then. I ought to add that they are most respectable, and even I understand, amiable and intelligent Ladies,—perhaps the very wisest we have of that advanced Progress-of-the-species sort, which prudent persons in this country are shy of having much to do with:—Mary Gillies, who came here last Saturday to "burn" those Papers along with me, quite gained our hearts by her mild wise ways and manners; a tall, serene, really beautiful old-maid of five-and-forty; [2] and I understand her sister the Paintress (whom owing to Progress of the Species I have hitherto not seen) is an equally brave gentle and superior lady. To Margaret Fuller's Packet of Papers their conduct has been that of Priestesses towards a sacred relic,—truly such, I do believe;—and it is very clear to me, if Mrs Fuller wrote them *objurgatiously* on the subject, it was much undeserved, and ought to be loyally retracted, and replaced by *thanks,* on the first opportunity. As indeed I have predicted that it would.

To these guardian Ladies I have urged, in writing, orally, and again in writing, with all my eloquence: that M. Fuller's "order" with regard to these Papers (if we will look beyond the mere letter of it, and into the real spirit of it) *cannot* now be fulfilled by any power human or divine; that there was attached to it a tacit but most vital condition, of *silence* to be observed concerning it and them, so that complete anni-hilation might ensue; whh condition having now been irretrievably violated, the very gods cannot "annihilate" these Papers. "Miss Mary and I," I have urged, "can burn the Papers in 2 minutes or less; any-body can so easily destroy the Papers: but who of gods or men can destroy the the melancholy Ghost (or wailing, suspecting, imagining Memory) of them, which will walk the world as goblin in a distracted manner till all memory of Margaret herself die?" Her real will can only be complied with now, and her Papers annihilated so far as *now* possible, by their being completely *examined* before burning, and pro-nounced to be of no importance, and to deserve and need the fire. On the whole, her Mother is the heir of them; her Mother, and such a Council of Friends, Emerson, Channing, Mrs Channing, these of all persons discoverable under this sun are the real tribunal to sit in judgt on them: to decide on burning them unseen, or with what *degree* of

---

[2] Mary Gillies was, or was to become, a writer of historical novels and children's books (John Foster Kirk, *A Supplement to Allibone's Critical Dictionary*).

sight and examination, it is fit to burn them. I urged also, "Be *speedy!* The Papers probably are of *no* moment whatever: if a churchyard spectre is threatening to walk the parish, and developing itself into pale valleys of Jehosophat and Battles of Armageddon,[3]—walk instantly up to it, tumble the pole and white sheet about their business, if you wd end it."

These considerations I have urged with emphasis, I cannot say with much success; at length finding the matter unlike to end that way, and every Note at present costing *me* a headache,—I announced to Miss Gillies 3 days ago that her sister's final proposal of Saturday last shd be adopted; viz. that the whole matter shd be referred to Margaret Fuller's *Mother* & her Council at Concord; that whatever that venerable Lady, so advised, shd decide upon, I wd *endeavour* to get done for her (with which I hoped Miss Gs wd cooperate); and that *till* such decision arrived, there shd be absolute silence on the subject. I gave Miss G. *your* Addresses at Concord, and directed all her farther pleadings, if any, to go thither: my judgt was quite made up, no Notes or headaches farther needed from me.— —Tell me, then, what to do. I *think* Mrs Fuller's order will produce compliance from Miss G.; I will try my best to bring it so about; and only yield to some absolute *Pike's case,* or Female Denunciation fronting me with arms a-kimbo. The Papers, I guess after all, are probably of little or no moment; but my thot is as above that they *shd* be examined a little in order to annihilate the "ghost" of them too. Do as you find good;—forget not to send back Margaret's scrap of paper to Miss Gillies, and some acknowledgment that she has behaved, been loyally eager to behave, with fidelity and piety in the matter.

I have a vile influenza for the last week; which lames me from all work, especially from all *speaking,*—or from writing a word beyond what is indispensable. About Fredk the Great and other high matters shortly. Adieu dear Friend: good be with you always.   T. Carlyle.

Concord, May [?], 1852.[1]

You make me happy with your loving thoughts and meanings towards me. I have always thanked the good star which made us early

---

[3] Cf. Joel 3: 2; Rev. 16: 16.

[1] Norton's text—"from an imperfect rough draft," as his note says. This fragment may be placed in time by the date of the Landor poem to which it refers and the

neighbors, in some sort, in time and space. And the beam is twice warmed by your vigorous good-will, which has steadily kept clear, kind eyes on me.

It is good to be born in good air and outlook, and not less with a civilization, that is, with one poet still living in the world. O yes, and I feel all the solemnity and vital cheer of the benefit.—If only the mountains of water and of land and the steeper mountains of blighted and apathized moods would permit a word to pass now and then. It is very fine for you to tax yourself with all those incompatibilities. I like that Thor should make comets and thunder, as well as Iduna apples, or Heimdal his rainbow bridge, and your wrath and satire has all too much realism in it, than that we can flatter ourselves by disposing of you as partial and heated. Nor is it your fault that you do a hero's work, nor do we love you less if we cannot help you in it. Pity me, O strong man! I am of a puny constitution half made up, and as I from childhood knew,—not a poet but a lover of poetry, and poets, and merely serving as writer, &c. in this empty America, before the arrival of the poets. You must not misconstrue my silences, but thank me for them all, as a true homage to your diligence which I love to defend. . . . .

She had such reverence and love for Landor that I do not know but at any moment in her natural life she would have sunk in the sea, for an ode from him; [2] and now this most propitious cake is offered to her Manes. The loss of the notes of Browning and of Mazzini, which you confirm, astonishes me.

Chelsea, 25 June, 1852—

Dear Emerson,

Your magnanimous Letters came; I forwarded Mrs Fuller's, and your smaller ostensible one, without delay; Miss Gillies's answer came before very long, *accepting* her Hobson's choice; and now so soon as this Note is thrown off, I sail off with it, and with the Parcel itself, to

---

Carlyle letter of June 25, 1852, which answers it. For the contents of the letter see below, C.6.25.52, n. 1. The ellipsis at the end of paragraph two represents, says Norton's note, a "break in continuity . . . in the rough draft."

[2] Landor's "On the Death of M. D'Ossoli and his Wife Margaret Fuller" was published in *The Examiner*, May 8, 1852.

John Chapman's whom I have appointed to be in readiness; and so, enclosing his *receipt* for you here by post, and delivering the *Mss* to their place in his big general Hamper, I hope the same steamer will prosperously convey both messages, and so this little business will be well finished.[1] I have had *no* farther trouble with it; and indeed never had any that was worth speaking a word upon,—much less so many kind words as you are misled into speaking, and attaching meaning to! You are a born *enthusiast,* as quiet as you are; and it will continue so, at intervals, to the end. I admire your sly low-voiced sarcasm too;—in short, I love the sternly-gentle close-buttoned man very well, as I have always done, and intend to continue doing!—Pray observe, therefore, and lay it to heart as a practical fact, that you are bound to persevere in writing to me from time to time; and will never get it given up, how sulky soever you grow, while we both remain in this world. Do not I very well understand all that you say about "apathized moods" &c? The gloom of approaching old age (approaching, nay arriving with some of us) is very considerable upon a man; and on the whole, one contrives to take the very ugliest view, now and then, of all beauti-fullest things; and to shut one's lips with a kind of grim defiance, a kind of imperial sorrow which is almost like felicity,—so completely and composedly wretched, one is equal to the very gods! These too are necessary moods to a man. But the Earth withal is verdant, sun-be-shone; and the Son of Adam has his place on it, and his tasks and re-compenses in it, to the close;—as one remembers by and by, too. On the whole, I am infinitely solitary; but not more heavy-laden than I have all along been, perhaps rather less so; I could fancy even old age to be beautiful, and to have a real divineness: for the rest, I say always, I cannot part with *you;* and so, in brief, you must get into the way of holding yourself obliged as formerly to a kind of *dialogue* with me; and speak, on paper since not otherwise, the oftenest you can. Let that be a point settled.

I am not *writing* on Frederic the Great; nor at all practically con-

---

[1] On this day Carlyle wrote to his brother John about the Gillies affair: "I have happily got thro' that for them and am this day to give the Packet itself into John Chapman's hands for despatch by the steamer: so *that* ends. I had a very kind Letter from Emerson this week, chiefly about that; I wd send it today (instead of next time) except for the weight of other enclosures" (NLS, MS 514). On August 16 Emerson wrote to Chapman that the "parcel of manuscript" had not been seen (*Let RWE,* IV, 304).

templating to do so. But, being in a reading mood after those furious *Pamphlets* (which have procured me showers of abuse from all the extensive genus Stupid in this country, and not done me any other mischief, but perhaps good), and not being capable of reading except in a train and *about* some object of interest to me,—I took to reading, near a year ago, about Frederick, as I had twice in my life done before; and have, in a loose way, tumbled up an immense quantity of shot rubbish on that field, and still continue. Not with much decisive approach to Frederick's *self*, I am still afraid! The man looks brilliant and noble to me; but how *love* him, or the sad wreck he lived and worked in? I do not even yet *see* him clearly; and to try making others see him—?—Yet Voltaire and he *are* the celestial element of the poor 18th Century; poor souls. I confess also to a real love for F.'s dumb followers: the Prussian *soldiery*—I often say to myself, "Were not *here* the real priests and virtuous martyrs of that loud-babbling rotten generation!" And so it goes on; where to end, or in what to end, God knows.

Adieu, dear Emerson. A blockhead (by mistake) has been let in, and has consumed all my time. Good be ever with you and yours.

T. Carlyle

1853

Concord
19 April 1853

My dear friend,

As I find I never write a letter except at the dunning of the Penny Post,—which is the pest of the Century,—I have thought lately of crossing to England to excuse to you my negligence of your injunction which so flattered me by its affectionateness a year ago. I was to write once a month. My own disobedience is wonderful & explains to me all the sins of omission of the whole world. The levity with which we can let fall into disuse such a sacrament as the exchange of greetings at short periods, is a kind of magnanimity, & should be an astonishing argument of the "Immortality"; & I wonder how it has escaped the notice of philosophers. But what had I, dear wise man, to tell you? What, but that life was still tolerable; still absurdly sweet; still promising, promising, to credulous idleness—but step of mine taken in a true direction, or clear solution of any the least secret,—none whatever. I scribble always a little,—much less than formerly,—and I did within a year or eighteen months write a chapter on Fate, which,—if we all live long enough, that is, you, & I, & the chapter, I hope to send you in fair print.[1] Comfort yourself—as you will—you will survive the reading,—& will be a sure proof that the nut is not cracked. For when we find out what Fate is, I suppose, the Sphinx & we are done for; and Sphinx, Oedipus, & world, ought, by good rights, to roll down the steep into the sea.[2]

But I was going to say, my neglect of your request will show you how little saliency is in my weeks & months. They are hardly distinguished in memory other than as a running web out of a loom, a bright stripe for day, a dark stripe for night, &, when it goes faster, even these run together into endless grey. Want want of battery. Give us big heads, big bodies. Fault of fulcrum & *abgrund*,[3] I cannot resist the foolish

---

[1] Not published until 1860, in *Conduct of Life.*   [2] Cf. Mark 5: 13.
[3] Norton wisely omitted the passage "Want . . . so."

invitations; so I went lately to St. Louis, & saw the Missisippi again. The powers of the river, the insatiate craving for nations of men to reap & cure its harvests, the conditions it imposes, for it yields to no engineering,—are interesting enough. The Prairie exists to yield the greatest possible quantity of adipocere. For corn makes pig, pig is the export of all the land, & you shall see the distant dependence of aristocracy & civility on the fat fourlegs. Workingmen, ability to do the work of the River, abounded, nothing higher was to be thought of. America is incomplete. Room for us all, since it has not ended, nor given sign of ending, in bard or hero. Tis a wild democracy, the riot of mediocrities, & none of your selfish Italies and Englands, where an age sublimates into a genius, and the whole population is made into paddies to feed his porcelain veins, by transfusion from their brick arteries. Our few fine persons are apt to die. Horatio Greenough, a sculptor, whose tongue was far cunninger in talk, than his chisel to carve, & who inspired great hopes, died two months ago at 47 years. Nature has only so much vital force, & must dilute it, if it is to be multiplied into millions. "The beautiful is never plentiful." [4] On the whole, I say to myself, that our conditions in America are not easier or less expensive than the European. For the poor scholar everywhere must be compromise or alternation, &, after many remorses, the consoling himself that there has been pecuniary honesty, & that things might have been worse. But no we must think much better things than these. Let Lazarus believe that Heaven does not corrupt into maggots, & that heroes do not succumb. Clough is here, & comes to spend a Sunday with me, now & then. He begins to have pupils, & if his courage holds out, will have as many as he wants.[5] I have given a letter to you, at Dr D's request, to a very modest but very worthy & truehearted gentleman, Dr Dalton of Lowell.[6] I doubt, if he leaves it. If he do, it only needs to sit with him a few minutes. There is a lady going presently to England, & through England to Italy, for the second time, a painter, Sarah Clarke, who perhaps may send you her card: if she does, you must also entreat her kindly. She was one of Margaret's friends, &

[4] I have been unable to find the source of this quotation.

[5] Clough had come to America the preceding October. He was working in Cambridge as a private tutor of Greek.

[6] Probably John Call Dalton, father of the distinguished physiologist of the same name.

benefactors.[7] One more American you may meet, Mr O. M. Mitchell, of Cincinnati, an astronomer who is a good specimen of western energy. He is an excellent observer (in his observatory), and an inventor of telegraphic clock, &c. Known to your Airy, & Adams.[8] He visits London now, on behalf of a railroad Company in Ohio; [9]—which has made him rich. He knows the Missisippi River; and if you have opportunity to say to Mr Owen, or Mr Forbes, or other Somerset House gentlemen, that Mr Mitchell is a lecturer of very considerable talent & should be heard at Albemarle Street,[10] I think you will please him & them. He sent, or his friends sent, to me, for any letters I might give him, before he went away; but too late for me to send to N.Y. But neither did I know the savans to whom he should go. Perhaps he is already on his return. I have written hundreds of pages about England & America, & may send them to you in print. And now be good & write me once more, & I think I will never cease to write again. And give my homage to Jane Carlyle. Ever yours,   R. W. Emerson

Concord, 12 May, 1853.[1]

My dear Carlyle,

Miss Bacon of New Haven, Connecticut, goes to London to prosecute certain literary enquiries, which she has much at heart. She is herself a lady of great worth, and is good scholar & writer enough to make the best statement of her opinions. Her studies respect English history, & mainly Shakspeare, & his times. Have you not a friend—Mr Spedding,

[7] The sister of James Freeman Clarke. Emerson wrote in his journal nineteen years later of her "repeated sisterly aid to Margaret Fuller, in old times, in her cruel headaches" (*Journal*, X, 385).

[8] Presumably George Biddell Airy, astronomer royal, and John Couch Adams, then president of the Royal Astronomical Society.

[9] Ormsby MacKnight Mitchel, soldier, professor, and director of the Cincinnati Observatory, had been chief engineer of the Little Miami Railroad.

[10] In London in 1848 Emerson had met the distinguished naturalists Richard Owen and Edward Forbes (*Let RWE*, IV, 41–42). Owen was at this time professor of comparative anatomy in the Royal College of Surgeons and conservator of the Hunterian Museum; Forbes was professor of botany in King's College, which then occupied the eastern wing of Somerset House. Albemarle Street was the location of the Royal Institution's library and lecture hall (Karl Baedeker, *London*, pp. 178 and 278).

[1] MS owned by the Folger Shakespeare Library.

who writes, or was writing Lord Bacon's Life? [2] If he is near you, & accessible, can you not obtain for Miss Bacon an interview with him? If to this you will add any instructions to Miss B., that will facilitate her access to the Library of the British Museum, you will effectually serve her.   Yours affectionately,   R W Emerson.

Chelsea, 13 May, 1853—

Dear Emerson,

The sight of your handwriting was a real blessing to me, after so long an abstinence. You shall not know all the sad reflexions I have made upon your silence within the last year. I never doubted your fidelity of heart; your genial deep and friendly recognition of my bits of merits, and my bits of sufferings, difficulties and obstructions; your forgiveness of my faults; or in fact that you ever would forget me or cease to think kindly of me: but it seemed as if practically *Old Age* had come upon the scene here too; and as if upon the whole one must make up one's mind to know that all this likewise had fallen silent, and could be possessed henceforth only on those new terms. Alas, there goes much over, year after year, into the region of the Immortals; inexpressibly beautiful, but also inexpressibly sad. I have not many voices to commune with in the world. In fact I have properly no voice at all; and yours, I have often said, was the *unique* among my fellow creatures, from which came full response, and discourse of reason: [1] the *solitude* one lives in, if one has any spiritual thought at all, is very great in these epochs!—The truth is, moreover, I bought spectacles to myself about two years ago (bad print in candle-light having fairly become troublesome to me); much may lie in that! "The buying of your first pair of spectacles," I said to an old Scotch gentleman, "is an important epoch; like the buying of your first razor."—"Yes," answered he, "but not quite so joyful perhaps!"— —Well, well, I have heard from you again; and you promise to be again constant in writing. Shall I believe you, this time? Do it, and shame the Devil! I am really persuaded it will do

[2] James Spedding, with R. L. Ellis and D. D. Heath, had been engaged since 1847 on a complete edition of the works of Francis Bacon. The relationship of Delia Bacon with Emerson and Carlyle is recounted fully in *Prodigal Puritan: a Life of Delia Bacon* by Vivian C. Hopkins.

[1] *Hamlet*, act I, scene ii, line 150.

yourself good; and to me I know right well, and have always known, what it will do. The gaunt lonesomeness of this Midnight Hour, in the ugly universal *snoring* hum of the overfilled deep-sunk Posterity of Adam, renders an articulate speaker precious indeed! Watchman, what sayest thou, then? Watchman, what of the night? [2]—

Your glimpses of the huge unmanageable Missisippi, of the huge do Model Republic, have here and there something of the *epic* in them, —*ganz nach meinem Sinne.* I see you do not dissent from me in regard to that latter enormous Phenomenon, except on the outer surface, and in the way of peaceably instead of *un*peaceably accepting the same. Alas, all the world is a "republic of the mediocrities," [3] and always was; —you may see what *its* "universal suffrage" is and has been, by looking into all the ugly mud-ocean (with some old weathercocks atop) that now *is:* the world wholly (if we think of it) is the exact stamp of men wholly, and of the *sincerest* heart-tongue-and hand- "suffrage" they could give about it, poor devils!— —I was much struck with Plato, last year, and his notions about Democracy: mere Latter-day Pamphlet *saxa et faces* [4] (read *faecas,* if you like) refined into empyrean radiance and lightning of the gods!—I, for my own part, perceive the use of all this too, the inevitability of all this; but perceive it (at the present height it has attained) to be disastrous withal, to be horrible and even damnable. That Judas Iscariot should come and slap Jesus Christ on the shoulder in a familiar manner; that all the heavenliest nobleness should be flung out into the muddy streets there to jostle elbows with all thickest-skinned denizens of chaos, and get itself at every turn trampled into the gutters and annihilated:—alas, the *reverse* of all this was, is, and ever will be, the strenuous effort and most solemn heart-purpose of every good citizen in every country of the world,— and will *reappear* conspicuously as such (in New England and in Old, first of all, as I calculate), when once this malodorous melancholy "*Uncle-Tommery*" [5] is got all well put by! Which will take some time yet, I think.—And so we will leave it.

[2] Isa. 21: 11.

[3] This phrase might well have appeared in the *Latter-Day Pamphlets,* but I do not find it there; "universal suffrage" does appear, in mocking capital letters rather than mocking quotation marks (*Works TC,* XX, 272).

[4] Cf. Vergil, *Aeneid,* I, 149–50: ". . . saevitque animis ignobile volgus/ iamque faces et saxa volant . . .".

[5] On January 19, 1853, Carlyle had written to his sister Jean: "*Uncle Tom's Cabin*

I went to Germany last Autumn; not *seeking* anything very definite; rather merely flying from certain troops of carpenters, painters, brick-layers, &c &c, who had made a lodgement in this poor house, and have not even yet got their incalculable riot quite concluded. Sorrow on them,—and no return to these poor premises of mine till I have quite left!—In Germany I found but little; and suffered, from 6 weeks of sleeplessness in German beds &c &c, a great deal. Indeed I seem to myself never yet to have quite recovered. The Rhine which I honestly as-cended from Rotterdam to Frankfort was, as I now find, my chief con-quest: the beautifullest river in the earth, I do believe;—and my first idea of a world-river. It is many fathoms deep, broader twice over than the Thames here at high water; and rolls along, mirror-smooth (except that in looking close, you will find ten thousand little eddies in it), voiceless, swift, with trim banks, thro' the heart of Europe, and of the Middle Ages wedded to the Present Age: such an image of calm *power* (to say nothing of its other properties) I find I had never seen before. The old Cities too are a little beautiful to me, in spite of my state of nerves; honest kindly people too, but sadly short of our and your *despatch-of-business* talents,—a really painful defect in the long run. I was on two of Fritz's Battlefields, moreover: Lobositz in Bohemia, and Cunersdorf by Frankfort on the Oder: but did not, especially in the latter case, make much of that. Schiller's death-chamber, Goethe's sad Court-environment; above all, Luther's little room in the *Wartburg* (I believe I actually had tears in my eyes there, and *kissed* the old oak-table, being in a very flurried state of nerves), my belief was that under the Canopy there was not at present so *holy* a spot as that same. Of human souls I found none specially beautiful to me at all, at all,— such my sad fate! Of learned professors, I saw little; and that little was more than enough. Tieck at Berlin an old man, lame on a sofa, I did love, and do; he is an exception, could I have seen much of him.[6] But on the whole *Universal Puseyism* seemed to me the humour of German, especially of Berlin, thinkers;—and I had some portentous specimens of that kind,—unconscious specimens of 400 quack power! Truly and

is the mania of *this* season; what will that of the *next* be? . . . to me for one, it seemed a pretty perfect sample of Yankee-Governess Romance, & I fairly could not and would not read beyond the first 100 pages of it" (NLS, MS 515).

[6] Carlyle had translated fiction by Ludwig Tieck for his anthology *German Romance* of 1827.

really the Prussian Soldiers, with their intelligent *silence,* with the touches of effective Spartanism I saw or fancied in them, were the class of people that pleased me best.— —But see my sheet is out! I am still reading, reading, most nightmare Books ab^t Fritz; but as to writing —Ach Gott! Never, never.—Clough is coming home, I hope.—Write soon, if you be not enchanted!

Yours ever   T Carlyle.

Concord, August 10, 1853

My dear Carlyle,

Your kindest letter, whose date I dare not count back to—perhaps it was May,—I have just read again, to be deeply touched by its noble tragic tone of goodness to me, not without new wonder at my perversity, & terror at what bolt may be a-forging to strike me. My slowness to write is a distemper that reaches all my correspondence, & not that with you only, though the circumstance is not worth stating, because if I ceased to write to all the rest, there would yet be good reason for writing to you. I believe the reason of this recusancy is, the fear of disgusting my my friends, as with a book open always at the same page. For I have some experiences, that my interest in thoughts,—& to an end, perhaps, only of new thoughts & thinking,—outlasts that of all my reasonable neighbors, & & offends, no doubt, by unhealthy pertinacity. But, though rebuked by a daily *reduction to an absurd* solitude, & by a score of disappointments with intellectual people, & in the face of a special hell provided for me in the Swedenborg Universe, I am yet confirmed in my madness by the scope & satisfaction I find in a conversation once or twice in five years,—if so often; & so we find or pick what we call our proper path, though it be only from stone to stone, or from island to island, in a very rude stilted & violent fashion. With such solitariness & frigidities, you may judge I was glad to see Clough here, with whom I had established some kind of robust working-friendship, & who had some great permanent values for me. Had he not taken me by surprize & fled in a night, I should have done what I could to block his way. I am too sure he will not return The first months comprise all the shocks of disappointment that are likely to disgust a newcomer. The sphere of opportunities opens slowly, but to a man of his abilities & culture,—rare enough here—with the sureness of chemistry. The giraffe entering Paris wore the label, "Eh bien, messieurs, il n'y a qu'une bete de plus!"[1] And Oxonians are cheap in London; but here, the eternal economy of sending things where they are wanted makes a commanding claim. Do not suffer him to relapse into London. He had made himself already cordially welcome to many good people, & would have soon made his own place. He had just established his valise at my house, & was to come,—the gay deceiver—once a fortnight, for his Sunday; & his individualities & his nationalities are alike valuable to me. I beseech you not to commend his unheroic retreat.[2]

I have lately made one or two drafts on your goodness,—which I hate to do, both because you meet them so generously, & because you never give me an opportunity of revenge,—and mainly in the case of Miss Bacon, who has a private history that entitles her to high respect, & who could be helped only by facilitating her Shakspeare studies, in which she has the faith & ardour of a discoverer. Bancroft was to have given her letters to Hallam, but gave one to Sir H. Ellis. Everett, I believe, gave her one to Mr Grote; [3] & when I told her what I remembered hearing of Spedding, she was eager to see him; which access I knew not how to secure, except through you. She wrote me that she prospers in all things, & had just received at once a summons to meet Spedding at your house. But do not fancy that I send any one to you heedlessly; for I value your time at its rate to nations, & refuse many more letters than I give. I shall not send you any more people without good reason.

Your visit to Germany will stand you in stead, when the annoyances of the journey are forgotten, & in spite of your disclaimers, I am preparing to read your history of Frederic. You are an inveterate European, & rightfully stand for your polity & antiquities & culture: and I have long since forborne to importune you with America, as if it were a humorous repetition of Johnson's visit to Scotland. And yet since Thackeray's adventure, I have often thought how you would bear the

[1] Perhaps a memory of Emerson's Paris visit of 1833. See *Let RWE*, I, 390.

[2] Clough had been offered, in July, an examinership in the educational office of the Privy Council and had sailed for England so abruptly that he left "items of clothing" at Concord which he asked Emerson to keep "as an auspice of a future coming" (*Correspondence*, ed. Frederick L. Mulhauser, II, 457–58).

[3] Henry Hallam, whose *Middle Ages* had established him in 1818 among the first of English historians; Sir Henry Ellis, chief librarian of the British Museum; George Grote, the eleventh volume of whose *History of Greece* had just been published.

pains & penalties; & have painted out your march triumphal. I was at New York, lately, for a few days, & fell into some traces of Thackeray, who has made a good mark in this country, by a certain manly blurting out of his opinion in various companies, where so much honesty was rare & useful. I am sorry never once to have been in the same town with him, whilst he was here. I hope to see him, if he comes again. New York would interest you; as I am told, it did him; *you* both less & more. The "society" there, is at least selfpleased, & its own; it has a contempt of Boston, & a very modest opinion of London. There is already all the play & fury that belongs to great wealth. A new fortune drops into the city, every day; no end is to palaces, none to diamonds, none to dinners & suppers. All Spanish America discovers that only in the U. States, of all the continent, is safe investment; & money gravitates therefore to New York. The Southern naphtha, too, comes in as an ingredient, & lubricates manners & tastes to that degree, that Boston is hated for stiffness, & excellence in luxury is rapidly attained. Of course, dining, dancing, equipaging, &c. are the exclusive beatitudes—and Thackeray will not cure us of this distemper. Have you a physician that can? Are you a physician, & will you come? If you *will* come, cities will go out to meet you. And now I see, I have so much to say to you that I ought to write once a month & I must begin at this point again incontinently.

Ever yours,   R. W. Emerson

Chelsea, London, 9 Sept^r, 1853—

Dear Emerson,

Your Letter came ten days ago; very kind, and however late, surely right welcome! You ought to stir yourself up a little, and actually begin to speak to me again. If we are getting old, that is no reason why we should fall silent, and entirely abstruse to one another. Alas, I do not find as I grow older that the number of articulate-speaking human souls increases around me, in proportion to the inarticulate and palavering species! I am often abundantly solitary in heart; and regret the old days when we used to speak oftener together.

I have not quitted Town this year at all; have resisted calls to Scotland both of a gay and a sad description (for the Ashburtons are gone to John of Groat's House, or the Scottish *Thule,* to rusticate & hunt; and, alas, in poor old Annandale a tragedy seems preparing for me, and the thing I have dreaded all my days is perhaps now drawing nigh, ah me!) [1]—I felt so utterly broken and disgusted with the jangle of last year's locomotion, I judged it would be better to sit obstinately still, and let my thoughts *settle* (into sediment and into clearness, as it might be); and so, in spite of great and peculiar noises moreover, here I am and remain. London is not a bad place at all in these months,—with its long clean streets, green parks, and nobody in them, or nobody one has ever seen before. Out of La Trappe, which does not suit a Protestant man, there is perhaps no place where one can be so perfectly alone. I might study even: but, as I said, there are noises going on; a *last* desperate spasmodic effort of building,—a new top-story to the house, out of which is to be made one "spacious room" (so they call it, tho' it is under 20 feet square) where there shall be air *ad libitum,* light from the sky, and no *sound,* not even that of the Cremorne Cannons,[2] shall find access to me any more! Such is the prophecy; may the gods grant it! We shall see now in about a month;—then adieu to mortar-tubs to all Eternity:—I endure the thing, meanwhile, as well as I can; might run to a certain rural retreat nearby, if I liked at any time; but do not yet: the worst uproar here is but a trifle to that of German inns, and horrible squeaking choking railway trains; and one does not go to seek this, *this* is here of its own will, and for a purpose! Seriously, I had for 12 years had such a soundproof inaccessible apartment schemed out in my head; and last year, under a poor helpless builder, had finally given it up; but Chelsea, as London generally, swelling out as if it were mad, grows every year noisier; a *good* builder turned up, and with a last paroxysm of enthusiasm, I set him to. My notion is, he will succeed; in which case, it will be a great possession to me for the rest of my life. Alas, this is not the kind of *silence* I could have coveted, and could once get,—with green fields and clear skies to accompany it! But one must take such as can be had,—and thank the gods. Even so, my friend. In the course of about a year of that garret sanctuary, I hope to have swept away much litter from my existence: in fact I am already, by dint of mere obstinate quiescence in such circumstances as these are, intrinsically growing fairly sounder in nerves. What a business a poor human

---

[1] In July Carlyle's aged mother had been near to death but had recovered (*Letters and Memorials,* II, 14).

[2] In Cremorne Gardens in Chelsea there was at this time a public amusement park (Baedeker, *London,* p. 357). Froude mentions fireworks there during the summer of 1853 (*Thomas Carlyle: Life in London,* II, 111).

being has with those nerves of his, with that crazy clay tabernacle of his! Enough, enough: there will be all Eternity to rest in, as Arnauld [3] said: "Why in such a fuss, little sir?" [4]—

You "apologize" for sending people to me: O you of little faith! [5] Never dream of such a thing: nay, whom *did* you send? The Cincinnati Lecturer I had provided for with Owen; they would have been glad to hear him, on the Cedar forests, on the pigs making rattlesnakes into brawn, and the general adipocere question, under any form, at the Albemarle Street rooms;—and he never came to hand. As for Miss Bacon we find her, with her modest shy dignity, with her solid character and strange enterprise, a real acquisition; and hope we shall now see more of her, now that she has come nearer us to lodge. I have not in my life seen anything so tragically *quixotic* as her Shakspeare enterprise: alas, alas, there can be nothing but sorrow, toil, and utter disappointment in it for her! I do cheerfully what I can;—which is far more than she *asks* of me (for I have not seen a prouder silent soul);—but there is not the least possibility of truth in the notion she has taken up: and the hope of ever proving it, or finding the least document that countenances it, is equal to that of vanquishing the windmills by stroke of lance. I am often truly sorry about the poor lady: but she troubles nobody with her difficulties, with her theories; she must try the matter to the end, and charitable souls must further her so far.[6]

Clough is settled in his Office; [7] gets familiarized to it rapidly (he says), and seems to be doing well. I see little of him hitherto; I did not, and will not, try to influence him in his choice of countries; but I think

---

[3] Antoine Arnauld, the Jansenist theologian.

[4] Cf. Emerson's "So hot? my little Sir" (*Works*, II, 135).   [5] Cf. Matt. 6: 30.

[6] On June 11, 1853, Carlyle wrote to W. E. Forster: "Emerson has sent me from Yankee-land a female Enthusiast for Shakespeare,—who has discovered (in her own *head* chiefly, I doubt) an entirely new Biography of Shakespeare, thinks his Plays, so thrice-miraculous are they, were *not* written by *him*, but by—the Lord knows whom:—and, in brief, has come to England with the hope of supporting that sublime notion by investigation in the old country! For the rest, rather a clever Damsel—of mature age, probably 40; of good manners, tho' with the most amazing Yankee drawl; and on the whole, shrewd, veracious, notwithstanding this in[con]ceivable hypothesis of hers. Name, 'Miss Delia L. Bacon'; lodges at Chapman's 142 Strand—We saw her here last night . . . an excellent soul, and almost pretty." Carlyle had invited James Spedding to his house that evening to meet Miss Bacon; his purpose in writing Forster was to get her an introduction to John Payne Collier, "the learned Editor of Shakespeare." (MS owned by the Victoria and Albert Museum.)

[7] See above, E.8.10.53, n. 1.

he is now likely to continue here, and here too he may do us some good. Of America, at least of New England, I can perceive he has brought away an altogether kindly, almost filial impression,—especially of a certain man who lives in that section of the Earth. More power to his elbow!— —Thackeray has very rarely come athwart me since his return: he is a big fellow, soul and body; of many gifts and qualities (particularly in the Hogarth line, with a dash of Sterne superadded), of enormous *appetite* withal, and very uncertain and chaotic in all points, except his *outer breeding,* which is fixed enough, and *perfect* according to the modern English style. I rather dread explosions in his history. A *big,* fierce, weeping, hungry man; not a strong one. *Ay de mi!* —But I must end, I must end. Your Letter awakened in me, while reading it, one mad notion. I said to myself, "Well, if I live to finish this Frederic impossibility, or even to fling it fairly into the fire, why should not I go, in my old days, and see Concord, Yankeeland, and that man again, after all!"—Adieu, dear friend; all good be with you & yours always.   T. Carlyle

                                                    Chelsea, 2 dec^r, 1853—
Dear Emerson,

Let me now present to you Mr S. Lawrence an Artist of great talent and accomplishment in the way of Portrait Painting (to whom I have repeatedly sat); and a truly worthy amiable and honourable man, whom I have long known as such. Being on a Tour in America for certain months (with more than one object), he will take Sitters as the occasion may offer. He is sincerely and highly esteemed by the best judges here; has in fact painted most of our best faces (Tennyson, Thirlwall [1] &c &c) as no other man among us can paint them. I think you will find in him truly a good friend of tacit (unconscious) intelligence; presumably adequate for that and other tasks;—and not unbeautiful to you and others that can recognise it.—In a word, please to receive Lawrence as a good man, of good gifts, is sure to be received by you;—and if you can in any way forward him, do not neglect to do it.
                    I am always   Yours sincerely   T. Carlyle
Ralph Waldo Emerson Esq
Concord, Boston, Masstts.
By Samuel Lawrence Esq

[1] Connop Thirlwall, historian of Greece and bishop of St. David's.

1854

Concord, 11 March, 1854.

My dear Carlyle,

The sight of Mr Sam. Laurence,—the day before yesterday, in New York, & of your head among his sketches,[1] set me on thinking which had some pain where should be only cheer. For Mr L. I hailed his arrival, on every account. I wish to see a good man whom you prize; and I like to have good Englishmen come to America, which of all countries, after their own, has the best claim to them. He promises to come & see me, & has begun most propitiously in New York. For you, —I have too much constitutional regard and—, not to feel remorse for my shortcomings & slowcomings, and I remember the maxim which the French stole from our Indians,—and it was worth stealing—"Let not the grass grow on the path of friendship!" Ah my brave giant, you can never understand the silence & forbearances of such as are not giants. To those to whom we owe affection, let us be dumb until we are strong, though we should never be strong. I hate mumped & measled lovers. I hate cramp in all men,—most in myself.

And yet I should have been pushed to write without Samuel Laurence: for I lately looked into "Jesuitism," a Latter Day Pamphlet, & found why you like those papers so well. I think you have cleared your skirts; it is a pretty good minority of one; enunciating with brilliant malice what shall be the universal opinion of the next edition of mankind. And the sanity was so manifest, that I felt that the overgods had cleared their skirts also to this generation, in not leaving themselves without witness, though, without this single voice, perhaps, I should not acquit them. Also I pardon the world that reads the book as though it read it not, when I see your inveterated humours. It required courage & required conditions that feuilletonists are not the persons to name or qualify, this writing Rabelais in 1850. And to do this alone!—You

[1] Laurence made at least four sketches of Carlyle (Dyer, *A Bibliography of Thomas Carlyle's Writings and Ana*, pp. 537-38).

must even pitch your tune to suit yourself. We must let Arctic naviga-
tors and deep-sea-divers wear what astonishing coats, & eat what meats
—wheat or whale—they like, without criticism. I read further, sidewise
& backwards, in these pamphlets, without exhausting them. I have not
ceased to think of the great warm heart that sends them forth, & which
I, with others, sometimes tax with satire, & with not being warm
enough—for this poor world;—I too,—though I know its meltings to
me ward.[2] Then I learned, that the newspapers had announced the
death of your mother, (which I heard of casually on the Rock River,
Illinois,) and that you & your brother John had been with her, in
Scotland.[3] I remembered what you had once & again said of her to me,
& your apprehensions of the event which has now come. I can well believe you were grieved. The best son is not enough a son. My mother
died in my house in November, who had lived with me all my life, &
kept her heart & mind clear, & her own until the end. It is very necessary that we should have mothers,—we that read & write, to keep us
from becoming paper. I had found that age did not make that she
should die without causing me pain. In my journeying lately, when I
think of home, the heart is taken out.

Miss Bacon wrote me in joyful fulness of the cordial kindness & aid
she had found at your hands, & at your wife's: [4] and I have never
thanked you, & much less acknowledged her copious letter,—copious
with desired details. Clough, too, wrote about you, & I have not written
to him since his return to England. You will see how total is my ossifi-
cation. Meantime I have nothing to tell you that can explain this mild
palsy. I worked for a time on my English Notes with a view to printing,
but was forced to leave them to go read some lectures in Philadelphia
& some Western towns. I went out northwest to great countries which
I had not visited before; rode one day, fault of broken railroads, in a
sleigh, 65 miles through the snow, by Lake Michigan, (seeing how
prairies & oak-openings look in winter) to reach Milwaukee "the world
there was done up in large lots" as a settler told me. The farmer as he
is now a colonist and has drawn from his local necessities great doses of
energy, is interesting, & makes the heroic age for Wisconsin. He lives

---

[2] Emerson usually hyphenated such phrases as this: see below, E.5.17.58.

[3] Carlyle's mother died on Christmas Day, 1853 (Froude, *Thomas Carlyle: Life in
London*, II, 156).

[4] The following January, Delia Bacon wrote to her sister of an evening with the
Carlyles: ". . . it was *very very pleasant*. . . . I have real cosy pleasant times when
I go there" (Theodore Bacon, *Delia Bacon*, p. 75).

on venison & quails. I was made much of, as the only man of the pen within 500 miles, & by rarity worth more than venison & quails. Greeley of the New York Tribune is the right spiritual father of all this region he prints & disperses 110 000 newspapers in one day, multitudes of them in these very parts. He had preceded me by a few days, & people had flocked together, coming 30 & 40 miles to hear him speak; as was right, for he does all their thinking & theory for them, for two dollars a year. Other than colonists I saw no man. "There are no singing birds in the prairie," I truly heard. All the life of land & water had distilled no thought. Younger & better, I had no doubt been tormented to read & speak their sense for them. Now I only gazed at them & their boundless land.

One good word closed your letter in September, which ought to have had an instant reply, namely, that you might come westward, when Frederic was disposed of! Speed Frederic, then, for all reasons and for this! America is growing furiously, town & state, new Kansas new Nebraska looming up in these days, vicious politicians seething a wretched destiny for them already at Washington.[5] the politicians shall be sodden, the states escape, please God! The fight of slave & freeman drawing nearer, the question is properly, whether slavery or whether freedom shall be abolished. Come & see. Wealth, which is always interesting, for from wealth power refuses to be divorced, is on a new scale. Californian quartz mountains dumped down in New York to be repiled architecturally along shore from Canada to Cuba, & thence west to California again. John Bull interests you at home, & is all your subject. Come & see the Jonathanization of John. What, you scorn all this? Well then, come see a few good people, impossible to be seen on any other shore, who heartily & always greet you. There is a very serious welcome for you here. And I too shall wake from sleep. My Wife entreats that an invitation shall go from her to you.

Faithfully yours,   R. W. Emerson

Chelsea, 8 April, 1854—

Dear Emerson,

It was a morning not like any other which lay round it, a morning to be marked with white, that one, about a week ago, when your Letter

---

[5] Congress was now approaching the end of its debate over the question of slavery in the territories of Kansas and Nebraska.

came to me; a word from you yet again, after so long a silence! On the whole, I perceive you will not utterly give up answering me, but will rouse yourself now and then to a word of human brotherhood on my behalf, so long as we both continue in this Planet. And I declare, the Heavens will reward you; and as to me, I will be thankful for what I get, and submissive to delays and to all things: all things are good compared with flat *want* in that respect. It remains true, and will remain, what I have often told you, that properly there is no voice in this world which is completely human to me, which fully understands all I say, and with clear sympathy and sense answers to me, but your voice only. That is a curious fact, and not quite a joyful one to me. The solitude, the silence of my poor soul in the centre of this roaring whirlpool called Universe, is great always, and sometimes strange and almost awful. I have two million talking bipeds without feathers,[1] close at my elbow, too; and of these it is often hard for me to say whether the so-called "wise" or the almost professedly foolish are the more inexpressibly unproductive to me. "Silence, silence!" I often say to myself: "Be silent, thou poor fool; and prepare for that Divine Silence which is now not far!"— —On the whole, write to me whenever you can; and be not weary of welldoing.[2]

I have had sad things to do and see since I wrote to you: the loss of my dear and good old Mother, which could not be spared me forever, has come more like a kind of total bankruptcy upon me than might have been expected, considering her age and mine. Oh those last two days, that last Christmas Sunday! She was a true pious brave and noble mother to me; and it is now all over; and the Past has all become pale and sad and sacred;—and the all-devouring potency of Death, what we call Death, has never looked so strange, cruel and unspeakable to me. Nay not *cruel* altogether, let me say: huge, profound, *unspeakable,* that is the word.—You too have lost your good old Mother, who staid with you like mine clear to the last: alas, alas, it is the oldest Law of Nature; and it comes on every one of us with a strange originality, as if it had never happened before.—Forward, however; and no more lamenting; no more than cannot be helped. "Paradise is under the shadow of our swords," said the Emir: "Forward!"[3]—

[1] Cf. Diogenes Laertius, *The Lives and Opinions of Eminent Philosophers,* trans. C. D. Yonge (London, Bohn's Classical Library, 1895), p. 231.

[2] II Thess. 3: 13.

[3] Attributed to Mohammed in the *Sahih Bukhari.* See Maulana Muhammad Ali, *A Manual of Hadith* (Lahore, 1944), p. 261.

I make no way in my Prussian History; I bore and dig toilsomely thro' the unutterablest mass of dead rubbish, which is not even English, which is German and inhuman; and hardly from ten tons of learned inanity is there to be riddled an old rusty nail. For I have been back as far as Pytheas (who first of speaking creatures) beheld the Teutonic Countries; and have questioned all manner of extinct German shadows, —who answer nothing but mumblings. And on the whole Fritz himself is not sufficiently divine to me, far from it; and I am getting old, and heavy of heart;—and in short, it oftenest seems to me I shall never write any word about that matter; and have again fairly got into the element of the IMPOSSIBLE. Very well: could I help it? I can at least be honestly silent; and "bear my indigence with dignity," as you once said.[4] The insuperable difficulty of *Frederic* is, that he, the genuine little ray of Veritable and Eternal that was in him, lay imbedded in the putrid Eighteenth Century, such an ocean of sordid nothingnesses, shams, and scandalous hypocrisies, as never weltered in the world before; and that in everything I can find yet written or recorded of him, he still, to all intents and purposes, most tragically *lies* THERE;— and ought not to lie there, if any use is ever to be had of him, or at least of *writing* about him; for as to *him,* he with his work is safe enough to us, far elsewhere.—Pity me, pity me; I know not on what hand to turn; and have such a Chaos filling all my Earth and Heaven as was seldom seen in British or Foreign Literature! Add to which, the sacred Entity, Literature itself is not growing more memorable to me, but less and ever less: good Heavens, I feel often as if there were no madder set of bladders tumbling on the billows of the general Bedlam at this moment than even the Literary ones,—dear at twopence a gross, I should say, unless one could *annihilate* them by purchase on those easy terms! But do not tell this in Gath; [5] let it be a sad family-secret.

I smile, with a kind of grave joy, over your American speculations, and wild dashing portraitures of things as they are with you; and recognise well, under your light caricature, the outlines of a right true picture, which has often made me sad and grim in late years. Yes, I consider that the "Battle of Freedom and Slavery" is very far from ended; and that the fate of poor "Freedom" in the quarrel is very

<hr/>

[4] Probably in conversation. But there is a similar statement in Emerson's lecture "The Transcendentalist," which was published in *The Dial* for January, 1843: ". . . though we had few virtues or consolations, we bore with our indigence . . ." (*Works*, I, 354).

[5] Cf. II Sam. 1: 20.

questionable indeed! Alas, there is but one *Slavery,* as I wrote somewhere; [6] and that, I think, is mounting towards a height, which may
bring strokes to bear upon it again! Meanwhile, patience; for us there
is nothing else appointed.—Tell me, however, what has become of your
Book on England? We shall really be obliged to you for that. A piece
of it went thro' all the Newspapers, some years ago; which was really
unique for its quaint kindly insight, humour and other qualities; like
an etching by Hollar [7] or Dürer, amid the continents of vile smearing
which are called "pictures" at present. Come on, come on; give us the
Book; and don't loiter!—

Miss Bacon has fled away to *St Albans* (the *Great* Bacon's place) 5 or
6 months ago; and is *there* working out her Shakspeare Problem, from
the depths of her own mind, disdainful apparently, or desperate and
careless, of all *evidence* from Museums or Archives; I have not had an
answer from her since before Christmas, and have now lost her address.
Poor Lady: I sometimes silently wish she were safe home again; for
truly there can no madder enterprise than her present one be well
figured.—Adieu, my Friend; I must stop short here. Write soon, if you
have any charity. Good be with you ever   T. Carlyle

[6] In "The Nigger Question" (1849) Carlyle had asserted that "the one intolerable
sort of slavery is the slavery of the strong to the weak; of the great and noble-
minded to the small and mean . . . of Wisdom to Folly" and that this kind of
slavery is imposed by ballot-boxes and universal suffrage.

[7] Wenceslaus Hollar's seventeenth-century English portraits and views of towns
would have been of great interest to Carlyle during the Cromwell period.

1855

Concord   17 April 1855

My dear friend!

On this delicious spring day, I will obey the beautiful voices of the winds, long disobeyed, & address you; nor cloud the hour by looking at the letters in my drawer to know if a twelvemonth has been allowed to elapse since this tardy writing was due. Mr Everett sent me one day a letter he had received from you, containing a kind message to me, which gave me pleasure & pain.[1] I returned the letter with thanks, & with promises that I would sin no more. Instantly I was whisked, "by the stormy wing of Fate"[2] out of my chair, & whirled, like a dry leaf, through the State of New York. Now at home again, I read English Newspapers, with all the world, & claim an imaginary privilege over my compatriots, that I revolve therein my friend's large part. Ward said to me yesterday, that Carlyle's star was daily rising. For C. had said, years ago, when all men thought him mad, that which the rest of mortals, including the Times Newspaper have at last got near enough to see with eyes, & therefore to believe.[3] And one day, in Philadelphia, you should have heard the wise young Philip Randolph[4] defend you against objections of mine. But when I hear such testimony, I say to myself, the high seeing austerely exigent friend whom I elected, & who elected me, twenty years & more ago, finds me heavy & silent, when all the world elects & loves him. Yet I have not changed. I have the same pride in his genius, the same sympathy with the Genius that governs

[1] In a letter to Everett of December 22, 1854, Carlyle wrote: "Emerson never writes to me, or not once in many months, the sinful man; please give him my regards if he ever comes athwart you" (*Let RWE*, IV, 486*n*).

[2] I have been unable to find the source of this quotation.

[3] *The Times* early in April contained many editorials and letters which were highly critical of the conduct of the war in the Crimea.

[4] Philip Physick Randolph, whom Emerson later wrote of as the best chess player in Philadelphia and "the grandson of the celebrated Dr Physic" (*Let RWE*, V, 538). "Dr Physic" was Philip Syng Physick, who, according to *The American Cyclopedia* (1879), "has been called the father of American surgery."

his. the old love with the old limitations, tho' love & limitation be all untold. And I see well what a piece of Providence he is, how material he is to the times, which must always have a solo Soprano to balance the roar of the Orchestra. The solo sings the theme; the orchestra roars antagonistically but follows.—And have I not put him into my Chapter of "English Spiritual Tendencies," with all thankfulness to the Eternal Creator,—though the Chapter lie unborn in a trunk.[5]

Tis fine for us to excuse ourselves, & patch with promises. We shall do as before and science is a fatalist. I follow, I find, the fortunes of my country, in my privatest ways. An American is pioneer & man of all work, & reads up his newspaper on Saturday night, as farmers & foresters do. We admire the μεγαλοψυχια, & mean to give our boys the grand habit; but we only sketch what they may do. No leisure except for the strong, the nimble have none.—I ought to tell you what I do, or I ought to have to tell you what I have done. But what can I? the same concession to the levity of the times, the noise of America comes again. I have even run on wrong topics for my parsimonious muse, & waste my time from my true studies.[6] England I see as a roaring volcano of Fate, which threatens to roast or smother the poor literary Plinys[7] that come too near for mere purpose of reporting.

I have even fancied you did me a harm by the valued gift of Antony Wood;[8]—which, & the like of which, I take a lotophagous pleasure in eating. Yet this is measuring after appearance, measuring on hours & days. the true measure is quite other, for life takes its color & quality not from the days, but the dawns. The lucid intervals are like drowning men's moments, equivalent to the foregoing years. Besides Nature *uses* us We live but little for ourselves, a good deal for our children, & strangers. Each man is one more lump of clay to hold the world together It is in the power of the Spirit meantime to make him rich

[5] Probably the chapter of *English Traits* which was later called "Literature."

[6] Perhaps a reference to the January 25 lecture on slavery (Cabot, *A Memoir of Ralph Emerson*, II, 759); if so, this is one of the last of Emerson's above-the-battle utterances. Perhaps also, as the next sentence suggests, a comment on *English Traits*.

[7] Pliny lost his life while observing the eruption of Vesuvius which buried Pompeii.

[8] In 1848 Carlyle gave Emerson a copy of Wood's seventeenth-century biographical dictionary *Athenae Oxonienses* (see below, E.1.23.70). This was probably the book about which Carlyle wrote to Forster on July 15, 1842: ". . . whether six guineas be a fair price for one that is offered to me . . . 'half-bound in Russia' " (MS owned by the Victoria and Albert Museum).

reprisals,—which he confides will somewhere be done.—Ah, my friend, you have better things to send me word of, than these musings of indolence. Is Frederic recreated? Is Frederic the Great? Forget my shortcomings & write to me. Miss Bacon sends me word again & again of your goodness. Against hope & sight she must be making a remarkable book. I have a letter from her, a few days ago, written in perfect assurance of success! Kindest remembrances to your wife & to your brother.   Yours faithfully,   R. W. Emerson

Chelsea, 13 May, 1855—

Dear Emerson,

Last Sunday, Clough was here; and we were speaking about you (much to your discredit, you need not doubt), and how stingy in the way of Letters you were grown; when, next morning, your Letter itself made its appearance. Thanks, thanks. You know not in the least, I perceive, nor can be made to understand at all, how indispensable your Letters are to me. How you are, and have for a long time been, the one of all the sons of Adam who, I felt, completely understood what I was saying; and answered with a truly *human* voice,—inexpressibly consolatory to a poor man, in his lonesome pilgrimage, towards the evening of the day! So many voices are not human; but more or less bovine, porcine, canine; and one's soul dies away in sorrow in the sound of them, and is reduced to a dialogue with the "Silences" which is of a very abstruse nature!—Well, whether you write to me or not, I reserve to myself the privilege of writing to you, so long as we both continue in this world! As the beneficent Presences vanish from me, one after the other, those that remain are the more precious, and I will not part with them, not with the chief of them, beyond all.

This last year has been a grimmer lonelier one with me than any I can recollect for a long time. I did not go to the Country at all in summer or winter; refused even my Christmas at The Grange with the Ashburtons,—it was too sad an anniversary for me;—I have sat here in my garret, wriggling and wrestling on the worst terms with a Task that I cannot do, that generally seems to me not worth doing, and yet *must* be *done*. These are truly the terms. I never had such a business in my life before. Frederick himself is a pretty little man to me, veracious, courageous, invincible in his small sphere; but he does not rise into the empyrean regions, or kindle my heart round him at all; and his history, upon which there are waggon loads of dull bad books, is the most dislocated, unmanagably incoherent, altogether dusty, barren and beggarly production of the modern Muses, as given hitherto. No man of *genius* ever saw him with eyes, except twice Mirabeau, for half an hour each time. And the wretched Books have no *indexes,* no precision of detail; and I am far away from Berlin & the seat of information;—and, in brief, shall be beaten miserably with this unwise enterprise in my old days; *and* (in fine) will consent to be so, and get thro' it if I can before I die. This of obstinacy is the one quality I still shew; all my other qualities (hope, among them) often seem to have pretty much taken leave of me; but it is necessary to hold by this last. Pray for me; I will complain no more at present. General Washington gained the freedom of America chiefly by this respectable quality I talk of; nor can a History of Fᵏ be written, in Chelsea in the year 1855, except as *against* hope, and by planting yourself upon it in an extremely dogged manner.

We are all woolgathering here, with wide eyes and astonished minds, at a singular rate, since you heard last from me! "Balaklava," I can perceive, is likely to be a substantive in the English language henceforth: it in truth expresses compendiously what an earnest mind will experience everywhere in English life; if his soul rise at all above cotton and scrip, a man has to pronounce it all a *Balaklava* these many years. A Balaklava now *yielding,* under the pressure of rains and unexpected transit of heavy waggons; champing itself down into mere mud-gulphs, —towards the bottomless Pool, if some flooring be not found. To me it is not intrinsically a new phenomenon, only an extremely hideous one. *Altum silentium,*[1] what else can I reply to it at present? The Turk war, undertaken under pressure of the mobility,[2] seemed to me an enterprise worthy of Bedlam from the first; and this method of carrying it on, *without* any general, or with a mere sash and cocked-hat for one,[3] is of the same block of stuff. *Ach Gott!* Is not Anarchy, and parliamentary eloquence instead of work, continued for half a century everywhere, a beautiful piece of business? We are in alliance with Louis Napoleon (a gentⁿ who has shewn only *housebreaker* qualities hitherto, and is required now to shew heroic ones, *or* go to the Devil); and,

[1] Vergil, *Aeneid,* X, 63. [2] I.e., "mob."

[3] Presumably Carlyle refers here to Lord Raglan, the British commander in the Crimea, whose conduct of the war had been much condemned.

under Meréchal Saint-Arnaud (who was once a dancing-master in this city, and continued a *thief* in all cities) a commander of the Playactor-Pirate description, resembling a *General* as Alex^r Dumas does Dante Alighieri,—we have got into a very strange problem indeed! [4]— —But there is something almost grand in the stubborn thickside patience and persistence of this English People; and I do not question but they will work themselves thro' in one fashion or another; nay probably get a great deal of benefit out of this astonishing slap on the nose to their self-complacency before all the world. They have not *done* yet, I calculate, by any manner of means: they are, however, admonished, in an ignominious and convincing manner, amid the laughter of nations, that they are altogether on the wrong road this great while (200 years, as I have been calculating often),—and I shudder to think of the plunging and struggle they will have to get into the approximately right one again. Pray for them also, poor stupid overfed heavy laden souls!— —

Before my paper quite end, I must in my own name, and that of a silent company of others inquire rigorously of R. W. E. why he does not *give* us that little Book on England he has promised so long? I am very serious in saying, I myself want much to see it;—and that I can see no reason why we all should not, without delay. Bring it out, I say, and print it, *tale quale*. You will never get it in the least like what *you* wish it, clearly no! But I venture to warrant, it is good enough,—far too good for the readers that are to get it. Such a pack of blockheads, and disloyal and bewildered unfortunates who know not their right hand from their left,[5] as fill me with astonisht, and are more and more forfeiting all respect from me. Publish the Book, I say; let us have it and so have done!— —Adieu my dear friend for this time. I had a thousand things more to write, but have wasted my sheet, and must end. I will take another before long, whatever you do. In my lonely thoughts you are never long absent: *Valete* all of you at Concord!

T. Carlyle

---

[4] During this period, Carlyle made a point of not reading the newspapers and so was perhaps unaware that Saint-Arnaud had been dead since September 29, 1854.

[5] Cf. Jonah 4: 11.

1856

Concord, 5 May, 1856.[1]

My dear Mrs Carlyle,

Will you let me recall my old name to your remembrance, on the occasion of the visit of a dear & honored friend to London, Mrs Ward of Boston, whom I especially wish to present to your kind regards. Mrs Ward is the wife of my friend Sam. G. Ward, Esq. whose name I know is known to your husband,—though they have never met,[2]—& is herself the most beloved & valued of all American women. I shall not trust myself to say the least of all the good I know of her; since we at home here who have seen her through many brilliant years may easily doubt whether the new friends she may meet in passing can feel as we do. But I send her to the best, & I shall gladly know that you who know all that is excellent in English society, have seen our joy & pride. Her health is bad, her physicians advise travel, I wish neuralgic pains were not permitted to assail such good nerves. Mrs Ward is on her way to Switzerland, where her son is at school, & stops in London a few days. I trust you shall not be ailing, nor in the country, as I have set my heart on her seeing you.

And so, with best thoughts & grateful remembrances, I remain your affectionate servant,   R. W. Emerson

Mrs Jane Carlyle

Concord, 6 May, 1856.

Dear Carlyle,

There is no escape from the forces of time & life, & we do not write letters to the gods or to our friends, but only to attorneys landlords & tenants. But the planes or platforms on which all stand remain the

---

[1] Manuscript owned by the National Library of Scotland, MS 3218.

[2] For Mrs. Ward, see below, E.5.6.56. For her husband and the visit to Carlyle which he did not make, see above, C.11.4.50.

same, & we are ever expecting the descent of the heavens, which is to put us into familiarity with the first named. When I ceased to write to you for a long time, I said to myself,—If any thing really good should happen here,—any stroke of good sense or virtue in our politics, or of great sense in a book,—I will send it on the instant to the formidable man; but I will not repeat to him every month, that there are no news. Thank me for my resolution, & for keeping it through the long night. One book, last summer, came out in New York, a nondescript monster which yet has terrible eyes & buffalo strength, & was indisputably American,—which I thought to send you; but the book throve so badly with the few to whom I showed it, & wanted good morals so much, that I never did. Yet I believe now again, I shall. It is called "Leaves of Grass," —was written & printed by a journeyman printer in Brooklyn, N. Y. named Walter Whitman; and after you have looked into it, if you think, as you may, that it is only an auctioneer's inventory of a warehouse, you can light your pipe with it.

By tomorrow's steamer goes Mrs Anna Ward to Liverpool & to Switzerland & Germany by the advice of physicians, and I cannot let her go without praying you to drop your pen, & shut up German history for an hour, & extend your walk to her chambers, wherever they may be.[1] *There's* a piece of republicanism for you to see & hear! That person was, ten or fifteen years ago, the loveliest of women, & her speech & manners may still give you some report of the same. She has always lived with good people, and in her position is a centre of what is called good society, wherein her large heart makes a certain glory & refinement. She is one of nature's ladies, & when I hear her tell I know not what stories of her friends, or her children, or her pensioners, I find a pathetic eloquence which I know not where to match. But I suppose you shall never hear it. Every American is a little displaced in London, & no doubt, her company has grown to her. Her husband is a banker connected in business with your Barings, and is a man of elegant genius & tastes, and his house is a resort for fine people. Thorwaldsen distinguished Anna Ward in Rome, formerly, by his attentions. Powers the Sculptor made an admirable bust of her; Clough & Thackeray will tell

---

[1] Carlyle was, characteristically, annoyed at what seemed the vagueness of Emerson's directions. On May 25, 1856, he wrote to his brother John: "Letter from Emerson (after above a year), which you shall see, when we have got settled about the *message* or request in it. Request to *call* on some Yankee Lady of distinction; whose address is not yet discovered" (NLS, MS 516).

you of her. Jenny Lind like the rest was captivated by her, & was married at her house.[2] Is not Henry James in London? he knows her well. If Tennyson comes to London, whilst she is there, he should see her for his "Lays of Good Women." [3] Now please to read these things to the wise & kind ears of Jane Carlyle, and ask her if I have done wrong in giving my friend a letter to her? I could not ask more than that each of those ladies might appear to the other what each has appeared to me.

I saw Thackeray, in the winter, & he said he would come to see me here, in April or May; but he is still, I believe, in the South & West.[4] Do not believe me for my reticency less hungry for letters. I grieve at the want & loss, and am about writing again, that I may hear from you.

Ever affectionately yours,   R. W. Emerson

Chelsea, 20 July, 1856—

Dear Emerson,

Welcome was your Letter to me, after the long interval; as welcome as any human Letter could now well be. These many months and years I have been sunk in what disastrous vortexes of foreign wreck you know, till I am fallen sick and almost broken-hearted, and my life (if it were not this one interest, of doing a problem which I see to be impossible, and of smallish value if found doable!) is burdensome and without meaning to me. It is so rarely I hear the voice of a magnanimous Brother Man addressing any word to me: ninety-nine hundredths of the Letters I get are impertinent clutchings of me by the button, concerning which the one business is, How to get handsomely loose again; What to say that shall soonest *end* the intrusion,—if saying Nothing will not be the best way. Which last I often, in my sorrow, have recourse to, at whatever known risks. "We must pay our tribute to

[2] Anna Barker Ward had been a close friend of Margaret Fuller and had seemed, in Emerson's fancy, the Recamier of Transcendentalism (*Let RWE*, II, 205n, 338n). On February 5, 1852, in a private ceremony at the Wards' house, Jenny Lind was married to her accompanist, Otto Goldschmidt; Edward Everett was one of the witnesses (P. R. Frothingham, *Edward Everett*, p. 312).

[3] Tennyson's "A Dream of Good Women," in the 1833 *Poems*, contained a reference to Chaucer's *Legend of Good Women* which may have contributed to this confusion.

[4] Thackeray was by this time embarked for England.

Time": [1] ah yes, yes;—and yet I will believe, so long as we continue together in this sphere of things, there will always be a *potential* Letter coming out of New England for me, and the world not fallen irretrievably dumb.— —The best is, I am about going into Scotland, in two days, into deep solitude, for a couple of months beside the Solway sea: I absolutely need to have the dust blown out of me, and my mad nerves rested (there is nothing else quite gone wrong): this unblessed *Life of Fred^k* is now actually to get along into the Printer's hand;—a good Book being impossible upon it, there shall a bad one be done, and one's poor existence rid of it:—for which great object, two months of voluntary torpor are considered the fair preliminary. In another year's time (if the Fates allow me to live), I expect to have got a great deal of rubbish swept into Chaos again. Unlucky it should ever have been dug up, much of it!—

Your Mrs Ward should have had our best welcome, for the sake of him who sent her, had there been nothing more: but the Lady never showed face at all; nor could I for a long time get any trace,—and then it was a most faint and distant one as if by *double* reflex,—of her whereabouts: too distant, too difficult for me, who do not make a call once in the six months lately. I did mean to go in quest (never had an *Address*); but had not yet rallied for the Enterprise; when Mrs W. herself wrote that she had been unwell, that she was going directly for Paris, and would see us on her return. So be it:—pray only I may not be absent next! I have not seen or distinctly heard of Miss Bacon for a year and half past: I often ask myself, what has become of that poor Lady, and wish I knew of her being safe among her friends again.[2] I have even lost the address (wh^h at any rate was probably not a lasting one); perhaps I could find it by the eye,—but it is five miles away; and my *non-plus-ultra* for years past is not above half that distance. Heigho! —But let me get to business; for I have a little piece of actual business again to burden you with; and my Paper is rapidly wasting away.

Chapman the Bookseller (in addition to *Fred^k*, about which we have yet made no bargain) has at length resolved on a "Collective Edition of Carlyle's Works"; to be printed in a cheap but handsome and im-

---

[1] I have been unable to find the source of this quotation.

[2] Delia Bacon was soon to leave London for Stratford and the last act of her tragedy. Within a year, her book was published and her monomania became insanity (Bacon, *Delia Bacon*, p. 308).

maculately correct form: 16 handy little volumes (big 12mo; no, fools-cap 8vo I should think) to sell at 6/ each, and be published monthly, —first of them will come out probably in Novr, and so last for 15 months more (French Revn makes the first *two* volumes). The Book is to be stereotyped; I have got a loyal friend to do the correcting, to do an Index &c &c;[3] the printer is the excellent Robson (acquainted with that peculiar article): in short I believe the thing will be *well* done, in all points. The Stereotyped Plates, after Chapman has printed his 2,000 or 4,000 are to be *mine*.

Well, you perceive now what I am at. If an American Publisher has liberty to import British Stereotype Plates (and to send them back *soon*, for that too will be needed), he might, if his mind lay towards such an adventure, have the chance of doing a "Carlyle's Works" for Americans, on terms both of cheapness and correctness defying all competition. What I want of you is to make some inquiry on the matter;—or perhaps set E. P. Clark, upon it, if he still stand true? Do not take too much trouble. I have a real wish (real if not very vivid) that my American friends could read me *without* the foul errors all their Editions abound with. *Item* a wish (real, but neither is this very vivid) to secure all the *peculium* there actually does lie in this Enter-prise at home and abroad,—at least to give myself the chance of trying for it. And this is all the length I have gone, or (if your answer be negative) have any intention to go. Pardon! Pardon!

My time is all up and more; and Chaos come again[4] is lying round me, in the shape of 'packing'; in a thousand shapes!—Browning is coming tonight to take leave. Do you know Browning at all? He is abstruse; but worth knowing.—And what of the *Discourse on England* by a certain man? Shame! We always hear of it again as "out"; and it continues obstinately *in*. Adieu, my friend.

Ever yours,   —T. Carlyle

Concord, August 22, 1856.[1]—

Dear Carlyle:—Here is the proposal in full of Phillips, Sampson & Co.,

[3] Henry Larkin, a young neighbor employed on the Chelsea steamers, gave Carlyle such assistance with all the volumes of *Frederick* (*Letters and Memorials*, II, 114).

[4] Cf. *Othello*, act III, scene iii, line 92.

[1] Text from Conway, *Autobiography*, II, 375. This letter was one of four which Conway copied in 1882: see above, Introduction, pp. 65–66.

in reply to my explanation of your design. It looks fair and fruitful to me, though I am a bad judge. The men Phillips and Sampson are well esteemed here, have great confidence in themselves (which always goes far with me), and I believe will keep their word as well as any of their kind, though in all my experience of mortal booksellers there are some unlooked-for deductions in the last result. I have neither a right nor a wish to throw any doubt on these particular booksellers, who mean the best. I hasten to send the letter, before yet any steamer from Liverpool can bring me any growl of wrath from my dear old lion. Stifle the roar, and let me do penance by appointing me to negotiations and mediations with P., S & Co. and the printers, which I will gladly and faithfully execute.

Success to the history of Frederic! I read a slight recent life of Voltaire by Eugene Noel, which touched Frederic; a far better book, "L'Eglise et les Philosophes," by Lanfrey; but wait for you. Ellery Channing, a dear gossip of mine, told me that he had read your 'French Revolution' 'five times'! Send the new edition with more speed.

Ever yours,   R. W. Emerson

The Gill, Cummertrees, Annan N. B.
28 Aug^t, 1856—

Dear Emerson,

Your Letter [1] alighted here yesterday, like a winged Mercury, bringing "airs from Heaven" [2] (in a sense) along with his news. I understand very well your indisposition to write; we must conform to it, as to the Law of *Chronos* (oldest of the gods); but I will murmur always, "It is such a pity as of almost no other man!"—You are citizen of a "republic," and perhaps fancy yourself republican in an eminent degree: nevertheless I have remarked there is no man of whom I am so certain to get something *kingly*:—and whenever your huge inarticulate America gets settled into *Kingdoms*, of the New Model, fit for these Ages which are all upon the *Moult* just now, and dreadfully like going to the Devil in the interim,—then will America, and all nations thro' her, owe the man Emerson a *debt*, far greater than either they or he are in the least aware of at present! That, I consider (for myself) to be an

---

[1] Missing: evidently the answer to C.7.20.56.
[2] *Hamlet,* act I, scene iv, line 41. See above, p. 101.

ascertained fact. For which I myself at least am thankful and have long been.

It pleases me much to know that this English, so long twinkling in our expectations and always drawn back again, is at last verily to appear: [3] I wish I could get hold of my Copy; there is no Book that would suit me better just now. But we must wait for four weeks till we get back to Chelsea,—unless I can find some trusty hand to extract it from the rubbish that will have accumulated there, and forward it by post. You speak as if there were something dreadful said of my own sacred self in that Book: Courage, my friend, it will be a most miraculous occurrence to meet with any said by you that does me *ill;* whether the immediate taste of it be sweet or bitter, I will take it with gratitude, you may depend,—nay even with pleasure, what perhaps is still more incredible. But an old man, deluged for half a century with the brutally nonsensical vocables of his fellow-creatures (which he grows to regard soon as *rain,* "rain of frogs" [4] or the like, and lifts his umbrella agt with indifference,—such an old gentn, I assure you, is grateful for a word that he can recognise perennial sense in; as in this case is his sure hope. And so be the little Book thrice welcome; and let all England understand (as some choice portion of England will) that there has not been a man talking about us these very many years whose words are worth the least attention in comparison.

"Post passing!" I must end, in mid course; so much still untouched upon. Thanks for Sampson & Co, and let them go their course upon me. If I can see Mrs Ward "about the end of Septr" or after, I shall be right glad:—but I fear she will have fled before that?—

I am here in my native Country, riding, sea-bathing, living on country diet,—uttering no word,—now into the 5th week; have had such a "retreat" as no La Trappe [. . .] [5] could have offered me. A "retreat" *witht cilices,* thistle-mattresses; and with *silent* devotions (if any) instead of blockhead spoken ones to the Virgin and others!—There is still an Excursion to the Highlands ahead, whh cannot be avoided;— then home again to *peine forte et dure.*—Good be with you always, dear friend.

T. Carlyle

[3] The publication of *English Traits* on August 6 (*Let RWE,* V, 29n) and the dispatch of copies to England were doubtless announced in the missing letter.

[4] The sudden appearance on land in damp weather of a multitude of young frogs was popularly believed to be the result of a *rain* of the creatures.

[5] There is a word here which I cannot read. It looks like "hardly."

Kinloch Luichart
Dingwall, N. B. 16 Septr 1856

Dear Emerson,

Your second Letter [1] finds me up here, aloft among the Highland
mountains (a Hunting seat of Lord Ashburton's) whither I have been
tossed out of my snug Border solitude,—nor in good hour. The Mountains and Lakes are very beautiful; but the storms, in this equinoctial
time, are already very loud, and I can do nothing with Deer, not even
eat them.—In a fortnight hence I hope to be back at Chelsea; but in
the meantime will answer your magnanimous Bibliopolical Proposal
(yours or Sampson's thro' you, is all one, in the haste I am in—just
waiting for the "Skye Mail" which passes once in two days),—some
word of answer or acknowledgement, not to lose more time than we
can help.

I say then that the Project of Mm. Phillips Sampson & Co, so far as
I in my ignorance can judge of it, seems very rational; and that, once in
London, I will make farther investigation into the practical particulars,
and prepare myself to say Yes or No when the time comes for that
finality. Meanwhile let Mm. Ph^s & S^n do one thing as preliminary,
Tell me *how much,* in current money, they will give for a cast of those
potential Stereotypes, to the extent of 2, 4, 6, or as many *thousands* as
they w^d like to purchase at once;—*how much per thousand,* in fact?
For it would not be convenient to *sell* the Stereotypes otherwise, I
think;—and I suppose there are ways of making certain that the uses
of them should be *restricted* to the Thousands covenanted for, & that
the Plates could be put under lock and key till wanted again. Once
knowing what the value per thousand from Messrs Sampson will be,
and what the cost in London to myself as preliminary, I shall know the
whole matter, and be able to pronounce some decision or other.— —I
am much ashamed to trouble *you* with this matter; but what can I do
at the present stage of it.

---

[1] Missing. On this day Carlyle wrote to his wife, who was at Ecclefechan: "A Letter from Emerson came thro' John,—that is to say enclosed in a Letter from John
at London. It ought to be answered today: but how answer it, at such a table, with
such a pen, and 4 people all busy writing around me!" (NLS, MS 614). He enclosed
the answer in a letter to John which indicates something of the content of Emerson's letter: "The Yankee Booksellers (whom Emerson approves) want me to make
a *second* set of *Stereotypes,* and send them to America for their use. I ask, *What
will you give?*" (NLS, MS 516).

Your Book is to be here tomorrow by post. You shall hear soon all the faults I have against it. An Irish Newspaper (the *Nation*) brought me some notice of it the other day, wh^h somewhat raises my interest. A *medicinal* intention, then, on the Author's part? [2] God knows there was hardly ever such a Hospital of Lepers. More power to such a Doctor, if that is his part!

Adieu, dear Friend, there is the Skye mail.

Yours ever   T. Carlyle.

Chelsea, 2 Decr 1856—

Dear Emerson,

I am really grieved to have hurt the feelings of Mr Phillips; [1] a gentleman to whom I, on my side, had no feelings but those of respect and good will! I pray you smooth him down again, by all wise methods, into at least good-natured indifference to me. He may depend upon it I could not mean to irritate him; there lay no gain for me in that! Nor is there anything of business left now between us. It is doubly and trebly evident those Stereotype Plates are *not* to him worth their prime-cost here,—still less, their prime-cost *plus* any vestige of definite motive for me to concern myself in them:—whereupon the Project falls on its face, & vanishes forever, with apologies all round. For as to that other method, that is a game I never thought, and never should think, of playing at!—

You may also tell him this little Biographical fact, if you think it will anyway help. Some ten or more years ago, I made a similar Bargain with a New-York House (known to you, and now I believe extinct): [2] "10" or something "per cent," of selling price on the Copies Printed,

---

[2] The Dublin *Nation* of September 6, 1856, reported that Emerson was as "impartial as Cicero upon Athens. . . . He finds the Englishman a mighty worker but a deadly blockhead. He admires them as he does ants. . . . The American spiritualist arraigns the hideous materialism of England—her commercial cynicism—her political infidelity—her desperation of 'Dissent'—her Atheism, which does not take even the forlorn French form of a faith in Humanity."

[1] At this point yet another Emerson letter seems to be missing from the correspondence. Some light is thrown upon the episode by a passage in a letter from Emerson to James Elliot Cabot of February 21, 1860: "I once established some correspondence between Phillips & Sampson, & Carlyle—when they were able to fight the Harpers for him, but, for I know not what reason, he was very churlish & Scottish & suspicious, & would not treat for this very book" (*Let RWE*, V, 203).

[2] Wiley & Putnam: see above, C.4.18.46 ff.

was to be my return—not for 4 or £500 money laid out, but for various
things I did, which gratis would by no means have been done; in fine
it was ther own Offer, made and accepted in due form: "10 per cent
on the copies printed." And how many were "printed," thinks Mr
Phillips? I saw one set; dreadfully ugly Books, errors in every page:—
and to this hour I have never heard tell of any other! The account remains *zero* net;—and it would appear there was simply one Copy
"printed," the ugly one sent to myself, whʰ I instantly despatched
again some whither!— —On second thoughts perhaps you had better
not tell Mr P. this story, at least not in this way. *His* integrity I would
not even question by insinuation nor need I, at the point where we
now are. I perceive he sees in extraordinary brilliancy of illumination
his own side of the bargain, and thinks me ignorant of several things
which I am well enough informed about. In brief, make a perfect
peace between us, O friend, and man of peace; and let the wampums
be all wrapped up, and especially the tomahawks entirely buried, and
the thing *end* forever!—To you also I owe apologies; but not to you do
I pay them, knowing from of old what you are to me. Enough, enough!

I got your Book by post in the Highlands; and had such a day over
it as falls rarely to my lot! Not for seven years and more have I got hold
of such a Book;—Book by a real *man,* with eyes in his head; nobleness,
wisdom, humour and many other things in the heart of him. Such
Books do not turn up often in the decade, in the century. In fact I
believe it to be worth all the Books ever written by New England upon
Old. Franklin might have written such a thing (in his own way); no
other since!—We do very well with it here and the wise part of us
best. That Chapter on the Church is inimitable; "the Bishop asking a
troublesome gentⁿ to take wine," ³—you shᵈ see the kind of grin it
awakens here on our best kind of faces. Excellent the manner of that,
and the matter too dreadfully *true* in every part. I do not much seize
your idea in regard to "Literature," tho' I do details of it, and will try
again. Glad of that too, even in its half state; not "sorry" at *any* part
of it,—you sceptic! On the whole write *again,* and ever again at greater
length: there lies your only fault to me. And yet I know, that also is a
right noble one, and rare in our day.—Oh my friend, save always for

³ In the chapter "Religion" of *English Traits* Emerson had written: "If a bishop
meets an intelligent gentleman and reads fatal interrogations in his eyes, he has
no resource but to take wine with him."

me some corner in y^r memory: I am very lonely in these months and years,—sunk to the centre of the Earth, like to be throttled by the Pythons and Mudgods in my old days;—but shall get out again, too; and be a better boy! No "hurry" equals mine, and it is in permanence.

Yours ever

T. Carlyle

1857

Concord—
4 November, 1857.[1]

My dear Carlyle,

The bearer, Mr John C. King,[2] is a sculptor of good fame among us for his portrait busts, and has resided in this country for many years. He is a countryman of of yours, & is now on his way to England, & is ambitious to make a cast of your head. You shall tell him whether he shall have that success. He is favorably known to some of your friends, having taken, I believe, a bust of Webster, for the late Lord Ashburton. He has lately made, under difficult circumstances, a successful bust in marble of a venerable townsman & friend of mine, Mr Samuel Hoar.[3]

Ever yours affectionately,   R. W. Emerson.

Thomas Carlyle, Esq.

[1] MS owned by the Houghton Library. The envelope carries, besides the address, a notation in Carlyle's hand: "Introducing Mr *King* a Sculptor (Decr 1857)—"

[2] "John Crookshanks King was a native of Ayrshire, but had long resided in the United States. Among his best-known busts are those of Webster and Emerson."— Rusk's note.

[3] "Hoar had died on Nov. 2 of the preceding year."—Rusk's note. Hoar was a lawyer and congressman and the father of Elizabeth and Rockwood.

1858

Concord
17 May 1858

My dear Carlyle,

I see no way for you to avoid the Americans but to come to America. For, first or last, we are all embarking, and all steering straight to your door. Mr & Mrs Joseph Longworth of Cincinnati are going abroad on their travels. Possibly, the name is not quite unknown to you: Their father, Nicholas Longworth, is one of the founders of the city of Cincinnati, a bigger town than Boston, where he is a huge land lord, & planter, & patron of sculptors & painters. And his family are most favorably known to all dwellers & strangers in the Ohio valley, as people who have well used their great wealth. His chief merit is to have introduced a systematic culture of the wine-grape & wine manufacture, by the importing & settlement of German planters in that region, and the trade is thriving to the general benefit.

His son Joseph is a well-bred gentleman of literary tastes, whose position & good heart make him largely hospitable. His wife is a very attractive & excellent woman, and they are good friends of mine. It seems, I have at some former time hold her, that, when she went to England, she should see you. And they are going abroad, soon, for the first time. If you are in London, you must be seen of them.

But I hailed even this need of taxing once more your often taxed courtesy, as a means to break up my long contumacy to-you-ward. Please let not the wires be rusted out, so that we cannot weld them again, & let me feel the subtle fluid streaming strong. Tell me what is become of "Frederic," for whose appearance I have watched every week for months? I am better ready for him, since one or two books about Voltaire, Maupertuis, & Company, fell in my way.

Yet that book will not come which I most wish to read, namely, the culled results, the quintessence of private conviction, a *liber veritatis*, a few sentences, hints of the final moral you drew from so much penetrating inquest into past & present men. All writing is necessitated to be exoteric, & written to a human *should,* instead of to the terrible *is.* And I say this to you, because you are the truest & bravest of writers. Every writer is a skater who must go partly where he would, & partly where the skates carry him, or a sailor who can only land where sails can be safely blown. The variations to be allowed for in the surveyor's compass are nothing like so large as those that must be allowed for in every book. And a friendship of old gentleman who have got rid of many illusions, & blushes, & passion for euphony, & surface harmonics, & tenderness for their accidental literary stores, but have kept all their curiosity & awe touching the problems of man & fate & the cause of causes,—a friendship of old gentlemen of this fortune is looking more comely & profitable than anything I have read of love. Such a dream flatters my incapacities for conversation, for we can all play at monosyllables, who cannot attempt the gay pictorial panoramic styles. So, if ever I hear that you have betrayed the first symptom of age, that your back is but a twentieth of an inch from the perpendicular I shall hasten to believe you are shearing your prodigal overgrowths, and are calling in your troops to the citadel, and I may come in the first steamer to drop in of evenings & hear the central monosyllables. Be good now again & send me quickly—though it be the shortest autograph certificate of . . .[1]

Chelsea, 2 June, 1858—

Dear Emerson,

Glad indeed I am to hear of you on any terms, on any subject! For the last 18 months I have pretty much ceased all human correspondence,—writing no Note that was not in a sense wrung from me, my one society the *Nightmares* (Prussian and other) all that while:—but often and often the image of you, and the thought of old days between us,

---

[1] The remainder of this letter is lost. A first draft, dated May 15, 1858, begins: "I am afraid to go on any longer in this contumacy. There came to me a little while ago an agreeable gentleman, Mr Probym, with a letter from you, dated, to be sure, a year before. I gladly greeted the letter & the bearer, but found that he did not know you but one of your friends. He made himself very welcome to all who saw him, & I carried him to our Club, where are Agassiz Longfellow Lowell & other good people . . ." The first draft contains other interesting variations from the letter of May 17; it is printed in full in *Let RWE,* V, 108.

has risen sad upon me; and I have wanted to get loose from the Night-mares to appeal to you again, to *edacious* Time and you. Most likely in a couple of weeks you wd have heard from me again at any rate.— Your friends shall be welcome to me; no friend of yours can be other at any time. Nor in fact did anybody ever sent by you prove other than pleasant in this house; so pray no apologies on that small score. —If only these Cincinnati Patricians can find me here when they come? For I am off to the deepest solitudes discoverable (native Scotland probably) so soon as I can shake the final tag-rags of Printer people off me;—"surely within three weeks now!" I say to myself. But I shall be back, too, if all prosper; and your Longworthys will be back; and Madam will stand to her point, I hope.

That Book on Friedrich of Prussia,—first *half* of it, two swoln un-lovely volumes, which treat mainly of his Father &c, and leave him at his Accession,—is just getting out of my hands. One packet more of Proofs, and I have done with it,—thanks to all the gods! No job ap-proaching in ugliness to it was ever cut out for me; nor had I any motive to go on, except the sad negative one, "Shall we be beaten in our old days, then?"—But it has thoroughly humbled me,—trampled me down into the *mud,* there to wrestle with the accumulated stupid-ities of Mankind, German, English, French and other, for *all* have borne a hand in these sad centuries;—and here I emerge at last, not *killed,* but almost as good. Seek not to look at the Book,—nay in fact it is "not to be *published* till Septr" (so the man of affairs settles with me yesterday, "owing to the political &c, to the season" &c); my only stipulation was that in ten days I shd be entirely out of it,—not to hear of it again till the Day of Judgement, and if possible not even then!— In fact it is a bad Book, poor, misshapen, feeble, *nearly* worthless (thanks to *past* generations and to me); and my one excuse is, *I* could not make it better, all the world having played such a game with it. Well, well!— —How true is that that you say about the Skater; and the rider too depending on his vehicles, on his roads, on his etceteras! Dismally true have I a thousand times felt it, in these late operations; never in any so much. And in short the business of writing has alto-gether become contemptible to me; and I am become confirmed in the notion that nobody ought to write,—unless sheer Fate force him to do it;—and then he ought (if *not* of the mountebank genus) to beg to be shot rather. That is deliberately my opinion,—or far nearer it than you will believe.

Once or twice I caught some tone of you in some American Magazine: [1] utterances highly noteworthy to me; in a sense, the only thing that is *speech* at all among my fellow-creatures in this time. For the years that remain, I suppose we must continue to grumble out some occasional utterance of that kind: what can we do at this late stage? But in the *real* "model Republic," [2] it w^d have been different with two good boys of this kind!—

Tho' shattered and trampled down to an inhuman degree, I do not think any bones are broken yet,—tho' age truly *is* here, and you may engage your berth in the steamer whenever you like. In few months I expect to be sensibly improved: but my poor Wife suffers sadly the last two winters; and I am much distressed by that item of our affairs. Adieu, dear Emerson: I have lost many things; let me not lose you till I must in some way!

Yours ever   T. Carlyle

If you read the Newspapers (which I carefully abstain from doing) they will babble to you about Dickens's "Separation from Wife" &c &c: fact of Separat^n (Lawyer's *Deed* &c) I believe is true; but all the rest is mere lies and nonsense. No crime or misdeameanour specificable on either side: *unhappy* together, these good many years past, and they at length end it.— —Sulzer said, "—men are by nature *good.*" "*Ach, mein lieber Sulzer, Er kennt nicht diese verdammte Race!*" [3] ejaculated Fritz, at hearing such an axiom.

---

[1] Probably Carlyle refers to the new *Atlantic Monthly*, to which Emerson contributed three anonymous but characteristic essays: "Society and Solitude" (December, 1857); "Books" (January, 1858); and "Persian Poetry" (April, 1858).

[2] See above, C.5.13.53, and the *Latter-Day Pamphlet* called "The Present Time": "There is one modern instance of Democracy nearly perfect, the Republic of the United States, which has actually subsisted for threescore years or more, with immense success as is affirmed; to which many still appeal, as to a sign of hope for all nations, and a 'Model Republic.'" (*Works TC,* XX, 19).

[3] This speech was translated by Carlyle in Ch. X of Bk. XVI of *Frederick:* "Alas, dear Sulzer, I see you don't know that damned race of creatures as I do!" (*Works TC,* XVI, 337). Johann Georg Sulzer was a Swiss aesthetician whom Frederick had made inspector of schools.

Cummertrees, Scotland [1]
(for Chelsea, London
30 June, 1858—

Dear Emerson,

I do not remember, if, while you were among us, you heard much of
Mr Scott,[2] or made any personal acquaintance with him: but the truth
is, he has been conclusively known, this long while, to a select and ever-
widening circle as one of the few distinguished thinkers of his time;
a man of real intellect, earnestness, originality and depth;—prevented
(or perhaps *preserved*), by intricasies of position, by uncertain health,
and other causes (*merits,* many of them) from being known so universally as he might well one day still be, and as many persons not worth
naming along with him already are, in our loud time. He by no means
tells all his secret at once; but it is certain he has his secret, many
curious secrets, abstrusely wrestled for, as he came thus far; and so
much as he will impart of them, I have always considered to be extremely well worth listening to, and taking with me. His utterance, by
Lecture or otherwise, which the cursory hearer considers free and
felicitous in a high degree, will strike the considerate ear as still more
remarkable by the much it hints at as being left *un*said.

Circumstances, of a legitimate nature, not an illegitimate as is com-
moner, bring him to lecture among you this Autumn; and if, by coun-

---

[1] MS owned by the Berg Collection of the New York Public Library.

[2] Alexander John Scott, Presbyterian clergyman. A friend of Edward Irving and
a preacher of extraordinary eloquence, he had been unfrocked for heresy and had
become a professor of English at the University of London and later principal of
Owens College, Manchester. He is identified in other letters of introduction owned
by the Berg Collection as "A. J. Scott" and "Professor Scott." From these letters,
among them a general recommendation "To all my American friends who take interest in Lecturing," it can be seen that Scott planned to lecture on Dante; from a
letter to Scott, of June 30, 1858, also in the Berg Collection, it is clear that the lecturer intended to travel mainly for his health: "Dear Scott,—It wd give me pleasure
to help in this American Enterprise; whh I perceive to be a very rational one. Unhappily I am in a kind of abeyance with the vocal public of that country; and have
not for years answered a Letter if by chance some Letter still came, nor had the
least Correspondence with anybody in that country,—except (and that a very little)
with Emerson alone. The fact, I suppose is, there are still many people well affected to me; but they have the dignity to hold their tongue in the presence of
such unmusical balderdash from other parties:—that is the sad lot of a literary
man and his real friends and hearers in these times. . . . Emerson you will find a
genuinely good man, and capable of spiritual discourse so as no other living is."

tenance, by good advice, by honest human welcome to a scene wh^h you know and wh^h he does not, you can in any way smooth the road for him, I doubt not, for my sake, for his, and for your own, it will be of the nature of a pleasure to you.

Yours ever truly,   T. Carlyle

Concord
Oct. 5, 1858

Dear Carlyle,

If Elizabeth Hoar comes where you are, I pray you to receive her as a lady of the highest worth. She is the friend of many excellent persons, yet an adorer of truth above all persons. You will find none who knows your genius better, yet the mould in which she was made will hardly allow the finest genius in the world to warp her. She has in her blood & family eminent claims to honor; & not less in herself. She should have been my sister, if my brother Charles had lived, & has been as my sister all my life. I hope Mrs Carlyle may see her, & think better of us New England people than her husband does.

Ever yours,   R. W. Emerson

T. Carlyle Esq.

1859

Chelsea, London, 9 April, 1859

Dear Emerson,—Long months ago there was sent off for you a Copy of *Friederich* of Prussia, two big red volumes [1] (for wh^h Chapman the Publisher had found some "safe swift" vehickle); and *now* I have reason to fear they are still loitering somewhere, or at least have long loitered: sorrow on them! This is to say: If you have not *yet* got them, address a line to "Saml F. Flower Esq,[2] Librarian of Antiquarian Society *Worcester* Mass." (forty miles from you, they say); and that will at once bring them. In the Devil's name!—

I never in my life was so near choked; swimming in this mother of Dead Dogs, and a long spell of it still ahead! I profoundly *pity myself* (if no one else does). You shall hear of me again if I survive;—but really that is getting beyond a joke with me; and I ought to hold my peace (even to you) and swim what I can.

Your little Touch of Human Speech on *Burns* was charming; had got into the Papers here (and been clipt out by me) before y^r Copy came;—and has gone far & wide since: Neuberg was to give it me in German from the *Allgemeine Zeitung;* [3] but lost the leaf.— —Adieu, my Friend; very dear to me, tho' dumb.

T. Carlyle (in such haste as
seldom was)— [4]

[1] The first two volumes of *Frederick* were published in September, 1858 (Dyer, *Bibliography* . . . , p. 80).

[2] This is presumably a misreading, by Carlyle or by someone in the Chapman organization, of the name of Samuel F. Haven. See below, E.5.1.59.

[3] Emerson's speech on Burns delivered at the centennial celebration in Boston on January 25 of this year was printed in *Celebration by the Burns Club* (Boston, 1859). A translation, almost complete, appeared in the *Allgemeine Zeitung*, IX (February, 19, 1859), 798.

[4] "The preceding letter was discovered in 1893, in a little package of letters put aside by Mr. Emerson and marked 'Autographs' "—Norton's note.

[May 1, 1859] [1]

Dear Carlyle,

Three weeks ago came to me Mr Haven's [2] letter from Worcester, announcing the arrival there of King Friedrich and, after a fortnight, the good book came to my door. A week later came your letter. Well I was heartily glad to get the Crimson Book itself. I had looked for it with the first ships As it came not I had made up my mind to that hap also. It was quite right I had disentitled myself. He the true friend had every right to punish me for my sluggish contumacy,— backsliding, too, after penitence. So I read with resignation our American reprint, & I enclose to you a leaf from my journal at the time, which leaf I read the other night in one of my lectures at the "Music Hall," in Boston. [3] But the Book came. He did not punish me. He is loyal, but royal as well, &, I have always noted, has a whim for dealing *en grande monarque*. The book came, with its irresistible inscription, [4] so that I am all tenderness & all but tears We think you the true inventer of the stereoscope, as having exhibited that art in style, long before we had yet heard of it in drawing. Lowell & Ward & even Agassiz (who never reads anything but Zoology drawn this time from his tortoises & squids) exchanged their greetings over this extraordinary history.

The letter came also. Every child of mine knows from far that handwriting, & brings it breathless home. I read without alarm your pathetical hints of your sad plight in the German labyrinth. I know too well what invitations & assurances brot you *in* there to fear any

---

[1] The manuscript of the final form of this letter is missing, although Norton printed a copy of it made by Alexander Ireland. The present text is from the first draft, which is in some ways fuller and more interesting than Norton's version. On May 25, 1859, Carlyle wrote to Neuberg of "A fine Letter from Emerson, whh you shall see" (NLS, MS 553).

[2] The *Worcester Almanac and Directory* for 1859 lists Samuel F. Haven as librarian of the American Antiquarian Society.

[3] Emerson's Music Hall lecture of April 13 was entitled "Art and Criticism" (*Let RWE*, V, 139n); that lecture, as printed in *Works*, XII, 298, contains a long paragraph on *Frederick* which is very similar to a passage in the journal for 1859 (IX, 195).

[4] "To R. Waldo Emerson Esq/ (Concord, Massachusetts):/ From an old Friend/ Chelsea, 6 Decr, 1858—": this inscription appears on the flyleaf of Volume III of the set of *Frederick* now in Emerson's study in the museum of the Concord Antiquarian Society. The set has presumably been rebound.

lack of guides to bring you out More presence of mind & easy change from the microscopic to the telescopic view, does not exist. I await peacefully your issue from your pretended afflictions.

What to tell you of my coop & byre? Ah! you are a poor fellow, & must be left with your glory. You hug yourself on missing the illusion of children, & must be pitied as having one glittering toy the less. I am fooled by my young people & grow old contented. I am victim all my days to certain graces of form & behavior, & can never come into equilibrium. The children suddenly take the keenest interest in life, & foolish papas cling to the world on their account, as never on their own. Out of sympathy we make believe to value the prizes of their hope & ambition. My two girls,—pupils once or now of Agassiz,[5]—are good apprehensive healthy decided young people who love life. My boy divides his time between Cicero & cricket knows his boat, the birds, & Walter Scott through & through, prose & verse, & will go to College next year

But on the whole I mean to write you letters We shall not know each other on this platform as long as we have known. A correspondence of 25 years should not be disused unless by some fatal event. Life is too short, & with all our poetry & morals too indigent to allow such sacrifices. School girls fill their folio sheets each day, & eyes so wary & which have learned to shut on so much are gathering an hourly harvest; & I cannot spare what on any terms is offered me. My only reason for not writing is the disbelief that our things which suffice us will interest you for we believe that the best of Europeans lie under terrible cockneyism [6]

I flatter myself I see some emerging of our people from the poison of their politics the insolvency of slavery begins to show, & we shall perhaps live to see that putrid Black Vomit extirpated by mere diking & planting. Another ground of contentment is the mending of the race here. My friend Sam Ward thinks the new Amers a marked improvement on their parents.[7]

[5] From 1855 to 1863 Agassiz ran a school for girls in the upper part of his house in Cambridge (Agassiz, *Louis Agassiz*, pp. 526–27).

[6] "My . . . cockneyism" does not appear in the Ireland-Norton copy.

[7] The Ireland-Norton copy here reads: "Sam Ward and I tickled each other the other day, in looking over a very good company of young people, by finding in the new-comers a marked improvement on their parents." The copy concludes: "With congratulations to Jane Carlyle on the grandeur of the Book,/ Yours affectionately,/ R. W. Emerson."

1860

Concord, 16 April, 1860—

My dear Carlyle,

Can booksellers break the seal which the gods do not, & put me in communication again with the loyalest of men? On the ground of Mr Wight's [1] honest proposal to give you a benefit from his edition, I, tho' unwilling, allowed him to copy the Daguerre of your head. The publishers ask also some expression of your good will to their work. I am not sure that this can be. Carey & Hart, it is true, have long since retired, & sold their edition & rights to other parties, who have sold again, nor do I know how long & far the good-will which they paid for can be made to extend. Have you an opinion?

Elliot Cabot, when I saw him, was waiting to hear from you on the matter of the Harpers' pretended property in the American edition of "Frederick." [2] Do not let him wait; that Harper at least may be forced to speak the truth, which we think he does not. No bookseller here now appears able to fight the Harpers. Phillips & Sampson, who once could, are now dead, & the firm, since their death, bankrupt. I saw, in Toronto, in the winter, two stalwart Carlyles, nephews of yours, sons of John Carlyle of Mohawk, Canada West; one of them Headmaster of the "Model School" in Toronto. [3] They do credit to the

[1] On March 14 the Boston publishers Brown and Taggard had written to Emerson, enclosing "a letter from Prof. O. W. Wight of New York (who is having 'Carlyle's Essays' stereotyped and of which we shall be the Publishers) in reference to the suggestions of allowing Mr Carlyle a part of the profit accruing from the sale of his work . . ." (MS owned by the Houghton Library). Orlando Williams Wight was a Universalist minister who had done much translating and editing for New York publishers.

[2] The Harpers had already published the first two volumes of *Frederick* and had evidently claimed, in a letter to Cabot or in an advertisement, that they had some right to the rest (*Let RWE*, V, 204).

[3] Emerson lectured in Toronto on January 27 (*Let RWE*, V, 192n). This John Carlyle was an elder half-brother, known in the family, before his emigration, as "John of Cockermouth"; his son James had written to Carlyle eight years before and had received a long letter of advice on "the trade of Teaching" (Wilson, *Life of Carlyle*, I, 19; IV, 404).

name. I commend you to the Gods who love & uphold you, & who do not like to make their great gifts vain but teach us that the best life insurance is a great task. I hold you to be one of those to whom all is permitted, & who carry the laws in their hand. Continue to be good to your old friends. Tis no matter whether they write to you, or not. If not, they save your time. When Friedrich is once dispatched to gods & men,—there was once some talk that you should come to America! You shall have an ovation such, & on such sincerity, as none have had.   Ever affectionately yours,   R. W. Emerson

I do not know Mr Wight, but he sends his open letter, which, I see, is already old, for me to write in: & I will not keep it lest it lose another steamer.

Chelsea   London, 30 April, 1860

Dear Emerson,

It is a special favour of Heaven to me that I hear of you again by this accident; and am made to answer a word *de Profundis.* It is constantly among the fairest of the few hopes that remain for me on the other side of this Stygian Abyss of a Friedrich (shd I ever get thro' it alive,) that I *shall then* begin writing to you again, who knows if not see you in the body before quite taking wing! For I feel always, what I have sometimes written, that there is (in a sense) but one completely human voice to me in this world, and that you are it, and have been, thanks to you, whether you speak or not! Let me say also while I am at it, that the few words you sent me about those first Two Volumes are present with me in the far more frightful darknesses of these last Two; and indeed are often almost my one encouragement. That is a fact, and not exaggerated, tho' you think it is. I read some criticisms of my wretched Book, and hundreds of others I in the gross refused to read; they were in praise, they were in blame; but not one of them looked into the eyes of the object, and in genuine human fashion responded to its human strivings, and recognized it,—completely right, tho' with generous exaggeratn! That was well done, I can tell you: a human voice, far out in the waste deeps, among the inarticulate sea-krakens and obscene monsters, loud-roaring, inexpressibly ugly, dooming you as if to eternal solitude by way of wages,

—"hath exceeding much refreshment in it," as my friend Oliver used to say.

Having not one spare moment at present, I will ans^r to *you* only the whole contents of that Letter; you in your charity will convey to Mr Wight and to Mr Cabot what portions respectively belong to them. Wight, if you have a chance of him, is worth knowing: a genuine bit of metal, too thin and ringing for my tastes (hammered, in fact, upon the Yankee anvils) but recognizably of steel and with a keen fire-edge.—Pray signify to him that he has done a thing agreeable to me, and that it will be pleasant if I find it will not hurt *him*. Profit to *me* out of it, except to keep his own soul clear and sound (to his own sense, as it always will be to mine) is perfectly indifft:—and on the whole I thank him heartily for showing me a chivalrous human brother, instead of the usual vulturous malodorous and much avoidable phenomenon, in Transatlantic Bibliopoly! This is accurately true;—and so far as his Publisher & he can extract encouragement from this, in the face of vested interests wh^h I cannot judge of,—it is theirs without reserve.

To Mr Cabot be so good as say that Harper of New-York is to me Harpy, odious, rapacious, not lovely or beneficent at all; that he has not, nor shall ever have if I can help it, the least vestige of a "bargain" with me in regard to these two expected volumes of *Friedrich;* —and that in fact I will rather give them frankly away for *Zero* to any honest Bookseller whom you or Cabot may recommend, than consign them to Harpydom on the terms their predecessors had. The wretched mortal wrote to me again and again, while the question with me was not of lucre but of life or death; and in every letter you saw the mingled physiognomy of owl, raven and unclean birds,—creating a certain horror! To be rid of him I said "£100 per volume, and no farther talk!" He held back, corresponded with Chapman, made me sensible of his evil presence in secondary ways; at length offered while I was in the agonies "£50 per volume." I bid Chapman, "Close with him, for God's sake, and let *him* disappear!"— —That is the exact state of it;—and my wish then strongly was, and still is, that I could in some way signify to him, "Avaunt, unclean bird, come not between the wind and me again! Be so extremely obliging as to steal any property of mine you can find not guarded by the gallows, and to hold your tongue about it, and not trouble me with any dialogue at all!"—

I am very glad I have got this written down for Mr Cabot; and pray tell him I do not wish that he should take any action farther on the subject,—except it were to point me out a man to whom, as above described, I could send the sheets gratis; if that were the way of shutting Harpy's beak, whh perhaps it isn't? In short, that latter is the one result I am ambitious of. And by simply doing nothing, I suppose it will be pretty much secured. The £100 from all America is nearly the same as what Tauchnitz yields in the name of all Germany: seems not vital to me "at all at all,"—and *worse* than zero if there has to be speech of unclean birds about them first!— —You will need to translate all that into rational deliberate speech; and deliver it mildly, with my gratitude, and other good human feelings (whh are not wanting, had I time to state them) to Mr Cabot. Nay the poor devil Harper, he too ought to have justice; and I am not the least angry at him, while he keeps wide of me! Besides I remember, it was not he at all that wrote; but some hungry feathered being (probably in moult at the time) whom he keeps here in London.[1] God give us patience with all creatures feathered and unfeathered,—at least till we can get a chance to suppress (and extinguish by good methods) the intolerable kinds of them!—

Adieu my friend; I have not written so much in the Letter way, not, I think, since you last heard of me. In my despair it often seems as if I shd never write more; but be sunk here, and perish miserably in the most undoable, least worthy, most disgusting and heart-breaking of all the labours I ever had. But perhaps also not, not quite. In whh case—Yours ever truly at any rate   T. Carlyle

[No time to re-read; I suppose you can decipher.] [2]

[1] The publisher Sampson Low was from 1847 to 1886 the London agent of Harper & Brothers (Harper, *The House of Harper,* p. 131).

[2] Carlyle's brackets.

1861

Chelsea, 29 Jany, 1861—

Dear Emerson,

The sight of my handwriting will, I know, be welcome again. Tho' I literally do not write the smallest Note once in a month, or converse with anything but Prussian Nightmares of a hideous, and with my Horse (who is human in comparison), and with my poor Wife (who is altogether human, and heroically cheerful to me, in her poor weak state),—I must use the five minutes, whh have fallen to me today, in acknowledget, *due* by all laws terrestrial and celestial, of the last Book that has come from you.

I read it a great while ago, mostly in sheets, and again read it in the finely printed form,[1]—I can tell you, if you do not already guess, with a satisfaction given me by the Books of no other living mortal. I predicted to yr English Bookseller a great sale even, reckoning it the best of all your Books. What the sale was or is I nowhere learned; but the *basis* of my prophecy remains like the rocks, and will remain. Indeed, except from my Brother John, I have heard no criticism that had much rationality,—some of them incredibly irrational (if that matter had not altogether become a barking of dogs among us);—but I always believe there are in the mute state a great number of thinking English souls, who can recognise a Thinker, and a Sayer, of perennially human type, and welcome him as the rarest of miracles, in "such a spread of knowledge"[2] as there now is:—one English soul of that kind there indubitably is; and I certify hereby, notarially if you like, that such is emphatically his view of the matter. You have grown older, more pungent, piercing;—I never read from you before such

---

[1] *Conduct of Life* was published in Boston by Ticknor and Fields on December 8, 1860 (*Let RWE*, V, 233n). Since the British edition of Smith, Elder, and Co. also appeared in that year, the American firm must have sent sheets in advance of publication.

[2] I think Carlyle is here quoting himself, but I do not remember where in his works I have seen the phrase.

lightning-gleams of meaning as are to be found here. The finale of all, that of "Illusions" falling on us like snow-showers, but again of "the gods sitting stedfast on their thrones" [3] all the while,—what a *Fiat Lux* is there, into the deeps of a philosophy, whh the vulgar has not, whh hardly 3 men living *have,* yet dreamt of! *Well done,* I say; and so let that matter rest.

I am still 12 months or so from the end of my Task; very uncertain often whether I can, even at this snail's pace, hold out so long. In my life I was never worn nearly so low, and seem to get *weaker* monthly. Courage! If I do get thro', you shall hear of me again.

Yours forever T. Carlyle

Concord, 16 April, 1861.

My dear Carlyle,

My friend—almost my sister,—Elizabeth Hoar, embarks again tomorrow for England. She takes with her, her niece, to whom your climate has been recommended for health's sake. Miss Hoar did not see you when in London, last year She called at your house, & saw Mrs Carlyle. You were away: I wish now she may be fortunate in seeing you also. You have not many readers with eyes so apprehensive & clear, & a moral verdict so unerring. I commend her a little proudly to your heroic regards, & to the kind counsels of my friend, Mrs Carlyle. Her brother, Judge Hoar, now of our Supreme Bench, well remembers you, and Dr Jacobson, to whom you sent him at Oxford.

I have to thank you for the cordial note which brought me joy many weeks ago. It was noble & welcome in all but its boding account of yourself & your task. But I have had experience of your labors, & these deplorations I have long since learned to distrust. We have settled it in America, as I doubt not it is settled in England, that "Frederick" is a history which a beneficent Providence is not very likely to interrupt. And may every kind & tender influence near you & over you keep the best head in England from all harm.

Affectionately, R. W. Emerson

T. Carlyle, Esq.

---

[3] An approximate quotation from the last sentence of the essay "Illusions."

1862

Concord
December 8 1862

My dear friend,

Long ago as soon as swift steamers could bring the new book across the sea, I received the 3d Volume of Friedrich, with your autograph inscription,[1] & read it with joy. Not a word went to the beloved author, for I do not write or think. I would wait perhaps for happier days, as our President Lincoln will not even emancipate slaves, until on the heels of a victory, or the semblance of such. But he waited in vain for his triumph, nor dare I in my heavy months expect bright days. The book was heartily grateful, & square to the author's imperial scale. You have lighted the glooms & engineered away the pits, whereof you poetically pleased yourself with complaining, in your sometime letter to me, clean out of it, according to the high Italian rule, & have let sunshine & pure air enfold the scene. First, I read it honestly through for the history; then I pause & speculate on the muse that inspires, & the friend that reports it. Tis sovereignly written, above all literature, dictating to all mortals what they shall accept as fated & final for their salvation. It is mankind's Bill of Rights & Duties, the royal proclamation of Intellect ascending the throne, announcing its good pleasure, that, hereafter, *as heretofore,* & now once for all, the world shall be governed by Commonsense & law of Morals, or shall go to ruin.

But the manner of it!—the author sitting as Demiurgus, trotting out his manikins, coaxing & bantering them, amused with their good performance, patting them on the back, and rating the naughty dolls when they misbehave; & communicating his mind ever in measure,

[1] The book had arrived early in June (Let **RWE, V,** 279), inscribed "To Ralph Waldo Emerson Esq/ with many regards:/ **T** Carlyle/ Chelsea, 17 May 1862." The flyleaf bearing the inscription has since, it would seem, been rebound in Volume **IV** of the set of *Frederick* now in Emerson's study in the museum of the Concord Antiquarian Society.

just as much as the young public can understand, hinting the future, when it would be useful; recalling now & then illustrative antecedents of the actor, impressing the reader that he is in possession of the entire history centrally seen, that his investigation has been exhaustive; and that he descends too on the petty plot of Prussia from higher & cosmical surveys. Better I like the sound sense & the absolute independence of the tone, which may put kings in fear. And, as the reader shares, according to his intelligence, the haughty *coup d' oeil* of this genius, & shares it with delight, I recommend to all governors, English, French, Austrian, & other, to double their guards, & look carefully to the censorship of the press. I find, as ever in your books, that one man has deserved well of mankind for restoring the Scholar's profession to its highest use & dignity. I find also that you are very wilful, & have made a covenant with your eyes that they shall not see anything you do not wish they should. But I was heartily glad to read somewhere that your book was nearly finished in the manuscript, for I could wish you to sit & taste your fame, if that were not contrary to law of Olympus. My joints ache to think of your rugged labor. Now that you have conquered to yourself such a huge kingdom among men, can you not give yourself breath, & chat a little, an Emeritus in the eternal university, and write a gossiping letter to an old American friend or so? Alas, I own that I have no right to say this last—I who write never.

Here we read no books. The war is our sole & doleful instructer. All our bright young men go into it, to be misused & sacrificed hitherto by incapable leaders. One lesson they all learn—to hate slavery, *teterrima causa*.[2] But the issue does not yet appear. We must get ourselves morally right. Nobody can help us. Tis of no account what England or France may do. Unless backed by our profligate parties, their action would be nugatory, and, if so backed, the worst. But even the war is better than the degrading & descending politics that preceded it for decades of years, & our legislation has made great strides, and if we can stave off that fury of trade which rushes to peace at the cost of replacing the South in the *status ante bellum*, we can, with something more of courage, leave the problem to another score of years—free labor to fight with the Beast, & see if bales & barrels &

---

[2] Horace, *Satires*, I, 3, 107–8: "Nam fuit ante Helenam cunnus teterrima belli/ causa."

baskets cannot find out that they pass more commodiously & surely to their ports through free hands, than through barbarians.[3]

I grieved that the good Clough, the generous, susceptible scholar should die.[4] I read over his "Bothie" again, full of the wine of youth at Oxford. I delight in Matthew Arnold's fine criticism in two little books.[5] Give affectionate remembrances from me to Jane Carlyle, whom Elizabeth Hoar's happiness & accurate reporting restored to me in brightest image.

Always faithfully yours, R. W. Emerson [6]

T. Carlyle, Esq.

[3] Carlyle sent this letter to his brother on December 28, 1862, with the following comment: "Emerson's Letter will rather disappoint you; nothing in it, abt the Practical State of America, that is not more or less chimerical,—conquering the South, and becoming celestial by emancipating Niggers, and so forth. But I find him entirely sincere: where he says I have made a covnt with my eyes;—not true, I hope, but evidtly sincere" (NLS, MS 525).

[4] Clough had died in November, 1861, at the age of forty-two.

[5] One of these was *On Translating Homer: Last Words* (London, 1862), which Arnold sent, as he said, "because of the passage about Clough at the end" (*Let RWE*, V, 361n); the other presumably was *On Translating Homer* (London, 1861).

[6] The Library of Congress owns an interesting fragment of a rough draft of this letter, written presumably in October. Words in brackets were deleted by Emerson. "I was charmed with Matthew Arnold's tracts about Homer & criticism; glad to have Clough's [little] Oxford [Poem] hexameters printed again; grieved that that susceptible author should die. We have a good club where we [sometimes] occasionally see an [sensible] Englishman & sometimes a sensible one. But the war has forced the 'unexpressive' Englishman to show his hand & his caste dislike to the American Tis very insular & shoppish. We are much ashamed of them, finding the high ones incapable of public regards & not as the rest.
"I admire Frederic's portrait of the Frenchman. When Prince Napoleon was here, last winter, I saw him at a dinner, [& his company] & had a short conversation about—religion, Ernest Renan, Michelet, &c.
"I go easily [down, or say,] *along*, [for there has been no up,] never much attached to life though I know well how to warm myself with my children. My boy I sent overland, a year ago, to California. He has just come back by sea in firmer health, & has entered college, though, like all the good boys, he wished to go to the war. My best bower anchor at the club is Lowell & Elliot Cabot whose chapter on art you shall read in the 'Atlantic Monthly' next month
"The war is a chief instructor here. We read no books, but our bright young men all go into it in some capacity, [& many are killed—almost] where they all suffer from bad generals. Many are killed, all are sobered, & tried by famine, fatigue, fever, defeat, wounds, & those who come home will be wiser; all come home haters of slavery. Whilst their rich papas had, all their lives, propitiated the beast
"Our future looks doubtful The swing of parties is so incalculable, & because of 'the brute part' & weight which always attaches itself to an incoming party The

Cause of Mankind requires either the humiliation of the slave-interest, either by exclusion or by conquest,—I do not think it makes great difference which; anything but reconstruction of the Union with [advantages to the] sops to the slavers. For the veins & arteries of the Federal govt would then organize instantly all the beast force in the North into place"

The return of Edward Emerson referred to above took place on October 6 (*Let RWE*, V, 290*n*); J. Elliot Cabot's article "House-Building" appeared in the *Atlantic Monthly* for October.

1864

Chelsea   8 March
1864

Dear Emerson,

This will be delivered to you by the Hon. Lyulf Stanley, an excellent, intelligent young gent[n] whom I have known ever since his infancy,—his Father and Mother being among my very oldest friends in London: "Lord and Lady Stanley *of Alderley*" (not *of Knowesley,* but a cadet branch of it), whom perhaps you did not meet while here.[1]

My young Friend is coming to look with his own eyes at your huge and hugely travailling Country;—and I think will agree with you, better than he does with me, in regard to that latter phenomenon.[2] At all events, he regards "Emerson," as intellig[t] Englishmen all do; and you will please me much by giving him your friendliest recept[n] & furtherance,—wh[h] I can certify that he deserves for his own sake, not counting mine at all.

Probably *he* may deliver you the Vol IV of *Fred[c];* he will tell you our news (part of wh[h], what regards my poor Wife, is very bad, tho' God be thanked, not yet the worst); [3]—and, in some six months, he may bring me back some human tidings from Concord, a place wh[h] always inhabits my memory—tho' it is so dumb latterly!

Yours ever   T. Carlyle

[1] Lord Edward Stanley of Alderley was postmaster-general under Palmerston; the famous parliamentary orator, Lord Edward Stanley of Knowsley, had been twice prime minister and had become the fourteenth Earl of Derby.

[2] For Carlyle's views on the American Civil War, see above, Introduction, pp. 46–48.

[3] Late in September, 1863, Jane Carlyle suffered a minor street accident which somehow resulted in partial paralysis and extreme pain that the doctors could diagnose only as neuralgia (Froude, *Thomas Carlyle: Life in London,* II, 230–34).

Concord, 26 Sept. 1864

Dear Carlyle,

Your friend, young Stanley, brought me your letter now too many days ago.[1] It contained heavy news of your household,—yet such as in these our autumnal days we must await with what firmness we can. I hear with pain that your Wife, whom I have only seen beaming goodness & intelligence, has suffered & suffers so severely. I recall my first visit to your house, when I pronounced you wise & fortunate in relations wherein best men are often neither wise nor fortunate. I had already heard rumors of her serious illness. Send me word, I pray you, that there is better health & hope. For the rest, the Colonna motto would fit your letter, "Though sad I am strong." [2]

I had received in July, forwarded by Stanley, on his flight through Boston, the fourth volume of "Friedrich," and it was my best reading in the summer, & for weeks my only reading. One fact was paramount in all the good I draw from it, that whomsoever many years had used & worn, they had not yet broken any fibre of your force:—a pure joy to me, who abhor the inroads which time makes on me & on my friends. To live too long is the capital misfortune, and I sometimes think, if we shall not parry it by better art of living, we shall learn to include in our morals some bolder control of the facts. I read once, that Jacobi [3] declared, that he had some thoughts, which,—if he should entertain them,—would put him to death: and perhaps we have weapons in our intellectual armory that are to save us from disgrace & impertinent relation to the world we live in. But this book will excuse you from any unseemly haste to make up your accounts nay, holds you to fulfil your career with all amplitude & calmness. I found joy & pride in it, & discerned a golden chain of continuity not often seen in the works of men, apprising me, that one good head &

[1] Emerson, pleased that Stanley was "on *our* side in politics" (*Let RWE*, V, 382), provided very distinguished company for him when he came to Concord: Wendell Phillips, Agassiz, Channing, and Alcott (*Journals*, X, 60). Stanley wrote from London, December 14, 1864: "Since I came back to England I have seen the Carlyles but once. They were very glad to hear news of you, though I am afraid that I can not tell you of any clearer understanding on their part of the merits of your great struggle" (MS owned by RWEMA).

[2] According to the *Enciclopedia Storico-Nobiliare Italiana,* the motto of the Colonna family is "Frangimur non flectimur undis."

[3] The philosopher F. H. Jacobi, presumably.

great heart remained in England, immoveable,—superior—to his own
eccentricities & perversities,—nay, wearing these, I can well believe, as
a jaunty coat or red cockade to defy or mislead idlers, for the better
securing his own peace, & the very ends which the idlers fancy he
resists. England's lease of power is good during his days.

I have in these last years lamented that you had not made the visit
to America, which in earlier years you projected or favored. It would
have made it impossible that your name should be cited for one moment on the side of the enemies of mankind. Ten days' residence in
this country would have made you the organ of the sanity of England
& of Europe to us & to them, & have shown you the necessities and
aspirations which struggle up in our Free States, which, as yet, have
no organ to others, & are ill & unsteadily articulated here. In our today's division of Republican & Democrat, it is certain that the American nationality lies in the Republican party (mixed & multiform
though that party be;) & I hold it not less certain, that, viewing all
the nationalities of the world, the battle for Humanity is, at this hour,
in America. A few days here would show you the disgusting composition of the party which within the Union resists the national action.
Take from it the wild Irish element, imported in the last twenty five
years into this country, & led by Romish priests, who sympathize, of
course, with despotism, & you would bereave it of all its numerical
strength. A man intelligent and virtuous, is not to be found on that
side. Ah! how gladly I would enlist you with your thunderbolt, on
our part! How gladly enlist the wise, thoughtful, efficient pens &
voices of England! We want England & Europe to hold our people
staunch to their best tendency. Are English of this day incapable of
a great sentiment? Can they not leave cavilling at petty failures, &
bad manners, & at the dunce part, (always the largest part in human
affairs,) and leap to the suggestions & fingerpointings of the gods,
which, above the understanding, feed the hopes & guide the wills of
men? This war has been conducted over the heads of all the actors in
it: and the foolish terrors—"what shall we do with the negro?" "the
entire black population is coming north to be fed," &c. have strangely
ended in the fact, that the black refuses to leave his climate; gets his
living *and* the living of his employers there, as he has always done; is
the natural ally & soldier of the Republic, in that climate; now takes
the place of 200 000 white soldiers; & will be, as this conquest of the

country proceeds, its garrison, till peace, without slavery, returns. Slaveholders in London have filled English ears with their wishes & perhaps beliefs; and our people, generals, & politicians, have carried the like, at first, to the war, until corrected by irresistible experience. I shall always respect War hereafter. The cost of life, the dreary havoc of comfort & time are overpaid by the Vistas it opens of Eternal Life, Eternal Law, reconstructing & uplifting Society,—breaks up the old horizon, & we see through the rifts a wider. The dismal Malthus, the dismal De Bow,[4] have had their night.[5] Our Census of 1860, and the War, are poems,[6] which will, in the next age, inspire a genius like your own.

I hate to write you a newspaper, but, in these times, tis wonderful what sublime lessons I have once & again read on the Bulletin-boards in the streets. Everybody has been wrong in his guess, except good women who never despair of an Ideal right.

I thank you for sending to me so gracious a gentleman as Mr Stanley, who interested us in every manner, by his elegance, his accurate information of that we wished to know, & his surprising acquaintance with the camp & military politics on our frontier. I regretted that I could see him so little. He has used his time to the best purpose, & I should gladly have learned all his adventures from so competent a witness. Forgive this long writing, and keep the old kindness which I prize above words.[7] My kindest salutations to the dear invalid!

R. W. Emerson

[4] The dismalness of the New Orleans editor J. D. B. De Bow must have lain for Emerson not in his economic opinions, which were much influenced by the anti-Malthusianism of Henry Carey, but in his advocacy of slavery and secession. See Skipper, *J. D. B. De Bow: Magazinist of the Old South.*

[5] Here the first draft reads: ". . . have had their day."

[6] Emerson may have found poetry in the combination of increased population— eight and a quarter million in a decade—and increased prosperity which was reported by the Census of 1860.

[7] Carlyle read this letter to Conway and expressed astonishment at Emerson's political opinions, but to the last sentence he said: "No danger but that will be kept." And "never again," wrote Conway, "did I hear Carlyle speak with his former confidence concerning the issue in America" (Conway, *Thomas Carlyle,* p. 102).

1865

Cummertrees, Annan, Scotland
14 June 1865—

Dear Emerson,

Tho' my hand is shaking (as you sadly notice), I determine to write you a little Note today. What a severance there has been these many sad years past!—In the first days of February I ended my weary Book; a totally worn-out man, got to shore ag^n after far the ugliest seas he had ever swam in. In April or the end of March, when the Book was published, I duly handed out a Copy for Concord & you: it was to be sent by Mail; but, as my Publisher (a *new* Chapman,[1] very unlike the *old*), discloses to me lately an incredible negligence on such points, it is quite possible the dog may *not,* for a long while, have put it in the Post-Office (tho' he faithfully charged me the postage of it, and was paid), and that the poor Waif may never yet have reached you! Patience; it will come soon enough,—there are two thick volumes, & they will stand you a great deal of reading, stiff, rather than "light."

Since February last, I have been sauntering ab^t, in Devonshire, in Chelsea, hither, thither: *idle* as a dry bone,—in fact, a creature sinking into deeper & deeper *collapse,* after 12 years of such mulish pulling & pushing; creature now good for nothing seemingly, and much indifferent to being so in permanence, if that be the arrang^t come upon by the Powers that made us. Some three or four weeks ago, I came rolling down hither, into this old nook of my Birthland, to see poor old Annadale ag^n with eyes, and the poor remnants of kindred & loved ones still left me there. I was not at first very lucky (lost *sleep* &c); but am now doing better, pretty much got adjusted to my new element, new to me since ab^t six years past,—the longest absence I ever had from it before. My Work was getting desperate at that time;

---

[1] Frederic Chapman in 1864 succeeded his cousin Edward Chapman as head of the firm of Chapman and Hall.

and I silently said to myself, "We won't return till *it* is done, or *you* are done, my man!"

This is my oldest living sister's[2] house; one of the most rustic Farmhouses in the world, but abounding in all that is needful to me, especially in the truest *silently* active affectn, the humble generosity of whh is itself medicinal balm. The place is airy, on dry waving knolls cheerfully (with such *water* as I never drank elsewhere, except at Malvern): all around me are the mountains, Cheviot & Galloway (3 to 15 miles off), Cumberland & Yorkshire (say 40 & 50, with the Solway brine & sands intervening): I live in total solitude, sauntering moodily in thin checkered woods, galloping abt, once daily, by old lanes & roads,—oftenest latterly on the wide expanses of Solway shore (when the tide is *out!*) where I see bright busy Cottages far off, houses over even in Cumberland, & the beautifullest amphitheatre of eternal Hills,—but meet no living creature; and have endless thots as loving & as sad & sombre as I like. My youngest Brother[3] (whom on the whole I like best, a rustic man, the express image of my Father in his ways of living & thinking) is within 10 miles of me; Brother John "the Dr" has come down to Dumfries to a Sister (12 miles off), & runs down over to me by rail now & then in few minutes. I have Books; but can hardly be troubled with them. Pitiful temporary babble and balderdash, in comparison to what the silences can say to one. Enough of all that: you perceive me suffictly, at this point point of my Pilgrimage, as withdrawn to *Hades* for the time being; intending a month's walk there, till the muddy semi-solutions settle into sediment according to what laws they have, & there be perhaps a partial restoratn of clearness. I have to go deeper into Scotland by & by, perhaps to try *sailing* whh generally agrees with me: but till the end of Septr I hope there will be no London farther. My poor Wife, who is agn poorly since I left (& has had frightful sufferings, last year especially) will probably join me in this region before I leave it:—and see here, this is authentically the way we figure in the eye of the Sun; and something like what yr spectacles, cd they reach across the Ocean

---

[2] Mary Austin.

[3] James Carlyle, who bore the same name as his father, worked the farm at Scotsbrig, near Ecclefechan, which for nearly forty years had been the headquarters of the Carlyle family (Wilson, *Carlyle at His Zenith*, p. 195).

into these nooks, wd teach you of us. There are 3 Photographs[4] whh I reckon fairly *like; these* are properly what I had to send you today, —little thinking that so much surplusage wd accumulate abt them; to whh I now at once put an end. Yr friend Conway,[5] who is a boundless admirer of yrs, used to come our way regularly now & then; and we always liked him well. A man of most gentlemanly, ingenious ways; turn of thot always loyal & manly, tho' tending to be rather *winged* than solidly ambulatory. He talked of coming to Scotland too; but it seems uncertn whether we shall meet. He is clearly rather a favte among the London people,—& tries to explain America to them; I know not if with any success.—As for me, I have entirely lost count & reckoning of yr enormous element, and its do[6] affairs & procedures, for some time past; & can only wish (whh no man more heartily does) that all may issue in as blessed a way as you hope. Fat Trollope (if you know Trollope & his fat commonplace at all) amused me much by a thing he had heard of yrs in some Lecture a year or two ago: "the American Eagle is a mighty bird; but what is he to the American Peacock!"[7]—at whh all the audience had exploded into laughter. Very good.—Adieu, old Friend.

Yrs ever   —T. Carlyle

[4] On this day Carlyle wrote to his wife, "I have spent the morning (nr 2 hours of it; shame on me, but my hand *shook* so, for a long while) in writing to Emerson. I meant merely to send him two Photographs; but the matter spread into detail. —The Phs I sent are the big wide-awake (Watkins, of *self*) and the beautiful *preferred* Elliot of you: I had but that one (came 29 May; send me 2 or 3 more of *it*); I cd not think of sending poor Goody otherwise than with her best foot foremost into Yankeeland" (NLS, MS 617).

[5] Moncure Daniel Conway, journalist and Unitarian minister, had come to England in 1863 as an unofficial propagandist for American abolitionism and had stayed on as minister to a London congregation (Burtis, *Moncure Conway*, pp. 93–107, 116).

[6] "Ditto."

[7] Trollope's own version of the remark, reported in his travel book, *North America* (1862), was "Your American eagle is very well. Protect it here and abroad. But beware of the American peacock." The lecture was "American Nationality," delivered in Boston on November 12, 1861. See Smalley and Booth's edition of *North America* (New York, 1951), p. 223.

1866

Concord, 7 Jany 1866—

Dear Carlyle,

Is it too late to send a letter to your door to claim an old right to enter, & to scatter all your convictions that I had passed under the earth? You had not to learn what a sluggish pen mine is. Of course, the sluggishness grows on me, & even such a trumpet at my gate as a letter from you heralding-in noble books, whilst it gives me joy, cannot heal the paralysis. Yet your letter deeply interested me, with the account of your rest so well-earned. You had fought your great battle, & might roll in the grass, or ride your pony, or shout to the Cumberland or Scotland echoes, with largest leave of men & gods. My lethargies have not dulled my delight in good books. I read these in the bright days of our new peace, which added a lustre to every genial work. Now first we had a right to read, for the very bookworms were driven out of doors whilst the war lasted. I found in the book no trace of age, which your letter so impressively claimed. In the book, the hand does not shake, the mind is ubiquitous. The treatment is so spontaneous, selfrespecting defiant,—liberties with your hero, as if he were your client, or your son, & you were proud of him, & yet can check & chide him, & even put him in the corner when he is not a good boy,—freedoms with kings, & reputations, & nations, yes, & with principles too—that each reader, I suppose, feels complimented by the confidences with which he is honored by this free-tongued masterful Hermes.—Who knows what the Δαῖμων will say next? This humor of telling the story in a gale,—bantering, scoffing, at the hero, at the enemy, at the learned reporters,—is a perpetual flattery to the admiring student,—the author abusing the whole world as mad dunces,—all but you & I, reader! Ellery Channing borrowed my Volumes V & VI., worked slowly through them,—midway came to me for vols. 1, 2, 3, 4, which he had long already read, & at last returned all with this word, "If you write to Mr Carlyle, you may say to him, that I have read these books, & they have made it impossible for me to read any other books but his."

Tis a good proof of their penetrative force, the influence on the new Sterling, who writes "The Secret of Hegel"[1] He is quite as much a student of Carlyle to learn treatment, as of Hegel for his matter, & plays the same game on his essence-dividing German, which he has learned of you on Friedrich. I have read a good deal in this book of Sterling's, & have not done with it.

One or two *errata* I noticed in the last vols. of Friedrich, though the books are now lent, & I cannot indicate the pages. Fort Pulaski, which is near Savannah, is set down as near Charleston.—Charles*ton*, S. Carolina, your printer has twice called Charles*town*, which is the name of the town in Massachuetts in which Bunker Hill stands.—Bancroft told me that the Letters of Montcalm are spurious.—We always write & say Ticonder*oga*.[2]

I am sorry that Jonathan looks so unamiable seen from your island.[3] Yet I have too much respect for the writing profession to complain of it. It is a necessity of rhetoric that there should be shades, &, I suppose, geography & government always determine even for the greatest wits where they shall lay their shadows. But I have always the belief that a trip across the sea would have abated your despair of us. The world is laid out here in large lots, & the swing of natural laws is shared by the population, as it is not,—or not as much, in your feudal Europe. My countrymen do not content me, but they are susceptible of inspirations. In the war, it was humanity that showed itself to advantage,— the leaders were prompted & corrected by the intuitions of the people, —they still demanding the more generous & decisive measure, & giving

---

[1] James Hutchison Stirling's two-volume exposition and defense of Hegel (1865) is written in a vigorous, exclamatory, personal style.

[2] Carlyle had twice spelled the word *Ticonderago*. In later editions this error and the Charleston-Charlestown-Savannah errors are corrected. The letter of Montcalm, which predicted the American revolution, Carlyle allowed to remain, but he added in a footnote of July, 1868: "In the Temple Library, London, I have since found a Copy: and, on strict survey, am obliged to pronounce the whole Pamphlet a *Forgery* . . ." (*Works TC*, XVIII, 146–47).

[3] Emerson perhaps refers to this passage: "In 1775, again, there began, over seas, another Anarchy . . . calling itself Liberty, Rights of Man; and singing boundless Io-Paeans to itself, as is common in such cases; an Anarchy . . . which has, at last, flamed up as an independent Phenomenon, unexampled in the hideously *suicidal* way;—and does need much to get burnt out" (*Works TC*, XIX, 3).

their sons & their estates, as we had no example before. In this heat, they had sharper perceptions of policy, of the ways & means, & the life of nations, & on every side we read or heard fate-words in private letters, in railway cars, or in the journals. We were proud of the people & believed they would not go down from this height But Peace came, & every one ran back into his shop again, & can hardly be won to patriotism more, even to the point of chasing away the thieves that are stealing not only the public gold, but the newly won rights of the slave, & the new measures we had contrived to keep the planter from sucking his blood.

Very welcome to me were the photographs—your own, & Jane Carlyle's. Hers, now seen here for the first time, was closely scanned, & confirmed the better accounts that had come of her improved health. Your earlier tidings of her had not been encouraging. I recognized still erect the wise friendly presence first seen at Craigenputtock. Elizabeth Hoar likes it well. Of your own—the hatted head is good, but more can be read in the head leaning on the hand, & the one in a cloak.[4]

At the end of so much writing, I have little to tell you of myself.[5] I am a bad subject for autobiography. As I adjourn letters, so I adjourn my best tasks. My youngest girl, Edith, was happily married, in October, to a good youth who had done three years' valiant service in the field, a Lieut. Colonel of Cavalry in the Masstts Volunteers.[6] She sends you the homage of her card. Her sister Ellen makes my house glad, day by day. Edward is spending his last year at Cambridge. My Wife joins me in very kind regards to Mrs Carlyle. Use your old magnanimity to me, & punish my stony ingratitudes by new letters from time to time.

Ever affectionately & gratefully yours,[7]

R. W. Emerson

Thomas Carlyle, Esq.

[4] Plates IV and V reproduce the first and third photographs of Carlyle and the photograph of Jane Carlyle.

[5] In the first draft, this paragraph begins: "But I did not mean to write sheets but only as our army men reported dead anxiously write home once with particulars. It is not too late for you to come here. I am not quite yet allowed the privileges of old age, but read lectures from time to time." Two days later, Emerson set out on a six-week lecture tour which took him as far west as Wisconsin (*Let RWE*, V, 447).

[6] William Hathaway Forbes (Rusk, *Life*, p. 430).

[7] In a letter from Carlyle to his brother John, of January 22, 1866, there appears

Concord
16 May 1866

My dear Carlyle,

I have just been shown a private letter from Moncure Conway to one of his friends here, giving some tidings of your sad return to an empty home.[1] We had the first news last week. And so it is. The stroke long-threatened has fallen at last, in the mildest form to its victim, & relieved to you by long & repeated reprieves. I must think her fortunate also in this gentle departure, as she had been in her serene & honored career. We would not for ourselves count covetously the descending steps, after we have passed the top of the mount, or grudge to spare some of the days of decay. And you will have the peace of knowing her safe, & no longer a victim. I have found myself recalling an old verse which one utters to the parting soul,—

"For thou hast passed all change of human life,
And not again to thee shall beauty die." [2]

It is thirty three years in July, I believe, since I first saw her, & her conversation & faultless manners gave assurance of a good & happy future. As I have not witnessed any decline, I can hardly believe in any, & still recall vividly the the youthful wife & her blithe account of her letters & homages from Goethe, & the details she gave of her intended visit to Weimar, & its disappointment.[3] Her goodness to me & to my friends was ever perfect, & all Americans have agreed in her praise. Elizabeth Hoar remembers her with entire sympathy & regard.

I could heartily wish to see you for an hour in these lonely days. Your friends, I know, will approach you as tenderly as friends can; and I can believe that labor,—all whose precious secrets you know,—will prove a consoler,—though it cannot quite avail,—for she was the rest that rewarded labor. It is good that you are strong, & built for endurance. Nor will you shun to consult the aweful oracles which in

---

this passage: "Since I began writing, this Letter has come from Emerson, long waited for, whh I enclose at once, for yr behoof and Jean's. You can return it at once, for even Jane has not yet seen it ('too busy' she ansrd, & is since gone out)." But a postscript, written in blue pencil and circled, says: "On the whole I will delay the Emerson till tomorrow!" (NLS, MS 526).

[1] Jane Carlyle died April 19, 1866 (Froude, IV, 265).

[2] I have been unable to find the source of this quotation.

[3] See above, Introduction, p. 12.

these hours of tenderness are sometimes vouchsafed. If to any, to you.

I rejoice that she stayed to enjoy the knowledge of your good day at Edinburgh, which is a leaf we would not spare from your book of life. It was a right manly speech [4] to be so made, & is a voucher of unbroken strength—and the surroundings, as I learn, were all the happiest,—with no hint of change. I pray you bear in mind your own counsels. Long years you must still achieve, and, I hope, neither grief nor weariness will let you "join the dim choir of the bards that have been," [5] until you have written the book I wish & wait for,—the sincerest confessions of your best hours. My wife prays to be remembered to you with sympathy & affection.

Ever yours faithfully,   R. W. Emerson

Thomas Carlyle, Esq.

[4] On the day before his wife's death, Carlyle, still in Scotland, had been sending out copies of the *Inaugural Address* which he had delivered at Edinburgh University April 2; one copy went to Emerson; the first copy, mailed on the 17th, had gone to Jane (TC to Jane, April 18, 1866 [NLS, MS 617]).

[5] I have been unable to find the source of this quotation.

1867

Mentone (France, Alpes Maritimes)
27 Jan^{ry}, 1867

My dear Emerson,

It is a long time since I last wrote to you; and a long distance in space and in fortune,—from the shores of the Solway in summer 1865, to this niche of the Alps and Mediterranean today, after what has befallen me in the interim! A longer interval, I think, and surely by far a sadder, than ever occurred betw^n us before, since we first met in the Scotch moors, some five and thirty years ago. You have written me various Notes,[1] too, and Letters, all good and cheering to me,—almost the only truly *human* speech I have heard from anybody living;—and still my stony silence c^d not be broken; not till now, tho' often looking forward to it, c^d I resolve on such a thing. You will think me far gone, and much bankrupt in hope and heart;—and indeed I am, as good as without hope and without fear; a gloomily serious, silent and sad old man; gazing into the final chasm of things, in mute dialogue with "Death Judgement and Eternity"[2] (dialogue *mute* on *both* sides!) not caring to discourse with poor articulate-speaking fellow creatures on *their* sorts of topics. It is right of me;—& yet also it is not right. I often feel that I had better be dead than thus indiff^t, contemptuous, disgusted with the world and its roaring nonsense, wh^h I have no tho^t farther of lifting a finger to help, and only try to keep out of the way of, and shut my door ag^t. But the truth is, I was nearly killed by that hideous Book on Friedr^h,—12 years in continuous wrestle with the nightmares and the subterranean hydras;—nearly *killed,* and had often tho^t I sh^d be altogether, and must die leaving the monster not so much as finished! This is one truth, not so evid^t to any friend or onlooker as it is to myself: and then there is another, known to myself alone, as it were; and of wh^h I am best not to speak to others, or to speak

---

[1] These notes, if Carlyle remembered correctly, are missing.
[2] Three of the seven "last things."

to them no farther. By the calamity of April last, I lost my little all in this world; and have no soul left who can make any corner of this world [3] into a *home* for me any more. Bright, heroic, tender, true and noble was that lost treasure of my heart, who faithfully accompanied me in all the rocky ways & climbings; and I am forever poor witht her. She was snatched from me in a moment,—as by a death from the gods. Very beautiful her death was; radiantly beautiful (to those who understood it) had all her life been: *quid plura?* I shd be among the dullest & stupidest if I were not among the saddest of all men. But not a word more on all this.

All summer last, my one solacement in the form of work was writing, and sorting of old documents and recollectns; summoning out agn into clearness old scenes that had now closed on me witht return.[4] Sad, and in a sense sacred; it was like a kind of *worship;* the only *devout* time I had had for a great while past. These things I have half or wholly the intentn to burn out of the way before I myself die:— but such continues still mainly my employt,—so many hours every forenoon; what I call the "work" of my day:—to me, if to no other, it is useful; to reduce matters to writing means that you shall know them, see them in their origins & sequences, in their essential lineaments, considerably better than you ever did before. To set abt writing my own *Life* wd be no less than horrible to me; and shall of a certainty never be done. The common impious vulgar of this earth, what has it to do with my Life or me? Let dignified oblivion, silence, and the vacant azure of Eternity swallow *me;* for my share of it, that, verily is the handsomest or one handsome way of settling my poor acct with the canaille of mankind extant and to come. "Immortal glory," is not that a beautiful thing, in the Shakespeare Clubs & Literary Gazettes of our improved Epoch?—I did not leave London, except for 14 days in August, to a fine and high old Lady-friend's in Kent; where, riding abt the woods & by the sea-beaches and chalk cliffs, in utter silence, I felt sadder than ever, tho' a little less *miserably* so, than in the intrusive babblets of London, whh I cd not quite lock out of doors. We read, at first, Tennyson's *Idyls,* with profound recognitn of the finely elaborated executn, and also of the inward perfectn of *vacancy,* —and, to say truth, with considerable impatience at being treated so

---

[3] Cf. Horace, *Odes,* II, vi, 13.
[4] These were some of the posthumously published *Reminiscences.*

very like infants, tho the lollipops were so superlative. We gladly changed for one Emerson's *English Traits;* and read that, with increasing satisfactn every evg; blessing Heaven that there were still Books for grown-up people too! That truly is a Book all full of thots like winged arrows (thanks to the Bowyer from us both):—my Lady-friend's name is Miss Davenport Bromley; it was at Wooton, in her Grandfather's House, in Staffordshire, that Rousseau took shelter in 1760; [5] and 106 years later she was reading Emerson to me, with a recognitn that wd have pleased the man, had he seen it.

Abt that same time, my health and humours being evidtly so the Dowr Lady Ashburton (*not* the high Lady you saw, but a Successor of Mackenzie-Highland type),[6] who wanders mostly abt the Continent since her widowhood, for the sake of a child's health, began pressing & inviting to spend the black months of Winter, here in her Villa with her;—all friends warmly seconding and urging; by one of whom I was at last snatched off, as if by the hair of the head (in spite spite of my violent No, no!) on the eve of Xmas last,[7] and have been here ever since,—really with improved omens. The place is beautiful as a very Picture, the climate superlative (today a sun & sky like very June); the *hospitality* of usage beyond example. It is likely I shall be here another six weeks at longest. If you plan to write me, the address is on the margin; and I will answer!

Adieu.   T. Carlyle

T. Carlyle Esqr
Aux soins de Mylady Ashburton/ Menton/ France.

[5] Rousseau was at Wootton for about a year, in 1766 and 1767, during which he wrote most of the *Confessions.*

[6] The second Lady Ashburton was Louisa Caroline Stewart Mackenzie, member of a distinguished Highland family.

[7] Carlyle left London on December 22 in the company of John Tyndall (Wilson, *Carlyle in Old Age,* p. 111).

1869

5 Cheyne Row, Chelsea,[1]
18 November 1869.

Dear Emerson,

It is near 3 years since I last wrote to you; from Mentone, under the Ligurian Olive and Orange trees, and their sombre foreign shadows, and still *more* sombre suggestings and promptings; the saddest, probably, of all living men. That you made no answer I know right well means only, "Alas, what can I say to him of consolatory that he does not himself know!" Far from a fault, or perhaps even a mistake on your part;—nor have I felt it otherwise. Sure enough, among the lights that have gone out for me, and are still going, one after one, under the inexorable Decree, in this now dusky and lonely world, I count with frequent regret that our Correspondence (*not* by absolute hest of Fate) should have fallen extinct, or into such abeyance: but I interpret it as you see; and my love and brotherhood to you remain alive and will while I myself do. Enough of this. By lucky chance, as you perceive, you are again to get one written Letter from me, and I a reply from you, before the final silence come! The case is this.

For many years back, a thought, which I used to check again as fond and silly, has been occasionally present to me, of testifying my gratitude to New England (New England, acting mainly through one of her Sons called Waldo Emerson), by *bequeathing to it my poor Falstaff Regiment, latterly two Falstaff Regiments, of Books,* those purchased and used in writing *Cromwell,* and do those on *Friedrich the Great.* "This could be done," I often said to myself; "this *could* per-

---

[1] In a letter of July 15, 1869, from Carlyle to his brother John, there appears this parenthesis, in pencil, following a scratched and blotted passage in pen: "[I must try pencil agn:—this hand, this hand; many days it absolutely won't write at all; but I *am* learng to write by dictatn, *must* alas!] (NSL, MS 526). The present letter is written except for the signature and a few corrections in the hand of Carlyle's niece, Mary Aitken, who since 1868 had been his secretary. The first two thirds of the rough draft, in Carlyle's hand, is owned by the National Library of Scotland.

haps; and this would be a real satisfaction to me! But who then would march through Coventry with such a set!" [2] The extreme insignificance of the Gift—this and nothing else, always gave me pause.

Last Summer, I was lucky enough to meet with your friend C. E. Norton, and renew many old Massachusets recollections, in free talk with so genial, gracefully social, intelligent and cheerful a man: to him I spoke of the affair; candidly describing it, especially the above questionable feature of it, so far as I could: and his answer, then and more deliberately afterwards, was so hopeful, hearty and decisive, that —in effect it has decided me; and I am, this day, writing to him that such is the poor fact, and that I need farther instructions on it so soon as you two have taken counsel together.[3]

To say more about the infinitesimally small value of the Books would be superfluous: Nay, in truth, many or most of them are not without intrinsic value, one or two are even excellent as Books: and all of them, it may perhaps be said, have a kind of *symbolic* or *biographic* value; and testify (a thing not useless) *on what slender commissariat stores* considerable Campaigns, 12 years long or so, may be carried on in this world. Perhaps you already knew of me, what the *Cromwell* and *Friedrich* collection might itself intimate, that much *buying* of Books was never a habit of mine,—far the reverse, even to this day!

Well, my Friend, you will have a meeting with Norton so soon as handy; and let me know what is next to be done. And that, in your Official Capacity, is all I have to say to you at present.

Unofficially there were much,—much that is mournful, but perhaps also something that is good and blessed, and though the saddest, also the highest, the lovingest and best; as beseems Time's Sunset, now coming nigh. At present I will say only that, in bodily health, I am not to be called ill, for a man who will be 74 next month; nor, on the spiritual side, has anything been laid upon me that is quite beyond

---

[2] Cf. *Henry IV, Part I:* act IV, scene ii, line 42.

[3] Carlyle had mentioned the bequest to Norton in a conversation of early May: "I should like when I die to leave these books to some institution in New England." Norton advised, in a letter of May 24: "I believe that your wishes would be best carried out were you to leave the books . . . to the Library of Harvard College" (*Letters*, I, 336, 339). A later letter from Carlyle to Norton described the bequest as "a proof of my grateful, loving, and hopeful feelings to New England . . . —of my true, essentially kind and deep regard to the great *New English Nation* named America" (MS owned by the Houghton Library).

my strength. More miserable I have often been; though as solitary, soft of heart, and sad, of course never.

Publisher Chapman, when I question him whether you for certain *get* your Monthly Volume of what they call "The Library Edition," assures and again assures me that "it is beyond doubt":—I confess I should still like to be *better* assured. If all is *right,* you should, by the time this Letter arrives, be receiving or have received your 13th volume, last of the *Miscellanies.* Adieu, My Friend:

Ever truly yours   T. Carlyle

R. Waldo Emerson, Concord, Mass.

1870

Chelsea, 4 Jany, 1870.

Dear Emerson,—A month ago or more I wrote, by the same post to you and to Norton ab^t those Books for Harvard College; and in late days have been expecting y^r joint ans^r. From Norton yesternight I receive what is here copied for y^r perusal;[1] it has come round by

---

[1] Copy

To Thomas Carlyle Esq., Chelsea

> Villa d'Elsi
> fuori di porta San Gallo
> Florence, Dec. 31, 1869.

Dear Sir

Your kind Note of November 18th., returned from America, reaches me here today,—and gives an unexpected pleasure to the end of this year. Doubtless you have heard from Emerson ere this, and learned from him that, owing to my continued absence from home, he and I have been unable to take counsel together as to the precise mode in which your good intention toward Harvard may be best carried out. But he will advise the right way, and the help I would gladly give is little needed. This, however, occurs to me to say, that if your precious gift take the form of a testamentary bequest, it will be best that it should be made directly to the University itself, under such conditions as you may deem best,—not merely that it may have a certain dignity as a species of public act,—but also because the University is entitled under our laws to receive such a gift without payment of taxes or import duties. If the books were left to Emerson as your Trustee, to be given in your name to the Library of the University, he might have some trouble to free himself from the payment of duties upon them. We are so unwise as to levy an import duty upon foreign wisdom when it comes to us in the form of books. The legal title of the University is "Harvard College in the city of Cambridge, in the State of Massachusetts." The agents of the College in England are Messrs. Baring Brothers & Co. 8 Bishopsgate St within London. It might save trouble if a memorandum were made giving directions that when the books are to be sent they should be put in the hands of the agents to be forwarded.

Your intention toward the University which embodies the best spirit of New England, touches me very deeply,—and hereafter will move many others as it now moves me. You could not, I am sure, place these books anywhere where such intrinsic worth & literary interest as they may have would be more highly appreciated, or where they would be regarded from their association with your life, with more grateful & reverent honour, than among the students and scholars of Cambridge. Such a pledge of confidence is no slight bond between the people of the two Englands.

Florence as you see, and given me real pleasure & instructn. From you, who are possibly also away from home, I have yet nothing; but expect now soon to have a few words. There did arrive one evg lately, yr Two pretty *volumes* of *Collected Works*,[2] a pleast salutatn from you —whh set me upon reading again what I thot I knew well before:— but the Letter is still to come.

Norton's hints are such a complete instructn to me that I see my way straight thro' the busss, and might by Note of "Bequest," and *memm for the Barings,* finish it in half an hour: nevertheless I will wait for yr Letter and punctually do nothing till yr directns too are before me. Pray write, therefore, all is lying ready here. Since you heard last, I have got *Two Catalogues* made out, approximately correct; one is to lie here till the Bequest be *executed;* the other I thot of sending to you agt the day? This is my own inventn in regard to the affair since I wrote last. Approve of it, and you shall have yr copy by Book-post at once. *"Approximately* correct"; absolutely I cannot get it to be. But I need not doubt the Pious Purpose will be piously & even sacredly *fulfilled;*—& yr Catalogue will be a kind of evidence that it is[3]

Adieu, dear Emerson till yr letter come.

Yrs ever   T. Carlyle

Concord, 23 January 1870 [1]

My dear Carlyle,

Tis a sad apology that I have to offer for delays which no apology can retrieve. I received your first letter with pure joy, but in the midst

---

I am sorry that you speak of "sick langours" &c &c—I shall be here with my family for some months longer. It would please me greatly to be of service to you.
I am, with great respect,

Gratefully & Sincerely Yours   Charles Eliot Norton

[2] *The Prose Works of Ralph Waldo Emerson* (Boston, 1869). Emerson noted in his journal on October 19, 1869, that a copy had been sent to Carlyle (Typescript Journals, vol. NY, p. 194).

[3] The catalogue, in Emerson's words, "enumerates the authors translators or editors of the books & in some instances adds a distinct opinion from Mr Carlyle on the literary value of the book" (*Let RWE,* VI, 107).

[1] This letter exists, so far as I know, only in incomplete rough drafts. The present text is made from a MS owned by the Library of Congress which seems to be the semi-final version. Another rough draft, owned by the RWEMA, is fully printed and annotated by Rusk in *Let RWE,* VI, 97–98. What seems to be yet another, also owned by the RWEMA, carries this notation in Emerson's hand: "piece of a let-

of extreme inefficiency. I had suddenly yielded to a proposition of Fields & Co to manufacture a book for a given day. The book was planned, & going on passably, when it was found better to divide the matter, & separate & postpone the purely literary portion (criticism chiefly), & therefore to modify & swell the elected part.[2] The attempt proved more difficult than I had believed, for I only write by spasms, & these ever more rare,—and daemons that have no ears. Meantime the publication-day was announced, & the printer at the door. Then came your letter in the shortening days. When I drudged to keep my word, *invita Minerva* [3]—I could not write in my book, & I could not write a letter. Tomorrow & many morrows made things worse—for we have indifferent health in the house, &, as it chanced, unusual strain of affairs,—which always come when they should not: for one thing— I have just sold a house which I once built opposite my own. But I will leave the bad month, which I hope will not match itself in my lifetime. Only tis pathetic & remorseful to me that any purpose of yours, especially a purpose so inspired, should find me imbecile.

Heartily I delight in your proposed disposition of the books. It has every charm of surprise & nobleness & large affection. The act will deeply gratify a multitude of good men who will see in it your real sympathy with the welfare of the country. I hate that there should be a moment of delay in the completing of your provisions,—& that I of all men should be the cause! Norton's letter is perfect on his part, & needs no addition I believe from me. You had not in your first letter named *Cambridge,* & I had been meditating that he would probably have divided your attention between Harvard, & the Boston Public Library—now the richest in country, at first founded by the gifts of

---

ter to Carlyle. I know not if it were ever sent." It reads as follows: "I can hardly tell how it lay still. I had got unwarily into a book. Five new Chapters & some old ones printed already—its publication day announced by Fields's trumpets, & I unready, & the printer at the door. That for the superficial reason; but also how can I write to you? Your mood is not mine & you choose to sit like Destiny at the door of nations, & predict calamity, & contradict with irresistible wit your own morale, & ridicule shatter the attempts of little men at humanity & charity & uphold the offender But strength is strength & comes always from God & so is at base divine & so issues divine."

[2] The book was *Society and Solitude.* E. W. Emerson suggests that the "purely literary portion" consisted of the essays "Poetry and criticism" and "Persian Poetry" which appeared in 1875 in the volume entitled *Letters and Social Aims (Works* VII, 344).

[3] See above, C.12.8.37, n. 8.

Joshua Bates (of London,) & since enriched by the city & private do-
nors, Theodore Parker among them. But after conversation with two
or three friends, I had decided that Harvard College was the right
beneficiary, as being the mother real or adoptive of a great number
of your lovers & readers in America, & because a College is a seat of
sentiment & cosmical relations. The Library is outgrown by other libraries in the country, counts only 119,000 bound volumes in 1868;
the several departments of Divinity, Law, Medicine, & Nat. Science
in the University having special libraries that together add some 40,000
more. The College is newly active (with its new President Eliot,[4] a
cousin of Norton's) & expansive in all directions. And the Library will
be relieved [5] through subscriptions now being collected among the
alumni with the special purpose of securing to it an adequate fund
for annual increase.

I shall then write to Norton at once that I concur with him in the
destination of the books to Harvard College, & approve entirely [6] his
advices in regard to details [7] And so soon as you send me the catalogue [8] I shall if you permit, communicate your design to President
Eliot & the Corporation. One thing I shall add to the catalogue now
or later (perhaps only by bequest,) your own prized gift to me, in 1848,
of Wood's *Athenae Oxonienses,* which I have lately had re-bound, &
in which every pen & pencil mark of yours is notable.[9]

The stately books of the New Edition have duly come from the
unforgetting friend.[10] I have Sartor, (Schiller), Fr. Revolution 3 Vols
Miscellanies Numbers 1, 2, 3, 4, 5, ten volumes in all, excellently printed
& [11] dressed & full of memories & [12] electricity and I shall add to the
inventory now or later, (perhaps only, by bequest,) your own prized
gift to me of "Wood's *Athenae Oxonienses,*" which I have lately re-
bound, & in which every pencil mark of yours is notable.

[4] Charles W. Eliot was inaugurated October 19, 1869.

[5] The phrase "& enriched" has been deleted here by Emerson.

[6] The word "the" has been deleted by Emerson.

[7] Here the words "given in his letter" have been deleted by Emerson.

[8] Emerson has deleted the words "you have made."

[9] Eventually the Wood volume was bequeathed to James Elliot Cabot (*Let RWE*
VI, 49*n*).

[10] This paragraph originally began "You ask me if I have the the new books. Yes."
Emerson deleted these words.

[11] Here Emerson substituted "dressed" for "bound."

[12] Emerson here substituted "electricity" for "sparks."

The [13] stately books of the New Edition [14] have duly come 10 volumes I have Sartor, Schiller, French Revolution I, II, III. Miscellanies 1, 2, 3, 4 5 ten volumes in all, excellently printed & full of memories & of power still vital My son is reading the French Revolution between the hours of the Medical College and I am contented with the variety of opinions maintaining that Friedrich or French Rev. or Sterling or the [15] critical papers on German & French heads are the best and the preferred report of critical readers from far or near.

I have much to say but not of things not opportune at this moment, & in spite of my long contumacy dare believe that I shall quickly write again my proper letter to my friend whose every word I watchfully read & remember.

> Letter to Carlyle
> on the Books for
> Cambridge.
> Jan 1870

> Melchet Court, Romsey [1]
> 14 February 1870

Dear Emerson,

Three days ago I at last received your Letter;—with very great pleasure and thankfulness, as you may suppose.[2] Indeed it is quite strangely interesting to see face to face my old Emerson again, not a feature of him changed, whom I have known all the best part of my life.

I am very glad, withal, to find that you agree completely with Norton and myself in regard to that small Harvard matter.

[13] The word "For" was deleted by Emerson, who then began the sentence with "The."

[14] Emerson deleted the words "the stately" following "New Edition" and inserted "stately" as it here appears, before "books."

[15] Here Emerson deleted the phrase "German & French."

[1] For Melchet Court, see below, C.2.24.70. This letter was dictated.

[2] Carlyle had waited impatiently for an answer to his letter of November 18. On January 6, he wrote to his brother: "From Emerson nothing has come"; on January 22: "From Emerson I still hear nothing—and begin rather to wonder. N'importe, howr, N'importe du tout"; on January 28: "No Letter has yet come from Emerson; I begin to conjecture he must be from home: I have never yet ansd Norton,—waiting till the Emerson come" (NLS, MS 527).

This is not Chelsea, as you perceive, this is a hospitable Mansion in Hampshire; but I expect to be in Chelsea within about a week: once there I shall immediately dispatch to you one of the three Catalogues I have, with a more deliberate Letter than I at present have the means of writing or dictating.

You probably have written to Mr Norton; when you do again, fail not to express to him my lively gratitude; as I shall myself take the first good opportunity of doing.

Yours ever truly   T. Carlyle

Chelsea, 24 Feby 1870

Dear Emerson,

At length I have got home from those sumptuous tumults ("Melchet Court" is the Dow^r Lady *Ashburton's* House, whose late Husband, an estimable friend of mine, and *half American,* you may remember here): and I devote to ending of our small Harvard Bus^ss,—small enough, but true and kindly—the first quiet hour I have.

Y^r Copy of the Catalogue, wh^h accompanies by *Book Post* of today, is the correctest I c^d manage to get done; all the Books mentioned in it I believe to be now here (and indeed, except 5 or 6 *tiny* articles, have *seen* them all, in one or other of the 3 rooms where my Books now stand, and where I believe the insignif^t trifle of "tinies" to be): all these will be punctually attended to, when the time comes, and proceeded with accord^g to Norton's scheme & yours;—and if any more "tinies," wh^h I c^d not even remember, sh^d turn up (wh^h I hardly think there will), these also will *class* themselves (as *Cromwelliana* or *Fred^cana*), and be faithfully sent on with the others. For benefit of my *Survivers* and *Representatives* here, I retain an exact *Copy* of the Catalogue now put into y^r keeping; so that everything may fall out square bet^n them and you, when the Time shall arrive.

I mean to conform in every partic^r to the plan sketched out by Norton & you,—unless, in y^r next Letter, you have something other or farther to advise:—and so soon as I hear from you that Harvard accepts my poor widow's mite of a *Bequest,* I will proceed to put it down in due form, and so finish this small matter, wh^h for long years has hovered in my tho^ts as a thing sh^d like to do. And so enough for this time.

I meant to write a longish Letter, touching on many other points,—tho' you see I am reduced to *pencil!* [1] & "write" with such difficulty (never yet c^d learn to "dictate," tho' my little Niece here is promptitude itself, and is so swift and legible,—useful here as a cheerful *rushlight* in this now sombre element, sombre, sad, but also beautiful and tenderly solemn more & more, in wh^h she bears me company, good little "Mary"!) But, in bar of all such purposes, Publisher Chapman has come in, with Cromwell *Engravings* & their hindrances, with money acc^ts &c &c; and has not even left me a moment of *time,* were nothing else needed!

Vol XIV (*Cromwell,* I) ought to be at Concord ab^t as soon as this. In our Newspap^s I notice y^r Book announced, "half of the Essays new"; [2] wh^h I hope to get *quam primum,* and illuminate some ev^gs with,—*so* as nothing else can, in my pres^t common mood.

Adieu, dear old Friend. I am & remain

Y^rs always   T. Carlyle

Concord, 21 March, 1870 [1]

My dear Carlyle,

On receiving your letter & catalogue I wrote out a little history of the benefaction [2] & carried it, last Tuesday, to President Eliot at Cambridge, who was heartily gratified, & saw everything rightly, & expressed an anxiety (most becoming in my eyes after my odious shortcomings,) that there should be no moment of delay on our part.—"The Corporation would not meet again for a fortnight:—but he would not wait—would call a special meeting *this week* to make the communication to them" He did so: the meeting was held on Saturday, & I have received this (Monday) morning from him enclosed letter & record.

It is very amiable & noble in you to have kept this surprise for us in your older days. Did you mean to show us that you could not be

[1] All subsequent Carlyle letters which were not dictated were written in pencil.

[2] *Society and Solitude* was not published until March 5 (*Let RWE,* VI, 110n).

[1] MS owned by the Houghton Library. Above the heading there is this notation in the hand of Charles Eliot Norton: "(With Carlyle's endorsement on fourth page. C.E.N.) Sent to me by Mrs. Alex. Carlyle, August, 1882."

[2] Emerson's "history of the benefaction" is a letter to Eliot, dated March 14 and consisting mainly of extracts from the letters of Carlyle and Norton (*Let RWE,* VI, 104–8). The enclosed letter was Eliot's acceptance of the bequest; the record was of the vote of the Harvard Corporation (*Journals,* X, 315).

old, but immortally young? & having kept us all murmuring at your Satires & sharp homilies, will now melt us with this manly & heartwarming embrace? Nobody could predict & none could better it. And you shall even go your own gait henceforward with a blessing from us all, & a trust exceptional & unique. I do not longer hesitate to talk to such good men as I see of this gift, & it has in every ear a gladdening effect. People like to see character in a gift, & from rare character the gift is more precious. I wish it may be twice blest in continuing to give you the comfort it will give us.

I think I must mend myself by reclaiming my old right to send you letters. I doubt not I shall have much to tell you, could I overcome the hesitation to attempt a reasonable letter when one is driven to write so many sheets of mere routine as 66 (nearly 67) years enforce. I shall have to prate of my daughters—Edith Forbes, with her two children at Milton; Ellen Emerson at home, herself a godsend to this house day by day; & my son Edward studying medicine in Boston,— whom I have ever meant & still mean to send that he may see your face when that professional curriculum winds up.

I manage to read a few books & look into many more. Herman Grimm sent me lately a good one, Goethe's *Unterhaltungen* with Müller,—which set me on Varnhagen & others.[3] My Wife sends old regards, & her joy in this occasion.

Yours ever,   R W Emerson

Thomas Carlyle, Esq.

Mr Eliot took my rough counting of Volumes as correct.[4] When he sends me back the Catalogue, I shall make it exact.—I sent you last week a little book by Bookpost.

Emerson's 2ᵈ Letter abᵗ *Harvard* recᵈ, April 4th 1870 [5]

[3] *Goethe's Unterhaltungen mit dem Kanzler F. von Müller,* just published. Hermann Grimm, eldest son of Wilhelm, was a historian of art, with whom Emerson had been in correspondence since 1856 (*Correspondence between . . . Emerson and . . . Grimm,* ed. F. W. Holls). On March 23, Emerson copied into his Journal (X, 316) a passage dealing with Goethe from Vol. X of K. A. Varnhagen von Ense's *Tagebücher.*

[4] Emerson had written to Eliot: "There appear to be in all about 325 volumes" (*Let RWE,* VI, 107).

[5] This is a notation in Carlyle's hand.

5 Cheyne Row, Chelsea,[1]
24 March 1870

My dear Emerson,

The day before yesterday, I heard incidentally of an unfortunate Mail Steamer, bound for America, which had lost its screw or some essential part of it; and so had, instead of carrying its Letters forward to America, been drifting about like a helpless log on the shores of Ireland till some three days ago, when its Letters and Passengers were taken out, and actually forwarded thither. By industrious calculation, it appears probable to us here that my Letter to you may have been tumbling about in that helpless Steamer, instead of getting to Concord; where, if so, said Letter cannot now arrive till the lingering of it have created some astonishment there.

I hastily write this, however, to say that a Letter was duly forwarded a few days after yours arrived,—Enclosing the *Harvard Catalogue*, with all necessary etceteras; endorsing all your proposals; and signifying that the matter should be authentically completed the instant I should hear from you again. I may add now that the thing *is* essentially completed,—all signed and put on paper, or all but a word or two, which, for form's sake, waits the actual arrival of your Letter.

I have never yet received your *Book;* and, if it linger only a few days more, mean to provide myself with a copy such as the Sampson & Low people have on sale everywhere.

I had from Norton, the other day, a very kind & friendly Letter.

This is all of essential that I had to say. I write in utmost haste. But am always, Dear Emerson,

Yours sincerely   T. Carlyle

Chelsea, 6 April, 1870—

Dear Emerson,

The day before yesty yr welcome Letter came to hand with the welcome news in it; yesty I put into my poor Documt here the few words still needed; locked everything into its still repository (yr Letter, Presidt Eliot's, Norton's &c &c); and walked out into the sunshine,

[1] This letter was dictated.

piously thankful that a poor little whim, wh^h had long lain fondly in my heart, had realised itself with an emphasis I c^d never hope, and was become (thanks to generous enthusiasm on New Engl^d's part) a beautiful little fact, lying done there, so far as I had to do with it. Truly y^r acc^t of matters threw a glow of life into my tho^{ts} wh^h is very rare there now; altogether a gratifying little Transaction to me,—and I must add a surprising, for the enthusiasm of good-will is evid^{tly} great, and the occasion is almost infinitesimally small! Well, well; it is all finished off and completed,—(you can tell Mr Eliot, with many thanks from me, that I did introduce the proper style, "Presid^t and Fellows" &c, and have forgotten nothing of what he said, or of what he *did*):—and so we will say only, *Faustum sit,* as our last word on the subject;—and to me it will be, for some days yet, under these vernal skies, something that is itself connected with THE SPRING in a still higher sense; a little white and red-lipped bit of *Daisy*, pure and poor, scattered into TIME's Seedfield,[1] and struggling above ground there, uttering *its* bit of prophecy withal, among the ox-hoofs and big jungles that are everywhere ab^t and not prophetic of much:—

One thing only I regret, that you *have* spoken of the affair! For God's sake don't; and those kindly people to whom you have,—swear them to silence for love of me! The poor little *Daisy*kin will get into the Newspap^{rs}, and become the nastiest of Cabbages:—silence, silence, I do beg of you to the utmost stretch of y^r power! Or is the case already irremediable? I will hope not. Talk ab^t such things, especially Penny Editor's talk, is like vile coal-smoke filling y^r poor little world; silence alone is azure, and has a *sky* to it.—But, enough now.

The "little Book" never came; and, I doubt, never will: it is a fate that seems to await 3 fourths of the Books that attempt to reach me by the *American* Post; owing to some *informality in wrapping* (I have heard);—it never gave me any notable *regret* till now. How^r, I had already bo^t myself an English Copy, rather gaudy little volume (probably intended for the *railways*, as if *it* were a Book to be read there), but perfectly printed, ready to be read anywhere by the open eye and earnest mind;—wh^h I read here, accordingly, with great attent^n, clear assent for most part, and admiring recognit^n. It seems to me you are all y^r old self here, and something *more*. A calm insight, piercing to

[1] Cf. Goethe's "Die Zeit ist mein Besitz, mein Acker ist die Zeit," in *West-östlicher Divan* (*Werke*, V, 55).

the very centre, a beautiful sympathy, a beautiful *epic* humour; a soul peaceably irrefragable in this loud-jangling world, of whh it sees the ugliness, but *notices* only the huge new *opulences* (still so anarchic); knows the electric telegraph, with all its vulgar botheratn and impertinences, accurately for what it is, and do do the oldest eternal Theologies of men. All this belongs to the Highest Class of thot (you may depend upon it); and agn seemed to me as, in several respects, the one perfectly *human* voice I had heard among my fellow creatures for a long time. And then the "style," the treatt & expressn,—yes, it is inimitable, best-Emersonian thro'out. Such brevity, simplicity, softness, homely grace; with such a penetrating meaning, *soft* enough, but irresistible, going down to the depths and up to the heights, as *silent electricity* goes. You have done *very well;* and many will know it even better by degrees.—Only one thing farther I will note: How you go as if altogr on the "Over-Soul," the Ideal, the Perfect or Universal & Eternal in this Life of ours; and take so little heed of the frightful quantities of *friction* and perverse *impediment* there everywhere are; the reflections upon whh in my own poor life made me now & then very sad, as I read you. Ah me, ah me; what a vista it is, mournful, beautiful, *unfathomable* as Eternity itself, these last 50 years of Time to me!—

Let me not forget to thank you for that *fourth* page of yr Note; I shd say it was almost the most interestg of all, News from yrself at first hand; a momentary glimpse into the actl Household at Concord, face to face, as in years of old! True, I get vague news of you from time to time; but what are these in comparison?—If you *will,* at the eleventh hour, turn over a new leaf, and write me Letters agn,—but I doubt *you won't.* And yet were it not worth while, think you? Νύξ ερχεται; [2] will be here *anon.*— —My kindest regards to yr Wife. Adieu my ever-kind Old Friend.

Yrs faithfully always,   T. Carlyle

Concord, April 8, 1870

My dear Carlyle,

Wo is me when you are anxious,—& more & worse when on account of me. I know myself the slowest of men yet did not suspect the vice

[2] Cf. John 9: 4.

in the sending of my last letter. Yet I believe it took ship only on the very day on which your new letter of inquiry is dated. That missive went not, I hope, in any foundering bark but in a good mail-bearing steamer respected by men & the sea-gods. I can not now recall on what day your letter accompanying the "Catalogue" arrived in this house but I sat down gladly as soon as a sinful man might to write out a fitting recital to the Corporation of the College of the message with which I was charged. I remember that I had to think before I went to Cambridge whether it were a day on which the President would be surely at home & I may have lost a day on such a contingency. But the interview with Mr Eliot was entirely satisfactory, & since the Corporation then stood advised not to meet for a forthnight, he decided that he would not wait, but wd. call a special meeting in the next week, that he might communicate your proffer to them. I came home & waited for his Report, & as soon he sent me the Corporation's vote, I wrote you a letter saying these things I am now repeating, & enclosed the Report & the President's letter to me, which I hope & trust you have received safely. Nay, I confide that I shall myself have your own word to that effect ten days hence. I hate that you should have grief & trouble growing out of your excellent deed, & that I should be the cause of it more than once—were unpardonable. I sent you my little book by aid of Fields & Co (I should think on the 7th March) & you must tell me if it failed to reach you. I had three days ago your Inverness newspaper which my wife reads with due interest.[1]

Yours affectionately,   R. W. Emerson

Thomas Carlyle, Esq.

I thank & prize my new correspondent, Mary Carlyle Aitken [2]

[1] In *The Inverness Advertiser* of March 12, 1870, there is this paragraph: "On Thursday evening the Rev. Walter Smith, of Glasgow, gave a lecture . . . 'The Light of Life, as viewed by Arnold, Emerson, and Carlyle.' . . . Mr Smith began the subject by giving an outline of Carlyle's philosophy, afterwards passing to that of Emerson and of Arnold (not the celebrated Arnold of Rugby, but his son Matthew), and winding up by comparing the views of these men with the system of Christianity and the character of Jesus Christ, the true and sole 'light of the world.' The lecture was characterized by great grasp of thought and critical discrimination, especially in the case of Carlyle, whose moral system—or no-system—was described and analyzed with competent width and acuteness, and with much vivid power and eloquence. Emerson, also, that 'pocket edition' of his master, was well hit off, —brilliant, showy, but unreal and unsubstantial."

[2] This postscript seems to imply a letter or an enclosure, now missing, from Miss Aitken to Emerson.

Chelsea, 31 May 1870—

Dear Emerson,—In great haste, fruit of my miserable & scandalous indolence and dreamy waste of this fine last May morng, I do manage to announce, in one brief word to you, That the first copy of y^r *Solitude & Society* has never come to hand, but that a *second* duly has,[1]— three days ago, all safe & right; a much handsomer copy, and better for my old eyes: wh^h shall enjoy that in time coming, to exclusion of the other, perhaps to *benefiting* of some third party by the other. Thanks; double thanks for this double punctuality.

Some ten days ago, having fallen in with a brand new *Chapman's Homer* (2 voll. just out, *improved* or not), and finding a bit of reference to y^{r}self,[2] I betho^t me that there was an older copy here, suffic^t & more for all my wants with it, and that I c^d send *you* this new one. The *Piccadilly* Chapman people got it accordingly; it was to go (infallibly, *these* Chapm^{ns} said, but only the Pope is infallible!)[3] *along* with y^r *4th vol of Cromwell;* and I hope it will,—if only as a punish^t for y^r praise of that monstrous *Homeric* individ^l; whom, after repeated trials, I have found that I cannot stand at all. More like a *leprosy* of Homer than a new skin to him; the most intolerable of all the "translations" I have seen.

I hear of you lecturing at Harvard College,[4] with immense acceptance, *well*-merited, I do believe. Good speed, good speed!—My own days here are fallen weak and empty; seems as if the fewer days I had to live, the more inane they grew! Filled only with sombre solemn recollection, and d^o d^o dreamy contemplat^{ns}; nothing of worth in them except the sorrowing *Love* wh^h Time only strengthens, and (I think) only Death Eternal c^d kill.

Adieu, dear Friend   Yours ever as before   T. Carlyle

---

[1] Probably the first copy did come: the one now in Carlyle's library is inscribed in Emerson's hand, "To the General in Chief from his Lieutenant, March, 1870."

[2] Evidently a new and improved version of Richard Hooper's 1857 edition of Chapman's *Iliad*. Hooper had quoted (p. xxxii) a passage of praise for Chapman from the chapter "Race" of *English Traits* by "Mr Ralph Waldo Emerson, the well-known American writer."

[3] The Vatican Council was at this time discussing the doctrine, soon to become dogma, of Papal Infallibility.

[4] See below, E.6.17.70.

Concord
June 17, 1870

My dear Carlyle,

Two unanswered letters filled & fragrant & potent with goodness will not let me procrastinate another minute, or I shall sink & deserve to sink into my dormouse condition. You are of the Anakim, & know nothing of the debility & postponement of the blonde constitution. Well, if you shame us by your reservoir inexhaustible of force, you indemnify & cheer some of us or one of us by charges of electricity.

Your letter of April came, as ever—more than ever, if possible— full of kindness, & making much of our small doings & writings, & seemed to drive me to instant acknowledgment; but the oppressive engagement of writing & reading 18 lectures on Philosophy to a class of graduates in the College, & these in six successive weeks, was a task a little more formidable in prospect & in practice than any foregoing one. Of course, it made me a prisoner, took away all rights of friendship, honor, & justice, & held me to such frantic devotion to my work as must spoil *that* also.

Well, it is now ended, & has no shining side but this one, that materials are collected & a possibility shown me how a repetition of the course next year,—which is appointed,—will enable me partly out of these materials, & partly by large rejection of these, & by large addition to them, to construct a fair report of what I have read & thought on the Subject. I doubt the experts in Philosophy will not praise my discourses;—but the topics give me room for my guesses, criticism, admirations & experiences with the accepted masters, & also the lessons I have learned from the hidden great. I have the fancy that a realist is a good corrector of formalism, no matter how incapable of syllogism or continuous linked statement. To great results of thought & morals the steps are not many, & it is not the masters who spin the ostentatious continuity.

I am glad to hear that the last sent book from me arrived safely. You were too tender & generous in your first notice of it, I fear. But with whatever deductions for your partiality, I know well the unique value of Carlyle's praise.

Many things crowd to be said on this little paper. Though I could see no harm in the making known the bequest of books to Cambridge

—no harm, but sincere pleasure, & honor of the donor from all good men, yet on receipt of your letter touching that, I went back to President Eliot,—& told him your opinion on newspapers. He said it was necessarily communicated to the seven persons composing the Corporation, but otherwise, he had been very cautious, & it would not go into print.

You are sending me a book, & Chapman's Homer it is? Are you bound by your Arabian bounty to a largess whenever you think of your friend? And you decry the book too. Tis long since I read it, or in it, but the apotheosis of Homer in the dedication to Prince Henry, "thousands of years attending" &c is one of my lasting inspirations [1] The book has not arrived yet, as the letter always travels faster, but shall be watched & received & announced. But since you are all bounty & care for me, where are the new volumes of the Library Edition of Carlyle? I received duly, as I wrote you in a former letter 9 volumes,— Sartor; Life of Schiller; 5 vols. Miscellanies; French Revolution; these books oddly addressed to my name, but at CINCINNATI, Masstts. Whether they went to Ohio, & came back to Boston, I know not. Two vols came later, duplicates of two already received, & were returned at my request by Fields & Co. with an explanation. But no following volume has come. I write all this because you said in one letter that Mr Chapman assured you that every month a book was despatched to my address.

But what do I read in our Boston Newspapers twice in the last 3 days? that "Thomas Carlyle is coming to America,"—& the tidings cordially greeted by the Editors.[2] Though I had just received your letter silent to any such point. Make that story true, though it had never a verisimilitude since thirty odd years ago, & you shall make many souls happy & perhaps so many needs and opportunities for beneficent power that you cannot be allowed to grow old or withdraw. Was I not once promised a visit? This house entreats you ear-

[1] In "The Epistle Dedicatorie" Chapman writes, with reference to Homer's muse: ". . . see how like the Phoenix she renues/ Her age, and starrie feathers in your sunne;/ Thousands of years attending . . ." .

[2] On June 13 the Boston *Daily Evening Transcript* announced, on the authority of the "British Cable": "Thomas Carlyle will soon sail for the United States." Two days later it carried an announcement from a less authoritative source: "The New York Commercial says there is no truth in the story that Mr. Carlyle intends visiting this country for the purpose of 'shooting Niagara.'"

nestly & lovingly to come & dwell in it. My Wife & Ellen & Edward E. are thoroughly acquainted with your greatness & your loveliness. And it is but ten days of healthy sea to pass.

So wishes heartily & affectionately   R. W. Emerson
T. Carlyle, Esq.

5 Cheyne Row Chelsea [1]
28 September 1870.

Dear Emerson,

Your Letter, dated 15th June, never got to me till about ten days ago; when my little Neice and I returned out of Scotland, and a long, rather empty Visit there! It had missed me here only by two or three days; and my highly *in*felicitous Selectress of Letters to be forwarded had left *it* carefully aside as undeserving that honour,—good faithful old Woman, one hopes she is greatly stronger on some sides than in this literary-selective one. Certainly no Letter was forwarded that had the hundredth part of the right to be so; certainly, of all the Letters that came to me, or were left waiting here, this was, in comparison, the one which might *not* with propriety have been left to lie stranded forever or to wander on the winds forever!—

One of my first journeys was to Chapman, with vehement *rebuke* of this inconceivable "Cincinnati-Massachusetts" business—*Stupiditas stupiditatum;* I never in my life, not even in that unpunctual House, fell in with anything that equalled it. Instant amendment was at once undertaken for, nay it seems had been already in part performed: "Ten voll., following the nine you already had, were dispatched in Field & Co's box above two months ago," so Chapman solemnly said and asseverated to me; so that by this time you ought actually to have in hand 19 voll.; and the 20th (first of *Friedrich*), which came out ten days ago, is to go in Field & Co's Box this week, and ought, not many days after the arrival of this Letter, to be in Boston waiting for you there. The *Chapman's Homer* (2 volumes) had gone with that first Field Packet; and would be handed to you along with the ten voll., which were overdue. All this was solemnly declared to me as on Affidavit; Chapman also took extract of the Massachusetts passage in your Letter, in order to pour it like ice-cold water on the head of

[1] This letter was dictated.

his stupid old Chief-Clerk, the instant the poor creature got back from his rustication: alas, I am by no means certain that it will make a new man of him, nor, in fact, that the whole of this amendatory programme will get itself performed to equal satisfaction! But you must write to me at once if it is not so; & done it shall be in spite of human stupidity itself. Note, withal, these things: Chapman sends no Books to America *except* through Field & Co; he does not regularly send a Box at the middle of the month; but he does "almost monthly send one Box"; so that if your monthly Volume do not start from London about the 15th, it is due by the very *next* Chapman-Field do; and if it at any time don't come, I beg of you very much to make instant complaint through Field & Co, or what would be still more effectual, direct to myself. My malison on all Blockheadisms and torpid stupidities and infidelities; of which this world is full!—

Your Letter had been anxiously enough waited for, a month before my departure; but we will not mention the delay in presence of what you were engaged with then. *Faustum sit;* that truly was and will be a Work worth doing your best upon; and I, if alive, can promise you at least one reader that will do his best upon your Work. I myself often think of the Philosophies precisely in that manner. To say truth, they do not otherwise rise in esteem with me at all, but rather sink. The last thing I read of that kind was a piece by Hegel, in an excellent Translation by Stirling, right well translated, I could see, for every bit of it was intelligible to me; but my feeling at the end of it was:—"Good Heavens, I have walked this road before many a good time; but never with a Cannon-ball at each ankle before!" Science also, Science falsely so called, is—But I will not enter upon that with you just now.

The Visit to America, alas, alas, is pure Moonshine. Never had I, in late years, the least shadow of intention to undertake that adventure; and I am quite at a loss to understand how the rumor originated. One Boston Gentleman (a kind of universal Undertaker, or Lion's Provider [2] of Lecturers, I think) informed me that *"the Cable"* had told him; and I had to remark "And who the devil told the Cable?" Alas, no, I fear I shall never dare to undertake that big Voyage; which has so much of romance and of reality behind it to me; *zu spät, zu spät.* I do sometimes talk dreamily of a long Sea-Voyage, and the good

[2] See above, C.4.1.40, n. 5.

the Sea has often done me,—in times when good was still possible. It may have been some vague folly of that kind that originated this rumour; for rumours are like dandelion-seeds; and *the Cable*, I daresay, welcomes them all that have a guinea in their pocket.

Thank you for blocking up that Harvard matter, provided it *don't* go into the Newspapers, all is right. Thank you a thousand times for that thrice-kind potential welcome, and flinging wide open of your doors and your hearts to me at Concord. The gleam of it is like sunshine in a subterranean place. Ah me, ah me! May God be with you all, dear Emerson.   Yours ever   T. Carlyle

R. Waldo Emerson Esq.
    &c &c

Concord, 15 October, '70

My dear Carlyle,

I am the ignoblest of all men in my perpetual shortcomings to you. There is no example of constancy like yours, & it always stings my stupor into temporary recovery & wonderful resolution to accept the noble challenge. But "the strong hours conquer us," [1] & I am the victim of miscellany,—miscellany of designs, vast debility & procrastination. Already many days before your letter came, Fields sent me a package from you, which he said he had found a little late, because they were covered up in a box of printed sheets of other character, & this treasure was not at first discovered. They are,

    1. Life of Sterling
    1 Latter Day Pamphlets
    1 Past & Present
    1 Heroes
    5 Vols. Cromwell's Letters & Speeches

Unhappily, Vol. 2d of Cromwell is wanting, and there is a duplicate of Vol. 5th instead of it. Now, two days ago came your letter, & tells me that the good old gods have also inspired you to send me Chapman's Homer! & that it came—heroes with heroes—in the same enchanted box.

I went to Fields yesterday & demanded the book. He ignored all—

---

[1] I have been unable to find the source of this quotation.

even to the books he had already sent me; called Osgood to council, & they agreed that it must be that all these came in a box of sheets of Dickens from Chapman, which was sent to the Stereotypers at Cambridge; and the box shall be instantly explored. We will see what tomorrow shall find. As to the duplicate, I will say here, that I have received two; 1. the above mentioned Vol. II. of Cromwell; and, 2ᵈ.ly, long before, a second copy of *Sartor Resartus,* apparently instead of the Vol. I of the *French Revolution,* which did not come. I proposed to Fields to send back to Chapman these two duplicates. But he said, "No, it will cost as much as the price of the books" I shall try to find in New York *who* represents Chapman & sells these books, & put them to his credit there, in exchange for the volumes I lack. Meantime, my serious thanks for all these treasures go to you,—steadily good to my youth & my age.

Your letter was most welcome, & most in that I thought I read in what you say of not making the long promised visit hither, a little willingness to come. Think again, I pray you, of that Ocean Voyage, which is probably the best medicine & restorative which remains to us at your age & mine. Nine or ten days will bring you (& commonly with unexpected comfort & easements on the way,) to Boston. Every reading person in America holds you in exceptional regard, & will rejoice in your arrival. They have forgotten your scarlet sins before or during the war. I have long ceased to apologise for or explain your savage sayings about American or other republics or publics, and am willing that anointed men bearing with them authentic charters shall be laws to themselves, as Plato willed. Genius is but a large infusion of Deity, & so brings a prerogative all its own. It has a right & duty to affront & amaze men by carrying out its perceptions defiantly, knowing well that time & fate will verify & explain what time & fate have through them said. We must not suggest to Michel Angelo, or Machiavel, or Rabelais, or Voltaire, or John Brown of Ossawottomie, (a great man,) or Carlyle, how they shall suppress their paradoxes & check their huge gait to keep accurate step with the procession on the street sidewalk. They are privileged persons, & may have their own swing for me.

I did not mean to chatter so much, but I wish you would come out hither & read our possibilities now being daily disclosed, & our actualities which are not nothing. I shall like to show you my near neighbors, topographically or practically, a near neighbor & friend E. Rockwood

Hoar whom you saw in his youth is now an inestimable citizen in this State & lately, in President Grant's Cabinet, Attorney-General of the U. S. He lives in this town & carries it in his hand. Another is John M. Forbes, a strictly private citizen, of great executive ability, & noblest affections, a motive power & regulator essential to our City,—refusing all office, but impossible to spare; [2] & these are men whom to name the voice breaks, & the eye is wet. A multitude of young men are growing up here of high promise, & I compare gladly the social poverty of my youth with the power on which these draw. The Lowell race, again, in our war yielded three or four martyrs so able & tender & true, that James Russell L. cannot allude to them in verse or prose but the public is melted anew.[3] Well, all these know you well, have read & will read you, yes, & will prize & use your benefaction to the College; and I believe it would add hope health & strength to you to come & see them. In my much writing I believe I have left the chief things unsaid. But come! I & my house wait for you.

Affectionately,   R. W. Emerson

Thomas Carlyle, Esq.[4]

[2] John Murray Forbes, the father-in-law of Emerson's daughter Edith, was an important railroad capitalist. During the war he had been quietly active in public affairs, especially in the organization of Negro regiments for the state of Massachusetts.

[3] Five young relatives of James Russell Lowell, among them three nephews, were killed in the war (Edward Everett Hale, *James Russell Lowell and His Friends*, pp. 180–81); for one of them, see below, E.4.10.71. Emerson was probably thinking of "Mr. Hosea Biglow to the Editor of the Atlantic Monthly," No. X of the second series of *Biglow Papers*, which alludes thus to the nephews: "why, hain't I held 'em on my knee?/ Didn't I love to see 'em growin',/ Three likely lads ez wal could be,/ Hahnsome an' brave an' not tu knowin'?" He may also have had in mind the stanza of "Memoriae Positum: R. G. Shaw" which begins "I write of one,/ While with dim eyes I think of three."

[4] On November 12, 1870, Carlyle wrote to his brother John: "I also enclose a letter from Emerson; which you will return" (NLS, MS 527).

1871

Concord, 10 April, 1871.

My dear friend,

I fear there is no pardon from you, none from myself, for this immense new gap in our correspondence. Yet no hour came from month to month to write a letter, since whatever deliverance I got from one web in the last year, served only to throw me into another web as pitiless. Yet what gossamer these tasks of mine must appear to your might! Believe that the American climate is unmanning, or that one American whom you know is severely taxed by Lilliput labors. The last hot summer enfeebled me till my young people coaxed me to go with Edward to the White Hills, & we climbed or were dragged up Agiochook, in August, & its sleet & snowy air nerved me again for the time But the booksellers whom I had long ago urged to reprint "Plutarch's Morals," claimed some forgotten promise, & set me on reading the old patriarch again, & writing a few pages about him, which no doubt cost me as much time & *pottering* as it would cost you to write a History.[1] Then an "Oration" was due to the New England Society in New York, on the 250th Anniversary of the Plymouth Landing,—as I thought myself familiar with the story, & holding also some opinions thereupon. But in the Libraries I found alcoves full of books & documents reckoned essential; and, at New York, after reading for an hour to the great assembly out of my massy manuscript, I refused to print a line until I could revise & complete my papers;—risking, of course, the nonsense of their newspaper reporters.[2] This pill swallowed & forgotten, it was already time for my Second "Course on Philosophy" at Cambridge,—which I had accepted again that I might repair the faults of the last year. But here were Eighteen lectures, each to be read

---

[1] Emerson's introduction to W. W. Goodwin's edition of the *Morals* is reprinted in *Works,* X, 293–322.

[2] The address was finally published in 1901 in *The New England Society Orations,* ed. Cephas and Eveline Brainerd, II, 373–93, but Emerson never succeeded in completing or revising it (*Let RWE,* VI, 138n).

sixteen miles away from my house, to go & come,—& the same work & journey twice in each week, & I have just got through the doleful ordeal. I have abundance of good readings & some honest writing on the leading topics,—but in haste & confusion they are misplaced & spoiled—I hope the ruin of no young man's soul will here or hereafter be charged to me as having wasted his time or confounded his reason.

Now I come to the raid of a London bookseller, Hotten, (of whom I believe I never told you) on my forgotten papers in the old "Dials," & other pamphlets here. Conway wrote me that he could not be resisted,—would certainly steal good & bad,—but might be guided in the selection. I replied, that the act was odious to me, & I promised to denounce the man & his theft to any friends I might have in England: but if, instead of printing then, he would wait a year, I would make my own selection, with the addition of some later critical papers, & permit the book. Mr Ireland in Manchester, & Conway in London, took the affair kindly in hand, & Hotten acceded to my change. And that is the next task that threatens my imbecility.[3] But now ten days ago, or less, my friend, John M. Forbes, has come to me with a proposition to carry me off to California, the Yosemite, the Mammoth trees, & the Pacific, &, after much resistance, I have surrendered for six weeks, & we set out tomorrow and hence this sheet of confession,—that I may not drag a lengthening chain.[4] Meantime, you have been monthly loading me with good for evil. I have just counted 23 vols. of Carlyle's Library Edition, in order on my shelves, besides 2, or perhaps 3, which Ellery Channing has borrowed. Add, that the precious Chapman's Homer came safely, though not till months after you had told me of its departure, & shall be guarded henceforward with joy.

—Wednesday [5] 13. Chicago. Arrived here & can bring this little sheet to the Post Office here. My daughter Edith Forbes, & her husband William H. Forbes, & three other friends accompany me & we shall overtake Mr Forbes Senior tomorrow at Burlington, Iowa. Effie Lowell, widow of one of the noblest of our young martyrs in the War, Col. Lowell, cousin of James Russell Lowell sends me word that she wishes

---

[3] John Camden Hotten had already published Lowell, Holmes, Harte, and other Americans. The book appeared in 1875, after Hotten's death, as *Letters and Social Aims* (*Works*, VIII, ix).

[4] Cf. Goldsmith, *The Traveller*, line 9.

[5] "The '*Wednesday*' of second date line is clearly an error" (Rusk's note).

me to give her a note of introduction to you, confiding to me that she has once written a letter to you which procured her the happiest reply from you,[6] and I shall obey her, & you will see her & own her rights. Still continue to be magnanimous to your friend   R. W. Emerson

Thomas Carlyle, Esq.

5 Cheyne Row, Chelsea,[1]
4 June 1871

Dear Emerson,

Your Letter gave me great pleasure. A gleam of sunshine after a long tract of of lowering weather. It is not you that are to blame for this sad gap in our correspondence; it is I, or rather it is my misfortunes, and miserable inabilities, broken resolutions &c &c. The truth is the winter here was very unfriendly to me; broke ruinously into my sleep; and through that into every other department of my businesses, spiritual and temporal; so that from about New-Year's Day last I have been, in a manner, good for nothing,—nor am yet, though I do again feel as if the beautiful Summer weather might perhaps do something for me. This it was that choked every enterprize; and postponed your Letter, week after week, through so many months. Let us not speak of it farther!

Note, meanwhile, I have no disease about me; nothing but the gradual decay of any poor digestive faculty I latterly had,—or indeed ever had since I was three and twenty years of age. Let us be quiet with it; accept it as a mode of exit, of which always there must be *some* mode.

---

[6] Charles Russell Lowell, a brigadier-general of cavalry under Sheridan, was killed in the Shenandoah Valley campaign of 1864 (E. W. Emerson, *Life and Letters of Charles Russell Lowell*, p. 482). His widow, Josephine, the sister of Robert Gould Shaw, sent Carlyle the *Harvard Memorial Biographies, of Men Who Died in the Civil War*, which included lives of her husband and brother, in an effort to change his opinion of the Civil War. Carlyle wrote to Norton, March 2, 1870: "A Lady in New York has sent me the other day a couple of big handsome voll. . . . with a few pretty and affectte words,—to whh I am giving due compliance, namely reading at least the Biographies she has put a *mark* to." The books filled him, he said, "with reflexns manifold, and emotions manifold" (MS owned by the Houghton Library). He replied, graciously, on March 10 (W. R. Stewart, *The Philanthropic Work of Josephine Shaw Lowell*, p. 50).

[1] This letter, except for the postscript, was dictated.

I have got done with all my press-correctings, editionings and paltry bother of that kind: vol 30 will embark for you about the middle of this month; there are then to follow ("uniform," as the printers call it, though in smaller type) a little vol. called *General Index* and 3 more voll. of *Translations from the German;*—after which we two will reckon and count; and if there is any *lacuna* on the Concord shelf, at once make it good. Enough, enough on that score.

The Hotten who has got hold of you here is a dirty little pirate who snatches at everybody grown fat enough to yield him a bite (paltry unhanged creature); so that in fact he is a symbol to you of your visible rise in the world here; and, with Conway's vigilance to help, will do you good and not evil. Glad am I, in any case, to see so much new spiritual produce still ripening around you; and you ought to be glad too. Pray Heaven you may long *keep your right hand* steady: you, too, I can perceive, will never any more than myself, learn to "write by dictation" in a manner that will be supportable to you. I rejoice also to hear of such a magnificent adventure as that you are now upon. Climbing the backbone of America; looking into the Pacific Ocean too, and the gigantic wonders going on there. I fear you wont see see Brigham Young, however? He also to me is one of the products out there; and indeed I may confess to you that the doings in that region are not only of a big character, but of a great;—and that in my occasional explosions against "Anarchy," and my inextinguishable hatred of *it,* I privately whisper to myself, "Could any Friedrich Wilhelm, now, or Friedrich, or most perfect Governor you could hope to realise, guide forward what is America's essential task at present faster or more completely than 'anarchic America' herself is now doing?" *Such* "Anarchy" has a great deal to say for itself,—(wd to Heaven ours of England had as had as much!—) and points towards grand ANTI-Anarchies in the future; in fact, I can already discern in it huge quantities of Anti-Anarchy in the "impalpable-powder" condition; and hope, with the aid of centuries, immense things from it, in my private mind!

Good Mrs. Lowell has never yet made her appearance; but shall be welcome whenever she does.—Did you ever hear the name of an aged, or elderly, fantastic fellow-citizen of yours, called J. Lee Bliss, who designates himself O. F. and A. K., *i.e.* "Old Fogey" and "Amiable Kuss?" He sent me the other night, a wonderful miscellany of symbolical shreds and patches;[2] which considerably amused me; and

[2] *Hamlet,* act III, scene iv, line 102.

withal indicated good-will on the man's part; who is not without humour, insight and serious intention or disposition. If you ever did hear of him, say a word on the subject next time you write.

And above all things write. The instant you get home from California, or see this, let me hear from you what your adventures have been and what the next are to be. Adieu, dear Emerson.

Yours ever affectionately,   T. Carlyle

Mrs Lowell sends a Note from Picadilly *this* new morning (June 5th); *call* to be made there today by Niece Mary, card left, &c &c. Promises to be an agreeable Lady.

Did you ever hear of such a thing as this suicidal Finis of the French "Copper Captaincy"; [3] gratuitous attack on Germany, and dᵒ Blowing-up of Paris by its own hand! An event with meanings unspeakable,— deep as the *Abyss.*— —

If you ever write to C. Norton in Italy, send him my kind remembrances.

T. C. (with abt the velocity of Engraving—on lead!)

Concord, 30 June, 1871

My dear Carlyle,

Tis more than time that you should hear from me whose debts to you always accumulate. But my long journey to California ended in many distractions on my return home. I found Varioloid in my house, (which my son had ignorantly brought home from his Medical Hospital,) & I was not permitted to enter it for many days, & could only talk with wife, son, & daughter, from the yard. Even now Edward is not quite healed of the *Sequelae.* I had crowded & closed my Cambridge lectures in haste, & went to the land of Flowers invited by John M. Forbes one of my most valued friends, father of my daughter Edith's husband. With him & his family & one or two chosen guests, the trip was made under the best conditions of safety, comfort & company,[1] I measuring for the first time one entire line of the Country. California surprises with a geography, climate, vegetation, beasts, birds, fishes even, unlike ours; the land immense; the Pacific Sea; Steam

---

[3] A copper captain, says the *NED*, is "a sham captain who assumes the title without any right": this was Carlyle's usual epithet for Louis Bonaparte.

[1] Between Chicago and San Francisco the company traveled in a private Pullman car (J. B. Thayer, *A Western Journey with Mr. Emerson*, p. 9).

brings the near neighborhood of Asia; and South America at your feet; the mountains reaching the altitude of Mont Blanc; the State in its 600 miles of latitude producing all our Northern fruits, & also the fig, orange, & banana. But the climate chiefly surprised me. The Almanac said April; but the day said June;—& day after day for six weeks uninterrupted sunshine. November & December are the rainy months The whole Country was colored with flowers, and all of them unknown to us except in greenhouses. Every bird that I know at home is represented here, but in gayer plumes. On the plains we saw multitudes of antelopes, hares, gophers—even elks, & one pair of wolves on the plains; the grizzly bear only in a cage. We crossed one region of the Buffalo, but only saw one captive. We found Indians at every railroad station,—the squaws & papooses begging, and the "bucks" as they wickedly call them, lounging. On our way out, we left the Pacific RR. for 24 hours to visit Salt Lake: called on Brigham Young—just 70 years old—who received us with quiet uncommitting courtesy, at first, —a strong-built, self-possessed, sufficient man with plain manners. He took early occasion to remark that "the one-man-power really meant all-mens-power." Our our interview was peaceable enough, & rather mended my impression of the man; &, after our visit, I read in the Deseret newspaper his Speech to his people on the previous Sunday. It avoided religion, but was full of Franklinian good sense. In one point, he says—"Your fear of the Indians is nonsense. The Indians like the white men's food; feed them well, & they will surely die." He is clearly a sufficient ruler, & perhaps civilizer of his kingdom of blockheads *ad interim;* but I found that the San Franciscans believe that this exceptional power cannot survive Brigham.

I am glad that Mrs Lowell has outrun me by months, that she has seen you & I hope that you have seen her as I do; for the Shaws, of which she is one, are a remarkable family for their character & grace. One of them, her father's sister, Mrs Russell, was one of our California Party. Your odd man, Lee Bliss, is wholly unknown to me even by name.

I have been surprised—but it is months ago,—by a letter from Lacy Garbett, the Architect, whom I do not know, but one of whose books about "Design in Architecture" [2] I have always valued. This letter,

[2] Edward Lacy Garbett, *Rudimentary Treatise on the Principles of Design in Architecture as Deducible from Nature and Exemplified in the Works of the Greek and Gothic Architects* (London, 1850).

asking of me that Americans shall join Englishmen in a Petition to Parliament against pulling down ancient Saxon buildings, is written in a way so wild as to suggest insanity, & I have not known how to answer it. At my "Saturday Club" in Boston I sat at dinner by an English lord— —, whose name I have forgotten,—from whom I tried to learn what laws Parliament had passed for the repairs of old religious Foundations, that could make them the victims of covetous Architects. But he assured me there were none such, & that he himself was President of a Society in his own County for the protection of such buildings.[3] So that I am left entirely in the dark in regard to the fact of Garbett's letter. He claims to speak both for Ruskin & himself.

I grieve to hear no better account of your health than your last letter gives. The only contradiction of it, namely, the power of your pen in this reproduction of thirty books, & *such* books, is very important & very consoling to me. A great work to be done is the best insurance, & I sleep quietly,—notwithstanding these sad bulletins,—believing that you cannot be spared.

George Bradford, an early & late friend of mine, who once stopped at your door, & values himself on having seen you, will bring this letter. He is a teacher or tutor of private pupils, for many many years, goes now & then to Europe, to Athens, to Constantinople, &c. & this time only to Switzerland He is a good scholar, and a most worthy man, but sadly a victim of *the blues*. With him is his niece & my cousin, Miss Ripley, of this town, an excellent woman, and, (if you have ever seen Hawthorne's books,) is the owner & occupant of "The Manse" in Concord.[4] Let your face shine on her for a moment.

Fare well dear friend,   R. W. Emerson.

Thomas Carlyle, Esq.

---

[3] Ruskin had called for the establishment of such a society in his pamphlet "The Opening of the Crystal Palace" (1854); but it was not until 1877 that Morris's Society for the Protection of Ancient Buildings came into existence (*The Athenaeum,* April 28, 1877). Probably Emerson's aristocrat was a member of the Society of Antiquaries.

[4] Emerson had been a guest of Elizabeth Ripley at the Manse while his own house was under quarantine (*Let RWE,* VI, 163). George Bradford had lived there as a boy, under the care of his sister, Elizabeth's mother, who was the daughter-in-law of Emerson's step-grandfather, Ezra Ripley (Rusk, *Life,* p. 557).

                                                    Concord
                                                3 July, 1871.
Dear Carlyle,

   Mr George P. Bradford, an old friend of mine, & whom I had the
pleasure of introducing to you many years ago,[1] is now on his way
to Switzerland, & neither his will nor mine will permit him to pass
through London without paying his respects to you.
                        Always yours,   R. W. Emerson
Thomas Carlyle, Esq.

                                                    Concord
                                                September 4 1871
My dear Carlyle,

   I hope you will have returned safely from the Orkneys[1] in time to
let my son Edward W. E. see your face on his way through London
to Germany, whither he goes to finish his medical studies—no, not
finish but prosecute.[2] Give him your blessing & tell him what he should
look for in his few days in London, & what in your Prussia. He is a
good youth, & we can spare him only for this necessity. I should like
well to accompany him as far as to your hearthstone, if only so I could
persuade you that it is but a ten-days ride for you thence to mine,—
a little farther than the Orkneys, & the outskirts of land as good, &
bigger. I read gladly in your letters some relentings toward America,
—deeper ones in your dealing with Harvard College, & I know you
could not see without interest the immense & varied blossoming of our
possibilities here,—of all nationalities, too, besides our own.

   I have heard from Mrs Lowell twice lately, who exults in your kindness to her.   Always affectionately, Yours,   R. W. Emerson

Thomas Carlyle, Esq.

   [1] In 1854, probably (*Let RWE*, IV, 435, 459); but no letter of introduction sur-
vives, so far as I am aware.
   [1] Emerson had heard from Moncure Conway that Carlyle was on his way back
from the Orkneys (*Let RWE*, VI, 179n).
   [2] Edward Waldo Emerson finished his medical studies at Harvard in 1874.

1872

Baltimore, Md.
5 January, 1872.

My dear Carlyle,

I received from you through Mr Chapman, just before Christmas, the last rich instalment of your Library Edition; viz.

Vols. 4, 5, 6, 7, 8, 9, 10	Life of Friedrich.
" 1, 2, 3,	Translations from German
" 1 volume	General Index,

eleven volumes in all,—& now my stately collection is perfect. Perfect too is your Victory. But I clatter my chains with joy, as I did forty years ago, at your earliest gifts. Happy man you should be, to whom the Heaven has allowed such masterly completion. You shall wear your crown at the Pan Saxon Games [1] with no equal or approaching competitor in sight,—well earned by genius & exhaustive labor, & with nations for your pupils & praisers. I count it my eminent happiness to have been so nearly your contemporary, and your friend—permitted to detect by its rare light the new star almost before the easterners had seen it, & to have found no disappointment, but joyful confirmation rather, in coming close to its orb. Rest, rest, now for a time, I pray you, & be thankful Meantime, I know well all your perversities, & give them a wide berth. They seriously annoy a great many worthy readers, nations of readers sometimes—but I heap them all as style, & read them as I read Rabelais's gigantic humors which astonish in order to force attention, & by & by are seen to be the rhetoric of a highly virtuous gentleman who *swears*. I have been quite too busy with fast succeeding *jobs* (I may well call them,) in the last year, to have read much in these proud books; but I begin to see daylight coming through my fogs, & I have not lost in the least my appetite for reading,

[1] See above, C.8.18.41.

—resolve, with my old Harvard professor, "to retire & read the Authors." [2]

I am impatient to deserve your grand volumes by reading in them with all the haughty airs that belong to seventy years which I shall count if I live till May 1873. Meantime I see well that you have lost none of your power & I wish that you would let in some good Eckermann to dine with you day by day, & competent to report your opinions,—for you can speak as well as you can write, & what the world to come should know;—& let it not be Conway, who (this in your private ear,) cannot, in my experience, report a fact or speech as it fell. It suffers a strange distortion in his mind.[3] But he is a good fellow, & bright, & I owe him only good will. So pray burn this note or blot it.

Affectionately,   R. W. Emerson

Concord

19 January '72

My dear Carlyle,

I send my son-in-law, Col. William H. Forbes, & my daughter Edith, his wife, to see your face, & crave your blessing. Colonel Forbes was an officer in the Mass^tts Cavalry, & did good service in Virginia, in the War of the Rebellion. His father is one of the best men in Massachusetts, with whom your friends the Amberleys [1] were well acquainted, & the son is very dear to us. Edith has known you all her life as one of our Penates, & I trust she will find you in London, & that you will go & bless her babes. They are on their way to France & Germany, & Italy, & I have charged them to see you, and if not now, then on their return to London. They will appreciate any counsel you shall give them as to places & things in London, or out of it, which they ought

[2] A marginal note in James Russell Lowell's copy of the 1883 edition of the *Correspondence*, the property of the Houghton Library, identifies this professor as "Popkin." John Snelling Popkin (1771–1852) was a teacher of Greek at Harvard College until his retirement in 1833.

[3] Conway's public reputation for inaccuracy and rashness was the result of his inexpert amateur diplomacy during the Civil War, but Emerson was perhaps also thinking of his more recent political and literary journalism (Burtis, *Moncure Conway*, pp. 93–107, 147–48).

[1] In 1867 the Amberleys had been guests of John Murray Forbes in Milton (*Let RWE*, V, 535). Viscountess Amberley was the daughter of Carlyle's friend Baron Stanley of Alderley.

to see: and I believe I shall give Edith a secret counsel, which, if she obeys, I hope you will be good, & permit her to carry out.[2]

I wrote you a note, the other day, from Baltimore, to assure you of my reception of the entirety of the "Library Edition," which now greets my eyes proudly yet kindly at home again. I have just now counted them over again, and find 31 vols. and the Index; 32 in all. I am not sure that this agrees with my former count. As I approach my freedom, I shall count them more inwardly.

After reading some lectures to the George "Peabody Institute" in Baltimore, I spent a few days in Washington, with Sumner, & saw many men & some good ones, but am gladly home again.

Always affectionately yours, R. W. Emerson
Thomas Carlyle, Esq.

5 Cheyne Row, Chelsea, 2 April 1872.
Dear Emerson,—I am covered with confusion, astonishment and shame to think of my long silence. You wrote me two beautiful letters; none friendlier, brighter, wiser could come to me from any quarter of the world; and I have not answered even by a sigh. Promptly and punctually my poor heart *did* answer; but to do it outwardly,—as if there had lain some enchantment on me,—was beyond my power. The one thing I can say in excuse or explanation is, that ever since Summer last, I have been in an unusually dispeptic, peeking, pining and dispirited condition; and have no right hand of my own for writing, nor for several months, had any other that was altogether agreeable to me.[1] But in fine I don't believe you lay any blame or anger on me at all; and I will say no more about it, but only try to repent and do better next time.

Your letter from the far West was charmingly vivid and free; one seemed to attend you personally and see with one's own eyes the *notabilia,* human and other, of those huge regions, in your swift flight

---

[2] Perhaps a request that she persuade Carlyle to be photographed with her son: this photograph is reproduced in Plate VII. On August 2, 1872, she wrote Carlyle an affectionate letter of goodbye from the steamer. She had asked her father, she said, whether she might give extra copies of the photograph to some gentlemen who had asked for them, but she had learned that he "preferred that his treasure should be his alone" (NLS, MS 1770).

[1] This letter is in the hand of Carlyle's niece.

through them to and from. I retain your little etching of Brigham
Young as a bit of real likeness; I have often thought of your transit
through Chicago since poor Chicago itself vanished out of the world
on wings of fire. There is something huge, painful and almost appall-
ing to me in that wild Western world of yours; and especially I wonder
at the gold-nuggeting there while plainly every gold-nuggeter is no
other than a criminal to Human Society, and has to *steal* the exact
value of his gold nugget from the pockets of all the posterity of Adam,
now and for sometime to come, in this world. I conclude it is a bait
used by All-wise Providence to attract your people out thither, there
to build towns, make roads, fell forests (or plant forests), and make
ready a Dwelling-place for New Nations, who will find themselves
called to quite other than nugget-hunting. In the hideous stew of
Anarchy in which all English Populations present themselves to my
dismal contemplation at this day, it is a solid consolation that there
will verily, in another fifty years, be above a hundred million men and
women on this Planet who can all read Shakespeare and the English
Bible and the (also for a long time biblical and noble) history of their
Mother Country,—and proceed again to do, unless the Devil *be* in
them, as their forebears did, or better, if they have the heart!—

Except that you are a thousand times too kind to *me,* your second
Letter also was altogether charming. You may depend on it, I will not
employ Conway, should I need a Boswell (which I never shall): my
opinion of him is completely your own, and indeed I see less and less
of him, though never absolutely nothing, as the years roll on. He has
one merit, that of a great deep and as if almost exclusive admiration
for you; I think there is nothing so fixed in his mind as that. For the
rest a windy, easy-going *fluff* of a creature; content with crudities
everywhere, as if they were purities; and talking a great deal of stuff
that has only half meaning in it: but he is very sociable, good-natured,
guileless, and is a general favourite I think among the people he fre-
quents. Peace be with him, poor soul; only not too much of him; and
—let his visits be more and more like those of angels, short and far
between!—

Do you know Ruskin's *Fors Clavigera,* which he cheerily tells me
gets itself reprinted in America? If you don't, *do,* I advise you. Also
his *Munera Pulveris,* Oxford-*Lectures* on Art, and whatever else he
is now writing,—if you can manage to get them (which is difficult here,

owing to the ways he has towards the bibliopolic world!). There is nothing going on among us as notable to me as those fierce lightning-bolts Ruskin is copiously and desperately pouring into the black world of Anarchy all round him. No other man in England that I meet has in him the divine rage against iniquity, falsity and baseness that Ruskin has and that every man ought to have. Unhappily he is not a strong man; one might say a weak man rather; and has not the least prudence of management; though, if he can hold out for another 15 years or so, he may produce, even in this way, a great effect. God grant it, say I. Froude is coming to you in October. You will find him a most clear, friendly ingenious solid and excellent man; and I am very glad to find you among those who are to take care of him when he comes to your New Country.[2] Do your best and wisest towards him, for my sake, withal. He is the valuablest Friend I now have in England, nearly tho' not quite altogther the one man in talking with whom I can get any real profit or comfort. Alas, alas here is the end of the paper, dear Emerson; and I had still a whole wilderness of things to say. Write to me, or even do not write, *and* I will surely write again.

I remain as ever Your Affectionate Friend,   T. Carlyle.

[2] For about a year, Emerson had been, through Conway, advising Froude about a proposed American lecture tour (*Let RWE*, VI, 150, 222).

1873

My dear Carlyle,

An old friend of mine from childhood up to this day,—Mr George P. Bradford,—leaves this town tomorrow on his way to England, and as he knows your mind better than most Americans, though he has never seen your face,[1] I trust he will find you at home & at liberty. Mr Bradford is the lineal descendant of William Bradford, first Governor of Plymouth Colony, & has inherited I believe all the virtues of his ancestor, & more. As he is a far better scholar than I, & is one of the three companions I find in Concord, I trust you will treat him kindly, & send him home soon.   Affectionately,   R. W. Emerson

Thomas Carlyle, Esq.

[1] See above, E.6.30.71 and E.7.3.71.

BIBLIOGRAPHY

PRINTED WORKS

Adams, Raymond. "Emerson's House at Walden," *The Thoreau Society Bulletin,* July, 1948 (Bulletin 24), pp. 3–8.

Agassiz, Elizabeth Cary. *Louis Agassiz.* Boston, 1886.

Alcott, Bronson. *The Journals of Bronson Alcott,* ed. Odell Shepard. Boston, 1938.

Allingham, William. *A Diary.* London, 1908.

Arnold, Matthew. *Discourses in America.* London, 1912.

—— *Letters,* ed. G. W. E. Russell. London, 1904.

—— *On Translating Homer.* London, 1861.

—— *On Translating Homer: Last Words.* London, 1862.

Austin, Sarah. *Characteristics of Goethe.* London, 1833.

Bacon, Theodore. *Delia Bacon.* Boston, 1888.

Baedeker's London and Its Environs. Leipzig, 1898.

Barnard, H. C. *A Short History of English Education.* London, 1947.

Barrus, Clara. *The Life and Letters of John Burroughs.* 2 vols. Boston, 1925.

Bates, William. *The Maclise Portrait Gallery.* New York, 1883.

Blair, Hugh. *Lectures on Rhetoric and Belles Lettres.* 3 vols. Dublin, 1783.

Browning, Robert. *The Letters of Robert Browning,* ed. T. L. Hood. New Haven, 1933.

—— *Robert Browning and Alfred Domett,* ed. Frederick G. Kenyon. New York, 1906.

Burroughs, John. "Carlyle and Emerson," *The Critic,* II (1882), 140.

Burtis, Mary Elizabeth. *Moncure Conway.* New Brunswick, N. J., 1952.

Cabot, James Elliot. *A Memoir of Ralph Waldo Emerson.* 2 vols. Boston, 1887.

Cameron, Kenneth E. *Emerson the Essayist.* Raleigh, N. C., 1945.

Carlyle, Jane Welsh. *Letters and Memorials of Jane Welsh Carlyle,* ed. J. A. Froude. London, 1883.

—— *New Letters and Memorials of Jane Welsh Carlyle,* ed. Alexander Carlyle. 2 vols. London, 1903.

Carlyle, Thomas. *The Correspondence of Thomas Carlyle and Ralph Waldo Emerson,* ed. Charles Eliot Norton. 2 vols. Boston, 1883.

—— "The Diamond Necklace," *Fraser's Magazine,* XV (January–February, 1837), 1–19 (January); 172–89 (February).

Carlyle, Thomas. "Dr. Francia," *The Foreign Quarterly Review*, XXXIII (July, 1843), 544–56.

—— *Early Letters*, ed. Charles Eliot Norton. London, 1886.

—— Essay on German literature (review of "Reinecke der Fuchs"), *The Foreign Quarterly Review*, XIII (October, 1831), 347–91.

—— *Letters to His Wife*, ed. Trudy Bliss. Cambridge, Mass., 1953.

—— *Letters . . . to John Stuart Mill, John Sterling, and Robert Browning*, ed. Alexander Carlyle. London, 1923.

—— "Mirabeau," *The London and Westminster Review*, XXVI (January, 1837), 382–439.

—— *New Letters*, ed. Alexander Carlyle. 2 vols. London, 1904.

—— "Parliamentary History of the French Revolution," *London and Westminster Review*, XXVII (April, 1837), 233–47.

—— *Reminiscenses of My Irish Journey in 1849*. London, 1882.

—— "The Sinking of the Vengeur," *Fraser's Magazine*, XX (July, 1839), 76–84.

—— *Works*, Centenary Edition, ed. H. D. Traill. 30 vols. London, 1896–1901.

——, tr. *Wilhelm Meister's Apprenticeship*. London, 1824.

—— *See also* Goethe.

Catalogue of the Harvard Chapter of Phi Beta Kappa. Cambridge, Mass., 1912.

Channing, William Ellery (the younger). *Poems*. Boston, 1843.

—— "Carlyle's French Revolution," *Boston Quarterly Review*, I (October, 1838), 407–17.

Channing, William Henry. *Memoir of William Ellery Channing*. 3 vols. Boston, 1860.

Chapman, John. *Human Nature*. London, 1844.

Clarke, James Freeman. *Autobiography, Diary, and Correspondence*, ed. E. E. Hale. Boston, 1891.

Clough, Arthur Hugh. *The Correspondence of Arthur Hugh Clough*, ed. Frederick L. Mulhauser. 2 vols. London, 1957.

Conway, Moncure. *Autobiography*. 2 vols. London, 1904.

—— *Emerson at Home and Abroad*. Boston, 1882; London, 1883.

—— *Thomas Carlyle*. New York, 1881.

Cooke, George Willis. *An Historical and Biographical Introduction to Accompany "The Dial."* 2 vols. Cleveland, 1902.

—— *A Bibliography of Ralph Waldo Emerson*. Boston, 1908.

—— *John Sullivan Dwight*. Boston, 1898.

"Correspondence of Carlyle and Emerson, The," *The Nation*, XXXVI (April 12, 1883), 324.

"Correspondence of Carlyle and Emerson, The," *The Saturday Review*, LV (March 24, 1883), 367–68.

"Correspondence of Carlyle and Emerson, The," *The Spectator*, LVI (March 24, 1883), 386–87.

Cromwell, Oliver. *Oliver Cromwell's Letters and Speeches: With Elucidations by Thomas Carlyle.* 2 vols. New York, 1845.

Dall, Caroline H. *Transcendentalism in New England: A Lecture Delivered before the Society of Philosophical Enquiry, Washington, D. C., May 7, 1895. . . .* Boston, 1897.

Donaldson, J. W. *The New Cratylus.* Cambridge, 1839.

Duffy, Charles Gavan. *Conversations with Carlyle.* New York, 1892.

Dwight, John Sullivan. *Select Minor Poems Translated from the German of Goethe and Schiller, with Notes.* Boston, 1839.

Dyer, Isaac Watson. *A Bibliography of Thomas Carlyle's Writings and Ana.* Portland, Maine, 1928.

Eckermann, Johann Peter. *Eckermann's Conversations with Goethe in the Last Years of His Life,* ed. S. M. Fuller. 4 vols. Boston, 1839.

Eidson, John Olin. *Charles Stearns Wheeler.* Athens, Ga., 1951.

Ellis, George E. Introductory note to Emerson's "Impressions of Thomas Carlyle in 1848," *Scribner's Monthly,* XXII (1881), 89–92.

Eliot, George. *The Letters,* ed. Gordon S. Haight. 7 vols. New Haven, 1954–55.

Emerson, Edward W. *Life and Letters of Charles Russell Lowell.* Boston, 1907.

—— *Emerson in Concord.* Boston 1889.

Emerson, Ralph Waldo. *The Early Lectures of Ralph Waldo Emerson,* vol. 1, ed. Stephen E. Whicher and Robert E. Spiller. Cambridge, Mass., 1959.

—— *Correspondence between Emerson and Grimm,* ed. F. W. Holls. Boston, 1903.

—— *Journals,* ed. Edward Waldo Emerson and Waldo Emerson Forbes. 10 vols. Boston, 1909–14.

—— *Letters,* ed. Ralph L. Rusk. 6 vols. New York, 1939.

—— *Uncollected Writings.* New York, 1913.

—— *Works,* ed. Edward Waldo Emerson. 12 vols. Boston, 1903–4.

——, William Henry Channing, and James Freeman Clarke. *Memoirs of Margaret Fuller Ossoli.* 2 vols. Boston, 1852.

——, and William Henry Furness. *Records of a Lifelong Friendship,* ed. H. H. Furness. Boston, 1910.

—— See also Carlyle, Thomas; Sterling, John.

Emerson Scrapbook, containing clippings about Emerson, 1903–19, in Columbia University Libraries.

Espinasse, Francis. *Literary Recollections and Sketches.* London, 1893.

Everett, Edward. *Eulogy on Lafayette, Delivered in Faneuil Hall . . . September 6, 1834.* Boston, 1834.

Faulkner, H. U. *American Economic History.* New York, 1924.

Federn, Karl. *Essays zur Amerikanischen Literatur.* Halle, 1899.

Ferrier, James Frederick. "An Introduction to the Philosophy of Consciousness," *Blackwood's Magazine,* XLIII–XLV (February, 1838–March, 1839), 187–201, 437–52, 784–91 (XLIII); 234–44, 539–50 (XLIV); 201–11, 419–30 (XLV).

Fitzgerald, Edward. *Letters and Literary Remains,* ed. William Aldis Wright. 7 vols. London, 1903.

Forster, John. *W. Penn and T. B. Macaulay: Brief Observations on the Charges in Macaulay's History of England, Against the Character of Penn.* Philadelphia, 1850.

Fox, George. *Journal,* ed. John L. Nickalls. Cambridge, 1952.

Frothingham, N. L. "Sartor Resartus," *Christian Examiner,* XII (September, 1836), 74–84.

Frothingham, O. B. *George Ripley.* Boston, 1882.

Frothingham, Paul Revere. *Edward Everett.* Boston, 1925.

———— *Memoir of William Ellery Channing.* Boston, 1886.

Froude, James Anthony. *Thomas Carlyle: A History of the First Forty Years of His Life.* 2 vols. New York, 1882.

———— *Thomas Carlyle: A History of His Life in London.* 2 vols. New York, 1884.

Fuller, Margaret, tr. *Eckermann's Conversations with Goethe.* Boston, 1839.

Garbett, Edward Lacy. *Rudimentary Treatise on the Principles of Design in Architecture as Deducible from Nature and Exemplified in the Works of the Greek and Gothic Architects.* London, 1850.

Garnett, Richard. *Life of Thomas Carlyle.* London, 1887.

Gilfillan, George. *A Gallery of Literary Portraits.* Edinburgh, 1845.

Gladstone, William Ewart. *The State and Its Relations with the Church.* London, 1838.

Goethe, Johann Wolfgang von. *Correspondence between Goethe and Carlyle,* ed. Charles Eliot Norton. London, 1887.

———— *Sämtliche Werke.* 40 vols. Stuttgart, 1902–7.

Gohdes, Clarence L. F. *The Periodicals of American Transcendentalism.* Durham, N. C., 1931.

Greenwood, Grace [Sarah Jane Clarke Lippincott]. *Haps and Mishaps of a Tour in Europe.* New York, 1854.

Griswold, Rufus. *The Poets and Poetry of America.* Philadelphia, 1842.

Hale, Edward Everett. *James Russell Lowell and His Friends.* Boston, 1899.

———— Review of *Cromwell, Boston Daily Advertiser* (January 21, 1846).

———— *Works.* 10 vols. Boston, 1901.

Hale, Edward Everett, Jr. *Life and Letters of Edward Everett Hale.* 2 vols. Boston, 1917.

Hanson, Lawrence, and Elisabeth Hanson. *Necessary Evil: The Life of Jane Welsh Carlyle.* New York, 1952.

Harper, J. Henry. *The House of Harper.* New York, 1912.

Harrison, Frederic, ed. *Carlyle and the London Library.* London, 1906.

Hazlitt, William. *Literary Remains.* London, 1836.

Hedge, F. H. "The Correspondence of Carlyle and Emerson," *The Christian Register,* LXII (March 15, 1883), 164.

Higginson, T. W. *Carlyle's Laugh and Other Surprises.* Boston, 1909.

Holmes, O. W. *Ralph Waldo Emerson.* Boston, 1884.

Hooper, Richard, ed. *The Iliad,* tr. George Chapman. London, 1857.

Hopkins, Vivian C. *Prodigal Puritan: A Life of Delia Bacon*. Cambridge, Mass., 1959.

Horne, Richard, ed. *A New Spirit of the Age*. London, 1844.

Howe, M. A. De Wolfe. *Life and Letters of George Bancroft*. 2 vols. New York, 1908.

Howitt, Mary. *An Autobiography*. Boston, 1889.

Hunt, Leigh. Review of Carlyle's *French Revolution*, *The Examiner*, No. 1546 (September 17, 1837), p. 596.

Hutcheson, Francis. *An Inquiry into . . . Beauty and Virtue*. London, 1726.

Ilbert, Courtenay. *Parliament: Its History, Constitution and Practice*. London, 1911.

Illustrated Memorial Volume of the Carlyle's House Purchase Fund Committee with Catalogue. . . . London, 1896.

Ireland, Alexander. "The Correspondence of Thomas Carlyle and Ralph Waldo Emerson, 1834–1872," *Academy*, XXIII (April 7, 1883), 231–33.

——— *In Memoriam: Ralph Waldo Emerson*. London, 1882.

James, Henry, Jr., "The Correspondence of Carlyle and Emerson," *The Century Magazine*, XXVI (June, 1883), 265–72.

Jameson, Anna Brownell. *Winter Studies and Summer Rambles in Canada*. London, 1838.

Jefferson, Thomas. *Writings*, ed. A. E. Bergh. 20 vols. Washington, 1907.

Johnson, Samuel. *Selections from Samuel Johnson*, ed. R. W. Chapman. Oxford, 1955.

Joyce, James. "Ibsen's New Drama," *The Fortnightly Review*, XLVII (1900), 575–90.

"Jung-Stilling—Religious Literature of Germany," *Foreign Quarterly Review*, XLII, 247–83.

Kirk, John Foster. *A Supplement to Allibone's Critical Dictionary*. Philadelphia, 1896.

Knox, Vicesimus. *Elegant Extracts . . . Prose*. London, 1797.

Kull, Irving S. *A Short Chronology of American History*. New Brunswick, N. J., 1952.

Landor, Walter Savage. *Complete Works*, ed. T. Earle Welby. 16 vols. London, 1929.

——— "On the Death of M. D'Ossoli and His Wife Margaret Fuller," *The Examiner*, No. 2310 (May 8, 1852), p. 294.

Lane, Charles. "Cromwell," *The Dial*, III (October, 1842), 238–64.

Laughton, J. K. *Memoirs of the Life and Correspondence of Henry Reeve, C. B., D. C. L.* 2 vols. London, 1898.

Lee, Eliza Buckminster. *The Life of Jean Paul Frederic Richter*. Boston, 1842.

Lowell, James Russell. *A Fable for Critics*. New York, 1848.

Lyell, Charles. *Principles of Geology*. Philadelphia, 1837.

MacCormac, E. I. *James K. Polk*. Berkeley, Calif., 1922.

Maginn, William. "Gallery of Literary Characters," *Fraser's Magazine*, VII (June, 1833), 706.

Mann, Mary Peabody. *Life of Horace Mann*. Boston, 1888.

Marheineke, Philip Konrad. *Geschichte der deutschen Reformation*. Berlin, 1816.

Martineau, Harriet. *Eastern Life, Past and Present*. 3 vols. London, 1848.

────── *Harriet Martineau's Autobiography*, ed. M. W. Chapman. 3 vols. Boston, 1877.

────── *How to Observe: Morals and Manners*. London, 1838.

────── "Mesmerism," *The Athenaeum*, No. 891 (November 23, 1844), p. 1070.

────── *Retrospect of Western Travel*. London, 1838.

────── Review of Dartmouth Oration, *The London and Westminster Review*, XXXII (April, 1839), 261–81.

Maurice, Frederick. *The Life of Frederick Denison Maurice*. New York, 1884.

Mill, John Stuart. *Letters*, ed. H. S. R. Elliott. London, 1910.

────── Review of Carlyle's *French Revolution*, *The London and Westminster Review*, XXVII (July, 1837), 17.

Milnes, Richard Monckton. *Poems of Many Years*. London, 1838.

Montègut, Emile. "Du Culte des Héros: Carlyle et Emerson," *Revue des Deux Mondes*, VII (1850), 722–37.

Muhammad Ali, Maulawl. *A Manual of Hadith*. Lahore, 1944.

Neff, Emery. *Carlyle*. New York, 1932.

Norton, Andrews. "The New School in Literature and Religion," *Boston Daily Advertiser*, August 27, 1913.

Norton, Charles Eliot. *Letters*, ed. Sara Norton and M. A. De Wolfe Howe. 2 vols. Boston, 1913.

Origo, Iris. "The Carlyles and the Ashburtons," *The Cornhill Magazine*, CLXIV (Autumn, 1950), 441–83.

Packe, Michael St. John. *The Life of John Stuart Mill*. New York, 1954.

Parker, Theodore. *A Discourse of Matters Pertaining to Religion*. Boston, 1842.

Parsons, Thomas William, tr. *The First Ten Cantos of the Inferno of Dante Alighieri*. Boston, 1843.

Phillips, George Searle, *see* Searle, January.

Pierce, E. L. *Memoir and Letters of Charles Sumner*. 4 vols. Boston, 1893.

Powers, Horatio Nelson. "A Day with Emerson," *Lippincott's Monthly Magazine*, XXX (November, 1882), 476–84.

Pückler-Muskau, Prince Hermann. *A Regency Visitor: The Letters of Prince Pückler-Muskau*, ed. E. M. Butler. New York, 1958.

Putnam, George Haven. *A Memoir of George Palmer Putnam*. 2 vols. New York, 1903.

Reid, Stuart J. *A Sketch of the Life and Times of the Rev. Sydney Smith*. New York, 1885.

Reid, T. Wemyss. *The Life, Letters, and Friendships of Richard Monckton Milnes*. 2 vols. London, 1890.

Richards, Irving T. "Longfellow in England," *PMLA*, LI (1936), 1129.

Ripley, George. *Discourses on the Philosophy of Religion*. Boston, 1836.

────── *Letters to Andrews Norton on "The Latest Form of Infidelity."* Boston, 1840.

—— *Specimens of Foreign Standard Literature.* 12 vols. Boston, 1830–42.

Rusk, Ralph L. *The Life of Ralph Waldo Emerson.* New York, 1949.

Ruskin, John. *Letters . . . to Charles Eliot Norton.* 2 vols. Boston, 1905.

Sanborn, F. B. *Ralph Waldo Emerson.* Boston, 1901.

——, and William T. Harris. *Amos Bronson Alcott: His Life and Philosophy.* Boston, 1893.

Schubarth, K. C. *Über Goethe's Faust, Vohlesungen.* Berlin, 1830.

—— *Zur Beurtheilung Goethe's mit Beziehung auf verwandte Literatur und Kunst.* 2 vols. Breslau, 1820.

Schütz, F. K. J. *Müllner's Leben, Charakter und Geist.* Meissen, 1830.

Schuyler, Montgomery. "Carlyle and Emerson," *The Atlantic Monthly,* LI (June, 1883), 774.

Searle, January [George Searle Phillips]. *Emerson, His Life and Writings.* London, 1855.

Sedgwick, Catherine Maria. *Letters from Abroad to Kindred at Home.* 2 vols. New York, 1841.

—— *Clarence, or, A Tale of Our Own Times.* Philadelphia, 1830.

—— *The Linwoods, or, "Sixty Years Since" in America.* New York, 1835.

Sewall, William. "On Carlyle," *Quarterly Review,* LXVI (1840), 446–503.

Shepard, Odell. *Pedlar's Progress: The Life of Bronson Alcott.* Boston, 1937.

Shepherd, Richard Herne. "The Correspondence of Carlyle and Emerson," *The Gentleman's Magazine,* CCLIV (April, 1883), 415–27.

—— *Memoirs of the Life and Writings of Thomas Carlyle.* London, 1881.

Skipper, Ottis Clark. *J. D. B. De Bow: Magazinist of the Old South.* Athens, Ga., 1958.

Slater, Joseph. "George Ripley and Thomas Carlyle," *PMLA,* LXVII (June, 1952), 341–49.

—— "Goethe, Carlyle, and the Open Secret," *Anglia,* LXXVII (1958), 422–26.

Smalley, George W. *London Letters.* 2 vols. London, 1890.

Snider, Denton J. *A Biography of Ralph Waldo Emerson.* St. Louis, 1921.

Sterling, John. *A Correspondence between John Sterling and Ralph Waldo Emerson,* ed. E. W. Emerson. Boston, 1897.

—— "Montaigne and His Writings," *The London and Westminster Review,* XXIX (August, 1838), 321–52.

—— "The Onyx Ring," *Blackwood's Magazine,* XLIV (November, 1838), 665–89; XLIV (December, 1938), 741–68; XLV (January, 1839), 17–46.

—— "On the Writings of Thomas Carlyle," *The London and Westminster Review,* XXXIII (1839), 1–68.

—— Review of F. G. Schneidewin's edition of Simonides, *The London and Westminster Review,* XXXII (1838), 99–136.

—— "The Sexton's Daughter," *Blackwood's Magazine,* XLIV (July, 1838), 1–20.

Stewart, W. R. *The Philanthropic Work of Josephine Shaw Lowell.* New York, 1911.

Stirling, James Hutchison. *The Secret of Hegel.* London, 1865.

Swift, Jonathan. *The Correspondence of Jonathan Swift, D.D.,* ed. F. E. Ball. 6 vols. London, 1912.

Thayer, J. B. *A Western Journey with Mr. Emerson.* Boston, 1884.

Thoreau, Henry David. *The Writings of Henry David Thoreau.* 20 vols. Boston, 1906.

Tyndall, John. *New Fragments.* London, 1892.

Very, Jones. *Essays and Poems.* Boston, 1839.

Voss, Johann Heinrich, tr. *Homer's Werke.* 2 vols. Stuttgart, 1844.

Wade, Mason. *Margaret Fuller.* New York, 1940.

Whipple, E. P. "Emerson and Carlyle," *The North American Review,* CXXXVI (1883), 431–45.

———— "Some Recollections of Ralph Waldo Emerson," *Harper's New Monthly Magazine,* LXV (September, 1882), 580.

Wilson, David Alec. *Carlyle till Marriage, 1795–1826.* London, 1923.

———— *Carlyle to "The French Revolution," 1826–1837.* London, 1924.

———— *Carlyle on Cromwell and Others, 1837–1848.* London, 1925.

———— *Carlyle at His Zenith, 1848–1853.* London, 1927.

———— *Carlyle to Three Score and Ten, 1853–1865.* London, 1929.

———— *Carlyle in Old Age, 1865–1881.* London, 1934.

Woodberry, G. E. "Carlyle and Emerson," *The Atlantic Monthly,* LI (April, 1883), 560–64.

Wright, Elizur. *Perforations in the "Latter-Day Pamphlets" by one of the "Eighteen Millions of Bores."* Boston, 1850.

———— "A Visit to Thomas Carlyle," *The Weekly Chronotype,* March 18, 1846.

MANUSCRIPT LETTERS

Abbreviations

NLS	The National Library of Scotland
NYPL	New York Public Library
RWE	Ralph Waldo Emerson
RWEMA	Ralph Waldo Emerson Memorial Association
TC	Thomas Carlyle
V&A	The Victoria and Albert Museum

Writer	Recipient	Date	Owner
Aitken, Mary Carlyle	Charles Eliot Norton	2/2/76	Houghton Library
	Charles Eliot Norton	5/11/79	Houghton Library
	Charles Eliot Norton	3/26/81	Houghton Library
	Charles Eliot Norton	9/26/82	Houghton Library
Ballantyne, Thomas	RWE	12/3/42	RWEMA
Carlyle, Jane	TC	9/25/47	NLS
	John Forster	11/22/47	V&A
	TC	9/6/50	NLS
Carlyle, John	TC	10/2/48	NLS

Writer	Recipient	Date	Owner
Carlyle, Thomas	his mother	9/12/34	NLS
	John Carlyle	12/2/36	NLS
	John Carlyle	5/30/37	NLS
	his mother	2/15/38	NLS
	John Carlyle	12/26/38	NLS
	his mother	6/19/39	NLS
	John Carlyle	7/28/39	NLS
	Joseph Newberg	12/21/39	NLS
	his mother	5/20/40	NLS
	David Aitken	2/22/41	U. of Edinburgh
	Jane Carlyle	4/14/41	NLS
	Jane Carlyle	4/17/41	NLS
	his mother	9/?/41	NLS
	Jean Aitken	10/2/41	NLS
	John Sterling	7/28/42	NLS
	Henry Colman(?)	6/?/43	Hist. Soc. of Penna.
	Wm. Macready	8/27/43	Berg Collection, NYPL
	his mother	5/13/44	NLS
	John Forster	10/4/44	V&A
	Edward Chapman	12/7/45	Pierpont Morgan Library
	Edward Chapman	12/29/45	Pierpont Morgan Library
	Jane Carlyle	4/15/46	NLS
	John Carlyle	5/3/46	NLS
	John Carlyle	10/8/46	NLS
	John Carlyle	11/8/46	NLS
	E. P. Clark	3/18/47	Houghton Library
	Jean Aitken	3/25/47	NLS
	E. P. Clark	5/18/47	Houghton Library
	Jean Aikten	10/26/47	NLS
	his mother	11/8/47	NLS
	Jane Carlyle	1/17/48	NLS
	Jane Carlyle	3/26/48	NLS
	John Forster	7/?/48	V&A
	James Marshall	7/9/48	British Museum
	Jane Carlyle	9/18/48	NLS
	John Carlyle	10/18/48	NLS
	Edward Chapman	8/9/49	Pierpont Morgan Library
	his mother	5/11/50	NLS
	Jane Carlyle	8/30/50	NLS
	Jane Carlyle	8/31/50	NLS

Writer	Recipient	Date	Owner
Carlyle, Thomas	Jane Carlyle	9/2/50	NLS
	J. S. Blackie	11/12/51	NLS
	John Carlyle	6/25/52	NLS
	John Forster	6/11/53	V&A
	John Carlyle	5/25/56	NLS
	Jane Carlyle	9/16/56	NLS
	John Carlyle	9/16/56	NLS
	Jane Carlyle	7/11/58	NLS
	John Forster	10/7/60	V&A
	John Carlyle	1/22/66	NLS
	John Carlyle	1/6/70	NLS
	John Carlyle	1/22/70	NLS
	John Carlyle	1/28/70	NLS
	Charles Eliot Norton	3/2/70	Houghton Library
	John Carlyle	11/12/70	NLS
	John Carlyle	11/13/72	NLS
	John Carlyle	4/12/73	NLS
	Charles Eliot Norton	4/18/73	Houghton Library
	John Carlyle	5/7/73	NLS
	Charles Eliot Norton	4/23/74	Houghton Library
	John Carlyle	3/25/76	NLS
Channing, William Ellery	RWE	nd	RWEMA
Child, Lydia Maria	TC	4/7/38	NLS
Conway, Moncure	RWE	9/19/78	RWEMA
Dewey, Orville	RWE	4/21/42	RWEMA
Emerson, Ellen	Lidian Emerson	11/8/72	RWEMA
	Lidian Emerson	5/1/73	RWEMA
	Charles Eliot Norton	2/26/81	Houghton Library
Emerson, Lidian	RWE	11/25/72	RWEMA
Emerson, Ralph Waldo	S. G. Ward	11/29/72	Houghton Library
	Moncure Conway	9/12/82	Columbia U. Library
Forbes, Edith Emerson	TC	8/?/72	NLS
	TC	10/6/79	NLS
	Moncure Conway	2/7/83	Columbia U. Library
Greeley, Horace	RWE	10/14/45	RWEMA
	RWE	12/10/45	RWEMA
	RWE	3/17/46	RWEMA
Harper and Brothers	RWE	5/9/43	RWEMA
Helps, Arthur	TC	12/3/48	V&A
Ireland, Alexander	RWE	1/8/78	RWEMA
Martineau, Harriet	RWE	2/25/52	RWEMA

Writer	Recipient	Date	Owner
Sinclair, James Leask	RWE	10/28/69	RWEMA
Stephen, Leslie	Charles Eliot Norton	7/5/83	Houghton Library
Walker, James	Charles Chauncy Emerson	4/15/36	RWEMA
Wheeler, Charles Stearns	RWE	6/21/38	RWEMA

INDEX

DATE DUE

#47-0108 Peel Off Pressure Sensitive